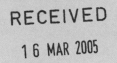
Innovation Management and
New Product Development

Visit the *Innovation Management and New Product Development*,
third edition, Companion Website at **www.pearsoned.co.uk/trott** to
find valuable **student** learning material including:

- Multiple choice questions to help test learning

We work with leading authors to develop the
strongest educational materials in business and
management, bringing cutting-edge thinking and
best learning practice to a global market.

Under a range of well-known imprints, including
Financial Times Prentice Hall, we craft high quality print and
electronic publications which help readers to understand
and apply their content, whether studying or at work.

To find out more about the complete range of our
publishing, please visit us on the World Wide Web at:
www.pearsoned.co.uk

Innovation Management and New Product Development

Third Edition

Paul Trott

University of Portsmouth Business School

FT Prentice Hall
FINANCIAL TIMES

An imprint of **Pearson Education**

Harlow, England • London • New York • Boston • San Francisco • Toronto
Sydney • Tokyo • Singapore • Hong Kong • Seoul • Taipei • New Delhi
Cape Town • Madrid • Mexico City • Amsterdam • Munich • Paris • Milan

Pearson Education Limited
Edinburgh Gate
Harlow
Essex CM20 2JE
England

and Associated Companies throughout the world

Visit us on the World Wide Web at:
www.pearsoned.co.uk

First published 1998
Third edition published 2005

© Pearson Professional Limited 1998
© Pearson Education Limited 2002, 2005

ISBN 0 273 68643 7

British Library Cataloguing-in-Publication Data
A catalogue record for this book is available from the British Library

Library of Congress Cataloging-in-Publication Data
Trott, Paul.
    Innovation management and new product development / Paul Trott. — 3rd ed.
      p. cm.
    Includes bibliographical references and index.
    ISBN 0-273-68643-7 (pbk.)
    1. Technological innovations — Management. 2. Industrial management. 3. Product management.
    I. Title.
    HD45.T76 2004
    658.5′75—dc22

                                             2004053300

10 9 8 7 6 5 4 3 2 1
08 07 06 05

Typeset in 10/12pt Times by 35
Printed by Ashford Colour Press Ltd, Gosport

The publisher's policy is to use paper manufactured from sustainable forests.

Contents

Ufuk M. Çakmakçi, Department of Business,
Istanbul Bilgi University, Turkey

Supporting resources

Visit **www.pearsoned.co.uk/trott** to find valuable
online resources

Companion Website for students
● Multiple choice questions to help test learning

OneKey
OneKey is
all you need

Convenience. Simplicity. Success.

For instructors
● Complete, downloadable Instructor's Manual
● PowerPoint slides that can be downloaded and used as OHTs

For more information please contact your local Pearson Education sales
representative or visit **www.pearsoned.co.uk/trott**

Preface

To the student

Welcome to this third edition of *Innovation Management and New Product Development*. Whether you are a student of business or technology I hope you will find the book enjoyable and that it will give you some insight into the problems faced by firms as they try to develop innovative products that will help them survive and prosper.

Many of you may be wondering how this subject relates to other subjects. The answer, as usual, depends on which perspective is taken: marketing, technology, legal, strategic management, the question of commercialisation, or a multiple-perspective approach that incorporates all of these. In any event, the management of innovation in general, and the development of new products in particular, require expertise in all areas – finance, manufacturing, human resources, marketing and business strategy. The management of innovation is not a functional activity, solely the preserve of a single department. It is imperative to view innovation and product development as a *management process* rather than as a functional activity. This is the view taken by this book (*see* Figure 1.1). Indeed, many would argue that product innovation suffers seriously when it is subdivided into separate specialisations.

Objective of book

The objective of this book is to present a contemporary view of innovation management that focuses on the links and overlaps between groups (*see* the corners of the triangle on Figure 1.1) rather than on a single perspective from, say, marketing or research and development. It attempts to do this from a business management perspective, and aims to provide students with the knowledge to understand how to manage innovation. It is designed to be accessible and readable and was the first textbook to bring together the areas of innovation management and new product development for the student of business.

The book is designed with one overriding aim: to make this exciting and highly relevant subject as clear to understand as possible. To this end, the book has a number of important features.

Unique features

- A clear and straightforward writing style enhances learning comprehension.
- Extensive up-to-date references and relevant literature help you find out more and explore concepts in detail.

- Clear chapter openers set the scene for each chapter and provide a chapter contents list which offers page references to all the sections within the chapter.
- Learning objectives at the beginning of each chapter explicitly highlight the key areas that will be explored in the chapter.
- Topical articles from the *Financial Times* illustrate how the subject is being discussed in the context of the wider business world.
- Summaries at the end of each chapter provide a useful means of revising and checking understanding.
- **NEW!** *Pause for thought* questions integrated within the text. These are designed to help you reflect on what you have just read and to check your understanding. Answers to all *Pause for thought* questions are given on the book's website (www.booksites.net/trott).
- Comprehensive diagrams throughout the book illustrate some of the more complex concepts.
- Plentiful up-to-date examples within the text drive home arguments. This helps to enliven the subject and places it in context.
- A comprehensive index, including references to all defined terms, enables you to look up a definition within its context.
- **NEW!** A new two-colour design enlivens the text and makes the structure easy to follow.
- A substantial case study at the end of each chapter shows the subject in action within actual firms.
- A comprehensive set of web references at the end of each chapter guides the reader to further resources.

Good luck with your studies, and enjoy reading and exploring this exciting subject.

To tutors

I am grateful for the substantial amount of feedback that I have received both from tutors who use the book and students who have read it. Since the first edition of this book was published in 1998 innovation has continued to be at the forefront of economic and political debate about how to improve the competitiveness of economies and firms. It has been a growing subject of interest, with many more text books on this subject now available. In the light of feedback this third edition has been substantially rewritten and restructured.

At the level of the firm, management research continues to confirm that innovative firms outperform their competitors (*see* Chapter 8). Fundamental questions remain, however, such as:

- How can firms best transform exciting technology into successful new products?
- How can firms capture knowledge and creativity and develop successful new products?
- How can firms improve the speed at which they get products into the market?

- What organisational structures and systems are appropriate for innovation and new product development?
- How can incumbent firms overcome their difficulty with disruptive technologies and compete with newcomers?

Changes in content and pedagogy of the third edition

In an effort to make the book more accessible, there has been a major change to the structure with emphasis now being placed on the three key areas of innovation, technology and new products. The three parts can be clearly seen from the plan of the book on p. xxi. This framework is intended to operate as a navigational map to help students through the book. The three parts are:

1 Innovation management;
2 Managing technology and knowledge;
3 New Product Development.

Part One explores the concept of innovation management and what needs to be managed. Part Two discusses the wide issue of managing technology and knowledge and in particular how companies can use it to develop new products. Part Three examines the process of developing new products and many of the new product management issues faced by companies.

Several of the chapters have been completely rewritten. There is also an additional new chapter on the role of packaging in new product development and there are four new substantial case studies. At the beginning of each chapter is a chapter contents list that lists all the sections and subsections of that chapter. This allows the student to get a clear picture of how the chapter is set out and how the various parts relate to each other. It also serves as a page index for the chapter. Every chapter now uses several *Pause for thought* questions that help the student reflect on what they have just read to check their understanding. Finally, every chapter has been updated in terms of new articles from the *Financial Times*, new examples and illustrations and new references.

Key features

- Substantial free-standing chapters that explore a subject in detail and provide plenty of material for exciting lectures to be developed.
- Emphasis on a strong underpinning of the academic literature.
- A multiple-perspective approach links the key areas of R&D, marketing and technology.
- Engaging narrative provides clarity and readability for students.

- Key phrases' and key words' boxes at the end of every chapter help students with revision.
- End of chapter discussion questions reinforce learning.
- A substantial case study at the end of each chapter showcases the subject in action within actual firms.
- Separate case study questions at the end of each chapter enhance understanding.
- Chapter structure allows the flexibility to teach chapters in different sequences.
- Increased and updated illustrations provide excellent visual learning tools.
- Increased use of real-world examples from the *Financial Times* drive home real-world applications.

Web products

Log on to **www.pearsoned.co.uk/trott** to access learning resources which include:

For students:

- Study materials designed to help you improve your results.
- Self-test multiple-choice questions, organised by chapter.
- Answers to all *Pause for thought* questions, to allow you to check understanding as you progress.
- Chapter links and Hot links to key companies and internet sites.

For Tutors (password protected):

- Lecture notes and PowerPoint slides.
- All figures and tables from the book in PowerPoint colour slides.
- Key models as full-colour animated PowerPoint slide shows.
- Teaching/learning case studies.
- Answers to all end of chapter discussion questions.
- Multiple choice questions, organised by chapter for use in assessments.

I hope that your students will find this an exciting and interesting text that is relevant to today's issues.

Acknowledgements

I am indebted to many for their ideas and assistance. My primary thanks go to the many academics who have advanced our knowledge of innovation and new product development. The following reviewers provided feedback for this new edition: Susan

Hart, Strathclyde University; Jon Sundbo, Roskilde University, Denmark; Helen Perks, UMIST; Fiona Lettice, Cranfield University; Niki Hynes, Napier University Business School; Mark Godson, Sheffield Hallam Univerity; Paul Oakley, University of Birmingham; David Smith, Nottingham Business School, Nottingham Trent University; Fritz Sheimer, FH Furtwagen; Claus J. Varnes, Copenhagen Business School; Roy Woodhead, Oxford Brookes University.

It has been a pleasure to work with my editor Thomas Sigel who provided many new insights and valuable suggestions in seeing this exciting new edition to its completion. The task of writing has been made much easier by the support I have had from many people. First and foremost, a massive thanks to my family and especially to my wife Alison.

Thanks to the team at Pearson Education and especially to Thomas who has given the book increased support.

Foreword

Innovation and product development have deservingly become popular topics in many fields, including business administration. However, it is mostly taught and researched into as a purely scientific, technological phenomenon. Innovation is seen as R&D laboratory work related to fundamental university research. Or it is seen as individual entrepreneurship that depends on entrepreneurs who can innovate and develop new products from start to finish.

Reality is more complex. Innovations and new products are developed through a managed organisational process in which technological R&D and individual entrepreneurship are mixed with strategic leadership, the involvement of employees and important market considerations. Innovation and product development can be managed, which means that the manager has several alternatives for increasing innovativeness and he or she needs to choose among these. Thus, it will be necessary to have a guide for choosing and assessing what the consequences of the choice will be.

Dr Paul Trott's book is one of the few guides available. This book places innovation in a strategic and management perspective. Technology development, product development, and the organisation of activities relating to innovation are integrated with one another, and models and tools for assessing and implementing each element are presented. This gives managers and aspiring managers practical instruments with which to deal with the innovation process. The book is, however, not only a practical guide, it also presents the latest results from research to provide an understanding of why firms behave as they do. A special characteristic of Trott's book is that it unites the 'push' factors – technology and product development from scientific and internal firm processes – with the 'pull' or market factors. Technology and new products are discussed in relation to market possibilities, which are the crucial factor in innovation but which are so often forgotten in books on innovation.

Innovation Management and New Product Development thus has a mission, which is unlike that of many other books on the market. This third edition is most welcome and it includes new topics that research has highlighted as being important to the innovation processes. Among these are market behaviour, such as branding, modulisation and packaging. This also makes the book more relevant to service firms, which more often turn to the market rather than to technology to gain their competitive advantages.

I hope this book will be useful to the increasing numbers of students and managers who need to focus on market-based innovation to improve their own qualifications and their present or coming firms' competitiveness.

Professor Jon Sundbo
Professor of Business Administration and Innovation
Roskilde University
Copenhagen
Denmark

Acknowledgements

We are grateful to the following for permission to reproduce copyright material:

NI Syndication for extracts from 'Inventor cleans up with profits' by N. Graham published in *The Sunday Times* 1 March 1998 and 'A little miracle' by M. Dobson published in *Sunday Times Magazine* 19 October 1997; The European Commission for extracts from *ESPRIT (1997) First Open Interconnects for Clustered Systems No. 12*; TV Choice Limited for the case study 'The role of design in the development of a wheelchair for cerebral palsy sufferers', from the film *Designing for the Market* www.tvchoice.uk.com; Copyright Clearance Center for an extract from 'FDA gives approval for generic versions of Eli Lilly's Prozac' by Jill Carroll published in *Wall Street Journal* 3 August 2001 © 2001 Dow Jones & Company, Inc.; and BMJ Publishing Group for extracts from 'Pharmaceutical packaging can induce confusion', a letter to the editor by M Rigby, published in *British Medical Journal* vol.324, 679, 2002.

Figures 4.1 and 4.5 from *Operations Management*, Pearson Education (Slack N. *et al.* 2001); Table 5.2 from *UNAIDS*, (UNAIDS 2000), www.UNAIDS.org; Figure 7.2 from 'Nike Just Did It – International Sub-Contracting and Flexibility in Athletic Footwear Production', in *Regional Studies*, Taylor & Francis (Donaghu, M. and Barff, R. 1990), www.tandf.co.uk/journals; Figure 9.8 from *Pharma Facts and Figures*, Association of the British Pharmaceutical Industry (1993 ABPI); Figure 10.2 from *Architect or Bee? The Human Price of Technology*, Hogarth Press, Random House Group Ltd (Cooley, M. 1987); Figure 11.4 from 'Brand First Management, in *Journal of Marketing Management* (Rubenstein, H. 1966), Westburn Publishers Ltd; Table 12.1 from *The Role of Marketing Specialists in Product Development*, The Marketing Education Group (Johne, F.A. and Snelson, P.A.; Figure 12.13 from *New Products Management*, McGraw-Hill (Crawford, M. 1997).

We are grateful to the Financial Times Limited for permission to reprint the following material:

Illustration 1.1 GSK promises 20 'blockbusters', © *Financial Times*, 4 December 2003; Illustration 1.4 Competition and innovation too much of a good thing: Innovation increases in a competitive market – but only up to a point, says a new study CHRIS GILES THEORY AND PRACTICE, © *Financial Times*, 14 May 2002; Illustration 2.1 Microsoft takes antitrust case to Supreme Court, FT.com, © *Financial Times*, 8 August 2001; Illustration 2.2 A last, last chance for Turkey, © *Financial Times*, 23 May 2001; Illustration 2.3 Graft clean-up key to success of Turkish bail out, © *Financial Times*, 29 May 2001; Illustration 3.1 A most harmonious collaboration: LEADERSHIP, © *Financial Times*, 10 January 2002; Illustration 4.7 Use the power of the net to divide and rule FT Summer School, © *Financial Times*, 18 August 2003; Illustration 5.1 Levi sings the blues over jeans, © *Financial Times*, 16 January 2001; Illustration 5.2 Pfizer sues rivals to protect Viagra patent, FT. com, © *Financial Times*, 23 October 2002; Illustration 5.7 Trademark view likely to allow sports stars to play own brand of name game, © *Financial Times*, 19 January 2004; Illustration 5.8 On the prowl for copycats,

© *Financial Times*, 3 March 1994; Illustration 5.9 If technology switches to the side of copyright, © *Financial Times*, 10 January 2002; Illustration 6.1 If downsizing, protect the corporate memory, © *Financial Times*, 16 October 2001; Illustration 7.3 Steered into a commanding lead, © *Financial Times*, 15 January 1988; Illustration 7.4 Prescription for cutting costs, © *Financial Times*, 12 January 1998; Illustration 7.5 Setback for Disney as Pixar alliance ends, FT.com, © *Financial Times*, 29 January 2004; Illustration 8.3 Seeking to bridge the science gap, © *Financial Times*, 25 February 2002; Illustration 9.1 Quick-hit chemistry becomes elusive, © *Financial Times*, 12 September 2001; Illustration 10.2 Science brought down to earth, © *Financial Times*, 15 March 1994; Case study: Ericsson and Sony explore tie-up, © *Financial Times*, 20 April 2001; Ericsson plans microelectronics division sell-off, © *Financial Times*, 20 August 2001; Sony-Ericsson seeks success with new phones, FT.com, © *Financial Times*, 3 March 2003; Ambitious expansion loses its shine, © *Financial Times*, 2 October 2001; Sony-Ericsson to raise control, © *Financial Times*, 10 March 2004; Ericsson nears surrender in handset battle, © *Financial Times*, 26 January 2001; Illustration 11.2 Apple iPod: from product to platform: *Apple Computer declined to comment for this article*, FT.com, © *Financial Times*, 18 January 2004; Illustration 11.4 Dasani recall leaves Coke dangling over murky water, © *Financial Times*, FT.com, © *Financial Times*, 20 March 2004; Illustration 12.1 New products crucial to success, FT.com, © *Financial Times*, 21 May 2002; Illustration 13.4 Laundry, with a minor in linguistics, © *Financial Times*, 10 June 2000; Illustration 14.3 Stay tuned to consumer taste, © *Financial Times*, 31 March 1998; Illustration 15.3 Coke cans plan for Dasani in France, © *Financial Times*, 25 March 2004.

We are grateful to the following for permission to use copyright material:

Illustration 11.3 The importance of 'brand value', FT.com, *The Financial Times Limited*, 19 May 2003, © Stephen Overell; Illustration 14.5 How to discover the unknown market, *The Financial Times Limited*, 6 May 1999, © W. Chan Kim, Bruce D Henderson and Renee Mauborgne.

In some instances we have been unable to trace the owners of copyright material, and we would appreciate any information that would enable us to do so.

Plan of the book

Part 1: The Concept of Innovation Management

Chapter 1 Innovation management: an introduction	Chapter 2 The context of innovation and the role of the state	Chapter 3 Managing innovation within firms

Chapter 4 Innovation and operations management	Chapter 5 Managing intellectual property

Part 2: Managing Technology and Knowledge

Chapter 6 Managing organisational knowledge	Chapter 7 Strategic alliances and networks	Chapter 8 Management of research and development: an introduction

Chapter 9 Managing R&D projects	Chapter 10 The role of technology transfer in innovation

Part 3: New Product Development

Chapter 11 Product and brand strategy	Chapter 12 New product development	Chapter 13 Packaging and product development

Chapter 14 Market research and its influence on new product development	Chapter 15 Managing the new product development team

Part One

The Concept of Innovation Management

The purpose of this part of the book is to introduce and explore the concept of innovation management. Particular emphasis is placed on the need to view innovation as a management process. A conceptual framework is introduced which emphasises the importance of internal processes and external linkages. This raises the issue of the context of innovation and Chapter 2 demonstrates that innovation cannot be separated from the wider political and social processes. The United States is often cited as a good example of a system that enables innovation to fburish: hence it is necessary to explore the economic, social and political institutions that facilitate innovation.

Chapter 3 explores the issue of the organisational context and it is from this vantage point that the subject of managing innovation within frms is addressed. Virtually all major technological innovations occur within organisations, hence it is necessary to look at organisations and their management.

Given that many new product ideas are based on existing products and may be developed from within the production or service operations function, Chapter 4 considers the role of operations within innovation. Many new product ideas may be modest and incremental rather than radical but the combined effect of many, small, innovative ideas may be substantial.

A major part of the process of innovation is the management of a frm's intellectual effort and this is the focus of Chapter 5. Patents, trademarks, copyright and registered designs are all discussed.

The principal message of this part is this: innovation is a management process that is heavily influenced by the organisational context and the wider macro system in which the organisation exists.

1

Innovation management: an introduction

There is extensive scope for examining the way innovation is managed within organisations. Most of us are well aware that good technology can help companies achieve competitive advantage and long-term financial success. But there is an abundance of exciting new technology in the world and it is the transformation of this technology into products that is of particular concern to organisations. There are numerous factors to be considered by the organisation, but what are these factors and how do they affect the process of innovation?

Chapter contents

Learning objectives

When you have completed this chapter you will be able to:

- recognise the importance of innovation;
- explain the meaning and nature of innovation management;
- provide an introduction to a management approach to innovation;
- appreciate the complex nature of the management of innovation within organisations;
- describe the changing views of innovation over time;
- recognise the role of key individuals within the process; and
- recognise the need to view innovation as a management process.

The importance of innovation

Corporations must be able to adapt and evolve if they wish to survive. Businesses operate with the knowledge that their competitors will inevitably come to the market with a product that changes the basis of competition. The ability to change and adapt is essential to survival.

Today, the idea of innovation is widely accepted. It has become part of our culture – so much so that it verges on becoming a cliché. For example, in 1994 and 1995, 275 books published in the the United States had the word 'innovation' in their title (Coyne, 1996). But even though the term is now embedded in our language, to what extent do we fully understand the concept? Moreover, to what extent is this understanding shared? A scientist's view of innovation may be very different from that of an accountant in the same organisation.

The GlaxoSmithKline story in Illustration 1.1 puts into context the subject of innovation and new product development. Innovation is at the heart of many companies' activities. But to what extent is this true of all businesses? And why are some businesses more innovative than others? What is meant by innovation? And can it be managed? These are questions that will be addressed in this book.

'. . . not to innovate is to die' wrote Christopher Freeman (1982) in his famous study of the economics of innovation. Certainly companies that have established themselves as technical and market leaders have shown an ability to develop successful new products. In virtually every industry from aerospace to pharmaceuticals and from motor cars to computers, the dominant companies have demonstrated an ability to innovate (*see* Table 1.1).

A brief analysis of economic history, especially in the United Kingdom, will show that industrial technological innovation has led to substantial economic benefits for the innovating *company* and the innovating *country*. Indeed, the industrial revolution of the nineteenth century was fuelled by technological innovations (*see* Table 1.2). Technological innovations have also been an important component in the progress of human societies. Anyone who has visited the towns of Bath, Leamington and Colchester will be very aware of how the Romans contributed to the advancement of human societies. The introduction over 2,000 years ago of sewers, roads and elementary heating systems is credited to these early invaders of Britain.

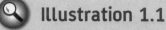 **Illustration 1.1**

FT

GSK promises 20 'blockbusters'

GlaxoSmithKline said yesterday that it had more than 20 potential blockbuster drugs in its pipeline with likely annual sales of more than $1 billion, but has yet to convince investors it is on track for a new period of high growth.

Unveiling the drugs in its research labs for the first time since the 2000 merger that formed the company, GSK said it had a 'wall of products coming forward', including treatments in areas such as cancer and heart disease.

The chief executive of the Anglo-American pharmaceuticals group said GSK had 147 different projects undergoing clinical trials, including 82 genuinely new drugs.

Despite the upbeat comments investors remained uncertain about the group's long-term prospects and the shares fell 1.4 per cent. The drop in the share price also reflected disappointment that a cancer treatment known as 572016 had been delayed a year while more trials were conducted.

GSK desperately needs new products to replace sales being lost to generic competition to three of its former top-selling drugs.

Source: *Financial Times*, 4 December 2003. Reprinted with permission.

Table 1.1 Market leaders in 2004

Industry	Market leaders	Innovative new products
Aerospace	Airbus Ind; Boeing	Passenger aircraft
Pharmaceuticals	Pfizer; GlaxoSmithKline	Impotence; ulcer treatment drug
Motor cars	Toyota; DaimlerChrysler; Ford	Car design and associated product developments
Computers and software development	Intel; IBM and Microsoft; SAP	Computer chip technology, computer hardware improvements and software development

Pause for thought

Not all firms develop innovative new products, but they still seem to survive. Do they thrive?

Table 1.2 Nineteenth-century economic development fuelled by technological innovations

Innovation	Innovator	Date
Steam engine	James Watt	1770–80
Iron boat	Isambard Kingdom Brunel	1820–45
Locomotive	George Stephenson	1829
Electromagnetic induction dynamo	Michael Faraday	1830–40
Electric light bulb	Thomas Edison and Joseph Swan	1879–90

The study of innovation

Innovation has long been argued to be the engine of growth. It is important to note that it can also provide growth almost regardless of the condition of the larger economy. Innovation has been a topic for discussion and debate for hundreds of years. Nineteenth-century economic historians observed that the acceleration in economic growth was the result of technological progress. However, little effort was directed towards understanding *how* changes in technology contributed to this growth.

Schumpeter (1934, 1939, 1942) was among the first economists to emphasise the importance of *new products* as stimuli to economic growth. He argued that the competition posed by new products was far more important than marginal changes in the *prices* of existing products. For example, economies are more likely to experience growth due to the development of products such as new computer software or new pharmaceutical drugs than to reductions in prices of existing products such as telephones or motor cars. Indeed, early observations suggested that economic development does not occur in any regular manner, but seemed to occur in 'bursts' or waves of activity, thereby indicating the important influence of external factors on economic development.

This macro view of innovation as cyclical can be traced back to the mid-nineteenth century. It was Marx who first suggested that innovations could be associated with waves of economic growth. Since then others such as Schumpeter (1934, 1939), Kondratieff (1935/51), Abernathy and Utterback (1978) have argued the long-wave theory of innovation. Kondratieff was unfortunately imprisoned by Stalin for his views on economic growth theories, because they conflicted with those of Marx. Marx suggested that capitalist economies would eventually decline, whereas Kondratieff argued that they would experience waves of growth and decline. Abernathy and Utterback (1978) contended that at the birth of any industrial sector there is radical product innovation which is then followed by radical innovation in production processes, followed, in turn, by widespread incremental innovation. This view was once popular and seemed to reflect the life cycles of many industries. It has, however, failed to offer any understanding of *how* to achieve innovative success.

Illustration 1.2: A review of the history of economic growth

The classical economists of the eighteenth and nineteenth centuries believed that technological change and capital accumulation were the engines of growth. This belief was based on the conclusion that productivity growth causes population growth, which in turn causes productivity to fall. Today's theory of population growth is very different from these early attempts at understanding economic growth. It argues that rising incomes slow the population growth because they increase the rate of opportunity cost of having children. Hence, as technology advances productivity and incomes grow.

Joseph Schumpeter was the founder of modern growth theory and is regarded as one of the world's greatest economists. In the 1930s he was the first to realise that the development and diffusion of new technologies by profit-seeking entrepreneurs formed the source of economic progress. Robert Solow, who was a student of Schumpeter, advanced his professor's theories in the 1950s and won the Nobel Prize for economic science. Paul Romer has developed these theories further and is responsible for the modern theory of economic growth, sometimes called neo-Schumpeterian economic growth theory, which argues that sustained economic growth arises from competition among firms. Firms try to increase their profits by devoting resources to creating new products and developing new ways of making existing products. It is this economic theory that underpins most innovation management and new product development theories.

Source: Adapted from M. Parkin *et al.* (1997) *Economics*, 3rd edn, Addison-Wesley, Harlow.

After the Second World War economists began to take an even greater interest in the causes of economic growth (Harrod, 1949; Domar, 1946). One of the most important influences on innovation seemed to be industrial research and development. After all, during the war, military research and development (R&D) had produced significant technological advances and innovations, including radar, aerospace and new weapons. A period of rapid growth in expenditure by countries on R&D was to follow, exemplified by US President Kennedy's 1960 speech outlining his vision of getting a man on the moon before the end of the decade. But economists soon found that there was no *direct* correlation between R&D spending and national rates of economic growth. It was clear that the linkages were more complex than first thought (this issue is explored more fully in Chapter 8).

There was a need to understand *how* science and technology affected the economic system. The neo-classical economics approach had not offered any explanations. A series of studies of innovation were undertaken in the 1950s which concentrated on the internal characteristics of the innovation process within the economy. A feature of these studies was that they adopted a cross-discipline approach, incorporating economics, organisational behaviour and business and management. The studies looked at:

- the generation of new knowledge;
- the application of this knowledge in the development of products and processes;
- the commercial exploitation of these products and services in terms of financial income generation.

In particular, these studies revealed that firms behaved differently (*see* Simon, 1957; Woodward, 1965; Carter and Williams, 1959). This led to the development of a new theoretical framework that attempted to understand how firms managed the above, and why some firms appeared to be more successful than others. Later studies in the 1960s were to confirm these initial findings and uncover significant differences in organisational characteristics (Myers and Marquis, 1969; Burns and Stalker, 1961; Cyert and March, 1963). Hence, the new framework placed more emphasis on the firm and its internal activities than had previously been the case. The firm and how it used its resources was now seen as the key influence on innovation.

Neo-classical economics is a theory of economic growth that explains how savings, investments and growth respond to population growth and technological change. The rate of technological change influences the rate of economic growth, but economic growth does not influence technological change. Rather, technological change is determined by chance. Thus population growth and technological change are exogenous. Also, neo-classical economic theory tends to concentrate on industry or economy-wide performance. It tends to ignore differences among firms in the same line of business. Any differences are assumed to reflect differences in the market environments that the organisations face. That is, differences are not achieved through choice but reflect differences in the situations in which firms operate. In contrast, research within business management and strategy focuses on these differences and the decisions that have led to them. Furthermore, the activities that take place within the firm that enable one firm seemingly to perform better than another, given the same economic and market conditions, has been the focus of much research effort since the 1960s.

The Schumpeterian view sees firms as different – it is the way a firm manages its resources over time and develops capabilities that influences its innovation performance. The varying emphasis placed by different disciplines on explaining how innovation occurs is brought together in the framework in Figure 1.1. This overview of the innovation process includes an economic perspective, a business management strategy perspective and organisational behaviour which attempts to look at the internal activities. It also recognises that firms form relationships with other firms and trade, compete and cooperate with each other. It further recognises that the activities of individuals within the firm also affect the process of innovation.

Each firm's unique organisational architecture represents the way it has constructed itself over time. This comprises its internal design, including its functions and the relationships it has built up with suppliers, competitors, customers, etc. This framework recognises that these will have a considerable impact on a firm's innovative performance. So too will the way it manages its individual functions and its employees or individuals. These are separately identified within the framework as being influential in the innovation process.

Recent and contemporary studies

As the twentieth century drew to a close there was probably as much debate and argument concerning innovation and what contributes to innovative performance as a hundred years ago. This debate has, nonetheless, progressed our understanding of the area of innovation management. It was Schumpeter who argued that modern firms

| Figure 1.1 | Overview of the innovation process |

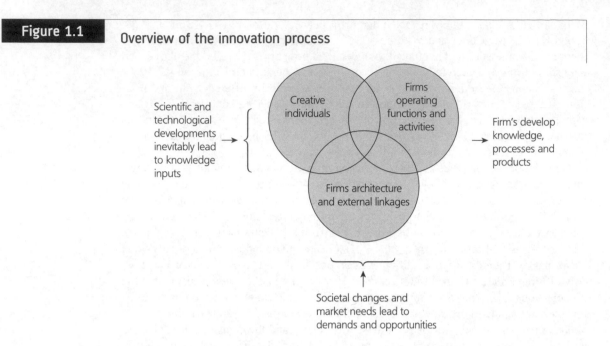

equipped with R&D laboratories have become the central innovative actors. Since his work others have contributed to the debate (Chandler, 1962; Nelson and Winter, 1982; Cohen and Levinthal, 1990; Prahalad and Hamel, 1990; Pavitt, 1990; Patel and Pavitt, 2000). This emerging Schumpeterian or evolutionary theory of dynamic firm capabilities is having a significant impact on the study of business and management today. Success in the future, as in the past, will surely lie in the ability to acquire and utilise knowledge and apply this to the development of new products. Uncovering how to do this remains one of today's most pressing management problems.

The importance of uncovering and satisfying the needs of customers is the important role played by marketing and these activities feed into the new product development process. Recent studies by Hamel and Prahalad (1994) and Christensen (2003) suggest that listening to your customer may actually stifle technological innovation and be detrimental to long-term business success. Ironically, to be successful in industries characterised by technological change, firms may be required to pursue innovations that are not demanded by their current customers. Christensen (2003) distinguishes between 'disruptive innovations' and 'sustaining innovations' (radical or incremental innovations). Sustaining innovations appealed to existing customers, since they provided improvements to established products. For example, the introduction of new computer software usually provides improvements for existing customers in terms of added features. Disruptive innovations tend to provide improvements greater than those demanded. For example, while the introduction of 3.5-inch disk drives to replace 5.25-inch drives provided an enormous improvement in performance, it also created problems for users who were familiar with the previous format. These disruptive innovations also tended to create new markets, which eventually captured the existing market (see Chapter 14 for much more on this).

The need to view innovation in an organisational context

During the early part of the nineteenth century manufacturing firms were largely family oriented and concentrated their resources on one activity. For example, one firm would produce steel from iron ore, another would roll this into sheet steel for use by, say, a manufacturer of cooking utensils. These would then be delivered to shops for sale. Towards the latter part of the century these small enterprises were gradually replaced by large firms who would perform a much wider variety of activities. The expansion in manufacturing activities was simultaneously matched by an expansion in administrative activities. This represented the beginnings of the development of the diversified functional enterprise. The world expansion in trade during the early part of the twentieth century saw the quest for new markets by developing a wide range of new products (Chandler, 1962).

Unfortunately, many of the studies of innovation have treated it as an artefact that is somehow detached from knowledge and skills and not embedded in know-how. This inevitably leads to a simplified understanding, if not a misunderstanding, of what constitutes innovation. This section shows why innovation needs to be viewed in the context of organisations and as a process within organisations.

The diagram in Figure 1.1 shows how a number of different disciplines contribute to our understanding of the innovation process. It is important to note that firms do not operate in a vacuum. They trade with each other, they work together in some areas and compete in others. Hence, the role of other firms is a major factor in understanding innovation. As discussed earlier, economics clearly has an important role to play. So too does organisational behaviour as we try to understand what activities are necessary to ensure success. Studies of management will also make a significant contribution to specific areas such as marketing, R&D, manufacturing operations and competition.

As has been suggested, in previous centuries it was easier in many ways to mobilise the resources necessary to develop and commercialise a product, largely because the resources required were, in comparison, minimal. Today, however, the resources required, in terms of knowledge, skills, money and market experience, mean that significant innovations are synonymous with organisations. Indeed, it is worthy of note that more recent innovations and scientific developments, such as significant discoveries like cell phones or computer software and hardware developments, are associated with organisations rather than individuals (*see* Table 1.3). Moreover, the increasing depth of our understanding of science inhibits the breadth of scientific study. In the early part of the twentieth century, for example, ICI was regarded as a world leader in chemistry. Now it is almost impossible for chemical companies to be scientific leaders in all areas of chemistry. The large companies have specialised in particular areas. This is true of many other industries. Even university departments are having to concentrate their resources on particular areas of science. They are no longer able to offer teaching and research in all fields. In addition, the creation, development and commercial success of new ideas require a great deal of input from a variety of specialist sources and often vast amounts of money. Hence, today's innovations are associated with groups of people or companies. Innovation is invariably a team game. This will be explored more fully in Chapters 3, 6 and 15.

Pause for thought

If two different firms, similar in size, operating in the same industry spend the same on R&D, will their level of innovation be the same?

Table 1.3 More recent technological innovations

Date	New product	Responsible organisation
1930s	Polythene	ICI
1945	Ballpoint pen	Reynolds International Pen Company
1950s	Manufacturing process: fbat glass	Pilkington
1970/80s	Ulcer treatment drug: Zantac	GlaxoSmithKline
1970/80s	Photocopying	Xerox
1980s	Personal computer	Apple Computer
1980/90s	Computer operating system: Windows 95	Microsoft
1995	Impotence drug: Viagra	Pfizer
2000s	Cell phones	Nokia

Individuals in the innovation process

Figure 1.1 identifies individuals as a key component of the innovation process. Within organisations it is individuals who define problems, have ideas and perform creative linkages and associations that lead to inventions. Moreover, within organisations it is individuals in the role of managers who decide what activities should be undertaken, the amount of resources to be deployed and how they should be carried out. This has led to the development of so-called key individuals in the innovation process such as inventor, entrepreneur, business sponsor, etc. These will be discussed in detail in Chapter 3.

Problems of definition and vocabulary

While there are many arguments and debates in virtually all fields of management, it seems that this is particularly the case in innovation management. Very often these centre on semantics. This is especially so when innovation is viewed as a single event.

When viewed as a *process*, however, the differences are less substantive. At the heart of this book is the thesis that innovation needs to be viewed as a process. If one accepts that inventions are new discoveries, new ways of doing things, and that products are the eventual outputs from the inventions, that process from new discovery to eventual product is the innovation process. A useful analogy would be education, where qualifications are the formal outputs of the education process. Education, like innovation, is not and cannot be viewed as an event.

Arguments become stale when we attempt to define terms such as new, creativity or discovery. It often results in a game of semantics. First, what is new to one company may be 'old hat' to another. Second, how does one judge success in terms of commercial gain or scientific achievement? Are they both not valid and justified goals in themselves? Third, it is context dependent – what is viewed as a success today may be viewed as a failure in the future. We need to try to understand how to encourage innovation in order that we may help to develop more successful new products (this point is explored in Chapters 11 and 12).

Entrepreneurship

In the United States the subject of innovation management is often covered in terms of 'entrepreneurship'. Indeed, there are many courses available for students in US business schools on this topic. In a study of past and future research on the subject of entrepreneurship, Low and MacMillan (1988) define it as 'the process of planning, organising, operating, and assuming the risk of a business venture'.

It is the analysis of the role of the individual entrepreneur that distinguishes the study of entrepreneurship from that of innovation management. Furthermore, it is starting small businesses and growing them into large and successful businesses that is the focus of attention of those studying entrepreneurship. For example, the *Sunday Times* reported how the founder of *The Source*, Daniel Mitchell, developed and grew his business from zero to sales of £35 million. Mitchell argues that 'success is about customers, but it is also about the people you employ' (*Sunday Times*, 2004).

Design

The definition of design with regard to business seems to be widening ever further and encompassing almost all aspects of business (*see* The Design Council, www.Designcouncil.com). For many people design is about developing or creating something, hence we are into semantics regarding how this differs from innovation. Hargadon and Douglas (2001: 476) suggest design is concerned with the emergent arrangement of concrete details that embody a new idea. A key question however, is how design relates to research and development? Indeed, it seems that in most cases the word *design* and the word *development* mean the same thing. Traditionally design referred to the development of drawings, plans and sketches. Indeed, most dictionary definitions continue with this view today and refer to a designer as a 'draughtsman who makes plans for manufacturers or prepares drawings for clothing or stage productions' (Oxford English Dictionary, 2003). In the aerospace industry engineers and designers would have previously worked closely together for many years developing drawings

| Figure 1.2 | The interaction between development activities and design environment |

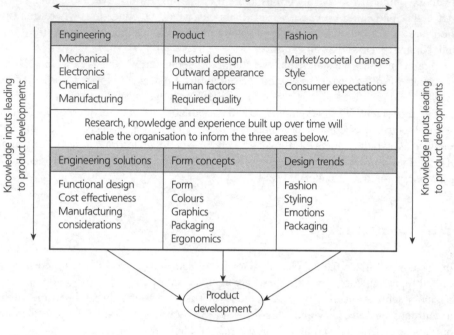

The spectrum of design activities

Knowledge inputs leading to product developments

Engineering	Product	Fashion
Mechanical Electronics Chemical Manufacturing	Industrial design Outward appearance Human factors Required quality	Market/societal changes Style Consumer expectations

Research, knowledge and experience built up over time will enable the organisation to inform the three areas below.

Engineering solutions	Form concepts	Design trends
Functional design Cost effectiveness Manufacturing considerations	Form Colours Graphics Packaging Ergonomics	Fashion Styling Emotions Packaging

Product development

for an aircraft. Today the process is dominated by computer software programmes that facilitate all aspects of the activity; hence the product development activities and the environments in which design occurs have changed considerably. Figure 1.2 shows, along the horizontal axis, the wide spectrum of activities that design encompasses from clothing design to design within electronics. The vertical axis shows how the areas of design feed into outputs from choice of colour to cost effectiveness; all of which are considered in the development of a product. The view taken by this book is to view design as an applied activity within research and development, and to recognise that in certain industries, like clothing for example, design is the main component in product development. In other industries, however, such as pharmaceuticals design forms only a small part of the product development activity.

Innovation and invention

Many people confuse these terms. Indeed, if you were to ask people for an explanation you would collect a diverse range of definitions. It is true that innovation is the first cousin of invention, but they are not identical twins that can be interchanged. Hence, it is important to establish clear meanings for them.

Innovation itself is a very broad concept that can be understood in a variety of ways. One of the more comprehensive definitions is offered by Myers and Marquis (1969):

Innovation is not a single action but a total process of interrelated sub processes. It is not just the conception of a new idea, nor the invention of a new device, nor the development of a new market. The process is all these things acting in an integrated fashion.

It is important to clarify the use of the term 'new' in the context of innovation. Rogers and Shoemaker (1972) do this eloquently:

It matters little, as far as human behaviour is concerned, whether or not an idea is 'objectively' new as measured by the lapse of time since its first use or discovery . . . If the idea seems new and different to the individual, it is an innovation [emphasis added].

Most writers, including those above, distinguish innovation from invention by suggesting that innovation is concerned with the *commercial and practical application* of ideas or inventions. Invention, then, is the conception of the idea, whereas innovation is the subsequent translation of the invention into the economy (US Dept of Commerce, 1967). The following simple equation helps to show the relationship between the two terms:

Innovation = theoretical conception + technical invention
                + commercial exploitation

However, all the terms in this equation will need explanation in order to avoid confusion. The *conception* of new ideas is the starting point for innovation. A new idea by itself, while interesting, is neither an invention nor an innovation, it is merely a concept or a thought or collection of thoughts. The process of converting intellectual thoughts into a tangible new artefact (usually a product or process) is an *invention*. This is where science and technology usually play a significant role. At this stage inventions need to be combined with hard work by many different people to convert them into products that will improve company performance. These later activities represent *exploitation*. However, it is the *complete* process that represents *innovation*. This introduces the notion that innovation is a process with a number of distinctive features that have to be managed. This is the view taken by this book. To summarise, then, innovation depends on inventions but inventions need to be harnessed to commercial activities before they can contribute to the growth of an organisation. Thus:

Innovation is the management of all the activities involved in the process of idea generation, technology development, manufacturing and marketing of a new (or improved) product or manufacturing process or equipment.

This definition of innovation as a management process also offers a distinction between an innovation and a product, the latter being the output of innovation. Illustration 1.3 should help to clarify the differences.

It is necessary at this point to cross-reference these discussions with the practical realities of managing a business today. The senior vice-president for research and development at 3M, one of the most highly respected and innovative organisations, recently defined innovation as:

Creativity: the thinking of novel and appropriate ideas.
Innovation: the successful implementation of those ideas within an organisation.

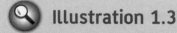

Illustration 1.3

An example of an invention

Scientists and development engineers at a household cleaning products company had been working for many months on developing a new lavatory cleaning product. They had developed a liquid that when sprayed into the toilet pan, on contact with water, would fizz and sparkle. The effect was to give the impression of a tough, active cleaning product. The company applied for a patent and further developments and market research were planned.

However, initial results both from technical and market specialists led to the abandonment of the project. The preliminary market feedback suggested a fear of such a product on the part of consumers. This was because the fizz and sparkle looked too dramatic and frightening. Furthermore, additional technical research revealed a short shelf-life for the mixture. This is a clear example of an invention that did not progress beyond the organisation to a commercial product.

Successful and unsuccessful innovations

There is often a great deal of confusion surrounding innovations that are not commercially successful. A famous example would be the Kodak Disc Camera or the Sinclair C5. This was a small, electrically driven tricycle or car. Unfortunately for Clive Sinclair, the individual behind the development of the product, it was not commercially successful. Commercial failure, however, does not relegate an innovation to an invention. Using the definition established above, the fact that the product progressed from the drawing board into the marketplace makes it an innovation – albeit an unsuccessful one.

Pause for thought   ❓

In 2003 the BBC ran a series of television programmes exploring the innovation route from idea to retail shelf. Viewers were asked to cast their vote on a selection of innovative prototype products; the winning three products would receive financial and technical backing to develop and market their idea. Some of the winning ideas were: revolutionary swimming goggles; a new type of ink pen; a collapsing waste basket. Which of these are inventions and which are innovations?

Different types of innovations

Industrial innovation not only includes major (radical) innovations but also minor (incremental) technological advances. Indeed, the definition offered above suggests that successful commercialisation of the innovation may involve considerably wider organisational changes. For example, the introduction of a radical, technological innovation, such as digital cameras by Kodak and Fuji, invariably results in substantial internal organisational changes. In this case substantial changes occurred with the manufacturing, marketing and sales functions. Both of these firms decided to concentrate on the rapidly developing digital photography market. Yet, both Fuji and Kodak were the market leaders in supplying traditional 35mm film cartridges. Their market share of the actual camera market was less significant. Such strategic decisions forced changes on all areas of the business. For example, in Kodak's case the manufacturing function underwent substantial changes as it began to substantially cut production of 35mm film cartridges. Opportunities existed for manufacturing in producing digital cameras and their associated equipment. Similarly, the marketing function had to employ extra sales staff to educate and reassure retail outlets that the new technology would not cannibalise their film-processing business. While many people would begin to print photographs from their PCs at home many people would continue to want their digital camera film processed into physical photographs. For both Fuji and Kodak the new technology has completely changed the photographic industry. Both firms have seen their revenues fall from film cartridge sales, but Kodak and Fuji are now market leaders in digital cameras whereas before they were not.

Hence, technological innovation can be accompanied by additional managerial and organisational changes, often referred to as innovations. This presents a far more blurred picture and begins to widen the definition of innovation to include virtually any organisational or managerial change. Table 1.4 shows a typology of innovations.

Innovation was defined earlier in this section as the application of knowledge. It is this notion that lies at the heart of all types of innovations, be they product, process or

Table 1.4 A typology of innovations

Type of innovation	Example
Product innovation	The development of a new or improved product
Process innovation	The development of a new manufacturing process such as Pilkington's fbat glass process
Organisational innovation	A new venture division; a new internal communication system; introduction of a new accounting procedure
Management innovation	TQM (total quality management) systems; BPR (business process re-engineering); introduction of SAPR3*
Production innovation	Quality circles; just-in-time (JIT) manufacturing system; new production planning software, e.g. MRP II; new inspection system
Commercial/marketing innovation	New fhancing arrangements; new sales approach, e.g. direct marketing
Service innovation	Internet-based fhancial services

SAP is a German software fm and R3 is an Enterprise Resource Planning (ERP) product.

service. It is also worthy of note that many studies have suggested that product innovations are soon followed by process innovations in what they describe as an industry innovation cycle (*see* Chapter 12). Furthermore, it is common to associate innovation with physical change, but many changes introduced within organisations involve very little physical change. Rather, it is the activities performed by individuals that change. A good example of this is the adoption of so-called Japanese management techniques by automobile manufacturers in Europe and the United States.

It is necessary to stress at the outset that this book concentrates on the management of product innovation. This does not imply that the list of innovations above are less significant; this focus has been chosen to ensure clarity and to facilitate the study of innovation.

Technology and science

We also need to consider the role played by *science and technology* in innovation. The continual fascination with science and technology at the end of the nineteenth century and subsequent growth in university teaching and research have led to the development of many new strands of science. The proliferation of scientific journals over the past 30 years demonstrates the rapidly evolving nature of science and technology. The scientific literature seems to double in quantity every five years (Rothwell and Zegveld, 1985).

Science can be defined as systematic and formulated knowledge. There are clearly significant differences between science and technology. Technology is often seen as being the application of science and has been defined in many ways (Lefever, 1992). It is important to remember that technology is not an accident of nature. It is the product of deliberate action by human beings. The following definition is suggested:

> Technology is knowledge applied to products or production processes.

No definition is perfect and the above is no exception. It does, however, provide a good starting point from which to view technology with respect to innovation. It is important to note that technology, like education, cannot be purchased off the shelf, like a can of tomatoes. It is embedded in knowledge and skills.

In a lecture given to the Royal Society in 1992 the former chairman of Sony, Akio Morita, suggested that, unlike engineers, scientists are held in high esteem. This, he suggested, is because science provides us with information which was previously unknown. Yet technology comes from employing and *manipulating science* into concepts, processes and devices. These, in turn, can be used to make our life or work more efficient, convenient and powerful. Hence, it is technology, as an *outgrowth of science*, that fuels the industrial engine. And it is *engineers* and not scientists who make technology happen. In Japan, he argued, you will notice that almost every major manufacturer is run by an engineer or technologist. However, in the United Kingdom, some manufacturing companies are led by chief executive officers (CEOs) who do not understand the technology that goes into their own products. Indeed, many UK corporations are headed by chartered accountants. With the greatest respect to accountants, their central concerns are statistics and figures of *past* performance. How can an accountant reach out and grab the future if he or she is always looking at *last* quarter's results (Morita, 1992)?

The above represents the personal views of an influential senior figure within industry. There are many leading industrialists, economists and politicians who would concur (Hutton, 1995). But there are equally many who would profoundly disagree. The debate on improving economic innovative performance is one of the most important in the field of political economics.

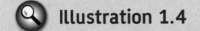

Illustration 1.4

FT

Theory and Practice

Too much of a good thing: innovation increases in a competitive market – but only up to a point, says a new study

'Competition good, market power bad' is as close as popular economics gets to a religious belief.

The faith is perhaps best articulated in Adam Smith's *Wealth of Nations* (1776), the bible of free-market economists.

'To widen the market and to narrow the competition is always the interest of the dealers . . . The proposal of any new law or regulation of commerce which comes from this order, ought always to be listened to with great precaution, and ought never to be adopted, till after having been long and carefully examined, not only with the most scrupulous, but with the most suspicious attention.'

But if competition so clearly works wonders by reducing costs, providing incentives for efficient production and eliminating vested interests, it has generated a surprising number of powerful critics over the years.

The main complaint, echoed in work from Joseph Schumpeter, one of the most famous economists of the last century, to Bill Gates, chairman of Microsoft, is that these notions fail to take account of the dynamic forces in markets.

If entrepreneurs cannot protect their ideas and inventions from competitors, innovation will be stifled and the progress of capitalism undermined.

Adam Smith's suspicion of laws or regulations that are in the interests of 'the dealers' still dominates the thrust of competition policy.

But the disbelievers have had success in transforming theory into competition policy in some areas. Politicians have created patents to protect new ideas; trademarks outlaw the copying of brands, designs, words and phrases; and copyright laws protect the original way an idea is expressed, for example in books, cinema or music.

In each case, the idea was to encourage innovation, to ensure that the benefits of progress accrue to those with the original idea, not to those who are good at reproducing it. Restrictions on all-out competition have been tolerated in the hope of generating innovation and a more dynamic economy.

So who is right, Smith or Schumpeter? In the mid-1990s, a serious problem emerged with the Schumpeterian view so beloved by drugs companies and Bill Gates: many studies found little connection between more innovative industries and markets where competition was restricted.

This work has now been extended by an international team of academic economists who have developed a theory from evidence relating innovation to competition. The study* concludes that innovation is least likely in the most and the least competitive industries.

Where competition is rife, companies refuse to spend money on innovation for fear that they will not be able to profit from their ideas. And where companies have lots of market power, they become lazy and do not bother to innovate.

Rachel Griffith, one of the authors, says: 'The theory appeals to common sense and fits the evidence well.'

►

It is probably in its painstaking use of data that the research itself is most innovative. The team collected information on a panel of 461 companies listed on the London Stock Exchange between 1968 and 1996, from which they measured the degree of competition each company faced. They combined this data with information from the US patent office to determine how innovative each company had been. Because some patents are trivial, the team considered not just the number of patents received by a company but also how often it was subsequently cited in other successful patents.

The results are striking. Companies in highly competitive and monopolistic industries were much less innovative than companies in the middle. Using profit margins as a proxy for competition, companies with margins of about 10 per cent on average produced 40 per cent more patents than companies with margins of 3 per cent or 20 per cent.

The research also evaluated the importance of other details of market structure on innovation. Where companies were neck and neck – for example Procter & Gamble and Unilever in the soap powder market – more innovation would occur than if one company was a clear leader, with many laggards. The research concludes that in neck-and-neck markets, the advantages of getting ahead (and so achieving a quieter life) encourages more innovation in all companies, while less innovation occurs overall if one company has a clear advantage.

These results seem to give rather awkward policy prescriptions for competition authorities: try to encourage competition, particularly if companies are evenly matched, but only up to a point – after which it can become counter-productive.

But Dr Griffith says it is possible to draw a more subtle conclusion. 'You must strive to encourage competition to drive down profits in the absence of innovation, while allowing companies just enough protection to profit in the future from their current ideas.'

The moral is that, as long as the cost of innovation can be recovered, competition should be encouraged. It suggests that existing protection of innovative ideas that generate large profit margins, for example in software and pharmaceuticals, has gone too far and is encouraging laziness not dynamism. Adam Smith would be pleased.

* *Source*: 'Aghion *et al.*, 'Competition and innovation: an inverted U relationship', www.ifs.org.uk/workingpapers/ wp0202.pdfchris.giles@www.FT.com; C. Giles, 'Theory and practice', *Financial Times*, 14 May 2002. Reprinted with permission.

Popular views of innovation

Science, technology and innovation have received a great deal of popular media coverage over the years, from Hollywood and Disney movies to best-selling novels (*see* Figure 1.3). This is probably because science and technology can help turn vivid imaginings into a possibility. The end result, however, is a simplified image of scientific discoveries and innovations. It usually consists of a lone professor, with a mass of white hair, working away in his garage and stumbling, by accident, on a major new discovery. Through extensive trial and error, usually accompanied by dramatic experiments, this is eventually developed into an amazing invention. This is best demonstrated in the blockbuster movie *Back to the Future*. Christopher Lloyd plays the eccentric scientist and Michael J. Fox his young, willing accomplice. Together they are involved in an exciting journey that enables Fox to travel back in time and influence the future.

Cartoons have also contributed to a misleading image of the innovation process. Here, the inventor, an eccentric scientist, is portrayed with a glowing lightbulb above

The popular view of science

Figure 1.3

his head, as a flash of inspiration results in a new scientific discovery. We have all seen and laughed at these funny cartoons.

This humorous and popular view of inventions and innovations has been reinforced over the years and continues to occur in the popular press. Many industrialists and academics have argued that this simple view of a complex phenomenon has caused immense harm to the understanding of science and technology.

Models of innovation

Traditional arguments about innovation have centred around two schools of thought. On the one hand the social deterministic school argued that innovations were the result of a combination of external social factors and influences, such as demographic changes, economic influences and cultural changes. The argument was that *when* the conditions were 'right' innovations would occur. On the other hand the individualistic school argued that innovations were the result of unique individual talents and such innovators are born. Closely linked to the individualistic theory is the important role played by serendipity; more on this later.

Over the past 10 years the literature on what 'drives' innovation has tended to divide into two schools of thought: the market-based view and the resource-based view. The market-based view argues that market conditions provide the context which facilitate or constrain the extent of firm innovation activity (Slater and Narver, 1994; Porter, 1980, 1985). The key issue here, of course, is the ability of firms to recognise opportunities in the market place. Cohen and Levinthal (1990) and Trott (1998) would argue that few firms have the ability to scan and search their environments effectively.

The resource-based view of innovation considers that a market-driven orientation does not provide a secure foundation for formulating innovation strategies for markets which are dynamic and volatile; rather a firm's own resources provide a much more stable context in which to develop its innovation activity and shape its markets in accordance to its own view (Penrose, 1959; Wernerfelt, 1984; Wernerfelt, 1995; Grant, 1996; Prahalad and Hamel, 1990; Conner and Prahalad, 1996; Eisenhardt and Martin, 2000). The resource-based view of innovation focuses on the firm and its resources, capabilities and skills. It argues that when firms have resources that are valuable, rare and not easily copied they can achieve a sustainable competitive advantage – frequently in the form of innovative new products. Chapter 6 offers a more detailed overview of the resource-based theory of the firm.

Serendipity

Many studies of historical cases of innovation have highlighted the importance of the unexpected discovery. The role of serendipity or luck is offered as an explanation. As we have seen, this view is also reinforced in the popular media. It is, after all, everyone's dream that they will accidentally uncover a major new invention leading to fame and fortune.

On closer inspection of these historical cases, serendipity is rare indeed. After all, in order to recognise the significance of an advance one would need to have some prior knowledge in that area. Most discoveries are the result of people who have had a fascination with a particular area of science or technology and it is following extended efforts on their part that advances are made. Discoveries may not be expected, but in the words of Louis Pasteur, 'chance favours the prepared mind'.

Linear models

It was US economists after the Second World War who championed the linear model of science and innovation. Since then, largely because of its simplicity, this model has taken a firm grip on people's views on how innovation occurs. Indeed, it dominated science and industrial policy for 40 years. It was only in the 1980s that management schools around the world began seriously to challenge the sequential linear process. The recognition that innovation occurs through the interaction of the science base (dominated by universities and industry), technological development (dominated by industry) and the needs of the market was a significant step forward (*see* Figure 1.4). The explanation of the interaction of these activities forms the basis of models of innovation today.

There is, of course, a great deal of debate and disagreement about precisely what activities influence innovation and, more importantly, the internal processes that affect a company's ability to innovate.

Nonetheless, there is broad agreement that it is the linkages between these key components that will produce successful innovation. Importantly, the devil is in the detail. From a European perspective an area that requires particular attention is the linkage between the science base and technological development. The European Union (EU) believes that European universities have not established effective links with industry, whereas in the United States universities have been working closely with industry for many years.

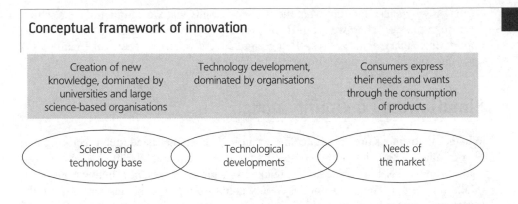

Figure 1.4

Conceptual framework of innovation

As explained above, the innovation process has traditionally been viewed as a sequence of separable stages or activities. There are two basic variations of this model for product innovation. First, and most crudely, there is the technology-driven model (often referred to as 'technology push') where it is assumed that scientists make unexpected discoveries, technologists apply them to develop product ideas and engineers and designers turn them into prototypes for testing. It is left to manufacturing to devise ways of producing the products efficiently. Finally, marketing and sales will promote the product to the potential consumer. In this model the marketplace was a passive recipient for the fruits of R&D. This technology-push model dominated industrial policy after the Second World War (*see* Figure 1.5). While this model of innovation can be applied to a few cases, most notably the pharmaceutical industry, it is not applicable in many other instances; in particular where the innovation process follows a different route.

It was not until the 1970s that new studies of actual innovations suggested that the role of the marketplace was influential in the innovation process (von Hippel, 1978). This led to the second linear model, the 'market-pull' model of innovation. The customer need-driven model emphasises the role of marketing as an initiator of new ideas resulting from close interactions with customers. These, in turn, are conveyed to R&D for design and engineering and then to manufacturing for production. In fast-moving consumer goods industries the role of the market and the customer remains powerful and very influential. The managing director of McCain Foods argues that knowing your customer is crucial to turning innovation into profits:

Figure 1.5

Linear models of innovation

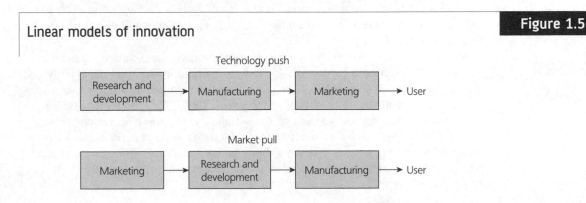

'Its only by understanding what the customer wants that we can identify the innovative opportunities. Then we see if there's technology that we can bring to bear on the opportunities that exist', he says. 'Being innovative is relatively easy – the hard part is ensuring your ideas become commercially viable' (Murray, 2003).

Simultaneous coupling model

Whether innovations are stimulated by technology, customer need, manufacturing or a host of other factors, including competition, misses the point. The models above concentrate on what is driving the downstream efforts rather than on *how* innovations occur (Galbraith, 1982). The linear model is only able to offer an explanation of *where* the initial stimulus for innovation was born, that is, where the trigger for the idea or need was initiated. The simultaneous coupling model shown in Figure 1.6 suggests that it is the result of the simultaneous coupling of the knowledge within all three functions that will foster innovation. Furthermore, the point of commencement for innovation is not known in advance.

| Figure 1.6 | The simultaneous coupling model |

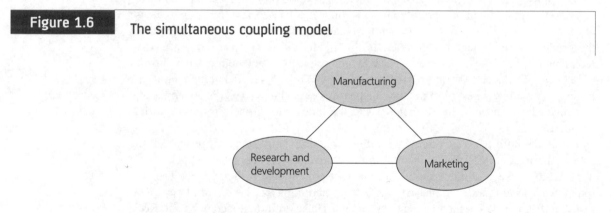

Interactive model

The interactive model develops this idea further (*see* Figure 1.7) and links together the technology-push and market-pull models. It emphasises that innovations occur as the result of the interaction of the marketplace, the science base and the organisation's capabilities. Like the coupling model, there is no explicit starting point. The use of information flows is used to explain how innovations transpire and that they can arise from a wide variety of points.

While still oversimplified, this is a more comprehensive representation of the innovation process. It can be regarded as a logically sequential, though not necessarily continuous, process that can be divided into a series of functionally distinct but interacting and interdependent stages (Rothwell and Zegveld, 1985). The overall innovation process can be thought of as a complex set of communication paths over which knowledge is transferred. These paths include internal and external linkages. The innovation process outlined in Figure 1.7 represents the organisation's capabilities and its linkages with both the marketplace and the science base. Organisations that are able to manage this process effectively will be successful at innovation.

Interactive model of innovation

Figure 1.7

Source: Adapted
from B. Rothwell and
W. Zegveld (1985)
*Reindustrialisation and
Technology*, Longman,
London.

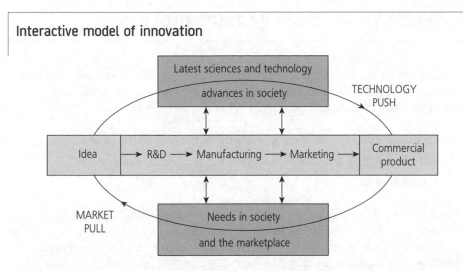

At the centre of the model are the organisational functions of R&D, engineering and design, manufacturing and marketing and sales. While at first this may appear to be a linear model, the flow of communication is not necessarily linear. There is provision for feedback. Also, linkages with the science base and the marketplace occur between all functions, not just with R&D or marketing. For example, as often happens, it may be the manufacturing function which initiates a design improvement that leads to the introduction of either a different material or the eventual development by R&D of a new material. Finally, the generation of ideas is shown to be dependent on inputs from three basic components (as outlined in Figure 1.4): organisation capabilities; the needs of the marketplace; the science and technology base.

Table 1.5 summarises the historical development of the dominant models of the industrial innovation process.

Table 1.5 The chronological development of models of innovation

Date	Model	Characteristics
1950/60s	Technology push	Simple linear sequential process; emphasis on R&D; the market is a recipient of the fruits of R&D
1970s	Market pull	Simple linear sequential process; emphasis on marketing; the market is the source for directing R&D; R&D has a reactive role
1980s	Coupling model	Emphasis on integrating R&D and marketing
1980/90s	Interactive model	Combinations of push and pull
2000s	Network model	Emphasis on knowledge accumulation and external linkages

Source: Based on R. Rothwell (1992) 'Successful industrial innovation: critical factors for the 1990s', *R&D Management*, Vol. 22, No. 3, 221–39.

Innovation as a management process

The preceding sections have revealed that innovation is not a singular event, but a series of activities that are linked in some way to the others. This may be described as a process and involves (Kelly and Kranzberg, 1978):

1 a response to either a need or an opportunity that is context dependent;
2 a creative effort that if successful results in the introduction of novelty;
3 the need for further changes.

Usually in trying to capture this complex process the simplification has led to misunderstandings. The simple linear model of innovation can be applied to only a few innovations and is more applicable to certain industries than others. The pharmaceutical industry characterises much of the technology-push model. Other industries, like the food industry, are better represented by the market-pull model. For most industries and organisations innovations are the result of a mixture of the two. Managers working within these organisations have the difficult task of trying to manage this complex process.

A framework for the management of innovation

Industrial innovation and new product development have evolved considerably from their early beginnings outlined above. However, establishing departmental functions to perform the main tasks of business strategy, R&D, manufacturing and marketing does not solve the firm's problems. Indeed, as we have seen, innovation is extremely complex and involves the effective management of a variety of different activities. It is precisely how the process is managed that needs to be examined. Over the past 50 years there have been numerous studies of innovation attempting to understand not only the ingredients necessary for it to occur but what levels of ingredients are required and in what order. Table 1.6 captures some of the key studies that have influenced our understanding.

A framework is presented in Figure 1.8 that helps to illustrate innovation as a management process. This framework does not pretend to any analytical status, it is simply an aid in describing the main factors which need to be considered if innovation is to be successfully managed. It helps to show that while the interactions of the functions inside the organisation are important, so too are the interactions of those functions with the external environment. Scientists and engineers within the firm will be continually interacting with fellow scientists in universities and other firms about scientific and technological developments. Similarly, the marketing function will need to interact with suppliers, distributors, customers and competitors to ensure that the day-to-day activities of understanding customer needs and getting products to customers are achieved. Business planners and senior management will likewise communicate with a wide variety of firms and other external institutions, such as government departments, suppliers and customers. All these information flows contribute to the wealth of

Table 1.6 Studies of innovation management

	Study	Date	Focus
1	Carter and Williams	1957	Industry and technical progress
2	Project Hindsight – TRACES, (Isensen)	1968	Historical reviews of US government-funded defence industry
3	Wealth from knowledge (Langrish *et al.*)	1972	Queens Awards for technical innovation
4	Project SAPPHO (Rothwell *et al.*, 1974)	1974	Success and failure factors in chemical industry
5	Minnesota Studies (Van de Ven)	1989	14 case studies of innovations
6	Rothwell	1992	25 year review of studies
7	Sources of innovation (Wheelwright and Clark)	1992	Different levels of user involvement
8	MIT studies (Utterback)	1994	5 major industry-level cases
9	Project NEWPROD (Cooper)	1994	Longditudinal survey of success & failure in new products
10	Radical innovation (Leifer *et al.*)	2000	Review of mature businesses

knowledge held by the organisation. Recognising this, capturing and utilising it to develop successful new products forms the difficult management process of innovation.

Within any organisation there are likely to be many different functions. Depending on the nature of the business, some functions will be more influential than others. The framework shown in Figure 1.8 identifies three main functions: marketing, research and manufacturing and business planning. Historical studies have identified these functions as the most influential in the innovation process. Whether one lists three or seven functions misses the point, which is that it is the interaction of these internal functions and the flow of knowledge between them that needs to be facilitated (Trott, 1993). Similarly, as shown on the framework, effective communication with the external environment also requires encouragement and support (Mason *et al.*, 2004).

Pause for thought

Surely all innovations start with an idea and end with a product, does that not make it a linear process?

Figure 1.8 Innovation as a management process

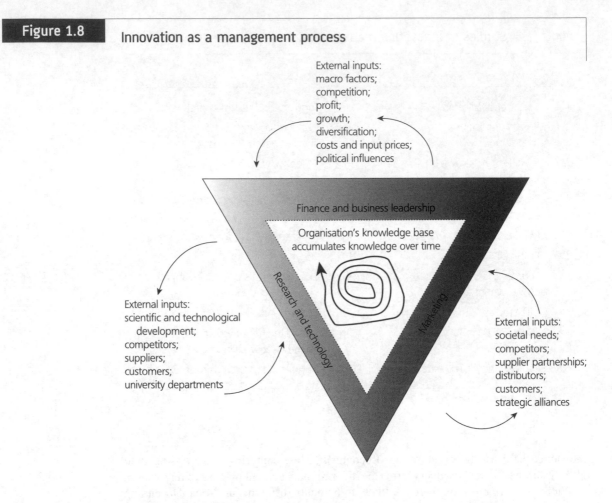

The need to share and exchange knowledge (network models)

The framework in Figure 1.8 emphasises the importance placed on interaction (both formal and informal) within the innovation process. Indeed, innovation has been described as an information–creation process that arises out of social interaction. In effect, the firm provides a structure within which the creative process is located (Nonaka and Kenney, 1991).

These interactions provide the opportunity for thoughts, potential ideas and views to be shared and exchanged. However, we are often unable to explain what we normally do; we can be competent without being able to offer a theoretical account of our actions (Polanyi, 1966). This is referred to as 'tacit knowledge'. A great deal of technical skill is know-how and much industrial innovation occurs through on-the-spot experiments, a kind of action-oriented research with *ad hoc* modifications during step-by-step processes, through which existing repertoires are extended. Such knowledge can only be learned through practice and experience. This view has recently found support from a study of Japanese firms (Nonaka, 1991) where the creation of new knowledge within an organisation depends on tapping the tacit and often highly subjective insights, intuitions and hunches of individual employees and making those insights available for testing and use by the organisation as a whole. This implies that certain knowledge and skills, embodied in the term 'know-how', are not easily understood; moreover they are less able to be communicated. This would suggest that to gain access to such knowledge one may have to be practising in this or related areas of knowledge. Cohen and Levinthal (1990: 130) refer to this condition as 'lockout', suggesting that failure to invest in research and technology will limit an organisation's ability to capture technological opportunities: 'once off the technological escalator it's difficult to get back on'.

In addition to informal interactions, the importance of formal interactions is also highlighted. There is a substantial amount of research stressing the need for a 'shared language' within organisations to facilitate internal communication (Allen, 1977; Tushman, 1978). The arguments are presented along the following lines. If all actors in the organisation share the same specialised language, they will be effective in their communication. Hence, there needs to be an overlap of knowledge in order for communication to occur. Such arguments have led to developments in cross-functional interfaces, for example between R&D, design, manufacturing and marketing. Concurrent engineering is an extension of this; in this particular case a small team consisting of a member from each of the various functional departments manages the design, development, manufacture and marketing of a product (*see* Chapter 15 for more on concurrent engineering).

Such thinking is captured in the framework outlined in Figure 1.8. It stresses the importance of interaction and communication within and between functions and with the external environment. This networking structure allows lateral communication, helping managers and their staff unleash creativity. This framework emphasises the importance of informal and formal networking across all functions.

This introduces a tension between the need for diversity, on the one hand, in order to generate novel linkages and associations, and the need for commonality, on the other, to facilitate effective internal communication. Clearly, there will be an organisational trade-off between diversity and commonality of knowledge across individuals.

Introducing organisational heritage

Finally, the centre of the framework is represented as organisational heritage, sometimes referred to as the organisational knowledge base. This does not mean the culture of the organisation. It represents a combination of the organisation's knowledge base (established and built up over the years of operating) and the organisation's unique architecture (see p. 9). This organisational heritage represents for many firms a powerful competitive advantage that enables them to compete with other firms. For the UK retail giant Tesco it is its distribution efficiencies and customer service, developed and built up over decades, that provides the company with a powerful competitive advantage. Siemens' organisational heritage is dominated by its continual investment over almost 100 years in science and technology and the high profile given to science and technology within its businesses. For Unilever, its organisational heritage can be said to lie in its brand management skills and know-how developed over many years. These heritages cannot be ignored or dismissed as irrelevant when trying to understand how companies manage their innovative effort.

This framework will be used as a navigational map to help guide readers through this complex field of study. Very often product innovation is viewed from a purely marketing perspective with little, if any, consideration of the R&D function and the difficulties of managing science and technology. Likewise, many manufacturing and technology approaches to product innovation have previously not taken sufficient notice of the needs of the customer. Finally, the organisational heritage of the firm will influence its future decisions regarding the markets in which it will operate. The point here is that firms do not have a completely free choice. What they do in the future will depend to some extent on what they have done in the past.

Case study

European Innovation Scoreboard (European Commission, 2003)[1]

Introduction

In a response to increased competition and globalisation the European Council argued for increased and enhanced efforts to improve the Union's performance in innovation. In March 2000 in the picturesque city of Lisbon the Union set itself the goal of becoming the most competitive and dynamic, knowledge-based economy in the world within the next decade. Fine words one may say, but precisely how does one set about achieving this laudable goal? A strategy was developed and presented in Stockholm in March 2001. The strategy was to build on the economic convergence that had been developed over the past 10 years within the EU single market and to coordinate an 'open method' of developing policies for creating new skills, knowledge and innovation. To support this approach the European Commission stated that there was a need for an assessment of how member countries were performing in the area of innovation. The idea of a 'Scoreboard' was launched to indicate the performance of member states. This would be conducted every year as a way of assessing the performance of member countries. It is essentially a benchmarking exercise where the European Union can assess its performance against other countries, most notably Japan and the United States.

This is an extremely ambitious project to try to assess innovative ability. There have been many studies over the past two decades that have tried to identify the factors necessary for innovation to occur (see Table 1.6), and while many factors have been identified many of these are necessary but not sufficient in themselves. Moreover, some governments have attempted to develop 'innovation tool-kits' and 'scorecards' to try to help firms in their own countries to become more innovative (UK Department of Trade and Industry). Most of these have not been successful. This ambitious project by the European Union is full of limitations and is generally regarded as over-simplistic. This is largely because the economic conditions of the member countries are so very different and all have a wide variety of strengths and weaknesses. None the less, in order to assess where the European Union should target help and the precise type of help required by each member it is necessary to analyse the innovative performance of countries. The scoreboard is an initial attempt at a very challenging exercise.

The 2003 Innovation Scoreboard

The Innovation Scoreboard is designed to complement the structural indicators. These are

[1] This case has been written as a basis for class discussion rather than to illustrate effective or ineffective managerial or administrative behaviour. It has been prepared from a variety of published sources, as indicated, and from observations.

things like education systems, financial systems for raising capital, levels of employment, etc., which the EU Commission currently assesses through other mechanisms and statistical analysis. To minimise the additional statistical burden, the Innovation Scoreboard mainly uses official Eurostat data, if official data is not available. It analyses statistical data on 17 indicators in four areas, depicts achievements and trends, highlights strengths and weaknesses and examines the extent of convergence in innovation. The four key areas are as follows:

1 *Knowledge creation*. The three indicators used for the creation of new knowledge are public R&D expenditure, business R&D expenditure and patenting activity.

2 *Human resources*. The scale and quality of human resources are major determinants of both the creation of new knowledge and its use throughout the economy. The indicators used are the education of scientists and engineers, the skill level of the working-age population and a measure of life-long learning. In addition employment indicators are used such as the share of the workforce in technology-intensive industries.

3 *Transmission and application of new knowledge*. This area covers the activities outside formal innovation. It is more concerned with the extent of adoption and use of new technology and knowledge. The indicators on in-house innovation and cooperative innovation are limited to small and medium-sized enterprises (SMEs). These, however, provide a better picture of innovation within small and medium-sized firms than R&D expenditure which is more prevalent among large firms. Moreover, SMEs form the majority of firms in most countries and play a vital role in innovation: linking public and large-firm research to practical applications within industrial settings.

4 *Innovation finance, output and markets*. This group includes indicators that cover the supply of finance to industry.

For the European Union as a whole analysis of changes over the past four years shows improvements in many areas and importantly in some areas countries within the Union lead the world, indicating that there is potential for member states to learn and replicate best practice. It is this idea of learning from other member countries that lies at the heart of the unique policy approach being applied to the coordination of improving innovative performance within the Union. The so-called 'open-method' approach to coordination is different from the usual EU policies which are based on establishing targets that all EU countries have to achieve over a period of time. For example, the European Union has a policy on clean bathing water within the Union, and all countries have been given targets to bring their bathing waters to the required standard. Depending on the initial state of cleanliness, countries have been given time-scales within which they must achieve these targets or face the risk of fines. The innovation policy, however, required a different approach and the 'open method of coordination' was developed. This is based on the premise that countries will progressively develop their own policies by spreading best practice.

Findings

Table 1.7 presents, for every indicator, the overall mean, the three leading member states with the best results for each indicator, and the results for the United States and Japan where available.

Since the first Innovation Scoreboard most countries have been improving their performance. Among the three largest EU economies (France, Germany and the United Kingdom) the United Kingdom has improved the fastest. Some countries have been improving much quicker than others. Most notably Denmark and Finland have been moving ahead of other countries.

▶

Table 1.7 Innovation Index Indicator results (2003)

No.	Indicator	EU mean	EU leader (1)	EU leader (2)	EU leader (3)	United States	Japan
1.1	Science and Engineering graduates	11	21 (IRL)	19 (UK)	16 (FR)	10	11*
1.2	Population with tertiary education	21	32 (FIN)	29 (UK)	27 (DK)	37	34
1.3	Participation in life-long learning	8	22 (UK)	19 (FI)	18 (DK/S)	–	–
1.4	Employed in medium/high-tech manufacturing	7	11 (D)	8 (FI)	8 (I)	–	–
1.5	Employed in high-tech services	4	5 (S)	5 (FIN)	4 (UK)	–	–
2.1	Public R&D/GDP	1	1 (FIN)	0.9 (S)	0.9 (NL)	0.8	0.8
2.2	Business R&D/GDP	1	3 (S)	2 (FIN)	2 (D)	2	2
2.3.1	High-tech EPO patents/population	31	136 (FIN)	100 (S)	68 (NL)	57	45
2.3.2	High-tech USPTO patents/population	12	47 (S)	41 (FIN)	22 (DK)	91	80
2.4.1	EPO patent applications	161	366 (S)	337 (FIN)	309 (DE)	170	174
2.4.2	USPTO patents granted	80	213 (S)	156 (FIN)	147 (DE)	322	265
3.1	SMEs innovating in-house (manufacturing)	37	46 (BE)	42 (NL)	41 (FIN)	–	–
3.1	SMEs innovation in-house (services)	28	44 (DE)	40 (LU)	38 (PT)	–	–
3.2	SMEs innovation cooperation (manufacturing)	9	22 (FIN)	14 (S)	12 (FR)	–	–
3.2	SMEs innovation cooperation (services)	7	18 (FIN)	13 (S)	13 (DK)	–	–
3.3	Innovation expenditure manufacturing	3	6 (S)	5 (BE)	5 (DE)	–	–
3.3	Innovation expenditure services	2	19 (S)	3 (PT)	2 (DE)	–	–
4.1	High-tech venture capital	0.1	0.3 (UK)	0.2 (S)	0.2 (B)	–	–
4.2	Early stage venture capital	0.04	0.1 (S)	0.1 (FIN)	0.1 (DK)	0.2	–
4.3.1	New-to-market products manufacturing	10	27 (FIN)	19 (I)	18 (PT)	–	–
4.3.1	New-to-market products services	7	18 (EL)	14 (ES)	12 (FIN)	–	–
4.3.2	New-to-frm products manufacturing	28	40 (DE)	32 (S)	31 (FIN)	–	–
4.3.2	New-to-frm products services	19	26 (ES)	24 (BE)	24 (S)	–	–
4.4	Home Internet access	0.5	0.97 (S)	0.93 (DK)	0.76 (FIN)	0.73	0.88
4.5	ICT markets/GDP	7	10 (S)	9 (UK)	8 (LU)	8	9
4.6	High-tech value added in manufacturing	14	30 (IRL)	25 (FIN)	19 (UK)	23	19
4.7	Volatility manufacturing	13	16 (UK)	14 (ES)	13 (PT)	–	–
4.7	Volatility services	17	21 (DE)	20 (S)	19 (NL)	–	–

EPO, European Patent Offce; GDP, Gross Domestic Product; SME, Small and medium enterprises; USPTO, United States Patent and Trademark Offce.

* This fgure is a 2001 Scoreboard fgure.

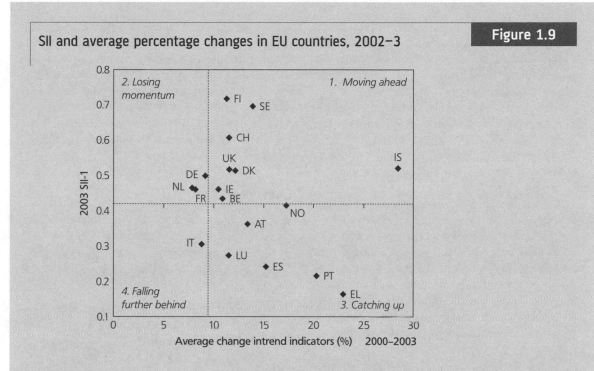

Figure 1.9

SII and average percentage changes in EU countries, 2002–3

The ranking of countries by their innovative performance was never the intention behind the Innovation Scoreboard, but this is precisely what many people have been doing with the results produced by the survey. Indeed, many newspapers have presented the findings accompanied with dramatic headlines to support or defend their arguments. The EU Commission recognised that this was how many analysts and commentators liked to see the findings; hence it produced a tentative summary innovation index (SII). This helps to address the need for a comparison of countries and performance. Several cautions are necessary when studying the SII. First, the SII is a relative rather than absolute index. An index of zero means there is no meaningful difference from the EU average. Second, the SII is not fully comparable between countries because of missing indicators for seven countries. The SII is based on only eight indicators for Japan and nine for the United States. Third, minor differences in the SII between countries are unlikely to be meaningful due to limitations

with some of the indicators. With these limitations in mind Figure 1.9 summarises the conditions in each country by giving the SII and the average percentage change.

Discussion

Innovation varies greatly from industry to industry and from firm to firm. For example, some industries are far more competitive than others; hence it is context dependent. Innovation is also complex and not fully understood, but we know that it is important to have certain things in place. All the things in the scoreboard are necessary but not sufficient in themselves to ensure innovation occurs. For example, the next chapter in this book looks at a late-industrialising country on the edge of Europe. A country with a population of 60 million, already a member of the North Atlantic Treaty Organisation (NATO) and a prospective member of the European Union. Turkey is that country and it is a good example of a late-industrialising economy. Sitting on the edge of Europe and bestriding two continents, Turkey should be in a position to develop a successful economy. However, in Turkey, there seems to be a missing link in terms of the innovative intention and capabilities of enterprises. Turkey needs to put in place many of the things detailed in the Scoreboard. This would surely help to develop enterprise in the country, but it will not convert Turkey into a Finland overnight.

By identifying, comparing and disseminating best practices in financing and technology transfer, Europe can improve its innovation performance. One area that needs particular attention is the overall perception of the entrepreneur. The image of the entrepreneur needs to have greater value, as in the United States where the drive to try to market new products, with the in-built risk of failure, is seen much more positively than in Europe.

The Scoreboard may be helpful to governmental policy makers in deciding where to invest substantial sums of money. However, this chapter has emphasised that firms behave differently given similar circumstances and that some firms appeared to be more successful than others. Given this, the Scoreboard's practical help is likely to be extremely limited. We have seen that innovation is extremely complex and involves the effective management of a variety of different activities within the organisation. Indeed, it is precisely how the process of innovation is managed that needs to be examined.

Questions

1 In the case study what are the limitations of such types of 'league tables'?

2 In the case study why are the factors listed on the Scoreboard necessary but not sufficient?

3 In the case study there are four key areas being assessed. What other areas do you think should be included?

4 In the case study what do the findings from Table 1.7 show?

5 In the case study why is the Scoreboard likely to be of little practical help?

Chapter summary

This initial chapter has sought to introduce the subject of innovation management and place it in context with the theory of economic growth. One can quickly become ensnarled in stale academic debates of semantics if innovation is viewed as a single event, hence the importance of viewing it as a process. The chapter has also stressed the importance of understanding how firms manage innovation and how this can be better achieved by adopting a management perspective.

The level of understanding of the subject of innovation has improved significantly over the past half a century and during that time a variety of models of innovation have emerged. The strengths and weaknesses of these were examined and a conceptual framework was presented that stressed the linkages and overlaps between internal departments and external organisations.

 ## Discussion questions

1 Many innovations today are associated with companies as opposed to individuals. Why is this, and what does it tell us?

2 What is wrong with the popular view of innovation in which eccentric scientists develop new products?

3 Explain how organisational heritage influences the innovation process.

4 Explain how technology differs from science, yet still does not equal innovation.

5 What is the difference between an unsuccessful innovation and an invention?

6 To what extent do you agree with the controversial view presented by the chairman of Sony?

7 To what extent are industry standards (such as the VHS format) beneficial?

8 Explain the Managing Director of McCain Food's view that invention is easy but innovation is difficult?

Key words and phrases

Economic growth 8	Network models of innovation 28
Firm's architecture 9	Organisational heritage 29
Innovation as a management process 26	Resource-based theory of the frm 21

Websites worth visiting

Business Link www.businesslink.gov.uk

Chemical Industries Association www.cia.org.uk

Confederation of British Industry www.cbi.org.uk

The Design Council www.Designcouncil.com

The Engineering Council (EC UK) www.engc.org.uk

European Industrial Research Management Association (EIRMA) www.eirma.asso.fr

European Union, Enterprise & Innovation www.europa.eu.int/comm/enterprise/innovation

European Union, Innovation Directorate www.cordis.lu/fp6/innovation.htm

Intellect UK www.intellectuk.org

Institute of Directors (IOD) www.iod.com

Patent Office www.patent.gov.uk

Quoted Companies Alliance (QCA) www.qcanet.co.uk

The R&D Society www.rdsoc.org

The Royal Academy of Engineering www.raeng.org.uk

Stanford University, explaining innovation www.Manufacturing.Stanford.edu

UK Government, Department of Trade and Industry www.Dti.gov.uk/innovation

References

Abernathy, W.J. and Utterback, J. (1978) 'Patterns of industrial innovation', in Tushman, M.L. and Moore, W.L. *Readings in the Management of Innovation*, 97–108, HarperCollins, New York.

Allen, T.J. (1977) *Managing the Flow of Technology*, MIT Press, Cambridge, MA.

Burns, T. and Stalker, G.M. (1961) *The Management of Innovation*, Tavistock, London.

Carter, C.F. and Williams, B.R. (1957) 'The characteristics of technically progressive firms', *Journal of Industrial Economics*, March, 87–104.

Chandler, A.D. (1962) *Strategy and Structure: Chapters in the History of American Industrial Enterprise*. MIT Press: Cambridge, MA.

Christensen, C.M. (2003) *The Innovator's Dilemma: When New Technologies Cause Great Firms to Fail*, 3rd edn, HBS Press, Cambridge, MA.

Cohen, W.M. and Levinthal, D.A. (1990) 'A new perspective on learning and innovation', *Administrative Science Quarterly*, Vol. 35, No. 1, 128–52.

Conner, K.R. and Prahalad, C.K. (1996) 'A resource-based theory of the firm: knowledge versus opportunism', *Organisation Science*, Vol. 7, No. 5, 477–501.

Cooper, R. (1994) 'Third generation new product processes', *Journal of Product Innovation Management*, Vol. 11, No. 1, 3–14.

Coyne, W.E. (1996) Innovation lecture given at the Royal Society, 5 March.

Cyert, R.M. and March, J.G. (1963) *A Behavioural Theory of the Firm*, Prentice-Hall, Englewood Cliffs, NJ.

Domar, D. (1946) 'Capital expansion, rate of growth and employment', *Econometra*, Vol. 14, 137–47.

Eisenhardt, K.M. and Martin, J.A. (2000) 'The knowledge-based economy: from the economics of knowledge to the learning economy', in Foray, D. and Lundvall, B.-A. (eds) *Employment and Growth in the Knowledge-Based Economy*, OECD, Paris.

European Commission (2001) European Innovation Scoreboard 2001, Cordis Focus supplement, document SEC 1414.

European Commission (2003) European Innovation Scoreboard, Technical Paper No. 1: Indicatives and Definitions, 11 November 2003.

Freeman, C. (1982) *The Economics of Industrial Innovation*, 2nd edn, Frances Pinter, London.

Galbraith, J.R. (1982) 'Designing the innovative organisation', *Organisational Dynamics*, Winter, 3–24.

Grant, R.M. (1996) 'Towards a knowledge-based theory of the firm', *Strategic Management Journal*, Summer Special Issue, Vol. 17, 109–22.

Hamel, G. and Prahalad, C.K. (1994) 'Competing for the future', *Harvard Business Review*, Vol. 72, No. 4, 122–8.

Hargadon, A. and Douglas, Y. (2001) 'When innovations meet institutions: Edison and the design of the electric light', *Administrative Science Quarterly*, Vol. 46, 476–501.

Harrod, R.F. (1949) 'An essay in dynamic theory', *Economic Journal*, Vol. 49, No. 1, 277–93.

Isenson R. (1968) 'Technology in retrospect and critical events in science' (Project Traces). Illinois Institute of Technology/National Science Foundation, Chicago IL.

Kelly, P. and Kranzberg, M. (eds) (1978) *Technological Innovation: A Critical Review of Current Knowledge*, San Francisco Press, San Francisco, CA.

Kondratieff, N.D. (1935/51) 'The long waves in economic life', *Review of Economic Statistics*, Vol. 17, 6–105 (1935), reprinted in Haberler, G. (ed.), *Readings in Business Cycle Theory*, Richard D. Irwin, Homewood, IL (1951).

Langrish, J., Gibbons, M., Evans, W.G. and Jevons, F.R. (1972) *Wealth from Knowledge*, Macmillan, London.

Lefever, D.B. (1992) 'Technology transfer and the role of intermediaries', PhD thesis, INTA, Cranfield Institute of Technology.

Leifer, R., Colarelli O'Connor, G., Peters, L.S., (2000) *Radical Innovation*, Harvard Business School Press, Boston, MA.

Low, M.B. and MacMillan, I.C. (1988) 'Entrepreneurship: past research and future challenges', *Journal of Management*, June, 139–59.

Mason, G., Beltram, J. and Paul, J. (2004) 'External knowledge sourcing in different national settings: a comparison of electronics establishments in Britain and France', *Research Policy*, Vol. 33, No. 1, 53–72.

Morita, A. (1992) ' "S" does not equal "T" and "T" does not equal "I" ', paper presented at the Royal Society, February 1992.

Murray, S. (2003) 'Innovation: A British talent for ingenuity and application', www.FT.com, 22 April.

Myers, S. and Marquis, D.G. (1969) 'Successful industrial innovation: a study of factors underlying innovation in selected firms', National Science Foundation, NSF 69–17, Washington, DC.

Nelson, R.R. and Winter, S. (1982) *An Evolutionary Theory of Economic Change*, Harvard University Press, Boston, MA.

Nonaka, I. (1991) 'The knowledge creating company', *Harvard Business Review*, November–December, 96–104.

Nonaka, I. and Kenney, M. (1991) 'Towards a new theory of innovation management: a case study comparing Canon, Inc. and Apple Computer, Inc.', *Journal of Engineering and Technology Management*, Vol. 8, 67–83.

Parkin, M., Powell, M. and Matthews, K. (1997) *Economics*, 3rd edn, Addison-Wesley, Harlow.

Patel, P. and Pavitt, K. (2000) 'How technological competencies help define the core (not the boundaries) of the firm', in Dosi, G., Nelson, R. and Winter, S.G. (eds) *The Nature and Dynamics of Organisational Capabilities*, Oxford University Press, Oxford, 313–33.

Pavitt, K. (1990) 'What we know about the strategic management of technology', *California Management Review*, Vol. 32, No. 3, 17–26.

Penrose, E.T. (1959) *The Theory of the Growth of the Firm*, Wiley, New York.

Polanyi, M. (1966) *The Tacit Dimension*, Routledge & Kegan Paul, London.

Porter, M.E. (1985) *Competitive Strategy*, Harvard University Press, Boston, MA.

Prahalad, C.K. and Hamel, G. (1990) 'The core competence of the corporation', *Harvard Business Review*, Vol. 68, No. 3, 79–91.

Rogers, E. and Shoemaker, R. (1972) *Communications of Innovations*, Free Press, New York.

Rothwell, R. and Zegveld, W. (1985) *Reindustrialisation and Technology*, Longman, London.

Rothwell, R. (1992) 'Successful industrial innovation: critical factors for the 1990s', *R&D Management*, Vol. 22, No. 3, 221–39.

Rothwell, R., Freeman, C., Horlsey, A., Jervis, V.T.P., Robertson, A.B. and Townsend, J. (1974) 'SAPPHO updated: Project SAPPHO phase II', *Research Policy*, Vol. 3, 258–91.

Schumpeter, J.A. (1934) *The Theory of Economic Development*, Harvard University Press, Boston, MA.

Schumpeter, J.A. (1939) *Business Cycles*, McGraw-Hill, New York.

Schumpeter, J.A. (1942) *Capitalism, Socialism and Democracy*, Allen & Unwin, London.

Simon, H. (1957) *Administrative Behaviour*, Free Press, New York.

Slater, S.F. and Narver, J. (1994) 'Does competitive environment moderate the market orientation performance relationship', *Journal of Marketing*, Vol. 58 (January), 46–55.

Sunday Times (2004) 'Quick learner who staked his claim in computer insurance', *Business Section* 3, 18 January.

Trott, P. (1993) 'Inward technology transfer as an interactive process: a case study of ICI', PhD thesis, Cranfield University.

Trott, P. (1998) 'Growing businesses by generating genuine business opportunities', *Journal of Applied Management Studies*, Vol. 7, No. 4, 211–22.

Tushman, M.L. (1978) 'Task characteristics and technical communication in research and development', *Academy of Management Review*, Vol. 21, 624–45.

Utterback, J. (1994) *Mastering the Dynamics of Innovation*, Harvard Business School Press, Boston, MA.

Van de Ven, A.H. (1999) *The Innovation Journey*, Oxford University Press, New York.

von Hippel, E. (1978) 'Users as innovators', *Technology Review*, Vol. 80, No. 3, 30–4.

Wernerfelt, B. (1995) 'The resource-based view of the firm: ten years after', *Strategic Management Journal*, Vol. 16, No. 3, 171–4.

Wheelwright, S. and Clark, K. (1992) *Revolutionising Product Development*, The Free Press, New York.

Woodward, J. (1965) *Industrial Organisation: Theory and Practice*, 2nd edn, Oxford University Press, Oxford.

Further reading

For a more detailed review of the innovation management literature, the following develop many of the issues raised in this chapter:

Byron, K. (1998) 'Invention and innovation', *Science and Public Affairs*, Summer, Royal Society.

Shavinina, L. V. (ed.) (2003) *The International Handbook on Innovation*, Elsevier, Oxford.

Sundbo, J. and Fuslang, L. (eds) (2002) *Innovation as Strategic Reflexivity*, Routledge, London.

Tidd, J. (2000) *From Knowledge Management to Strategic Competence: Measuring technological, market and organisational innovation*, Imperial College Press, London.

Tidd, J., Bessant, J. and Pavitt, K. (2001) *Managing Innovation*, 2nd edn, John Wiley & Sons, Chichester.

2

The context of innovation and the role of the state

Ufuk M. Çakmakçi

This chapter aims to demonstrate that the process of innovation has a much wider context than is readily acknowledged. Indeed, innovation cannot be separated from political and social processes. The nationality of innovation has been a widely accepted characteristic of the capitalist development process (Dicken, 1998; Freeman and Soete, 1997; Nelson, 1993). The United States, in particular, is frequently cited as a good example of a nation where the necessary conditions for innovation to fburish are in place. This includes both tangible and intangible features, including, on the one hand, economic, social and political institutions, and, on the other, the way in which knowledge evolves over time through developing interactions and networks. It is this much wider context and in particular the role of the state that will be explored now.

Chapter contents

Learning objectives

When you have completed this chapter you will be able to:

- understand the wider context of innovation and the key influences;

- recognise that innovation cannot be separated from its local and national context and from political and social processes;

- understand that the role of national states considerably influences innovation;

- identify the structures and activities that the state uses to facilitate innovation; and

- identify the factors that have contributed to the lack of innovation in the 'late-industrialising' state of Turkey.

Innovation in its wider context

According to many, the process of innovation is the main engine of (continued) economic growth. As far back as 1943 Joseph Schumpeter emphasised that

> *the fundamental impulse that sets and keeps the capitalist engine in motion comes from the new consumers' goods, the new methods of production or transportation, the new markets, the new forces of industrial organisation that capitalist enterprise creates. (1943: 10)*

However, such potential to create new products, processes, markets or organisations are path-dependent in the sense that there are certain nations and locations which seem to have acquired that capability over time, for innovation relies upon the accumulation and development of a wide variety of relevant knowledge (Dicken, 1998).

The view that much needs to be in place for innovation to occur and that there is a significant role for the state is confirmed by Alfred Marshall, whose ideas were responsible for the rebuilding of Europe after the Second World War. He commented on both the tangible and intangible aspects of the Industrial Revolution and suggested that 'the secrets of Industry are in the air'. Marshall (cited in Dickens, 1998: 20) recognised a number of characteristics that influenced innovation:

- the institutional set-up;
- the relationship between the entrepreneurs and financiers;
- society's perception of new developments;
- the openness to science and technology;
- networks between scientific and academic communities and business circles;
- the productive forces and financial institutions;
- the growing liberal–individualist economic paradigm;
- the role played by the state in accommodating and promoting capitalistic changes and preparing the framework for the development of capitalism.

The process of innovation has so far been treated as an organisational issue. We have seen, and will continue to see over the course of the book, that within the organisation, management of the innovation process is an extremely demanding discipline, for converting a basic discovery into a commercial product, process or service is a long-term, high-risk, complex, interactive and non-linear sequence. However, the capability of organisations in initiating and sustaining innovation is to a great extent determined by the wider local/national context within which they operate. This is essentially why 'innovation within' requires a favourable 'context outside'. That is, economic and social conditions will play a major role in whether the organisations or corporate actors will take the risk and establish the longer-term vision that innovation is key to competitiveness, survival and sustained growth. To get a better understanding of this, it is necessary to 'look out of the window' at the business environment in which economic actors strive to get an upper hand in the marketplace in a mix of competition and cooperation through network, market and hierarchical relations. This notion is reinforced by the interactions between the organisation and the external environment, which is emphasised in Figure 1.7.

The development of science and technology in the West opened a wide gap between the so-called industrialised nations and their followers, 'late-industrialisers'. Late-industrialisers refer to countries with no or limited indigenous technology development capacity. Some states, including Japan and some east Asian countries, have managed to close that gap with strategies which focus mainly on industrialisation. In these countries, economic growth was achieved through imitation by diffusion of technology, development of new technology and efforts to develop their own capacities. So the cycle that began with imitation was later turned into a creative and broader basis upon which economic transformation could be achieved. This transformation required continual efforts by entrepreneurs and businesses and a collaborative framework promoted by the state. However, to reach maturity in today's economy, i.e. to be able to create high-value-added and knowledge-based products and services, would appear to be a gigantic task for the states and societies of the latecomers. Apart from its regulatory and redistribution functions, the state must play a significant role through strategic intervention into infrastructure development and technological capacity formation as well as into human capital formation.

This wider view of the economic environment is referred to as *integral economics*, where the economic processes are viewed in their social and political entirety. As pointed out by Dicken (1998: 50), 'technology is a social process which is socially and institutionally embedded'. In this context, it would be useful to remind ourselves that innovation cannot be separated from its local and national (as well as global) contexts and from political and social processes, let alone main economic trends.

Given the nature of 'the game', however, there is always the risk that entrepreneurs and businesses may only focus on high-return opportunities in the short term, marginalise strategic and innovative perspective and ignore the long-term implications of such behaviour (as will be seen in Chapter 14). Economies dominated by this type of philosophy will have serious difficulties in moving beyond commercial activities (that is, in current popular business discourse, 'moving boxes'). This has so far been Turkey's story. In this context, we find that the businesses themselves and the business philosophy were progressively created by the Republican state within a modernist approach only to observe that the so-called entrepreneurs opted to become rich rather than entrepreneurs. So, the act of 'business-making' was only undertaken on the surface; and policy changes such as liberalisation only led the entrepreneurs and businesses to seek their ends in the short run with no calculated risk-taking in business. Thus, business in Turkey developed its own weakness by becoming dependent on the weaknesses of the Turkish state, e.g. using high and growing budget deficits as a money-making opportunity. In this chapter, we will try to highlight why the situation for economies such as the Turkish economy remain unchanged, while some societies and economies enjoyed sustained growth over several decades and have become powerful players in the global economy.

> ## Pause for thought
>
> For Schumpeter the idea of being entrepreneurial was not simply buying some-thing cheap and selling it for a quick profit. It was bound up with new products and new methods of production; by implication it was long-term rather than short-term in nature. Is our understanding of entrepreneurship different now?

The role of the state and national 'systems' of innovation

To support our understanding of the process of innovation within the capitalist enter-prise we must also grasp a basic understanding of the way the economy interrelates with global and regional economies on local and national levels. Not only do national eco-nomies tend to be dominated by a form of economic organisation (e.g. the *Chaebol* in South Korea or *Keiretsu* in Japan), it is also the case that the relationship between state and business differs radically from one national space to the other. Such interrelation-ships in society generate a business environment with a unique business value system, attitude and ethic. Historically, this difference created advantages and disadvantages for business organisation across a range of activities, the most important of which may be perceived as the process of innovation. This would seem to be the case given the cru-cial role played by innovation in the history of capitalism.

The answer to the question of whether there is a role for the state in the process of innovation has been addressed in different contexts (e.g. Porter, 1990; Afuah, 2003). The literature on the subject has attracted attention to the following points, where state action may be necessary:

1 *The 'public' nature of knowledge that underpins innovation.* This refers to the role that can be played by the government in the process of idea generation and its subsidisation and distribution. This way, economic actors may be stimulated to work on new ideas, alongside state organisations, and may endeavour to convert such ideas into marketable goods or services. For instance, by granting intellectual property rights to producers of knowledge and by establishing the necessary legal infrastructure to support those rights, the state may promote knowledge generation.

2 *The uncertainty that often hinders the process of innovation.* Macro-economic, technological or market uncertainties may hinder innovation. When the companies are risk-averse in investing funds in innovation projects, then the state may promote such activities through subsidising, providing tax advantages and supporting firms to join R&D projects. Forming a stable economic environment, where funds could be extended by the banking system to productive firms, also creates a favourable long-term perspective, for one of the first preconditions of strategy making is economic stability. Thus, expectations of low inflation, low interest rates and stable growth will encourage firms to invest in entrepreneurial activity (particularly given that other areas, e.g. portfolio investments, are less profitable to invest in).

3 *The need for certain kinds of complementary assets.* Provision of electricity, roads and water has historically assisted industrial development; recently, the establishment of communication systems (e.g. communication superhighways), legal infrastructure and the formation of industrial districts have been issues where state action has led to favourable outcomes with tangible and intangible conditions created for enterprises.

4 *The need for cooperation and governance, resulting from the nature of certain technologies.* For the development of possible networks, which will enhance and promote the diffusion of new technologies and innovations, the state may set the vision and enhance the possibilities for better communication and joint decision making.

5 *Politics.* Lastly, in terms of politics, national states still have a key role in foreseeing and contributing to international and regional standards of business making within the system of 'national states' and in creating consent and cohesion in the national arena among domestic forces. Such standards are increasingly becoming environmental, safety and human rights standards in industrial or business activities.

How national states can facilitate innovation

Figure 2.1 highlights the possible roles that can be played by national states. It takes Porter's industry attractiveness framework and develops the role the state can play in relation to innovation. It underlines a firm's relationship with the buyers, factor conditions (e.g. labour, capital, raw materials), related and supporting industries (e.g. technology providers, input providers, etc.) and other institutions that help facilitate strategic orientation and innovative capabilities. These will determine to a great extent the firm's opportunities – notwithstanding the fact that its inner strengths, i.e. its strategy-making capabilities and structural features, will clearly affect this potential.

As a financier of R&D and major purchaser, the state has a significant impact on strategic direction toward critical industries and encouraging entrepreneurial spirit. For instance, in 1995, the United States committed to a budget for R&D spending of $71.4 billion, which was spent on defence, health, space, general science, energy, transportation, energy, environment and agriculture. Most of the funds went to industrial research laboratories, universities, non-profit laboratories and federally funded research R&D centres. There are also indirect ways of financing R&D, such as tax exemptions, subsidies, loan guarantees, export credits and forms of protection. For example, Boeing paid no taxes between 1970 and 1984, and also received a tax refund amounting to $285 million (Afuah, 2003). As a major purchaser, the state will also reduce uncertainty and create favourable cash flows for firms by its willingness to pay higher (monopolistic) prices for early models.

Through education, information dissemination, governance and other societal actions, the state can impact upon the way the society perceives discoveries and adapts new technologies at the same time as creating cohesion in the society and making strategic interventions to promote, for instance, the formation of a highly qualified workforce. Interdependency between state and society may create a favourable national culture which welcomes scientific development, and remove the potential for conflict between leading sectors and traditional sectors, economic interests and social forces and cultural traditions and new trends. By incubating a form of unity between state and society, the state may set in motion an overall vision and dynamic in the society and for the industry.

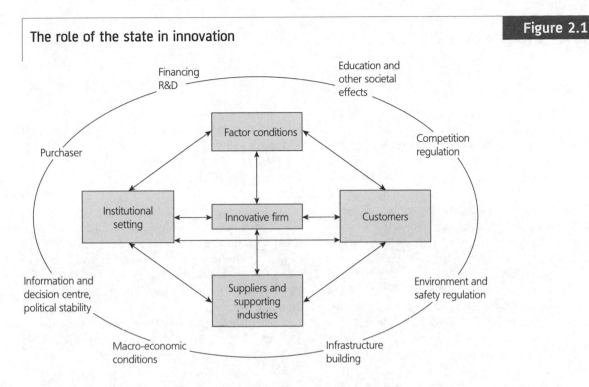

Figure 2.1

The role of the state in innovation

Regulation of competition is another critical area for the reproduction/expansion of the capitalist system, as the state can promote the system by preventing monopolies that can result in under-innovation and by protecting the society against possible abuse by companies. Microsoft's very high-profile antitrust case with the US government is a good illustration (*see* Illustration 2.1). A summary of the complex way in which the state can impact upon the behaviour of capitalist firms and how they manage their economic and social relationships is shown in Figure 2.1.

Fostering innovation in the United States and Japan

Although local characteristics also play a very significant role in the innovation process, the overall tendencies of nations and nation states are linked to success on a very local level. While some states, such as Japan, provided extensive support and subsidies to promote industrial innovation, others, such as the United States, have aimed to create positive effects in the economy by letting the market achieve the most efficient allocation of resources with minimal possible intervention. The so-called Chicago School paradigm for promoting competitiveness and innovation, which created a belief in the free market to maximise innovation and productivity (Rosenthal, 1993), has, for more than two decades, been the dominant perspective in the United States. At this instance, we can cite the impact on the industry of public R&D with such expected transformative effects as provided by the Internet's later commercial application, initially a military project initiated by the state. In fact, the United States is leading the way in performing half of the world's basic research, making most of the seminal discoveries, thanks to the trillion-dollar investment in US universities and government laboratories.

Illustration 2.1

FT

Microsoft takes antitrust case to Supreme Court

Microsoft on Tuesday asked the US Supreme Court to take up the software giant's landmark antitrust battle with the government, urging the nation's highest court to throw out all legal rulings the trial judge made against the company.

In its petition, Microsoft argued that a federal appeals court made a critical mistake when it failed to throw out the findings of Thomas Penfield Jackson, the judge who presided over the 4-month trial.

In June, the seven-judge appeals court found that Judge Jackson had 'destroyed the appearance of impartiality' by conducting interviews with newspaper reporters before his final judgment, and then disparaging Microsoft executives after the trial had concluded.

But the appeals court only disqualified Judge Jackson from future proceedings, ruling that his 1999 findings of fact against the company should stand because he did not show any actual bias in his conduct during the case.

In its appeal to the Supreme Court, Microsoft argued that the judge should have been retroactively disqualified to September 1999, the time when he began interviews with reporters, a move that would eviscerate his findings of guilt against the company.

'Had Microsoft learned in September 1999 about [the interviews] . . . Microsoft would have immediately moved for disqualification,' the company argued in its brief. 'As the court of appeals noted, there is "little doubt" that such a motion would have been granted.'

The Justice Department said it would argue against a Supreme Court review: 'This was an issue addressed by the court of appeals.'

'We think it is best to get this case going forward again at the district court, as the court of appeals ordered', said Iowa Attorney General Tom Miller, who is leading state prosecutors who have joined the Justice Department in the case.

In a separate filing on Tuesday, Microsoft asked the court of appeals to delay sending the case to a new trial judge. The lower court is scheduled to take up the suit by the end of the week, but Microsoft argued that such a move would allow the new trial judge to make rulings before the Supreme Court had a chance to hear the appeal.

Antitrust experts have been sceptical of the Supreme Court's likelihood of taking up the case, saying the June appeals court ruling, which found the company guilty of abusing its monopoly power in computer operating systems, was unanimous. 'The Supreme Court generally doesn't get involved in the application of ethics' rules', said Ernest Gellhorn, an antitrust expert at George Mason University.

Some experts argued that Tuesday's move was a delaying tactic, with the company hoping to tie the case up in appeals until it can release the new version of its operating system, Windows XP, scheduled to be shipped in October.

Vivek Varma of Microsoft said the company was only asking the Supreme Court to reconsider the actions of Judge Jackson and not the antitrust issues.

Source: P. Spiegel, 'Microsoft takes antitrust case to Supreme Court', *Financial Times*, 8 August 2001. Reprinted with permission.

In the case of more interventionist states, incentives were provided either as direct support (e.g. subsidies, location provision, etc.) or in the form of 'governance' assuming a coordinating and leading role in the management of innovation projects. In this instance governance refers to the efforts at creating cohesion and complementarity, which are directed to the realisation of a joint objective that is deemed to be mutually beneficial to the various parties involved. A good example of the latter was the role played by the Japanese state in bringing universities, state organisations (primarily the Ministry of International Trade and Industry (MITI)), sector organisations and business enterprises together for research on the development of the Trinitron television (a technology that dominated home electronics for more than two decades) with financial support attached. Although the Japanese model has come under severe criticism, particularly by Porter *et al.* (2000), as a result of the recent economic slowdown, the weaknesses mainly attributed to the lack of concern for strategy in Japanese companies and being stuck in between two competitive strategies of cost and quality, as well as low profitability, the success of the model has been long acknowledged (*see*, for instance, Johnson, 1982; Hart, 1992; Castells, 1992). In the case of innovation, governance requires the establishment of a proper framework for the smooth flow of knowledge between universities, state institutions, private sector organisations and corporations until the end result takes some form of a marketable commodity. In this framework, while some economies are better placed with innovation capabilities, some are at a disadvantage because of their characteristics.

The concept of 'developmental states' is used to show the way in which some states achieved a major transformation of the economy and society. At the other end of the spectrum there are the 'predatory states', which capture most of the funds in the economy and reallocate them in the form of rents to a small group of the population, thus impeding the growth potential in the state (Evans, 1989). This development was found in particular to be a major characteristic of some east Asian states, especially the so-called Tigers of Korea, Taiwan, Singapore and Hong Kong (Castells, 1992). Although such states were not immune to corruption, fraud and other forms of inefficiency, they brought about major changes in the economy, particularly in upgrading the potential of the industry from imitation toward innovation and technology development, which is by no means an easy task.

Pause for thought

Is it true that in a developed market economy the role of the state is a minor one? Why is it NOT surprising that many consumer products such as in-car satellite navigational guidance, mobile telephones and computers have their origins in defence research?

The right business environment is key to innovation

Schumpeter preached technology as the engine of growth but also noted that to invest in technology there had to be spare resources and long time-horizons. So the business environment must give the 'right' signals to the business units for them to invest in such operations. In this regard, not only does macro-economic stability play a significant role but also the availability of quick (short-term) returns and opportunistic trends needs to be suppressed so that the money can flow into basic research and R&D. Likewise, the approach of business would differ if it faced strong (external or internal) competition. A protected domestic market more often than not amounts to signalling to business units that they should seek monopolistic or oligopolistic returns by not making enough investment into new product development or even product improvement.

The next chapter explores the organisational characteristics that need to be in place for innovation to occur. From the preceding discussion one can already begin to see what these characteristics might be.

Waves of innovation and growth in capitalism: historical overview

When we investigate the history of capitalist development, there is a pattern of economic growth. The work of Kondratieff and Schumpeter have been influential in identifying the major stages of this development. The five waves, or growth cycles, are identified in Figure 2.2. This highlights that technological developments and innovations have a strong spatial dimension; however, leadership in one wave is not necessarily maintained in the succeeding waves. So one can observe shifts in the geography of innovation through time. The leaders of the first wave were Britain, France and Belgium. The second wave brought new players into the game, namely the United States and Germany. Wave three saw the strengthening of the positions of the United States and Germany. In wave four, Japan and Sweden joined the technology and innovation race. More recently, in wave five, Taiwan and South Korea are becoming key players in the global economy.

Figure 2.2 Kondratieff waves of growth and their main features

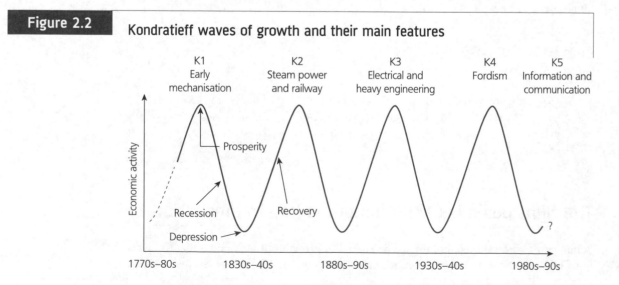

In these Kondratieff waves, the capitalist economy grew on the basis of major innovations in product, process and organisation with accompanying shifts in the social arena. Kuhn's theory on the nature of scientific revolutions has been justified: each wave comes to an end due to its major shortcomings and the successive wave fundamentally restructures and improves those weaknesses. Each major phase of innovation produced a 'star' industry or industry branch, which seemed to affect the way the economy was organised. The leap forward provided by such industry(ies) resulted in a major transformation of the economy and economic relations – given that other factors such as demand, finance, industrial and social conditions were favourable. Products, processes and organisations created by technological development became universal and cheaply available to a vast population, which, in turn, created the economic shift. These Kondratieff waves took place in the order of early mechanisation, steam power and railways, electrical and heavy engineering, 'Fordism' (i.e. use of mass-production methods), and information and communication. The last of these waves is currently underway with what is now termed the information revolution. Almost every day we are presented with a number of 'new' ways in which we can do business, search for information, communicate and socialise with other people or carry out our bank operations. This means that the new developments deeply affect not only economic relations but also our private (home and relations) and work (public) spheres.

In the very first Kondratieff wave, the rise of the factory and mechanisation in textiles was only part of the story. The need to produce in greater quantities to start serving the growing overseas markets with the improved transport methods now available was complemented by the abundance of finance with the money flowing in from the colonies, particularly the United States. Universally and cheaply available input (i.e. cotton), improving nation-wide transport infrastructure (with rising investment in canals and roads by landlords), the advent of the so-called adventurers (now widely recognised as entrepreneurs), pools of labour available for employment in some local markets, the growing education infrastructure, the role played by academic and scientific societies and the attitude of the state towards manufacturing interests were the other complementary factors affecting change (Freeman and Soete, 1997).

With the decline of the previous techno-economic paradigm, the next one starts to take shape with features that offer solutions to the weaknesses of the earlier phase. As Marx foresaw, capitalism has always found a way of reproducing itself with changes in the way factors of production were organised. For instance, the organisational characteristics have changed from the first through to the fifth wave, and the early emphasis on individual entrepreneurs has given way to small firms, then to the monopolists, oligopolists and cartels of the third wave, centralised TNCs (transnational corporations) of the fourth wave and, finally, to the so-called 'network' type, flexible organisations of the information age (*see* Table 2.1 for an overview of the waves of growth).

Pause for thought

The Kondratief theory suggests that networks constitute a key organisational attribute to the current wave of economic growth. Does this mean it is not possible for a firm to be innovative on its own?

Table 2.1 Characteristics of the five waves of growth

	Wave 1	Wave 2	Wave 3	Wave 4	Wave 5
Main branches	Textiles Textile machinery Iron working Water power Pottery	Steam engines Steamships Machine tools Iron and steel Railway equipment	Electrical engineering Electrical machinery Cable and wire Heavy engineering Steel ships Heavy chemicals	Automobiles Trucks/tractors/planes Consumer durables Process plant Synthetic materials Petrochemicals	Computers Electronic capital goods Telecommunications Robotics Information services
Universal and cheap key factors	Cotton	Coal, iron	Steel; electricity	Oil; plastics	Gas; oil; microelectronics
Infrastructure	Trunk canals Turnpike roads	Railways Shipping	Electricity supply and distribution	Highways; airports/airlines	Digital networks; satellites
Limitations of previous techno-economic paradigm; solutions	Limitations of scale, process control and mechanisation in 'putting out' system; solutions offered through mechanisation and factory organisation towards productivity and profitability	Limitations of water power: inflexibility of location, scale of production, reliability; solutions offered through steam engine and transport system	Limitations of iron as an engineering material (strength, durability, precision, etc.) overcome by steel and alloys; limitations of steam engine overcome by unit and group electrical machinery, power tools, permitting layout improvement and capital saving; standardisation	Limitations of batch production overcome by flow processes and assembly line; full standardisation and replaceability of components and materials; universal availability and cheapening of mass consumption goods	Inflexibility of dedicated assembly line and process plant overcome by flexible manufacturing systems, networking and economies of scope; electronic control systems and networking provide for necessitated flexibility
Organisation of firms	Individual entrepreneurs and small firms (<100 employees); partnership between technical innovators and financial circles	Small firms dominate but large firms and large markets emerge; limited liability and joint stock companies emerge	Emergence of giant firms, cartels, trusts, mergers; regulation of or state ownership of natural monopolies; concentration of finance and banking capital; emergence of middle management	Oligopolistic competition; TNCs; 'arm's-length' subcontracting or vertical integration; bureaucratic control and bureaucratisation	Networks of large and small firms based increasingly on computers; trust-based networks with close cooperation in technology, quality control, training and production planning (e.g. JIT)
Geographical focus	Britain, France, Belgium	Britain, France, Belgium, Germany, United States	Germany, United States, Britain, France, Belgium, The Netherlands, Switzerland	United States, Germany, other EU, Japan, Switzerland, other EFTA, Canada, Australia	Japan, United States, Canada, Germany, Sweden, other EU and EFTA, Taiwan, Korea,

Sources: Reproduced and adapted from P. Dicken (1998) *Global Shift: Transforming the World Economy*, Paul Chapman, London, 148; C. Freeman and L. Soete (1997) *The Economics of Industrial Innovation*, 3rd edn, Pinter, London.
EFTA, European Free Trade Association; JIT, just-in-time; TNC, transnational corporation.

Fostering innovation in 'late-industrialising' countries

We have already noted that there is no guarantee for continued technological leadership. The geography of innovation has shown regional, national or local variations in time. One proof in this regard has been the case of south-east Asia. Although the late developers followed more or less similar paths towards industrialisation, some managed significant achievements, particularly in the attitude of the private sector to innovation and technology development (for example, Taiwan, Malaysia and Korea). Almost all latecomers started with the exports of basic commodities, and through the application of a mix of policies in different periods, they aimed for industrialisation. When innovation is considered, the focus of entrepreneurs and businesses was initially on imitative production (so-called 'reverse engineering') in relatively unsophisticated industries. When the business environment became conducive to business activity, after initial capital accumulation in key industries, then an upward move was observed along the ladder of industrialisation. In many countries such a transformation required an envisioning state, actively interfering with the functioning of the private enterprise system. In some cases, it set 'the prices wrong' deliberately (Amsden, 1989) to protect and promote infant industries; in others, it created enterprises itself in order to compensate for the lack of private initiative in the economy (Toprak, 1995).

Although there are significant differences between the cases of Latin American countries and their south Asian counterparts, their paths of industrialisation also bear similarities. Initially, all were exporters of raw materials and importers of higher-technology products. In achieving the transformation, the move from simple technology sectors towards higher-value-added and heavy industries seems to be the key to their successes. This was achieved with the complementary use of (inward-looking) import-substituting industrialisation (ISI) and (outward-looking) export-oriented (EOI) economic policies. The main difference in south Asian economies, which, in retrospect, seems to be their main advantage, was that after the initial phase of ISI, they opened up to international competition through an EOI regime in contrast particularly to Latin American countries and Turkey.

Attempting to achieve innovation and sustained growth in the late-industrialising Turkish economy

Already a member of the North Atlantic Treaty Organisation (NATO) and a prospective member of the European Union, Turkey is a good example of a late-industrialising economy. Sitting on the edge of Europe and bestriding two continents, Turkey should be in a position to develop a successful economy. With a population of 60 million and growing (unlike many countries in Europe, most notably Germany), Turkey offers a large underdeveloped market opportunity to businesses in Europe. However, in

Turkey, there seems to be a missing link in terms of the innovative intention and capabilities of enterprises. In this section, we will try to explore the root causes of this weakness by providing a historical analysis. The structural tendencies and socio-economic trends will also be considered in exploring what is *not* happening in the Turkish context. Illustration 2.2 highlights the genuine economic problems faced by Turkey.

 ## Illustration 2.2

FT

A last, last chance for Turkey

The IMF has taken a huge gamble in yet again rescuing the country from a crisis created by the follies of its leaders

On May 15, the International Monetary Fund decided to reward failure. With the agreement of its shareholders, it added Special Drawing Right 6.4bn ($8bn) to the amounts it was prepared to lend Turkey. This brought IMF credit available to the country to $19bn. If Turkey were to draw this, it would become the IMF's largest debtor.

At first glance, this is a clear case of throwing good money after bad in a country with a long history of failed attempts at stabilisation. It is the second rescue of a programme initiated in December 1999, with a stand-by of $3.7bn. The first rescue followed a currency crisis in November 2000. An additional credit of $7.3bn was advanced in December under the supplemental reserve facility.

The operation also seems a clear violation of the emerging consensus on the IMF's role in the world. The Fund is no longer supposed to save lenders from the costs of taking amply rewarded risks or to rescue countries from the consequences of their governments' folly. How then can this possibly be justified?

One justification – that Turkey is vital to the stability of a critical region of the world – should be put to one side. It is true – but provides a weak argument for IMF involvement. This is an argument for bilateral assistance. Fund programmes should be grounded in economics, not just in politics.

Fortunately, it is possible to make an economic case. The negative point is that Turkey would almost certainly default on its foreign and domestic public debt or experience something close to hyperinflation, in the absence of a rescue. The positive one is that judicious assistance may bring stability at last.

If these arguments are to persuade doubters, the country has to possess a workable programme. It may well do so. While Turkey retains the same coalition government as before, it has in the minister for the economy, Kemal Dervis, a former vice-president of the World Bank – someone who understands what needs to be done and why. He is popular, at present. Moreover, as he has argued (*FT*, May 15), he can provide the co-ordination lacking previously. His new programme is certainly superior to the old one. As laid out in the government's letter of intent, it covers everything that matters.*

Structural reform includes the elimination of the huge overnight exposures of the state banks, their recapitalisation and an overhaul of their corrupted governance. It also includes closure or resale of insolvent private banks and strengthening of those still solvent. In addition, the government has agreed to privatise many state companies and reform the markets in which they operate, including those for telecommunications, electricity and natural gas.

Fiscal targets include a primary budget surplus (balance before interest payments) for the public sector as a whole of 5.5 per cent this year and 6.5 per cent in 2002. If achieved, this would represent a big improvement on the primary deficit of 2 per cent in 1999 and surplus of 2.8 per cent in 2000. Moreover, the failed exchange-rate peg regime is replaced, first, by a system of domestic monetary targeting and then, later this year, by fully fledged inflation targeting.

Yet the question remains whether the programme, strong though it seems to be, is strong enough. Unfortunately there is a high chance of failure, whatever the intentions of those in charge.

The most obvious risk lies in the dynamics of debt. After a long history of fiscal and financial profligacy and entrenched inflation, Turkey has reached the limits of debt manageability. Net public sector debt is forecast to jump from 58 per cent of gross national product at the end of 2000 to 79 per cent by the end of this year, falling to 70 per cent in 2002 and 65 per cent in 2003. In making these forecasts, the government assumes that forward-looking domestic real interest rates will fall from 36 per cent this year to 20 per cent in 2002. While not hugely optimistic, this assumes some return of confidence among people who have been brutally punished for trusting the government.

Debt manageability also depends on a strong rebound from a relatively weak recession. GNP is forecast to decline by only 3 per cent this year, followed by growth of 5 per cent in 2002 and 6 per cent in 2003. Also crucial is achievement of the fiscal targets. Yet these demand an 8 per cent real reduction in government spending (excluding interest payments) between 2000 and 2001, to bring it back almost to where it was in 1998.

Voluntary roll-over, on supportable terms, of the huge quantities of short-term debt is vulnerable to any disruption in confidence. The new official money will be a big help. But the overall public sector borrowing requirement is forecast at 17 per cent of GNP this year and 10 per cent

in 2002. Financing this is bound to impose heavy demands on the fragile domestic financial system.

Confidence will also depend on political developments. A big risk is that the combination of real cuts in spending with structural reforms and a deeper than forecast recession will generate job losses and fierce political resistance. Another is that, with the IMF money already agreed (albeit available only in tranches), Turkey's politicians will return to their populist ways, destroying monetary and fiscal credibility again.

Whether the IMF was right to take these risks is a matter of judgment. That there is moral hazard does not mean there should be no insurance. Similarly, that an operation is risky is not an argument against assistance. If the IMF were to do only safe operations, it would have no reason for existence. Yet if the worst occurred, the Turkish people could end up not just with a collapsed economy and a discredited political regime but with a still heavier foreign currency debt burden than the one they bear today. If so, it would have been better not to have made the new loan.

Many informed official observers do think the programme is indefensible. I am prepared to give the IMF the benefit of the doubt, even though an argument can be advanced for having made debt restructuring a condition for further official assistance on this scale.

Yet these now are bygones. From now on, the Turkish authorities need to be told, forcefully, that this is their last, last chance, however strategically important their country remains. Rescuing Turkey from one failure after another is bad for the country, bad for the financial markets and bad for the IMF. This programme must be the end of it.

* Turkey Letter of Intent and Memorandum on Economic Policies, 3 May 2001 and IMF Approves Augmentation of Turkey's Stand-By Credit to US$19bn, press release, 15 May 2001, www.imf.org.martin.wolf@ft.com

Source: M. Wolf, 'A Last, Last Chance for Turkey', www.FT.com, 23 May 2001. Reprinted with permission.

The economic history of Turkey

The Industrial Revolution created a gap between those who led the modernisation project and those who were slow to adapt. Such was the case of the Ottoman Empire. Henceforth the Turkish economy lagged behind with an increasing dependence on the technologies, knowledge and products created in the West. As a 'peripheral economy' Turkey imported capital and intermediate goods along with some consumer goods; and the economy was mainly based on commerce and foreign investment. In parallel, production was mainly limited to agriculture, and besides, commerce was undertaken by the minorities (Greeks, Armenians and Jews). In consequence, the Turks' approach towards business had at best been neutral.

The strategies and objectives of the Turkish policy makers and overall economic trends since the beginning of the twentieth century are summarised in Table 2.2. Beginning with the implementation of the first constitutional regime in 1908, the political elite has aimed for national development through industrialisation. Such an industrialisation effort was enacted during the 1840s, based on the industries of textiles, iron castings, porcelain production, gunpowder and arms production in an industrial district on the west side of Istanbul (Clark, 2000). In line with twentieth-century trends, almost all the machinery was imported from the West.

Under the circumstances, at the dawn of the twentieth century, Turkey had developed a preference for building its national economy. Particularly given the losses faced in the Balkan Wars and the First World War, the political elite was seemingly behind the idea that there would be 'no political independence unless economic independence' was achieved. In fact the changes started with the announcement of *Tanzimat* (introduction of the constitutional regime and political reforms) in 1908 and the law on the encouragement of industry in 1913. The Turkish state now took production seriously and showed a tendency to move away from its characteristics as a fiscal state (that aimed to balance the budget to finance its military expenses). In retrospect, however, Turkey started the twentieth century as a 'late-industrialising country' with very limited or no domestic technology production capability (and in fact with not much of a production philosophy or capacity), and the gap was not easy to bridge.

This transformation in the minds of the political elite was also manifested by certain trends in the economy. While the attitude of the Muslim public and elite was positive towards employment opportunities in the state bureaucracy and military, the same group had always overlooked commerce and business as a profession. However, with this drastic mentality change, the state officials and bureaucrats themselves started to take part in business affairs as board members of enterprises. This, in a way, constructed a bridge between the budding economy and the state tradition in Turkey. In other words, the link between public policy making and private economic interests was established right at the outset of the formation of the capitalist economy in Turkey. However, whether this has created a favourable atmosphere for the private sector for the coming years is a different story.

Table 2.2 The Turkish economy in the twentieth century

Period: Economy	Goals	Means/strategies
1900–12	National economic development	'Ottoman bourgeoisie' Liberal trade policies
1913–23	National economy – National identity	Creation of a Muslim-based private sector Strong state presence and intervention
1923–32	National economic development	Private sector-led Liberal trade policies
1933–45	National economic development	State-led Protectionist policies Experiment with planning (1st and 2nd Plans)
1946–53	National economic development	Liberal trade policies 'The Vaner Plan'
1954–60	National economic development	Mixed economy Planning dismissed Protectionist policies Emphasis on infrastructure Emphasis on agriculture
1961	National economic development	Preparation of a framework for planned industrialisation
1962–7	National economic development	State-led 1st 5-Year Plan Protectionist policies
1968–80	National economic development	Private sector led 2nd and 3rd Plans Protectionist policies Macro-economic crisis after 1975
1980–95	Articulation into the world economy and completion of CU (Customs Union) with EU	Private sector-led Gradual trade and financial liberalisation; emphasis on infrastructure
1994–2000s	Articulation into the world economy	Ongoing financial crises?

Sources: Developed from G.L. Yalman (1997) 'Bourgeoisie and the state: changing forms of interest representation within the context of economic crisis and structural adjustment: Turkey during the 1980s', unpublished PhD thesis, Manchester University; U.M. Çakmakçi (1997) 'The political economy of governance: an integral economic analysis of textile and apparel sectors in Turkey', unpublished PhD thesis, Lancaster University.

A weak business system

So far, it can be seen that the nation-building project of the Turkish state incorporated a significant economic dimension. While the minorities were deliberately distanced from their enterprises, Muslim Turks were to replace them. As the Armenians gave up supporting the Congress for Union and Progress during the Balkan War and took 'the Armenian Problem' to the international arena, and as Turkish Greeks supported Venizelos and his Great Hellenic ideals, there was a response within the Turkish community that only Muslim Turks should form the basis of a national economy and society. In other words, the leaders of Union and Progress and later the Republican People's Party regarded the 'Turkification' of the economy as a precondition of the nation-building project. However, the strong and symbiotic relations that were established at the outset continued throughout the century to characterise the Turkish business essentially as state-dependent (Bura, 1994). Thus, creating a business class from scratch had its costs: entrepreneurs and businesses, which are expected to invest their funds into business activities along the value chain were seeking easy and quick returns or invested their funds in luxury goods. In a favourable environment, such funds could have meant the strengthening of the economy. However, the case of Turkey proved that lack of a proper legal and institutional framework, social code, established business values and ethic resulted in a sluggish business system.

The missing link in innovation: 'petty' entrepreneurship and rent-seeking

During the twentieth century the Turkish state has created a business class dependent on itself. The orientation of business turned out to be to follow the opportunities created by the state and seek high returns in the short run. This form of activity was centred on a value system that involved money making in whatever way and in the shortest time possible, so instead of creating a business outlook in the country the Turkish state contributed to the formation of a 'rentier' capitalist class. The values and attitudes of the business community, on the other hand, were such that they aimed to get rich regardless of the societal costs. The implications of this for capitalist enterprises turned out to be negative in terms of their approach to business, productivity, specialisation, innovation and competitiveness.

There is a spectrum of such short-termist, speculative behaviour of Turkish economic actors in history. Even if we disregard the so-called war-time profiteers of the First and Second World Wars, there is evidence of the developing values and norms in relation to business as early as 1950s, noted by Kerwin (1951):

> *Turkish businessmen demand abnormal returns and rapid amortisation, and their tendency to sink a large portion of funds in inventory seems to indicate that objectives of a speculative nature often dominate the goal of enhanced efficiency and profitability of industrial production.*

In this context, the state project of building a national economy by creating a national business was confused with the idea of creating riches. The universally used mechanisms of subsidies, preferential credits and new lines of business activity promoted through state purchases, which could under favourable circumstances and in balanced conditions promote a strong productive sector, resulted in 'petty entrepreneurialism' as a consequence of the signals conveyed to the business community. The 1950s were quite representative in this regard not only because these were years during which most private sector enterprises were established but also because of the nature of business attitude promoted. The motto of the day was 'A millionnaire in each neighbourhood' (as opposed to 'a businessman in each neighbourhood').

Short-termism and corruption

Such ends were usually sought by the use of illicit means and particular relations with state officials, politicians and bureaucrats. When these issues were covered by the press, Adrian Menderes, the prime minister in the troubled 1950s, suggested that, 'They steal. I know they steal; but what can I do? I am the prime minister, not an inspector.' The powerlessness of the state officials in this regard was later converted into a draft bill proposing that such forms of economic behaviour should be punishable by death, a proposal which the parliament refused after heated debates. Hence, although those were years when economic activity reached historical peaks in a liberal epoch, it is widely accepted that the 1950s fostered the spirit of profit in place of the spirit of entrepreneurialism. Illustration 2.3 shows how even today corruption is still considered to be a major hindrance in Turkey's economic development.

The times of import-substitution industrialisation, i.e. the 1960s and the 1970s, introduced a new notion of rent-seeking to the Turkish economic literature: 'fictitious trading' either through exaggerating the value of commodities exported (to obtain subsidies) or minimising the value of imports (to reduce taxes payable). The 1980s witnessed the late prime minister and president Turgut Özal, for the establishment of private television channels, declare that 'bypassing the constitution once' would not harm the country. So the basic values and principles upon which the private enterprise system was founded shifted to a slippery context, where becoming rich through bypassing laws and moral norms itself became an accepted standard.

However, rent-seeking in this context does not refer one-sidedly to corruption and the like; more importantly it refers to any other affair that lacks a business perspective that may be morally and economically acceptable to a wider population, one that would focus on strategies and structures to enforce competitive advantages, create a larger customer base, attune to the needs and requirements of customers, quality, organisational characteristics that may foster innovation and change, and so on. This was particularly manifest in the annual reports of the Istanbul Chamber of Industry on the largest 500 companies in Turkey. These reports, starting from 1993, reflected a basic fact that 30–60 per cent of large-scale enterprises' revenues came from operations outside their line of business activity, namely portfolio investments (ISI 1993, 1994, 1995, etc.). These investments were most often made into tax-free treasury bonds with the money borrowed abroad through open positions, capturing the easy arbitrage opportunity (with high interest rates and an overvalued domestic currency). However, given that this was a vicious circle, as increasing state indebtedness was being financed with more expensive internal borrowing (i.e. continually rising interest rates to keep treasury bonds attractive), the (economic and social) costs of continuing with the status quo

Illustration 2.3

Corruption and economic troubles

On February 12 this year representatives of nine Turkish companies arrived at the Ministry of Public Works in Ankara bearing sealed envelopes containing bids for a new road in the earthquake zone south of Istanbul.

One by one the envelopes were opened and the quotes noted. But there was no excitement because the winner was known weeks before. The bids were rigged. The tenders were by invitation only and the participants knew that they were there to make it look as if competitive bidding was taking place.

Huseyin Gundogdu, an Ankara-based contractor who has been waging a one-man battle against corruption at the ministry, was not one of the participants. But, he says, more than six weeks earlier he had learned on the industry grapevine who would win the tender and at what price.

'In January I wrote to the Ministry of Finance and informed them that the tender was rigged', says Mr Gundogdu, who became a whistle-blower after the public works ministry shut him out of an earlier deal he had expected to win. Mr Gundogdu petitioned every government body that could be interested, from the Ministry of Public Works itself to the country's Supreme Auditing Board – but to no avail. He also informed Kuwait, which was providing the $22m (GBP15.4m) loan for the cost of the road. He told the newspapers, and two leading dailies carried the news prominently. But still nothing happened. On April 4 the contract was awarded to a company called Tasyapi – as Mr Gundogdu had predicted. He has submitted all his documents to a court in Ankara and is still waiting.

'The insensitivity is just incredible', he said in an interview before the ministry finally responded by inviting him to discuss the case with them this month. 'I feel like tearing my hair out and running through the streets screaming.'

Corruption in Turkey affects not just public procurement, but almost every aspect of the economy and the state apparatus, ranging from top politicians to lowly customs officials. Turkey has been ranked the world's 50th most corrupt country out of a total of 90 surveyed by Transparency International, a non-governmental organisation.

But the problem is compounded by a Byzantine bureaucracy and legal system, prompting PWC, the international accountancy firm, to rank Turkey the world's fourth least transparent country after China, Russia and Indonesia.

A clean-up is critical because Turkey, a member of Nato, key strategic ally of the US and aspirant member of the European Union, has just secured a $15.7bn bailout from the International Monetary Fund and World Bank to help overcome its worst economic crisis in two decades. The country's ability to combat pervasive corruption is vital if the economy is to be saved from debt default or hyperinflation – and foreign assistance is not to be wasted.

The reforms to which the money's disbursement is tied would automatically reduce scope for corruption by curbing state interference in the economy through privatisation and market-based regulation. Yet Kemal Dervis, the respected new economy minister, describes resistance from 'vested interests and rent-seeking mechanisms' as the biggest threat to success of the reforms.

'Corruption has become a way of life', said one of Turkey's most senior public auditors on condition of anonymity. 'We have turned into a country where no civil servant will do anything without baksheesh. There is no sector that is immune from baksheesh, corruption, illicit gain or kickback.'

'In the public administration there is a bribe connection everywhere. When I was young, civil servants who took bribes were disgraced. Now if you don't take a bribe, people think you are a fool. It's so widespread that people don't even try to hide it.'

The costs of corruption are hard to separate from the costs of mismanagement and waste by a bloated state. But the most pressing reason for Turkey's international support is to help plug a $40bn hole in the banking system caused, as Ajay Chhibber, the World Bank's director for Turkey, puts it, by 'a combination of corruption and populism'.

Separately, a World Bank report reckons that Turkey has recently spent between 16 and 18 per cent of GDP on public procurement a year, or $32bn to $38bn. Of that amount, according to an Ankara Chamber of Industry survey quoted by the World Bank, 'payments in the form of donations to political parties, especially the ones in power, in the amount of up to 15 per cent of the contract value, ensures that a contractor wins'.

In addition, untold sums are wasted because work is often overpriced, late, or simply superfluous. 'A contractor claims he has found a bed of rocks where there was in fact soil. Or he charges the government for removing 900 truck loads of dirt when the real figure is 90', said the senior auditor. 'The government agency in question goes along and shares the surplus profit with the contractor.'

It was Turgut Özal, the late reformist prime minister and president, who paved the way for large-scale corruption when he introduced market reforms in the 1980s without modernising the state bureaucracy and the 'No sector is immune from baksheesh' judiciary. In remarks taken to sanction corruption, he famously commented: 'My civil servant knows how to look after himself.'

A recent survey by the Social and Economic Studies Foundation of Turkey showed that a large majority of the population come into contact with corruption in their daily dealings with officialdom. Many were aware of 'widespread corruption' at customs, tax offices, the real estate registry, state hospitals and law courts.

Rising public pressure to tackle corruption recently forced the resignation of the energy minister. Cumhur Ersumer stepped down three days after a public prosecutor charged 15 officials and businessmen with bribery and conspiracy in state energy tenders.

The indictment, concluding the White Energy investigation by public prosecutors working with the paramilitary gendarmerie, painted a picture of widespread irregularities in a variety of state energy tenders, including bribery of officials by private sector executives seeking to win lucrative deals. Former employees of international consortia led by Atomic Energy of Canada and by NPI, a Franco-German joint venture between Framatome and Siemens, are among 15 people charged as a result of the White Energy indictment for alleged corruption in a $2.4bn–$4bn tender to build Turkey's first nuclear power plant.

For a long time the authorities were able to hide from the public the true cost of official misdemeanours and to ignore warnings from Turkey's Supreme Audit Board, which since 1995 has refused to certify the accounts of the Treasury in areas such as the state banks. But only until banking sector weaknesses triggered two financial crises in a row. The latest crisis, which led to a devastating devaluation on February 22, began in the state banking sector. Accounting for around 40 per cent of the banking system's total assets of $100bn, three state banks – Ziraat, Halk and Emlak – were established decades ago with a mandate to subsidise farmers, small and medium-sized traders and public housing.

They accumulated $20bn in recent years in 'duty losses' incurred in fulfilling those obligations. But further unknown sums were lost in 'bad loans' to politically connected individuals such as Murat Demirel, a nephew of Suleyman Demirel, the previous president. He was arrested on banking fraud charges last October, after his privately owned Egebank had to be taken over by the authorities.

►

The full extent of non-performing assets in the Turkish banking system is still not clear. But Vural Akisik, the private banker now in charge of restructuring the state banks, estimates bad loans at Halk, the second largest, at $600m, with perhaps less than $100m at Ziraat, the largest state bank. This may be an understatement. Mr Dervis has said that of every 100 lira loaned by Emlak Bank, 47 constituted a non-performing loan.

What is clear, however, is that as the state banks borrowed more and more heavily from depositors and other banks to finance their mismanagement, a growing threat loomed over Turkey's entire financial system. Although the 'duty losses' were technically public debt, they were not recorded as such, enabling the government to present an artificially rosy picture of the public finances. Instead of being included in the government's budget, the duty losses were booked on banks' balance sheets as receivables from the Treasury.

Such practices continued until early this year with the grudging consent of the IMF, which believed that the problems of the state-owned banks could be tackled over the medium term. 'There was a definite desire by the government to cover this up while we were urging greater transparency,' recalls one western official. 'But what everyone misjudged was the amount of time we had to sort out the problem.'

The complacency was shattered when a public flare-up between Bulent Ecevit, prime minister, and President Ahmet Necdet Sezer – over corruption in state-owned banks, no less – precipitated a run on the lira and a surge in interest rates. This in turn led state banks to default on their obligations and play a big role in the collapse of Turkey's previous IMF-backed programme in February.

An overhaul of state banks is now central to the latest reform programme drawn up by Mr Dervis who has replaced their previous managers with financially independent professionals, such as Mr Akisik. Mr Dervis, a former World Bank economist, who is personally seen as 'pure' for having spent the past 22 years working outside Turkey, has also promised a switch to total transparency in public expenditure. Much now will depend on the government's ability to keep its reform promises. An early test is provided by public procurement. After leaving the drafting of a new public procurement law to 'the medium term' as part of preparations for membership of the EU, the government has promised the IMF to bring that change forward to October. But as Mr Gundogdu waits for the outcome of his complaint, there is widespread scepticism about whether the same politicians who presided over past abuses will be able to clean them up.

Like many Turks, Nesrin Nas, a deputy for Motherland, the party founded by Mr Ozal and now the junior coalition partner, hopes that the depth of the current crisis will provide the catalyst to 'restructure the existing system from scratch'.

'In our [old] system everybody expected to receive something from the state', she says. 'But now that the money has run out, everybody is unhappy.'

Source: L. Boulton and M. Munir, 'Graft clean-up key to success of Turkish bail out', www.FT.com, 29 May 2001. Reprinted with permission.

were not calculated by the business community, resulting in regular financial crises (as in April 1994, November 2000 and February 2001).

Going beyond the business community, a similar discourse and understanding can be found in the wider society, reflecting the perception of a patrimonial state. It seems to be a natural thing to ask for assistance from a 'strong state', in helping out family problems, local problems, etc. Similar examples can be found from local neighbourhoods, schools, mosques or business associations. A recent case concerns Turkish farmers. After the application of direct support programmes to agriculture in the United States and Europe, the World Bank also supported the adaptation of a similar scheme in Turkey, where producers would be entitled to $5 per one-tenth of a hectare. The result produced by the incentive is not surprising in the Turkish context. From an area with 2,000 inhabitants, 8,000 applications came in; and the claimed land size for receiving subsidy was larger than the registered size of villages in one region (www.ntvmsnbc.com/news/85507.asp, 29 May 2001).

Fostering innovation in the future

So far, we have identified the values and intentions of the business community in Turkey in relation to entrepreneurship and business making. We have suggested that while the business environment did not convey favourable signals to the business community to seek their well-being in deeper business activities, the economic agents themselves contributed to the ongoing mentality with the intention of benefiting significantly from the situation. Although in Turkey studies on innovation lack the required depth and quantity, it would not be surprising for us to find out that a few recent studies would be indicative of the 'sightless' approach of business and society toward innovation.

One such study is that of Uzun (2001). Based upon a study of 2,100 firms of differing sizes in the Turkish manufacturing industry, he concludes (p. 190) that

> *Turkey has to rely basically on technology transfer in the development of industry. In the meantime indigenous technology development will accelerate as it develops its own technology generating capability . . . Transferred technologies are maintained, adopted, improved and renewed with the support of the existing scientific and technological knowledge.*

This also confirms Kirim and Ales' previous findings in relation to the Turkish textile industry: that firms developed capacities for the local adaptation and improvement of technologies imported from the West (Kirim and Ales, 1989). Although the number of firms undertaking innovation has shown a remarkable increase since the early 1980s, factors such as high costs, lack of financial sources, perceived high risks and limited business foresight seem to impede innovation. However, in terms of patented innovations (by the European Patent Office), Turkey is at the bottom of the list, along with Iceland, with a 0.01 per cent share of total issued patents (OECD, 1999). This is reflected locally with only 19 per cent of firms having pursued patent applications (Uzun, 2001). This is in line with the suggestion that Turkey continues to be a late industrialiser with *limited* capability in adapting and improving imported technologies (and coming nowhere near for the production of generic technologies).

The quality of formal education and depth of research undertaken by universities, along with institutionalised and informal networks between sectors and universities, have been determined as the key ingredients of the innovation process. Whereas ties were formed between academic institutions and the business community during the Industrial Revolution in the West and were later strengthened, this link in the context of Turkey remained rather weak. As a result of organisational isomorphism, academic institutions have focused on undergraduate (mass) teaching at the expense of basic scientific research (Üsdiken, 1996; Uzun, 2001).

In this framework, it would not be wrong to put forth the argument that the capability and intentions of business enterprises cannot be separated from the very societal conditions within which they are embedded. Although limited in terms of representation and sample size, Öner's findings on the Turkish attitudes towards innovativeness and adaptiveness in work situations and interpersonal relations are also telling. Based upon semi-structured interviews with 20 adults (10 male and 10 female), she found that the concept of innovation that is assimilated in the Turkish culture has its limits (Öner, 2000). That is, when it comes to considering the relationship between efficiency and innovation, there seems to be a social demand on individuals toward being 'efficient innovators'. Despite being an oxymoron, this is in fact in stark contrast to the literature on creativity and innovation, where the organisational context is usually found to allow for a certain amount of slack for innovators to pursue their individual aspirations and goals (cf. Kirton, 1989; Kanter *et al.*, 1997; Dougherty and Hardy, 1996). Moreover, in the Turkish context, it is also found that innovativeness is sometimes perceived as clashing seriously with traditions and social norms, and hence is rejected as the basis of family or interpersonal relations.

Pause for thought

In order to compete much emphasis is placed on the need to cut costs and improve efficiency. Why would an emphasis on efficiency alone be bad for businesses and economic growth in general?

Innovation requires more than technology and good management

We have explored the reasons why some state contexts are more conducive to deeper levels of entrepreneurial activity and innovation; while some others promote 'petty entrepreneurialism' with short-term, accumulation-ridden intentions. Indeed, some answers have been provided by specifically focusing on the case of Turkey (this is further illustrated in the case study at the end of this chapter). This chapter has also tried to explain how some nations achieved a strong transformation from basic industries and joined the vanguard of technology development. In that respect, it was suggested that although knowledge accumulation is a socially and spatially focused process, geographical shifts have occurred throughout history when 'state–societal arrangements' were conducive and there may be possible openings for late-developing nations in the future. This, however, is by no means a simple process.

Case study

Turkey and its lack of innovation

This case study briefly examines the development of the Turkish economy and assesses the factors that may have contributed to its current position. It considers the business system that now prevails in Turkey and discusses how this can be transformed into a business system that fosters innovation.

Introduction

Turkey's path of industrialisation is similar to those of Latin American and south-east Asian economies. Figure 2.3 highlights that, similar to its counterparts in Latin America and south-east Asia, Turkey also combined inward-looking and outward-oriented economic policies during different phases of capitalist development. The main differences arose because of the timing of policy shift, nature of business–state and society–

state interrelations (that produced the attitude widely adopted in the economy and society), and the state of the world economy at the period of transition. The main difference between Turkey and the noted countries has so far been the lack of any industrial deepening phase before or after the initial opening up of the economy to international competition. In Turkey's case, the trend is still one of exporting unsophisticated products like clothing and textiles.

Whether the country has been locked into the so-called traditional, labour-intensive industries is a question recently raised by a number of industry representatives, strategists and academics. This issue, also known as 'the Heckscher–Ohlin trap', highlights the risks of trying to compete in the international market in these industries. The case of Turkey between 1980 and the mid-1990s does not negate this

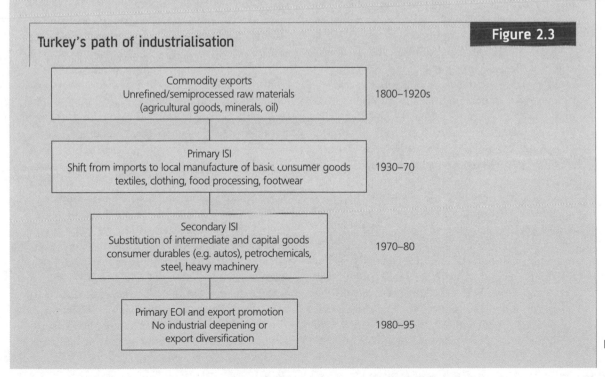

Turkey's path of industrialisation

Figure 2.3

Commodity exports — Unrefined/semiprocessed raw materials (agricultural goods, minerals, oil)	1800–1920s
Primary ISI — Shift from imports to local manufacture of basic consumer goods textiles, clothing, food processing, footwear	1930–70
Secondary ISI — Substitution of intermediate and capital goods consumer durables (e.g. autos), petrochemicals, steel, heavy machinery	1970–80
Primary EOI and export promotion — No industrial deepening or export diversification	1980–95

▶

pattern. Clothing and textile manufactures still account for 30–40 per cent of all exports leaving the country. Given the trends towards globalisation and regionalisation, such sectors as clothing face increasing competition from the rest of the world (e.g. China), which will lead to the declining prices of such products (compared to the prices of qualified-labour/capital-intensive, sophisticated goods). This, ultimately, implies a worsening in terms of trade for such sectors. This is true even though the Turkish clothing industry showed a remarkable upgrade in its competitive position. Its structure is predominantly based on networking, with long-term relations with sub-contractors; and strategically, it has been moving along the value-added chain towards quality and differentiation, collection-creation and recently brand-name formation (Çakmakç, 1997). However, the success in these strategies has so far been limited; and Turkish producers seem to continue imitating new Western product developments, and style and fashion (partly a result of major weaknesses in textile woven fabrics and the dyeing–processing and finishing phases of the textile value chain); and face strong competition from Asian suppliers.

After the implementation of the Customs Union with the European Union in 1995, however, there is seemingly a positive trend to higher-value-added sectors. It is highlighted that there are positive signs of shifting from the clothing industry into sectors like transport equipment, vehicles (i.e. coaches and buses), motorcycles, televisions and some durables such as refrigerators and cookers (Lohrmann, 2000). There is also some R&D activity in telecommunications and computer industries (Uzun, 2001). This signifies that Turkey's role in the international (or regional/EU) division of labour may be redefined and this will eventually bring the long-awaited industrial broadening in the economy. However, this does not overrule the observation that the economy is knowledge and technology-dependent on 'the West'; and one of the determinants of technology development

domestically (i.e. through Foreign Direct Investment (FDI)) is still weak in the wake of macro-economic instability.

The business system in Turkey

In the Turkish context, one can safely argue that the economy is dominated by Holdings, the counterparts of *Keiretsu* in Japan and *Chaebol* in Korea. Since the early years of the republic, large enterprises were always promoted through state policy and development plans ('large was beautiful for the Turkish state'). In other words, Turkey's case has been a justification of the statement that, historically, no country has entered into modern economic growth without the state's targeted intervention or collaboration with large-scale private sector entities.

After consolidation during the 1950s, 1960s were the years that first saw the birth of the Holding company in Turkey. A comparison of Turkish company Holding with *Chaebols* and *Keiretsu* in Table 2.3 clarifies that one of the key distinguishing features of Turkish Holding is that there is almost no specialisation in a line of activity. Although we observe this commitment to a line of activity in both Japan and Korea (be it through economic dynamics or state enforcement), the Turkish Holding always sought the most profitable areas, where returns are possibly short-term and require little risk taking. So we can find a Holding operating in as diverse areas as restaurant management, car production, food processing, banking, university establishment, telecommunications and Internet services, supermarket management and textile production.

The representation of the interests of large-scale establishments and access to state policy have taken an institutional turn after the establishment of the Turkish Industrialists and Businessmen's Association (TÜSAD) in 1971 with a distinct break from other commercial and business interests dominating the Union of Chambers of Commerce and Industry. In the Turkish context, the access to policy making and state

Table 2.3 A comparative framework for the Turkish Holding company

	Japanese Keiretsu	*Korean* Chaebol	*Turkish Holding*
History	Post-Second World War: restructuring of Old-Zaibatsu	1970s–80s: subsidies for heavy industry and chemicals in export-led policy	Republican Creation: Law on Creation of Independence1950s, 1960s, 1970s, 1980s TSKB, tax rebates, FTCs, etc.
Business specialisation	High (esp. in production *Keiretsu*) Toyota: vehicles	Low Hyundai: ship and vehicle. The state limits activities to three main sectors (1980s)	Very low: multi-activity Koç: restaurants, cars, supermarkets, university, banks, food processing, etc.
Bank	Yes (central to all)	No: state-owned banks (8 per cent ownership)	Yes
Foreign trade Company	Sogo Sosho	Yes: after 1975	FTCs: 1980s
Relational Subcontracting	High: risk sharing with suppliers through long-term trust-based contracts: logic of JIT	Low: self-sufficient, vertically integrated	Low: self-sufficient, vertically integrated
Ownership	Intercompany shareholding arrangements: councils	Family-based	Family-based
Personal authority	Low	High	High: HQ makes strategic decisions, quasi-autonomous subsidiaries
Managers	Well-educated elite	Wealthy well-educated elite (cross-marriage)	Prestigious universities and US-educated elite
Relations with the state	State guidance: MITI R&D, SMEs, new industries, new markets, some periodical protectionism	Dependence/favouritism: financing, taxation, protectionism, political affliation, rent-seeking	Dependence/favouritism: financing, taxation, protectionism, initiation of enterprise, connection with state officials, rent-seeking
Relations with labour	Dissolution of powerful unions in the 1960s; consensual relations based on loyalty, life-long employment, multi-skilled workers	Coercive military regime in post-1970: low labour costs and disciplined workers and labour unions, General Park	Coercive military regime in post-1980: low labour costs and disciplined workers and labour unions, General Evren
Strategies	Commitment to development objectives and long-term company growth (lack of shareholders)	Growth pattern reflects the opportunities provided by politicians and state officials	Growth pattern reflects the opportunities provided by politicians and state officials in line with short-term profitability: entry into industries and rent-seeking

▶

officials has always had an informal dimension, where particular relations with officials, members of parliament, ministers and the prime minister has been the norm for industrialists and business executives to raise issues with the state and promote certain proposals (Gülfidan, 1993). Now with the introduction of TÜSAD to the institutional setting, the relations with the state have formed a dual structure. Through the increasing influence of TÜSAD and employers' unions, the 1980s in Turkey saw an example of 'corporatism without labour', where the 'Iron Triangle'* worked with minimal influence from organised labour, which suffered serious losses after the military coup of 1980 (Çakmakç, 1997). What the 1980s could at least provide for businesses was a peaceful working environment and declining real labour wages, in contrast to the strife- and crisis-ridden years of the 1970s.

Discussion

Turkey's present and future has been largely determined by its past. It may be useful here to quote Karl Marx:

> *Men make their own history, but they do not make it just as they please; they do not make it under circumstances chosen by themselves, but under circumstances directly encountered, given and transmitted from the past. The tradition of all the dead generations weighs like a nightmare on the brain of the living.*

(Marx, *The Eighteenth Brumaire of Louis Bonaparte: 245*)

Given the complexities of the global economy today and the requirements of new technologies,

the weight on late-industrialising states and societies is heavier than ever before. What is to be done? First, analyse the historical trends and structures, inherited in these countries. Second, act upon major weaknesses and set up a vision for the future.

In a similar pattern, Turkey's 'Transition to a Strong Economy' programme seems to have addressed the difficulties of the past and the way forward. However, much remains to be done to achieve the desired results, particularly given the dominance and volatility of money and finance sectors.

It is very well understood that to become a strong and respectable state in the twenty-first century requires a productive and strong private sector; this facilitates the healthy operation of a market economy, which can mobilise social support and undertake legal supervision. A strong economy will be created by a private sector working in a confident environment, an effective state and wide social consensus. Entrepreneurs and businesses should be able to divert their energy away from rent-seeking from the state into production, exporting, technological development and creating employment.

Questions

1 From the case study discuss the strengths of the Turkish economy.

2 Given these strengths why has it struggled to develop?

3 From the case study characterise the Turkish Holding company.

4 To what extent is Turkey's past responsible for its current position?

5 What needs to be done to improve economic growth in Turkey?

---

* At one corner of the triangle are interest groups (constituencies). The interest group brings issues and policies to the attention of legislators in Government and suggests policies they want. At another corner sit members of Government who also seek to align themselves with a constituency for political and electoral support. These Government members support legislation that advances the interest group's agenda. Occupying the third corner of the triangle are bureaucrats for whom the benefits of implementing interest group policies include the appropriation of sizable chunks of government funds as well as the chance to exercise their expertise by fleshing out skeletal or ambiguously worded legislation. The result is a three-way, stable alliance that is sometimes called a sub-government because of its durability, impregnability and power to determine policy.

Chapter summary

This chapter has explored the wider context of innovation, in particular the role of the state. It has shown that innovation cannot be separated from political and social processes. The case study of Turkey demonstrates the importance of having in place the necessary business environment. For innovation to flourish a nation needs to put in place the necessary conditions. This includes both tangible and intangible features, including economic, social and political institutions, and processes and mechanisms that facilitate the flow of knowledge between industries and firms. The lack of innovation within the Turkish economy illustrates the importance of these features and in many ways provides an example to other developing countries of pitfalls to avoid.

Discussion questions

1 Discuss the tangible features that it is necessary for the state to put in place to foster innovation.

2 How can the state encourage entrepreneurs and businesses to invest in longer time horizons?

3 Explain Schumpeter's view of entrepreneurial behaviour and economic growth?

4 Discuss the evidence for the fifth Kondratieff wave of growth.

5 What are the specific problems facing the Turkish economy?

6 How has Turkey's economic history contributed to its current problems?

7 What is meant by a 'weak business system'?

Key words and phrases

Business system   56

Corruption   57

Entrepreneurship   56

Kondratieff waves of growth   48

National systems of innovation   43

Schumpeterian theory   48

Short-termism   57

Websites worth visiting

Confederation of British Industry www.cbi.org.uk

The Engineering Council (EC UK) www.engc.org.uk

European Industrial Research Management Association (EIRMA) www.eirma.asso.fr

Intellect UK www.intellectuk.org

Quoted Companies Alliance (QCA) www.qcanet.co.uk

The R&D Society www.rdsoc.org

The Royal Academy of Engineering www.raeng.org.uk

UK Government, Department of Trade and Industry www.Dti.gov.uk/innovation

References

Afuah, A. (2003) *Innovation Management: Strategies, Implementation and Profits*, 2nd edn, Oxford University Press, Oxford.

Amsden, A. (1989) *Asia's Next Giant: South Korea and Late Industrialisation*, Oxford University Press, Oxford.

Bura, A. (1994) *State and Business in Modern Turkey: A Comparative Study*, State University of New York Press, Albany, NY.

Çakmakç, U.M. (1997) 'The political economy of governance: an integral economic analysis of textile and apparel sectors in Turkey', unpublished PhD thesis, Lancaster University.

Castells, M. (1992) 'Four Asian Tigers with a dragon head: a comparative analysis of the state, economy, and society in the Asian Pacific Rim', in Appelbaum, R.P. and Henderson, J. (eds) *States and Development: The Asian Pacific Rim*, Oxford University Press, Oxford, 33–70.

Clark, E.C. (2000) 'The Ottoman Industrial Revolution', *Çerçeve*, January.

Dicken, P. (1998) *Global Shift: Transforming the World Economy*, Paul Chapman, London.

Dougherty, C. and Hardy, M. (1996) 'Sustained innovation in large and mature firms', *Academy of Management Journal*, Vol. 39, No. 5, 1120–53.

Evans, P.B. (1989) 'Predatory, developmental, and other apparatuses: a comparative political economy perspective on the Third World state', *Sociological Forum*, Vol. 4, No. 4, 561–87.

Freeman, C. and Soete, L. (1997) *The Economics of Industrial Innovation*, 3rd edn, Pinter, London.

Gülfidan, S. (1993) *Big Business and the State in Turkey: The Case of TÜSIAD*, Boğaziçi University, Istanbul.

Hart, J.A. (1992) *Rival Capitalists: International Competitiveness in the United States, Japan, and Western Europe*, Cornell University Press, London.

ICI (1993–96) ICI 500 *Largest Firm Analysis*, Istanbul Chamber of Industry, Istanbul.

Jessop, B. (1982) *The Capitalist State*, Martin Robertson, Oxford.

Jessop, B. (1990) *State Theory: Putting Capitalist States in their Place*, Polity Press, Cambridge.

Johnson, C. (1982) *MITI and the Japanese Miracle: The Growth of Industrial Policy 1925–75*, Stanford University Press, Stanford, CA.

Kanter, R.M., Kao, J. and Wiersema, F. (eds) (1997) *Innovation: Breakthrough Thinking at 3M, DuPont, GE, Pfizer, and Rubbermaid*, Harper Businessmasters Series, New York.

Kerwin, R.W. (1951) 'Private enterprise in Turkish economic development', *Middle East Journal*, Vol. 5, No. 1, 1120–53.

Kirton, M.J. (1989) *Adaptors and Innovators: Styles of Creativity and Problem-Solving*, Routledge, London.

Kirim, A. and Ales, H. (1989) 'Technical change and technological capability in the Turkish textile sector', *METU Studies in Development*, Vol. 16, Nos. 1–2, 1–30.

Lohrmann, A. (2000) 'Development effects of the customs union between Turkey and the European Union: catching-up or the Heckscher–Ohlin trap?' *Russian and East European Finance and Trade*, Vol. 36, No. 4, 26–44.

Marx, K. (1972) *The Karl Marx Library*, Vol. 1: *The Eighteenth Brumaire of Louis Bonaparte*, Padover, S.K. (ed.), McGraw Hill, New York, pp. 245–6.

Nelson, R.R. (ed.) (1993) *National Innovation Systems*, Oxford University Press, Oxford.

OECD (1999) *Patent Counts as Indicators of Technology Output*, OECD, Paris.

Öner, B. (2000) 'Innovation and adaptation in a Turkish sample: a preliminary study', *Journal of Psychology*, Vol. 134, No. 6, 671–6.

Porter, M. (1990) *The Competitive Advantage of Nations*, Macmillan, London.

Porter, M., Takeuchi H. and Sakakıbara, M. (2000) *Can Japan Compete*? Perseus Pub., Cambridge, MA.

Rosenthal, D.E. (1993) 'Reevaluating the Chicago School paradigm for promoting innovation and competitiveness', *Canada–United States Law Journal*, Vol. 19, 97–104.

Schumpeter, J. (1943) *Capitalism, Socialism and Democracy*, Allen & Unwin, London.

Toprak, Z. (1995) *National Economics-National Bourgeoisie: Economy and Society in Turkey 1908–1950* (in Turkish: *Milli Iktisat-Milli Burjuvazi: Türkiye'de Ekonomi ve Toplum 1908–1950)*, Türkiye Toplumsal ve Ekonomik Tarih Vakfı, Istanbul.

Üsdiken, B. (1996) 'Importing theories of management & organization', *International Studies of Management and Organization*, Vol. 26, No. 3, 33.

Uzun, A. (2001) 'Technological innovation activities in Turkey: the case of manufacturing industry, 1995–1997', *Technovation*, Vol. 21, 189–96.

Yalman, G.L. (1997) 'Bourgeoisie and the state: changing forms of interest representation within the context of economic crisis and structural adjustment: Turkey during the 1980s', unpublished PhD thesis submitted to Manchester University.

Further reading

For a more detailed review of the role of the state in innovation management, the following develop many of the issues raised in this chapter:

Dicken, P. (1998) *Global Shift: Transforming the World Economy*, Paul Chapman, London.

Dougherty, C. and Hardy, M. (1996) 'Sustained innovation in large and mature firms'.

Patel, P. and Pavitt, K. (2000) 'How technological competencies help define the core (not the boundaries) of the firm', in Dosi, G., Nelson, R. and Winter, S.G. (eds) *The Nature and Dynamics of Organisational Capabilities*, Oxford University Press, Oxford, 313–33.

Shavinina, L. (2003) *The International Handbook on Innovation*, Elsevier, Oxford.

Tidd, J. (2001) 'Innovation management in context, organisation and performance', *International Journal of Management Reviews*, Vol. 3, No. 3, 169–83.

3

Managing innovation within firms

Virtually all innovations, certainly major technological innovations such as pharmaceutical and automobile products, occur within organisations. The management of innovation within organisations forms the focus for this chapter. The study of organisations and their management is a very broad subject and no single approach provides all the answers. The identifcation of those factors and issues that affect the management of innovation within organisations is addressed here.

Chapter contents

Learning objectives

When you have completed this chapter you will be able to:

- identify the main trends in the development of the management of organisations;
- explain the dilemma facing all organisations concerning the need for creativity and stability;
- recognise the difficulties of managing uncertainty;
- identify the activities performed by key individuals in the management of innovation; and
- recognise the relationship between the activities performed and the organisational environment in promoting innovation.

Theories about organisations and innovation

Chapter 1 outlined some of the difficulties in studying the field of innovation. In particular, it emphasised the need to view innovation as a management process within the context of the organisation. This was shown to be the case especially in a modern industrialised society where innovation is increasingly viewed as an *organisational activity*. This chapter tackles the difficult issue of managing innovation within organisations. To do this, it is necessary to understand the patterns of interaction and behaviour which represent the organisation.

The theory of organisations is a set of ideas drawn from many disciplines and lies beneath much of the study of innovation. In many ways organisation theory bridges pure social and behavioural sciences and management practices at the level of the organisation. As an applied science it examines the behaviour of organisations and provides useful information about how organisations respond to different management techniques and practices, hence its importance in understanding how the process of innovation is managed.

Given the diversity of the literature in this field, there are few clear prescriptions on what organisations need to do in order to manage innovation successfully. None the less, there are numerous analytical frameworks and organisation-specific models of innovation. The literature can be classified into four dominant strands (Perrow, 1970) as shown in Figure 3.1.

| Figure 3.1 | The importance of a multiple-perspective approach |

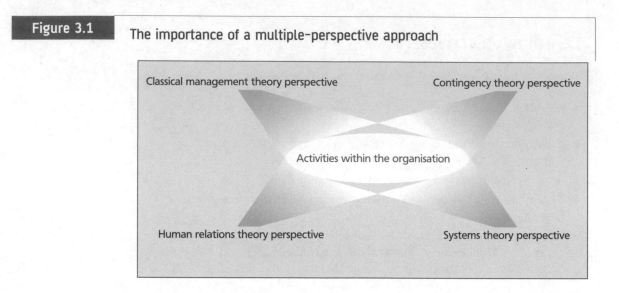

Classical or scientific management perspective

The classical view of organisations took hold after the Industrial Revolution and the huge increase in world trade at the beginning of the twentieth century. It is built around traditional management concepts, bureaucratic theory (Weber, 1964) and scientific management (Taylor, 1947). This school of thought tends to view the organisation as an instrument for achieving established goals, in which members of the organisation can be made to serve these goals by management's use of reward and motivation techniques. It assumes that all tasks confronting the organisation can be rationalised. Hence, organisations should be designed to ensure a predictable flow of work. Specialisation of tasks is employed to maximise efficiency and there is emphasis on rules to achieve coordination between units. This view assumes that people can be combined with machines to produce an orderly output. Within this framework innovation is a series of rational decisions leading to a clearly defined outcome. Indeed, this school of thought contributed to the dominance of the 'technology-push' model of innovation (*see* Chapter 1).

Human relations approach

It was following extensive questioning of the classical view in the 1930s that the human relations school evolved. Much of the original impetus was provided by the Hawthorn Studies at Western Electric (Roethlisberger and Dickinson, 1939). These new approaches identified informal and non-legitimised group processes within the organisation. Informal communications and activities were unearthed by social scientists and found to influence organisational behaviour. This school of thought also led to the development of the contingency theory (*see* below).

A slightly different perspective views the organisation as a political system and suggests that change will result in some conflict between different units in the organisation when a unit perceives that the innovation or change might reduce its influence (Harvey and Mills, 1970). This also introduces the notion of routine and innovative solutions. It is argued that problem situations and problem solutions are arranged along a routine–innovative dimension. A routine solution is defined as 'a solution that has been used before', while an innovative solution is defined as 'a solution that has not been used before and for which there are no precedents in the organisation' (pp. 189–90). Harvey and Mills argue that an organisation will tend to impose routine solutions unless there is pressure on the organisation's structural arrangements. These arrangements reinforce the continuation of routine patterns around which interests have formed. Innovative solutions will only be imposed when the organisation is in a higher stress-threat situation, which is more likely to demand innovative behaviour if the organisation is to adapt. This model builds on the work of Burns and Stalker (1961) (*see* below), who indicate that there are different types of solutions, mechanistic routine and organic innovative, that are appropriate for different situations.

Contingency approach

The third main strand of literature is represented by organisation contingency theories. These posit the view that there is not necessarily a *single best* organisational structure, but rather that the structure should be adapted to the activities being performed. Organisational activities or tasks are the things that individuals do as part of groups in order for the organisation to achieve its purposes. This emphasis on internal activities rather than structure is an important factor with regard to innovation. This book takes the view that the process of innovation is made up of a *series of linked activities within an organisation*.

Research in this field (Thompson, 1967; Perrow, 1970; Hull, 1981) has identified a range of different characteristics that organisations have exhibited that, it is argued, more accurately describe the range of different organisational environments. The following list represents a typology of characteristics that have been identified within certain organisations:

- certainty versus uncertainty
- stability versus instability
- uniform versus non-uniform
- few exceptions versus many exceptions
- many repetitive events versus few repetitive events

In general, contingency theory argues that tasks that are certain, stable, uniform, have few exceptions and many repetitive events are compatible with bureaucratic organisational forms, which stress formality. At the other end of the task continuum, tasks that are uncertain, unstable, non-uniform, have many exceptions and few repetitive events are compatible with organic flexible organisational forms (*see* Table 3.1).

Table 3.1 Issues identified by systems theory that need to be managed

Issue	Characteristics
Adaptation	The ability to alter ways of working to meet the changing environment
Coordination	Enabling the different parts of the organisation to function as one
Integration	The ability to harmonise a diverse range of activities and people
Strain	Coping with friction between organisational parts
Output	Achieving purposes and goals
Maintenance	Keeping elements in the system active

Systems theory

The fourth set of ideas developed concurrently with contingency theory during the 1960s and 1970s. However, systems theory emphasises processes and dynamic analysis rather than characteristic and structural analysis (Checkland, 1989; Thompson, 1967; Katz and Khan, 1966). The origins of the theory can be traced back to the 1950s when Ludvig von Bertalanffy, a biologist, first used the term 'systems theory' (Bertalanffy, 1951). Systems theorists analyse the commercial organisation from the perspective of complex organic systems.

A system is defined as any set of elements linked in a pattern which carries information ordered according to some pre-determined rules. Organisations are seen as goal-directed systems. All systems have both structures and processes. Structures are the relatively stable elements, whereas processes are the dynamic relationships among system elements over time.

This school of thought has led to a richer and better understanding of organisational activities. For example, the issues in Table 3.2 are said to be continually addressed by organisations. They should be viewed as issues that need to be managed rather than problems that can be solved.

In addition, systems theory has also highlighted the importance of the organisation's interaction with the external world. Indeed, this interaction is identified as an important element of the innovation process. It is precisely the way in which organisations manage and capture the benefits from the knowledge flows, which are the product of these interactions, that will affect their ability to innovate.

Together these four schools of thought have contributed enormously to the understanding of the management of innovation. Some of the more significant issues will now be addressed in more detail.

Table 3.2 Organisational characteristics that facilitate the innovation process

Organisational requirement	Characterised by
1 Growth orientation	A commitment to long-term growth rather than short-term profit
2 Vigilance	The ability of the organisation to be aware of its threats and opportunities
3 Commitment to technology	The willingness to invest in the long-term development of technology
4 Acceptance of risks	The willingness to include risky opportunities in a balanced portfolio
5 Cross-functional cooperation	Mutual respect among individuals and a willingness to work together across functions
6 Receptivity	The ability to be aware of, to identify and to take effective advantage of externally developed technology
7 'Slack'	An ability to manage the innovation dilemma and provide room for creativity
8 Adaptability	A readiness to accept change
9 Diverse range of skills	A combination of specialisation and diversity of knowledge and skills

Pause for thought

If we know what organisational characteristics are required for innovation why are not all firms innovative?

The dilemma of innovation management

Within organisations there is a fundamental tension between the need for stability and the need for creativity. On the one hand, companies require stability and static routines to accomplish daily tasks efficiently and quickly. This enables the organisation to compete today. For example, the processing of millions of cheques by banks every day, or the delivery of food by multiples to their retail outlets all over the country, demands high levels of efficiency and control. On the other hand, companies also need to develop

Figure 3.2   Managing the tension between the need for creativity and efficiency

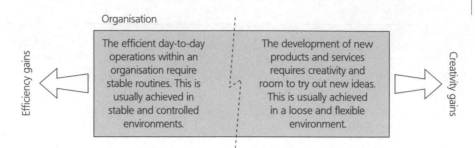

new ideas and new products to be competitive in the future. Hence they need to nurture a creative environment where ideas can be tested and developed. This poses one of the most fundamental problems for management today (*see* Figure 3.2).

Take any medium to large company and examine its operations and activities. From Mars to Ford, and from P&G to Sony, these companies have to ensure that their products are carefully manufactured to precise specifications and that they are delivered for customers on time day after day. In this hectic, repetitive and highly organised environment the need to squeeze out any slack or inefficiencies is crucial to ensure a firm's costs are lower than their competitors'. Without this emphasis on cost reductions a firm's costs would simply spiral upwards and the firm's products and services would become uncompetitive. But we have already seen in the previous chapter that long-term economic growth is dependent on the ability of firms to make improvements to products and manufacturing processes. This means that firms need to somehow make room for creativity and innovation, that is, allow slack in the system. Here then is the dilemma: how do firms try to reduce costs and slack to improve competitiveness on the one hand and then try to provide slack for innovation on the other? As usual with dilemmas the answer is difficult and has to do with balancing activities. The firm needs to ensure there is a constant pressure to drive down costs and improve efficiency in its operations. At the same time it needs to provide room for new product development and improvements to be made. The most obvious way forward is to separate production from research and development (R&D) but while this is usually done there are many improvements and innovations that arise out of the operations of the firm as will be seen in the next chapter. Indeed, the operations of the firm provide enormous scope for innovation. Consider for one moment the packaging of a product. It is not possible to create a new product in isolation of the operations required to get the product from manufacture to retailer and then on to consumer. These all need to be considered as can be seen from Chapter 13, which explores the role of packaging.

Pause for thought

To resolve the innovation dilemma, why do not firms simply separate the creative side of their business from the operational side?

Managing uncertainty

It is becoming clear that product innovation is a complex process. Figure 1.5 highlighted the main areas of attention, but each of these represents a complex area in itself. Innovation involves numerous factors acting separately but often influencing one another. Organisations have to respond to internal and external events, some of which are beyond their control. While management in general involves coping with uncertainty, sometimes trying to reduce uncertainty, the *raison d'être* of managers involved in innovation is to develop something different, maybe something new. The management of the innovation process involves trying to develop the creative potential of the organisation. It involves trying to foster new ideas and generate creativity. Managing uncertainty is a central feature of managing the innovation process.

Pearson's uncertainty map

Pearson's uncertainty map (Pearson, 1991) provides a framework for analysing and understanding uncertainty and the innovation process. The map was developed following extensive analysis of case studies of major technological innovations, including Pilkington's float glass process, 3M's Post-It Notes and Sony's Walkman (Henry and Walker, 1991). In these and other case studies a great deal of uncertainty surrounded the project. If it involves newly developed technology this may be uncertainty about the type of product envisaged. For example, Spencer Silver's unusual adhesive remained unexploited within 3M for five years before an application was found. Similarly, if a market opportunity has been identified the final product idea may be fairly well established, but much uncertainty may remain about how exactly the company is to develop such a product. For example, the case study at the end of Chapter 1 discussed the development of a new range of aqueous-based cleaning products. Here the market was identified but at the time there was uncertainty about how to develop a product for this market.

So Pearson's framework divides uncertainty into two separate dimensions:

● uncertainty about ends (what is the eventual target of the activity or project); and
● uncertainty about means (how to achieve this target).

The case study at the end of Chapter 8 deals with the development of Guinness's 'In-can system'. This clearly highlights the problems of managing uncertainty about means. Several projects were unsuccessful and there were probably several occasions where decisions had to be taken regarding future funding. Decisions had to be made such as whether to cancel, continue or increase funding. In these situations, because the degree of uncertainty is high, senior managers responsible for million-dollar budgets have to listen carefully to those most closely involved and those with the most information and knowledge. Further information and knowledge are usually available with the passage of time, so time is another element that needs to be considered. Indeed, it is because time is limited that decisions are required. It is clear, however, that many decisions are made with imperfect knowledge, thus there is usually an element of judgement involved in most decisions.

| Figure 3.3 | Pearson's uncertainty map |

Source: A.W. Pearson (1991) 'Managing innovation: an uncertainty reduction process', in *Managing Innovation*, J. Henry and D. Walker, eds, Sage/OU.

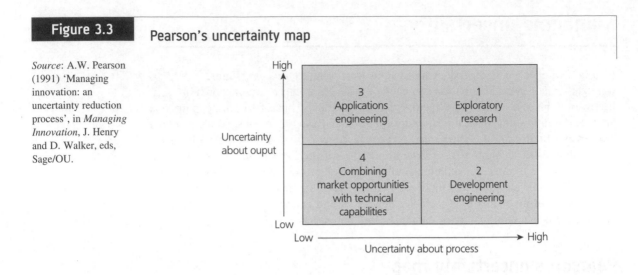

Pearson's framework, shown in Figure 3.3, addresses the nature of the uncertainty and the way it changes over time. The framework is based on the two dimensions discussed above, with uncertainty about ends on the vertical axis and uncertainty about means on the horizontal axis. These axes are then divided, giving four quadrants.

Quadrant 1

Quadrant 1 represents activities involving a high degree of uncertainty about means and ends. The ultimate target is not clearly defined and how to achieve this target is also not clear. This has been labelled 'exploratory research' or 'blue sky' research, because the work sometimes seems so far removed from reality that people liken it to working in the clouds! These activities often involve working with technology that is not fully understood and where potential products or markets have also not been identified. This is largely the domain of university research laboratories, which are usually removed from the financial and time pressures associated with industry. Some science-based organisations also support these activities, but increasingly it is only large organisations who have the necessary resources to fund such exploratory studies. For example, Microsoft conducts the majority of its research in Seattle, United States. Interestingly it calls this center a 'campus'.

Quadrant 2

In this area the end or target is clear. For example, a commercial opportunity may have been identified but as yet the means of fulfilling this has yet to be established. Companies may initiate several different projects centred around different technologies or different approaches to try to achieve the desired product. Also additional approaches may be uncovered along the way. Hence, there is considerable uncertainty about precisely how the company will achieve its target. This type of activity is often referred to as development engineering and is an on-going activity within manufacturing companies which are continually examining their production processes, looking for efficiencies and ways to reduce costs. A good example of a successful development in this area is the Guinness 'In-can system'. The company was clear about its target – trying to make the taste of Guinness from a can taste the same as draught Guinness. Precisely how this was to be achieved was very uncertain and many different research projects were established.

Quadrants 3 and 4 deal with situations where there is more certainty associated with how the business will achieve the target. This usually means that the business is working with technology it has used before.

Quadrant 3

In this area there is uncertainty regarding ends. This is usually associated with attempting to discover how the technology can be most effectively used. Applications engineering is the title given to this area of activity. Arguably many new materials fall into this area. For example, the material kevlar (used in the manufacture of bullet-proof clothing) is currently being applied to a wide range of different possible product areas. Many of these may prove to be ineffective due to costs or performance, but some new and improved products will emerge from this effort.

Quadrant 4

This area covers innovative activities where there is most certainty. In these situations activities may be dominated by improving existing products or creating new products through the combination of a market opportunity and technical capability. With so much certainty, similar activities are likely to be being undertaken by the competition. Hence, speed of development is often the key to success here. New product designs that use minimal new technology but improve, sometimes with dramatic effect, the appearance or performance of an existing product are examples of product innovations in this area. A good exponent of this is Nokia. It has demonstrated an ability to introduce new cell phones incorporating new designs rapidly into the market, thereby maintaing its position as market leader.

Applying the uncertainty map to avoid promising success and delivering failure

The uncertainty map's value is partly the simplicity with which it is able to communicate a complex message, that of dealing with uncertainty, and partly its ability to identify the wide range of organisational characteristics that are associated with managing uncertainty with respect to innovation. The map conveys the important message that the management of product and process innovations is very different. Sometimes one is clear about the nature of the target market and the type of product required. In contrast, there are occasions when little, if anything, is known about the technology being developed and how it could possibly be used. Most organisations have activities that lie between these two extremes, but such differing environments demand very different management skills and organisational environments. This leads the argument towards the vexed question of the organisational structure and culture necessary for innovation, which will be addressed in the following section. First, it is necessary to explore the innovation process through the uncertainty map.

The map helps managers to consider how ideas are transformed into innovations; a very simplistic view of the innovation process. Moreover, it provides a way of identifying the different management skills required. Quadrant 1 highlights an area of innovative activity where ideas and developments may not be immediately recognisable as possible commercial products. There are many examples of technological developments that occurred within organisations that were not recognised. In Xerox's Palo Alto laboratories, the early computer software technology was developed for computer graphical interface as far back as the early 1970s. Xerox did not recognise the possible future benefits of this research and decided not to develop the technology further. It was later exploited by Apple Computer and Microsoft in the 1980s. This raises the question of how to evaluate research in this area. Technical managers may be better able to understand the technology, but a commercial manager may be able to see a wide range of commercial opportunities. Continual informal and formal discussions are usually the best way to explore all possibilities fully, in the hope that the company will make the correct decision regarding which projects to support and which to drop. This is a problem that will be returned to in Chapter 9.

At the other extreme is Quadrant 4, where scientists often view this type of activity as merely tinkering with existing technology. However, commercial managers often get very excited because the project is in a 'close-to-market' form with minimal technical newness.

Between these two extremes lie Quadrants 2 and 3. In the applications engineering quadrant where the business is exploring the potential uses of known technology, management efforts centre on which markets to enter; whereas in the development engineering quadrant special project-management skills are required to ensure that projects either deliver or are cancelled before costs escalate.

In all of the above particular organisational environments and specialist management skills are required depending on the type of activity being undertaken. These will be determined by the extent of uncertainty involved.

Pause for thought

If most new products are minor modifications of existing products why do firms continue with high-risk, high-cost projects?

Organisational characteristics that facilitate the innovation process

The innovation process, outlined at the end of Chapter 1, identified the complex nature of innovation. It also emphasised the need to view innovation within the context of the organisation. Table 3.3 represents a classification of the main *organisational characteristics* that are continually identified in the literature as necessary for successful innovation.

Table 3.3 Organic versus mechanistic organisational structures

Organic	Mechanistic
1 Channels of communication Open with free information fbw throughout the organisation	1 Channels of communication Highly structured, restricted information flow
2 Operating styles Allowed to vary freely	2 Operating styles Must be uniform and restricted
3 Authority for decisions Based on the expertise of the individual	3 Authority for decisions Based on formal line management position
4 Free adaptation By the organisation to changing circumstances	4 Reluctant adaptation With insistence on holding fast to tried and true management principles despite changes in business conditions
5 Emphasis on getting things done Unconstrained by formally laid out procedures	5 Emphasis on formally laid down procedures Reliance on tried and true management principles
6 Loose, informal control With emphasis on norm of cooperation	6 Tight control Through sophisticated control systems
7 Flexible on-job behaviour Permitted to be shaped by the requirements of the situation and personality of the individual doing the job	7 Constrained on-job behaviour Required to conform to job descriptions
8 Decision-making Participation and group consensus used frequently	8 Decision-making Superiors make decisions with minimum consultation and involvement of subordinates

Source: D.P. Slevin and J.G. Covin (1990) 'Juggling entrepreneurial style and organizational structure: how to get your act together', *Sloan Management Review*, Winter, 43–53.

Growth orientation

It is sometimes surprising to learn that not all companies' first and foremost objective is growth. Some companies are established merely to exploit a short-term opportunity. Other companies, particularly family-run ones, would like to maintain the company at its existing size. At that size the family can manage the operation without having to employ outside help. Companies that are innovative are those companies whose objective is to grow the business. This does not imply that they make large profits one year then huge losses the next, but they actively plan for the long term. There are many companies who make this explicit in their annual reports, companies such as Nokia, Siemens, BMW and Microsoft.

Vigilance

Vigilance requires continual external scanning, not just by senior management but also by all other members of the organisation. Part of this activity may be formalised. For example, within the marketing function the activity would form part of market research and competitor analysis. Within the research and development department scientists and engineers will spend a large amount of their time reading the scientific literature in order to keep up to date with the latest developments in their field. In other functions it may not be as formalised but it still needs to occur. Collecting valuable information is one thing, but relaying it to the necessary individuals and acting on it are two necessary associated requirements. An open communication system will help to facilitate this.

Commitment to technology

Most innovative firms exhibit patience in permitting ideas to germinate and develop over time. This also needs to be accompanied by a commitment to resources in terms of intellectual input from science, technology and engineering. Those ideas that look most promising will require further investment. Without this long-term approach it would be extremely difficult for the company to attract good scientists. Similarly, a climate that invests in technology development one year then decides to cut investment the next will alienate the same people in which the company encourages creativity. Such a disruptive environment does not foster creativity and will probably cause many creative people to search for a more suitable company with a stronger commitment to technology.

Acceptance of risks

Accepting risks does not mean a willingness to gamble. It means the willingness to consider carefully risky opportunities. It also includes the ability to make risk-assessment decisions, to take calculated risks and to include them in a balanced portfolio of projects, some of which will have a low element of risk and some a high degree of risk.

Cross-functional cooperation

Inter-departmental conflict is a well documented barrier to innovation. The relationship between the marketing and R&D functions has received a great deal of attention in the research literature. This will be explored further in Chapter 15, but generally this is because the two groups often have very different interests. Scientists and technologists can be fascinated by new technology and may sometimes lose sight of the business objective. Similarly, the marketing function often fails to understand the technology involved in the development of a new product. Research has shown that the presence of some conflict is desirable, probably acting as a motivational force (Souder, 1987). It is the ability to confront and resolve frustration and conflict that is required.

Receptivity

The capability of the organisation to be aware of, identify and take effective advantage of externally developed technology is key. Most technology-based innovations involve a combination of several different technologies. It would be unusual for all the technology to be developed in-house. Indeed, businesses are witnessing an increasing number of joint ventures and alliances (Hinton and Trott, 1996), often with former competitors. For example, Sony and Ericsson have formed a joint venture to work on the development of cell phone handsets (*see* the case study on Sony-Ericsson in Chapter 10 for more details). Previously these two companies fought ferociously in the battle for market share in the cell phone handset market.

'Slack'

While organisations place great emphasis on the need for efficiency, there is also a need for a certain amount of 'slack' to allow individuals room to think, experiment, discuss ideas and be creative (Cordey-Hayes *et al.*, 1997). In many R&D functions this issue is directly addressed by allowing scientists to spend 10–15 per cent of their time on the projects they choose. This is not always supported in other functional areas.

Adaptability

The development of new product innovations will invariably lead to disruptions to established organisational activities. Major or radical innovations may result in significant changes, although the two are not necessarily linked. The organisation must be ready to accept change in the way it manages its internal activities. Otherwise proposed innovations would be stifled due to a reluctance to alter existing ways of working or to learn new techniques. In short, organisations need the ability to adapt to the changing environment.

Diverse range of skills

Organisations require a combination of specialist skills and knowledge in the form of experts in, say, science, advertising or accountancy and generalist skills that facilitate cross-fertilisation of the specialist knowledge. In addition they require individuals of a hybrid nature who are able to understand a variety of technical subjects and facilitate the transfer of knowledge within the company. Similarly, hybrid managers who have technical and commercial training are particularly useful in the area of product development (Wheelwright and Clark, 1992). It is the ability to manage this diversity of knowledge and skills effectively that lies at the heart of the innovation process. This is wonderfully illustrated below in the analysis of conducting or managing an orchestra. On the one hand great individual musical talent is required and yet at the same time individuals must play as part of the team. The parallel between an orchestra and a business is portrayed in Illustration 3.1.

Illustration 3.1

FT

A most harmonious collaboration: LEADERSHIP

The Orpheus Orchestra has no conductor. Its consensual management may have lessons for business

The Orpheus Chamber Orchestra is a success by any standard. The New York-based ensemble commands the highest fees for an orchestra of its size on the international concert circuit.

Its intelligent, transparent playing has won four Grammy awards. Its musician members also appear to be extremely happy, with average tenure of 20 years.

Yet it is the only orchestra that consistently rehearses and performs without a conductor, having developed a form of internal democracy known as 'the Orpheus process'.

Are there management lessons to be learnt from this? CUS business schools certainly think so. The orchestra has extended its repertoire by staging demonstrations and performances for MBA students. Its latest gig was an afternoon session at the Haas School of Business at the University of California, Berkeley.

The parallel between an orchestra and a business is not as far-fetched as it sounds. The Orpheus consists of 27 highly skilled knowledge workers who co-operate to solve complex problems. Discord can ruin a performance and damage the corporate brand. Commitment and involvement by every member of the team can produce award-winning results.

J. Richard Hackman, professor of social and organisational psychology at Harvard University, suggests that the success of the Orpheus points to a new model of leadership in knowledge-based organisations.

In 1988, Peter Drucker, the management guru, said that businesses would start to be managed more like symphony orchestras, with a conductor/chief executive dealing direct with highly skilled professionals rather than working through layers of middle management. The chief executive's job, he proposed, would be to focus the talents of each team member on the joint performance.

The success of the Orpheus raises a different possibility, says Prof Hackman. In the foreword to *Leadership Ensemble,** a book in which Harvey Seifter, the orchestra's executive director, describes the Orpheus process, Prof Hackman writes: 'Rather than relying on a charismatic, visionary leader who both calls the shots and engages members' motivation, might it be possible for all members to share responsibility for leadership and for differences and disagreements to be sources of creativity, rather than something that should be suppressed in the interest of uniformity and social harmony?'

David Pottruck, co-chief executive at Charles Schwab, the financial group based in San Francisco, was sufficiently intrigued to attend the Haas school demonstration. He observes: 'In

* Harvey Seifter, *Leadership Ensemble, Lessons in Collaborative Management from the World's Only Conductorless Orchestra*, published in the US by Times Books, US$25.

most business groups there is an authority figure but that model of leadership works very badly at the highest level. I have eight senior executives reporting to me at Schwab and the John Wayne style of leadership will not work.'

Under the Orpheus process, a core group of six to 12 musicians is selected to set the artistic tone for each performance. Each instrumental section elects a representative. This group works intensively on the detailed, bar-by-bar decisions that turn sheet music into a symphony or a concerto.

Within the core group there is a 'concert master', usually from the instrumental group with the lead role in the piece. But this is not a position of authority. While the concert master is expected to get the rehearsal going, discussions among the core group are detailed, open and frank.

'No one takes a vision of the piece and imposes it on the group', says Mr Seifter. 'Rehearsals for us are a process of discussion and consensus building. It puts power and responsibility in the hands of the people who are doing the work.'

Once a basic interpretation has been thrashed out, the full orchestra is assembled. Again, there is considerable debate. Decisions made by the core group can be overridden if the wider group disagrees. It is rare that decisions are put to a formal vote. But it does happen.

A demonstration of the rehearsal process – in this case Joseph Haydn's symphony number 63 in C major – shows that the Orpheus process is open and inter-active. Ideas and interpretations are discussed and put to the test until a consensus is reached. A suggestion that wins the day is as likely to come from the woodwind section as from the first violins.

The clarinettist is unhappy with the group's phrasing between bars 88 and 100 in the first movement. He suggests an interpretation, while the group listens. The first violin, acting as concert master, disagrees and suggests a less mannered approach. A debate ensues among the core group. The clarinettist's suggestion appears to attract the strongest support. The first violin concedes and the rehearsal continues.

Mr Seifter believes that a number of factors are required to make the process work. First, each member of the team needs to be able to work as a specialist in his or her own instrument and as a generalist making contributions to the direction of the wider group.

Second, each team member needs to learn the art of making 'respectful but direct criticism'. This is something that many people in business fail to master. Says Mr Pottruck: 'In so many organisations there is so much politics and jockeying for position that the notion of respect goes out of the window.'

Third, there needs to be passionate commitment to the project – both the music and the principle of making work an orchestra based on non-hierarchical principles. This overriding commitment is what helps the musicians overcome reservations about decisions with which they may disagree.

You do not need to be profoundly versed in counterpoint to hear how the process contributes to the lucid quality of the orchestra's music. The performance of Haydn that resulted from the demonstration at the Haas school was open and transparent, as if every member of the ensemble understood not only how to play the music in harmony but also why they were taking a particular route.

This is not to say that the Orpheus process is perfect or can be applied to every business situation. As a rule, says Mr Seifter, it takes the orchestra twice as long to rehearse a piece of music as an orchestra led from the front by a conductor who imposes an interpretation. This implies a dramatic cost in terms of productivity.

Moreover, the process does not scale easily. It is doubtful that the model would work with a full-scale symphony orchestra, perhaps double the size of the Orpheus. And not every musician has the right personality to fit in with the process. Organisational democracy demands commitment and patience.

▶

This helps explain why the Orpheus remains the world's only conductorless orchestra despite its 30 successful years in business. Watching the Orpheus process at work does provide a lesson in the functioning of expert teams.

Terry Pearce, a former International Business Machines executive turned leadership coach, points to research that shows that technical skills alone do not explain the difference between great teams and the merely competent. The magic ingredient appears to be personal relationships between team members. This 'social glue' enables them to overcome setbacks and work around obstacles while keeping everyone engaged in the process.

'It is the culture that differentiates this group: the listening skills, the respect, the group emotional intelligence', he says of the Orpheus musicians.

Ronnie Bauch, a violinist and one of three artistic directors who lead the setting of the orchestra's repertoire, puts it another way:

'Everybody has to be able to lead at any given moment and everybody has to be able to follow. You need to be able to sell your idea to the group and then be flexible enough to accept rejection.'

This is a tall order. People at the highest level in business do not necessarily want to be collaborators as well as leaders. Even if they want to behave democratically, it is difficult to remain true to such ideals when decisions need to be made quickly or under intense external pressure. Perhaps the biggest lesson of the Orpheus is that it is worth making the extra effort to try.

'What I have learnt over the years is that the group really is more intelligent than any one of us', says Mr Pottruck. '[Schwab] cannot afford the inefficiencies of the Orpheus process. But the sublimation of individual roles to group processes is incredibly important.'

Source: S. London, 'A most harmonious collaboration: LEADERSHIP', *Financial Times*, 10 January 2002. Reprinted with permission.

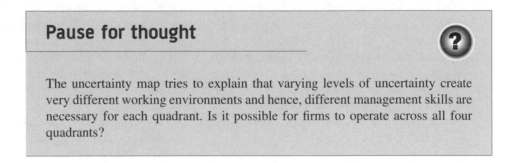

Pause for thought ?

The uncertainty map tries to explain that varying levels of uncertainty create very different working environments and hence, different management skills are necessary for each quadrant. Is it possible for firms to operate across all four quadrants?

Industrial firms are different: a classification

A brief look at companies operating in your town or area will soon inform you that industrial firms are very different. You may say that this is axiomatic. The point is, however, that in terms of innovation and product development it is possible to argue that some firms are users of technology and others are providers. For example, at the simplest level most towns will have a range of housebuilding firms, agricultural firms,

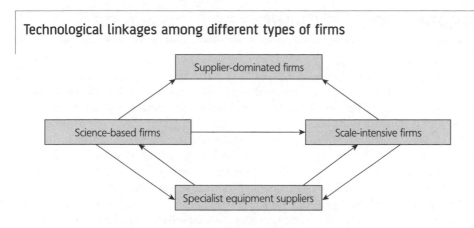

Technological linkages among different types of firms

Figure 3.4

Source: K. Pavitt
(1994) 'Sectoral
patterns of
technological change:
towards a taxonomy
and theory', *Research
Policy*, Vol. 13,
343–73.

retail firms and many others offering services to local people. Such firms tend to be small in size, with little R&D or manufacturing capability of their own. They are classified by Pavitt (1994) as *supplier-dominated firms*. Many of them are very successful because they offer a product with a reliable service. Indeed, their strength is that they purchase technologies in the form of products and match these to customer needs. Such firms usually have limited, if any, product or process technology capabilities. Pavitt offers a useful classification of the different types of firms with regard to technology usage; this is shown in Figure 3.4.

At the other end of the scale are *science-based firms* or technology-intensive firms. These are found in the high-growth industries of the twentieth century: chemicals, pharmaceuticals, electronics, computing, etc. It is the manipulation of science and technology usually by their own R&D departments that has provided the foundation for the firms' growth and success. Unlike the previous classification, these firms tend to be large and would include corporations such as Bayer, Hoechst, Nokia, GlaxoSmithKline, Sony and Siemens.

The third classification Pavitt refers to as *scale-intensive firms*, which dominate the manufacturing sector. At the heart of these firms are process technologies. It is their ability to produce high volumes at low cost that is usually their strength. They tend to have capabilities in engineering, design and manufacturing. Many science-based firms are also scale-intensive firms, so it is possible for firms to belong to more than one category. Indeed, the big chemical companies in Europe are a case in point.

The final classification is *specialist equipment suppliers*. This group of firms is an important source of technology for scale-intensive and science-based firms. For example, instrumentation manufacturers supply specialist measuring instruments to the chemical industry and the aerospace industry to enable these firms to measure their products and manufacturing activities accurately.

This useful classification highlights the flows of technology between the various firms. This is an important concept and is referred to in later chapters to help explain the industry life cycle in Chapter 12, the acquisition of technology in Chapter 9, the transfer of technology in Chapter 10 and strategic alliances in Chapter 7.

Organisational structures and innovation

The structure of an organisation is defined by Mintzberg (1978) as the sum total of the ways in which it divides its labour into distinct tasks and then achieves coordination among them. One of the problems when analysing organisational structure is recognising that different groups within an organisation behave differently and interact with different parts of the wider external environment. Hence, there is a tendency to label structure at the level of the organisation with little recognition of differences at group or department level. None the less, there have been numerous useful studies exploring the link between organisational structure and innovative performance.

The seminal work by Burns and Stalker (1961) on Scottish electronic organisations looked at the impact of technical change on organisational structures and on systems of social relationships. It suggests that 'organic', flexible structures, characterised by the absence of formality and hierarchy, support innovation more effectively than do 'mechanistic' structures. The latter are characterised by long chains of command, rigid work methods, strict task differentiation, extensive procedures and a well defined hierarchy. Many objections have been raised against this argument, most notably by Child (1973). Nevertheless, flexible rather than mechanistic organisational structures are still seen, especially within the business management literature, as necessary for successful industrial innovation. In general, an organic organisation is more adaptable, more openly communicating, more consensual and more loosely controlled. As Table 3.4 indicates, the mechanistic organisation tends to offer a less suitable environment for managing creativity and the innovation process. The subject of organisation structures is also discussed in Chapter 15 in the context of managing new product development teams.

Formalisation

Following Burns and Stalker, there have been a variety of studies examining the relationship between formalisation and innovation. There is some evidence of an inverse relationship between formalisation and innovation. That is, an increase in formalisation of procedures will result in a decrease in innovative activity. It is unclear, however, whether a decrease in procedures and rules would lead to an increase in innovation. Moreover, as was argued above, organisational planning and routines are necessary for achieving efficiencies.

Complexity

The term complexity here refers to the complexity of the organisation. In particular, it refers to the number of professional groups or diversity of specialists within the organisation. For example, a university, hospital or science-based manufacturing company would represent a complex organisation. This is because within these organisations there would be several professional groups. In the case of a hospital, nurses, doctors and a wide range of specialists represent the different areas of medicine. This contrasts

Table 3.4 Key individual roles within the innovation process

Key individual	Role
Technical innovator	Expert in one or two fields. Generates new ideas and sees new and different ways of doing things. Also referred to as the 'mad scientist'.
Technical/ commercial scanner	Acquires vast amounts of information from outside the organisation, often through networking. This may include market and technical information.
Gatekeeper	Keeps informed of related developments that occur outside the organisation through journals, conferences, colleagues and other companies. Passes information on to others, finds it easy to talk to colleagues. Serves as an information resource for others in the organisation.
Product champion	Sells new ideas to others in the organisation. Acquires resources. Aggressive in championing his or her cause. Takes risks.
Project leader	Provides the team with leadership and motivation. Plans and organises the project. Ensures that administrative requirements are met. Provides necessary coordination among team members. Sees that the project moves forward effectively. Balances project goals with organisational needs.
Sponsor	Provides access to a power base within the organisation: a senior person. Buffers the project team from unnecessary organisational constraints. Helps the project team to get what it needs from other parts of the organisation. Provides legitimacy and organisational confidence in the project.

Source: Based on E.B. Roberts and A.R. Fushfeld (1981) 'Staffing the innovative technology-based organisation', *Sloan Management Review*, Spring, 19–34.

sharply with an equally large organisation that is, for example, in the distribution industry. The management of supplying goods all over the country will be complex indeed; but it will not involve the management of a wide range of highly qualified professional groups.

Centralisation

Centralisation refers to the decision-making activity and the location of power within an organisation. The more decentralised an organisation the fewer levels of hierarchy are usually required. This tends to lead to more responsive decision making closer to the action.

Organisational size

Size is a proxy variable for more meaningful dimensions such as economic and organisational resources, including number of employees and scale of operation. Below a certain size, however, there is a major qualitative difference. A small business with fewer than 20 employees differs significantly in terms of resources from an organisation with 200 or 2,000 employees.

The role of the individual in the innovation process

The innovation literature has consistently acknowledged the importance of the role of the individual within the industrial technological innovation process (Rothwell *et al.*, 1974; Langrish *et al.*, 1972; Utterback, 1975; van de Ven, 1986; Wolfe, 1994; Martins and Terblanche, 2003). Furthermore, a variety of *key roles* have developed from the literature stressing particular qualities (*see* Table 3.4).

Rubenstein (1976) went further, arguing that the innovation process is essentially a *people process* and that organisational structure, formal decision-making processes, delegation of authority and other formal aspects of a so-called well run company are not necessary conditions for successful technological innovation. His studies revealed that certain individuals had fulfilled a variety of roles (often informal) that had contributed to successful technological innovation.

In a study of biotechnology firms, Sheene (1991) explains that it is part of a scientist's professional obligation to keep up to date with the literature. This is achieved by extensive scanning of the literature. However, she identified feelings of guilt associated with browsing in the library by some scientists. This was apparently due to a fear that some senior managers might not see this as a constructive use of their time. Many other studies have also shown that the role of the individual is critical in the innovation process (Allen and Cohen, 1969; Allen, 1977; Wheelwright and Clark, 1992; Hauschildt, 2003).

IT systems and their impact on innovation

The impact of large IT systems on firms and the way they operate has been one of the most noticeable changes within organisations of the late 1990s and early twenty-first century. Enterprise Resource Planning (ERP) business software has become one of the most successful products in the world. For many firms such as Microsoft, Owens–Corning, ICI, UBS and Procter & Gamble, it has changed the way they work (Gartner, 2002). Indeed, substantial claims are made about the software's capabilities. A complete system could take several years and several hundred million dollars to deploy. The market leaders in this highly lucrative business-to-business market are SAP, Oracle,

Baan and PeopleSoft. SAP has over 20,000 R/3 products installed world-wide and Oracle has installed databases in nearly every one of the world's top 500 companies. However, the impact of these systems on a firm's innovative capability is now under scrutiny. In some creative working environments, where previously autonomous and creative minds were free to explore, they are now being restricted to what's on offer via 'pull-down' menus.

ERP systems have been adopted by the majority of large private sector firms and many public sector organisations in the United Kingdom, Europe and the industrialised world in general. This growing trend towards ERP systems would not materialise unless significant advantages were to be expected from its introduction. Although there may some isomorphic effects at work that facilitate the spread of perceived best practice and help the marketing efforts of key players in the industry to succeed, these factors on their own would not be able to explain the widespread adoption of ERP systems in the absence of real benefits.

The principal benefits that can arise from ERP systems are linked to expected gains in the efficiency and effectiveness of business processes that come about with the availability of more accurate and timely information. ERP offers integration of business functions and can reduce data collection and processing duplication efforts.

In summary some of the potential benefits of implementing ERP systems are:

- more efficient business processes;
- reduction of costs to several business procedures;
- better coordination and cooperation between functions and different company departments;
- better management monitoring and controlling functions;
- modification and adaptation abilities accordingly to company and market requirements;
- more competitive and efficient entrance to electronic markets and electronic commerce;
- possible redesigning of ineffective business functions;
- access to globalisation and integration to the global economy;
- inventory visibility and better decision support;
- active technology for market research and media environment; and
- improving communication between partners of the channel.

Business managers of organisations with significant ERP experience suggest that ERP systems introduction into an organisation amounts to a near reinvention of the organisation. ERP systems do not easily fit any organisation. ERP systems offer significant advantages, but, in order to work efficiently and effectively, they require that organisational processes be made to fit their system demands. As we will discuss below, the price to be paid for efficiency and effectiveness comes with a prescribed rigidity that may hinder innovation and creativity.

There is also a problem with the impact of ERP on the innovative climate in organisations and on the existent company operations (Johannessen et al., 2001). In short, ERP systems very often require a reconfiguration of work processes and routines. Many people, however, feel unhappy when they are asked to change established 'ways of doing things' and they may rightly feel that new standardised work processes may undermine their autonomy enjoyed in current non-standardised operations. ERP systems, however, can only deliver the promised efficiency gains with a standard information set and leave no alternatives to a standardised approach. But it is not only that information processing and work routines have to be standardised; with an integrated system everyone's performance and achievements become much more visible. Information sharing can easily be perceived as serving the purpose of tightening management control if the organisational climate has deteriorated in the ERP implementation process. If employees feel that they are losing their autonomy and that they are subjected to a culture of instant accountability, then this may have dramatic effects on their productivity and creativity and may nullify some of the potential ERP gains.

There are several ways in which ERP systems operations may have a negative impact on individual creativity. First of all, ERP systems may reduce the richness of information content when informal communication processes get increasingly replaced by standardised data exchanges made available through ERP systems. The previous section noted the role of tacit knowledge with respect to innovation and that it is embedded in social processes. If ERP becomes the key communication medium and information has to be made palatable to its data requirements, then tacit knowledge outside the system may be sidelined (Johannessen *et al.*, 2001; Nonaka, 1991). As a consequence, explicit knowledge may get preference over tacit knowledge. But individual and group creativity is not only dependent on rich information. There are motivational factors at work as well. If ERP leads to a culture of instant control and accountability, then this may undermine the intrinsic motivation of employees and may lead to a culture where risk taking and experimentation becomes increasingly less desirable. It will always be safer to use the available ERP data than to look elsewhere for inspiration. Diligent users of the ERP system are more difficult to blame for their mistakes or lack of achievement. ERP can become a very useful legitimating tool.

More significantly, firms must recognise that ERP systems (like any database) are driven from master data such as customer records, Bill of material records (BoM), and like other databases are unforgiving. Get a field entry wrong and it can cause serious problems. Most likely the internal logic of ERP systems will require large amounts of time being devoted to ensuring the correct entry is made. This is yet another example of how the IT infrastructure impacts on people's working practices. A simple example may be useful here. Consider the activities of an architect working for a major property developer in Europe. The architect develops a variety of homes for consideration and specifies the building design and materials required. While in the past the architect may have flicked through some trade catalogues or contacted suppliers for what might be available, now all possible options available are prescribed via a pull-down menu. The advantages are clear to see: reduced time searching, order processing at the press of a few keys. But what about the impact on the creativity of the design of the building?

Unlike other IT management information systems, ERP has a dramatic impact on the way people work. Indeed, such business intelligence systems force change on an organisational structure, working practices, policies and procedures. The interdependence of the organisational components is never more clearly illuminated. Indeed, it is the knock-on effects of ERP in other aspects of the organisation such as staff skills, budgets, performance measurement procedures and so on that frequently cause most angst.

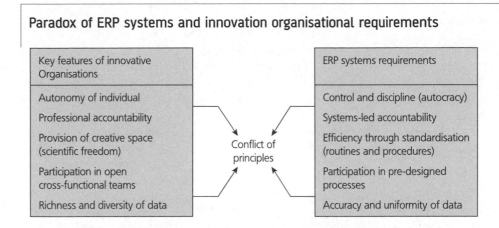

Figure 3.5

Paradox of ERP systems and innovation organisational requirements

The level of personal autonomy individuals have and perceived to hold is frequently cited as one of the key people issues during the implementation of ERP systems (Sauer, 1993). There is much more emphasis on correct routines and prescribed ways of working; indeed individual peculiar working practices have to be removed for ERP to be effective. Staff may find their daily activities dominated by highly prescriptive procedures on their computer screens. The overall perception is often one of the enterprise moving towards a more autocratic, centralised management style. There are a significant number of conflicts between the demands on the organisation of an ERP system and the necessary characteristics that have been identified within the literature for innovation to occur. For example, ERP requires discipline and aids managerial control, whereas freedom and creativity in the form of professional autonomy is continually cited as necessary for innovation to occur. Figure 3.5 provides an overview over some of the key fundamental clashes of organising principles between ERP systems requirement and the success factors of innovative organisations (Trott and Hoecht, 2004).

Establishing an innovative environment and propagating this virtuous circle

This chapter has highlighted the role of the organisational environment in the innovation process. It has also shown how many different factors influence this environment. Given the importance of innovation, many businesses have spent enormous sums of money trying to develop an environment that fosters innovation. Each year *Fortune* produces a list of the most innovative companies in the United States. For the past few years the following companies have finished at or near the top: 3M, Rubbermaid, Dell, Microsoft, Siemens and Motorola (*Fortune*, 2004). Developing a reputation for innovation helps propagate a virtuous circle that reinforces a company's abilities (*see* Figure 3.6).

| Figure 3.6 | Propagating a virtuous circle of innovation |

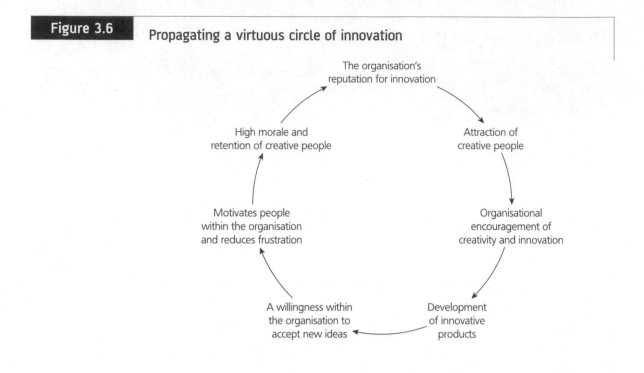

The concept of a virtuous circle of innovation can be viewed as a specific example of Michael Porter's (1985) notion of competitive advantage. Porter argued that those companies who are able to achieve competitive advantage – that is, above-average performance in an industry sector – are able to reinvest this additional profit into the activities that created the advantage in the first place, thus creating a virtuous circle of improvement, or so-called competitive advantage.

Reputation of the organisation

The reputation of a company for innovation takes many years to develop. It is also strongly linked to overall performance. However, within a selection of successful companies there will inevitably be some that are regarded as more innovative than others. This may be due to several factors, including recent product launches, recent successful programmes of research and high levels of expenditure on R&D. Depending on topical media events at the time, some companies are able to achieve wide exposure of new products or new research. Such exposure is often dependent on effective publicity but also serendipity.

Attraction of creative people

Creative people will be attracted to those companies that themselves are viewed as creative. In much the same way as undergraduates apply for positions of employment with those companies viewed as successful, top scientists will seek employment from those companies which have a reputation for innovation and scientific excellence (Jones, 1992).

Organisation encourages creativity

Many organisations pay lip service to creativity without putting in place any structures or plans to encourage innovation. It has to be supported with actions and resources. The organisation has to provide people with the time to be creative. This can be in a formalised way, as used in much of the chemical industry. For example, 15 per cent of a research scientist's time may be dedicated to projects of personal interest. Alternatively, organisations can try to build sufficient slack into the system to allow for creative thinking (*see* p. 78).

In addition, the organisation should try to build an environment that tolerates errors and mistakes. This will encourage people to try new ideas and put forward suggestions. Successful new ideas need to be rewarded in terms of publicity for the people involved. This is usually most easily achieved through internal newsletters or company magazines. In addition, financial rewards – promotions, gifts or holidays – may be offered.

Some organisations also use creativity-stimulation techniques such as a weekend away at a country retreat to discuss new ways of working, new ideas, etc. These activities collectively will help send a clear message that the organisation is serious about innovation.

Development of innovative products

This does not mean the ability to develop products incorporating the latest technology, although this may be an output. It means developing new products that are genuine improvements compared with products currently available. Moreover, it is success in the marketplace that very often leads to further success.

A willingness to accept new ideas

Many organisations suffer from an inability to implement changes and new ideas, even after rewarding the people involved in developing the new idea. Once a new product idea has been accepted it is important that it is carried through to completion.

Increased motivation and reduced frustration

If individuals within the organisation can see their ideas and efforts contributing to the performance of the business, they will be encouraged still further. On the other hand, if seemingly good ideas are constantly overlooked, this will lead to increased frustration.

High morale and retention of creative people

All of the proceeding activities will help contribute to increased morale within the organisation. A rewarding and enjoyable working environment will help to retain creative people. This in turn should reinforce the company's innovative capabilities.

Case study

Gore-Tex® and W.L. Gore & Associates: An innovative company and a contemporary culture[1]

This case study explores the role of organisational management and culture within a very innovative firm, which is responsible for some very well known products such as the famous Gore-Tex fabric, and yet few people know very much about this remarkable organisation. It is operated in a similar way to that of a co-operative such as the John Lewis Partnership in the United Kingdom, where the employees are also owners. In addition the organisation seeks to minimise management with the emphasis on action and creativity. Today this enigmatic firm employs approximately 7,000 people in more than 45 plants and sales locations world-wide. Manufacturing operations are clustered in the United States, Germany, Scotland, Japan and China. Proprietary technologies with the versatile polymer polytetrafluoroethylene (PTFE) have resulted in numerous products for electronic signal transmission; fabrics laminates; medical implants; as well as membrane, filtration, sealant and fibres technologies for a range of different industries. Today the organisation divides its products into four main groupings: medical products; fabric products; electronic products; and industrial products. Gore has approximately 650 US patents and thousands world-wide. Further details of these can be found by visiting the US Patent & Trademark office website at www.uspto.gov.

Introduction

W.L. Gore & Associates is probably best known in Europe for its Gore-Tex product (that piece of material in your coat that keeps you dry yet allows your body to breathe), yet few people know very much about this privately owned and relatively secret company. Fewer still realise the very innovative and contemporary way the organisation is run – it seeks to have an 'unmanagement style'. Annual revenues top $1 billion. W.L. Gore is a privately held company ranking in the top 200 of the Forbes top 500 privately held companies for 2002. Indeed, W.L. Gore would rank in the Fortune 500 companies in terms of profits, market value and equity value. Given that the firm is a privately held corporation many details of the company's operations and strategies are not widely known. Unlike publicly listed firms it does not need to share information on such topics as marketing strategies, manufacturing processes or technology development. The company is owned primarily by its employees (known as associates) and the Gore family. W.L. Gore enterprises is comprised of more than 7,000 associates at over 45 locations around the world.

W.L. Gore & Associates was founded in 1958 in Newark, Delaware, when Bill and Vieve Gore set out to explore market opportunities for fluorocarbon polymers, especially polytetrafluoroethylene (PTFE). First developed by Bill Gore when he worked as a scientist for the Dupont Corporation. Gore could not get anyone at Dupont to invest in his new idea, so he bought the patent and went into business on his own. Within the first decade alone, W.L. Gore wire and cables landed on the moon (the firm supplied cables for the 1969 lunar missions); the company opened divisions in Scotland and Germany; and a venture partnership took root in Japan.

W.L. Gore has introduced its unique technical capabilities into hundreds of diverse products.

[1] This case has been written as a basis for class discussion rather than to illustrate effective or ineffective managerial or administrative behaviour. It has been prepared from a variety of published sources, as indicated, and from observations.

It has defined new standards for comfort and protection for work-wear and active-wear (Gore-Tex); advanced the science of regenerating tissues destroyed by disease or traumatic injuries; developed next-generation materials for printed circuit boards and fibre optics; and pioneered new methods to detect and control environmental pollution.

Gore-Tex®, a breathable fabric

In 1969, Bob Gore discovered that rapidly stretching PTFE created a very strong, microporous material (this became known as expanded PTFE, or ePTFE), which offered a range of new, desirable properties. To be effective a waterproof fabric needs to be able to prevent moisture getting from the outside to the inside. Furthermore, a waterproof fabric must have the ability to withstand water entry in active conditions such as walking in wind-driven rain and sitting or kneeling on a wet surface. In the case of garments for wear especially in active conditions, perspiration is a common problem. If perspiration vapour becomes trapped inside our clothing, it can condense into liquid moisture that causes dampness – and wet heat loss is 23 times faster than dry heat loss. A fabric that would enable moisture to escape and at the same time prevent moisture from entering would seem unachievable, but that is precisely what the Gore-Tex® fabric does. Rain coats incorporating the Gore-Tex® fabric were first introduced way back in 1976, hence the patent for the breathable fabric expired in 1996. However, new patents are still active on improved methods of making Gore-Tex® fabric. There are now many generic versions of breathable fabric on the market. The success of the product has largely been witnessed in the 1990s as outdoor pursuits grew rapidly in popularity during this period. This led to an explosion in sales of Gore-Tex related products, such as coats, back-packs, shoes and trousers. Indeed, clothing manufacturers who used the Gore-Tex fabric in their garments, such as Berghaus, Karrimor and North Face, became household names as this once esoteric specialised clothing market became mainstream.

Working within W.L. Gore Associates

The very unusual organisational structure and management sets this firm apart from its competitors. Moreover, there is some evidence to support its claim to be highly creative and innovative as Gore – US has made all six annual lists of the '100 Best Companies to Work for' in *Fortune* magazine from 1998 to 2003. Its UK firm was ranked among the '100 Best Places to Work in the U.K.' (McCall, 2002). Gore – Italy ranked among the '35 Best Places to Work in Italy' (2003). Gore – Germany ranked among the '50 Best Places to Work in Germany' (2003). It is often cited as a model for effective management of innovation, and the firm is proud of its heritage and how it works:

We encourage hands-on innovation, involving those closest to a project in decision-making. Teams organize around opportunities and leaders emerge. Our founder, Bill Gore created a flat lattice organization. There are no chains of command nor pre-determined channels of communication. Instead, we communicate directly with each other and are accountable to fellow members of our multi-disciplined teams.

Associates are hired for general work areas. With the guidance of their sponsors (not bosses) and a growing understanding of opportunities and team objectives, associates commit to projects that match their skills. Everyone can quickly earn the credibility to define and drive projects. Sponsors help associates chart a course in the organization that will offer personal fulfilment while maximizing their contribution to the enterprise. Leaders may be appointed, but are defined by

▶

'followership.' More often, leaders emerge naturally by demonstrating special knowledge, skill, or experience that advances a business objective.

Associates are committed to four basic guiding principles articulated by Bill Gore:

fairness to each other and everyone with whom we come in contact;

freedom to encourage, help, and allow other associates to grow in knowledge, skill, and scope of responsibility;

the ability to make one's own commitments and keep them; and consultation with other associates before undertaking actions that could impact the reputation of the company by hitting it below the waterline.

(Gore, 2003)

Non-hierarchical corporate culture

The firm's unique structure was born out of Bill Gore's frustration with a large corporate bureaucracy; the W.L. Gore culture seeks to avoid taxing creativity with conventional hierarchy. The company encourages hands-on innovation, involving those closest to a project in decision making; hence decision making is based on knowledge rather than seniority. Teams organise around opportunities and leaders emerge based on the needs and priorities of a particular business unit. To avoid the traditional pyramid of bosses and managers, Bill created a flat lattice organisational structure in which there are no chains of command and no pre-determined channels of communication. Instead, employees communicate directly with each other and are accountable to fellow members of multi-disciplinary teams. The company bases its business philosophy on the belief that given the right environment, there is no limit to what people can accomplish.

The formula seems to have worked. In 40 years of business, W.L. Gore & Associates has developed hundreds of unique products that reflect an underlying commitment to fluoropolymer technologies. The company is passionate about innovation and has built a unique work environment to support it based on a corporate culture that encourages creativity, initiative and discovery. According to Gore:

you won't find the trappings of a traditional corporate structure here: no rigid hierarchy, no bosses, and no predictable career ladder. Instead, you'll find direct communication, a team oriented atmosphere, and one title – associate – that's shared by everyone. It's an unusual corporate culture that contributes directly to the business' success by encouraging creativity and opportunity.

(Gore, 2003)

The last principle is meant to protect the company from inappropriate risk. While employees are given wide latitude to pursue entrepreneurial opportunities, no one can initiate projects involving significant corporate financial commitments without thorough review and participation by qualified associates.

An individual starting at W.L. Gore is assigned three sponsors. A starting sponsor helps get the associate acquainted with W.L. Gore. An advocate sponsor makes sure the associate receives credit and recognition for their work and a compensation sponsor makes sure the associate is paid fairly. One person can fill all three sponsor roles. Compensation is determined by committees and relies heavily on evaluations by other associates as well as the compensation sponsor.

Employee ownership structure

The goal of Gore's highly flexible and competitive programme is to maximise freedom and fairness for each associate. The benefit plans consist of core benefits and flexible benefits. Core benefits are basic plans and services provided by Gore to all eligible associates. They include an Associate Stock Ownership Plan, vacation, holidays, profit sharing, sick pay, basic life insurance, travel accident insurance and adoption aid.

The Associate Stock Ownership Plan (ASOP) is the most valuable financial benefit. Its purpose is to provide equity ownership, and through this ownership, to provide financial security for retirement. All associates have an opportunity to participate in the growth of the company by acquiring ownership in it. Every year W.L. Gore contributes up to 15 per cent of pay to an account that purchases W.L. Gore stock for each participating associate. W.L. Gore contributes the same percentage of pay for each associate active in the plan. An associate is eligible for this benefit after one full year of employment and qualifies for full ownership of their accounts after five years of service, when they are fully vested. Valued quarterly, W.L. Gore stock is privately held and is not traded on public markets. The ASOP, although it does not own all of the W.L. Gore shares, does own a majority of them, with the remainder owned by the Gore family.

Associates also qualify for cash profit-sharing distributions when corporate profit goals have been reached. Profit-sharing distributions typically occur an average of twice a year. In addition, each pay period associates are provided with pre-tax benefits, called flex dollars, to use for the purchase of 'flexible benefits'. These include medical plans, dental plans, long-term disability insurance, personal days, supplemental individual life insurance, family life insurance and health care or dependent care spending accounts.

Unique characteristics of ownership culture

W.L. Gore believes that given the right environment, there is no limit to what people can accomplish. That is where the W.L. Gore lattice system comes in to play. It gives the associates the opportunity to use their own judgement, select their own projects and directly access the resources they need to be successful. Another unique aspect of the lattice system is the company's insistence that no single operating division become larger than 200 people in order to preserve the intimacy and ease of communications among smaller work groups. As divisions grow, they are separated into constituent parts to preserve that culture.

Discussion

This case illustrates some of the organisational characteristics that are necessary for innovation to occur. The unique organisational model seems to work for W.L. Gore. It is certainly contemporary and does seem to help to unleash creativity and to foster teamwork in an entrepreneurial environment that seeks to provide maximum freedom and support for its employees (associates). Many of the organisational characteristics are not, however, unique to W.L. Gore and there are many other firms where these characteristics can be found, such as 3M, Hewlett Packard, Corning, Dyson, BP and Shell. It does reinforce the need for firms wishing to be innovative to adopt these characteristics (*see* Table 3.2).

There are several key characteristics that help make the W.L. Gore company successful, both financially and as a place to work. First, the high-quality technology and heritage of the firm that encourages an emphasis on developing superior products. Second, the use of small teams encourages direct one-on-one communication, this contributes to the ability to make timely; informed decisions and get products to market very quickly. Third, the channels of communications are very open, the lattice structure allowing all employees the freedom to meet and discuss projects, situations, concerns and share congratulations with everyone. Fourth, W.L. Gore believes that providing equity compensation to its employees establishes a sense of ownership and increased commitment among its employees. The ASOP program at W.L. Gore is the majority owner of the company. Fifth, W.L. Gore provides a comprehensive set of employee benefits and is continually looking for ways to improve upon what is currently available. Sometimes that

▶

just means re-evaluating what the employees want and need. Finally, making sure that the individual work groups do not get too large to be effective is a key element of 'right-sizing' for the company culture. This way W.L. Gore maintains a sense of intimacy and ease of communications among its work groups.

While the employee share ownership sounds attractive, any decrease in performance and fall in value of the shares can cause enormous resentment within the firm as they see the value of their savings decrease. And unlike publicly listed firms these shareholders cannot remove the managers. W.L. Gore's competitors are varied and diverse: there is no single company which competes with Gore in every product area. Firms such as Bayer, Hoecht, Corning, Dow and Du-Pont all compete in Gore's product fields: medical, fabric, industrial and electronic applications.

Questions

1 Explain what happened to the Gore-Tex brand after the patent expired. What activity can firms use to try to maintain any advantage developed during the patent protection phase?

2 List some of the wide range of products where the Gore-Tex fabric has been applied?

3 It seems that Gore Associates is heavily oriented towards technology; what are some of the dangers of being too heavily focused on technology?

4 Cooperatives and share-ownership schemes provide many attractions and benefits, but there are also limitations; discuss these.

Sources: Gore (2003); L. Harrison (2002); A. McCall (2002); M. Milford (1996); D. Anfuso (1999).

Chapter summary

Before the Industrial Revolution many innovations were the result of lone inventors and entrepreneurs. Today the situation is very different. The overwhelming majority of innovations come from organisations and this was the focus of this chapter. In particular, it explored the organisational environment and the activities performed within it that are necessary for innovation to occur. These, of course, are dependent on the extent to which an organisation recognises the need for and encourages innovation.

All organisations have to manage the dilemma of innovation. It is not something that can be removed; it will always be present. Successful companies, however, are able to manage this dilemma. It was shown that successful companies also need to be able to manage uncertainty. In addition, several roles were identified as necessary for innovation to occur and it was stressed that these are often performed by key individuals.

 ## Discussion questions

1 Explain how the three main schools of thought have contributed to our understanding of managing innovation within organisations?

2 Can organisations operate across the entire spectrum of innovation activities?

3 Explain the fundamental dilemma facing organisations and the tensions it creates.

4 How can the uncertainty map help managers?

5 Discuss the challenges faced by a conductor of an orchestra and the extent to which these are similar to that of managing research in an organisation?

6 Discuss the main organisational characteristics that facilitate the innovation process.

7 Explain the key individual roles within the innovation process and the activities they perform.

Key words and phrases

Competitive advantage 96	Product champion 91
Dilemma of innovation 77	Receptivity 85
Exploratory research 80	Slack 85
Gatekeeper 91	Systems theory 76

Websites worth visiting

3M www.3m.com/about3M/pioneers/innovChron.jhtml

Chemical Industries Association www.cia.org.uk

Confederation of British Industry www.cbi.org.uk

The Design Council www.Designcouncil.com

The Engineering Council (EC UK) www.engc.org.uk

European Industrial Research Management Association (EIRMA) www.eirma.asso.fr

Intellect UK www.intellectuk.org

Quoted Companies Alliance (QCA) www.qcanet.co.uk

The R&D Society www.rdsoc.org

The Royal Academy of Engineering www.raeng.org.uk

Stanford University, explaining innovation www.Manufacturing.Stanford.edu

UK Government, Department of Trade and Industry www.Dti.gov.uk/innovation

References

Allen, T.J. (1977) *Managing the Flow of Technology*, MIT Press, Cambridge, MA.

Allen, T.J. and Cohen, W.M. (1969) 'Information flow in research and development laboratories', *Administrative Science Quarterly*, Vol. 14, No. 1, 12–19.

Anfuso, D. (1999) 'Core values shape W.L. Gore's innovative culture', *Workforce* magazine (US), March, 48–53.

Bertalanffy, L. von (1951) 'General systems theory: a new approach to unity of science', *Human Biology*, Vol. 23, No. 4, December, 303–61.

Burgelman, R.A. (1983) 'A process model of internal corporate venturing in the diversified major firm', *Administrative Science Quarterly*, Vol. 28, 225–44.

Burns, T. and Stalker, G.M. (1961) *The Management of Innovation*, Tavistock, London.

Checkland, P. (1989) 'Soft systems methodology', *Human Systems Management*, Vol. 8, 273–89.

Child, J. (1973) 'Predicting and understanding organisational structure', *Administrative Science Quarterly*, Vol. 18, 168–85.

Child, J. (1988) *Organisation: A Guide to Problems and Practice*, 2nd edn, Harper & Row, London.

Cordey-Hayes, M., Trott, P. and Gilbert, M. (1997) 'Knowledge assimilation and learning organisations', in Butler, J. and Piccaluga, A. (eds) *Knowledge, Technology and Innovative Organisations*, Guerini E. Associati, Milan.

European (1993) 'Golf's free wheeler laps up the quiet side of life', 14–17 October, 46.

Financial Times (1977) 'A cultural exchange', 8 May, 25.

Financial Times (1997) 'ICI to sell UK fertilisers business', 21 November, 19.

Fortune (2004) 'America's most admired companies', 7 February, 50–66.

Gartner (2002) How Proctor & Gamble runs its global business on SAP, CS-15-3473, Research Note, 25 February 2000.

Gore (2003) Extract from the W.L. Gore Associates website.

Harrison, L. (2002) 'We're all the boss,' *Time*, Inside Business edition, 8 April.

Harvey, E. and Mills, R. (1970) 'Patterns of organisational adaptation: a political perspective', in Mayer, N. Zald (ed.) *Power in Organisations*, Vanderbilt University Press, Nashville, TN.

Hauschildt, J. (2003) 'Promoters and champions in innovations: development of a research paradigm', in Shavinina, L. (ed.) (2003) *The International Handbook on Innovation*, Elsevier, Oxford.

Henry, J. and Walker, D. (eds) (1991) *Managing Innovation*, Sage/Oxford University Press, London.

Hinton, M. and Trott, P. (1996) 'The changing nature of R&D management and why I.T. is not a panacea', paper presented at *R&D Management Conference*, Switzerland, September.

Hull, J.K. (1981) 'Employee status within the company', *Company Lawyer*, Vol. 2, No. 5, 207–14.

Johannessen, J., Olaisen, J. and Olsen, B. (2001) 'Management of tacit knowledge: the importance of tacit knowledge, the danger of information technology, and what to do about it', *Journal of Information Management*, Vol. 21, No. 1, 3–20.

Jones, O. (1992) 'Postgraduate scientists and R&D: the role of reputation in organisational choice', *R&D Management*, Vol. 22, 4.

Katz, D. and Kahn, R.L. (1966) *The Social Psychology of Organisations*, John Wiley, New York.

Langrish, J., Gibbons, M., Evans, W.G. and Jevons, F.R. (1972) *Wealth from Knowledge*, Macmillan, London.

Martins, E. C. and Terblanche, F. (2003) 'Building organizational culture that stimulates creativity and innovation', *European Journal of Innovation Management*, Vol. 6, No. 1, 64–74.

McCall, A. (ed.) (2002) 'The firm that lets staff breathe', *Sunday Times* (London), 24 March, '100 Best Companies to Work For', special section.

Milford, M. (1996) 'A company philosophy in bricks and mortar', *New York Times*, 1 September, Sec. R, p. 5.

Mintzberg, H. (1978) 'Patterns in strategy formulation', *Management Science*, Vol. 24, 934–48.

Nonaka, I. (1991) 'The knowledge-creating company', *Harvard Business Review*, November–December, 96–104.

Pavitt, K. (1994) 'Sectoral patterns of technological change: towards a taxonomy and theory', *Research Policy*, 13, 343–73.

Pearson, A. (1991) 'Managing innovation: an uncertainty reduction process', in Henry, J. and Walker, D. (eds) *Managing Innovation*, Sage/Oxford University Press, London, 18–27.

Perrow, C. (1970) *Organisational Analysis: a Sociological View*, Tavistock, London.

Porter, M.E. (1985) *Competitive Advantage*, Harvard University Press, Boston, MA.

Roberts, E.B. and Fushfield, A.R. (1981) 'Staffing the innovative technology-based organisation', *Sloan Management Review*, Spring, 19–34.

Roethlisberger, F.J. and Dickinson, W.J. (1939) *Management and the Worker*, Harvard University Press, Boston, MA.

Rothwell, R., Freeman, C., Horlsey, A., Jervis, V.T.P., Robertson, A.B. and Townsend, J. (1974) 'SAPPHO updated: Project SAPPHO phase II', *Research Policy*, Vol. 3, 258–91.

Rubenstein, A.H. (1976) 'Factors influencing success at the project level', *Research Management*, Vol. 19, No. 3, 15–20.

Sauer, C. (1993) *Why Information Systems Fail: A Case Study Approach*, Alfred Waller, Henley-on-Thames.

Schock, G. (1974) 'Innovation processes in Dutch industry', TNO Industrial Research Organisation, Netherlands.

Sheene, M.R. (1991) 'The boundness of technical knowledge within a company: barriers to external knowledge acquisition', paper presented at R&D Management Conference on *The Acquisition of External Knowledge*, Kiel, Germany.

Slevin, D.P. and Covin, J.G. (1990) 'Juggling entrepreneurial style and organizational structure: how to get your act together', *Sloan Management Review*, Winter, 43–53.

Souder, W.E. (1987) *Managing New Product Innovations*, Lexington Books, Lexington, MA.

Szakasits, G.D. (1974) 'The adoption of the SAPPHO method in the Hungarian electronics industry', *Research Policy*, Vol. 3, No. 1, 18–28.

Taylor, F. (1947) *Scientific Management*, Harper & Row, New York.

Thompson, J.D. (1967) *Organisations in Action*, John Wiley, New York.

Trott, P. and Hoecht, A. (2004) 'Enterprise resource planning (ERP) and its impact on innovation', *International Journal of Innovation Management* (forthcoming).

Utterback, J.M. (1975) 'The process of technological innovation within the firm', *Academy of Management Review*, Vol. 12, 75–88.

van de Ven, A.H. (1986) 'Central problems: the management of innovation', *Management Science*, Vol. 32, No. 5, 590–607.

Weber, M. (1964) *The Theory of Social and Economic Organisation*, Collier Macmillan, London.

Wheelwright, S.C. and Clark, K.B. (1992) *Revolutionising product development*, The Free Press, New York, USA.

Wolfe, R.A. (1994) 'Organisational innovation: review and critique and suggested research directions', *Journal of Management Studies*, Vol. 31, No. 3, 405–31.

Further reading

For a more detailed review of the innovation management literature, the following develop many of the issues raised in this chapter:

Chesbrough, H.W. and Teece, D. (1996) 'When is virtual virtuous? Organising for innovation', *Harvard Business Review*, January–February, 65–73.

Gundling, E. (2000) *The 3M Way to Innovation: Balancing people and profit*, Kodansha International, New York.

Rothwell, R. (1992) 'Successful industrial innovation: critical factors for the 1990s', *R&D Management*, Vol. 22, No. 3, 221–39.

Shavinina, L. (2003) *The International Handbook on Innovation*, Oxford, Elsevier.

Sundbo, J. and Fuslang, L. (eds) (2002) *Innovation as Strategic Reflexivity*, Routledge, London.

Tidd, J. (2001) 'Innovation management in context, organisation and performance', *International Journal of Management Reviews*, Vol. 3, No. 3, 169–83.

Wolfe, R.A. (1994) 'Organisational innovation: review and critique and suggested research directions', *Journal of Management Studies*, Vol. 31, No. 3, 405–31.

4

Innovation and operations management

Richard Noble

Many new product ideas are based on existing products and may be developed from within the production or service operations function. A large number of these ideas may be modest and incremental rather than radical but the combined effect of many, small innovative ideas may be substantial. In considering innovation, it is necessary therefore to examine the role of operations and its management. Equally effective research and development (R&D) requires close links with the production operations.

Chapter contents

Learning objectives

When you have completed this chapter you will be able to:

- recognise the importance of innovation in operations management;
- recognise the importance of sales volume in product design;
- recognise the importance of design in the process of making and delivering a product or service;
- appreciate that the nature of design is context dependent;
- recognise that much innovation is not patentable;
- provide an understanding of a number of approaches to design and process management; and
- recognise the importance of e-commerce and its impact on operations.

Operations management

Most organisations provide items that are a combination of product and service elements – for example, a restaurant provides a product (the food) and a service (delivery to your table). The term operations management was coined to bring together the skills and techniques developed in the manufacturing and service sectors in order to help encourage the transfer of the best practices. In an age of global mass production and competition, it is often the service element of any purchase that gives the supplying operation its crucial competitive advantage. The case study at the end of this chapter shows how the production of a book is only part of the operation involved in publishing a book and getting it to the customer. Innovation within the operations function is therefore crucial in achieving the organisation's strategic objectives. Some commentators have peddled a popular line that manufacturing in advanced economies is no longer financially viable.

Operations management is about the control of a conversion process from an *input* to an *output* (*see* Table 4.1).

This chapter considers the design and management of the conversion processes given in Table 4.1. A large percentage of the asset base of the organisation normally lies within these boundaries, and it is essential that the assets be used to effect, to gain an advantage in this increasingly competitive world. In particular, the degree of innovation involving these expensive assets is crucial if the organisation is to prosper. Figure 4.1 illustrates the operation function and includes the elements of design, planning and control and improvement.

To this process (Figure 4.1) need to be added three other very important dimensions:

1 the customer who becomes part of the process as in self-service supermarkets or in the education process taking place in tutorials;

2 information from customers (complaints or compliments), market research or government agencies (standards, laws, EU directives, etc.); and

3 the physical and business environment in which the organisation operates.

Table 4.1 Operations inputs and outputs

Organisation	Input	Processes include	By-products	Output
A car producer	Material (steel, rubber, glass) People Skills Energy	Welding Painting Assembly	Material waste Heat waste	Cars Salaries
A university	Students Teachers Information Knowledge	Lectures Seminars Research Learning	Waste paper	Graduates Academic papers
A hospital	Doctors Patients Medicines Knowledge	Medical operations Radiotherapy	Clinical waste	Healthy patients
A publishing company	Paper Ink Author's work	Editing Binding Printing	Paper pulp Chemical waste	Books Royalties

Figure 4.1   The operations manager's role

Source: Adapted from N. Slack *et al.* (2001) *Operations Management*, 3rd edn, Pearson Education, London.

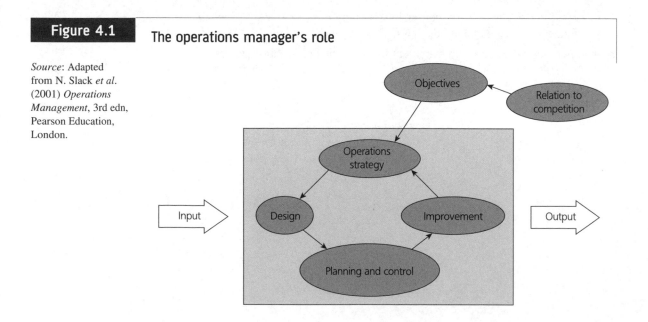

Pause for thought

?

How does a government get involved in design?

The nature of design and innovation in the context of operations

Some innovations are described as 'leading edge' and are based upon work from within the R&D laboratories and may involve patent applications. Innovation (as we saw in Chapter 1) may also be a new application of an existing technique to a different situation. Something that is new and innovative to one company may be a tried and tested procedure or product to another. Also, every innovative idea may not be suitable to patent but, to those concerned, the novelty, the ingenuity, the problems associated with its introduction and the cost–benefit to the organisation may be just the same.

Although in many companies designers quite frequently make inventions, designing and inventing are different in kind. Design is usually more concerned with the process of *applying* scientific principles and inventions (Roy and Weild, 1993). Design is a compromise between the different elements that constitute the design. For example, increasing the wall thickness of a product made from steel may increase the product's strength, reliability and durability but only with the consequential increase in product weight and cost.

Design requirements

The objective of design is to meet the needs and expectations of customers. Good design therefore starts and ends with the customer. Marketing gathers information from customers and *potential* customers to identify customer needs and expectations. Expectations differ from customer to customer – indeed they may vary from day to day from the same customer. For example, what would constitute the design of a good university lecture will vary from one student to another. The same student might also have a different need and expectation from the lecturer after a long lunch break in the union bar. Customer expectations vary.

Working with marketing, the product and service designer then designs a specification for the product and service. This is a complex task involving complex interrelating variables and aspects of the company's objectives. To help in the specification process Slack *et al.* (2004) remark that all products and services can be considered as having three aspects (the case study at the end of this chapter illustrates this point):

- a *concept* – the expected benefits the customer is buying;
- a *package* of component products that provides those benefits defined in the concepts, i.e. what the customer actually purchases and constitutes the ingredients of the design; and
- the *process*, which defines the relationship between the component product and services by which the design fulfils its concept.

A meal in a restaurant consists of products (the food and drink) and services such as the style of waitress service and background music. Some products or service elements are core to the operation and could not be removed without destroying the nature of the package. Other parts of the package serve to enhance the core. In a fast-food restaurant the food and the speed of delivery are essential core elements of the package while the ambience and layout of the restaurant supports the core (*see* Illustration 4.1).

By changing the core, or adding or subtracting supporting services, organisations can provide different packages and therefore design very different products and services. In a fast-food restaurant the customer may order the food at the counter (and possibly pay the bill) and stand for a moment or two until the choice is delivered in disposable containers. The service is substantially different from that purchased in an exclusive restaurant.

Another example of product design comes from Braun, a leading European manufacturer of small domestic appliances. Braun has over 60 per cent of its sales from products with less than five years from product launch. Given the design brief to combine together, and perform as least as well as, three specialist kitchen appliances, the designers applied 10 industrial design principles to the Braun Multimix product (*see* Illustration 4.2). For a similar list of design principles in the service sector *see* Van Looy *et al.* (2001).

The different examples of the design parameters considered illustrate the complexity of the process of design. The design brief depends on the market for which the product or service is created. For example, the aesthetics of a domestic water tap is not important when mounted out of sight under the kitchen sink. If, however, it were mounted in a visible application, the aesthetics of the tap would be very important.

Roy and Weild (1993) suggest a design spectrum, which ranges from the concept designer whose primary concern is ensuring technical excellence to the focus of the industrial designer on 'manufacturability' and the ease of use of the product.

For example, the design team involved in the manufacture of a hi-fi set would include:

- an electronics engineer concerned with the ability of the electrical circuits to faithfully produce sound from the CD – i.e. the function of the product;

Illustration 4.1

A fast-food restaurant

The success of fast-food restaurants like McDonald's could be due to a number of factors but among the most important would be in the design of its operating system that ensures consistency and uniformity of its *products* and *service* in all their premises. In London, New York, Vancouver and Hong Kong, the customer will be familiar with the layout and decor and will know the food to expect. This recipe for success has been duplicated and copied by competitive organisations the world over.

The original key innovation was to have a very simple menu of just three foods and six drinks. This simplicity allowed straightforward cooking and preparation procedures that ensured consistent product quality. McDonald's were able to influence and manage their supply chain to ensure uniformity of raw material, again helping the consistency of product produced.

Simple menu, simple procedures, standard facilities and good operations management combine to give a cost-effective operation.

Fast-food restaurants often have other operational characteristics that contribute to their success. If there is a counter to queue at it will be well away from the door – a *fast*-food restaurant would *not* want to advertise a queue. You pay for the food in advance avoiding the need to revisit the counter. Furthermore, they do not encourage you to linger – filling the place with customers who have been served and paid is not to their advantage. The seats, if they exist, tend to be uncomfortable.

Source: Based on D.M. Upton (1998) *Designing, Managing and Improving Operations*, Prentice-Hall, Englewood Cliffs, NJ, 114.

- the marketing department members who would be concerned about the look of the product, i.e. the aesthetics, incorporating views from channel members, etc.;
- an industrial engineer who will be concerned with the sales volume required; how the product is to be made and assembled, i.e. the operations tasks involved in creating the product; and
- consideration of the packaging requirements for items on display and those that were to be shipped to customers.

In this illustration the knowledge required in the design spectrum ranges from acoustics, electronics, mechanics, plastic processing technology, industrial engineering to ergonomics and is therefore so broad and complex that no one person can be professionally competent in the whole range of disciplines required. In addition to their own specific competence the designer also needs an appreciation of the problems of other elements of the design spectrum. Managing such a diverse range of disciplines is a complex matter.

Illustration 4.2

Design principles at Braun AG

1 *Usefulness*. The product was designed with the electric motor aligned vertically with the attachments (competitive products have horizontal motors and vertical attachments requiring a more complex gearbox).

2 *Quality*. Braun designers emphasised four aspects of quality:

   (a) Versatility – the design included the full range of expected tasks required in cooking: mixing, blending, kneading and chopping.

   (b) High mechanical efficiency providing high performance across the range of required tasks.

   (c) Safety features to prevent contact with moving parts.

   (d) Integrating injection moulding of the main housings into a single manufacturing tool.

3 *Ease of use*. Great emphasis was placed on the human engineering of the product to ensure ease of use and cleaning (*see* the cerebral palsy case study, Chapter 11).

4 *Simplicity*. What was relevant was stressed, what was superfluous was omitted.

5 *Clarity*. The need for complex instructions was avoided. For example, inserting attachments automatically set the required motor speed.

6 *Order*. All the details of the product had a logical and meaningful place.

7 *Naturalness*. The designers avoided any contrived or artificially decorative elements.

8 *Aesthetics*. Although not a primary objective it was achieved by simplicity, attention to detail and the quest for order and naturalness.

9 *Innovation*. Braun was committed to achieving long-lasting appeal for its design so the innovations involved were carefully developed and managed.

10 *Truthfulness*. The principle that 'only honest design can be good design' was applied avoiding any attempt to play on people's emotions and weaknesses.

This approach has been successful in producing many new products and the aesthetics of Braun's products have been recognised with samples on display in the Museum of Modern Art in New York.

Source: Adapted from N. Slack *et al.* (2001) *Operations Management*, 3rd edn, Pitman, London.

Design and volumes

All the operations management functions involve making decisions – some are tactical or structured and have short-term consequences while others are more strategic with longer-term implications for both the operations function and the organisation as a whole. One such major decision relates to the implications of the production *volume* required.

The highly skilled eighteenth-century craftsman making furniture at the rate of a few per year is a different type of person from the individual on a twenty-first-century assembly line making furniture at a production rate of hundreds per day. As well as a different type of person, the machinery, the processing techniques used, the materials and the design will also be very different. Choosing the most appropriate and cost-effective method of manufacture is critical to the continued success of the organisation.

When a designer first has an innovative idea for a product, he may have made (possibly make himself) a model to look at and to handle in order to help develop the idea. He may want to show this model to his colleagues or potential customers. Even with all the modern technology available (CAD/CAM, etc.) the 'one-off' models are frequently produced to refine the design or to help gauge customer interest in the product (as witnessed by the concept cars seen at motor shows). At this stage in the innovation process, detailed drawings may not be required or appropriate and highly skilled and expensive personnel therefore make the product. At this stage of a product life cycle the term used to describe the manufacturing process is the *project method of manufacture*. Projects are unique or 'one-off' and the required disciplines and techniques involved can be found in projects of all scales from an academic dissertation to that of building the Channel Tunnel.

To illustrate this point, consider the development of a simple product such as a toolbox. The design engineer (or innovator) after preliminary meetings with the marketing people and/or potential customers makes a scale model of the product. In the earliest stage of this product it is best made by the personnel, machinery and techniques involved in a *project* style of production process. The innovator or designer listens to the observations and is able to reflect on these points in the development of the design (*see* Figure 4.2).

The design is well received and after minor modifications the design team decides to have a sample batch made (using common fasteners) by the operations function to help evaluate the market. The toolbox is shown to a range of customers who are each keen to buy a large batch at a competitive price. The industrial design team recognises that by changing the design by avoiding the need for fasteners, investing in tools to shape the individual elements of the box and welding the components together, the assembly time will be reduced and substantial costs saved. *As the required volume increases the most appropriate method of manufacture changes.*

Another key point is that assembly skills required to produce the product have become *embedded in the process machinery* and the workers involved have become machine minders (see Illustration 4.3 on the production of blocks on HMS *Victory* below and Figure 4.3). If the volume required increases even more, by having robots on the assembly line the direct labour involved is further reduced. If the product demand rises even further it may be appropriate that the product is redesigned again and made out of a plastic material (lighter and stronger) requiring investment in a very different processing technology.

Figure 4.2   Design simplification

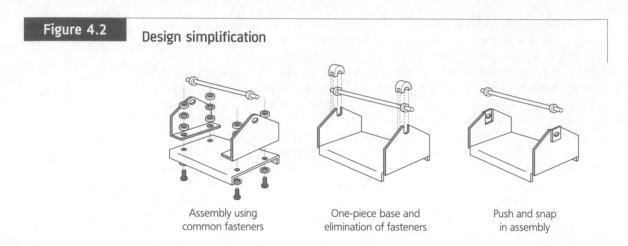

| Assembly using common fasteners | One-piece base and elimination of fasteners | Push and snap in assembly |

Figure 4.3   HMS *Victory*

Illustration 4.3

Innovation and design in the manufacturing process

The first use of machine tools in mass production was during the Napoleonic wars in the early 1800s. The British Navy, based in Portsmouth, had a need for 100,000 blocks (blocks house the sail ropes) per annum to both equip new ships and to provide spares. For example, HMS *Victory* alone required 900 blocks and each of these was individually carved by skilled craftsmen. Because the blocks were subject to storm, sea water, wind, ice and sun each ship would sensibly set sail with a full set of replacements and the many suppliers just could not cope with such a high demand.

Marc Brunel (born in France in 1769) was in 1798 dining with the British aide-de-camp in Washington, DC, a Major General Hamilton, when the conversation turned to ships and navies and to the particular problems with the manufacture of these wooden blocks. This was an opportunity to innovate in the process of manufacture and Brunel seized it. His idea was to simplify the manufacturing process into many more stages and to design specialist machines for each part of the operation of manufacture, thus enabling the large volume production of blocks.

In 1799 and with the help of an introduction from General Hamilton to Earl Spencer of Althorp, Brunel persuaded the British Navy to install the 43 Brunel-designed machine tools in factory in the naval dockyards in Portsmouth. By 1807 the facility was providing all the needs of the navy with only 10 unskilled men. Moreover, as the human element had been much removed from the process, the resulting blocks were far more likely to be consistent in dimensions and therefore of 'better' quality. The machines were still in use over 100 years later and seven are on display in the Portsmouth Naval Museum.

Brunel also applied the same innovative process design logic to other manufacturing problems. In 1809 he was shocked to see the damaged feet of returning war veterans that had been caused by their poorly made and fitted footwear. He, therefore, designed a set of machines that produced boots and shoes in nine different sizes with 24 disabled soldiers manning the machines. The boots and shoes were very successful and in 1812 the production volume was expanded to meet the army's *total* requirements.

Marc's son, Isambard Kingdom Brunel, designed and built steam ships, railways and many bridges for which he is correctly revered as one of most influential engineers in British history. However, most of what we consume and take for granted is based on the innovation in the processes of manufacture of 200 years ago by men such as Marc Brunel who introduced the concepts of mass production.

Source: www.brunelenginehouse.org.uk/people, 24 September 2003; and the Portsmouth Naval Museum, United Kingdom.

Craft-based products

Some products are craft based and will only ever be made in small volumes – for example, in products from the *haute couture* fashion houses. Unique gowns are hand-made by very skilled personnel and paraded at the fashion show (a new product launch). The designs are 'copied' by other organisations and there is a rush to get copies made and supplied to the high street retailers. These copies may look similar but are usually made from different materials using different techniques and are consequently less costly to make and to purchase. The operations management of the supplier to the high street has to be able to respond very quickly to get the goods to the market before the fashion changes. The flexibility and speed of response of the operation is therefore critical to the success of the organisation. In this illustration, good marketing is also vital to avoid the end-of-season excess stocks that ambitious and unrealised sales can cause.

Pause for thought

Is the illustration concerning block manufacture for HMS *Victory* the first example of a mass production system?

Design simplification

The purpose of design is to develop things that satisfy needs and meet expectations. By making the design such that the product is easy to produce the designer enables the operation to *consistently* deliver these features.

If the product is simple to make, the required quality management procedures will be less complex, easy to understand and, therefore, likely to be more effective. If a design is easy to make there will be fewer rejects during the manufacturing process and less chance that a substandard product reaches the customer. Referring to the toolbox illustration (Figure 4.2), the reduction in the number of components from over thirty to less than five, makes material control simpler. This in turn leads to simpler purchasing of components and less complex facility layouts. The same logic applies equally well in service sector applications (Brown *et al.*, 2001; Johnston and Clark, 2001).

The application of technology and techniques of 'concurrent engineering' where research, design and development work closely or in parallel rather than in sequence have made important contributions to this area of management (Waller, 1999). Innovation within the manufacturing function involves searching for new ways of saving costs and is a continual process, and the closer designers work with operations and marketing personnel, the more likely the organisation is to succeed. This point is developed in the quality function deployment (QFD) section below (p. 123).

It can take several years and cost millions of pounds to plan and build a major assembly facility such as a car plant. With such a huge investment it is essential that the design of the product is 'correct' at an early stage, as errors detected late can be prohibitively expensive to rectify.

Process design and innovation

The process design is based on the technology being used within the process. The metal-forming processes, the chemical processing industry, the plastic material processing and electronic assembly are all sophisticated subjects with their own literature.

The design of processes

Figure 4.4

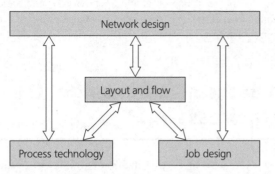

In order to illustrate a feature of innovation within process design, consider one of the important elements of operations – that of the design of the layout of the facility providing the goods or service. In service-type operations the customer may be inside the company's operations function and the significance of layout is even more important.

If an employee spends his working day assembling automotive car seats on an assembly line he quickly becomes expert in that area of manufacture and design. Most people spend the bulk of their 'awake' time involved with work and enjoy talking about their job if the opportunity arises. In all organisations it is the intellect of the employees that is the source of innovation and it is the role of senior managers to create an atmosphere to encourage appropriate intellectual activity if the organisation is to prosper. We go to art galleries or concerts to be entertained and inspired and so it should be in our place of work, in order that the elusive spark of innovation is encouraged.

The importance of the working environment is also recognised in the consideration given to the planning and layout of whole business areas and university campuses. The case study at the end of this chapter illustrates the importance of bookshop layout in influencing sales. The Chinese have feng shui, which is devoted to the impact of these factors on our working and personal environment. The design of the process is linked with the technology involved in the process and is fundamentally linked both to the organisation and job design.

Figure 4.4 models the relationship between the elements of process design and this is as applicable to the service sector as it is to the manufacturing sector. The flow of product within a factory operation may correspond to the flow of the customer (as with an airport design) or of information (as in the headquarters of a bank). The impact on the people involved in delivering the service is clear.

The product design engineer considers the ergonomics of the product such as a car seat (a key feature in a car purchase decision), while the process design engineer considers the ergonomics of a workstation on an assembly line.

In the service sector the process design parameters of minimising the flow of information are even more critical as the customer is often within the organisation itself. Customers may be made part of the process as in carrying their own luggage at airports or serving themselves in what is essentially the organisation's stock room at the supermarket. Clear signs and directions, easy-to-understand routes through the operation, understandable forms and approachable staff are all features of a well-designed service system. These are examples of *keeping things simple* – if the customer does not have to communicate with an employee to obtain the service there is less chance for communication and quality problems. Think of and compare the children's party game of 'Chinese Whispers' with the processing of paperwork or messages through several different departments in a large organisation. At every point of information transfer there is an opportunity for the quality of the information to be degraded.

Innovation in the management of the operations process

New, innovative ways of working within the operations process (including packaging and delivery) (*see* Chapter 13 on packaging) to gain competitive advantage is part of every operations manager's duties. Quality performance is a key operations management responsibility and innovation to help improve quality performance is critical to all organisations.

Quality circles and process improvement teams

A quality circle is a small group of voluntary workers who meet regularly to discuss problems (not necessarily restricted to quality matters) and determine possible solutions. The quality circle concept was developed from the ideas of Deming, Juran and Ishikawa in the 1960s. Most people are expert in their job and appreciate this being acknowledged. Members of quality circles are given training in quality control and evaluation techniques. An idea coming from a member of the quality circle is far more likely to be adopted than an idea imposed from above. Quality circles therefore reflect and exploit the advantages of the human resource theories embedded in employee participation and empowerment approaches. Furthermore, the recognition by senior managers that the employees are worth listening to helps to improve the total quality ethos of the company with beneficial effects on the company and its customers.

Since their introduction it is estimated that over 10 million Japanese workers have been part of a quality circle with an average saving of several thousand US dollars (Russel and Taylor, 2000). The later term 'process improvement team' was used (among others) to reflect the need to look at the whole business process being considered. There has been adoption of the quality circle approach by organisations in Europe and the United States but some argue that the cultural and adversarial differences between management and unions have inhibited the success of the approach in certain situations. However, quality circles can be a rich source of innovative solutions to problems and cost savings and patent applications may follow.

Pause for thought

Should 'to be innovative' be part of every job, especially a manager's?

Total quality management (TQM)

Most business texts have chapters on quality from their marketing, human resources or operations perspectives. It was the concept of total quality management that has been among the most significant in its effect. First introduced by Arm and Feigenbaum in the 1950s and then developed and refined by others (including Crosby, Deming, Ishikawa and Juran) TQM became defined as:

> *An effective system for integrating the quality development, quality maintenance and quality improvement efforts of the various groups in an organisation so to enable production and service at the most economical levels which allows for full customer satisfaction.*

(Feigenbaum, 1986)

The TQM philosophy stresses the following points:

- meeting the needs and expectations of customers;
- covering all the parts of the organisation;
- everyone in the organisation is included;
- investigating all costs related to quality (internal and external);
- getting thing right by designing in quality;
- developing systems and procedures which support quality improvements; and
- developing a continuous process of improvement.

Meeting expectations is difficult: as the quality level of products improves this in turn increases customer expectations. For example, in 1970 it was accepted that family-size cars required servicing every 3,000–6,000 miles and lasted for 60,000–70,000 miles. The automotive technical improvements now mean that a service interval of 12,000 miles and cars that last for over 100,000 miles are now the norm and are expected. Innovation in the ways to achieve what the customer expects in the combination of product and service provided is one way to gain sustainable advantage over your competition. The humorous example in Illustration 4.4 shows the different approaches to quality management.

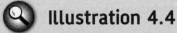 **Illustration 4.4**

Different approaches to quality

IBM of Canada ordered a batch of components from a Japanese supplier and specified that the delivery should have an acceptable quality level of three defective parts per thousand. When the parts arrived they were accompanied by a letter which expressed the suppliers' bewilderment at being asked to supply defective parts as well as good ones. The letter also explained that they had found it difficult to make parts that were defective but had done so and were included and wrapped separately with the delivery.

Source: Adapted from N. Slack *et al.* (2004) *Operations Management*, 4th edn, Pitman, London.

For a TQM approach to be successful all the staff in all departments have to be involved. Quality is the responsibility of everyone and not some other manager or department. Quality and employee improvements are therefore inextricably linked and should be part of a continuous cycle. If a modest innovative and improvement cycle continues, by embedding the approach in the culture of the organisation, the long-term and total result may exceed that of a radical solution. The 'knowledge' of the organisation has thereby increased. No organisation has the ability to recruit and retain all the very best brains and operation managers need to recognise that they need to exploit the skills and enthusiasm of all their people. The impact of small, relatively easy to achieve, improvements can be very positive. Much of the improvement in the reliability of cars over the past 20 years has been attributed to a very large number of incremental improvements initiated by thousands of employees in all the manufacturing companies involved.

TQM with its continuous improvement, employee involvement and process ownership has shown itself to be an effective policy in managing organisations not least because of the enthusiastic implementation (team building). However, if the idea meant that an element of the process was no longer needed and jobs were lost, what then of employee involvement? Many, if not most, employees would be unwilling to suggest losing jobs. Even in circumstances when alternative work was available to those displaced, many would be reluctant to vigorously pursue the idea. The very feeling of process ownership by the employees may *obstruct* all radical change, i.e. TQM may not support major innovation (Giaver, 1998).

Pause for thought

Artists and sculptors sign their work to give it provenance and because they are proud of their achievement. Would it be a good idea to make every worker that proud?

Quality function deployment (QFD)

Making design decisions concurrently rather than sequentially requires superior coordination among the parties involved – marketing, engineering, operations and, most importantly, the customer. Quality function deployment (QFD) is a structured approach to this problem that relates the *voice* of the customer to every stage of the design and the delivering process. In particular QFD:

- promotes better understanding of customer demands;
- promotes better understanding of design interactions;
- involves operations in the process at the earliest possible moment;
- removes the traditional barriers between the departments; and
- focuses the design effort.

Also known as the 'House of Quality' the technique is regarded by some as a highly complex technique only suitable for projects in large organisations. Others see QFD as a solution to the complex problems faced by designers and deserving of the persever- ance necessary. This was the case in the Japanese car component firm, Kayaba, who attempted to use the QFD systems of Toyota and initially suffered almost total failure. Kayaba went on to develop its own successful version, which it called 'Anticipatory Development' and won the company a Deming Prize for its quality achievements (Lowe and Ridgway, 2000).

The ISO 9000 approach

Many countries developed their own quality systems and standards and in 1994 these were 'combined' to become the International Standards Organisation ISO 9000 – a set of standards governing documentation of a quality programme. A qualified external examiner checks that the company complies with all the requirements specified and certifies the company. Once certified, companies are listed in a directory and this infor- mation is made available to potential customers. As many large organisations *insist* on all suppliers having the ISO quality standards, much time and effort was spent in new, innovative ways of controlling and developing processes to maintain the agreed and certified standards. Completing the certification process can be long and expensive (Krajewski and Ritzman, 2001, 267), however, compliance with ISO 9000 says nothing about the *actual quality* of the product.

In part to reflect this point the ISO 9000 (2000) developed to include four additional principles:

quality management should be customer focused;

quality performance should be measured;

quality management should be improvement driven; and

top management must demonstrate their commitment to maintaining and
   continually improving management systems.

Despite these revisions, ISO is not seen as beneficial by all parties (Slack *et al.*, 2004, 734).

The EFQM excellence model

In 1988, 14 leading western European companies formed the European Foundation for Quality Management and gave an award for the most successful application of TQM in Europe. In 1999 this idea and model was refined and developed into the *EFQM Excel- lence Model* that reflected the increased understanding and emphasis on the customer (and market) focus and is results oriented. The underlying idea is that *results* (people, customer, society and key performance) are achieved through a number of *enablers* (Figure 4.5) in managing and controlling the input/output transformation *processes* involved.

Performance measurement is by self-assessment which EFQM defines as 'a com- prehensive, systematic, and regular review of an organisatio's activities and results

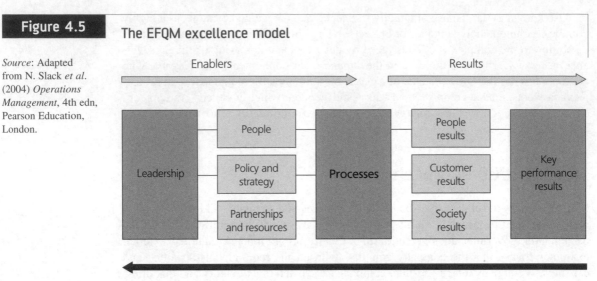

Figure 4.5

The EFQM excellence model

Source: Adapted from N. Slack *et al.* (2004) *Operations Management*, 4th edn, Pearson Education, London.

referenced against a model of business excellence'. It may be easier to understand *and apply* this approach than is the case with some of the more philosophical concepts within TMQ. Furthermore, the EFQM Excellence model also embeds *innovation and learning* in the performance of the organisation.

Pause for thought

How well does the EFQM business excellence model apply to service sector situations?

Design of the organisation and its suppliers

Figure 4.4 shows the relationships between network, process and job design while Figure 4.5 describes the whole supply chain and includes suppliers and customers.

Material (or information) flows through a series of operations to the end user (customer). The term supply chain management describes the system of managing the network across company boundaries in order to drive the whole chain towards the shared objective of satisfying the customers. The same objectives form part of most organisations' strategic plan (to deliver prompt, reliable product and services cost-effectively) and the holistic approaches within the supply chain management concept require useful network coordination mechanisms.

For a company to achieve its own quality goals it must include and consider the quality programmes of its suppliers and customers. Identifying the causes of uncertainty, determining how this affects other activities in the supply chain and formulating ways of reducing or eliminating the uncertainty is essential to the management of all the processes involved.

McDonald's built a restaurant in Moscow. To achieve its required and expected level of quality and service, the company set up an entire supply chain for growing, processing and distributing the food. McDonald's made sure that all parties along the whole chain understood its expectations of performance and closely monitored performance (Upton, 1998). The TQM team-based philosophy requires trust between all the parties involved for it to be effective. The same trust level needs to be present for successful supply chain management. As the supplying network expands across the world so does that of competitive organisations and the competition becomes the efficiency of one supply chain versus another. Only by *innovating* within the organisation's supply chain, in terms of product and service, will the organisation survive.

Business process re-engineering (BPR)

A contrast to the incremental ideas of process improvement is that of the radical breakthrough approach of business process re-engineering (BPR). First attributed to Hammer (1990), the technique is a blend of a number of ideas found within operations (process flow-charting, network management) and the need for customer focus. These were bought together to define BPR as:

> *The fundamental rethinking and radical redesign of business processes to achieve dramatic improvements in critical, contemporary measures of performance, such as cost, quality, service and speed.*
>
> (Slack *et al.*, 2004)

An existing organisation and its procedures reflect the way that business was conducted and may not support the core business in the future. For example, in the 1980s BPR techniques were used extensively in the IT industry when the cheap and progressively more powerful networked PC began to replace mainframes.

The approach is not without critics and certainly was used as one of the major 'downsizing' tools common in the 1980s and 1990s. The combination of radical downsizing and redesign can mean the loss of core experience from the operation. If taken too far (for example, if the short-term profit improvement was achieved at the expense of support for R&D expenditure) the resulting organisation could became 'hollow' and dic. Also, the core business has to be sound otherwise BPR is akin to 'flogging a dead horse'.

The BPR approach is similar to the ideas put forward by Peters (1997) who makes the case for the total destruction of company systems, hierarchy and procedures and replacing them with a multitude of single-person business units working as professionals. He argues that the small modest improvement enshrined in TQM detracts effort from the real need to reinvent the business, i.e. 'Incrementalism is an enemy of innovation'. Tom Peters argues that a radical approach is the only way organisations can be sufficiently innovative to survive in the twenty-first century.

Making the resources available to continuously innovate and improve the service to customers and developing new markets for products is a difficult and complex task. The emphasis on the need to understand and be close to customers has helped to improve organisations across the world. However, commercial history is littered with successful oganisations who failed to recognise the emergence of new technologies. Christensen (1999) develops the philosophy of *disruptive innovations* that introduce a very different package of attributes to the marketplace from the ones that mainstream customers have historically valued. Christensen argues that leading companies failed to maintain their position at the top of their sector when the technology or markets changed because they ignored the emerging disruptive technology. Chapter 14 discusses this issue in more detail.

Thus we have the radical breakthrough approach of Hammer, Christensen and Peters versus the diametrically opposite incremental methodologies enshrined in the philosophies of TQM. It may be possible, even necessary, to follow both at different times. Large and significant improvements can be followed by incremental and less spectacular innovations and improvements but senior managers and company directors must be aware of the strengths and weaknesses of both.

Operations and technology

The most significant technological advance that has impacted on operations has been the application of computers. Among the many applications was the work in the 1970s and 1980s with the transfer of information (later funds) electronically between elements of the secure private networks along the organisation's supply chains. For example, electronic data interchange (EDI) facilitated the application of the just-in-time (JIT) approach in manufacturing operations (*see* Table 4.2). The technology (the agreement on network protocols and software) and the innovative techniques they made possible were an integral part of the drive to generate business value across the supply chains. The phrase electronic commerce or e-commerce was coined to bring together a range of activities involved in the different industries and business sectors. E-commerce is defined as a transaction by which the order is placed – not the payment delivery

---

Table 4.2 The development of e-commerce and the impact on operations

Phase	Operations activities
Phase 1	Electronic data interchange (EDI) supporting innovations such as JIT
Phase 2	Establishing a web presence – sales information-based
Phase 3	Conducting e-commerce – progressive application across different sectors
Phase 4	Automation – customer-based

Illustration 4.5

How Dell has successfully adapted

Michael Dell founded the Dell Corporation in Texas, USA, in 1984 and was the pioneer in the direct selling of custom-built computers by mail order. By 1998 Dell had over 25 per cent of sales from the Internet and had become the largest manufacturer of business PCs in the world.

Dell's story is very impressive and analysts have searched for reasons for their success.

- Mass customisation
- SCM good links with flexible vendors
- Background in telemarketing
- Customer knowledge leading to 'premier pages' that have saved Ford $2m
- High reliability: Dell has received 174 awards for performance
- Delivery support 24/7
- Adaptive business strategy by moving up the value chain
- Concentrating on what customers wanted

Source: Adapted from E. Turban *et al*. (2000) *Electronic Commerce – A Managerial Perspective*, Prentice-Hall, Englewood Cliffs, NJ; and S. Brown *et al*. (2001) *Operations Management*, Butterworth-Heinemann, Oxford.

channels (www.statistics.gov.uk/themes/economy, 2004). The growth of e-commerce has been very rapid as companies and governments recognised the vast potential of this global technology that can integrate customers and content in highly innovative and previously impossible ways.

The second phase (Table 4.2) was the very rapid publication of product information on the Web and by the end of the 1990s most organisations in the United States and the United Kingdom had websites. Many were very extensive; for example, in 1999 General Motors Corporation offered 18,000 pages of information that included 98,000 links to the company's products and services (Turban *et al*., 2000).

The effect on some organisations has been dramatic. In the early 1990s, the *Encyclopaedia Britannica* was leather-bound and found on most library shelves. By the mid-1990s the same content was in CD form at less than 10 per cent of the bound volume price. In October 1999 the information was available free on the Web at Britannia.com, the required revenue coming from advertising alongside the data. Later, by 2001, the organisation withdrew the advertising and introduced a fee to access the Internet version. The products, the technology of the processes producing the product and the business strategy have all been changed in less than a decade. The organisation has clearly introduced change and innovation.

The Web technology allows you 'into' the supply chain and you are able to design and monitor the progress of your own product through the producing operating system. Dell Computers is a very good illustrative example (*see* Illustration 4.5).

Dell successfully adapted its processes to take advantage of the technology while remaining close to the fundamental of understanding the needs of its customers.

What is less obvious is the power of the Internet to unlock value by separating different types of systems, business processes and companies, and give organisations the ability to use their resources most effectively. Illustration 4.6 shows how companies are able to decouple their back-office operations from customer-facing activities so that common services can be centralised while customer-facing activities can be moved

Illustration 4.6

FT

Use the Internet's power to divide and rule

When we think about how the internet creates value, we naturally think about its power to connect systems, processes and companies to each other. That is how we define a network such as the internet: computer systems linked together in a way that makes it easier to share information.

What is less obvious is the power of the internet to unlock value by separating different types of systems, business processes and companies, and give organisations the ability to use their resources most effectively. The internet has ushered in an era of connectivity based on open standards where people, devices and applications can communicate regardless of their location.

This flexibility in location allows different types of functionality and expertise to be decoupled – separated from each other and relocated to make the most of specialisation.

Just as water finds its own level when disparate sources are connected with pipes, functionality and expertise can flow to their ideal locations when systems, business processes and companies are connected over a ubiquitous network.

Decoupling allows organisations to benefit from scale as well as specialisation, differentiation as well as vertical integration and centralisation as well as decentralisation. In the design of IT systems, the internet allows IT infrastructure to be decoupled from end-user applications, so systems can be agile and responsive at the level of applications, yet robust and scalable in their infrastructure.

It lets companies decouple their back-office operations from customer-facing activities so that common services can be centralised while customer-facing activities can be moved closer to clients. And by decoupling different activities in industry value chains, the internet enables companies to concentrate on their core skills while broadening their network of partners.

To understand how decoupling overcomes design compromises in IT systems, consider a simple example – designing a personal computer that is powerful yet user-friendly. In the absence of a network such as the internet, all functionality, applications and data need to be located on the same personal computer. This involves a hidden compromise.

On the one hand, you want your computer to be small, flexible and user-friendly – in a word, personal. On the other hand, you want it to be powerful, have lots of memory and be highly reliable – more like a mainframe computer. What you end up with is a computer that is neither user-friendly as an appliance, nor as powerful as a mainframe.

If we introduce a network such as the internet into the picture, the situation changes dramatically. Now you can move the mainframe-like functions of the computer, such as storage and processing, to a central server that is powerful, reliable and scalable. At the same time, you can allow the PC-like functions, such as displaying information and taking user input, to stay close to the user.

By separating the back-end infrastructure functions that belong on a large server from the front-end functions that are best housed on the client device, the internet breaks the design compromise inherent in co-location.

In fact, infrastructure-like functions can be delivered over a pipe, just like water, electricity and natural gas. This is the essence of the 'utility computing' idea that is currently animating International Business Machines and other computer vendors. But utility computing presents a paradox: infrastructure will become more centralised, while devices and user applications will become more decentralised.

I foresee the emergence of a few large information utility companies that will supply

IT infrastructure. At the same time, though, I predict the creation of billions of highly focused information appliances for end-users.

The decoupling logic also applies to the design of business processes in a company. For decades, companies have struggled to find the right balance between centralisation and decentralisation of their operations. On the one hand, centralisation allows for better economies of scale and improved coordination of activities across a company. On the other, it makes companies less responsive to their customers and local markets.

To see how decoupling can help resolve this dilemma, think about how a company's activities can be classified into 'front-office' activities (those that directly involve customers, such as sales, solution design and customer relationship management), and 'back-office' activities (those that provide support, such as administration, human resource management and accounting).

Front-office activities are most effective when they are tailored to the needs of specific customer segments. Conversely, back-office activities are most effective when they are standardised and centralised. The internet allows companies to decentralise front-end activities and move them closer to customers, while allowing back-end activities to be centralised into set of shared services.

Consider how General Electric is taking advantage of decoupling as it redesigns its global processes. GE's India-based GE Capital International Services provides 15 of the top GE businesses with services that include accounting, business analysis and software development. GECIS allows GE companies to manage their front-end activities closer to their markets while benefiting from improved scale and lower labour costs at the India-based back-end operations. The growth of IT-enabled business services in India is being fuelled by the realisation that companies can benefit by decoupling and relocating their back-office operations to lower-cost locations.

Decoupling is also reshaping the way companies decide the scope of their activities within the industry value chain.

In the days of Alfred Sloan, companies believed that competitive advantage was gained through vertical integration. However, it is difficult to be good at all activities in the value chain. Therefore, it makes sense for companies to focus on what they do best and to outsource the rest.

However, if you cannot communicate effectively with partners and suppliers, the benefits of specialisation are diluted because of the cost of coordinating activities across companies.

With the internet, companies no longer need to compromise between specialisation and integration. By reducing the cost of interaction between companies and their partners, the internet allows companies to limit their operations to what they do best, and to outsource non-core activities. The result: a disaggregation of industry value chains into networks of specialised companies called 'business webs' or 'value networks'.

Consider the value network that Cisco Systems, the networking company, has created to offer e-learning services to its enterprise customers. Cisco starts with a family of products and augments it with specialised products and services from a network of partners. The internet allows Cisco to benefit from the specialisation of its partners, while delivering an integrated solution to its customers.

The internet allows companies to resolve age-old debates between specialisation and generalisation, centralisation and decentralisation and scale versus focus through its ability to decouple systems, processes and companies. If you understand the power of decoupling, you can go beyond these seemingly irreconcilable conflicts and unlock new value for your company.

Mohanbir Sawhney, 'Use the power of the net to divide and rule FT Summer School', www.FT.com, 18 August 2003. Reprinted with permission.

closer to clients. And by decoupling different activities in industry value chains, the Internet enables companies to concentrate on their core skills while broadening their network of partners.

Pause for thought

How much of the success of Dell can be attributed to patents?

The final phase 4 (Table 4.2) includes auctions where companies publish their requirements on the Internet and organisations across the globe are invited to quote. Traditional competitors are coming together forming trading exchanges for their supplies. For example Ford, DaimlerChrysler and GM amalgamated elements of their supply chain in the *Covisint* exchange. They were later joined by Renault and Peugot Citroën (Turban *et al.*, 2000).

The impact of the Internet is present in all business areas. In education there is an increasing wealth of good quality information freely available on the Internet and there are increased opportunities for changing the processes involved in education. (for example distance learning). Consequently governments take e-commerce very seriously. At the EU summit in February 2000 the creation of 20 million new jobs were forecast (*The Independent*, 2000). Twenty million *different* jobs is a much more likely outcome as companies develop their systems and procedures to reflect the technology.

Pause for thought

If the forecast of 20 million different or new jobs is correct whose jobs are affected?

A common feature of global business forecasts is that the business-to-business e-commerce (B2B) is predicted to be substantially larger than Business to Consumer E-commerce (B2C). (See emarketer.com and forrester.com.) The EDI links between organisations in the 1980s were relatively easy to adapt to the web-based trading relationships possible in the 1990s. Within B2B e-commerce substantial savings in purchase and administration costs are reported (Turban *et al.*, 2000) in many, if not all business sectors. For example, paper-less cheques (e-checks) can provide industry-wide savings and benefits of $2–3 billion per year to the US economy (Turban *et al.*, 2004, 511). The 'losers' in these developments have been those intermediaries (people and organisations) no longer required.

The performance of this high-technology sector has been difficult and many 'dot-com' companies have failed to achieve the initial promise of the late 1990s. Being innovative always carries a risk. Being first to market has not been much of an advantage to many 'dot-com' companies (Leadbeater, 2001). Some car manufactures limit their involvement with the Web trading Covisint exchange to simple products (screws,

---

The design spectrum

Figure 4.4

| Product design | Process design | Service design | Supply chain management design | Organisation design | Business design | Business sector design |

Range of knowledge required

---

nuts and bolts, etc.), as perhaps they feel that the emphasis on price that is implicit in an auction would have a negative impact on quality and the working relationships between the participants (Cope, 2001; McMcracken, 2001). Business pragmatism has been applied to the over-hyped 'dot-com' revolution with focus being on the basics (Skapinker, 2001).

However, beyond an early cost saving achieved by Internet enabled technology, perhaps the longer lasting and more sustainable additional value of the Internet is when it facilitates a purchase that would not otherwise have happened.

Highly innovative strategic alliances have been taking place – for example, the collaboration of Amazon.com and Wal-Mart, i.e. the traditional high street retailer and cyber shopping combining (Rushe, 2001; Fiorina and London, 2001). With the impact of the technology on the supply chains and the creation of trading exchanges the re-design of business sectors is taking place. The Internet auction house, E-bay had a community of almost 50 million users, provided a living for thousands of people and transacted over $14 billion in sales in 2002. Some individuals have amassed a fortune in a marketplace that did not exist in 1995 (Turban *et al.*, 2004, 432)! The range of the various design competencies required within an organisation is therefore huge and may be represented by a spectrum of knowledge (*see* Figure 4.6).

There can be few individuals who fully understand the complexity of this range of expertise but a competent CEO or general manager must manage the diverse disciplines involved. They must at the very least understand how these disciplines overlap and relate.

Case Study

Novels, new products and Harry Potter[1]

This case study explores the world of publishing and examines how a new product in this industry reaches the customer. While many publishers spend enormous sums of money promoting their bestsellers (Bloomsbury and Harry Potter is an obvious example), sometimes little money, if any, is spent investing in the new publishing products and talents of tomorrow, that is, new

[1] This case has been written as a basis for class discussion rather than to illustrate effective or ineffective managerial or administrative behaviour. It has been prepared from a variety of published sources, as indicated, and from observations.

authors. In effect some publishers are simply printing books without the necessary promotion. This case illustrates that in this relatively straightforward new product there are many factors, some very surprising, that influence the success or not of a new book. The role of the publisher, the role of the agent, the role of the retailer, the role of the buyer, the role of the critic – all influence success in this industry. While all publishers would like to have the next Harry Potter, this case illustrates that this is unlikely to happen if they do not invest in new product development today.

Introduction

Record-breaking sales of *Harry Potter and the Order of the Phoenix* sent retailers world-wide calling on Bloomsbury (United Kingdom) and Scholastic (United States), the book's publishers, to speed up their orders to save leaving their shelves bare. Initial reports from retailers confirmed that copies of the fifth in J.K. Rowling's seven-part series about the boy wizard sold faster than any other book in history: 5m copies sold in the United States on the first day, which if confirmed would break publishing records. Scholastic's first print run was 6.8m, with a second of 1.7m. Amazon.com, the online retailer, said it had delivered 420,000 copies of the 768-page book in the United Kingdom and received 1.3m pre-orders world-wide, almost three times more than the previous record holder, *Harry Potter and the Goblet of Fire*, the fourth book in the series. Tesco, Britain's biggest retailer, originally ordered 500,000 copies, sold 317,400 books in the first 24 hours, In comparison, the group sold only 42,000 copies of the last Potter book over the whole of its first week. But, the sales phenomenon does not necessarily translate to big profits. Tesco and other groups slashed the prices of the book to drive sales and snatch market share from specialist retailers. Asda, the Leeds-based chain owned by Wal-Mart, sold 120,000 copies in the first 24 hours at one of the lowest prices £8.96 ($15). Waterstones, the specialist chain owned by HMV Group, said the scale of the launch was

unprecedented. At its flagship store in Piccadilly, central London, the group saw more than 2,000 people queueing many for hours to buy a copy (www.FT.com, 2003).

When it comes to considering the development of a new product one of the most identifiable and simple to imagine is a book. Compared to a new product in the aircraft or motor industries a new novel is simple and straightforward. Moreover, books have been produced for thousands of years, it is a mature industry and surely when it comes to publishing everything is thoroughly understood? In reality the industry continues to develop and continues to surprise even the most experienced publisher.

A book is published in the hope and expectation that it will sell thousands maybe even millions of copies for the author and publisher. Yet, despite the best efforts of many publishers, some books defy expectations and flop. Consider Anthea Turner's autobiography. Despite all the media hype, it sold just 451 copies in its first week and was soon piled high in the discount 'remainder' bookshops (Kean, 2001). Publishers are not eager to discuss such disappointing stories, yet the Waterstones bookseller suggests that 15 per cent of all books are returned to the publisher. In fact most books do not sell. In 2001 116,000 new titles were launched in the UK, that is, about 2000 new titles a week! As we have seen, even celebrity status is no guarantee of success, although it is usually a substantial help.

Success depends on many things including whether or not your publisher is willing to pay up to £10,000 to book retailers in order to have a book displayed at the front of the shop. Or even paying a retail chain up to £6,000 to have a book selected as 'read of the week'. This may all sound unfair and devious – welcome to the modern world of publishing, where the looks of the author count almost as much as the writing. Daunta Kean (Kean, 2001) argued that most books in the bestseller lists were there due to at least some money changing hands between retailers and publishers and by authors working hard to promote themselves. It should come as no surprise to the student of business that the role of the retailer is as important in books as it is in other consumer products. In many ways a novel is just another consumer product, a combination of product and service.

A growing and profitable industry, but only for the few

The world of publishing continues to be an exciting and profitable business. Sales continue to grow and more and more books are published each year. Table 4.3 shows the historical context and the rapid growth in the number of titles published in the last ten years. Yet few books make any significant amount of money for the author or the publisher. So why are so many more books being published? The answer, of course, is that you only need one J.K. Rowling out of a hundred or even a thousand new authors to justify the publisher's speculation, especially when the publisher, in this case, Bloomsbury only paid £2,500 for her first book (Burkeman, 2001). The film rights for Harry Potter were sold to Warner Brothers for over £50 million and J.K. Rowling has earned more than £40 million from the Harry Potter series. AOL–Time Warner settled on a single sponsor, Coca-Cola, which paid $150 million for exclusive marketing rights. The film

Table 4.3 Book titles published in thousands

Year	Book titles published
1850	2,200
1900	7,500
1960	20,000
1991	67,704
1995	95,064
2000	116,415

Sources: E.J. Hobsbawm (1990) *Industry and Empire*, Penguin, London; C. O'Grady, 'A book's life', *The Guardian*, 18 August, 9

will also help to increase sales still further, in the lucrative US market, from the current 19 million (Bloomsbury sold the US publishing rights to Scholastic Inc.). Mattel and Hasbro have recently bought the license to merchandise products from the film, all of which will be future profits for Bloomsbury and Rowling (*see* Illustration 4.7). The world-wide sales of Harry Potter books are now in excess of 115 million copies.

 Illustration 4.7

J.K. Rowling

Like that of her own character, Harry Potter, J.K. Rowling's life has the lustre of a fairy tale. Divorced, living on public assistance in a tiny Edinburgh flat with her infant daughter, Rowling wrote *Harry Potter and the Sorcerer's Stone* at a table in a café during her daughter's naps – and it was Harry Potter that rescued her. First, the Scottish Arts Council gave her a grant to finish the book. After its sale to Bloomsbury (UK), the accolades began to pile up. Harry Potter won the British Book Awards, Children's Book of the Year, and the Smarties Prize, and rave reviews on both sides of the Atlantic. Book rights have been sold to England, France, Germany, Italy, Holland, Greece, Finland, Denmark, Spain and Sweden.

Source: www.scholastic.com/harrypotter/author/index.htm

▶

The journey from manuscript to published book

Once the author, especially a new or unknown author, has completed a manuscript, the key task is to get it published. This is extremely difficult, as many prospective writers will tell you. Thousands of manuscripts land on the desks of publishers and agents every week. Most are 'binned' or returned to the author. Agents and publishers reject manuscripts that later turn out to be best-selling novels, but they will argue that this is the nature of the business. This, of course, is of little help to the author whose novel has been rejected for the fifth time. 'Don't give up', the agent will say, 'Harry Potter was rejected by several publishers.'

Most publishers will only work through agents and will not communicate directly with authors. This is because the agents understand the business and sometimes know the individual commissioning editors. The publishers view the agents as helpful in weeding out the 'rubbish' leaving the editors with the better manuscripts to consider.

The author–agent relationship is a business partnership. The specifics of the partnership will vary depending on the nature of the work in question, the author's needs, and the agent's policies and practices. In general, though, an agent will review his client's work and advise on quality and potential marketability and the possible strategy for securing its publication. For that work, the agent receives a commission (usually 15 per cent) against the author's advance and all subsequent income relevant to the sold product.

But even the best agent cannot sell inferior work. The commissioning editor is the buyer, and, as a rule, an author gets only one chance per editor. After an editor reads whatever is put before him or her, some deep, perhaps indelible impression is formed. This corresponds to quality management issues in other industries. If the author has written a second-rate book, and if the agent has not vetted it beforehand, the editor is likely not only to reject the work but to also refuse to see anything else from that author in future.

T. Colgan (1996), senior editor, Berkley Publishing, offers some frank advice on the role of a commissioning editor. There are many reasons why commissioning editors reject a manuscript and here are the most common ones:

- *The editor.* All people have likes and dislikes, and editors are no different. Most editors have deep-seated ideas about what their readers are looking for that go far beyond what the actual numbers show. That is why many editors insist on staying with an author after several bad outings or why they push to take on a talented new author in a category that is on the wane.

- *The market.* This is the trickiest consideration to gauge. It is not as simple as looking at the numbers. It is true, this will give you a pretty good idea of the market today, but when an editor buys a book he or she needs to be thinking about the market up to two years from now. After all, it is going to take the author six months to a year to finish his or her work. Once he or she delivers, it is going to be about a year before you can get the book in the schedule.

- *The house.* 'Thank you for submitting your material, but, unfortunately, this is not right for our list.' List in this instance refers to a publisher's portfolio of products. Anyone who's ever received a rejection letter is familiar with that sentence or something similar. Sure, a lot of times, it's just code for: 'Your manuscript stinks!' But there are plenty of times when it means just what it says. They may already have a mystery series that is similar to yours, or you may be writing in an area that is not one of their fortes. Each publishing house has its own strengths and weaknesses. Some publishing houses do well with true crime while others will not touch it. Some have great success with cosy mysteries, and others find them utter failures.

- *The author.* You should write because you want to, and you should write what you want to. Let the market take care of itself. Attempting to pattern yourself after a successful author is an almost certain way to strangle your own voice and collect an impressive number of rejection slips.

The publisher and the contract

At the initial stage of acceptance the publisher is as much interested with the looks of the author as with the writing. This may sound surprising but good looks can help with sales, especially if the author is young (O'Grady, 2001). Once another commissioning editor has read the manuscript, the original commissioning editor tries to convince other departments that they should make an offer to the agent. The agent will discuss this offer with the author, but royalties for first books are usually standard at between 7–15 per cent of the net price of the book. Any advance, which is taken out of future royalties, is also negotiated. Most first-time authors are simply relieved to get their work published. J.K. Rowling agreed an advance of £2,500 for the first Harry Potter book. The negotiations do not end here. For there are foreign and film rights to be discussed. If applicable, and they are usually not, these will produce more revenue than UK sales. Clearly the agent will want to retain these rights but frequently these are signed over to the publisher. An interesting footnote here is that J.K. Rowling's agent and not the publisher signed the film rights to Harry Potter, while the publisher signed the foreign publishing rights.

Drafts, revisions and presentation

The editor assigned to any book will work closely with the author once the contract has been signed. The original manuscript may need months or even years of reworking. This is a good example of the iterative process of new product development. Also the new word-processing software facilitates this process. Other editors may also make suggestions for changes to the plot or scenes or how the story could be improved. A copy-editor will also be involved checking the details, facts and consistency. Eventually it will be typeset and checked again for correctness, grammar, etc. Advanced proofs may even be sent to reviewers or trade buyers, in the hope of an advance order. This brings us to the next stage: the book jacket. The designers are briefed – they may even go so far as to read a chapter! Within a few weeks, several cover ideas are submitted before a design is chosen, usually by a combination of the editor and the marketing department. The author has little if any input.

The size of the final book is almost as important as the design of the jacket cover. For in the publishing industry size really does matter. First, there is the question of whether to publish in hardback and paperback or just paperback. Some critics argue that to be taken seriously a book needs to be published in hardback. This may sound slightly snobbish, but in some sections this view is taken seriously and it is certainly taken seriously by authors, all of whom it seems want to be seen in hardback. There are three main size formats: A, B and C. The A format measures 110mm × 178mm and is the typical size of most best-selling paperbacks. Format B is slightly larger at 130mm × 198mm and is considered to be slightly more up market and associated with more prestigious authors. Format C is 135mm × 216mm and is the size of many hardbacks. Industry insiders suggest that the format of the book is an indication to retailers and consumers about the type of book on the shelf. Few consumers may be aware of this but as a way of illustration almost all books being considered for the prestigious Booker prize are published in hardback first. To be fair, many years ago there was a significant difference in production costs but with the introduction of computer software into printing and design the difference in production costs are not as significant as they once were. ▶

Retailers

The number of book retailers has decreased over the past 20 years, yet the number of sales of books has increased. The market is now dominated by a few very large retailers; WH Smith and Waterstones handle 25 per cent of all book sales; book clubs account for a further 16 per cent (Amazon.com, an Internet bookseller, has had a significant impact on this industry). In addition, the multiples are now stocking and selling a narrow range of the best-selling books at discounted prices. The big retailers, like any other retailer, have to concentrate on books that will sell, whereas the specialist bookshops, frequently owned and operated by people for interest rather than profit, would be willing to stock a wider variety but cannot compete with the multiples who stock only best-selling titles.

To become a bestseller a book needs to be available in the large retail outlets, and it needs to be visible in these outlets. Publishers will go to great lengths to secure shelf space for a book they wish to promote. This includes entertaining the retail buyers with extravagant 'business trips', for example to the Wimbledon tennis championships or to a Formula One motor race, to try to influence the buyer's decision. According to Oliver Burkeman (2001) one year Collins bought all the available space in WH Smith for back-to-school dictionaries and sales of Oxford University Press dictionaries plummeted. High sales depend on shelf space: some publishers have argued that a bestseller is 70 per cent the book and 30 per cent the marketing.

The other major influence on the success of a book is the role played by 'critics' in the media. If a book receives the praise of one of the mainstream newspaper book critics this will have an enormous positive influence on sales, similarly from a radio book critic or even better a television book critic. The key issue here is getting the book in front of the critic and getting them to read it. Once again publishers will use some of the tactics used with buyers to try to further their cause.

Conclusions

The truth is sometimes painful and difficult to accept, but most authors do not earn very much money from their writing. A Society of Authors report stated that half of all writers earn less than the minimum wage (Kean, 2001). This may simply be due to the fact that what is written is not very good or not wanted, but the evidence seems to suggest that publishers are contributing to the problem. What is of concern is that increasingly publishers are selecting fewer books to promote, for without promotion a book is being only printed. Promotion is an integral part of publishing. Indeed, most dictionaries define publishing as 'to make widely known'. Printing a book and leaving it piled high in a warehouse is not making it widely known. Printing is only part of the activity of publishing. It is understandable that all publishers have limited promotional budgets, but to decide not to invest any promotion at all in a book is deceiving the author. If authors were aware that little if any effort was being targeted at his or her book they would surely be better advised to move to another publisher or to get it printed themselves.

The future of publishing depends on new authors. To be innovative, publishers need to nurture and find new talent. This is effectively the research and development (R&D) of publishing. Without this activity publishers will soon find they have no new products to sell. Supporting a best-selling author is fine and necessary but so is uncovering tomorrow's J.K. Rowling. The case highlights that the big retailers who, understandably, adopt a short-term market-pull approach increasingly dominate the market. This leads to fewer titles being promoted and made available (despite an increasing number of titles being printed) and stifles innovation. Consumers are not always able to communicate their needs; frequently consumers do not know whether they are going to enjoy a story about a child and his wizard-like powers until they have read it.

Questions

1 Explain why you think the Harry Potter series of books have been so successful.

2 In the case study explain how a new book has three aspects of a product (concept, package and process).

3 In the case study identify all the factors that influence the sale and success of a new book. Also weight the amount of influence you feel these factors have on a book's success.

4 How can publisher's exploit writers?

5 When it comes to developing new products for tomorrow; compare how football clubs try to invest in developing new products/players and how publishers try to invest in new products/authors.

6 In the case study, discuss the role of Internet sites to support book sales, such as the HarryPotter.com website.

Chapter summary

The quality of design and management within operations is thus seen as an essential part of innovation management. Often by understanding the basics of good design by perhaps 'keeping things simple' and looking at your products and services as your customers receive them will help to deliver a continual stream of new product and service improvements. Continuous redesign of the company (e.g. Dell) and its products and service, listening to your customers, watching your competitors, keeping aware of inventions and emerging technologies is a daunting task. We are not just talking about *fitting* the various departments and functions together as a team, but creating a *resonance* across all the constituents of the design spectrum.

Discussion questions

1 What do you understand by *innovation* within the education sector?

2 Apply Braun's principles to your university or college.

3 The vast improvements in stock minimisation made possible by the technology and combined with organised distribution from strategically located warehouses has reduced the stock holding of the combined operations of supermarkets to 20 from 45 days' sales. If customers pay with cash and the supermarkets pay their suppliers 30 days after delivery to the warehouse, who is funding the stock on the supermarket shelves?

4 Which elements of the TQM philosophy could you apply to your university or college? What might be the benefits?

5 Do you think the EFQM model of excellence could apply to your university? What might be the benefits?

6 Consider the innovation activities of the design spectrum. How much of the range would involve patents?

7   Can you think of any circumstances in which the philosophy of 'keeping things simple' would not apply?

8   'Technology changes. The laws of economics do not.' Discuss the implications and validity of this statement.

Key words and phrases

Websites worth visiting

The Design Council www.designcouncil.org.uk

E-commerce www.statistics.gov.uk/themes/economy

The EFQM model of excellence www.efqm.org/

For marketing information www.emarketer.com and www.forrester.com

Government Statistics www.statistics.gov.uk/

Journal of Operations Management www.sciencedirect.com/science

An Operations Management text book www.booksites.net/slack/

See how things are made www.manufacturing.stanford.edu

Sustainability www.sustainability.org

References

Brown, S., Blackmon, K., Cousins, P. and Maylor, H. (2001) *Operations Management*, Butterworth-Heinemann, Oxford.

Burkeman, O. (2001) 'Price wars', *The Guardian*, 18 August, 9.

Christenson, C.M. (1999) *Innovation and the General Manager*, McGraw-Hill, London.

Colgan, T. J. (1996) www.authorlink.com/index.html

Cope, N. (2001) 'B2B hubs in reverse spin', *The Independent*, 22 February.

EFQM (2003) *EFQM Excellence Model*, EFQM, Brussels.

Feigenbaum, A.V. (1986) *Total Quality Control*, McGraw-Hill, New York.

www.FT.com (2003) 'Harry Potter storms the bookstores', 23 June.

Fiorina, C. and London, S. (2001) 'Corporate restructuring', *Financial Times*, 22 August.

Giaever, H. (1998) *Does Total Quality Management Restrain Innovation?* DNV report no. 99–2036.

Hammer, M. (1990) 'Re-engineering work: don't automate, obliterate', *Harvard Business Review*, July/August, 104–12.

Hobsbawm, E.J. (1990) *Industry and Empire*, Penguin, London.

The Independent (2000) 'Internet reforms will help case for euro', 25 March.

Johnston, R. and Clark, G. (2001) *Service Operations Management*, Prentice Hall, London.

Kean, D. (2001) 'How to be a bestseller', *The Guardian*, 4 August, 8.

Krajewski L. J. and Ritzman L.P. (2001) *Operations Management*, Prentice Hall, London.

Leadbeater, C. (2001) 'Fallacies and first movers', *Financial Times*, 1 February.

Lowe, A. and Ridgway, K. (2000) 'UK user's guide to quality function deployment', *Engineering Management Journal*, June.

McMcracken, J. (2001) 'Southfield, Mich.-based online automotive exchange', *Detroit Free Press*, 11 August.

National Statistics website, www.statistics.gov.uk/themes/economy (accessed 27 August 2001).

O'Grady, C. (2001) 'A book's life': *Guardian*, 18 August, 9.

Peters, T. (1997) *The Circle of Innovation*, Hodder & Stoughton, London.

Roy, R. and Weild, D. (1993) *Product Design and Technological Innovation*, Open University Press, Milton Keynes.

Rushe, D. (2001) 'Amazon and Wal-Mart in alliance talks', *Sunday Times*, 3 March.

Russel, R. and Taylor, B. (2000) *Operations Management*, Prentice-Hall, Englewood Cliffs, NJ.

Skapinker, M. (2001) 'Death of the net threat', *Financial Times*, 12 March.

Slack, N., Chambers, S., Harland, C., Harrison, A. and Johnson, R. (2001) *Operations Management*, 3rd edn, Pitman, London.

Slack, N., Chambers, S., Harland, C., Harrison, A. and Johnson, R. (2004) *Operations Management*, 4th edn, Pitman, London.

Turban, E., Lee, U., King, D. and Chung, H.M. (2000) *Electronic Commerce – A Managerial Perspective*, Prentice-Hall, Englewood Cliffs, NJ.

Turban, E., Lee, U., King, D. and Chung, H.M. (2004) *Electronic Commerce – A Managerial Perspective*, Prentice-Hall, Englewood Cliffs, NJ.

Upton, D.M. (1998) *Designing, Managing and Improving Operations*, Prentice-Hall, Englewood Cliffs, NJ.

Van Looy, B., Gemmel, P. and Van Dierdonck, R. (2003) *Services Management*, Prentice-Hall, London.

Waller, D.L. (1999) *Operations Management – A Supply Chain Approach*, International Thomson Publishing, London.

Further reading

Brown, S. (1996) *Strategic Manufacturing for Competitive Advantage*, Prentice-Hall, Englewood Cliffs, NJ.

Christensen, C.M. (2003) *The Innovator's Dilemma: When New Technologies Cause Great Firms to Fail*, 3rd edn, HBS Press, Cambridge, MA.

Drucker, P.F. (2002) *Managing in the Next Society*, Butterworth Heinmann, Oxford.

Krajewski, L.J. and Ritzman, L.P. (1998) *Operations Management: Strategy and Analysis*, 5th edn, Addison-Wesley, Reading, MA.

Managing intellectual property

Intellectual property concerns the legal rights associated with creative effort or commercial reputation. The subject matter is very wide indeed. The aim of this chapter is to introduce the area of intellectual property to the manager of business and to ensure that they are aware of the variety of ways that it can affect the management of innovation and the development of new products. The rapid advance of the Internet and e-commerce has created a whole new set of problems concerning intellectual property rights. All these issues will be discussed in this chapter.

Chapter contents

Learning objectives

When you have completed this chapter you will be able to:

- examine the different forms of protection available for a firm's intellectual property;
- identify the limitations of the patent system;
- explain why other firms' patents can be a valuable resource;
- identify the link between brand name and trademark;
- identify when and where the areas of copyright and registered design may be useful; and
- explain how the patent system is supposed to balance the interests of the individual and society.

Intellectual property

The world of intellectual property changes at an alarming rate. The law, it seems, is always trying to keep up with technology changes that suddenly allow firms to operate in ways previously not considered. Illustration 5.1 shows how legal events over the past few years have fundamentally affected the activities of so-called grey marketers and the subsequent powers granted to the owners of a range of branded marks including famous lucrative names such as Levi's, Nike and Calvin Klein. The pronouncements from the European Court of Justice together with national court decisions have created a degree of confusion. The landmark Silhouette Case has proved immensely controversial with regard to the operation of trademark law throughout the European Union. The decision seems to prohibit the importation into the European Union of branded goods or services, unless such activity has been specifically consented to by the brand owner.

This chapter will explore this dynamic area of the law and illustrate why firms need to be aware of this increasingly important aspect of innovation.

Illustration 5.1

FT

Levi sings the blues over jeans in Tesco

Levi Strauss, the clothing company, will today tell the European Court of Justice that its jeans should not be sold in supermarkets because sales staff need special training to explain the different styles to customers. 'Customers need advice on what's on offer and the difference between loose and baggy, straight and slim', said Mark Elliott at Levi. 'We're not saying you need a university degree to sell jeans, but if a person is cutting bacon and filling shelves one minute, it's not possible for them to sell jeans as well.'

The company is bringing the case against Tesco, the UK retailer, which imported Levi's from outside the EU to sell at knock-down prices. The European Court will hear arguments from both companies today in an important case that could challenge rules on so-called grey-market imports of designer goods from outside the European Union. But a judgement is not expected for up to another year.

Tesco says Levi will not supply it so it buys from cheaper markets such as the US and eastern Europe. 'It's not rocket science to sell jeans . . . we don't think giving five minutes extra training than our staff get justifies an extra 20 pounds on the price and neither do our customers', said Simon Soffe, a Tesco spokesman.

'British customers are losing out . . . because the brands are trying to protect Fortress Europe and keep lower prices out', a Tesco statement said.

Levi says Tesco has never met the standard to become a licensed outlet, and lack of training is one of the main reasons. 'Staff have to explain how one blue is different from another blue. These things are important to jeans aficionados', Mr Elliott said.

Source: D. Hargreaves, 'Levi sings the blues over jeans', *Financial Times*, 16 January 2001. Reprinted with permission.

If you just happen to come up with a novel idea, the simplest and cheapest course of action is to do nothing about legal protection, just keep it a secret (as with the recipe for Coca-Cola). While this in theory may be true, in reality many chemists and most ingredients and fragrance firms would argue that science can now detect a droplet of blood in an entire swimming pool, and to suggest that science cannot analyse a bottle of cola and uncover its ingredients is stretching the bounds of reason. The keep-it-secret approach prevents anyone else seeing it or finding it. Indeed, the owner can take their intellectual property to their grave, safe in the knowledge that no one will inherit it. This approach is fine unless you are seeking some form of commercial exploitation and ultimately a financial reward, usually in the form of royalties.

One of the dangers, of course, with trying to keep your idea a secret is that someone else might develop a similar idea to yours and apply for legal protection and seek commercial exploitation. Independent discovery of ideas is not as surprising as one might first think. This is because research scientists working at the forefront of science and technology are often working towards the same goal. This was the case with Thomas Edison and Joseph Swan, who independently invented the light bulb simultaneously either side of the Atlantic. Indeed, they formed a company called Ediswan to manufacture light bulbs at the end of the nineteenth century.

Table 5.1 shows an overview of the different forms of intellectual property and rights available for different areas of creativity.

Table 5.1 An overview of the main types of intellectual property

	Type of intellectual property	Key features of this type of protection
1	Patents	Offers a 20-year monopoly
2	Copyright	Provides exclusive rights to creative individuals for the protection of their literary or artistic productions
3	Registered designs	As protected by registration, is for the outward appearance of an article and provides exclusive rights for up to 15 years
4	Registered trademarks	Is a distinctive name, mark or symbol that is identifed with a company's products

The issues of intellectual property are continually with us and touch us probably more than we realise. Most students will have already confronted the issue of intellectual property, either with recording pre-recorded music or copying computer software. The author is always the owner of his or her work and the writing of an academic paper entitles the student to claim the copyright on that essay. Indeed, the submission of an academic paper to a scientific journal for publication requires the author to sign a licence for the publisher to use the intellectual property. Patenting is probably the most commonly recognised form of intellectual property, but it is only one of several ways to protect creative efforts. Registered designs, trademarks and copyright are other forms of intellectual property. These will be addressed in the following sections.

Pause for thought   ?

Given the impressive advances made in science over the past 50 years, especially in the area of detecting substances and ingredients, scientists now claim to be able to detect one drop of blood in a swimming pool full of water. Does anyone still believe that the ingredients in Coca-Cola, for example, are secret and unknown?

Trade secrets

There are certain business activities and processes that are not patented, copyrighted or trademarked. Many businesses regard these as trade secrets. It could be special ways of working, price costings or business strategies. The most famous example is the recipe for Coca-Cola, which is not patented. This is because Coca-Cola did not want to reveal the recipe to their competitors. Unfortunately, the law covering intellectual property is less clear about the term *trade secret*. Indeed, Bainbridge (1996) argues there is no satisfactory legal definition of the term.

An introduction to patents

Illustration 5.2 dramatically illustrates the importance of patents to the business world. A patent is a contract between an individual or organisation and the state. The rationale behind the granting of a temporary monopoly by the state is to encourage creativity and innovation within an economy. By the individual or organisation disclosing in the patent sufficient detail of the invention, the state will confer the legal right to stop others benefiting from the invention (Derwent, 1998). The state, however, has no obligation to prevent others benefiting from it. This is the responsibility of the

---

 Illustration 5.2

FT

Pfizer sues rivals to protect Viagra patent

Pfizer, the world's largest drugs group, filed a patent infringement suit on Tuesday against rivals Bayer AG, GlaxoSmithKline and an Eli Lilly joint venture, seeking to protect its blockbuster male impotence drug Viagra from competition in the US.

The three defendants are on the verge of launching two rival treatments for male erectile dysfunction in the US that are not prohibited by Viagra's main patent, valid until 2011.

The company said US patent authorities on Tuesday granted it a broad patent until 2019 to use oral PDE-5 inhibitors – drugs that act on the body's PDE-5 enzyme and thus treat impotence. This patent does not cover Viagra's active ingredient, sildenafil.

Pfizer subsequently filed a lawsuit in federal court in Delaware claiming the three companies' potential products infringed its patent. The rival products threaten to cut into pricing power and revenues of one of the best known drugs in the world with about $1.7bn sales this year.

The lawsuit to preserve its 100 per cent market share in the US comes one day after President George W. Bush announced a new regulatory rule to speed generic competition.

The proposal seeks to keep brand-name drug groups from using extraneous patents to delay inexpensive generic rivals. Pfizer's Viagra patent case, however, does not involve generics.

The UK High Court struck down a similar broad patent Pfizer is invoking in the US enabling Viagra competition overseas.

The court ruled in November 2000 that scientific literature had widely reported the effects of inhibiting PDE-5 on male impotence before Pfizer filed for the patent in 1993.

'Pfizer's goal is to delay competitive entry for Viagra as long as possible, and if the patent were actually to stick, that would simply be gravy for Pfizer in our opinion', said Anthony Butler, analyst at Lehman Brothers.

Source: C. Bowe, 'Pfizer sues rivals to protect Viagra patent', www.FT.com; 23 October 2002. Reprinted with permission.

individual or organisation who is granted the patent. And herein lies a major criticism of the patent system. The costs of defending a patent against infringement can be high indeed. This point is explored later.

The UK Patent Office was set up in 1852 to act as the United Kingdom's sole office for the granting of patents of invention. The origins of patent system stretch back a further 400 years. The word patent comes from the practice of monarchs in the Middle Ages (500–1500) conferring rights and privileges by means of 'open letters', that is, documents on which the royal seal was not broken when they were opened. This is distinct from 'closed letters' that were not intended for public view. Open letters were intended for display and inspection by any interested party. The language of government in medieval England was Latin and the Latin for open letters is 'litterae patentes'. As English slowly took over from Latin as the official language the documents became known as 'letters patent' and later just 'patents'.

- *Monopoly for 20 years.* Patents are granted to individuals and organisations who can lay claim to a new product or manufacturing process, or to an improvement of an existing product or process, which was not previously known. The granting of a patent gives the 'patentee' a monopoly to make, use, or sell the invention for a fixed period of time, which in Europe and the United States is 20 years from the date the patent application was first filed. In return for this monopoly, the patentee pays a fee to cover the costs of processing the patent, and, more importantly, publicly discloses details of the invention.

- *Annual fees required.* The idea must be new and not an obvious extension of what is already known. A patent lasts up to 20 years in the United Kingdom and Europe, but heavy annual renewal fees have to be paid to keep it in force.

- *Patent agents.* The role of a patent agent combines scientific or engineering knowledge with legal knowledge and expertise and it is a specialised field of work. Many large companies have in-house patent agents who prepare patents for the company's scientists. They may also search patent databases around the world on behalf of the company's scientists.

The earliest known English patent of invention was granted to John of Utynam in 1449. The patent gave Mr Utynam a 20-year monopoly for a method of making stained glass that had not previously been known in England. For a patent to benefit from legal protection it must meet strict criteria:

- novelty;
- inventive step; and
- industrial application.

Novelty

The Patent Act 1977, section 2(1), stipulates that 'an invention shall be taken to be new if it does not form part of the 'state of the art'. A state of the art is defined as all matter, in other words, publications, written or oral or even anticipation (*Windsurfing International* v. *Tabar Marine*, Court of Appeal, 1985), will render a patent invalid.

Inventive step

Section 3 of the Patent Act status that 'an invention shall be taken to involve an inventive step if it is not obvious to a person skilled in the art'.

Industrial applications

Under the Patent Act an invention shall be taken to be capable of industrial application if it can be a machine, product or process. Penicillin was a discovery which was not patentable but the process of isolating and storing penicillin clearly had industrial applications and thus was patentable.

Pause for thought

If states and governments in particular are determined to outlaw monopolistic practices in industry and commerce, why do they offer a 20-year monopoly for a patent?

Exclusions from patents

Discoveries (as opposed to inventions), scientific theory and mathematical processes are not patentable under the 1988 Patent Act. Similarly, literary artistic works and designs are covered by other forms of intellectual property such as trademarks, copyright and registered designs.

The patenting of life

The rapid scientific developments in the field of biology, medical science and biotechnology has fuelled intense debates about the morality of patenting life forms. Until very recently there was a significant difference between the US patent system, which enabled the granting of patents on certain life forms, and the European patent system, which did not. Essentially the US system adopted a far more liberal approach to the patenting of life. This difference was illustrated in the 'Harvard oncomouse' case (Patent No. 4,581,847). The Harvard Medical School had its request for a European patent refused because the mouse was a natural living life form and hence, unpatentable. This European approach had serious implications for the European biotechnology industry. In particular, because the R&D efforts of the biotechnology industry could not be protected, there was a danger that capital in the form of intellectual and financial could flow from Europe to the United States, where protection was available. The other side of the argument is equally compelling; the granting to a company of a patent on certain genes may restrict other companies' ability to work with those genes. On 27 November 1997 the European Union agreed to Directive 95/0350(COD) and COM(97)446 which permits the granting of patents on certain life forms. This had a particular significance in the area of gene technology.

The subject of cloning a new life form from existing cells stirs the emotions of many. When Dolly, the first large mammal to be created from cells taken from other sheep, was announced it generated enormous controversy and publicity. This was especially so for the group of scientists from the Roslin Institute, a publicly funded institute and PPL Therapeutics, a biotechnology company that developed Dolly. The debate about the ethics of the science continues and related to this is the intellectual property of the gene technology involved (*see Financial Times*, 1997 and Rowan, 1997) for a full discussion of this debate).

Human genetic patenting

Five years ago this industry barely existed: today it is worth £30 billion. Across Europe there are now 800 small and medium-sized enterprises in the business of making something new from life itself. Public institutions and private enterprises have filed claims on more than 127,000 human genes or partial human gene sequences. All are seeking wealth from DNA. These organisations are searching for tests, treatments, cures and vaccines for thousands of diseases; they are looking for new ways of delivering and new ways of making medicines.

There are many, of course, who take a more pessimistic view of this new science and argue that scientists should not play with nature and even that it is a threat to the future of mankind. A brighter view is that science is on the edge of a new frontier and the future will be one where human suffering is relieved and where incurable illnesses are treated. Whichever view you take, it is worthy of note that many of these firms are small start-ups headed by one or two scientists who have staked the future of the firm on several patent applications. Indeed, the firms' capitalisation is often based on the future predictions of patent applications. This is a very precarious situation for investors. This raises the issue of whether the patent developed all those years ago is suitable for this type of industry or the twenty-first century in general.

In 1998 the European Union harmonised patent law to give European scientists and investors the chance to make one application for one big market, rather than separate applications to member states. It also gave European entrepreneurs the right to patent genes or life. In the past few years the biotechnology firms have been making numerous patent applications for genes or partial human gene sequences. This, of course, leads to the argument that human genes are being turned into intellectual property and licensed to the highest bidders. The key question is, will this property then be made widely available to help the hungry, the sick and the desperate? Or will a few rich firms profit from many years of publicly funded science and exploit the poor and vulnerable?

These are clearly difficult ethical questions that you may wish to debate among yourselves, but at the heart of this is patent law. This is illustrated in the case study at the end of this chapter. The purpose of any patent system is to strike a balance between the interests of the inventor and the wider public. At present many believe that US patent law is too heavily biased towards the needs of inventors and investors and does not take into account the poor and developing countries of the world.

The configuration of a patent

For a patent to be granted its contents need to be made public so that others can be given the opportunity to challenge the granting of a monopoly. There is a formal registering and indexing system to enable patents to be easily accessed by the public. For this reason patents follow a very formal specification. Details concerning country of origin, filing date, personal details of applicant, etc., are accompanied by an internationally agreed numbering system for easy identification (*see* the Appendix). The two most important sources of information relating to a patent are the *patent specification* and the *patent abstract*. Both of these are classified and indexed in various ways to facilitate search.

The specification is a detailed description of the invention and must disclose enough information to enable someone else to repeat the invention. This part of the document needs to be precise and methodical. It will also usually contain references to other scientific papers. The remainder of the specification will contain claims. These are to define the breadth and scope of the invention. A patent agent will try to write the broadest claim possible as a narrow claim can restrict the patent's application and competitors will try to argue that, for example, a particular invention applies only to one particular method. Indeed, competitors will scrutinise these claims to test their validity.

The patent abstract is a short statement printed on the front page of the patent specification which identifies the technical subject of the invention and the advance that it represents (*see* the Appendix). Abstracts are usually accompanied by a drawing. In addition these abstracts are published in weekly information booklets.

It is now possible to obtain a patent from the European Patent Office for the whole of Europe, and this can be granted in a particular country or several countries. The concept of a world patent, however, is a distant realisation. The next section explores some of the major differences between the two dominant world patent systems.

Patent harmonisation: first to file and first to invent

Most industrialised countries offer some form of patent protection to companies operating within their borders. However, while some countries have adequate protection others do not. Moreover, different countries are members of different conventions and some adopt different systems. The European and the US patent systems have many similarities, for example a monopoly is granted for 20 years under both systems. There is, however, one key difference. In the United States the patent goes to the researcher who can prove they were the first to invent it, not – as in Europe – to the first to file for a patent.

The implications of this are many and varied but there are two key points that managers need to consider.

1 In Europe, a patent is invalid if the inventor has published the novel information before filing for patent protection. In the United States there are some provisions which allow inventors to talk first and file later.

2 In Europe, patent applications are published while pending. This allows the chance to see what monopoly an inventor is claiming and object to the Patent Office if there are grounds to contest validity. In the United States the situation is quite different – applications remain secret until granted.

The issue of patent harmonisation has a long history. The Paris Convention for the Protection of Industrial Property was signed in 1883, and since then it has received many amendments. At present its membership includes 114 countries. European countries have a degree of patent harmonisation provided by the European Patent Convention (EPC) administered by the European Patent Office.

The sheer size of the US market and its dominance in many technology-intensive industries means that this difference in the patent systems has received, and continues to receive, a great deal of attention from various industry and government departments in Europe and the United States.

Some famous patent cases

- *1880: Ediswan.* It is rare that identical inventions should come about at the same time. But that is what happened with the electric light bulb, which was patented almost simultaneously on either side of the Atlantic by Thomas Edison and Joseph Swan. To avoid patent litigation the two business interests combined in England to produce lamps under the name of 'Ediswan', which is still registered as a trademark.

- *1930: Whittle's jet engine.* While Frank Whittle was granted a patent for his jet engine, his employers, the RAF, were unable to get the invention to work efficiently and could not manufacture it on an industrial scale. It was left to the US firms of McDonnell Douglas and Pratt and Witney to exploit the commercial benefits from the patents.

- *1943: Penicillin.* Alexander Fleming discovered penicillin in 1928 and 13 years later, on 14 October 1941, researchers at Oxford University filed Patent No. 13242. The complete specification was accepted on 16 April 1943 (*see* Illustration 5.3).

Illustration 5.3

BTG

Penicillin was discovered in a London hospital by Alexander Fleming in 1928. It was to take another 12 years (1940) before a team working at Oxford University discovered a method of isolating and storing the drug. However, as a result of the Second World War, which drained Britain of much of its financial resources, Britain did not have the capability to develop large-scale fermentation of the bacteria. Help was sought from the United States and the success of the technology is well known.

The UK government was concerned that it gave away valuable technology. By way of a response to this, following the end of the Second World War, it established the National Research Development Corporation (NRDC) in 1948 to protect the intellectual property rights of inventors' efforts which had been funded by the public sector. For example, this included research conducted in universities, hospitals and national laboratories.

From its very beginning the NRDC soon began generating funds. Oxford University developed a second generation of antibiotics called cephalosporins. They were patented world-wide and the royalties secured the financial base of the NRDC for many years.

The NRDC changed its name to the British Technology Group (BTG) and has continued to be successful in arranging and defending patents for many university professors. In 1994 BTG became an independent public limited company.

Historically BTG were involved only in UK intellectual property issues, but their activities have expanded. It was recently involved in litigation with the US Pentagon for patent infringement on the Hovercraft as well as another case concerning Johnson and Johnson, the US healthcare group. BTG were so successful in this case that Johnson and Johnson asked BTG to manage a portfolio of nearly 100 inventions to try to generate royalties.

Patents in practice

There are many industrialists and small business managers who have little faith in the patent system. They believe, usually as a result of first-hand experience, that the patent system is designed primarily for those large multinational corporations who have the finances to defend and protect any patents granted to them. The problem is that applying and securing a patent is only the beginning of what is usually an expensive journey. For example, every time you suspect a company may be infringing your patent you will have to incur legal expenses to protect your intellectual property. Moreover, there are some examples of large corporations spending many years and millions of dollars in legal fees battling in the courts over alleged patent infringement. One of the most well-known cases was *Apple Computer Inc.* v. *Microsoft*, where Apple alleged that Microsoft had copied its Windows operating system. The case lasted for many years and cost each company many millions of dollars in legal fees.

Many smaller firms view the patent system with dread and fear. Indeed, only 10 per cent of the UK patents are granted to small firms. Yet small firms represent 99 per cent of companies (*The Guardian*, 1998).

Illustration 5.4

Effective patents are dependent on the depth of your pocket!

James Dyson is now a household name across much of Europe and is responsible for designing and developing the bagless vacuum cleaner. He is, however, critical of the patent system. He has personal experience of the system and argues that it is prohibitively expensive. He explains that when he was filing for patents for his vacuum cleaner he did not have enough money to patent all the features of his product. Also, the costs of taking patents out in several countries is very expensive. Many of the costs involved are hidden. For example, there are translation fees to pay for different countries and languages. According to Mr Dyson the cost of taking out a patent in five countries is between £50,000 and £60,000. In addition, there are renewal fees to pay.

Source: N. Graham (1998) 'Inventor cleans up with profits', *Sunday Times*, 1 March, 4, 16.

In theory it sounds straightforward – £225 to apply for a UK patent. In practice, however, companies should be considering £1,000–£1,500 to obtain a UK patent. Furthermore, protection in a reasonable number of countries is likely to cost more like £10,000. Illustration 5.4 highlights many of the limitations of the patent system.

In some industries it seems the rules of intellectual property may need to change. Some have argued that reforming the intellectual property law may help to stimulate more innovation and that a growing part of the economy (e.g. services, information technology) is only weakly protected under current intellectual property law. One possible way to encourage innovation is by extending coverage to these products and broadening legal protection to cover new product ideas for a short period. Small companies and individual entrepreneurs would benefit most from this broader but shorter protection (Alpert, 1993).

Expiry of a patent and patent extensions

There is much written on the subject of patent application and the benefits to be gained from such a 20-year monopoly. There is, however, much less written about the subject of the effects of patent expiry. In other words, what happens when the patent protecting your product expires? A glance at the pharmaceutical industry reveals an interesting picture. Illustration 5.5 shows the reality for a firm when its patent expires.

For any firm operating in this science-intensive industry, the whole process of developing a product is based around the ability to protect the eventual product through the use of patents. Without the prospect of a 20-year monopoly to exploit many years of research and millions of dollars of investment, companies would be less inclined

Illustration 5.5

FDA gives approval for generic versions of Eli Lilly's Prozac

Washington – Federal regulators approved several generic versions of Eli Lilly & Co's popular antidepressant Prozac, ushering in one of the biggest generic-drug launches in history. The Food and Drug Administration approved Barr Laboratories Inc., of Pomona, NY, to market a 20-milligram capsule, the most common dosage. The FDA also approved an oral solution made by Teva Pharmaceutical Industries Ltd., of Jerusalem; a 40 mg capsule from Dr. Reddy's Laboratories Ltd, of Hyderabad, India; a 10 mg capsule from Geneva Pharmaceutical, of Broomfield, CO; and 10 mg and 20 mg tablets from Pharmaceutical Resources Inc., of Spring Valley, NJ Barr started shipping its version yesterday, when Prozac's patent and market protection expired. Because it was the first to file for approval with the FDA, Barr will be the only company allowed to offer the 20 mg for 180 days. Afterwards, others with FDA approval can market the drug in that form. Barr said its version will be widely available by next week, and as early as today for those who placed orders ahead

of time. Barr wouldn't say precisely how much its version would cost, but said it would be between 25% and 40% less than Prozac, which runs about $2.50 a day. Two other forms of Prozac – a weekly pill and one for women – remain under patent protection. Sales of the blockbuster drug, known generically as fluoxetine hydrochloride, totaled about $2.5 billion last year, according to Lilly, of Indianapolis. 'Millions of American consumers will immediately begin to benefit from savings, and millions more who might otherwise have had to forgo this medicine because of its high cost will have access to a more affordable version of Prozac', said Barr Chairman Bruce L. Downey. The generic approvals come one year after Barr won a court victory that cut nearly three years off Lilly's Prozac patent. At the time, Lilly predicted a significant drop in sales when generic versions hit the market.

Source: Jill Carroll, *Wall Street Journal*, 3 August 2001. Copyright © 2001 Dow Jones & Company, Inc.

to engage in new product development. (The case study at the end of Chapter 9 explores new product development in the pharmaceutical industry.) On expiry of a patent competitors are able to use the technology, which hitherto had been protected, to develop their own product. Such products are referred to as generic drugs (a generic sold on its chemical composition). When a generic drug is launched, the effect on a branded drug which has just come off-patent can be considerable. For example, Takeda is expecting a drop in sales of 90% when its $4-billion anti-ulcer treatment drug Prevacid comes off patent in 2009 (*see* Figure 5.1). Remarkably, market share falls of 85 per cent are typical (*Chemistry & Industry News*, 1995; Natamoto and Pilling, 2004). A generic drug is cheap to produce as no extensive research and development costs are incurred and pharmaceutical drugs are relatively easy to copy. It is in effect a chemical process. The principal forms of defence available to manufacturers are brand development and further research.

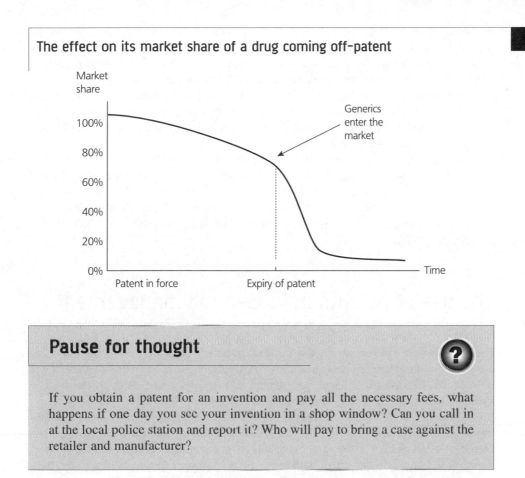

Figure 5.1

The effect on its market share of a drug coming off-patent

Pause for thought

If you obtain a patent for an invention and pay all the necessary fees, what happens if one day you see your invention in a shop window? Can you call in at the local police station and report it? Who will pay to bring a case against the retailer and manufacturer?

Developing a brand requires long-term development. Pharmaceutical companies with a product protected by patents will usually have between 10 and 20 years to develop a brand and brand loyalty, the aim being that even when the product goes off-patent customers will continue to ask for the branded drug as opposed to the generic drug. In practice, companies adopt a combination of aggressive marketing to develop the brand, and technical research on existing drugs to improve the product still further and file for additional patents to protect the new and improved versions of the product.

Patent extensions

Patent extensions are known in Europe as Supplementary Protection Certificates usually abbreviated to 'SPC'. They were introduced in Europe in the mid-1990s to compensate patent owners for regulatory delays in approving their pharmaceuticals and agrochemicals. The approvals sometimes took so long that the patent had reached the end of its 20-year life, thus opening the invention to all comers, before the inventor had had much chance to commercialise it.

The SPC was designed to provide a level playing field for all pharmaceuticals/agrochemicals patent owners who had suffered regulatory delay exceeding five years, to restore to them an effective 15-year term of protection. The SPC takes effect at the instant of patent expiry, and then lasts for the length of time by which regulatory approval exceeded five years. Each SPC therefore has its own fixed duration, but, to protect the public, the maximum duration is five years' effect.

The United States achieves a similar result by a different route, namely by directly extending the lifetime of those individual patents where the applicant can show regulatory delay in getting the product onto the market. Japan has been considering legislation to achieve broadly similar results (BTG, 2004).

Every month of patent extension can mean hundreds of millions of dollars in additional revenues for blockbuster products. A number of companies, including Bristol Myers Squibb, AstraZeneca, GlaxoSmithKline and Schering-Plough have been accused of using such tactics to boost profits. However, a Federal Trade Commission report found only eight instances of suspect patent extensions between 1992 and 2000 (Bowe and Griffith, 2002).

The use of patents in innovation management

Patent offices for each country house millions of patents. In the United Kingdom there are over 2 million British patents and all this information is available to the public. Each publication, because of the legal requirement that details of patents be disclosed, is a valuable source of technological knowledge. Indeed, the information provision activities of the Patent Office have increased in their function. For example, scientists working in a particular field will often search patent databases to see how the problems they face have been tackled in the past. They will also use previous patents to identify how their current area of work fits in with those areas of science and technology that have been developed and patented previously. Very often patents can provide a valuable source of inspiration.

In addition, many firms also use the patent publication register to find out what their competitors are doing. For example, a search of the world-wide patent databases may reveal that your major competitor has filed a series of patents in an area of technology that you had not considered previously. Armed with prior knowledge of the industry and the technology it may be possible to uncover the research direction in which your competitor is heading, or even the type of product line that it is considering developing. All this industrial intelligence can help research teams and companies to develop and modify their own strategy or to pursue a different approach to a problem.

Do patents hinder or encourage innovation?

According to Professor William Haseltine, the rush for patents did not hamper AIDS research. In the 1980s he worked for a team that deciphered the DNA of the HIV virus, worked out the sequences of its genes, and discovered some of the proteins those genes made. His name is on more than a dozen patents on the AIDS virus, but the patents are held by the cancer institute he then worked for at the Harvard Medical School. He makes a very strong case in favour of the patent system for fostering innovation. Indeed, he thinks the patents speeded up the assault on the virus itself.

> *I would guess there may be 1000 patents filed by now (for HIV tools), each one building on the other. You would be very hard pressed to make the case that a patent on the virus, a patent on the genome sequence, a patent on individual sequences, is in any way inhibiting rather than stimulating of productive research, both in academia and in companies. I can think of no case in which a patent has ever inhibited an academic scientist.*

(Professor W Haseltine, *The Guardian*, 2000)

Trademarks

Trademarks have particular importance to the world of business. For many companies, especially in the less technology-intensive industries where the use of patents is limited, trademarks offer one of the few methods of differentiating a company's products. The example of Coca-Cola is a case in point. Trademarks are closely associated with business image, goodwill and reputation. Indeed, many trademarks have become synonymous with particular products: Mars and chocolate confectionery, Hoover and vacuum cleaners and Nestlé and coffee. The public rely on many trademarks as indicating quality, value for money and origin of goods. Significant changes have been made to trademark law in the United Kingdom. The Trade Marks Act (1994) replaced the Trade Marks Act (1938), which was widely recognised as being out of touch with business practices today. The United Kingdom now complies with the EC directive on the approximation of the laws of member states relating to trademarks and ratified the Madrid Convention for the international registration of trademarks. The law relating to trademarks is complex indeed. For example, what is a trademark? Bainbridge (1996) offers a comprehensive review of law surrounding intellectual property. The following section offers a brief introduction to some of the key considerations for product and business managers.

The Trade Marks Act (1994, section 1(1)) defines a trademark as

> *being any sign capable of being represented graphically which is capable of distinguishing goods or services of one undertaking from those of other undertakings.*

This can include, for example, Apple Computers, the Apple logo and Macintosh all of which are registered trademarks. Some of the first trademarks were used by gold- and silversmiths to mark their own work. The first registered trademark, No. 1, was issued to Bass in 1890 for their red triangle mark for pale ale. Illustration 5.6 on the Mr Men offers an example of the effective and successful use of trademarks.

There are certain restrictions and principles with the use of trademarks. In particular, a trademark should:

- satisfy the requirements of section 1(1);
- be distinctive;
- not be deceptive; and
- not cause confusion with previous trademarks.

Should satisfy the requirements of section 1(1)

The much wider definition of a trademark offered by the 1994 Act opened the possibility of all sorts of marks that would not have previously been registrable. Sounds, smells and containers could now be registered. A number of perfume manufacturers have applied to register their perfumes as trademarks. Coca-Cola and Unilever have applied to register their containers for Coca-Cola and Domestos respectively.

 Illustration 5.6

Mr Hargreaves and the Mr Men

Many of you have probably seen this fellow before or one of his companions. If not, he is Mr Happy and is part of the Mr Men collection. Since 1973 Mr Happy and colleagues have appeared on everything from yoghurt pots to a Japanese commercial for a gas company. That is not including the TV series or the millions of books sold. All the characters are registered trademarks. After all, if you want to stop someone stealing your ideas it is an advantage if you can prove that you own them. That's why Roger Hargreaves registered his drawings with the UK Patent Office. To date, Mr Hargreaves has received over £1.5 million ($2 million).

Sources: Patent Office, *Financial Times* (1988).

Distinctive

A trademark should be distinctive in itself. In general this means that it should not describe in any way the product or service to which it relates. Usually words that are considered generic or descriptive are not trademarked. In addition, it should not use non-distinctive expressions which other traders might reasonably wish to use in the course of a trade. For example, to attempt to register the word beef as a trademark for a range of foods would not be possible since other traders would reasonably want to use the word in the course of their trade. It would, however, be acceptable to use beef in association with a range of clothing because this would be considered distinctive. Laudatory terms are not allowed, for example the word heavenly for a range of cosmetics would not be possible since it is a laudatory term. The law, however, concerning this aspect of distinctiveness looks set to change following a recent ruling in the European courts. Illustration 5.7 explains why famous people may at last be able to trademark their own surname.

Non-deceptive

A trademark should also not attempt to deceive the customer. For example, to attempt to register Orlwoola, as happened in 1900, as an artificial fibre would not be possible, since the very word could persuade people to believe the material was made of wool.

Illustration 5.7

Trademark view likely to allow sports stars to play own brand of name games

Sports personalities, entertainers and other public figures could find it easier to assert monopoly rights over their surnames after a European Court of Justice opinion, said lawyers yesterday.

Applications to register surnames have become increasingly frequent, particularly in sport where personalities have either been keen to launch own-brand merchandise or – as in the case of footballer David Beckham – prevent others from exploiting their fame.

Last year, there was even an unsuccessful attempt to trademark the name Jesus to sell jeans. Other names to have raised intellectual property issues in the past have included Elvis Presley and Paul McCartney.

But the UK Trade Marks Registry has consistently refused to 'register' ordinary surnames if there is a large number of operators in the market for the goods or services designated.

Its guidelines recommend that the 'commonness' of the surname should be a factor in deciding whether a trademark can be approved, with telephone directories providing a yardstick. Any name that appears more than 200 times in the London directory is usually classed as common, for example.

But now, in the context of a British case referred to the Luxembourg court for guidance, Dámaso Ruiz-Jarabo Colomer, an advocate-general, says there is no reason to treat surnames differently from any other trademark.

'There is nothing in the [trade mark] directive to justify treating surnames differently', he said in an opinion released last week.

The legal opinion came in the case of Nichols, a British company that wanted to trademark the surname for automatic vending machines, food and drinks.

The UK registry granted the vending machine application, but refused it for the other two categories.

It said the surname was common and that, in a market with large number of operators, it would be difficult for consumers to identify the commercial origin of the products from a common surname.

Advocate-generals' opinions are not binding on the ECJ but they are followed in most cases. If that happens here, lawyers say that trademark applicants are likely to benefit.

'I think it's a very sensible decision, and could result in change to UK Trade Mark Registry procedure', said Geoff Steward, partner at the Macfarlanes law firm.

Mr Steward pointed to the case of Wayne Rooney, the footballer, who is believed to have been applying to trademark his surname in respect of football merchandise, clothing and the like. 'This decision means he will probably succeed', he said.

Source: N. Tait, 'Trademark view likely to allow sports stars to play own brand of name games', *Financial Times*, 19 January 2004.

Not confusing

Finally, a trade or service mark will not be registered if it could be confused with the trademark of a similar product that has already been registered. For example, 'Velva-Glo' was refused as a trademark for paints because it was judged to be too near the word 'Vel-Glo' which was already registered.

Brand names

Increasingly the link between the brand name and the trademark is becoming closer and stronger. The literature tends to separate the two, with brands remaining in the sphere of marketing and trademarks within the sphere of law. In terms of a property right that is exploitable, however, brand names and trademarks are cousins. They both serve to facilitate identity and origin. That origin in turn indicates a certain level of quality, as reflected in the goods. Indeed, it is worthy of note that many brands have been registered as trademarks.

Like other capital assets owned by a firm such as manufacturing equipment or land, a brand can also be considered an asset, and a valuable one at that. 'Brand equity' is the term used to describe the value of a brand name. Accountants and marketers differ in their definitions and there have been a variety of approaches to define the term (Feldwick, 1996):

- the total value of a brand as a separable asset – when it is sold, or included on a balance sheet;
- a measure of the strength of consumers' attachment to a brand; and
- a description of the associations and beliefs the consumer has about the brand.

Brand equity creates value for both customers and the firm. The customers can clearly use brand names as simplifying heuristics for processing large amounts of information. The brand can also give customers confidence in the purchasing situation. Firms benefit enormously from having strong brand names. Investment in a brand name can be leveraged through brand extensions and increased distributions. High brand equity often allows higher prices to be charged; hence it is a significant competitive advantage.

A firm may decide to purchase a brand from another company rather than to develop a brand itself. Indeed, this may be less expensive and less risky. IKEA, for example, purchased the Habitat brand. Habitat had a strong UK presence in the furniture and household products market and enabled IKEA to increase its presence in the UK furniture market.

Using brands to protect intellectual property

Product managers, product designers and R&D managers all recognise that despite their best efforts sometimes the success of a product can be dependent on the brand. In the cigarette market, for example over 70 per cent of consumers are loyal to a particular brand (Badenhausen, 1995), and this makes entry to this market very difficult. Brands help buyers to identify specific products that they like and reduce the time required to purchase the product. Without brands, product selection would be random and maybe more rational, based on price, value and content of the product. It would certainly force consumers to select more carefully. If all the products in a store had the same plain white packaging but information was made available on ingredients, contents and details of the manufacturing process, consumers would spend an enormous amount of time shopping. Brands symbolise a certain quality level and this can be transferred to other product items. For example, Unilever extended the Timotei shampoo name to skin-care products. This clearly enabled the company to develop a new range of products and use the benefits of brand recognition of Timotei.

An area of branding that is growing rapidly is that of the licensing of trademarks. Using a licensing agreement, a company may permit approved manufacturers to use its trademark on other products for a licensing fee. Royalties may be as low as 2 per cent of wholesale revenues or as high as 10 per cent. The licensee is responsible for all manufacturing and marketing and bears the cost if the product fails. Today the licensing business is a huge growth industry. The All England Tennis and Croquet Club license their brand to a small group of companies each year. During the summer those companies use the association with Wimbledon to promote their products. Products such as Robinson's soft drinks, Wedgwood pottery, Slazenger sports goods and Coca-Cola have all signed licence agreements with the All England Club. For an organisation like the All England Club the advantages are obvious: increased revenue and, to a lesser extent, increased promotion of the tournament. To other firms like JCB, Jaguar Cars and Harley-Davidson, all of whom license their trademarks to clothing manufacturers, it clearly provides increased revenues, but also raises opportunities for diversification. The major disadvantages are a lack of control over the products, which could harm the perception and image of the brand. The All England Club, for example, have numerous committee meetings to consider very carefully the type of organisation and product that will bear its trademark.

Exploiting new opportunities

Product and brand managers must continually be vigilant about changes in the competitive market. This will help to realise new development opportunities for the brand. Some companies have developed reputations for exploiting the latest technology developments; indeed some of these firms are responsible for the breakthroughs. The following list of examples illustrates how pioneering firms have exploited opportunities and developed their brands:

- *New technology*. Sony and Rank Xerox are examples of firms that over the past 20 years have continually exploited new technology.

- *New positioning*. First Direct and The Body Shop uncovered and developed unique positions for themselves in the market. First Direct was one of the pioneers of telephone banking and continued to build on this position. Similarly The Body Shop was a pioneer of 'green' cosmetics and has exploited this position.

- *New distribution*. Direct Line and Argos Stores developed new channels of distribution for their products and services. Direct Line exploited the concept of telephone insurance and later expanded into other financial services, and Argos Stores developed the concept of warehouse-catalogue shopping.

Frequently, rival firms will develop generic products and services to rival the brand. Nowhere is this more apparent than in the pharmaceutical industry, as the previous section illustrated. One of the key issues for brand managers is whether the brand can sustain its strong market position in the face of such competition. It is possible to defend a brand through effective marketing communications, but this is rarely enough. Usually the brand will need to innovate in one or more of the areas listed above. Some brands have failed to innovate and have then struggled in the face of fierce competition. One example is the Kelloggs brand. Over the past ten years Kelloggs has seen its market share of the cereal market gradually decline in the face of strong competition from store brands. Critics of Kelloggs argue that its brand managers have failed to innovate and develop the brand.

Pause for thought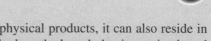

Intellectual property does not just lie in physical products, it can also reside in services and ways of operating. What role does the brand play in service-based industries such as airlines?

Brands, trademarks and the Internet

Nowhere is the subject of trademarks and brands more closely intertwined than on the Internet. Individuals and firms are linked up and identified through so-called 'domain names'. These are essentially an address, comprising four numbers, such as 131.22.45.06. The numbers indicate the network (131), an Internet protocol address (22 and 45) and a local address (06). Numeric addresses, however, are difficult to remember. Internet authorities assigned and designated an alphanumeric designation and mnemonic which affords the consumer user-friendly information with regard to identify and source – the 'domain name' (for example, microsoft.com and ports.ac.uk).

It can be seen then that domain names act as Internet addresses. They serve as the electronic or automated equivalent to a telephone directory, allowing Web browsers to look up their intended hits directly or via a search engine such as Alta Vista. One may argue at this point that domain names act as electronic brand names. Moreover, the characteristics of a domain name and a trademark are considerable. A recent US judgement has pronounced that domain names are protectable property rights in much the same way as a trademark (www.webmarketingtoday.com).

Duration of registration, infringement and passing off

Under the new Trade Marks Act (1994) the registration of a trademark is for a period of 10 years from the date of registration which may be renewed indefinitely for further 10-year periods. Once accepted and registered, trademarks are considered to be an item of personal property.

The fact that a trademark is registered does not mean that one cannot use the mark at all. In the case of *Bravado Merchandising Services Ltd* v. *Mainstream Publishing Ltd*, the respondent published a book about the pop group Wet Wet Wet under the title *A Sweet Little Mystery – Wet Wet Wet – The Inside Story*. Wet Wet Wet was a registered trademark and the proprietor brought an injunction against the use of the name. The court decided that the trademark had not been infringed because the respondent was using the mark as an indication of the main characteristic of the artefact which, in this instance, was a book about the pop group (Bainbridge, 1996).

Where a business uses a trademark that is similar to another or takes unfair advantage of or is detrimental to another trademark, infringement will have occurred. This introduces the area of passing off and is the common law form of trademark law. Passing off concerns the areas of goodwill and reputation of the trademark. In *Consorzio de Prosciutto di Parma* v. *Marks & Spencer plc* (1991) Lord Justice Norse identified the ingredients of a passing off action as being composed of:

- the goodwill of the plaintiff;
- the misrepresentation made by the defendant; and
- consequential damage.

Illustration 5.8 highlights many of the concerns expressed by businesses in what they see as unfair competition. This area of law has many similarities to trademark law and is considered to be a useful supplement to it (*see* Bainbridge, 1996 for a full explanation of the law of passing off).

Illustration 5.8

FT

On the prowl for copycats

The battle to stop retailers from selling products identical to famous brands

Consumer goods manufacturers in the UK are fighting to stop retailers selling own-label products that look almost identical to well-known brands.

A dozen of the biggest names have formed the British Producers and Brand Owners Group to press for a change in the law – which they say lags far behind those in other European countries when it comes to protecting their products from 'copycat' competition by retailers.

Members include Allied Lyons, Gillette, Guinness, Grand Met, ICI Paints, Kellogg, Mars, Nestlé, Procter & Gamble, SmithKline Beecham and Unilever.

They say own-label products are being designed deliberately to resemble manufacturers' brands – using similar bottles or packs, colours and typography, even similar names. But while manufacturers spend millions of pounds on research, development and marketing of brands, it costs retailers very little to copy them.

The issue, says Michael Mackenzie, director-general of the Food and Drink Federation, which represents manufacturers, is not so much that consumers might mistake the own-label product for the manufacturer's brand. Rather, look-alike brands may 'give the impression that the manufacturer of the proprietary brand has made the own-label product'.

Brand manufacturers may have contributed to the confusion in the past by actually making

▶

own-label products for supermarkets, but most no longer do so. Kellogg recently ran an advertising campaign based on the fact that it does not make cereal for anyone else.

While the big names believe the problem has worsened, they have nevertheless been reluctant to speak out. This is because their relations with retailers are delicate. 'The worst thing you can do is to pick a fight with your biggest customers', says Mackenzie. 'But the customers are giving them no option.'

What has prompted manufacturers to move now is the prospect of changing the law through the government's Trade Marks Bill, which was introduced first into the House of Lords and reached the report stage last week. It will get its third reading in about 10 days' time.

The bill is designed to harmonise UK laws on unfair competition with those in other EU countries, based on the Paris Convention on intellectual property. It aims to make it easier to register trademarks, as well as certain shapes, words and logos on packaging.

But manufacturers say it does not go far enough. They want protection against look-alike brands which imitate the overall appearance of their own brands, without directly copying logos or designs. Lord Reay last week introduced an amendment on behalf of the brand owners group extending such protection.

After a debate in the Lords last Thursday, Lord Reay withdrew his amendment when the government promised to review the issue, but the group may re-introduce its amendment if the government does not act during the passage of the bill.

Paul Walsh, partner at Bristows, Cooke & Carpmael, a law firm specialising in intellectual property, says the UK is out of line with most of Europe in not giving brands proper statutory protection. Germany has a statute on 'protection of get-up', and there are similar laws in France, Benelux and Greece.

The problem of look-alikes is particularly sensitive in the UK because supermarkets have worked hard to change consumers' perceptions of own-label products from inferior imitations to quality alternatives. Retailers make much higher margins on own-label products because they do not bear the same development costs as manufacturers. The big three UK grocers – Sainsbury's, Safeway and Tesco – have pushed own-label sales to more than 50 per cent of turnover, far higher than elsewhere in Europe.

But opponents of the amendment argue that the bill as it stands, coupled with existing safeguards, is adequate. The British Retail Consortium, which represents more than 200 retailers, says manufacturers are attempting to restrict shops' ability to introduce own-label products.

'Shoppers are not confused', the consortium said. 'they are very canny and read the label carefully.' The Consumers Association found in a survey last month that shoppers showed a preference for many own-label products in blind tastings. It warns that tighter restrictions on own-label products could lead to narrower choice for consumers.

Source: N. Buckley, 'On the prowl for copycats', *Financial Times*, 3 March 1994. Reprinted with permission.

Registered designs

A new product may be created which is not sufficiently novel or contain an inventive step so as to satisfy the exacting requirements for the granting of a patent. This was the situation faced by Britain's textile manufacturers in the early nineteenth century. They would create new textile designs but these would be later copied by foreign competitors. The Design Registry was set up in the early 1800s in response to growing demands from Britain's textile manufacturers for statutory protection for the designs of their products. Today, designs that are applied to articles may be protected by design law (*see* Illustration 5.7). There are two systems of design law in the United Kingdom. One is similar to that used for patent law and requires registration. The other system of design protection is design right and is provided along copyright lines. There is a large area of overlap between the two systems.

The registered designs system is intended for those designs intended to have some form of aesthetic appeal. For example, electrical appliances, toys and some forms of packaging have all been registered.

A design as protected by registration is the *outward appearance of an article*. Only the appearance given by its actual shape, configuration, pattern or ornament can be protected, not any underlying idea. The registered design lasts for a maximum of 25 years. Initially the proprietor is granted the exclusive right to a design for a fixed term of five years. This can be renewed for up to five further five-year terms.

To be registered a design must first be new at the date an application for its registration is filed. In general a design is considered to be new if it has not been published in the United Kingdom (i.e. made available or disclosed to the public in any way whatsoever) and if, when compared with any other published design, the differences make a materially different appeal to the eye. For example, if a company designed a new kettle that was very different from any other kettle, the company could register the design. This would prevent other kettle manufacturers from simply copying the design. Clearly, the kettle does not offer any advantage in terms of use, hence a patent cannot be obtained, but a good design is also worth protecting.

Copyright

This area of the law on intellectual property rights has changed significantly over the past few years, mainly because it now covers computer software. Computer software manufacturers are particularly concerned about the illegal copying of their programs. The music industry has also battled with this same problem for many years. It is common knowledge that this was an exceptionally difficult area of law to enforce and new technology may at last provide copyright holders with an advantage. Up to now they have fallen prey to copying technology, but Waldmeir (2002) suggests that compact discs will begin to include technology that prevents them from being copied. The impact of this may be to hinder creativity in the long term (*see* Illustration 5.9).

For the author of creative material to obtain copyright protection it must be in a tangible form so that it can be communicated or reproduced. It must also be the author's own work and thus the product of his or her skill or judgement. Concepts, principles, processes or discoveries are not valid for copyright protection until they are put in a tangible form such as written or drawn. It is the particular way that an idea is presented that is valid for copyright. This particular point, that ideas cannot be copyrighted, often causes confusion. If someone has written an article, you cannot simply rephrase it or change some of the words and claim it as your own. You are, however, entitled to read an article, digest it, take the ideas from that article together with other sources and

Illustration 5.9

FT

If technology switches to the side of copyright

Moves to stop music copying could leave copyright owners with far more power than was ever intended under US law

The recording industry has vowed to make 2002 the year of the copyright.

If the industry has its way, this will be the year when we all begin purchasing music in forms that cannot be stolen. Compact discs will begin to include technology that prevents them being copied (the first discs have already started to appear in music stores). And online, music will be sold through subscription services that stop unauthorised reproduction. 2002 could become the year when copyright fights back.

If the technology works, it could transform the fortunes of copyright holders. Up to now, they have fallen easy prey to any teenager who could type the characters 'MP3' into a search engine: the theft of copyrighted music online has been virtually effortless.

But if technology switches sides, if it now facilitates not theft but the perfect control of who listens to what, when, on the internet, US copyright owners could find themselves wielding far more power than was ever intended under US copyright law, or the constitution that inspired it.

Courts and lawmakers are facing that old question with new urgency: how much copyright is too much? How can copyright law reward creators without allowing them to monopolise their creation in ways that would chill future innovation?

Even the US Supreme Court, which intervenes only rarely in matters of intellectual property law, is this month considering the question of copyright. The justices are expected to announce shortly, perhaps next week, whether they will hear a case that challenges the ascendancy of copyright.

That case argues that the existing American social and legal bargain over copyright is flawed even without the intervention of technologies that could destabilise it even further.

Lawrence Lessig, Stanford University law professor and theorist of the digital society, has seized on the case to challenge the whole recent course of US copyright law, which has consistently expanded the scope and duration of copyright at the expense of public access to copyright works.

He filed the lawsuit on behalf of Eric Eldred, who wanted to compile an electronic archive of unusual and out-of-print works online but was prevented from posting some works by a 1998 law extending the term of copyright protection.

Prof Lessig argues that Congress has exceeded its constitutional authority by repeatedly extending the term of copyrights – 11 times in the past 40 years. The 1998 law alone extended copyright by 20 years: works copyrighted by individuals since 1978 were granted a term of 70 years beyond the life of the author; works made by or for corporations were protected for 95 years. The extension applied to existing works even if the author was dead or the work long out of print.

For Prof Lessig, these extensions violate the constitution's command to Congress that it 'promote the Progress of Science and useful Arts, by securing for limited Times to Authors and Inventors the exclusive Right to their respective Writings and Discoveries'.

Copyrights of such length are no longer 'limited', he argues; and Congress can scarcely claim to 'promote the Progress of Science and the useful Arts' when it extends the copyright of dead authors. Copyrights are meant not to reward authors but to serve as an incentive to creation. No incentive can make a dead writer resume production.

The problem is not just that, for example, Mickey Mouse gets 20 years' more copyright protection under the 1998 law. The issue is larger; as Prof Lessig wrote recently in *Wired* magazine: 'Our trend in copyright law has been to enclose as much as we can: the consequence of this enclosure is a stifling of creativity and innovation.'

Shakespeare would have known exactly what he meant: even the greatest creators build on previous creation. Many of Shakespeare's plays might never have been written if he had had to pay royalties to those inferior authors who wrote the dramas on which they were based.

So, Prof Lessig argues, every time Congress extends copyright it inexcusably impoverishes the public domain. Creativity builds on itself: without reasonable public access to copyrighted works, it has nothing to build on.

But if that situation is bad, how much worse a world in which copyrights are not just long but unlimited? Copy Protection technology can stop creative material from entering the public domain, not just until its copyright expires but for ever. Locked CDs may theoretically lose their copyright but that will not unlock them. Such technologies risk giving copyright owners an absolute monopoly over content for ever – a far cry from the limited monopoly outlined by the constitution.

US lawmakers have begun to ask whether record companies can guard against digital copying without violating US copyright law.

Last week Rick Boucher, who heads the Congressional internet caucus, sent a letter to record company executives asking whether anti-piracy technology might override consumers' legal right to copy music they had purchased for use in car tape-players or other devices.

These are early days but at least the issue of copyright ascendancy is on the table. Technologies of copyright control will almost certainly transform that debate beyond all recognition, if not this year, then some time very soon afterwards. At that point, tinkering with the existing legal regime may well not be enough.

In his recent book *The Future of Ideas*, Prof Lessig recommends a radical revision of copyright law: copyright protection should be cut to five years, renewable 15 times. Where copyrights were not renewed, the work would enter the public domain.

'The benefit for creativity from more works falling into the commons would be large', he argues. 'If a copyright isn't worth it to an author to renew for a modest fee, it isn't worth it to society to support through an array of criminal and civil statutes.'

US lawmakers may not like his suggestion but they ignore the looming copyright crisis at society's peril. Technology has precipitated the crisis; law cannot long ignore it.

Source: P. Waldmeir 'If technology switches to the side of copyright', *Financial Times*, 10 January 2002. Reprinted with permission.

weave them into your own material without any copyright problems. In most instances common sense should provide the answer.

Copyright is recognised by the symbol © and gives legal rights to creators of certain kinds of material, so that they can control the various ways in which their work may be exploited. Copyright protection is automatic and there is no registration or other formality.

Copyright may subsist in any of nine descriptions of work and these are grouped into three categories:

Illustration 5.10

Mickey Mouse is now past 75 and was to be out of copyright

This issue of copyright is currently causing great concern for one of the most famous organisations in the world and certainly the most famous cartoon character. In the USA copyright lasts for 75 years (for creations prior to 1978) and Mickey Mouse in 2003 was 75 years old. At this point, the first Mickey Mouse cartoon was to be publicly available for use by anyone. Plane Crazy was released in May 1928 and was to slip from the Disney empire in 2003. In the autumn of 1928 Disney released *Steam Boat Willie*, the world's first synchronised talking cartoon and soon after Disney copyrighted the film.

At first glimpse one may be tempted to have some sympathy for the Disney organisation. However, Walt Disney wisely registered Mickey Mouse as a trademark, recognising from an early date that Mickey Mouse had value far beyond the screen. Hence, the use by others of the character on numerous products produces large licensing revenues for the Disney Corporation.

The Disney Corporation managed to secure a twenty year extension from Congress under the 1998 Copyright law.

Source: James Langton, *Sunday Telegraph*, 15 February 1998; *Financial Times*, 10 January 2002. Reprinted with permission.

1 original literary, dramatic, musical and artistic works;

2 sound recordings, films, broadcasts and cable programmes; and

3 the typographical arrangement or layout of a published edition.

Each of these categories has more detailed definitions. For example, films in category 2 include videograms; and 'artistic work' in category 1 includes photographs and computer-generated work.

The duration of copyright protection varies according to the description of the work. In the United Kingdom for literary, dramatic, musical and artistic works copyright expires 70 years after the death of the author, in other cases 50 years after the calendar year in which it was first published. The period was for 75 years in the United States (but is now 50 years for all works created after 1978), but this issue is currently causing a great deal of concern for one of the most well-known organisations in the world (*see* Illustration 5.10).

Remedy against infringement

There are some forms of infringement of a commercial nature such as dealing with infringing copies that carry criminal penalties. Indeed, HM Customs have powers to seize infringing printed material. Also a civil action can be brought by the plaintiff for one or more of the following:

- damages;
- injunction; and
- accounts.

Damages

The owner of the copyright can bring a civil case and ask the court for damages, which can be expected to be calculated on the basis of compensation for the actual loss suffered.

Injunction

An injunction is an order of the court which prohibits a person making infringing copies of a work of copyright.

Accounts

This is a useful alternative for the plaintiff in that it enables access to the profits made from the infringement of copyright. This is useful especially if the amount is likely to exceed that which might be expected from an award of damages.

Pause for thought

Who owns the copyright on your essays you write? What can you do if you uncover sections of it in a newspaper or in a book?

Case study

Pricing, patents and profits in the pharmaceutical industry

This case study explains how the pharmaceutical industry uses the patent system to ensure it reaps rewards from the drugs that it develops. Increasingly, however, there is alarm at the high costs of these drugs to the underdeveloped world, especially against a backcloth of the AIDS epidemic in South Africa. While the pharmaceutical industry has responded with several concessions, the case against the industry is that it is enjoys a privileged position partly due to the patent system.

Introduction

There is a story about a pharmaceutical executive on a tour of the US National Mint who inquired how much it cost to produce each dollar

▶

bill. On hearing the answer, the man smiled. Making pills, it seemed, was even more profitable than printing money. Whether true or not, the three most profitable businesses in the world are reputed to be narcotics, prostitution and ethical pharmaceuticals. A recent Oxfam report showing the scale of the AIDS problem in Southern Africa has brought the pharma-companies into the spotlight. The allegation is that these companies exploit the poor in the developing world. With a median 35 per cent return on equity, pharmaceuticals is far and away the world's most profitable major industry. With profits of more than $6 billion, pharma-companies such as Pfizer and GlaxoSmithKline dwarf the likes of Unilever, BT or Coca-Cola. Yet every year in the developing world millions of people die from diseases, such as malaria and tuberculosis, which the rich developed world has eradicated. Table 5.2 shows the scale of the problem.

In the past the pharmaceutical industry has maintained that many of the drugs that could benefit the suffering in the underdeveloped world are expensive and have taken years to research and develop. The only way the pharmaceutical industry can claw back its expenditure on research and development is by patenting their drugs thereby providing them with a 20-year monopoly in which to generate sales and profits. The social contract underlying the patents system is based on an agreement that in return for such investment – and for publishing through patents the details of the research results – a company is entitled to an exclusive right to the sale of the resulting product for a limited period of time: 20 years.

The case against the pharmaceutical industry

Most drug prices bear no relation to the very small cost of production because the industry has a contract with society, enshrined in the patent system. For a limited period (usually 10 years not allowing for clinical trials, etc.) pharmaceutical companies charge monopoly prices for patented medicines. In return, they invest huge amounts of research dollars in pursuit of the next innovation.

At a time when the AIDS epidemic appears to have stabilised in most advanced countries, thanks largely to the use of sophisticated drugs, the disease is continuing to spread at an ever more alarming rate through developing countries (*see* Table 5.2).

Yet those countries now suffering the most from the disease are also those least able to afford the drugs necessary to control it. The issue, of course, challenges the whole patenting system.

It is not just the underdeveloped countries that are experiencing difficulties with intellectual property laws and medicine. A 30-year-old London woman contacted Bristol-Myers Squibb, a US pharmaceutical company, begging help to obtain Taxol. This drug could have controlled her breast cancer, but her National Health Service region did not prescribe it because of its exorbitant cost. There is no patent on Taxol as

---

Table 5.2 The scale of the AIDS epidemic in Southern Africa (% of adult population infected)

Botswana	35.8
Lesotho	23.5
Malawi	15.9
Mozambique	13.2
Namibia	19.5
South Africa	9.9
Swaziland	25.2
Tanzania	8.9
Zambia	19.9
Zimbabwe	25.6

Source: UNAIDS (2000) Reproduced by kind permission of *UNAIDS*, www.UNAIDS.org

the US government discovered it. But Bristol-Myers Squibb, because it performed minor work calculating dosage levels, holds the intellectual property rights on dose-related data, even though the data was originally collected by the government. Ultimately, the company was shamed into offering her free medicine if she moved to the United States. However, doctors concluded that the offer was probably too late.

> *In AIDS and breast cancer, the stricken North and South share a horrific commonality as the new landless peasantry in the apartheid of intellectual property rights.*
>
> *(The Guardian, 27 July, 2000)*

The developing countries are demanding changes. They argue that patent laws should be relaxed allowing, for example, either for their own companies to produce cheaper generic versions of the expensive anti-AIDS drugs, or for the import of such generic copies from other countries. In February 2001 the Indian company Cipla offered to make a combination of AIDS drugs available at about one-third of the price being asked by companies in developing countries. This price is already less than those in the West. If ever there was a good example of profiteering here it is. Worst of all, it seems to be profiteering at the expense of the poor. The charge of unethical behaviour seems to be ringing loudly. But for how long will the legal systems and courts in the world tolerate thousands of deaths before one of them decides enough is enough? The pharmaceutical industry is aware of the strength of public opinion and the mounting pressure it is under and has made significant concessions, including cutting the price of many of its drugs to the developing world. Will this, however, be enough? The whole industry, it seems, is now under pressure to justify the prices it charges for its drugs. If it fails to convince governments, it may see the introduction of legislation and price controls.

The case for the pharmaceutical industry

The pharmaceutical industry can claim that it has been responsible for helping to rid many parts of the world of dreadful diseases. It is able to claim that the enormous sums of money that it spends each year on research and development is only possible because of the patent system. Any change in the system will put at risk the billions of dollars that are spent on research into heart disease, cancer and other killers. This is usually enough for most governments and others to back away from this very powerful industry. Not surprisingly, the drugs industry is appalled at the prospect of price controls. Sidney Taurel, chief executive of the US drugs company Eli-Lilly, has warned 'If we kill free markets around the world, we'll kill innovation.'

The industry clearly has a unique structure and differs markedly from many others, but whether there is evidence for supra-normal profits is questionable. Professor Sachs, director of the Center for International Development at Harvard University, argues that if price controls were introduced, companies would simply scale back their investments in research. This is often seen by many as a 'threat' that the industry uses against governments. Once again there is limited evidence to suggest this would necessarily happen. Sachs suggests 'This is an extremely sophisticated, high cost, risky business with very long lead-in times and an extremely high regulatory hurdle', he says. 'My sense is that every rich country that has said, "You're making too much money" and has tried to control prices has lost the R&D edge.'

The pharmaceutical industry has a powerful voice. It is a large employer, invests large sums of money in science and technology and is without doubt an industry that will grow in this century. Most governments would like to have a thriving pharmaceutical industry and hence try to help and not hinder their efforts. Moreover, there are thousands of people in the developed world whose lives are being saved and extended from new sophisticated drugs that are being developed

▶

every month. The industry has many advocates and supporters.

Price cuts

In June 2001 Britain's biggest drugs company, GlaxoSmithKline, reduced the cost to the developing world of drugs for treating malaria, diarrhoea and infectious diseases. Merck and Bristol-Myers Squibb, two of the world's largest drugs companies, had already announced earlier in the year that they were supplying AIDS drugs at cost price or less to all developing countries. Bristol-Myers Squibb also announced that it would not be enforcing its patent rights in Southern Africa.

The field of pricing pharmaceutical products is complicated because in most countries prices are determined by what governments, the main buyers in the industry, are prepared to pay. The same pill made by the same company may cost half in Canada of what it does in the United States. In Mexico, it may cost still less. Such differential pricing is fundamental to the pharmaceutical industry. Because consumers are not paying for raw materials, but rather for intellectual property, drug companies charge what they can get away with and governments pay what they deem affordable. The United States, however, is the exception, as here prices are determined on the open market. However, it seems things are about to change, for the US upper house, the Senate, has challenged the existing market arrangements. It argues that US citizens should not be paying substantially more for patented drugs, while citizens in other countries get the same drugs at much lower prices because their government is only willing to pay a certain price. The Senate's amendment would allow drugs to be imported from any foreign factory approved by the Food and Drug Administration. As there are plenty of those in India and China, Senators are effectively demanding that US citizens get medicine at developing world prices. Clearly, social and economic pressures

are mounting on the industry. In December 2003 the National Health Service (NHS) in the United Kingdom launched a £30m lawsuit, which accuses seven firms of price-fixing by controlling and manipulating the market in penicillin-based antibiotics (Meikle, 2003).

Conclusions

It is the unique structure of the industry and the patent system that is at the crux of the problem. Europe, the United States and Japan account for virtually all the profits of the pharmaceutical companies. In most other markets profits are driven down by the power and price sensitivity of customers. But in pharmaceuticals, neither the patient who consumes the drugs nor the doctor who prescribes them is price sensitive. Customers for medicines are not price sensitive because they do not pay for them. In Europe it is the taxpayer who foots the bill.

Whereas most companies have profits capped by aggressive industry buyers, the pharmaceutical firms have to negotiate only with civil servants, and, argues Professor Doyle, 'when taxpayers' money is available, commercial disciplines frequently disappear' (Doyle, 2001). But, even in the United States where a free market exists, the pharmaceutical companies are able to charge even higher prices, hence the US Senate's proposed changes. Once again this is because the pharmaceutical companies are frequently selling to private health insurers. Many US employers offer health insurance as part of the employment package.

Competition is another key force that drives down prices in most industries. In electronics – an industry even more innovative than pharmaceuticals – excess profits from a new product soon disappear as competitors bring out copies. But, in the pharmaceutical business, it is the patent system that ensures high profits continue for an average of 10 years. The consequence of this ability to negotiate very high prices and the absence of competitive threat is that the giant pharmaceuticals have no incentive to compete on price. It also helps to explain why the pharma-companies have been unwilling to sell cheap medicines to the poor in Africa and Asia. The real worry is that dropping prices to the developing world would undermine the enormous margins being received in Europe and the United States. Buyers would soon be reimporting medicines at a fraction of the official price, which may be the case soon in the United States.

The industry's justification for its high prices and patent monopolies is that it encourages innovation, but to what extent is this true? In most other industries it is intense competition and a fight to survive and win market share that drives forward innovation. Without new and better products companies such as Hewlett-Packard and Canon know they will not maintain growth and market share. As we have seen in Chapters 1, 2 and 3, innovation is dependent on a collection of factors and the patent system alone cannot stimulate innovation. It is necessary but not sufficient.

The industry's most popular argument to defend the patent system is that it has unusually high cost structures due to the enormous sums of money it has to invest in science and technology. Increasingly, however, the industry is spending more on marketing existing products than it is on developing new ones. Professor Doyle argues

that marketing costs are now typically almost double the R&D spend. GlaxoSmithKline, for example, has 10,000 scientists but 40,000 sales-people! Even this well-rehearsed argument is now beginning to sound hollow.

The pharmaceutical industry has enjoyed 50 years of substantial growth and substantial profits and many people have benefited. The patent system is intended to balance the interests of the individual and society; increasing numbers of people are questioning this balance. The pharmaceutical companies need to consider every step carefully for they surely do not want to become the unacceptable face of globalisation.

Questions

1 Explain how the pricing of drugs contributes to the acquisition of supra-normal profits in the pharmaceutical industry.

2 It is because drugs are absolutely essential to life that the pharmaceutical industry is able to justify large profits. Discuss the merits of this argument. Consider also that bread and milk companies do not make huge profits.

3 Explain why drugs are not price-sensitive.

4 Explain why the patent system may not be working as originally intended.

Chapter summary

This chapter has explored the area of intellectual property and the different forms of protection available to a firm. This is a dynamic area of business. The operation of trademark law throughout the European Union is now controversial, as is the area of patents. It seems that the pharmaceutical industry is preparing itself for significant changes. This chapter also made it clear that the patent system has fierce critics, largely due to the associated costs involved with defending a patent against infringement. The patent system, however, was also highlighted as a valuable source of technological knowledge that is used by many companies.

Discussion questions

1 Explain why many research organisations are against the patenting of life forms.

2 Discuss the main forms of intellectual property protection available to companies.

3 Explain why discoveries are not patentable.

4 Discuss some of the limitations of the patent system.

5 Is the pharmaceutical industry the unacceptable face of globalisation (consider the anti-capitalist demonstrations of recent years)?

6 Explain with the use of examples when it would be appropriate to use trademarks and copyright to protect a firm's intellectual property.

Key words and phrases

Brands as intellectual property 161	Patent 146
Copyright 165	Patent extension 155
Generic products 149	Registered Design 164
Infringement of intellectual property 168	Trade mark 157

 ## Websites worth visiting

BTG www.BTGPLC.com

European Union, Enterprise and Innovation www.europa.eu.int/comm/enterprise/innovation

Intellect UK www.intellectuk.org

Inventions, designs, patents www.iacllc.com

National Endowment for Science and Technology www.NESTA.org.uk

Patent agents www.patent-faq.com

Patent Office www.patent.gov.uk

Pilkington PLC technology management: www.pilkington.com

Thomson Derwent patents directory www.Thomsonderwent.com

UK Government, Department of Trade and Industry www.Dti.gov.uk/innovation

 ## References

Alpert, F. (1993) 'Breadth of coverage for intellectual property law: encouraging product innovation by broadening protection', *Journal of Product and Brand Management*, 2, 2.

Badenhausen, K. (1995) 'Brands: the management factor', *Financial World*, 1 August, 50–69.

Bainbridge, D.I. (1996) *Intellectual Property*, 3rd edn, Financial Times Pitman Publishing, London.

Bowe, C. and Griffith, V. (2002) 'Proposal on patents set to hit revenues', *Financial Times*, 22 October.

BTG (2004) 'About patents', www.BTGPLC/info/patents

Chemistry & Industry News (1995) ci.mond.org/9521/952107.html

Court of Appeal (1985) Reports of Patent, Design and Trade Mark Cases (RPC), No. 59.

Derwent (1998) Derwent World Patents Index, Derwent Scientific and Patent Information: www.Derwent.com

Doyle, P. (2001) 'AIDS and the pharmaceutical industry', *The Guardian*, 10 March.

Feldwick, P. (1996) 'Do we really need brand equity?', *Journal of Brand Management*, Vol. 4, No. 1, 9–28.

Financial Times (1997) 'Gene is out of the bottle', 30 October, 15.

Graham, N. (1998) 'Inventor cleans up with profits', *Sunday Times*, 1 March, 4, 16.

The Guardian (1998) 'Keep your ideas to yourself', 17 February, 22.

The Guardian (2000) 'Patenting life', 15 November, 4.

Hargreaves, D. (2001) *Financial Times*, 16 January.

http://www.webmarketingtoday.com

Meikle, J. (2003) 'NHS seeks £30m from drug firms in price fixing claim', *The Guardian*, 23 December, 6.

Nakamoto, M. and Pilling, D. (2004) 'Tough tasks ahead at Takeda', *Financial Times*, 23 August.

Rowan, D. (1997) 'Signing up to a patent on life', *The Guardian*, 27 November, 19.

Waldmeir, P. (2002) 'If technology switches to the side of copyright', *Financial Times*, 10 January, 15.

Further reading

For a more detailed review of the intellectual property literature, the following develop many of the issues raised in this chapter:

Borg, Eric A. (2001) 'Knowledge, information and intellectual property: implications for marketing relationships', *Technovation*, Vol. 21, 515–24.

The Economist (2000) 'The knowledge monopolies: patent wars', 8 April, 95–9.

Shavinina, L. (2003) *The International Handbook on Innovation*, Elsevier, Oxford.

Part TWO

Managing Technology and Knowledge

New technologies are transforming markets, businesses and society at an ever-increasing rate. Businesses need somehow to manage their way through this new terrain. Given that virtually all firms are established to generate funds for their owners, one of the fundamental issues for them to address is how to transform technology into profits. In this second part of the book we turn our attention to this key factor in innovation knowledge and technology. Chapter 6 looks at how firms accumulate knowledge and utilise this to develop business opportunities. It is these opportunities that are at the heart of new product ideas. To profit from these technologies, however, firms need to offer products that are a lower price or different from their competitors, for long-term success they need to ensure what they offer is not easily copied by others.

A firm's capabilities lie not just within but also outwith the linkages and networks that it has established over time – Chapter 7 examines the subject of strategic alliances. It is not only large international companies that are using alliances to develop products and technology, small innovative companies also recognise the potential benefits of working with others.

Chapter 8 examines how companies manage research and development (R&D). It details the main activities performed by R&D departments and how these can influence the development of new products. Chapter 9 explores the challenges faced by R&D managers as they wrestle with project selection and evaluation. Important questions are raised concerning when to stop pouring money into struggling research projects. The extent to which a company can acquire technology developed outside of the organisation via technology transfer is studied in Chapter 10.

6

Managing organisational knowledge

The ability of firms to identify technological opportunities and exploit them is one of the most fundamental features that determines successful from unsuccessful firms. But, technology by itself will not lead to success. Firms must be able to convert intellect, knowledge and technology into things that customers want. The ability to use its assets to perform value-creating activities can lead to the development of firm-specific competencies. These competencies provide firms with the ability to generate profits from their technology assets. This chapter examines the role of competencies and how these determine the innovative potential of firms.

Chapter contents

Learning objectives

When you have completed this chapter you will be able to:

- explain the significance of technology trajectories for firms investing in technology;
- recognise the importance of firm-specific competencies in generating long-term profits;
- provide an understanding of the role of an organisation's knowledge base in determining innovative capability;
- provide an understanding of the concept of the learning organisation;
- recognise the importance of technical and commercial capabilities in innovation management; and
- recognise a variety of different innovation strategies.

The battle of Trafalgar

The battle of Trafalgar in 1805 may not seem like an appropriate place to begin the study of strategy and technological innovation. It does, however, provide an interesting historical example of how strategy (in this case military strategy) is often linked to new technological developments.

For those who are unable to recall their eighteenth- and nineteenth-century maritime history, Nelson defeated the French and Spanish fleets in the battle of Trafalgar. Today Nelson's ship, HMS *Victory*, stands in a drydock in Portsmouth harbour (*see* p. 117). The battle was fought off the south-west coast of Spain and the sailing ships of the day were armed with cannons that used gunpowder to launch cannon balls at the enemy's ships, the aim being to hole the ship so that it would ultimately sink. Failure to achieve this would either result in being 'holed' oneself or being invaded by the enemy's crew if they were able to get alongside.

Nelson's fleet, while composed of fewer vessels, had a crucial strategic advantage. It possessed a simple but important piece of technology that, arguably, was instrumental in securing victory. The Spanish and French armadas were armed with cannons, but theirs were fired by lighting a short fuse that burned and then ignited the gunpowder. There were several limitations to this ignition process. First, the fuse would not always burn, and second, valuable time was being wasted while waiting for it to burn. Nelson's ships, on the other hand, had overcome this limitation through the development of a simple hammer-action ignition system that ignited the gunpowder. The firing process involved placing a cannon ball in the cannon and rolling it into position, with its nose poking through the aperture in the side of the ship. A cord would be pulled to trigger the hammer action and ignite the gunpowder, causing an explosion that would force the cannon ball out towards the target. Nelson's ships were able to load and fire several cannon balls while the enemy's fleet were waiting for fuses to burn.

Technology trajectories and the dynamic capabilities of the firm

The battle of Trafalgar provides a useful illustration of the pivotal role of technology in competition. Nowhere is this more evident than in the world of business. Firms with superior technology have delivered spectacular financial rewards to their owners: Intel's microprocessors; Nokia's mobile telephones; Pfizer's Viagra to name only a few. But, as we have seen in Chapter 1, technology alone cannot deliver victory; technology, however, coupled with a market opportunity and the necessary organisational skills to deliver the product to the market will help significantly.

In Nelson's case the choice of where to deploy technological effort was far more limited than that open to firms today. Large firms and to a lesser extent small firms have a bewildering array of opportunities to exploit, especially when they have products operating in many markets across several industries. As one would expect, those given responsibility for charting the direction of the firm, the leaders, will have views on where the firm should be heading, but the technology capability of the firm frequently dictates what is possible and what can or cannot be achieved in a given time-frame. In other words, a firm's opportunities are constrained by its current position and current knowledge base, i.e. it is path-dependent. This introduces the notion of technological trajectories first put forward by Nelson and Winter (1982) and developed by Dosi (1982). For example, many firms may marvel at the huge profits generated by Pfizer from its Viagra drug, but few firms are in a position to develop a similar or superior product. Only those operating in the pharmaceutical industry will be in a position to respond and even then the possible entrants will be limited to those who have prior knowledge of the related fields of technology, determined by its range of research projects. Acquiring knowledge about technology takes time, involves people and experiments and requires learning. To exploit technological opportunities a firm needs to be on the 'technology escalator'. As we will see later in this chapter, firms cannot move easily from one path of knowledge and learning to another. According to David Teece and Gary Pisano (1994) the choices available to the firm in terms of future direction are dependent on its own capabilities, that is, the firm's level of technology, skills developed, intellectual property, managerial processes and its routines. Furthermore, they argue the choices made by any firm must take place in a changing environment, characterised by changing levels of technology, changing market conditions and changing societal demands. Teece and Pisano refer to this concept as the dynamic capabilities of firms.

Pause for thought

If technology trajectories are determined by a firm's past, how can it change trajectories and get on another one?

The acquisition of firm-specific knowledge

Arguing for knowledge and the need to acquire it is a bit like arguing for peace or education. Few can argue against such a laudable aim. But it is not any knowledge that is required, it is firm-specific knowledge; knowledge that is useful and applicable. Otherwise reading the telephone directory would constitute acquiring knowledge but this clearly has limited benefits. For example, 3M is often cited as having core competencies in coatings and adhesives, hence one would expect the firm to have a wide range of research projects related to these technologies. This then is the key, how do firms know what knowledge to acquire and when do they know when they have acquired it. This is clearly dependent on the firm's prior knowledge and introduces the notion of absorptive capacity. This refers to a firm's ability to acquire and utilise new knowledge. This notion is further explored in the chapters on R&D management and technology acquisition.

Dynamic competence-based theory of the firm

The *dynamic competence-based theory of the firm* sees both the external and internal environments as dynamic: the external environment is constantly changing as different players manoeuvre themselves and a company's internal environment is also evolving. The management of this internal process of change together with an understanding of the changes in the external environment offers a more realistic explanation of the challenges facing senior management. In addition, firms are seen as different (Nelson, 1991) and hence compete on the basis of competencies and capabilities (Tushman and Anderson, 1986; Nelson and Winter, 1982; Hamel and Prahalad, 1990, 1994; Pavitt, 1990; Cohen and Levinthal, 1990; Seaton and Cordey-Hayes, 1993). This literature presents a related theoretical view that centres around an organisation's ability to develop specific capabilities. These capabilities tend to be dependent on the organisation's incremental and cumulative historical activities. In other words, a company's ability to compete in the future is dependent on its past activities. This view of an organisation's heritage is developed by Cohen and Levinthal (1990) in the context of the management of research and development. In their research, they developed the notion of 'absorptive capacity'.

In their study of the US manufacturing sector Cohen and Levinthal reconceptualise the traditional role of R&D investment, which was viewed simply as a factor aimed at creating specific innovations. They see R&D expenditure as an investment in an organisation's absorptive capacity. They argue that an organisation's ability to evaluate and utilise external knowledge is related to its *prior knowledge* and expertise and that this prior knowledge is, in turn, driven by prior R&D investment. Similarly, the notion of 'receptivity', advocated by Seaton and Cordey-Hayes (1993), is defined as an organisation's overall ability to be aware of, identify and take effective advantage of technology. This is explored in Trott and Cordey-Hayes (1996), who present a process model of receptivity showing the activities necessary for innovation to occur.

The issue of an organisation's capacity to acquire knowledge was also addressed by Nelson and Winter (1982) who emphasised the importance of 'innovative routines'. They argue that the practised routines that are built into the organisation define a set

---

Figure 6.1   Tacit knowledge

A useful example of tacit knowledge is tying a shoelace. Virtually everyone knows how to tie a shoelace. However, it is extremely difficult to explain to someone in diagrams, words or speech how to perform this task. Hence, tacit knowledge may be described as knowledge that is acquired but difficult to explain to others.

---

of competencies that the organisation is capable of doing confidently. These routines are referred to as an organisation's core capabilities. It is important to note that the notion of routines here does not necessarily imply a mechanistic, bureaucratic organisational form (*see* Chapter 3). The potential for controversy is resolved by Teece (1986), who distinguishes between 'static routines', which refer to the capability to replicate previously performed tasks, and 'dynamic routines', which enable a firm to develop new competencies. Indeed, dynamic organisational routines are very often those activities that are not easily identifiable and may be dominated by tacit knowledge (*see* Figure 6.1).

The point here is that over long periods organisations build up a body of knowledge and skills through experience and learning-by-doing. In addition to these internal organisational processes, Kay (1993) suggests that the *external linkages* that a company has developed over time and the investment in this network of relationships (generated from its past activities) form a distinctive competitive capability. Moreover, this can be transformed into competitive advantage when added to additional distinctive capabilities such as technological ability and marketing knowledge (Casper and Whitley, 2003).

Developing firm-specific competencies

The ability of firms to identify technological opportunities and exploit them is one of the most fundamental features that determines successful from unsuccessful firms. Increasingly economists are using the notion that firms possess discrete sets of capabilities or competencies as a way of explaining why firms are different and how firms change over time. During the 1990s the management literature changed its emphasis from trying to understand what firms must do to position themselves in the competitive environment to exploring what capabilities are required for survival and change. The most influential analysts in this later field are Gary Hamel and C.K. Prahalad (1994). Their ideas have been readily embraced by business leaders around the world. To summarise they are: that competitive advantage resides not in a firm's products but in their competencies. These are defined as knowledge, skills, management processes and routines acquired over time that are difficult to replicate – this may be because they are constantly changing and updating them. Furthermore, they state that few companies are likely to develop world leadership in more than five or six fundamental competencies. The case study of Gore Inc. at the end of Chapter 3 illustrates how this firm has developed unparalleled knowledge and skills on the polymer polytetrafluoroethylene (PTFE). Indeed, this knowledge base has enabled the firm to develop a range of product applications for a variety of markets over 30 years. It is, however, not just physical technologies where firm can develop competencies. Tesco stores in the United Kingdom have developed a range of skills, know-how and routines in retailing and distribution with which their competitors find it difficult to compete. Furthermore, even after years of studying the Tesco approach competitors are struggling to replicate what it does. According to Hamel and Prahalad it is because firms are not readily able to replicate Tesco's activities that this would indicate that these competencies are at the core of the organisation's abilities, and are probably based on tacit knowledge and embedded routines. They use the metaphor of the tree to show the linkages between core competencies and end products. They suggest that a firm's core competencies are comparable to the roots of a tree, with the core products representing the trunk and business units smaller branches and final end products being flowers, leaves and fruit (*see* Figure 6.2). Technology in itself does not mean success; firms must be able to convert

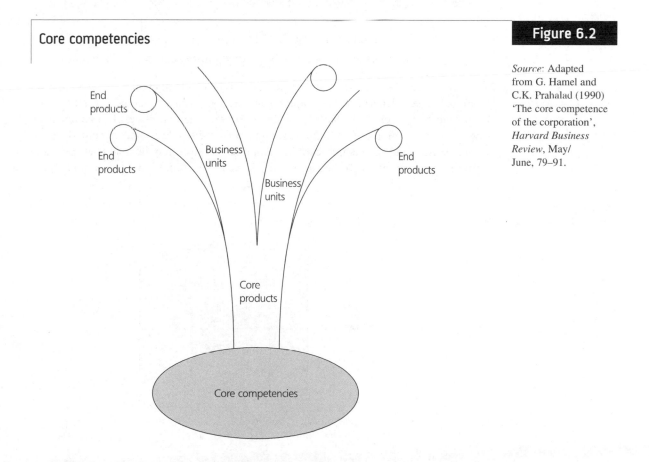

Core competencies

Figure 6.2

Source: Adapted from G. Hamel and C.K. Prahalad (1990) 'The core competence of the corporation', *Harvard Business Review*, May/June, 79–91.

intellect, knowledge and technology into things that customers want. This ability is referred to as a firm's competencies: *the ability to use its assets to perform value-creating activities*. This frequently means integrating several assets such as: product technology and distribution; product technology and marketing effort; and distribution and marketing.

Competencies and profits

According to Hamel and Prahalad a firm's ability to generate profits from its technology assets depends on the level of protection it has over these assets and the extent to which firms are able to imitate these competencies. For example, are competencies at the periphery or the centre of a firm's long-term success? If they are at the centre and difficult for firms to imitate, then long-term profits are assured, e.g. Honda and its ability to produce performance engines. Over the past 50 years few firms have been able to imitate Honda's success in developing engines. The following are examples of other firms that have been cited as having core competencies that are difficult to replicate:

- Intel's ability to develop microprocessors that exploit its copyrighted microcode;
- Coca-Cola's ability to develop products that people are willing to pay a premium for;
- Honda's ability to produce high quality and performance engines; and
- 3M's ability to develop a wide range of products from coatings and adhesives.

These firms can be placed in the uppermost right-hand quadrant of the matrix in Figure 6.3. These firms have been able to generate long-term profits based on their core competencies and few firms have been able to imitate their activities. If a competence is non-core and imitability is high, then one may not be able to make profits from it, all else being equal. If it is non-core but imitable, the firm may be able to make some negligible profits from it. If, however, the competence is core but easily imitated, the

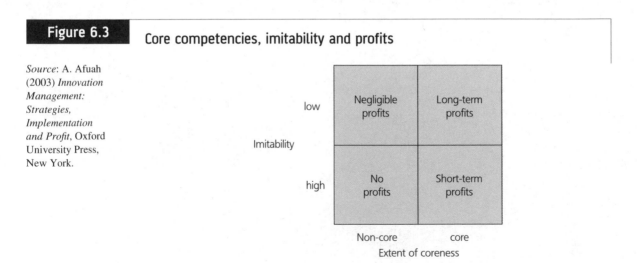

| Figure 6.3 | **Core competencies, imitability and profits** |

Source: A. Afuah (2003) *Innovation Management: Strategies, Implementation and Profit*, Oxford University Press, New York.

firm can make profits, but these are likely to be temporary as competitors will soon imitate.

Technology development and effort required

Foster (1986) and Abernathy and Utterback (1978) argue that the rate of technological advance is dependent on the amount of effort put into the development of the technology. As was pointed out in Chapter 1 with President's Kennedy's pledge to get a man on the moon, if unlimited resources are made available, as in the Kennedy example, there may well be very few limits. Under normal circumstances, however, technological progress starts off slowly then increases rapidly and finally diminishes as the physical limits of the technology are approached. This is diagrammatically referred to as an S-curve. Slow progress at the start equates to a horizontal line, rapid progress as knowledge is acquired equates to a vertical line and slow progress towards the end equates to a horizontal line. It is usually at this point that a new technology replaces the existing one; indeed it is necessary if advances are to continue. Figure 6.4 illustrates the development of supercomputers.

Pause for thought   ?

Other than through the use of patents and copyright how can a firm prevent its competencies from being imitated?

Technology life cycles and S-curves   Figure 6.4

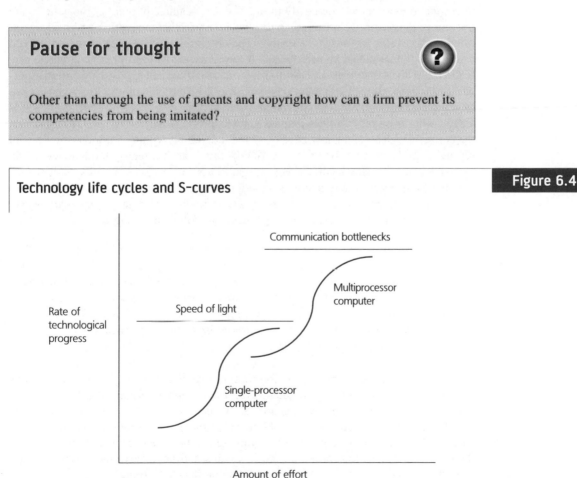

The knowledge base of an organisation

Many organisations have shown sustained corporate success over many years. This does not only mean unbroken periods of growth or profit, but also combinations of growth and decline that together represent sustained development and advancement. Research by Pavitt *et al.* (1991) on innovative success led him to remark:

> *Large innovating firms in the twentieth century have shown resilience and longevity, in spite of successive waves of radical innovations that have called into question their established skills and procedures . . . Such institutional continuity in the face of technological discontinuity cannot be explained simply by the rise and fall of either talented individual entrepreneurs or of groups with specific technical skills. The continuing ability to absorb and mobilise new skills and opportunities has to be explained in other terms.*

Pavitt identifies a number of properties of innovative activities in large firms. He places a great deal of emphasis on the concept of firm-specific competencies that take time to develop and are costly to initiate. Key features of these competencies are the ability to convert technical competencies into effective innovation and the generation of effective *organisational learning*. The observations made earlier suggest a need to analyse organisational knowledge and the processes involved in realising that knowledge rather than analysing organisational structure. If we can uncover the internal processes that determine a company's response to a given technology, this may help to explain the longevity of large innovating companies.

But what is meant by organisational knowledge? One may be tempted to think that the collective talents and knowledge of all the individuals within an organisation would represent its knowledge base. It is certainly the case that one individual within an organisation, especially within a large organisation, rarely sees or fully understands how the entire organisation functions. Senior managers in many large corporations have frequently said, with some amusement, when addressing large gatherings that they do not understand how the organisation operates! The following quote is typical:

> *I am constantly being surprised as I travel around the many different parts of this organisation; while I know that we are in the car production business I am constantly amazed at the wide range of activities that we perform and how we do what we do. We regularly convert our raw materials of steel and many different component parts into fine automobiles, and then get them all over the world all within a matter of days. It's amazing and difficult to explain how we do it.*
>
> (Senior executive from a US car producer)

This statement highlights the notion that *an organisation itself can seem to have knowledge*. That is, no one individual, even those people charting the course of the company, actually fully understands how all the internal activities and processes come together and function collectively. This concept of the organisation retaining knowledge is developed by Willman (1991), who argues that 'the organisation itself, rather than the individuals who pass through it, retains and generates innovative capacity, even though individuals may be identified who propagate learning'.

How the whole can be viewed as more than the sum of the parts

Figure 6.5

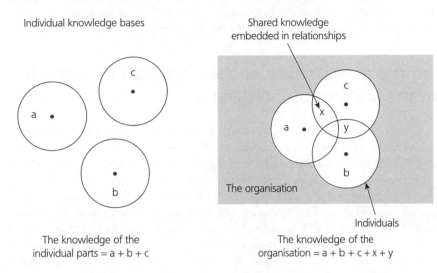

Individual knowledge bases

Shared knowledge embedded in relationships

The organisation

Individuals

The knowledge of the individual parts = a + b + c

The knowledge of the organisation = a + b + c + x + y

The whole can be more than the sum of the parts

It is important to recognise that the knowledge base of an organisation is not simply the sum of individuals' knowledge bases. If this were the case, and knowledge was only held at the individual level, then an organisation's expertise and acquired abilities would change simply by employee turnover. The wealth of experience built up by an organisation through its operations is clearly not lost when employees leave. The employment of new workers and the retirement of old workers does not equate to changing the skills of a firm. Figure 6.5 attempts to show how a collective knowledge base is larger than the sum of individual knowledge bases.

Organisational heritage

Organisational knowledge is distinctive to the firm. That is, it is not widely available to other firms. Hence, the more descriptive term organisational heritage. It is true that technical knowledge, in the form of patents, or commercial knowledge, in the form of unique channels of distribution, although used by an organisation are available to other firms. However, organisational knowledge includes these and more. For example, a vehicle manufacturer may use a wide variety of technologies and patents. This knowledge will not necessarily be unique to the organisation, that is, other companies will be aware of this technology. But the development and manufacture of the vehicle will lead to the accumulation of skills and competencies that will be unique to the organisation. Hence, it is the individual ways in which the technology is applied that lead to organisation-specific knowledge.

To explore the above example further, groups or teams of people will develop specific skills required in the manufacture of a product. Over time, the knowledge, skills and processes will form part of the organisation's routines, which it is able to perform repeatedly. Individuals may leave the organisation and take their understanding to other organisations. But even if large groups of people leave, it is likely that understanding will have been shared with others in the organisation and it will have been recorded in designs or production planning records for use by others.

When the performance of the organisation is greater than the abilities of individuals

The notion of organisational knowledge was popularised by Kay (1993) who puts forward the idea of 'architecture' as a source of distinctive capability. This builds on the work of Nelson and Winter (1982), Dosi (1982), Pavitt (1990) and Hamel and Prahalad (1994) referred to earlier. The image of a football team is often used at this point to illustrate the argument that a team such as say Charlton Athletic in the English Premier League has recently consistently performed well, but also better than the combined abilities of its players would seem to allow. This can also be said of many industrial organisations who have been able to generate exceptional long-term success from relatively ordinary employees. This, argues Kay (1993), is the result of the organisation's architecture. Whatever label one chooses, it seems clear that a firm's organisational knowledge plays a significant role in its firm's ability to innovate and survive in the long term.

Organisational knowledge represents internal systems, routines, shared understanding and practices (*see* Figure 6.6). In the past it was loosely described as part of an organisation's culture, along with anything else that could not be fully explained. Organisational knowledge, however, represents a distinctive part of the much broader concept of organisational culture.

There are several tangible representations of this knowledge, such as minutes of meetings, research notebooks, databanks of customers, operating procedures, manufacturing quality control measures, as well as less tangible representations such as tried and tested ways of operating. Nelson and Winter (1982) argue that such learning-by-doing

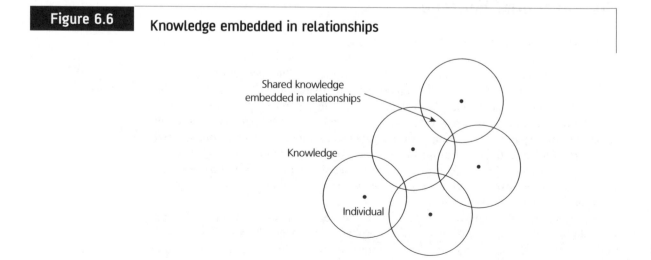

Figure 6.6 **Knowledge embedded in relationships**

is captured in organisational routines. It is evident that the knowledge base of an organisation will be greater, in most cases, than the sum total of the individual knowledge bases within it. Willman (1991) argues that this is because knowledge is also embedded in social and organisational relationships (*see* Figure 6.6). At its simplest level suggests Kay, organisational knowledge is where each employee knows one digit of the code which opens the safe; clearly, this information is only of value when combined in the correct sequence with the information held by all the others.

Japanese organisations and the role of organisational knowledge

It has been argued that Western managers fail to understand the nature and concept of organisational knowledge and consequently they are unable to manage it, let alone exploit it. This is because the traditions of Western management have become ingrained with writings and theories, from Frederick Taylor to Herbert Simon, which see the organisation as merely a machine to process information (Nonaka, 1991). According to this view, the only useful knowledge is formal and systematic: hard data and codified procedures. Similarly, the measurement of this knowledge is hard and quantifiable: increased efficiency, lower costs, improved return on investment, etc. Nonaka suggests that there is another way to consider organisational knowledge found most commonly in highly successful Japanese companies. He explains (p. 100):

> *The centre-piece of the Japanese approach is the recognition that creating knowledge is not simply a matter of processing objective information. Rather, it depends on tapping the tacit and often highly subjective insights, intuitions, and hunches of individual employees and making those insights available for testing and use by the company as a whole.*

The knowledge base of an organisation is defined in this view as 'the accumulation of the knowledge bases of all the individuals within an organisation *and* the social knowledge embedded in relationships between those individuals'. These relationships are often recognised as organisational processes and procedures (Kogut and Zander, 1992; Nonaka, 1991). The interactions and relationships between individuals may be said to represent a form of 'organisational cement' that performs two functions. First, it combines individual knowledge bases into a larger body of knowledge. Second, it enables individual knowledge bases to be accessed by the organisation, effectively via interaction with other individuals.

Characterising the knowledge base of an organisation

Discussions concerning the knowledge base of an organisation tend to focus on R&D activities and other technical activities. However, an organisation's ability to develop new products that meet current market needs, to manufacture these products using the appropriate methods and to respond promptly to technological developments, clearly involves more than technical capabilities. Nelson (1991) has argued that in industries

Figure 6.7	The knowledge base of an organisation

Source: Adapted from P.S. Adler and A. Shenhar (1990) 'Adapting your technological base: the organisational challenge', *Sloan Management Review*, Autumn, 25–37.

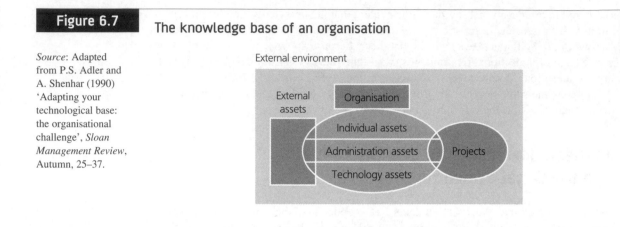

where technological innovation is important firms need more than a set of core capabilities in R&D:

> *These capabilities will be defined and constrained by the skills, experience, and knowledge of the personnel in the R&D department, the nature of the extant teams and procedures for forming new ones, the character of the decision making processes, the links between R&D and production and marketing, etc.*
>
> (Nelson, 1991: 66)

The wide range of skills mentioned by Nelson implies that the commonly held view of an organisation's knowledge base comprising only technical matters is too narrow. This is supported by Adler and Shenhar (1990), who suggest that an organisation's knowledge base is made up of several dimensions. The following five dimensions can be considered (*see* Figure 6.7):

- *Individual assets* – the skills and knowledge of the individuals that form the organisation. It is the application of these that influences corporate success.

- *Technological assets* – the most immediately visible elements of the technological base, the set of reproducible capabilities in *product*, *process* and *support areas*. Technological assets can be more or less reliably reproduced; the other elements are, by contrast, fundamentally relational, which makes them much more difficult to replicate.

- *Administration assets* – the resources that enable the business to develop and deploy individual and technological assets. These are specifically the skill profile of employees and managers, the *routines, procedures and systems* for getting things done, the organisational structure, the strategies that guide action and the culture that shapes shared assumptions and values.

- *External assets* – the relations that the firm establishes with current and potential allies, rivals, suppliers, customers, political actors and local communities, e.g. joint ventures, distribution channels, etc.

- *Projects* – the means by which technological, organisational and external assets are both deployed and transformed. Projects should be considered as part of the knowledge base in so far as the organisation's *modus operandi* is a learned behavioural pattern that can contribute to or detract from technological and business performance.

This more realistic assessment of an organisation's knowledge base shows how the various components of an organisation are inter-related. The inclusion of external networks is an important point. The formal and informal links an organisation has developed, often over many years, are a valuable asset. Pennings and Harianto (1992) include history of technological networking within the organisational skills necessary for innovation. At this point one may argue that it would be more appropriate to consider an organisation's knowledge base rather than select individual parts for analysis, which may be compared to trying to establish a racing car's performance by only analysing the engine. There are clearly other factors that will also have a dramatic impact on the car's performance.

The suggestion that an organisation's knowledge base is also time-dependent, that the acquisition of knowledge takes place over many years, introduces the notion of organisational heritage, discussed above. If we accept the notion of organisational knowledge, this leads to the question of whether it is possible for organisations to learn.

The learning organisation

The concept of the learning organisation has received an unprecedented level of attention in the management literature. A special edition of *Organisational Science* was dedicated to the subject and it has received the attention of mainstream economics (Malbera, 1992). The emphasis of much of the early literature on this subject was on the history of the organisation, and the strong influence of an organisation's previous activities and learning on its future activities. That is, the future activities of an organisation are strongly influenced by its previous activities and what it has learned (Pavitt *et al.*, 1991; Dosi, 1982; Nelson and Winter, 1982; Tidd, 2000).

Unfortunately, the term organisational learning has been applied to so many different aspects of corporate management, from human resources management to technology management strategies, that it has become a particularly vague concept. At its heart, however, is the simple notion that successful companies have an ability to acquire knowledge and skills and apply these effectively, in much the same way as human beings learn. Arguably, companies that have been successful over a long period have clearly demonstrated a capacity to learn. Cynics have argued that this is just another management fad with a new label for what successful organisations have been doing for many years. However, according to Chris Argyris (1977), organisations can be extremely bad at learning. Indeed, he suggests that it is possible for organisations to lose the benefits of experience and revert to old habits. It is necessary to engage in double-loop rather than single-loop learning, argues Argyris, since the second loop reinforces understanding. At its most simple level, single-loop learning would be the adoption of a new set of rules to improve quality, productivity, etc. Double-loop learning occurs when those sets of rules are continually questioned, altered and updated in line with experience gained and the changing environment.

A process of knowledge accumulation and application in innovative firms

The accumulation of knowledge and the effective assimilation and application of this knowledge are what appear to distinguish innovative firms from their less successful counterparts. This capability is popularly referred to as organisational learning. However, it is the internal processes that lead to this ability that need to be the focus of management attention. One would expect that a review of the organisational innovation literature would help in revealing these activities. However, this body of literature tends to use a structural approach when exploring the ability of organisations to innovate. Hence, discussions are dominated by how organisational structures and management strategies affect an organisation's ability to innovate. For example, Burns and Stalker (1961) supported the view that flexible organisational forms will sustain innovation but bureaucratic firms will not. Ansoff (1968) suggests the need for forecasting and environmental analysis techniques at the strategic management level. Daft (1982) emphasises the need for stable knowledge bases enhanced through stable communication. Rothwell (1975) discusses the importance of key individuals in the process, in this case the business innovator. Rothwell (1992) offers a list of 'critical success factors' necessary for successful industrial innovation, including company interaction with technology sources and markets; innovation as strategy; and internal control systems. All of these studies emphasise the presence or absence of certain factors rather than describing the actual activities or processes that are required. Recent studies by Japanese scholars on the development of new products have shown that to develop competencies companies have to uncover and understand their 'dynamic routines', which will invariably be built on tacit knowledge (Nonaka, 1991). These ideas are developed further by Trott (1993) who identifies an internal knowledge-accumulation model (*see* Figure 6.8). The process illustrated in this model highlights individual non-routine activities that contribute to the generation of genuine business opportunities.

Specialist functional departments in large organisations usually possess a wealth of idiosyncratic knowledge and experience. One of their important but unappreciated roles is constantly imparting specialist knowledge to colleagues concerning technical or commercial ideas. This 'informal internal consultancy' activity is often described as 'the informal testing of ideas on people in their functional capacity' (Trott, 1993). For example, a technical idea will often be informally discussed with colleagues from marketing to get informed commercial advice. This valuable informal activity is often unrecognised. The process has a dual role: not only does it serve as an informal testing device whereby ideas can be presented to a variety of in-house specialists who are then able to assess the idea, it is also a support-gathering device. If the general feedback is positive and sufficient people are made aware of the idea, this will increase the likelihood of its eventually receiving formal backing from the business team. If, on the other hand, the feedback is broadly negative, this will alert individuals to the fact that the idea will probably not receive formal support. They will either develop the idea further by gaining additional information or decide that it is not suitable, for whatever reason, as an opportunity for the business.

When companies lose personnel for whatever reason, the effects can be considerable. Maitland argues these effects can be reduced (see Illustration 6.1)

The internal knowledge accumulation process

Figure 6.8

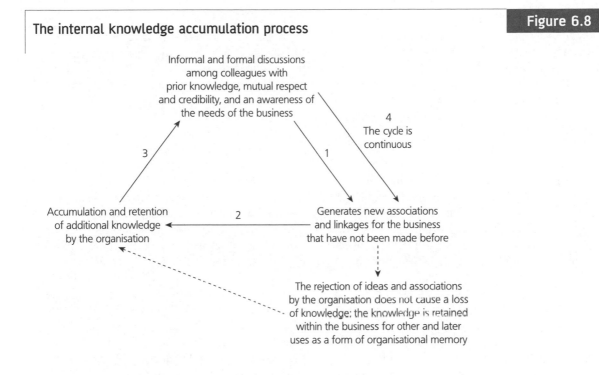

Informal and formal discussions among colleagues with prior knowledge, mutual respect and credibility, and an awareness of the needs of the business

4
The cycle is continuous

3

1

Accumulation and retention of additional knowledge by the organisation

2

Generates new associations and linkages for the business that have not been made before

The rejection of ideas and associations by the organisation does not cause a loss of knowledge; the knowledge is retained within the business for other and later uses as a form of organisational memory

Illustration 6.1

FT

If downsizing, protect the corporate memory

Many companies risk losing expertise through job cuts. But by analysing how staff interact, they may be able to minimise the damage

The costs can be enormous when job cuts cause companies to lose experienced people who know how things work. The Cullen inquiry into the rail crash at Ladbroke Grove in London in 1999, in which 31 people died, testified to that.

The inquiry heard evidence that specialists had lost their jobs after British Rail was privatised in 1996 and that middle managers who remained did not understand what their staff did each day. Many new recruits to jobs where safety was at stake were inexperienced or inadequately trained

and a loss of 'corporate memory' led to inconsistency and confusion over procedures for train drivers.

This may be an extreme example but many companies risk losing critical knowledge and expertise as the job cuts resulting from the economic downturn and the events of September 11 spiral into hundreds of thousands.

'Most companies are making the same mistakes they made during the last downsizing', says Dave Snowden of International Business Machines, who is European director of the Institute for Knowledge Management, a research consortium of more than 40 companies and government agencies. 'A lot of organisations used the back end of business process re-engineering as an excuse to get rid of people and had to hire employees back.' Many returned as consultants on higher pay.

What can companies do this time to avoid losing critical knowledge when people leave and to dissuade employees from hoarding their expertise in the face of possible job cuts?

First, they need to recognise the problem. The steep downturn is exposing many companies' lack of commitment to understanding and using their people's knowledge, says Jeanie Daniel Duck, senior vice-president at the Boston Consulting Group. 'When companies feel they're in a crisis, it is one of the things that goes by the board, unless they've made it a routine or suffered because of losing knowledge in the past.'

Next, any attempt to stop knowledge walking out of the door must be handled sensitively. Launching a knowledge-sharing initiative at a time when people are expecting redundancies would not be a good idea, says Laura Empson, a lecturer in management studies at the Said Business School in Oxford, who has done extensive research in this area. 'People will be extremely cynical and will see it as an attempt to extract their knowledge.'

When a US engineering and construction company introduced an online 'warehouse' for engineers to share their design ideas, it fell flat, as Thomas Davenport and Laurence Prusak recount in their book *Working Knowledge*. 'Having been through a period of lay-offs and fearing that more were coming, employees saw their unique knowledge as a source of job security and felt that sharing it would weaken their position.' Worse still, the company culture did not reward sharing and employees were expected to acquire knowledge in their own time. Strong incentives are needed to coax people into divulging their expertise when being dismissed. The price may be an increase in their redundancy package, provision of career counselling, or an agreement to hire them back as consultants.

Spotting just such an opportunity, Barnes Kavelle, a UK human resources consultancy, has launched an initiative called Corporate Skills Leaseback. The idea is to help companies prepare redundant employees for life as self-employed consultants, upon whom they can call when needed.

David Paget, who developed the service, says that not all employees are suited to such work. But he paints a rosy picture of the benefits: an instant reduction in employment costs of 20 per cent or more; retention of valuable corporate memory; and happy ex-employees with great work/life balance. But there must be risks in trying to retain knowledge this way. Any loyalty that ex-employees feel to the company that made them redundant is likely to last only as long as it takes to find more lucrative work elsewhere. Extracting knowledge from staff who are being permanently laid off will not be straightforward either. Not all knowledge can be captured by the organisation and turned into a process, despite the more exaggerated claims made about knowledge management, that buzzword of the 1990s boom. Technology has certainly helped companies to gather and disseminate information and procedures that once depended on individuals' know-how. But there have been many obstacles to getting employees to share knowledge and ideas on corporate intranets.

For one thing, people know more than they can tell in words and they can tell more than they can write down, says Mr Snowden. This is why they are generally better at explaining how they do their job in a videotaped interview than if they are asked to consign it to paper. People also know what they know only when they need to know it, he says. They may even forget they possess skills or experience that happen to be in short supply elsewhere in the organisation.

Far better, therefore, not to lose the valuable sources of knowledge at all. To find out where they reside, companies need to question their staff and analyse their social networks.

'You don't ask people what they know', he says. 'You ask them who they would ask if they wanted to know about different subjects. There are people who suck knowledge in and never give it out. There are people with a limited number of network relationships. And there are people who always know somebody who knows.'

The latter can be high on the list for redundancy because managers are unsure what they do, or because they appear to be weak performers. One member of a sales team was earmarked for redundancy because he barely met his sales quota each year. But a 'knowledge mapping' exercise revealed that he played a critical role as a mentor to the rest of the team.

People like this are often not ambitious but they can hold a company together, says Mr Snowden. 'The most valuable knowledge is often not possessed by the people you think are your star performers.' If those at the centre of knowledge networks come to be seen as the most valuable people, knowledge hoarders will look vulnerable when downsizing becomes necessary. Organisations that reward people for sharing knowledge will know who falls into these two opposing categories, says Ms Empson of the Said Business School. In such companies, the incentive to share

knowledge should be even greater when jobs are under threat.

That will not be the case in organisations where knowledge-sharing goes unrecognised and unrewarded. Here, any threat to jobs is likely to strengthen the belief that knowledge is power, says Tim Curry, global chief knowledge officer at Ernst & Young.

'I'm going to be much less inclined to share knowledge, trust others and operate collegiately if I think I'm going to be sacked tomorrow because of a relatively arbitrary management decision based on old-fashioned, one-dimensional performance criteria, such as how much I sell or how much time I'm engaged on client work', he says.

For some companies, it may be too late to salvage important knowledge. Building a culture where knowledge is understood, valued and shared can take a long time. This may be the time to prepare for the next downturn.

Source: A. Maitland, 'If downsizing, protect the corporate memory', *Financial Times*, 16 October 2001. Reprinted with permission.

Combining commercial and technological strengths: a conceptual approach to the generation of new business opportunities

In examining ways to generate new opportunities, the focus has been on recognising the importance of external organisational linkages, often called networks, as sources of external knowledge, *and* the process of associating these with the internal knowledge base of the company. It is this notion (shown diagrammatically in Figure 6.9) that helps identify a different approach to how companies can generate new business opportunities. It shows how these external linkages lower the threshold level for the process of 'osmosis' of external knowledge (Cohen and Levinthal, 1990). Figure 6.9 highlights the role played by the knowledge base of the company and the need to view this as a dynamic entity made up of skills, know-how and expertise, much of which is tacit, that is to say difficult to articulate and capture, but none the less present in all companies.

| Figure 6.9 | Conceptual framework for generating genuine business opportunities |

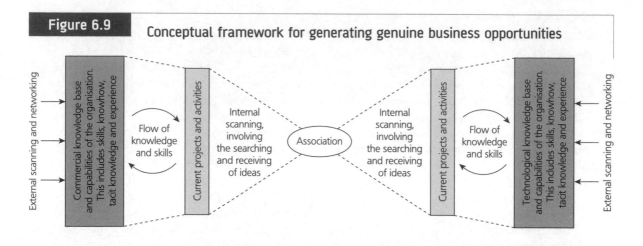

The conceptual framework shown in Figure 6.9 represents the role played by the knowledge bases of the firm in generating genuine business opportunities. A key activity is the continual external scanning undertaken by the organisation's commercial and technical arms shown at the furthest right- and left-hand sides. Towards the centre of the diagram is the process of assimilating internal knowledge from the organisation's knowledge bases. It is the assimilation of knowledge from the external environment via the company's external linkages with its internal capabilities that leads to new business opportunities being created. The successful combination of all of these activities can lead to the generation of genuine business opportunities (GBOs). This comprises a commercial opportunity (essentially commercial knowledge such as the identification of a new market, improving distribution through a strategic alliance, effective pricing strategies, etc.) with a technical opportunity (essentially technical knowledge such as the improvement in performance of a new material, the identification of an interesting new patent, the development of a new manufacturing process, etc.) where this is aligned with existing commercial and technical competencies to ensure that the company genuinely has the ability to turn the opportunity into a product (even if it decides not to). The complexity of the process may help to explain why creating genuine business opportunities is so difficult to achieve, since a wide range of activities need to be in place in order for associations to be made.

One company that seems not only to have recognised the importance of actively generating new business opportunities and new products but also to be extremely successful in this practice is Pfizer. It is widely known around the world for its Viagra drug. But, Pfizer has grown from a mid-ranking pharmaceutical firm in the 1990s to the largest pharmaceutical firm in the world. It has achieved rapid growth by exploiting technology developments better than its competitors. It is not that it conducts more R&D than its competitors, simply that it has been able to spot opportunities to exploit. Pfizer has long recognised the value of its internal R&D and its external linkages, including customers and suppliers, and has developed a range of competencies based on the ability to capture opportunities from these linkages, associate these with its knowledge base and generate business opportunities and new products. Pfizer's recent successful new products include: Lipitor, the world's top-selling drug with sales in 2003 of over $2 billion; Zoloft, an anti-depressant, Neurontin, an anticonvulsant;

and Zithromax, Pfizer's leading antibiotic; each of these achieved sales greater than $500 million (Firn, 2003).

The company has thus facilitated the creation of genuine business opportunities by increasing the richness of the information received in terms of detail and breadth.

It is necessary to counsel caution at this point, because the process of turning these genuine business opportunities into commercial success is one of the most long-standing and fundamental issues facing businesses. We do not have to look too hard to uncover examples where companies have developed ideas and identified business opportunities yet failed to turn these into commercial successes. Xerox, which over the years has created numerous new product ideas including much of the technology behind the icon-driven computer operating system, did not recognise the potential of the opportunities it had created and did not benefit financially from the commercial success of what has turned out to be one of the most important developments in computing. It is significant, however, that the company has continued to generate business opportunities for itself and commercial success, while others have not.

The degree of innovativeness

The framework outlined in Chapter 1 emphasises the interaction that any firm has with the external environment, both in terms of markets and science and technology. The developments taking place in these external environments will continue largely independent of the individual firm. Any firm's ability to survive is dependent on its capability to adapt to this changing environment. This suggests that a firm has a range of options open to it. A company will attempt to look ahead and try to ensure that it is prepared for possible forthcoming changes and in some instances a firm can modify world science and technology. But mostly the future is unknown – some firms will prosper; others will not. In virtually all areas of business it is not always clear who are the players in the innovation race. Very often contenders will emerge from the most unexpected places. Furthermore, companies often find themselves in a race without knowing where the starting and finishing lines are! Even when some of these are known, companies often start out with the aim of becoming a leader and end up being a follower (Pavitt *et al.*, 1991).

The development of new products and processes has enabled many firms to continue to grow. However, there is a wide range of alternative strategies which they may follow, depending on their resources, their heritage, their capabilities and their aspirations. Collectively these factors should contribute to the direction that the corporate strategy takes. Unfortunately, technology is rarely an explicit element of a firm's corporate strategy. This is so even in science- and technology-intensive firms. Very often, along with manufacturing, technology is the missing element in the corporate strategy. Until very recently technological competencies were not viewed as an integral part of the strategic planning process. They were seen as things to be acquired if required. As was discussed earlier, scientific knowledge cannot be bought like a can of tomatoes, off the shelf. By definition (*see* Chapter 1), technology is embedded in products and processes and, while it is possible to acquire a patent, for example, this does not necessarily mean that the company will also possess the technological capability to develop products

Table 6.1 Innovative strategies in the personal computer industry

Strategy	Characteristics	Examples of companies	Products
1 Leader/offensive	Science/technology intensive High risk	Intel Apple	Microchip Macintosh and graphical-user interface operating system
2 Follower/defensive	Strong technology base Agility in design and manufacturing	IBM HP	Personal computer (leader in mainframe) Regarded as market leader Largely due to its range of PCs and additional features
3 Cost minimisation/Imitative	Low-cost manufacture Limited technology base	Research Machines Research Machines	Low-cost PC Focus is on assembly of component parts
4 Market segmentation specialist/traditional	Niche market Minimal technological change	Apple n/a in this particular industry	Graphic design and education markets n/a

and processes from that patent. This has been an expensive lesson learned by many international chemical companies which have acquired licences from other chemical companies to develop a chemical process, only to experience enormous difficulties in producing the product. In one particular case the company abandoned the plant, having already sunk several million pounds into the project.

The innovation policy pursued cuts a wide path across functions such as manufacturing, finance, marketing, R&D and personnel, hence the importance attached to its consideration. The four broad innovation strategies commonly found in technology-intensive firms (Freeman, 1982; Maidique and Patch, 1988) are discussed below and in Table 6.1. These are not mutually exclusive or collectively exhaustive. A wide spectrum of other strategies is logically possible; indeed, very often a firm adopts a balanced portfolio approach with a range of products.

Leader/offensive

The strategy here centres on the advantages to be gained from a monopoly, in this case a monopoly of the technology. The aim is to try to ensure that the product is launched into the market before the competition. This should enable the company either to adopt a price-skimming policy, or to adopt a penetration policy based on gaining a high market share. Such a strategy demands a significant R&D activity and is usually accompanied by substantial marketing resources to enable the company to promote the new product. This may also involve an element of education about the new product, for example Polaroid's instant film and Apple's personal computer.

Fast follower/defensive

This strategy also requires a substantial technology base in order that the company may develop improved versions of the original, improved in terms of lower cost, different design, additional features, etc. The company needs to be agile in manufacturing, design and development and marketing. This will enable it to respond quickly to those companies that are first into the market. In the cell phone market Alcatel, Sagem and Samsung are able to get new cell phone handsets into the market quickly. None of these firms competes with Nokia, Motorola, Siemens and Sony-Ericsson in terms of innovative technology, but they have none the less delivered profits and a return for their investors (*see* Case study in Chapter 10). Without any in-house R&D their response would have been much slower, as this would have involved substantially more learning and understanding of the technology.

Very often both the first two strategies are followed by a company, especially when it is operating in fierce competition with a rival. Sometimes one is first to the market with a product development, only to find itself following its rival with the next product development. This is commonly referred to as healthy competition and is a phenomenon that governments try to propagate.

Cost minimisation/imitative

This strategy is based on being a low-cost producer and success is dependent on achieving economies of scale in manufacture. The company requires exceptional skills and capabilities in production and process engineering. This is clearly similar to the defensive strategy, in that it involves following another company, except that the technology base is not usually as well developed as for the above two strategies. Technology is often licensed from other companies. However, it is still possible to be extremely successful and even be a market leader in terms of market share. Arguably HP has achieved this position in the PC market. Originally its PCs were IBM clones but were sold at a cheaper price and are of a superior quality to many of the other competitors.

This is a strategy that has been employed very effectively by the rapidly developing Asian economies. With lower labour costs these economies have offered companies the opportunity to imitate existing products at lower prices, helping them enter and gain a foothold in a market, for example footwear or electronics. From this position it is then possible to incorporate design improvements to existing products.

Market segmentation specialist/traditional

This strategy is based on meeting the precise requirements of a particular market segment or niche. Large-scale manufacture is not usually required and the products tend to be characterised by few product changes. They are often referred to as traditional products. Indeed, some companies promote their products by stressing the absence of any change, for example Scottish whisky manufacturers.

A technology strategy provides a link between innovation strategy and business strategy

For each of the strategies discussed above there are implications in terms of the capabilities required. When it comes to operationalising the process of innovation, this invariably involves considering the technology position of the firm. Hence, the implementation of an innovation strategy is usually achieved through the management of technology.

Many decisions regarding the choice of innovation strategy will depend on the technology position of the firm with respect to its competitors. This will be largely based on the heritage of the organisation (*see* Chapter 1). In addition, the resource implications also need to be considered. For example, a manufacturer of electric lawn-mowers wishing to adopt an innovation leadership strategy would require a high level of competence in existing technologies such as electric motors, blade technology and injection moulding relative to the competition, as well as an awareness of the application of new technologies such as new lightweight materials and alternative power supplies. Adopting a follower strategy, in contrast, would require more emphasis on development engineering and manufacture.

In terms of resource expenditure, while the figures themselves may be very similar it is where the money is spent that will differ considerably, with the leader strategy involving more internal R&D expenditure and the follower strategy involving more emphasis on design or manufacturing. This area of technology strategy and the management of technology is explored in more detail in Chapters 8, 9 and 10.

Case study

Unilever garbage bags[1]

Although this case dates back to the mid-1970s, it is not widely known and is an excellent example of strategic planning, the generation of business opportunities and the evaluation of a business opportunity with respect to the stated corporate strategy.

Introduction

Unilever plc is an Anglo-Dutch international brand management organisation specialising in the development of world-wide international brands. In particular it focuses its activities on the management of commodity products in three main areas: food products, such as margarine and tea; personal care products, such as shampoo and toothpaste; and household cleaning products, such as detergents and lavatory cleaners.

The company was formed in 1930 with the merger of Lever Brothers of the United Kingdom and Unie of The Netherlands. Lever Brothers had a long history of manufacturing soap and soap powders and Unie had built up a portfolio of products around the manufacture of margarine.

[1] This case has been written as a basis for class discussion rather than to illustrate effective or ineffective managerial administrative behaviour. It has been prepared from a variety of published sources, as indicated, and from observations.

Since this time Unilever has built businesses on this heritage and developed new capabilities and strengths.

Background

During the 1960s UK government planning had seen a huge increase in the development of high-rise housing. Although viewed today as flawed, the idea behind the building of tower blocks was to provide much needed inexpensive accommodation on limited available land. In addition, the population explosion in the 1960s caused many people involved with public policy to express concern about the shortage of housing for the future. High-rise housing was seen as a possible solution to these problems. Numerous city councils, supported by central government, decided to develop housing of this type and the construction of high-rise tower blocks continued into the early 1970s.

It was at this time that a consumer research group at Unilever uncovered what at first seemed to be merely a latent consumer need. This later turned into a multi-million-pound business opportunity.

A variety of different techniques were used at the time by consumer research groups to garner information from housewives. (Although the use of such terms as housewife may be inappropriate today, in the mid-1970s dual-income families were rare and household cleaning was largely the preserve of the female partner in a marriage.) The Household Cleaning Products business within Unilever would either invite housewives into the research laboratories at Port Sunlight Village, near Liverpool, or visit consumers at home. At that time the business was responsible for several well-known brands including Flash floor cleaner and Domestos lavatory cleaner.

A wide range of consumers from across the socio-economic spectrum were involved in this research. However, it was during discussions with housewives in high-rise tower blocks that the need was uncovered. After several exchanges

about cleaning bathrooms and sinks, the women expressed their frustration with having to clean up food remains from around the toilet. This puzzled the researcher, who for a brief second thought she had misunderstood what had been said. Further questioning revealed that for this woman a common cleaning chore was having to clean up spilt food from around the base of the toilet. This was because any liquid/semi-liquid food that was not eaten by her family had to be disposed of down the toilet. The researcher continued to enquire further about what happened with solid food waste. This, replied the woman, could be dealt with in a much more satisfactory way by wrapping the food in old newspaper and placing it in the kitchen wastebasket.

The researcher explored this problem with other housewives in high-rise tower blocks who expressed similar concerns. They also showed additional frustrations, in particular about odours from food sitting in kitchen wastebaskets until the weekly refuse collection. This problem had not been mentioned by those living in more conventional single- or two-storey housing, largely because food waste was placed in dustbins outside the house.

A business opportunity

Extensive exploration of this issue was undertaken with consumers over the following few weeks. This revealed that this was an inconvenience for many and a problem for a few. One or two households explained that they placed plastic carrier bags inside their kitchen wastebasket to avoid having to clean it after each use. They acknowledged, however, that this was a luxury. This was due to the effect of the oil crisis of the early 1970s. Petroleum and petroleum-derivative products, such as polythene, were relatively expensive. At that time the multiples (such as Sainsbury, Tesco and the Co-op) charged consumers for carrier bags (equivalent to approximately 22p in 2002). Most households used cardboard boxes to carry their groceries home or

►

their own shopping bags, so unlike today, they did not have a drawer full of carrier bags.

The consumer research group presented their findings to a group of brand managers and R&D managers in the Household Cleaning Products business. Enormous excitement was generated as their thoughts immediately turned to a new product idea. Potentially the market was huge – virtually every household in the country. This was because, even though people in single- and two-storey housing did not currently identify kitchen wastebasket liners as a need, consumer products companies were experienced in highlighting problems to consumers and then offering solutions using sophisticated marketing communications. The meeting agreed to set up a new product group to explore the idea further. In particular, they looked at estimates of market size, manufacturing costs, technical input and marketing requirements.

Corporate strategy

A brief analysis of Unilever's history will reveal its consistent approach to the careful management and nurture of successful brands. Persil, Domestos and PG Tips have extremely long histories. The business has invested heavily over the years to build brand awareness and brand loyalty through a wide variety of promotional campaigns. This represents, albeit simplified, Unilever's corporate strategy – to build and develop international brands that will enable the group to provide added-value, long-term growth.

At the Household Cleaning Products division this translated into a portfolio of existing brands such as Flash, Domestos and Persil. The division had to decide whether the proposed new product concept would fit this strategy.

Evaluation of the opportunity

The results of the initial market research were placed in front of everyone. Around the table sat senior managers from the Household Cleaning division, senior research and development managers and the new product group (NPG). The initial discussions were very positive about the idea of a new business. This was largely due to the encouraging market research data which pointed to the enormous potential of such a product.

Discussions moved on to expected margins, that is, what were the expected costs and profits. At this point doubts began to creep into the minds of a few people – not because the margins were unhealthy, but because discussions began to focus on the manufacture of polythene, an area in which Unilever did not have a wealth of knowledge. The NPG began to realise that if this business opportunity was to develop it would be necessary to take the business into an area of technology with which it had little experience. However, as several people made clear, many companies have diversified into other areas with great success. The oil crisis and cost of polythene were also mentioned.

The discussions around the table switched to building a brand, the core of Unilever's strategy and the activity that is most readily associated with the company. It was at this juncture that several doubts emerged about the ability of the business to build a brand around such a product. One marketing manager argued that Bowater Scott had been able to build a brand around, of all things, toilet paper (Andrex). Surely Unilever could do it with liners for wastebaskets. Others in the group were not so certain. One senior research and development manager enquired about the group's preliminary technical investigations and in particular whether there were any possibilities of technical leadership. One member of the NPG explained that a research team had been established with the R&D department to look at this issue. Initial findings revealed the following technical possibilities:

- variety of different-size liners;
- variety of different colours;
- variety of different textures of material;

- limited scope for design, but sealing the opening of the liner presented a few opportunities; and
- possibilities of incorporating fragrances within the liner.

As the meeting drew to a close there were several other discussions about the enormous market potential. The final point concerned competition and most around the table agreed that it would be fast and fierce as soon as this market opportunity was discovered. The potential competitors were likely to be the chemical and polythene manufacturers and polythene product manufacturers.

Walking away from a huge business opportunity

It slowly began to dawn on the NPG that it was increasingly unlikely that the investment required for this new business would be forthcoming. Eventually the meeting was closed and the decision was taken not to develop a new business. The NPG was given the opportunity to continue with its investigations and present its findings a year later. Most realised, however, that over the year many additional business opportunities were likely to emerge and this was probably the end for wastebasket liners at Unilever.

Discussion

This case provides an interesting example of a seemingly excellent business opportunity not being developed further because of lack of 'fit' with the business's capabilities, both in terms of commercial and technical know-how. The lack of 'brand potential' and insufficient technical knowledge of the product area, in the end proved to be persuasive arguments. The role of the marketplace and the market research group in particular in generating business opportunities is clearly illustrated. Indeed, cooperation between marketing and R&D led to several suggestions for technical innovations and possible new product ideas.

Questions

1 Explain how Unilever's heritage influenced the decision not to develop further the wastebasket liner business opportunity.

2 Illustrate the commercial and technology aspects of the business opportunity.

3 Discuss the role of consumer research in the development of a new business opportunity for Unilever.

4 To what extent is it possible to judge whether the decision taken was the correct one?

5 Can you think of any other ways in which the business opportunity could be developed further?

Chapter summary

This chapter examined how business strategy affects the management of innovation. In so doing it introduced the notion of an organisation's knowledge base and how this links strategy and innovation. The heritage of a business was also shown to form a significant part of its knowledge base. Moreover, a firm's knowledge base largely determines its ability to innovate and certainly has a large influence on the selection of any innovation strategy.

Discussion questions

1 Explain the role played by core competencies in a firm's strategic planning.

2 What is meant by the technology escalator in the concept of technology trajectories?

3 Explain why a business's heritage needs to be considered in planning future strategy.

4 Try to plot two firms in each of the quadrants on the profit–competency matrix (Figure 6.3).

5 Explain the difference between individual knowledge and organisational knowledge and show how an organisation's knowledge can be greater than the sum of individual knowledge bases.

6 How would you compare the knowledge bases of two organisations?

Key words and phrases

Core competency 185	Learning organisation 193
Degree of innovativeness 199	Organisational heritage 189
Dynamic capabilities 182	Technology strategy 181
Knowledge base of an organisation 188	Technology trajectories 182

Websites worth visiting

BTG www.BTGPLC.com

Intellect UK www.intellectuk.org

Patent Office www.patent.gov.uk

References

Abernathy, W.J. and Utterback, J. (1978) 'Patterns of industrial innovation', *Technology Review*, Vol. 80, No. 7, 40–7.

Adler, P.S. and Shenhar, A. (1990) 'Adapting your technological base: the organizational challenge', *Sloan Management Review*, Autumn, 25–37.

Afuah, A. (2003) *Innovation Management: Strategies, Implementation and Profit*, Oxford University Press, New York.

Ansoff, H.I. (1968) *Corporate Strategy*, Penguin, Harmondsworth.

Bosman, A. and Storm, P.M. (eds) *Understanding and Managing Strategic Change*, North-Holland, New York, 83–109.

Burns, T. and Stalker, G.M. (1961) *The Management of Innovation*, Tavistock, London.

Casper, S. and Whitley, R. (2003) 'Managing competencies in entrepreneurial technology firms: a comparative institutional analysis of Germany, Sweden and the UK', *Research Policy*, Vol. 33, 89–106.

Cohen, W.M. and Levinthal, D.A. (1990) 'A new perspective on learning and innovation', *Administrative Science Quarterly*, Vol. 35, No. 1, 128–52.

Daft, R. (1982) 'Bureaucratic versus non-bureaucratic structures and the process of innovation and change', in Bacharach, S. (ed.) *Research in Sociology of Organisations*, JAI, Greenwich, CT, 129–66.

Dosi, G. (1982) 'Technical paradigms and technological trajectories: a suggested interpretation of the determinants and directions of technical change', *Research Policy*, Vol. 11, No. 3, 147–62.

Firn, D. (2003) 'Pfizer profits boosted by disposal gains', www.FT.com, 22 April.

Foster, R. (1986) *Innovation: The Attacker's Advantage*, New York: Summit Books.

Freeman, C. (1982) *The Economics of Industrial Innovation*, 2nd edn, Frances Pinter, London.

Hamel, G. and Prahalad, C.K. (1990) 'The core competence of the corporation', *Harvard Business Review*, May/June, 79–91.

Hamel, G. and Prahalad, C.K. (1994) 'Competing for the future', *Harvard Business Review*, Vol. 72, No. 4, 122–8.

Kay, J. (1993) *Foundations of Corporate Success*, Oxford University Press, Oxford.

Kogut, B. and Zander, U. (1992) 'Knowledge of the firm, combinative capabilities, and the replication of technology', *Organisation Science*, Vol. 3, No. 3, 495–7.

Maidique, M. and Patch, P. (1988) 'Corporate strategy and technology policy', in Tushman, M.L. and Moore, W.L. (eds) *Readings in the Management of Innovation*, HarperCollins, New York.

Malbera, F. (1992) 'Learning by firms and incremental technical change', *Economic Journal*, Vol. 102, 845–59.

Nelson, R.R. (1991) 'Why do firms differ, and how does it matter?' *Strategic Management Journal*, Vol. 12, No. 1, 61–74.

Nelson, R.R. and Winter, S. (1982) *An Evolutionary Theory of Economic Change*, Harvard University Press, Boston, MA.

Nonaka, I. (1991) 'The knowledge creating company', *Harvard Business Review*, Vol. 69, No. 6, 96–104.

Pavitt, K. (1990) 'What we know about the strategic management of technology', *California Management Review*, Vol. 32, No. 3, 17–26.

Pavitt, K., Robson, M. and Towsend, J. (1991) 'Technological accumulation, diversification and organisation in UK companies, 1945–1983', *Management Science*, Vol. 35, No. 1, 81–99.

Pennings, J.M. and Harianto, F. (1992) 'Technological networking and innovation implementation', *Organisational Science*, Vol. 3, No. 3, 356–82.

Rothwell, R. (1975) 'Intracorporate entrepreneurs', *Management Decision*, Vol. 13, No. 3, 246–56.

Rothwell, R. (1992) 'Successful industrial innovation: critical factors for the 1990's', *R&D Management*, Vol. 22, No. 3, 221–39.

Seaton, R.A.F. and Cordey-Hayes, M. (1993) 'The development and application of interactive models of technology transfer', *Technovation*, Vol. 13, No. 1, 45–53.

Teece, D. (1986) 'Profiting from technological innovation: implications for integration, collaboration, licensing and public policy', *Research Policy*, Vol. 15, 285–305.

Teece, D.J. and Pisano, G. (1994) 'The dynamic capabilities of firms: an introduction', *Industrial and Corporate Change*, Vol. 3, No. 3, 537–56.

Tidd, J. (2000) *From Knowledge Management to Strategic Competence: Measuring Technological Market and Organisational Innovation*, Imperial College Press, London.

Trott, P. (1993) 'Inward technology transfer as an interactive process: a case study of ICI', PhD thesis, Cranfield University.

Trott, P. and Cordey-Hayes, M. (1996) 'Developing a receptive R&D environment: a case study of the chemical industry', *R&D Management*, Vol. 26, No. 1, 83–92.

Tushman, M. and Anderson, M. (1986) 'Technological discontinuities and organisational environments', *Administrative Science Quarterly*, Vol. 31, No. 3, 439–65.

Willman, P. (1991) 'Bureaucracy, innovation and appropriability', paper given at ESRC Industrial Economics Study Group Conference, London Business School, November 22.

Further reading

For a more detailed review of the knowledge management literature, the following develop many of the issues raised in this chapter:

Argyris, C. (1977) 'Double loop learning in organizations', *Harvard Business Review*, September/October, 55.

Henry, J. and Walker, D. (eds) (1991) *Managing Innovation*, Sage/Oxford University Press, London.

Johnson, G. and Scholes, K. (2002) *Exploring Corporate Strategy*, Prentice Hall, Hemel Hempstead.

Kay, J. (1993) *Foundations of Corporate Success*, Oxford University Press, Oxford.

Kay, J. (1996) 'Oh Professor Porter, whatever did you do?' *Financial Times*, 10 May, 17.

Lynch, R. (1997) *Corporate Strategy*, Financial Times Pitman Publishing, London.

Nonaka, I. and Takeuchi, H. (1995) *The Knowledge Creating Company*, Oxford University Press, Oxford.

Shavinina, L. (2003) *The International Handbook on Innovation*, Elsevier, Oxford.

Stacey, R.D. (1993) *Strategic Management and Organisational Dynamics*, Financial Times Pitman Publishing, London.

7

Strategic alliances and networks

In strategic alliances frms cooperate out of mutual need and share the risks to reach a common objective. Strategic alliances provide access to resources that are greater than any single frm could buy. This can greatly improve its ability to create new products, bring in new technologies, penetrate other markets and reach the scale necessary to survive in world markets.

Collaboration with other frms, however, can take many forms. Virtually all frms have networks of suppliers, and in some cases this can form part of a frm's competitive advantage. This chapter will explore the area of frms' networks and the linkages that frms use.

Chapter contents

Learning objectives

When you have completed this chapter you will be able to:

- recognise the reasons for the increasing use of strategic alliances;
- recognise the role of embedded technology in strategic alliances;
- provide an understanding of the risks and limitations of strategic alliances;
- explain how the role of trust is fundamental in strategic alliances;
- examine the different forms an alliance can take;
- explain how the prisoner's dilemma game can be used to analyse the behaviour of firms in strategic alliances; and
- identify the factors that affect the success of an alliance.

Defining strategic alliances

Faced with new levels of competition many companies, including competitors, are sharing their resources and expertise to develop new products, achieve economies of scale, and gain access to new technology and markets. Many have argued that these strategic alliances are the competitive weapon of the next century (*see* Illustration 7.1 for a definition of a strategic alliance). One of the major factors that prevents many firms from achieving their technical objectives and, therefore, their strategic objectives, is the lack of resources. For technology research and development (R&D), the insufficient resources are usually capital and technical 'critical mass'. The cost of building

Illustration 7.1

Definition of strategic alliance

A strategic alliance is a contractual agreement among organisations to combine their efforts and resources to meet a common goal.

It is, however, possible to have a strategic alliance without a contractual agreement hence a more accurate definition would be:

A strategic alliance is an agreement between two or more partners to share knowledge or resources, which could be beneficial to all parties involved.

Source: P.S. Chan and D. Heide (1993) 'Strategic alliances in technology: key competitive weapon', *Advanced Management Journal*, Autumn, Vol. 58, No. 4, 9–18; N.M. Vyas, W.L. Shelburn and D.C. Rogers (1995) 'An analysis of strategic alliances: forms, functions and framework', *Journal of Business and Industrial Marketing*, Summer, Vol. 10, No. 3, 47.

and sustaining the necessary technical expertise and specialised equipment is rising dramatically. Even for the largest corporations leadership in some market segments they have traditionally dominated cannot be maintained because they lack sufficient technical capabilities to adapt to fast-paced market dynamics.

In the past, strategic alliances were perceived as an option reserved only for large international firms. Intensified competition, shortening product life cycles and soaring R&D costs mean that strategic alliances are an attractive strategy for the future. Moreover, Slowinski *et al.* (1996) argue that strategic alliances provide an opportunity for large and small high-technology companies to expand into new markets by sharing skills and resources. They argue it is beneficial for both parties since it allows large firms to access the subset of expertise and resources that they desire in the smaller firm, while the smaller company is given access to its larger partner's massive capital and organisational resources.

For many firms the thought of sharing ideas and technology in particular with another company is precisely what they have been trying to avoid doing since their conception. It is a total lack of trust that lies at the heart of their unwillingness to engage in any form of cooperation. The element of trust is highlighted through the use of the 'prisoner's dilemma'.

Technology partnerships between and in some cases among organisations are becoming more important and prevalent. From 1976 to 1987, the annual number of new joint ventures rose sixfold; by 1987, three-quarters of these were in high-technology industries (Faulkner, 1995; Kaufman *et al.*, 2000; Lewis, 1990). As the costs, including risk associated with R&D efforts, continue to increase, no company can remain a 'technology island' and stay competitive.

The term strategic alliance is used to cover a wide range of cooperative arrangements. The different forms of strategic alliances will be explored later in this chapter.

The fall of the go-it-alone strategy and the rise of the octopus strategy

Businesses are slowly beginning to broaden their view of their business environment from the traditional *go-it-alone* perspective of individual firms competing against each other. The formation of strategic alliances means that strategic power often resides in sets of firms acting together. The development of cell phones, treatments for viruses such as AIDS, aircraft manufacture and motor cars are all dominated by global competitive battles between groups of firms. For example, the success of the European Airbus strategic alliance has been phenomenal. Formed in 1969 as a joint venture between the German firm MBB and the French firm Aerospatiale, it was later joined by CASA of Spain and British Aerospace of the United Kingdom. The Airbus A300 range of civilian aircraft achieved great success in the 1990s securing large orders for aircraft ahead of its major rival Boeing.

Even IBM has forsaken the go-it-alone strategy. The company has teamed up with Cisco Systems to develop security systems and with Toshiba, Japan, to develop liquid crystal display (LCD) screens (Foremski, 2004; Nordwall, 1991).

| Alliances formed by IBM to strength elements of its business strategy | **Figure 7.1** |

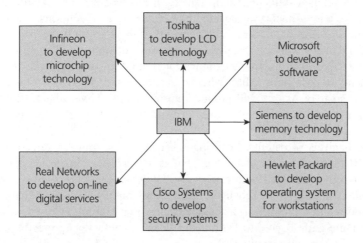

Source: B.D. Nordwall (1991) 'Electronic companies form alliances to counter rising costs', *Aviation Week and Space Technology*, 17 June, 151–2; T. Formenski (2003) 'Infineon, IBM set to unveil chips advance', *Financial Times*, 10 June; T. Formenski (2004) 'Cisco and IBM join forces in global security sector', *Financial Times*, 13 February.

The so-called octopus strategy (Vyas *et al.*, 1995) gets its name from the long tentacles of the eponymous creature. Firms often develop alliances with a wide range of companies. Figure 7.1 shows the alliances that IBM have formed to strengthen elements of its business strategy. Arguably JVC adopted an octopus strategy to try to ensure the VHS technology became the industry standard in the VCR industry. JVC entered alliances with Sharp, Toshiba and RCA.

It is not just large established firms that are rushing into new fields in which they are comparatively small and inexperienced. Many small and medium-sized firms are also entering strategic alliances with a variety of different firms. They are able to offer their existing skills, knowledge and technology, which together with other areas of expertise can create 'hybrid' technologies' such as bio-electronics, or by combining process and product innovations from different industries. Firms are increasingly finding they need an array of complementary assets (Teece, 1998).

Complementary capabilities and embedded technologies

The example of IBM above illustrates that even firms with a long and impressive heritage to defend see technology as the main determinant of competitive success. As a result they increasingly realise they need access to new technology. Moreover, they also realise they cannot develop it all themselves. Acquiring technology from outside using technology transfer (the subject of technology transfer is explored in much more detail in Chapter 10) and forming alliances with others is now regarded as the way forward.

Many large established firms such as Sony, IBM and Nokia have developed global brands and sophisticated distribution infrastructures, but these are of limited value in the computer hardware industry without a constant stream of new products and technologies. Hence, these firms have developed extensive linkages or networks around the world. Hamel (1991) argues that this is necessary because historically regions of the world have developed skills and competencies in certain areas. For example, European countries have a long history of developing science-based inventions, but suffer from a poor understanding of markets and frequently fail to capture the full commercial potential from their inventions. American firms have demonstrated an ability to generate significant profits from market innovations, but then do not make the continual improvements in cost and quality, whereas Japanese and Asian firms have extensive skills in the areas of quality and production efficiencies. Given this global spread of expertise firms have consequently developed linkages with a wide variety of firms all over the world.

The mechanisms of patents, licensing and technology transfer agreements help to create an efficient market for technology, but as we have seen in earlier chapters, technology is usually embedded with experience, know-how and tacit knowledge. Hence, alliances allow not only for exchange of technology but also for the exchange of skills and know-how often referred to as competencies. For example, General Motors used its joint venture with Toyota to learn about 'lean' manufacturing practices. Similarly Thompson, the French consumer electronics group, relied on its alliance with JVC, from Japan, to learn to mass produce the micromechanic subsystem key to successful videocassette recorder production (Doz and Hamel, 1997). The embedded nature of new technologies has forced firms to view technologies as competencies (clearly some technologies will be more embedded than others). This has resulted in an increasing number of alliances, whereas previously a technology licensing or purchase agreement may have been used (Nadler and Tushman, 1997).

Interfirm knowledge-sharing routines

The only way to ensure effective learning for both parties is to build knowledge-sharing routines (Nelson and Winter, 1982; Cohen and Levinthal, 1990; Trott and Cordey-Hayes, 1996; Day and Shoemaker, 2000). This will involve sharing information, know-how and skills. Information can readily be shared via hard copy and electronic data transfer, but know-how and skills are much more difficult as we have seen in Chapter 6. None the less, it is possible and many firms rely on individuals spending time within other firms, either on secondment for a set time or through exchanges of staff. It is the interpersonal interaction which facilitates the transfer of tacit knowledge. Design and manufacturing alliances such as those established by Nike (Illustration 7.2) are very effective at knowledge-sharing routines and hence become more innovative than their competitors. This then becomes a powerful competitive advantage which is extremely difficult to replicate and copy and may give a firm an advantage for many years. Moreover, it is an advantage that a firm may possess which does not require costly patent protection and avoids the risk of copycat branding.

Forms of strategic alliances

Strategic alliances can occur *intra-industry* or *inter-industry*. For example, the three US automobile manufacturers have formed an alliance to develop technology for an electric car. This is an example of an *intra-industry alliance*. This is in response to US legislation requiring a certain percentage of US cars to be gasoline-free by 2010. The UK pharmaceutical giant GlaxoSmithKline has established many *inter-industry* alliances with a wide range of firms from a variety of industries; it includes companies such as Matsushita, Canon, Fuji and Apple.

Furthermore, alliances can range from a simple handshake agreement to mergers, from licensing to equity joint ventures. Moreover, they can involve a customer, a supplier or even a competitor (Chan and Heide, 1993). Research on collaborative activity has been hindered by a wide variety of different definitions. There are six generic types of strategic alliance (Bleeke and Ernst, 1993; Gulati, 1995; Faulkner, 1995; Conway and Stewart, 1998):

1 licensing;

2 supplier relations;

3 joint venture;

4 collaboration (non-joint ventures);

5 R&D consortia;

6 industry clusters; and

7 innovation networks.

Licensing

Licensing is a relatively common and well-established method of acquiring technology. It may not involve extended relationships between firms but increasingly licensing another firm's technology is often the beginning of a form of collaboration. There is usually an element of learning required by the licensee and frequently the licensor will perform the role of 'teacher'. While there are clearly advantages of licensing such as speed of entry to different technologies and reduced cost of technology development, there are also potential problems, particularly the neglect of internal technology development. In the videocassette recording (VCR) industry JVC licensed its VHS recording technology to many firms including Sharp, Sanyo and Thompson. This clearly enabled these firms to enter the new growth industry of the time. But these firms also continued to develop their own technologies in other fields. Sharp, in particular, built on JVC's technology and developed additional features for its range of videocassette recorders.

Supplier relations

Many firms have established close working relations with their suppliers, and without realising it may have formed an informal alliance. Usually these are based on cost-benefits to a supplier. For example:

- lower production costs that might be achieved if a supplier modifies a component so that it 'fits' more easily into the company's product;

- reduced R&D expenses based on information from a supplier about the use of its product in the customer's application;

- improved material flow brought about by reduced inventories due to changes in delivery frequency and lot sizes; and

- reduced administration costs through more integrated information systems.

At its simplest level one may consider a sole-trader electrician, who over time builds a relationship with his equipment supplier, usually a wholesaler. This can be regarded as simply a 'good customer' relationship, where a supplier will provide additional discounts and services for a good customer such as obtaining unusual equipment requests, making special deliveries, holding additional stock, etc. The next level may involve a closer working relationship where a supplier becomes more involved in the firm's business and they share experience, expertise, knowledge and investment, such as developing a new product. For example, the French electronics firm, Thompson, originally supplied radiocassette players to the car manufacturer Citroën. This relationship developed further when Citroën asked Thompson if it could help with the development of radio controls on the steering wheel. This led to an alliance in the development of new products. Many manufacturing firms are increasingly entering into long-term relationships with their component suppliers. Often such agreements are for a fixed term, say five years, with the option of renewal thereafter. British Aerospace adopt this approach when negotiating component suppliers for its aircraft. Such five-year agreements may also include details of pricing, where British Aerospace will expect the price of the component to fall over time as the supplier benefits from economies of scale and manufacturing experience.

Joint venture

A joint venture is usually a separate legal entity with the partners to the alliance normally being equity shareholders. With a joint venture, the costs and possible benefits from an R&D research project would be shared. They are usually established for a specific project and will cease on its completion. For example, Sony-Ericsson is a joint venture between Ericsson of Sweden and Sony of Japan. It was established to set design manufacture and distribute cell phones. Previously both firms had been unsuccessful in the handset market (*see* case study at the end of this chapter). The intention of establishing a joint venture is generally to enable the organisation to 'stand alone'. Illustration 7.2 shows how the Corning Corporation has for many years followed a strategy of developing a range of joint ventures based on its technologies.

Collaboration (non-joint ventures)

The absence of a legal entity means that such arrangements tend to be more flexible. This provides for the opportunity to extend the cooperation over time if so desired. Frequently these occur in many supplier relationships, but they also take place beyond supplier relations. Many university departments work closely with local firms on a wide variety of research projects where there is a common interest. For example, a local firm may be using a carbon-fibre material in manufacturing. The local university chemistry department may have an interest in the properties and performance of the material.

Illustration 7.2

The Corning Corporation

Corning is unique among major corporations in deriving the majority of its turnover from joint ventures and alliances. The company has a long and impressive heritage: as a specialist glass manufacturer it had its own R&D laboratory as far back as 1908. In the 1930s it began combining its technologies with other firms in other industries, giving it access to a wide variety of growth markets. An alliance with PPG gave it access to the flat glass building market; an alliance with Owens provided access to the glass fibres market and an alliance with Dow Chemicals provided it with an opportunity to enter the silicon products market (recent lawsuits in the United States from people whose silicon breast implants that were unsuccessful have forced the Dow Corning alliance into financial difficulties). Corning now has a network of strategic alliances based on a range of different technologies. These alliances now deliver revenue in excess of its own turnover.

In addition Corning has established a separate division to further develop alliances with firms in the fibres and photonics technologies. Corning Innovation Ventures was established to provide Corning Incorporated with insight and visibility into new technologies and to build future customer partnerships. Corning's unique access to the market and technologies provides partners with guidance to help build and execute a better business plan. The Innovation Ventures team brings together a unique background of technical and marketing skills with 38 years of combined fibre optic and photonic experience within the market leader in optical communications.

In particular, Corning plans to form partnerships with large or small entrepreneurial firms. Such firms may wish to partner with Corning because it is the leader in the optical layer of telecommunications. By utilising its 1,600 scientists, engineers and five major research facilities dedicated to photonic research, any entrepreneur partners are guaranteed access to a wealth of knowledge and experience in photonics and optical fibre. Through the firm's vast network of marketing experience across all its optical product lines, and its extensive customer base at the OEM and carrier level, partners are also granted access to the insight, marketing and commercial experience that had led the firm to market leadership position.

Source: www.corning.com/innovationventures (2001).

Cooperation between the parties may produce benefits for both. Such collaboration is frequently extended and maintained for many years.

R&D consortia

A consortium describes the situation where a number of firms come together to undertake what is often a large-scale activity. The rationale for joining a research consortium includes sharing the cost and risk of research, pooling scarce expertise and equipment, performing pre-competitive research and setting standards (*see* 'Forms of external R&D' in Chapter 9 for a more detailed explanation of this form of strategic alliance).

Industry clusters

Michael Porter (1998) identified a number of very successful industry clusters. Clusters are geographic concentrations of interconnected companies, specialised suppliers, service providers and associated institutions in a particular field that are present in a nation or region. It is their geographical closeness that distinguishes them from innovation networks. Clusters arise because they increase the productivity with which companies can compete. The development and upgrading of clusters is an important agenda for governments, companies and other institutions. Cluster development initiatives are an important new direction in economic policy, building on earlier efforts in macroeconomic stabilisation, privatisation, market opening and reducing the costs of doing business.

Porter explains how clusters pose a paradox. In theory, location should no longer be a source of competitive advantage. Open global markets, rapid transportation and high-speed communications should allow any company to source any thing from any place at any time. But in practice, location remains central to competition. Today's economic map of the world is characterised by what Porter calls clusters: critical masses in one place of linked industries and institutions – from suppliers to universities to government agencies – that enjoy unusual competitive success in a particular field. The most famous examples are found in Silicon Valley and Hollywood (see case study at the end of this chapter), but clusters dot the world's landscape. Porter explains how clusters affect competition in three broad ways: first, by increasing the productivity of companies based in the area; second, by driving the direction and pace of innovation; and third, by stimulating the formation of new businesses within the cluster. Geographic, cultural and institutional proximity provides companies with special access, closer relationships, better information, powerful incentives and other advantages that are difficult to tap from a distance. The more complex, knowledge-based and dynamic the world economy becomes, the more this is true. Competitive advantage lies increasingly in local things – knowledge, relationships and motivation – that distant rivals cannot replicate.

Innovation networks

The use of the term network has become increasingly popular. To many it is the new form of organisation offering a sort of 'virtual organisation'. Terms such as 'web' or 'cluster' are also used to describe this or a similar phenomenon (Nadler and Tushman, 1997; DeBresson and Amesse, 1991). Others believe them to be nothing more than a new label for a firm's range of supplier and market relationships. For example, brand management firms like Nike are frequently regarded as network firms. This is because Nike essentially owns and manages the brand and relies on an established network of relationships to produce and distribute its products. It does not own all the manufacturing plant used to manufacture its shoes or all the retail outlets in which its products are sold. It undertakes research, design and development, but has a network of manufacturers in Asia, India and South America. Similarly it has a network of distributors in all the countries in which it operates. Figure 7.2 shows the supplier network of Nike. Nike classifies its suppliers into three different categories:

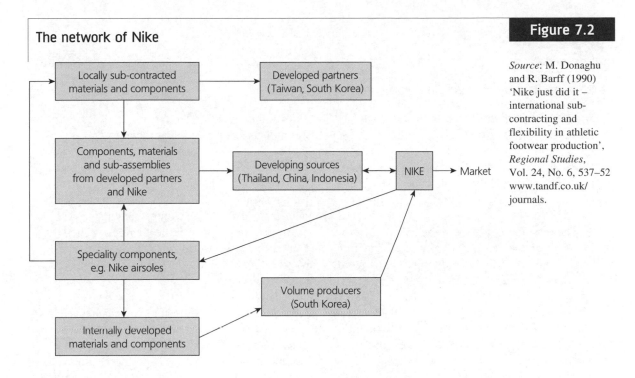

The network of Nike

Figure 7.2

Source: M. Donaghu and R. Barff (1990) 'Nike just did it – international sub-contracting and flexibility in athletic footwear production', *Regional Studies*, Vol. 24, No. 6, 537–52 www.tandf.co.uk/journals.

- volume producers, who produce for a variety of firms;
- developed partners, who are exclusive Nike suppliers, producing the most advanced and newest models of footwear; and
- developing sources, those suppliers that can produce shoes at very low cost.

There is little consensus in the literature about precisely what an innovation network is or indeed when an innovation network is said to exist, but there is some agreement that a network is more than a series of supplier and customer relationships (Tidd, 2001). Some networks have been described as federated in that a set of loosely affiliated firms work relatively autonomously but none the less engage in mutual monitoring and control of one another (Day and Schoemaker, 2000). Other networks can be viewed more as a temporary web, in which firms coalesce around one firm or a business opportunity. For example, following most natural disasters around the world, a collection of organisations including emergency services, government departments, charities and volunteer organisations quickly work together as a network to tackle the immediate problems. Other networks are sometimes referred to as strategic partnerships and usually evolve from long-standing supplier relationships. Through repeated dealings, trust and personal relationships evolve. For example, firms with an established track record in supplying materials, components, etc., to Nike may well find themselves becoming involved in additional activities such as concept testing and product development. This may also include universities, government agencies and competitors.

The United Kingdom's so-called 'motor sport valley', a 100-mile area across southern England centred on Oxford and stretching between Cambridge and Poole, is an

Illustration 7.3

Steered into a commanding lead

The UK's 'motor sport valley' is an industrial driving force

Why has the UK, whose car manufacturing industry was until recently a catalogue of disasters, become the undisputed world leader of motor sport?

The reasons could lie in its need for relentless innovation, imaginative design and engineering, and standard-setting production quality, all delivered at breakneck speed.

Nick Henry and Steven Pinch, economic geographers at Birmingham and Southampton universities, believe that the way these qualities have been developed could have lessons for the rest of UK industry. The two academics have just completed an 18-month study of the UK motor sport industry, funded by the Economic and Social Research Council, which involved talking to just about every Formula One team, every maker of the dominant IndyCar single-seaters, rally and touring car teams and industry associations.

The report depicts an industry operating at frantic pace, with employees driven more by enthusiasm than by pay, and where companies are set up and fail at a rate which is unmatched elsewhere but is seen as beneficial to the industry. It shows why the Department of Trade and Industry sees the sector as a flagship industry, and provides independent endorsement of the multi-million pound technology park being created at Silverstone motor racing complex.

Underpinning the report is the finding that 'Motor Sport Valley', a 100-mile area across southern England centred on Oxford and stretching between Cambridge and Poole, has many of the features of regionalised, flexible production seen as vital to economic growth in advanced economies. These include a geographical clustering of companies in the same sector; high rates of company formation; a strong focus on innovation; emphasis on exports; and flexibility of products and production processes.

The Valley's geographical cohesion has helped it become a world dominating force through its 'knowledge community', say the academics. Although the Valley now has a global industry, 'with finance, sponsorship, drivers, engineers, parts and expertise coming to the UK from all over the world', its organisational base is still networks of hundreds of small and medium-sized companies.

This allows the industry to benefit from the high creation and failure rate for businesses as the knowledge and experience of individuals is quickly reabsorbed into other companies when one business fails. 'Motor sport is very much a knowledge-based industry and although expensive equipment is needed, the crucial asset of a motor sport company is the knowledge possessed by its key personnel', says Mr Henry.

The authors say there is 'virtually no other industry in which the need for continual innovation and change is greater than in racing car construction', and that what they see as a surprising degree of flexibility of response at managerial and employee levels plays a large part in the industry's success in the UK.

What Mr Henry and Mr Pinch describe as 'a Darwinian-like struggle for survival' in motor sport involves a continuous striving for products and processes to give the winning edge, with knowledge transfer core to the process. Their mapping of the careers of 100 designers and engineers shows a transfer every 3.7 years. Proximity, within the Valley and at race meetings, also allows the transmission of knowledge through gossip, 'which plays a much more important role than most realise'.

That component suppliers typically work for several teams is seen as beneficial because of the rapid rate of innovation. 'As long as a team knows it can keep ahead of its rivals, it is not a problem if the ideas eventually get transferred throughout the industry . . . an individual team probably has more to gain than lose through the skills which components suppliers learn by servicing a number of different racing car companies.'

The ERSC report says 'there is no industry which better demonstrates what can be achieved by total dedication and supreme effort. In the case of motor sport, this dedication has not been self-consciously engineered by management gurus but is an integral part of the way the industry operates.'

Source: John Griffiths, 'Steered into a leading command', *Financial Times*, 15 January 1998. Reprinted with permission.

interesting example of a loose network or web of firms working within Formula One motor sport. It has a geographic clustering of companies in related industries, a strong focus on innovation and many small flexible manufacturing firms (*see* Illustration 7.3). The point at which a large cluster of firms becomes classified as a 'science park' is a moot point (*see* Chapter 10 for more on science parks). But, in this particular example, unlike 'Silicon Valley' that represents a cluster of firms operating in computer hardware and software industries, the focus of the 'motor sport valley' is on one market – Formula One motor sport.

The 'virtual company'

More recently the idea of a 'virtual company' has begun to emerge. This is where every aspect of the business is outsourced and run by unknown suppliers. Illustration 7.4 shows how the pharmaceutical industry is making progress in this radical way of

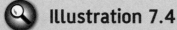

Illustration 7.4

FT

Prescription for cutting costs

Vanessa Houlder looks at how the pharmaceuticals industry is developing the 'virtual' company

Enthusiasm for the truly 'virtual' company – in which every single aspect of the business is run by autonomous suppliers – is mostly confined to management theorists. Practical examples have been difficult to find.

One sector that is making headway with this radical method of running a business is the pharmaceutical industry. Two years ago, Roche, one of the world's largest pharmaceutical companies, calculated that it could shave as much as 40 per cent off the cost of developing a drug – typically hundreds of millions of dollars – by adopting a virtual business model.

In the summer of 1996, Roche put this idea into practice. It set up a subsidiary, called Protodigm, with responsibility for taking three drugs – for Alzheimer's disease, traumatic shock and cancer – through clinical trials.

▶

After a year and a half, Protodigm believes it is on track to meet its targets. So far, every milestone has been met or bettered, according to Jon Court, Protodigm's managing director.

The company subcontracts its work out to as many as 20 suppliers for each drug. This is supervised by just eight directors and one administrator. Once the drugs have been submitted for regulatory approval, they will be handed back to the parent company for marketing.

How can this small group of managers hope to cut costs so significantly? For one thing, they can strike hard bargains with suppliers; for another, they can cut costs and time by keeping overheads and bureaucracy to a minimum.

These ideas are not new. Some industries have always tended to favour virtual structures. Property development, for example, has always depended on putting together small teams of contractors, surveyors and architects for individual projects.

But there is no doubt that these ideas are becoming increasingly popular.

In a survey by Andersen Consulting and the Economist Intelligence Unit last year, 42 per cent of the 350 respondents predicted that, in the future, their companies would operate in a wide network of alliances and relationships with other organisations.

The driving force behind this trend is companies recognising they cannot do everything for themselves when faced with greater competition, growing cost pressures, faster technological change and the increasing need for more marketing muscle internationally. They also believe that small, nimble suppliers save time and money by cutting out bureaucracy.

'We are faster because we are less bureaucratic and we live or die as a service company', says Edwin Moses, managing director of Oxford Asymmetry, a rapidly growing UK contractor to the pharmaceuticals industry.

Advances in information and communications technology have made it far easier for a network of autonomous companies to work together. The availability of high quality suppliers has increased as job losses in large organisations encourage experienced staff to leave and set up as independent suppliers.

Many of these trends have been particularly prevalent in the pharmaceuticals industry. Moreover, the pharmaceuticals industry's need to generate new products makes it susceptible to these ideas.

Over the course of this decade, hundreds of alliances have been forged between pharmaceutical and biotechnology companies, which offer skills and a culture of innovation that the pharmaceutical giants sometimes lack.

A survey by PA Consulting three years ago found that research and development outsourcing in the pharmaceuticals industry was expected to increase by 30 per cent over the next five years. 'Attitudes are changing', says Steve Bone, director of business innovation at Generics, a Cambridge-based consultancy. 'Some very large pharma companies are planning to do virtual R&D. It is an attempt to make their people more entrepreneurial and more outward-looking.'

But there are potential hazards with the virtual model. Can a very small staff offer enough expertise to guide a drug through trials? Dr Court is convinced that it can. 'Being able to ask the right questions is the key thing', he says. 'Between the nine of us we have 150 years of drug development experience.'

Vanguard, another virtual pharmaceutical company, started in 1992 with four people and has expanded to 50 people. Although it still contracts out all its work, it has needed to employ more managers to ensure it has sufficient in-house expertise to supervise the contracting-out process.

Intellectual property is another potential problem. Traditionally, pharmaceutical companies have been extremely secretive about the processes they use to make their drugs.

Dr Court says he has no reason to doubt the discretion of Protodigm's suppliers which, he points out, also have confidential information of their own. 'We want them to feel like partners. We have to trust each other.'

He thinks that, traditionally, pharmaceutical companies have failed to get the best out of their suppliers because they are 'hell bent on protecting their knowledge about the product'.

Security is not the only reason for restricting the sort of R&D that is farmed out to suppliers. A company may damage its long-term potential by outsourcing certain aspects of its work, instead of nurturing its own capabilities. When IBM launched its first PC in 1981, it outsourced its operating system development to Microsoft. This appeared sensible at the time – but proved costly in the long run.

Another factor that will influence the success of the virtual model is the state of the relationship between a large number of self-interested players.

Writing in the *Harvard Business Review* in 1996, Henry Chesbrough and David Teece of the Haas School of Business pointed out that coordinating a lot of different parties can be difficult, particularly if something goes wrong. By contrast, large organisations do not generally reward people for taking risks but they do have established processes for settling conflicts and coordinating all the activities necessary for innovation.

Virtual companies can move faster, work harder and take more risks than conventional organisations. But the incentives that make a virtual company powerful also leave it vulnerable, they argue.

'While there are many successful virtual companies, there are even more failures that don't make the headlines.'

Source: V. Houlder, 'Prescription for cutting costs', *Financial Times*, 12 January 1998. Reprinted with permission.

running a business. However, there are clearly aspects of control that may be lost in such organisations. Other aspects such as intellectual property, skills and know-how may also be lost if everything is outsourced. Figure 7.1 gives the chilling warning of the business opportunities that may be lost when activities are ousourced. When IBM launched its first PC in 1981 it outsourced the development of the operating system to a small firm called Microsoft!

Motives for establishing an alliance

Frequently alliances will have multiple objectives. For example, an alliance may seek to access technology, gain greater technical critical mass and share the risk of future technology development. The European Airbus is a good example of an alliance that has multiple objectives. Table 7.1 lists the most common reasons cited for entering a strategic alliance.

Research by Morrison and Mezentseff (1997) suggests that strategic business alliances will only achieve a sustainable competitive advantage if they involve learning and knowledge transfer (*see* Figure 10.7). They design a framework to help such partnerships develop a cooperative learning environment to achieve long-term success. The emphasis on learning helps to develop individual and organisational intelligence, thereby ensuring the future success of the strategic alliance.

Table 7.1 Reasons for entering a strategic alliance

	Reasons	Examples
1	Improved access to capital and new business	European Airbus to enable companies to compete with Boeing and MacDonnell Douglas
2	Greater technical critical mass	Industry alliance formed between US microchip manufacturers to compete with Japanese
3	Shared risk and liability	Sony-Ericsson, a joint venture between two electronics frms to try to dominate cell phone handset market
4	Better relationships with strategic partners	European Airbus
5	Technology transfer benefts	Customer supplier alliances, e.g. VW and Bosch
6	Reduce R&D costs	GEC and Siemens 60/40 share of telecommunications joint venture: GPT
7	Use of distribution skills	Pixar and Disney
8	Access to marketing strengths	NMB, Japan and Intel; NMB has access to Intel's marketing
9	Access to technology	Ericsson gained access to Sony's multi-media technology for third-generation cell phones
10	Standardisation	Attempt by Sony to get Beetamax technology as industry standard
11	By-product utilisation	GlaxoSmithKline and Matsushita, Canon, Fuji
12	Management skills	J Sainsbury and Bank of Scotland; Sainsbury accessed fnancial skills

Sources: D.A. Littler (1993) 'Roles and rewards of collaboration', in Tidd, J., Besant, J. and Pault, K. (eds) (2001) *Managing Innovation*, Wiley, Chichester, p. 51; P.S. Chan and D. Heide (1993) 'Strategic alliances in technology: key competitive weapon', *Advanced Management Journal*, Vol. 58, No. 4, 9–18; A. Harney (2001) 'Ambitious expansion loses its shine: analysts change their tune about Sony's dreams and begin to count the costs of the new mobile phone alliance with Ericsson, *Financial Times*, 2 October; R. Budden (2003) 'Sony-Ericsson seeks success with new phones', www.FT.com, 3 March.

The process of forming a successful strategic alliance

The formation of a strategic alliance is a three-step process (*see* Figure 7.3). It begins with the selection of the right partner. This will clearly depend on what is required and the motivation for the strategic alliance. This is usually followed by negotiations based on each partner's needs. The third and final stage is the management towards collaboration. This last step encompasses a wide range of activities, including joint goal-setting and conflict resolution. Moreover, this last stage needs constant work to keep the relationship sound. Aside from collaborative management, the success of a business alliance depends on the existence of mutual need and the ability to work together despite differences in organisational culture.

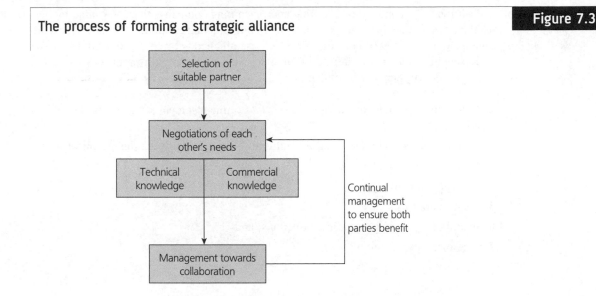

The process of forming a strategic alliance

Figure 7.3

Risks and limitations with strategic alliances

So far we have addressed only the potential benefits to be gained from strategic alliances. However, a strategic alliance also has a downside. It can lead to competition rather than cooperation, to loss of competitive knowledge, to conflicts resulting from incompatible cultures and objectives, and to reduced management control (Chan and Heide, 1993). A study of almost 900 joint ventures found that less than half were mutually agreed to have been successful by all partners (Harrigan, 1986; Dacin *et al.*, 1997; Spekman *et al.*, 1996). Illustration 7.5 shows how after more than eight successful years together Pixar and Disney decided to end the joint venture. While the future looks bright for Pixar – Disney's future is less assured.

The literature on the subject of technological cooperation presents a confusing picture. There is evidence to suggest that strategic alliances may harm a firm's ability to innovate. Arias (1995) argues that inter-firm networking may result not only in desired outcomes but also in negative consequences. The creation of closely structured networks of relationships may produce increased complexity, loss of autonomy and information asymmetry. These hazards may ultimately lead to a decreased ability to innovate and participate in technological change.

To avoid these problems, management should anticipate business risks related to partnering, carefully assess their partners, conduct comprehensive resource planning and allocation of resources to the network and develop and foster social networks. All parties should also ensure that the motives for participating are positive, that the networks are as formidable as the alliances within them and that there is a perception of equal contribution and benefits from the parties. Lastly, there should be communication, data sharing, goals and objectives.

The level and nature of the integration appears to be a crucial factor. In some cases the alliance is very tight indeed. For example, Motoman, a robotic systems supplier, and Stillwater Technologies, a tooling and machining company, share the same facility for their offices and manufacturing and their computer and communications systems are linked (Sheridan, 1997). For other firms a loose alliance is far more comfortable.

Research in the area of failure of alliances identifies seven different reasons (Vyas *et al.*, 1993; Duysters *et al.*, 1999):

1 failure to understand and adapt to new style of management required for the alliance;

2 failure to learn and understand the cultural differences between the organisations;

3 lack of commitment to succeed;

4 strategic goal divergence;

5 insufficient trust;

6 operational and or geographical overlaps; and

7 unrealistic expectations.

Illustration 7.5

FT

Setback for Disney as Pixar alliance ends

Michael Eisner's efforts to revive the fortunes of Walt Disney suffered a fresh blow on Thursday as his hugely successful alliance with Pixar, the animation studio behind *Finding Nemo* and *Toy Story*, collapsed.

The failure will trigger a scramble among other Hollywood studios, which have been angling to take over from Disney as distributor of Pixar's blockbuster movies.

The collapse of the talks with Pixar robs Disney of an important strategic alliance and analysts said it was a serious setback for Mr Eisner, the company's chairman.

Peter Mirsky, an analyst at Oppenheimer in New York, said the Pixar relationship not only generated income from movies but also plugged a hole left by the weakness in Disney's own animation division, for instance by supplying a new crop of popular characters for its theme parks.

The blow will offer further encouragement to Roy Disney and Stanley Gold, the former Disney directors who have been waging a vocal campaign against Mr Eisner. On Thursday night, the two men said they were 'dismayed but not surprised' by the failure of the Pixar talks.

'More than a year ago, we warned the Disney Board that we believed Michael Eisner was mismanaging the Pixar partnership and expressed our concern that the relationship was in jeopardy.'

Run by Steve Jobs, founder of Apple Computer, Pixar has had an unbroken run of five hit movies which has made it one of the hottest properties in the movie business. Its groundbreaking 3D animation combined with cute characters and storylines have brought comparisons with Disney's own impact on animation in its heyday.

Pixar and Disney had been locked in negotiations for the past 10 months over extending their alliance, which is due to expire after two more movies. On Thursday, though, Mr Jobs walked away from the talks, after rejecting proposed terms that Disney put forward early last week.

The negotiations foundered despite Disney's willingness to take a far smaller slice of the income from future Pixar films. Disney was also willing to agree a simple distribution deal that would have paid it a basic fee that is far lower than it has accepted on any similar arrangement before, said one person close to the company. At the moment it takes a 12 per cent distribution fee, shares half of the profits from the movies and keeps ownership of Pixar's movies.

In another concession to Mr Jobs, Disney was willing to give up part of its rights to pro-fits from the next two Pixar movies – *The Incredibles* and *Cars* – according to the person familiar with its stance. However, in a statement on Thursday Tom Straggs, Disney's chief fin-ancial officer, said that Pixar's demands would have cost 'hundreds of millions of dollars' and finally proved unacceptable.

In a brief statement, Mr Jobs said: 'We've had a great run together – one of the most successful in Hollywood history – and it's a shame that Disney won't be participating in Pixar's future success.'

Despite losing access to future Pixar films, Disney still has the rights to make sequels to the company's earlier movies, which include *Monsters Inc* and *A Bug's Life*.

Rival Hollywood executives, who were caught off guard by the news, were yesterday racing to put together offers to Pixar. Analysts said Warner Brothers, Twentieth Century Fox and Sony Pictures were the most likely partners for Pixar, which is expected to judge the contenders according to their global distribution clout – both at the box office and with DVD retailers.

Mr Jobs held a series of informal meetings with studio heads before beginning negotiations with Disney last year, but no serious talks have taken place.

Source: R. Waters and P.T. Larsen, 'Setback for Disney as Pixar alliance ends', *Financial Times*, 29 January 2004. Reprinted with permission.

The formation of strategic alliances by definition fosters cooperation rather than competition. Ensuring competition remains is a major implication of strategic alliances. The respective government departments of trade and commerce around the world need to be vigilant of the extent to which firms that cooperate are also capable of manipulat-ing the price of products.

The role of trust in strategic alliances

The business and management literature and accepted management thinking are pre-dominantly optimistic in their belief that there is much to gain from strategic alliances and collaborative technology development. This optimism remains largely robust despite substantial failures of high-profile alliances highlighting the difficulties and limitations of such strategic alliances (see Porter, 1987; Bleeke and Ernst, 1992).

According to the strategic management literature, firms with a global presence – in particular those operating in technology-intensive sectors – are increasingly reliant on collaborative technology development. They can no longer continue to rely on the use of traditional means to protect their 'secrets', such as internalisation and legal controls, because they need to become more 'outward-looking' and therefore more receptive in their technology development strategy. By its very nature, collaborative technology development means that sharing knowledge and 'openness' is a precondition for successful organisational learning. Openness and free exchange of information, however, make companies more vulnerable to risks of information leakage. It is in this specific context that the problem of trust emerges most clearly in collaborative technology development. In order to reap the benefits from collaborative technology development, companies or, more precisely, research managers need to be able to trust their partners (Hollis, 1998).

The concept of trust

All forms of collaboration involve an element of risk and require substantial amounts of trust and control. It is the leakage of sensitive information to competitors that is of most concern to firms. Innovative applied research often develops out of the collaboration of firms and research institutions, where this is initiated with the help of previous academic contacts of key players in firms and universities. In this case the selection of, and decision to trust, a partner is typically made on the basis of prior professional and or social knowledge (Liebeskind and Oliver, 1998; Zucker *et al.*, 1996). For example, scientists working at one large firm will have graduated from university with friends who took up similar positions in other large firms. Hence, every scientist will have a small network of scientists largely as a result of university. Firms recognise that all their scientists operate within networks and expect them to exercise their professional judgement. Usually personal knowledge and the desire to protect one's professional reputation are sufficient safeguards to justify a limited-scale disclosure of sensitive information. If the initial collaboration is successful, the scale of collaboration can be increased incrementally and higher levels of mutual trust will be reached (Lewicki and Bunker, 1996).

Trust is not the same as confidence. For example, supporters of football teams are confident that their team will work hard and win some games over the course of the season, but they trust their players, manager and club that collectively the organisation will try to win and that results are not 'fixed' through corruption. Both confidence and trust are based on expectations about the future, but trust entails the exposure to the risk of opportunistic behaviour by others. One can say that an agent exhibits trust when he or she has no reason to believe that the trusted other will exploit this opportunity (Giddens, 1990; Humphrey and Schmitz, 1998).

It is important to keep in mind that trust is practised and exercised between individuals, even if they represent an organisation. Trust is a personal judgement and carries an emotional as well as a cognitive dimension. While trust at the system level is similar to confidence – as there is no choice but to trust the currency to store value – trust in an institution or organisation depends on personal experience with individuals representing the organisation at its contact points (Giddens, 1990). This does not mean that the institutional dimension should be underestimated.

Trust, then, exists at the individual and organisational levels and research has attempted to distinguish different levels and sources of trust (Zucker, 1986; Sako, 1992; Hoecht and Trott, 1999). The bases of trust in alliances are identified in Table 7.2.

The sources of trust production are not mutually exclusive and often work in conjunction. For instance, while membership of an ethnic group (personal-based trust) can be a vital initial advantage for setting up a business, or having studied at a particular

Table 7.2 Types of trust

Type of trust	Characteristics
Process	Where trust is tied to past or expected exchange, such as reputation or gift exchange
Personal	Where trust is tied to a person, depending on family background, religion or ethnicity
Institutional	Where trust is tied to formal structures, depending on individual or firm-specifc attributes
Competence trust	Confidence in the other's ability to perform properly
Contractual trust	Honouring the accepted rules of exchange
Goodwill trust	Mutual expectations of open commitment to each other beyond contractual obligations

university for finding 'open doors', this will not be enough to sustain trust over time. Trust can be initiated as personal trust, but it will have to be 'earned' before long (Humphrey and Schmitz, 1998). Similarly, bestowing trust onto a person or an institution does not mean that methods of limiting the damage from potential 'betrayal' cannot be used. Contractual safeguards, access to legal redress and institutional assurances can have a very positive effect on collaborative business relations as Lane and Bachmann (1996) have shown in their comparison of the role of trust in UK and German supplier relations.

In the context of collaborative R&D, institutional sources of trust production will, however, be of limited use only. It is clearly not possible to rely on institutional-based trust and legal safeguards for the protection of intangible, pre-competitive knowledge against misuse (Sitkin and Roth, 1993). Even if such safeguards were workable, the necessity to incorporate each little step along the development path of a collaborative research project into a contractual arrangement would cause enormous delays and hence endanger its very success. The level of trust needed here is the one labelled 'goodwill trust' by Sako (1992), where the mutual commitment goes beyond honouring what is explicitly agreed and the trustee can be trusted to exercise the highest level of discretion, to take beneficial initiatives and to refrain from taking unfair advantage even if such opportunities arise (Hoecht and Trott, 1999).

The use of game theory to analyse strategic alliances

Research using game theory has suggested that some alliance structures are inherently more likely than others to be associated with a high opportunity to cheat, high behavioural uncertainty and poor stability, longevity and performance. Parkhe (1993) argues maintaining robust cooperation in interfirm strategic alliances poses special problems. The study by Parkhe looked at 111 interfirm alliances. The findings suggested the need for a greater focus on game-theoretic structural dimensions and institutional responses to perceived opportunism in the study of voluntary inter-firm cooperation.

The development of the VCR industry is littered with strategic alliances formed by various businesses to try to help ensure they gain access to the relevant technology. Unfortunately not all the alliances were successful. Sony embarked on several strategic alliances with competitors in an attempt to try to make its Beetamax technology the industry standard. When JVC, Toshiba and others refused, the alliance existed in name only (Baden-Fuller and Pitt, 1996). There are many other examples of alliances failing – some soon after inception, others after a long and successful relationship.

The issue of trust is a critical element in any strategic alliance. By its very nature an alliance, like a marriage, is dependent on all parties working together so that the total outcome is greater than any one party can achieve on its own. It is important to note that trust is usually established over a long period of time, in much the same way as courtship prior to marriage involves understanding one another and building confidence in the relationship. In order to lose trust, however, one must have gained it in the first place. A more serious proposition is that firms may enter a strategic alliance with a lack of trust in the other party. The issue of trust is the underlying theme of the prisoner's dilemma, which is discussed in the next section.

Game theory and the prisoner's dilemma

The extent to which two companies are going to cooperate is a key question for any strategic alliance. This question can be examined using the prisoner's dilemma. It graphically highlights the options facing companies when they embark on a strategic alliance. It illustrates that cooperation is the mutually advantageous strategy but that non-cooperation provides high-risk opportunities to both parties.

The basic form of this game is known as the prisoner's dilemma and gets its name from the following scenario. Suppose two criminals are arrested for drug dealing. The local police chief arrests them both and takes them to the cells for interrogation. They are placed in separate cells and face fierce questioning. The police chief, however, does not have sufficient evidence to gain a conviction. The chief asks Detective Holmes to offer a deal to both criminals. If either confesses, he will receive a minimal sentence for becoming an informer and helping the police. If neither confess they will both receive a sentence based upon some other lesser charge for which the police chief does have evidence. If they both confess, the court will take this cooperation into account and will probably pass a lighter sentence on both. The game matrix is represented in Figure 7.4, with the relevant years of sentence to be expected.

Both criminals A and B have a dominant strategy. No matter what the other does, both are better off if they confess. The option of 'do not confess' carries with it the risk of spending 10 years in prison. The maximum sentence for confessing is 6 years with a possibility of only 1 year. Given this payoff matrix both criminals should confess. This is the classic form of the prisoner's dilemma.

Prisoner's dilemma

Figure 7.4

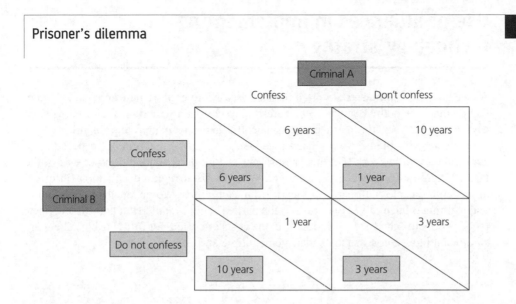

It has a close relative, which is the repeated game. This is a more realistic interpretation of reality, as few business relationships are one-off events. For example, BMW competes with Volkswagen in a variety of markets now and most likely in the future. With the knowledge that one is to repeat any game played, the options are likely to be different. To return to the criminals locked up in prison: if they both realise that 'squealing' on a fellow-prisoner may bring with it some form of revenge, such as death, from the prisoner's friends, the range of outcomes changes significantly. The dominant solution is now to play *do not confess*. Figure 7.5 shows the repeated game matrix.

The repeated game

Figure 7.5

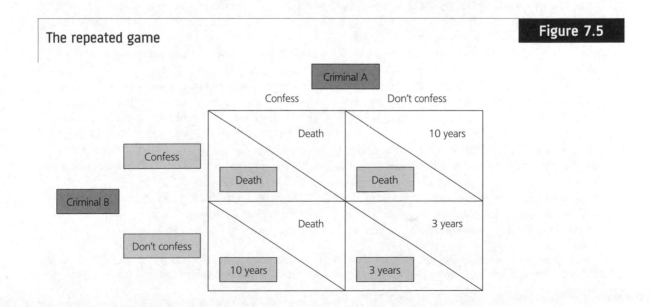

Use of alliances in implementing technology strategy

As we have seen, alliances are often pursued as ways to explore new applications, new technologies or both. By their very nature they confront uncertainty and knowledge asymmetry between the partners. Consequently there are many calls for full explicit agreements with plans to be signed in advance of any collaboration, especially by accountants and lawyers. Yet this can prevent and hinder collaboration because of the lack of familiarity between the partners. What is often required is a more informal approach to enable both parties to learn from each other. Moreover, the collaboration and learning often evolves over time as the parties begin to understand one another better. The benefits can be great indeed, but the costs are often not fully visible. There are significant hidden costs such as management time and energy.

Case study

The Hollywood film industry and the role of knowledge network organisations[1]

This case study explores the rise of project-based work and the creation of temporary organisations that undertake it. In knowledge-intensive professional services such as management consultancy, architecture and law, project-based employment is increasingly being used. For example, management consultancy firms secure work in the form of large projects that typically last for six months to two years. The management consultancy may have employees that they put on the project but in addition the project team will be made up of a variety of contract consultants with varying skills over the life of the project. This type of project-based work has been the norm in the construction industry for many years. Here the contractor leading the project will employ the skills required to construct the building. Similarly, in the film industry an enterprise is formed to make a film. This project-based enterprise grows and contracts in size over the life of the film. When the film is released the enterprise is closed. This is unlike other industries where the

principal company is expected to remain in business and seek new work.

Industry clusters and networks

Clusters are geographic concentrations of interconnected companies, specialised suppliers, service providers and associated institutions in a particular field that are present in a nation or region. Clusters arise because they increase the productivity with which companies can compete. Today's economic map of the world is characterised by what Michael Porter calls clusters: critical masses in one place of linked industries and institutions – from suppliers to universities to government agencies – that enjoy unusual competitive success in a particular field (for a fuller explanation of industry clusters see above, p. 218, for more details).

Over the past 100 years the area around Hollywood has developed a wide range of skills and services to meet the needs of the film

[1] This case has been written as a basis for class discussion rather than to illustrate effective or ineffective managerial or administrative behaviour. It has been prepared from a variety of published sources, as indicated, and from observations.

industry. Hollywood is a regional cluster of competencies in much the same way as Silicon Valley is in northern California or the Motorsport valley in the United Kingdom (*see* Illustration 7.3). There is no single firm or institution that is able to offer all the necessary skills required. But, all these skills are available from a variety of organisations and individuals. Access to these skills, however requires knowledge of the networks and it seems this is the key to unlocking the creative potential of the Hollywood film industry.

History of Hollywood

Since the development of sound to accompany the pictures, Hollywood has established a flexible system for regularly producing and distributing feature-length motion pictures. The diffusion of the Hollywood cinema, distribution and presentation throughout the world was successfully completed by the early 1920s. During the 1930s Hollywood was able to increase its control over the world market particularly because it exploited the development of sound. This also coincided with the establishment of five large film-making studios which dominated film making, distribution and exhibiting films. These were:

1 Paramount;
2 Loew's;
3 Fox Film;
4 Warner Bros; and
5 RKO.

During this era of film making the big five employed permanent staff to make films, such as scriptwriters, special effect technicians, costume designers and actors. Although difficult to imagine now, actors were employed by a studio and would act in films being made by the studio. There have always been independent film companies and one of the most successful during this early period of sound motion pictures was MGM. As an independent it did not have permanent staff and would bring people together to make a film on a short-term contract basis.

During the 1950s, the big five studios found the costs of maintaining groups of permanent employees prohibitively expensive. Eventually the studio system of film making gave way to the example set by the independents such as MGM. Today film making is dominated by short-term projects and short-term contracts.

Independent film making and the $60 billion porn industry in the San Fernando Valley

To the cinema-snob, there is no place for pornography in the discussion of independent film making. Yet, to anyone with even a passing knowledge of film history, there would be no independent cinema without our barely clad brothers and sisters in the skin flicks.

As an industry, pornography has enjoyed a truly pioneering effect which is rarely noted. Indeed, the adult entertainment industry always existed as independent productions, working far beyond the studio systems. Historically, the porn business set the groundwork for non-theatrical distribution channels, guerrilla marketing, breaking on-screen taboos (especially the unapologetic depiction of inter-racial and same-sex couplings), and challenging the status quo on censorship long before so-called serious film-makers bothered to get agitated. More recently, adult filmmakers were the first to embrace DV technology for shooting films, the first to use the Internet for the promotion and marketing of new titles, and the first to encourage a new wave of DIY filmmaking under the appealing moniker of 'amateur porn'. Indeed, adult films are very much an integral part of the ebb and flow of the indie film world (Helmore, 1999).

According to figures released recently by the Los Angeles County Economic Development Corporation, 10,000–20,000 jobs depend on the industry. The San Fernando Valley is where the bulk of the world's adult films are made and is home to the world's largest community of porn stars – about 1,600 of them – as well as 50 of the world's 85 top pornography companies. It is

▶

however, the Internet which has fuelled the more recent rapid growth of the adult entertainment industry. This is largely because it has made anonymity easier for people. People can access adult products without having to leave their home or deal with the embarrassment of going out to a video store.

The adult entertainment industry has also played a significant role in the growth and adoption of new technologies. The VCR industry is famously quoted as saying that in the early days it relied on the skin flicks to keep it going. It was certainly true that the video rental market began with adult video films. Similar parallels can be drawn with the Internet as 'it was porn businesses that were quick to offer short subscription terms and digital products in the form of image galleries, as well as the sale of hard goods,' says Mark Hardie, analyst at Internet tracking company Forrester Research, which estimates that $1 billion of the $7.8 billion spent online last year went on porn (Hardie; cited in Helmore, 1999).

Forrester forecasts that the market will grow at an annual rate of 20 per cent. The vast sums that can be made from Internet porn were shown earlier this year when Steve Cohen, owner of Sex.com, made a $3.6 billion bid for the Caesar's Palace chain of hotels and casinos. Sex.com claims to have 9 million subscribers paying $24.95 a month. Moreover, with the coming of broadband Internet delivery, video-on-demand services by cable TV companies and digital versatile disc (DVD) technology, the adult entertainment industry seems destined for further growth.

While corporate America may look down its nose at the adult entertainment industry, it has taken notice of the enormous profits to be made from it and associated activities such as distribution. Castle Superstores Corp, 'an adult version of Toys "Я" Us', operates outlets in 11 Wal-Mart stores in the mid-west; US cable and satellite companies make as much as $310 million a year from porn distribution; Hilton and Sheraton hotel chains profit from offering porn to their guests; and AT&T profits from connecting callers to sex chat lines. Indeed, as an indication of the size of revenues to be obtained two of the largest porn makers: Private Media Group and Metro Global Media, are already listed on Nasdaq. Forbes estimates the global porn market at $60 billion; as Steve Orienstein, president of Wicked Films, told the *Los Angeles Times*: 'You have to try really hard to lose money in this business.'

The nature of film making and the project-based enterprise

Like virtually all new products they start with an idea that grows in the minds of an individual or a group into a genuine business opportunity that is either supported or not. Take the recent case of Mystic River for which Sean Penn received an Academy Award for best actor in 2004. According to the director, Clint Eastwood, this project started after he read the novel by Dennis Lehane. Eastwood was so impressed by the novel he contacted the author and explained that he would like to make a film based on the book. One of the first key decisions for Eastwood was to appoint a screenwriter to convert the novel to a film. Notwithstanding the influence of the director in this case, this is typical of how film ideas are born. To move from idea to film however, requires resources and eventually a financial backer is involved (i.e. the producer) who is responsible for getting the film made. The artistic and creative input lies with the director and is separate from the financial responsibilities that lie with the producer.

A film company recruits all its personnel in similar ways to other industries. The producer recruits people with the business skills he requires and the director begins to recruit the artistic talent he believes he needs. With a big-budget film project it is common practice to hire crews that have worked together previously. Personal networks of contacts are crucial here and the producer and the director will appoint several key people to recruit the necessary teams required. So, for example, the director may appoint a number of assistant directors with

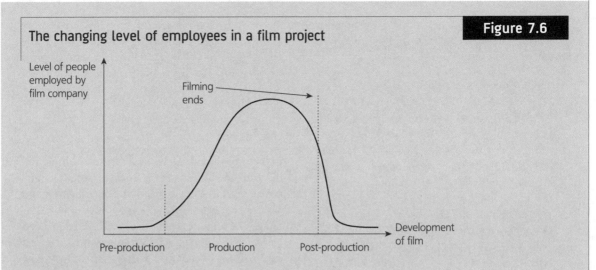

The changing level of employees in a film project

Figure 7.6

Level of people employed by film company

Filming ends

Pre-production   Production   Post-production

Development of film

particular responsibilities, such as visual effects, camera and photography. In many cases they are able to appoint small teams of people. Smaller, low-budget films will have the additional restraint of resources as a key influencing factor.

The levels of employment rise and fall dramatically as production of the film begins. One month 20 people may be employed and the next it could be 200. During filming the creative costs are extremely high as all sorts of skills are employed from camera crews, lighting engineers, costume designers, make-up artists, photographers, sound technicians, etc. Usually staffing follows a curve as shown in Figure 7.6, with a small core of people involved in pre-production, a large number during production and a small creative group in post-production. On the business and commercial side the producer may have to keep investors informed of the financial position on a monthly basis.

Another unique characteristic of film making are the delays and interruptions that seem to come from the most unanticipated quarters. The weather is a frequent cause of cost overruns and delays, sometimes hundreds of highly skilled people will be in place to record part of the film only for them to be unable to do so for several days due to poor weather. Frequently this will mean paying crews while they sit around waiting for the weather to change. The absence of a key cast member is another reason for significant cost overruns and schedule delays.

Learning during idleness

During the actual film shooting different groups of specialists alternate between periods of intense activity and forced idleness. Experienced crews can anticipate about how much time their services will be required in a day but cannot be certain. While learning by doing is well understood in the film industry there is much learning by watching. Indeed, the periods of idleness for the different crews enable them to exchange war stories and experiences of recent and sometimes not so recent projects. It is widely accepted that much learning and sharing of knowledge is undertaken during these periods. In this case the learning is being undertaken by individuals and will be transferred to their next project; what is worthy of note is that the 'organisation' does not appear to be learning.

Unemployment and skin flicks to the rescue

The nature of the film industry with the dominance of project-based work means that for almost everyone in the industry there are periods of intense activity, in other words employment and long periods of unemployment. This is where the 'skin flicks' industry plays another important role in Hollywood. It provides much needed

▶

work and ultimately money to film industry crews. As Dave Chrisman (2000) from the *Los Angeles Magazine* explains:

Like thousands of other L.A.-based crew members, Mark Wright who worked on **Titanic** *and other major mainstream films as a cameraman has found porn to be a reliable way to make ends meet. 'I've gotta pay the bills', says Wright, who refuses to do hard-core shoots but has done work for the Playboy Channel. 'There are lines I will not cross, but they keep getting pushed farther away as times get tougher.' Faced with unemployment or working in porn, hordes of out-of-work gaffers and production assistants are heading to the San Fernando Valley for their paychecks.*

Of course, dabbling in porn is nothing new for seasoned Hollywood pros. *Men in Black* and *Wild Wild West* director Barry Sonnenfeld got his start as a cameraman in skin flicks. The difference now is that this former sideline has become a lifeline.

'It's easy money', admits a spokesman for Local 80 of the International Alliance of Theatrical Stage Employees, which represents grips (camera-crews) and gaffers. 'And if you don't care about morals, it's still work.'

End of the film, end of the enterprise

Once post-production is complete the film is finished and the organisation has accomplished its task. The organisation is then closed. Many actors and actresses, especially those in demand, will complete shooting of a film and move on to another film project a long time before the film is released. The same is true for many of the other people involved. Indeed, if post-production takes a long time or there are problems securing distribution it may be many years after filming is complete that those involved actually see the film. And, of course, there are many films shot that never reach the big screen. In recent years part of the post-production phase has involved some market Eresearch activities such as showing previews to audiences to gauge their reactions, prior to finalising the film. Like in most other new product launches revenue generation can only begin on release of the film.

Conclusions

In the film-making industry at the end of making the film the organisation formed for this purpose ceases to exist any longer. Leaving no fixed assets, no structure and no structure for continued learning. Revenue success will be divided amongst the investors and any critical success in the form of awards will go to individuals. There is no firm like Microsoft, Toyota or Shell to absorb knowledge for future projects and products. So whereas Toyota will retain knowledge and experiences gained from the development of a new product this does not seem to happen in the project-based film industry. Indeed, the role of project-based enterprises seems to be at odds with the notion of firm-specific competencies that are developed over time. How can this occur when the organisation is renting skills for a short-period only? And how can such firms develop routines and embed knowledge into these routines with such an unstable workforce?

Another interesting aspect of this case is the role of networks: both social networks and technical knowledge networks. That is the key players forming the organisation, the producer and the director use both their social networks and work networks to locate the necessary skills as well as appoint leading players responsible for appointing all the necessary crews required.

For a variety of reasons the San Fernando Valley is not as well known as its Silicon Valley cousin. Yet it is as important to film making as the Silicon Valley in northern California is to the computer industry. It has been at the forefront of adopting new technologies and was hugely influential in the development of the VCR industry and the internet. Its significance should not be overlooked and it is time for the business world to embrace the successes of the adult film and leisure industry. Students of business can learn much from this $60 billion industry.

Sources: D. Chrisman (2000) 'Porn again: why mainstream film crew members work on pornography films', *Los Angeles Magazine*, January; M.E. Porter (1998) 'Clusters and the new economics of competition', *Harvard Business Review*, November–December, 77–90.

Questions

1 Characterise the advantages of independent film making.

2 Compare the industry network of Hollywood with that of the Motorsport Valley in the United Kingdom.

3 In this industry it seems that everyone involved in the project is a 'temp'. Explain.

4 If the organisation is dissolved after completing the making of the film what happens to the skills and competencies learnt and developed?

5 In what ways has the adult entertainment industry helped other industries?

Chapter summary

This chapter has explored the role of strategic alliances and how firms are increasingly recognising that alliances provide access to resources that are greater than any single firm could buy. The main purpose was to highlight their growing importance within the world of business. This is further reinforced by the concept of industry clusters and networks. In some knowledge-intensive industries, such as the film industry described in the case study, the role of alliances has been further developed. In these network industries loose alliances are formed to undertake a project, and when the project is finished the organisation ceases to exist. Linked to the issue of cooperation is the question of intellectual property and in particular the potential problem of information leakage. Many firms are understandably reticent about entering any form of collaboration for they fear losing the small advantage which they perceive they have over their competitors. Trust is frequently at the centre of any decision on whether a firm enters an alliance, and usually trust has to be established over a period of time before firms agree to enter an alliance.

Discussion questions

1 Discuss the increasing use of strategic alliances by firms to help achieve their objectives.
2 Why are some government departments concerned about the increasing use of strategic alliances?
3 What is an octopus strategy?
4 Discuss the wide range of reasons for entering a strategic alliance.
5 Explain some of the risks involved with all strategic alliances.
6 Explain why the repeated game of the prisoner's dilemma is considered to be more useful in predicting behaviour.

Websites worth visiting

3m.com **www.3m.com**
Corning corp **www.corning.com**
Pixar plc **www.pixar.com**
Sony-Ericsson **www.sonyericsson.com**

References

Arias, J.T.G. (1995) 'Do networks really foster innovation?' *Management Decision*, Vol. 33, No. 9, 52–7.

Baden-Fuller, C. and Pitt, M. (eds) (1996) *Strategic Innovation*, Routledge, London.

Bleeke, J. and Ernst, D. (1992) *Collaborating to Compete*, John Wiley, New York.

Budden, R. (2003) 'Sony-Ericsson seeks success with new phones', www.FT.com, 3 March.

Chan, P.S. and Heide, D. (1993) 'Strategic alliances in technology: key competitive weapon', *Advanced Management Journal*, Vol. 58, No. 4, 9–18.

Chrisman, D. (2000) 'Porn again: why mainstream film crew members work on pornography films', *Los Angeles Magazine*, January, www.lamag.com.

Cohen, W.M. and Levinthal, D.A. (1990) 'A new perspective on learning and innovation', *Administrative Science Quarterly*, Vol. 35, 128–52.

Conway, S. and Stewart, F. (1998) 'Mapping innovation networks', *International Journal of Innovation Management*, Vol. 2, No. 2, 223–54.

Dacin, M.T., Hitt, M.A. and Levitas, E. (1997) 'Selecting partners for successful international alliances', *Journal of World Business*, Vol. 32, No. 1, 321–45.

Day, G.S. and Schoemaker, P.J.H. (2000) *Wharton on Managing Emerging Technologies*, John Wiley, New York.

DeBresson, C. and Amesse, F. (1991) 'Networks of innovators: a review and introduction to the issues', *Research Policy*, Vol. 20, 363–73.

Donaghu, M. and Barff, R. (1990) 'Nike just did it – international sub-contracting and flexibility in athletic footwear production', *Regional Studies*, Vol. 24, No. 6, 537–52.

Doz, Y. and Hamel, G. (1997) 'The use of alliances in implementing technology strategies', in Tashman, M.L. and Anderson, P. (eds) *Managing Strategic Innovation and Change: A Collection of Readings*, Oxford University Press, New York.

Duysters, G., Kok, G. and Vaandrager, M. (1999) 'Crafting successful strategic technology partnerships', *R&D Management*, Vol. 29, No. 4, 343–51.

Faulkner, D. (1995) *International Strategic Alliances*, McGraw-Hill, Maidenhead.

Foremski, T. (2003) 'Infineon, IBM set to unveil chips advance', *Financial Times*, 10 June.

Foremski, T. (2004) 'Cisco and IBM join forces in global security sectory', *Financial Times*, 13 February.

Giddens, A. (1990) *The Consequences of Modernity*, Oxford University Press, Oxford.

Gulati, R. (1995) 'Does familiarity breed trust? The implications of repeated ties for contractual choice in alliances', *Academy of Management Journal*, Vol. 38, No. 1, 85–112.

Hamel, G. (1991) 'Competition for competence and inter-partner learning within international strategic alliances', *Strategic Management Journal*, Vol. 12, No. 1, 83–103.

Harney, A. (2001) 'Ambitious expansion loses its shine: analysts change their tune about Sony's dreams and begin to count the costs of the new mobile phone alliance with Ericsson', *Financial Times*, 2 October.

Harrigan, K.R. (1986) *Managing for Joint Venture Success*, Lexington Books, Lexington, MA.

Helmore, E. (1999) 'Porn waxes as movies wane', *Guardian Unlimited*, 12 September.

Hoecht, A. and Trott, P. (1999) 'Trust, risk and control in the management of collaborative technology development', *International Journal of Innovation Management*, Vol. 3, No. 3, 257–70.

Hollis, M. (1998) *Trust Within Reason*, Cambridge University Press, Cambridge.

Humphrey, J. and Schmitz, H. (1998) 'Trust in inter-firm relations in developing and transition economies', *Journal of Development Studies*, Vol. 34, No. 4, 32–61.

Kaufman, A., Wood, C.H. and Theyel, G. (2000) 'Collaboration and technology linkages: a strategic supplier typology', *Strategic Management Journal*, Vol. 21, 649–63.

Lane, C. and Bachmann, R. (1996) 'The social construction of trust: supplier relations in Britain and Germany', *Organisation Studies*, Vol. 17, No. 3, 365–95.

Lewicki, R.J. and Bunker, B.B. (1996), 'Developing and maintaining trust in work relationships', Kramer, R. and Tyler, T. (eds) *Trust in Organisations*, Sage, London, 114–39.

Lewis, J.D. (1990) *Partnerships for Profit*, The Free Press, New York.

Liebeskind, J. and Oliver, A. (1998) 'From handshake to contract: intellectual property, trust and the social structure of academic research', in Lane, C. and Bachmann, R. (eds) *Trust Within and Between Organisations: Conceptual Issues and Empirical Applications*, Oxford University Press, Oxford, 118–45.

Littler, D.A. (2001) 'Roles and rewards of collaboration', in Tidd J., Bessant J. and Pault K., *Managing Innovation: Integrating Technological, Market and Organisational Charge*, 2nd edn, Wiley, Chichester.

Morrison, M. and Mezentseff, L. (1997) 'Learning alliances – a new dimension of strategic alliances', *Management Decision*, Vol. 35, Nos. 5–6, 351.

Nadler, D.A. and Tushman, M. (1997) *Competing by Design: The Power of Organisational Architecture*, Oxford University Press, New York.

Nelson, R.R. and Winter, S. (1982) *An Evolutionary Theory of Economic Change*, Harvard University Press, Boston, MA.

Nordwall, B.D. (1991) 'Electronic companies form alliances to counter rising costs', *Aviation Week and Space Technology*, 17 June, 151–2.

Parkhe, A. (1993) 'Strategic alliance structuring: a game theoretic and transaction cost examination of interfirm cooperation', *Academy of Management Journal*, August, Vol. 36, No. 4, 794.

Porter, M.E. (1987) 'From competitive advantage to corporate strategy', *Harvard Business Review*, May–June, 43–59.

Porter, M.E. (1998) 'Clusters and the new economics of competition', *Harvard Business Review*, November–December, 10–24.

Sako, M. (1992) *Prices, Quality and Trust: Inter-firm Relations in Britain and Japan*, Cambridge University Press, Cambridge.

Sheridan, J. (1997) 'An alliance built on trust', *Industry Week*, Vol. 246, No. 6, 17 March, 67.

Sitkin, S. and Roth, N. (1993) 'Explaining the limited effectiveness of legalistic "remedies" for trust/distrust', *Organization Science*, Vol. 4, 367–92.

Slowinski, G., Seelig, G. and Hull, F. (1996) 'Managing technology-based strategic alliances between large and small firms', *Advanced Management Journal*, Vol. 61, No. 2, 42.

Spekman, R.E., Lynn, A.I., MacAvoy, T.C. and Forbes, I. (1996) 'Creating strategic alliances which endure', *Long Range Planning*, Vol. 29, No. 3, 122–47.

Teece, D. (1998) 'Capturing value from knowledge assets: the new economy, markets for know-how and intangible assets', *California Management Review*, Vol. 40, No. 3, 55–79.

Tidd, J. (2001) 'Innovation management in context, organisation and performance', *International Journal of Management Reviews*, Vol. 3, No. 3, 168–83.

Trott, P. and Cordey-Hayes, M. (1996) 'Developing a "receptive" environment for inward technology transfer: a case study of the chemical industry', *R&D Management*, Vol. 26, No. 1, 83–92.

Vyas, N.M., Shelburn, W.L. and Rogers, D.C. (1995) 'An analysis of strategic alliances: forms, functions and framework', *Journal of Business and Industrial Marketing*, Summer, Vol. 10, No. 3, 47.

Zucker, L. (1986) 'Production of trust: institutional sources of economic structure, 1840–1920', *Research in Organisational Behaviour*, Vol. 8, 53–111.

Zucker, L., Darby, M., Brewer, M. and Yusheng, P. (1996) 'Collaboration structure and information dilemmas in biotechnology: organisational boundaries of trust production', in Kramer, R. and Tyler, T. (eds) *Trust in Organisations. Frontiers of Theory and Research*, Sage, London, 90–113.

 # Further reading

For a more detailed review of the strategic alliances and innovation networks literature, the following develop many of the issues raised in this chapter:

Ahuja, G. (2000) 'Collaboration networks, structural holes, and innovation: a longitudinal study', *Administrative Science Quarterly*, Vol. 45, 425–55.

Brusoni, S., Prencipe, A. and Pavitt, K. (2001) 'Knowledge specialization, organizational coupling, and the boundaries of the firm: why do firms know more than they make?', *Administrative Science Quarterly*, Vol. 46, 597–621.

Coombs, R., Saviotti, P. and Walsh, V. (1996) *Technological Collaboration*, Edward Elgar, Aldershot.

Deeds, D.L., DeCarolis, D. and Coombs, J. (2000) 'Dynamic capabilities and new product development in high technology ventures: an empirical analysis of new biotechnology firms', *Journal of Business Venturing*, Vol. 15, No. 3, 211–29.

Faulkner, D. (1995) *Co-operating to Compete*, McGraw-Hill International, Maidenhead.

Mason, G., Beltram, J. and Paul, J. (2004) 'External knowledge sourcing in different national settings: a comparison of electronics establishments in Britain and France', *Research Policy*, Vol. 33, No. 1, 53–72.

Patel, P. and Pavitt, K. (2000) 'How technological competencies help define the core (not the boundaries) of the firm', in Dosi, G., Nelson, R. and Winter, S.G. (eds), *The Nature and Dynamics of Organisational Capabilities*, Oxford University Press, Oxford, 313–33.

Shavinina, L. (2003) *The International Handbook on Innovation*, Elsevier, Oxford.

Management of research and development

The management of research and development (R&D) was, and in some cases still is, viewed as a form of insurance policy. Those companies that did not perform any R&D were regarded as either poor or irresponsible. The *raison d'être* of industrial R&D was to generate opportunities that the business could exploit through the application of science and technology. Today, however, R&D is viewed in the much wider context of technology acquisition. Indeed, it is debatable how far a company can acquire technology without any internal technological research and development.

Chapter contents

Learning objectives

When you have completed this chapter you will be able to:

- recognise that R&D management is context dependent. The development of a new engine for an aircraft, for example, may take 10 years and involve many different component suppliers, the development of a new domestic cleaning product, however, may take only a few months;

- recognise that the R&D function incorporates several very different activities;

- explain that formal management techniques are an essential part of good R&D management; and

- recognise that certain factors are necessary but their presence alone is not sufficient to achieve successful management of R&D projects.

What is research and development?

To many, especially academics, the term research will mean the systematic approach to the discovery of new knowledge. Universities do not usually develop products – unless one considers teaching material as the product of the research. In industry, however, research is a much more generic term and can involve both new science and the use of old science to produce a new product. It is sometimes difficult to determine when research ends and development begins. It is probably more realistic to view industrial R&D as a continuum with scientific knowledge and concepts at one end and physical products at the other. Along this continuum it is possible to place the various R&D activities (*see* Figure 8.1). Later in this chapter we discuss the variety of R&D activities usually found within a large R&D department.

Technology is a commonly used word and yet not fully understood by all those who use it. Hickman (1990) offers a comprehensive classification of technology, used to describe both products and processes. Roussel *et al.* (1991) define technology as the application of knowledge to achieve a practical result. More recently, the term know-how has been used in the management literature to describe a company's knowledge base, which includes its R&D capability.

Research and development has traditionally been regarded by academics and industry alike as the management of scientific *research* and the *development* of new products; this was soon abbreviated to R&D. Twiss (1992) offers a widely accepted definition:

R&D is the purposeful and systematic use of scientific knowledge to improve man's lot even though some of its manifestations do not meet with universal approval.

The recent debates about scientific cloning of animal cells are a good example of what Twiss means by the results of R&D often delivering controversial outcomes. A more contemporary definition is offered by Roussel *et al.* (1991), who define the concept as:

To develop new knowledge and apply scientific or engineering knowledge to connect the knowledge in one field to that in others.

This definition reflects the more recent view that scientific knowledge is expanding so rapidly that it is extremely difficult for one company to remain abreast of all the technologies that it needs for its products. Companies pull together scientific knowledge from a wide variety of sources. For example, the manufacture of a personal computer will require technology from several different streams including microprocessor technology, visual display technology and software technology. It would be almost impossible for a company to be a technology leader in all of these fields.

Figure 8.1	The R&D continuum

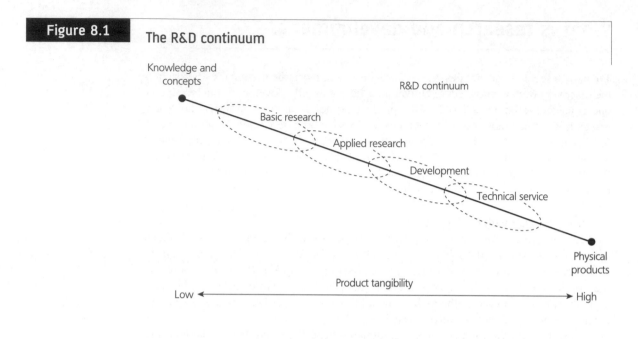

The traditional view of R&D

After the Second World War, research and development played an important role in providing firms with competitive advantage. Technical developments in industries such as chemicals, electronics, automotive and pharmaceuticals led to the development of many new products, which produced rapid growth. For a while it seemed that technology was capable of almost anything. The traditional view of R&D has therefore been overcoming genuine technological problems, which subsequently leads to business opportunities and a competitive advantage over one's competitors. The case study of the development of the smokeless cigarette highlights this traditional role of R&D which is still applied today.

President Kennedy's special address to the US Congress in 1961, in which he spoke of 'putting a man on the moon before the decade was out', captured the popular opinion of that time. Many believed anything was possible through technology. This notion helps to explain one of the major areas of difficulty with R&D. Traditionally, it has been viewed as a linear process, moving from research to engineering and then manufacture. That R&D was viewed as an overhead item was reinforced by Kennedy who pledged to spend 'whatever it costs' and indeed enormous financial resources were directed towards the project. But this was a unique situation without the usual economic or market forces at play. Nevertheless, industry adopted a similar approach to that used by the space programme. Vast amounts of money were poured into R&D programmes in the belief that the interesting technology generated could then be incorporated into products (*see* Illustration 8.1). In many instances this is exactly what happened, but there were also many examples of exciting technology developed purely because it was interesting, without any consideration of the competitive market in which the business operated. Hence, many business leaders began to question the value of R&D.

Illustration 8.1

The development of the smokeless cigarette

There are two big problems with cigarette smoking: it damages the smoker's health and it annoys those who dislike passive smoking. This presents companies involved in the manufacture of cigarettes with a genuine technological problem: how to produce a cigarette that overcomes these two key issues. For years now the big cigarette manufacturers, Philip Morris and R.J. Reynolds, have been thinking of ways to overcome the problem of passive smoking. The result has been the development of the smokeless cigarette.

There is enormous commercial logic in a cigarette that satisfies users without threatening their health or irritating others. It would have vast money-making potential. No wonder then that R.J. Reynolds has spent £325 million developing such a product.

Numerous prototype products have been developed and test-marketed, but none has been commercially successful. The latest product, called Eclipse, launched by R.J. Reynolds in 1996, uses a smouldering carbon tip to heat moist tobacco creating a vapour instead of smoke. The vapour quickly evaporates after it has been exhaled.

Hot on the heels of R.J. Reynolds has been Philip Morris, which has launched an electronic smoking machine. The system comes in two parts, a low-tar cigarette and an electronic 'puff' activated lighter which fits permanently around the cigarette. The device is intended to make smoking more socially acceptable by eliminating the smoke given off by the burning end of the cigarette.

Previous products of this type have failed because smokers thought they lacked flavour. Many analysts also suggest that part of the allure of smoking is the smoke! However, pressure on smokers is mounting and it is increasingly outlawed in many public places.

R.J. Reynolds is now part of Reynolds America which started trading on August 2, 2004. The new company has sales of $8.2bn and is the number 2 in the US tobacco market behind Altria's Philip Morris.

Sources: R. Tomkins (1994), 'Tobacco's Holy Grail', *Financial Times*, 2 December; Neil Buckley (2004), COMPANIES INTERNATIONAL: Reynolds American begins trading', *Financial Times*, 3 August 1997. Reprinted with permission.

R&D management and the industrial context

As will become clear, there is no single best way to manage R&D. There is no prescription, no computer model that will ensure its success. Each company and every competitive environment is unique and in its own state of change. R&D needs to be managed according to the specific heritage and resources of the company in its competitive industry. While the management of R&D in the aircraft industry is very different from the textile industry, there are, none the less, certain factors and elements that are common to all aspects of R&D management, almost irrespective of the industry. This chapter will draw on examples from across several different industries. This will help to highlight differences as well as identify commonalties in the management of R&D. Illustration 8.2, taken from a 1919 visit to the occupied territories of Germany, emphasises the very long history of industrial R&D.

Illustration 8.2

Industrial R&D has a long history

Many of Europe's largest chemical companies have a long history of funding industrial research. After the end of the First World War several reports were written examining the scope and nature of industrial research in German chemical companies. The following extract is taken from one of these reports:

One of the most striking features in the works visited is the application in the broadest sense of science to chemical industry. This is naturally very prominent in the triumvirate of the Bayer, Farbwerke Hoechst and the BASF, but it is equally noticeable in many of the smaller undertakings. The lavish and apparently unstinted monetary outlay on laboratories, libraries and technical staff implies implicit confidence on the part of the leaders of the industry in the ability to repay with interest heavy initial expenditure.

Source: ABCM (1919) Report of the British Chemical Mission on Chemical Factories in the Occupied Area of Germany.

At the beginning of this book we discussed one of the most fundamental dilemmas facing all companies, the need to provide an environment that fosters creativity and an inquisitive approach, while at the same time providing a stable environment that enables the business to be managed in an efficient and systematic way. Somehow businesses have to square this circle. Nowhere is this more apparent than in the management of research and development. For it is here that people need to question the accepted ways of working and challenge accepted wisdom.

One may be tempted to think that research, by definition, is uncertain, based around exploring things that are unknown. It cannot therefore be managed and organisations should not try to do so. There is, however, overwhelming evidence to suggest that industrial technological research can indeed be managed and that most of those organisations who spend large amounts of money on R&D, such as Microsoft, IBM, Sony, Siemens and Zeneca, do so extremely well (*see* Table 8.1). This table of Europe's leading firms in terms of R&D expenditure is part of the DTI's yearly *R&D Scoreboard*. It began in 1992 as a way of raising the profile of R&D in the UK and to try to give recognition to those companies who are investing in the future. The first *R&D Scoreboard* was sponsored by *The Independent* newspaper as a means of helping to promote the publication (*The Independent*, 1992).

Large organisations with more resources can clearly afford to invest more in R&D than their smaller counterparts. Therefore, in order to present a more realistic comparison than that derived from raw sums invested, R&D expenditure is frequently expressed as:

R&D as % of sales = (R&D expenditure/total sales income × 100%)

This not only allows comparisons to be made between small and large firms, but also gives a more realistic picture of R&D intensity within the organisation. Across industry sectors there are great differences in expenditure. Table 8.2 shows typical levels of R&D expenditure across different industry sectors. Some industries are technology intensive with relatively high levels of R&D expenditure. The case study at the end of

Table 8.1 Europe's R&D expenditure league (2002)

Rank	Company	R&D spend (£M)	R&D as a % of sales	R&D per employee (£000)	Industrial sector
1	DaimlerChrysler Germany	3,957	8.9	10.7	Engineering, vehicles
2	Siemens Germany	3,792	10.8	8.5	Electronic and electrical equipment
3	GlaxoSmithKline UK	2,936	18.7	27.7	Pharmaceuticals
4	Volkswagen Germany	2,849	12.4	9.3	Engineering, vehicles
5	Nokia Finland	2,261	12.9	42.9	Electronic and cell phones
6	Aventis France	2,229	21.4	28.5	Pharmaceuticals
7	Ericsson Telefon Sweden	2,090	22	28.5	Telecommunications
8	Philips Netherlands	1,983	13.2	11.9	Electronic and electrical equipment
9	Novartis Switzerland	1,951	18.5	26.4	Chemicals
10	Roche Switzerland	1,912	21.2	27.5	Pharmaceuticals
11	Astra-Zeneca UK	1,906	24.7	33.2	Pharmaceuticals
12	Bayer Germany	1,650	15.1	13.2	Chemicals
13	Robert Bosch Germany	1,621	12.8	7.2	Electronic and electrical equipment
14	Alcatel (France)	1,544	16.4	20.3	Electronic and electrical equipment
15	BMW Germany	1,520	12.9	15.4	Engineering, vehicles
16	EADS The Netherlands	1,366	14.3	13.1	Aerospace
17	Peugeot (PSA) (France)	1,215	12.9	6.1	Engineering, vehicles
18	Renault France	1,160	13.2	8.8	Engineering, vehicles
19	Institute Finanzianlo Industriale (Italy)	1,148	7.7	5.5	Telecommunications
20	BAE System	899	14.5	13	Aeorospace

Source: www.innovation.gov.uk/projects/rd_scoreboard(2003)

Table 8.2 R&D expenditure across industry sectors

Industry sector	R&D expenditure as % of sales
Pharmaceuticals	18
Aerospace	9
Automotive	9
Chemicals	7
Electrical and electronics	10
Food	1.5
Engineering	8
IT software	22
IT hardware	6

Source: www.innovation.gov.uk/projects/rd_scoreboard (2003)

this chapter shows that even in those industries not normally associated with R&D, the benefits of successful R&D can be large indeed.

The fact that some of the largest and most successful companies in the world spend enormous sums of money on R&D should not be taken as a sign that they have mastered the process. It is important to acknowledge that R&D management, like innovation itself, is part art and part science. Industry may not be able to identify and hire technological geniuses like Faraday, Pasteur or Bell, but many companies would argue that they already employ geniuses who, year after year, develop new patents and new products that will contribute to the future prosperity of the organisation. These same companies would also argue that they cannot justify spending several millions of dollars, pounds or Deutschmarks purely on the basis of chance and good fortune. This would clearly be unacceptable, not least to shareholders. So while companies appreciate that there is a certain amount of serendipity, there are also formal management techniques that over the years have been learnt, refined and practised and which are now a necessary part of good R&D management.

R&D investment and company growth

On a global scale, R&D investment has increased by an average of 23 per cent from 1991–2002. R&D expenditure now consumes a significant proportion of a firm's funds across all industry sectors. This is principally because companies realise that new products can provide a huge competitive advantage. Yet comparing national strengths in science and technology is a hazardous exercise, bedevilled by incompatible definitions. While it is relatively easy to measure inputs it is far harder to measure outputs in terms of quality (*see* the Innovation Scoreboard case study in Chapter 1). Figure 8.2 shows a

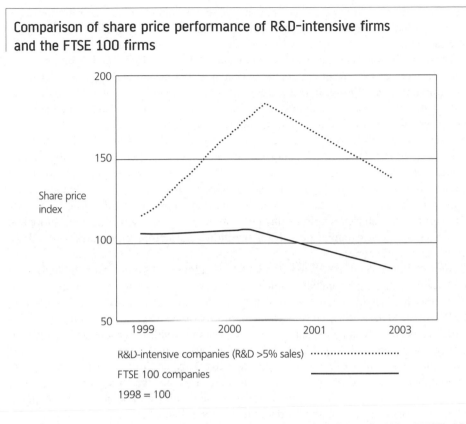

Figure 8.2

Comparison of share price performance of R&D-intensive firms
and the FTSE 100 firms

R&D-intensive companies (R&D >5% sales)   ··············
FTSE 100 companies   ────────
1998 = 100

comparison of share price performance of R&D-intensive firms and the FTSE 100
firms. Clearly the performance of a firm's share price is not necessarily a true guide of
performance, it is, none the less, one output. What is worthy of note is that the number
of R&D-intensive firms is increasing.

It is now widely recognised that competition can appear from virtually anywhere in
the world. Countries formerly viewed as receptacles for the outputs of factories across
Europe are now supplying products themselves. Mexico, Brazil, Malaysia, China and
India now supply a wide range of products to Europe, including car components, computer hardware and clothing. Globalisation provides opportunities for companies but it
also brings increased competition. The introduction of new products provides a clear
basis on which to compete, with those companies that are able to develop and introduce
new and improved products having a distinct advantage.

Firms are also uneasy about R&D, or to be more accurate a lack of R&D. Ever since
1982 when ICI completed a study into the effects of stopping product innovation, companies have viewed innovation and R&D investment with some anxiety. They fear that
should they stop investment in R&D, and product innovation in particular, the consequences would be severe. The results of the study showed that profits would decline
very slowly for around 15 years, before falling very sharply. It is worthy of note
that if a similar study were to be undertaken today it is almost certain that the 15-year
figure would be halved to approximately eight. The ICI study also posed another
important question. How long, it wondered, would it take for profits to recover, if after
the 15 years the company magically resumed its product innovation at three times its

previous rate? The study revealed that it would take another 25 years for profit to recover to the level achieved before the product innovation programme was stopped (Weild, 1986).

These findings reflect the conventional wisdom that has dominated thinking in this field for most of the twentieth century. That is, most companies assume that R&D investment is a good thing; like education, in general, it is surely a worthy investment. In the 1980s there was great interest in the concept of technology transfer and the belief that companies could buy in any technological expertise they required. More recent research has highlighted the folly of such arguments (Cohen and Levinthal, 1990; Quintas *et al.*, 1992) and the business community has returned to a view that fundamentally R&D investment is beneficial. The difficulty lies in where precisely to invest; which projects and technology to invest in; and when to stop pouring money into a project that looks likely to fail but could yet deliver enormous profits. The case study at the end of this chapter explores this point. It also shows how a major technological innovation led to substantial growth for the individual company in particular and the drinks industry in general.

Many international companies, including Unilever, ICI and British Aerospace (Lancaster, 1997), have conducted numerous studies attempting to justify R&D expenditure. This has not been easy because there is no satisfactory method for measuring R&D output. Many studies have used the number of patents published as a guide. This is mainly because it is quantifiable rather than being a valid measure. It is, however, quality not quantity of output that is clearly important. It is worthy of note that most companies would like to be able to correlate R&D expenditure with profitability. At present there is a lack of conclusive evidence to connect the two. Edwin Mansfield (1991) has undertaken many studies concerning the relationship between R&D expenditure and economic growth and productivity. He concludes that:

although the results are subject to considerable error, they establish certain broad conclusions. In particular, existing econometric studies do provide reasonably conclusive evidence that R&D has a significant effect on the rate of productivity increase in the industries and time periods studied.

Furthermore, a study by Geroski *et al.* (1993) did reveal a positive relationship between R&D expenditure and *long-term* growth. This raises an important point. R&D expenditure should be viewed as a long-term investment. It may even reduce short-term profitability. Company accountants increasingly question the need for large sums to be invested in an activity that shows no obvious and certainly no rapid return. Many argue that public money should be used for 'pure research' where there is no clear application. Its outputs could then be taken and used by industry to generate wealth. However, the UK government's recent initiatives to couple science to the creation of wealth, through such programmes as Technology Foresight, seems to suggest that even public money is being directed towards applied research.

This raises the issue of evaluating R&D. While few, if any, of the companies listed in Table 8.1 would question the value of R&D, this does not preclude the need for evaluation. How much money should companies invest in R&D? How much should be used for applied research and how much for pure research? These questions will be addressed later in this chapter and in Chapter 9.

Illustration 8.3

Seeking to bridge the science gap

Europe's spending on R&D is laggind far behind that of the US. Brussels has called for state and private investment to increase by 60 per cent over the next eight years but companies may not rush to meet the challenge

A knowledge gap has opened up over the Atlantic in research and development – one of the key motors of innovation and economic growth.

Europe has fallen well behind the US, as governments and businesses in the 15 countries of the European Union fail to keep pace with the expenditure on science and technology of their US counterparts.

Between 1995 and 1999, the latest period for which figures are available, the difference between US and European R&D investment more than trebled. By the end of the period, European innovators in industry and government were spending €76bn a year less than their US colleagues.

The result is that companies and economies in the EU have fewer, and less sophisticated, tools to go head to head with their rivals on the other side of the Atlantic.

Many in Europe fear that achievements such as last year's sequencing of the human genome, where European scientists made a huge contribution to the work of their US counterparts, could become ever rarer.

'[Lower R&D investment] has eroded our competitiveness and deteriorated our industrial and trade performance compared to the US. Taking action to reverse these trends is imperative', says Philippe Busquin, who, as European commissioner for research, is charged with bridging the transatlantic knowledge gap.

After years of warm words and few actions, the European authorities seem to have woken up to the fact that something radical needs to be done to turn the tide.

Last month, Mr Busquin made an almost unnoticed addition to the so-called 'Lisbon agenda' – the ambitious set of targets to make Europe the most competitive economy in the world by 2010, which was agreed in the Portuguese capital nearly two years ago. The amendment could have sweeping implications for businesses and governments across the region.

In a document outlining the priorities for next month's summit of heads of state in Barcelona, the EU pledged to increase Europe's state and private investment in R&D by nearly 60 per cent – from the current 1.9 per cent of gross domestic product to 3 per cent within eight years.

Such a rise would bring Europe in line with the US, where R&D investment is 2.6 per cent of GDP and rising fast, and Japan, which already spends 2.9 per cent of its national wealth on research.

Will the EU make it? Many in industry, academia and national governments believe such a rapid increase is not as realistic as Mr Busquin believes.

They warn that practical problems, such as recruiting trained scientists and engineers or building and equipping enough laboratory space, could make it impossible to achieve the goal, even if companies try their best.

The UK's finance ministry, for example, says it shares Brussels' vision, which was openly supported by Tony Blair, the prime minister, in a joint letter with Wim Kok, his Dutch counterpart, last week, but it casts doubt over the 3 per cent target.

'We are not sure that it is right to have an explicit target. What matters is that we have an innovation performance that will drive growth', says a ministry official.

▶

The EU is limited in what it can do directly to promote research. Its next R&D programme, known as Framework Six, will distribute €17.5bn-($15bn)-worth of grants to companies and universities over four years from 2003 – only 5 per cent of what national governments will spend on R&D over the period. At the same time, Mr Busquin is trying to remove the obstacles, such as national restrictions on research grants, which prevent scientists moving freely around Europe.

But the Belgian-born commissioner believes prime responsibility for the knowledge gap lies with businesses rather than governments. A recent study by the European Commission showed that businesses' expenditure on R&D in the US is 73 per cent higher than in the EU and grew nearly three times as fast between 1995 and 1999.

Such a lag in EU businesses' investments accounts for the vast majority of the €76bn R&D difference between the US and Europe. 'On current trends, the EU will fall further behind, compromising any chance of reaching the objective agreed at Lisbon', the study concludes. Getting businesses to spend more on R&D at a time of an economic downturn and uncertain stock market conditions is not going to be easy.

The Brussels authorities believe national governments should play their part by making investment in R&D more attractive to the private sector through four main instruments.

The first, and most direct, way of getting business people's minds focused on innovation is to pay them to innovate. For years, state subsidies have been Europe's traditional route to foster private R&D investment. Last year, EU governments dispensed about €4bn in state aid for R&D by means of various programmes.

However, this policy is being threatened by external and internal factors. Externally, the economic slowdown is putting pressure on governments to curb expenditure – R&D, with its promises of returns in the distant future, is an obvious target.

Internally, Mario Monti, the EU competition commissioner, is a sworn enemy of all forms of state aid. In its latest report on state aid, Mr Monti's department noted that countries with high state aid for R&D did not produce more patents or a more efficient labour force – remarks that did not go down well with Mr Busquin's experts.

But even if Mr Monti does not intervene, state aid will not make up the entire shortfall and indirect interventions, such as tax breaks, could play an important part in plugging the knowledge gap.

A number of EU countries already operate such schemes. In Sweden, for example, a quarter of the income of foreign researchers is tax free, while in the UK small and medium-sized companies have a credit of 150 per cent on R&D expenditure. The British government is now consulting on the final details of a new tax incentive that would apply to all companies.

Mr Busquin's study concludes that fiscal incentives 'could and should be applied in a more intensive way across the EU'.

Experts fear the commissioner's call could fall on deaf ears. Georges Haour, professor of technology management at IMD, the international business school in Lausanne, Switzerland, warns that governments 'will be reluctant to see their income decrease at a time when they have exploding costs in healthcare, retirement benefits and so on'.

Tim Bradshaw, senior policy adviser for technology and innovation at the Confederation of British Industry, notes that tax-break schemes and state aid are linked, as some fiscal incentives could incur Mr Monti's wrath and be classified as illegal subsidies.

'The EU may need to make changes to its rules restricting state aid to industry if governments are to give effective tax incentives for companies to increase R&D spending', he says.

Mr Busquin's third option is the use of so-called guarantee schemes – government guarantees to equity and loans provided by private sector banks for companies' investment in R&D.

But, although there are several such schemes across Europe, very few are used for research. 'This form of public support is clearly under-exploited and should be used far more extensively', the study says.

Some within the Commission argue that to catch up with the US something stronger is needed: Europe, they argue, should go the American way and build a large venture capital industry.

Across the Atlantic, risk capital has become a vital funding source for technology-based start-ups, while in Europe it accounts for a mere 0.04 per cent of EU GDP. The Commission wants governments to set up schemes to attract venture capital for start-ups.

But that is going to take time and even if the funds were flowing in, R&D start-ups would still be faced with a bureaucratic nightmare to protect their discoveries. The Commission has drawn up plans for an EU-wide patent, which would reduce costs and red tape, but these have been stalled by a wrangle over which language to adopt in the document and which courts should be responsible for enforcement.

For Philippe de Buck, secretary-general of Unice, the European employers' federation, a common patent would be a big incentive for businesses to invest in R&D.

'We have to ask ourselves, why aren't businesses investing enough in R&D? There are a number of difficult conditions. A competitive, enforceable and cheap patent would remove one of them.'

Source: F. Guerrera and C. Cookson, 'Seeking to bridge the science gap', *Financial Times*, 25 February 2002. Reprinted with permission.

Classifying R&D

Traditionally industrial research has focused on a variety of research activities performed *within* the organisation. This practice was modelled on the research undertaken within universities during the early part of the twentieth century. This was seen as public research financed by public money for the public good. In other words, research undertaken within universities was performed in the pursuit of new knowledge. Its results were publicly available and the commercial exploitation of this knowledge was largely disregarded. For example, Fleming's discovery of penicillin was initially not patented. Industrial research, on the other hand, was specifically intended for the benefit of the company funding the research. Industry's purpose was to grow and make profits and this was to be achieved through the development of new products and new businesses. Hence, industry's expectations of its own research expanded to include the development of knowledge into products (*see* Figure 8.3).

Over the years industrial research and development (R&D) has increasingly been guided by the aims of its financiers via its business strategy, and to a lesser extent by the pursuit of knowledge. The main activities of industrial R&D have included the following:

- discovering and developing new technologies;
- improving understanding of the technology in existing products;
- improving and strengthening understanding of technologies used in manufacturing; and
- understanding research results from universities and other research institutions.

| Figure 8.3 | Classification of areas of research emphasis in industry and university |

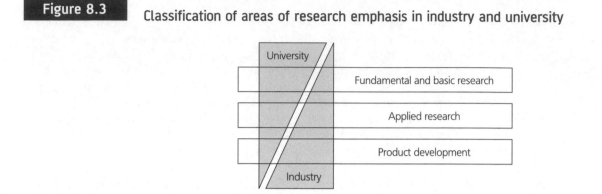

The management of R&D can be viewed as two sides of the same coin. On the one side there are research activities, often referred to as fundamental or basic research, and on the other development, usually the development of products. Many industries make a clear distinction between research and development and some companies even suggest that they leave all research to universities, engaging only in development. Figure 8.3 shows the areas of research emphasis in industry and universities. In between the discovery of new knowledge and new scientific principles (so-called fundamental research) and the development of products for commercial gain (so-called development) is the significant activity of transforming scientific principles into technologies that can be applied to products (*see* Illustration 8.4). This activity is called applied research. The development of the videocassette recorder (VCR) shows how over a period of almost 30 years industry worked with existing scientific principles to develop a product with commercial potential.

The operations that make up R&D

Figure 8.1 illustrated the R&D operations commonly found in almost every major research and development department. They may have different labels, but within Siemens, Nokia, BMW and Shell such operations are well documented. In smaller organisations the activities are less diverse and may include only a few of these operations. This section explains what activities one would expect to find within each type of R&D operation. To help put these activities in context Figure 9.5 shows how they relate to the product life cycle framework.

Basic research

This activity involves work of a general nature intended to apply to a broad range of uses or to new knowledge about an area. It is also referred to as fundamental science and is usually only conducted in the laboratories of universities and large organisations. Outputs from this activity will result in scientific papers for journals. Some findings will be developed further to produce new technologies. New scientific discoveries such as antibiotics in the 1940s belong to this research category.

Illustration 8.4

Manipulating known scientific principles through technological development: the VCR story

At the heart of virtually all technologically innovative products lies good fundamental science. The ability to manipulate known scientific principles through technological development is the main research activity of most companies. A good example of this is the VCR industry.

Although videocassette recorders (VCRs) were first introduced in the early 1970s, the story begins long before this date. It was during the 1950s that firms (already in the broadcast industry) began experimenting with existing broadcasting technology to develop a videotape recorder. The front runners were RCA and Ampex in the United States and Toshiba in Japan, all of which had knowledge and experience of television broadcasting technology. In the early 1950s, the RCA team developed a machine that moved a narrow tape at very high speeds past fixed magnetic heads. Meanwhile Toshiba developed a different approach, in which the recording head rotated at high speed while the tape moved past relatively slowly. Toshiba's breakthrough was patented in 1954. Ampex developed a transverse scanner in which four recording heads on a rapidly rotating drum scanned across a two-inch-wide tape.

Ampex was the first to succeed commercially and its videotape recording machine made a huge impact on the broadcasting industry, despite a price of $50,000. Within a few years Ampex had licensed the technology to RCA and Toshiba.

None of the original technology pioneers viewed the idea of producing a product for the mass market as a business opportunity. This baton was to be taken up by three other Japanese firms: JVC, Sony and Matsushita. Spurred on by the success of the other companies, independently they began numerous technical development projects to try to exploit the commercial opportunity of a mass market videotape recorder.

It was only after many failed projects and learning from the mistakes of others that a design emerged in the late 1960s. It was Sony who in 1969 announced the development of a 'magazine-loaded' videotape recorder. JVC soon announced its own slightly different magazine-loaded recorder using half-inch tape as opposed to Sony's one-inch tape. The first Betamax model was offered to the market in April 1975. JVC revealed its VHS technology to its parent company Matsushita and this was launched at the end of 1976.

The war of the formats is now folklore, especially in business schools around the world. It may be useful to highlight some of the key issues.

The key point is the recording time of the two formats. VHS had a recording time of two hours while Betamax had a recording time of only one hour. Industry experts suggest that technologically the formats were equal. That is, on home commercial television sets the difference in picture quality was nil. In the early years it was Sony and Betamax who pioneered most of the technical developments, but in less than a year the VHS manufacturers had caught up. Another common misconception is that Sony refused to license its Betamax technology. This is not true. It tried from the very beginning to license the technology and have it accepted as standard.

Sources: R.S. Rosenbloom and M.A. Cusumano (1988) 'Technological pioneering and competitive advantage: the birth of the VCR industry', in M.L. Tushman and W.L. Moore (eds) *Readings in the Management of Innovation*, HarperCollins, New York; 'The format war' (1988) *Video Magazine*, April.

Applied research

This activity involves the use of existing scientific principles for the solution of a particular problem. It is sometimes referred to as the application of science. It may lead to new technologies and include the development of patents. It is from this activity that many new products emerge. This form of research is typically conducted by large companies and university departments. The development of the Dyson vacuum cleaner involved applying the science of centrifugal forces first explained by Newton. Centrifugal forces spin dirt out of the air stream in two stages (or cyclones), with air speeds of up to 924 miles an hour. This technology led to the development of several patents.

Development

This activity is similar to applied research in that it involves the use of known scientific principles, but differs in that the activities centre on products. Usually the activity will involve overcoming a technical problem associated with a new product. It may also involve various exploratory studies to try to improve a product's performance. To continue with the Dyson vacuum cleaner example, the prototype product underwent many modifications and enhancements before a commercial product was finally developed. For example, the company has recently launched a cylinder model to complement its upright model.

Technical service

This activity, as its title suggests, focuses on providing a service to existing products and processes. This frequently involves cost and performance improvements to existing products, processes or systems. For example, in the bulk chemical industry it means ensuring that production processes are functioning effectively and efficiently. This category of R&D activity would also include design changes to products to lower the manufacturing costs. For Dyson Appliances extensive efforts will be employed in this area to reduce the cost of manufacturing its vacuum cleaner, leading to increased profit margins for the company.

R&D management and its link with business strategy

Planning decisions are directed towards the future, which is why strategy is often considered to be as much an art as a science. Predicting the future is extremely difficult and there are many factors to consider: economic, social, political, technological, natural disasters, etc. The R&D function also has to make some assessment of the future in order to perform effectively. Thus senior R&D managers have to build into their planning process a conscious view of the future. However imprecise, this will include:

- environmental forecasts;
- comparative technological cost-effectiveness;
- risk; and
- capability analysis.

Environmental forecasts

These are primarily concerned with changes in technology that will occur in the future. But this cannot be considered in isolation and other factors such as economic, social and political factors also have to be considered.

- Who will be our competitors in five or ten years' time?
- What technologies do we need to understand to avoid technological surprises?
- What will be the new competitive technologies and businesses?

Comparative technological cost-effectiveness

It is argued that technologies have life cycles and that after a period further research produces negligible benefit. When this stage is reached a new branch of technology is likely to offer far more promising rewards. This may require a significant shift in resources. Today, for example, many car manufacturers are increasing their research efforts in electrical power technology.

Risk

The culture of the organisation and its attitude to risk will influence decision making. Usually risk is spread over a portfolio of projects and will include some exploratory high-risk projects and some developmental low-risk ones. Planning cannot remove risk but it can help to ensure that decisions are reached using a process of rational analysis.

Capability analysis

It is fairly obvious to state, but companies have to consider their own strengths and weaknesses. This analysis should help them ensure that they have the necessary capabilities for the future.

Integration of R&D

The management of research and development needs to be fully integrated with the strategic management process of the business. This will enhance and support the products that marketing and sales offer and provide the company with a technical body of knowledge that can be used for future development. Too many businesses fail to integrate the management of research and technology fully into the overall business strategy process (Adler *et al.*, 1992). A report by the European Industrial Management Association (EIRMA, 1985) recognises R&D as having three distinct areas, each requiring

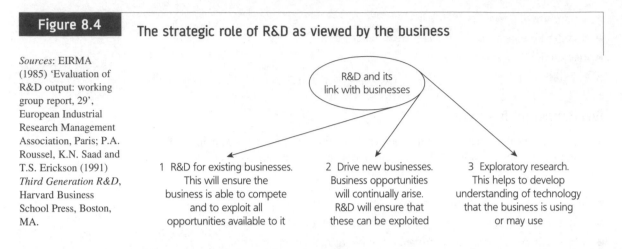

Figure 8.4

The strategic role of R&D as viewed by the business

Sources: EIRMA (1985) 'Evaluation of R&D output: working group report, 29', European Industrial Research Management Association, Paris; P.A. Roussel, K.N. Saad and T.S. Erickson (1991) *Third Generation R&D*, Harvard Business School Press, Boston, MA.

investment: R&D for existing businesses, R&D for new businesses and R&D for exploratory research (*see* Figure 8.4).

These three strategic areas can be broken down into operational activities.

Defend, support and expand existing businesses

The defence of existing businesses essentially means maintaining a business's current position, that is, keeping up with the competition and ensuring that products do not become outdated and ensuring that existing products can compete. For example, the newspaper industry has seen numerous technological changes dramatically alter the way it produces newspapers. In particular, the introduction of desktop publishing and other related computer software has provided increased flexibility in manufacturing operations as well as reducing production costs.

Drive new businesses

Either through identification of market opportunities or development of technology, new business opportunities will continually be presented to managers. Sometimes the best decision is to continue with current activities. However, there will be times when a business takes the decision to start a new business. This may be an extension of existing business activities, but sometimes it may be for a totally new product. For example, 3M's unexpected discovery of temporary adhesive technology led to the creation of a completely new business – the Post-It notes.

Broaden and deepen technological capability

The third area is more medium- to long-term strategy. It involves the continual accumulation of knowledge, not only in highly specialised areas where the company is currently operating, but also in areas that may prove to be of importance to the business in the future. For example, Microsoft initially concentrated its efforts on computer-programming technologies. The company now requires knowledge in a wide variety of technologies, including telecommunications, media (music, film and television), sound technology, etc.

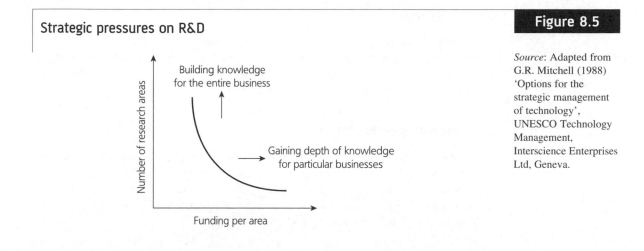

Strategic pressures on R&D

Figure 8.5

Source: Adapted from G.R. Mitchell (1988) 'Options for the strategic management of technology', UNESCO Technology Management, Interscience Enterprises Ltd, Geneva.

Strategic pressures on R&D

In technology-intensive industries much of the technological resources consumed by a particular business are in the form of engineering and development (often called technical service). These resources can be spread over a wide range of technical activities and technologies. In addition, a firm will have a number of specific areas of technology in which it concentrates resources and builds a technological competence. As one would expect, there is a significant difference between possessing general technical service skills and possessing scientific competence in a particular area. The building and development of technological knowledge competencies take time and demand a large amount of research activity.

Mitchell (1988) suggests there is a trade-off between concentrating resources in the pursuit of a strategic knowledge competence and spreading them over a wider area to allow for the building of a general knowledge base. Figure 8.5 shows the demands on technical resources. The growth of scientific and technological areas of interest to the firm (in particular the research department) pressurises research management to fund a wider number of areas, represented by the upward curve. The need for strategic positioning forces the decision to focus resources and build strategic knowledge competencies, represented by the downward curve. In practice, most businesses settle for an uneasy balance between the two sets of pressures.

The technology portfolio

From an R&D perspective the company's technology base can be categorised as follows:

● core technologies;
● complementary technologies;
● peripheral technologies; and
● emerging technologies.

Core technologies

The core technology is usually central to all or most of the company's products. Expertise in this area may also dominate the laboratories of the R&D department as well as strategic thinking. For example, in the photocopying industry photographic technologies are core.

Complementary technologies

Complementary technologies are additional technology that is essential in product development. For example, microprocessors are becoming essential in many products and industries. For the photocopying industry there are several complementary technologies, including microprocessor technology and paper-handling technology, which enables the lifting, turning, folding and stapling of paper.

Peripheral technologies

Peripheral technology is defined as technology that is not necessarily incorporated into the product but whose application contributes to the business. Computer software often falls into this category. The photocopying industry is increasingly using software to add features and benefits to its products, such as security.

Emerging technologies

These are new to the company but may have a long-term significance for its products. In the photocopying industry, telecommunications technologies may soon be incorporated as standard features of the product.

The difficulty of managing capital-intensive production plants in a dynamic environment

Many manufacturing operations involve the careful management of multi-million-pound production plants. Such businesses have a slightly different set of factors to consider than a company operating the manufacturing plant for say, shoes, which is labour- rather than technology-intensive. Hundreds of millions of pounds are invested in a new chemical plant and options open to it in terms of changes in products are limited. This is because a production plant is built to produce one chemical product. Moreover, the scrapping of an existing plant and the building of a new one may cost in excess of £300 million. There are few companies in the world who could continually build, scrap and rebuild chemical plants in response to the demands of the market and make a profit from such actions. Hence companies operating process plants cannot respond *completely* to market needs.

This particular dilemma faced by companies with large investments in production technology is frequently overlooked by those far removed from the production floor. Young marketing graduates may feel that a company should be able to halt production of one product in order to switch to the production of another offering better prospects.

The effect of such a decision may be to bankrupt the company! The chemical industry is increasingly developing smaller, more flexible plants rather than the large, single-purpose plants that have been common since the turn of the twentieth century.

In some industries where investment lies less in the technology and more in the human resources, changes to a production plant are possible. Toshiba UK completely switched one of its production plants from producing microwave ovens to industrial air conditioners. It had been making microwave ovens in its Plymouth factory since 1985, but unfortunately due to low-cost competition from Korea production was halted in 1990. The new product was far more complex and cost up to 20 times more. This involved substantial changes to production methods and training of staff. Following a £20-million investment and six years of development, the plant is seen as extremely successful with output valued at £30 million a year (Marsh, 1997).

Which business to support and how?

It is well understood that technological developments can lead to improved products and processes, reduced costs and ultimately better commercial performance and competitive advantage. The ability to capitalise on technological developments and profit from the business opportunities that may subsequently arise requires a business to be in an appropriate strategic position. That is, it must possess the capability to understand and use the technological developments to its own advantage. This requires some form of anticipation of future technological developments and also strategic business planning. Technological forecasting and planning are fraught with uncertainty. Figure 8.6 illustrates the iterative and continual process involved in the management of research and technology.

The effect of corporate strategy is usually most noticeable in the selection of R&D projects. For example, a corporate decision by Unilever to strengthen its position in the luxury perfume business may lead to the cancellation of several research projects, with more emphasis being placed on buying brands like Calvin Klein. Ideally, a system is required that links R&D decision making with corporate strategy decision making. However, it is common in R&D departments to make decisions on a project-by-project basis in which individual projects are assessed on their own merits, independent of the organisation. This is partly because the expertise required is concentrated in the R&D department and partly due to scientists' fascination with science itself. This used to be the case in many large organisations with centralised laboratories. Such a decision-making process, however, is only valid when funds are unlimited and this is rarely the case. In practice, funds are restricted and projects compete with each other for continued funding for future years. Not all projects can receive funding and in industrial R&D laboratories projects are cancelled week after week, frequently to the annoyance of those involved.

The flow diagram in Figure 8.6 highlights the need for integration of corporate and R&D strategy. The process of corporate planning involves the systematic examination of a wide variety of factors. The aim is to produce a statement of company objectives and how they are to be achieved. Essentially, a number of questions need to be considered.

| Figure 8.6 | The R&D strategic decision-making process |

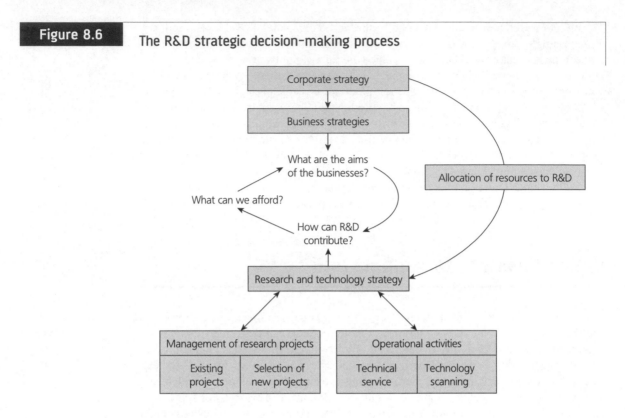

- What might the company do?
- What can the company do?
- What should the company do?

This leads to the development of business strategies. At the base of the diagram are the inputs from R&D activities, in particular existing R&D projects and potential projects that may be selected for funding. The organisation must repeatedly ask itself: What are the needs of the businesses? What should R&D be doing? What can R&D do? This process is neither a bottom–up nor a top–down process. What is required is continual dialogue between senior management and R&D management.

While it is tempting to say that technology influences the competitive performance of all businesses, in reality some businesses are more heavily influenced than others. In many mature and established industries, the cost of raw materials is much more of an influence on the competitive performance of the business than are technology developments. For example, the price paid for commodities like coffee, cocoa and sugar can dramatically influence profits in many food industries. Similarly, in the chemical industry the competitive position of petroleum-based plastics is determined by the price paid for the raw material, oil. Consequently, some businesses, especially those operating in mature industries, would be unable to influence their competitive position through technology alone. Even if the business was to substantially increase the level of R&D investment, its competitive position would still be determined by raw material prices.

Several attempts have been made by industry to quantify this factor when considering the level of R&D investment required. Scholefield (1993) developed a model using the concept of technology leverage. This is the extent of influence that a business's technology and technology base have on its competitive position. In general, technology leverage will be low when the influence of raw material and distribution costs and economic growth is high. High-volume, bulk commodity products would fall within this scenario.

Technology leverage and R&D strategies

The state of a business in terms of its markets, products and capabilities will largely determine the amount of research effort to be undertaken. Research by Scholefield (1993) suggests that there are essentially two forms of activity for a R&D department, growth and maintenance. Within these two groups it is possible to conduct significantly different types of activities. Hence, these categories can be subdivided into the four groups depicted in Figure 8.7.

Survival

This type of activity is conducted if the decision has been made to exit the business. In such circumstances the role of the R&D department is to ensure its interim survival against technological mishaps to process or product. This would be a reactive problem-solving role and may be termed 'survival research'.

Competitive

If the intention is to sustain the business, then the role of research is to maintain the relative competitive technological position by making improvements to both product and process. For example, in the automotive industry most manufacturers have invested heavily in their own processes and vehicle build-qualities have improved dramatically; so much so that reliability, although still improving, is almost taken for granted by car

---

Classifying the level of research using technology leverage   **Figure 8.7**

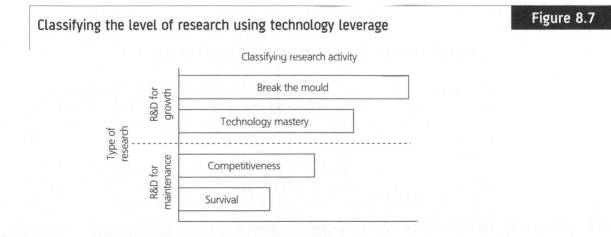

buyers. The process technologies involved have become widely accepted and used. However, if any one manufacturer allowed its process technologies to fall behind those of its competitors, it would almost certainly provide an advantage to them. The amount of research activity required to maintain a high-technology leverage position, however, will be significantly greater than that required to maintain a low-technology leverage position. Thus it seems reasonable to split this category in two: competitive (low-technology leverage) and competitive (high-technology leverage).

Technology mastery

Incremental growth of a business in a strong position involves improving the product and process relative to the competition. This will clearly involve a level of research activity greater than the competitive position outlined above. It will involve keeping abreast of all technological developments that may affect the business's products or processes. Hence, a much higher level of R&D expenditure will be required.

Break the mould

If the aim is to create a technological advantage then a much higher order of novelty and creativity is required. Following such a strategy will involve developing new patentable technology and may involve a higher level of basic scientific research.

Using the model

A business's expenditure on research activity would normally be reviewed annually or quarterly. The model is used as a guide to establish whether a business's research activity is appropriate for its position. Experience has shown that without such a guide research activity can drift over time, resulting in too much or too little activity appropriate for the business. The model provides the facility for business and research managers to monitor research activity. In practice this involves continual analysis, adjustment and realignment. For example, each quarter a business's executive would meet and discuss quarterly results. During these meetings, its strategic position could be reclassified according to performance and external environmental factors. That is, a business's category may change from, say, 3 to 4 or from 2 to 1.

Strengths and limitations of this approach

The model attempts to introduce some theory into what is often an arbitrary competition for research activity. It provides a framework within which discussions may take place. In practice, the model is used to check decisions made by research and business managers, as opposed to being used for dictating decisions. In addition, it includes a technological perspective for classifying a business's strategic position. Many strategic management tools, while paying lip service to the importance of technology, fail to accommodate a technological perspective in the decision-making process. There is an over-emphasis on the financial or marketing perspective (Ansoff, 1968; BCG, 1972; Porter, 1985).

It also shows how the role of strategic technology management and a business's selected growth strategy can influence the business climate within which managers operate. For example, if a strategic decision is taken to exit a business, this will clearly have a profound influence on the nature of activities. One would expect the activities of a business operating in a climate of growth to be different from those of one operating in a climate of decline.

Allocation of funds to R&D

Unlike many other business activities, successful R&D cannot be managed on an annual budgetary basis. It requires a much longer-term approach enabling knowledge to be acquired and built up over time. This often leads to tensions with other functions that are planning projects and activities. None the less, as was explained earlier in this chapter, R&D has to be linked to the business strategy.

It is unusual for unlimited funds to be available, hence business functions usually compete with other departments for funds. Marketing will no doubt present a very good case why extra money should be spent on new marketing campaigns; the IT department will request more funds for more equipment and valuable training for everyone; and the sales department will almost certainly ask for more salespeople to boost sales. It is a difficult circle to square. A great deal depends on the culture of the organisation and the industry within which it is operating (*see* Chapters 3 and 6). Pilkington, for example, spends proportionally large sums on R&D, many say too much, especially when one considers its more recent performance (*Financial Times*, 1998). Other companies spend very little on R&D but huge amounts on sales and marketing. This is the case for the financial services industry. So one of the most difficult decisions facing senior management is how much to spend on R&D. Many companies now report R&D expenditure in their annual reports. However, while the fact that it is now relatively easy to establish, for example, that Rubbermaid spent 14 per cent of sales on R&D in 1994, exactly how the company arrived at this figure is less clear.

Setting the R&D budget

In practice, establishing the R&D budget for a business is influenced by short-term performance fluctuations and availability of funds, which is, in turn, influenced by the setting of annual budgets. Additionally, budgets are also influenced by the long-term strategic technological needs of the business. It is extremely difficult to establish a basis for the allocation of funds that will be acceptable to all parties. A number of different approaches are used by different companies (*see* below). In practice, businesses use a combination of these methods. In addition, managerial judgement and negotiation will often play a significant role. The portfolio management approach, outlined earlier in this chapter, enables profits from today's successful businesses to be invested into what the company hopes will become the profitable businesses of tomorrow. Many businesses also invest in basic research. This is research that is perceived to be of interest to the company as a whole and of benefit to the organisation in the long term.

There are several key factors that need to be considered when allocating funds to R&D:

- expenditure by competitors;
- company's long-term growth objectives;
- the need for stability; and
- distortions introduced by large projects.

Six approaches can be used for allocating funds to R&D.

Inter-firm comparisons

While R&D expenditure varies greatly between industries, within similar industries there is often some similarity. It is possible to establish reasonably accurately a competitor's R&D expenditure, the number of research personnel employed, etc. By analysing the research expenditure of its competitors, a business is able to establish an appropriate figure for its own research effort. Table 8.3 would suggest that a company trying to establish its R&D budget should consider spending between 10 and 25 per cent of sales on R&D.

A fixed relationship to turnover

R&D expenditure can be based on a constant percentage. Turnover normally provides a reasonably stable figure that grows in line with the size of the company. As an example of this method, a company has decided to spend 2 per cent of its annual turnover on R&D. If its turnover is £10 million then its annual R&D expenditure would be £200,000. A criticism of this method is that it uses past figures for future investments.

A fixed relationship to profits

Fixing R&D expenditure to profits is highly undesirable. It implies that R&D is a luxury which can only be afforded when the company generates profits. This method

---

Table 8.3 Comparison of R&D expenditure within the European pharmaceutical industry

Company	R&D expenditure as % of sales
Novartis (Switz)	18.5
GlaxoSmithKline (UK)	18.7
Aventis (France)	21.4
Roche (Switz)	21.2
Astra-Zeneca (UK)	24.7

Source: www.innovation.gov.uk/projects/rd_scoreboard (2003)

completely ignores the role of R&D as an investment and the likely future benefits that will follow. Often, in fact, poor profits can be turned around with new products.

Reference to previous levels of expenditure

In the absence of any criteria for measurement, a starting point for discussions is likely to be the previous year's expenditure plus an allowance for inflation. In spite of its crudeness, this method is often used in conjunction with one or more of the other methods, especially during negotiations with other functional managers.

Costing of an agreed programme

An R&D manager is concerned with managing research projects, so the allocation of funds for each individual project may seem attractive. This allows him or her to add together the requirements for certain projects and arrive at a figure. Invariably the total will exceed what the department is likely to receive. Negotiations are then likely to ensue, focusing on which projects to cut completely or on which to reduce expenditure.

Internal customer–contractor relationship

In some large multinational companies, the individual business units may pay for research carried out on their behalf by the R&D function. In addition, there is usually some provision for building the knowledge base of the whole organisation. For example, each business manager within ICI manages his or her own R&D budget but each business must also contribute 10–12 per cent for long-term research. Shell operates a similar programme.

Level of R&D expenditure

Lord Lever's famous quote about advertising expenditure could equally be applied to R&D investment: 'half the money I spend on advertising is wasted, the problem is I don't know which half'. Scientists and technologists would rightly argue that even if the return on investment is not a profitable product, the investment in knowledge is not wasted. Without getting drawn into a philosophical debate on the acquisition of knowledge, the point is that an evaluation of a financial investment in R&D should be subject to the same criteria as evaluations of other investments made by the organisation. However, herein lies the difficulty. There are many short-term returns from an R&D investment, as was made clear above, but there is also a longer-term return. Often technological expertise is built up over many years through many consecutive short-term research projects. It is extremely difficult to apportion the profit to all contributing functions from a product developed over a period of several years. There is also considerable merit in the argument that without the R&D investment there would not have been a product at all. This subject has received a great deal of attention over the past four decades (Williams, 1969; Mansfield et al., 1972; Meyer-Krahmer, 1984; Cordero, 1990; McGrath and Romeri, 1994).

The R&D manager is under the same pressures as the senior management team. They have to ensure that the business has opportunities to exploit for future growth. In reality a few successful projects are usually sufficient to justify the investment.

Virtually all R&D managers are responsible for a portfolio of projects. The aim is to try to select those that will be successful and drop those which will not. The Guinness case study at the end of this chapter highlights the difficulty of project selection. Sometimes it is the project least likely to succeed that turns out to be the next Post-It notes business. One of the most dramatic examples of the high level of uncertainty involved in R&D project evaluations is demonstrated in Illustration 9.5 with the Viagra case.

Financial forecasts made at the time of R&D project selection are subject to gross errors, either because the development costs turn out to be much higher (rather than lower) or the financial benefits derived from the project are higher or lower than was originally forecast (Twiss, 1992). Such forecasts are clearly of limited value. None the less, some form of financial analysis cannot be avoided. It will certainly be demanded by senior management. Analyses which are unrealistic and have no credibility within the organisation are of limited value. This area of decision making is dominated by personal experience and historical case studies that the company has experienced.

A variety of quantitative and qualitative measurements have been developed to try to help business managers tackle the problem of project selection (Chiesa and Masella, 1996). It remains, however, a combination of uncertain science and experience. Chapter 9 explores how businesses attempt to evaluate R&D projects in terms of whether to continue funding or to drop the project.

Case study

Developing corporate success through successful R&D at Guinness plc[1]

Introduction

Guinness plc is one of the world's leading drinks companies, producing and managing an impressive portfolio of international brands such as Johnnie Walker, Bell's, Gordon's and the world's most distinctive beer. The merger of Guinness and Grand Metropolitan to form Diageo, has created one of the largest drinks groups in the world (Blair, 2000). Furthermore, the immediate future for the product that bears the company's name looks particularly bright. This is largely due to a major technological breakthrough which brought Guinness the Queen's Award for Technological Achievement, the first time that a drinks company has been presented with the award. This case study examines how this new product revolutionised the beer and lager industry. The Guinness 'in-can system', now referred to generically as 'widget technology' following heavy promotion by Courage, forces pressurised beer through a small aperture in the widget and into the beer when the can is opened. The effect is a foamy head.

Background

The Guinness company has a long history stretching back more than 230 years. Arthur

---

[1] This case has been written as a basis for class discussion rather than to illustrate effective or ineffective managerial or administrative behaviour. It has been prepared from a variety of published sources, as indicated, and from observations.

Guinness began brewing ale for the people of Dublin. In those days ale was brewed using a blend of several barrels. In the 1770s a new beer appeared in Dublin that was imported from London. It was known as Entire and contained roasted barley, which gave it a characteristically dark colour. In addition, unlike the traditional Dublin ale, it was served from a single barrel. As the popularity of this imported beer grew, Arthur Guinness, along with many other Dublin brewers, decided to tackle the English at their own game. Not all the brewers were successful in developing this new ale. However, Arthur Guinness soon had to choose between producing the traditional Dublin ale and this new brew. It would appear that he made the correct decision.

Labels are used by companies to help identify the contents of their products and promote particular brands. The famous Guinness trademark with its Irish harp emblem first appeared in Britain in 1862 and was registered as a trademark in 1876. Guinness supplied its labels to bottlers, but only to those bottlers which sold no other bottled stout except Guinness. Bottlers which sold their own stouts as well as Guinness had to provide their own labels which Guinness insisted on approving.

Over the years the label has changed, sometimes because of legislation and the need to provide information to the consumer, but mainly to give it a more contemporary feel. The trademark remains much the same as in 1862.

By 1920 production of Guinness was 3 million barrels a week, and in 1936 the Park Royal brewery opened in London to cope with the extra demand.

In these early days beer was sold in wooden casks. Glass was not used until after the tax on glass bottles was repealed in 1845. Guinness did not undertake the bottling itself. Instead, the beer was sold to a multitude of independent bottlers, ranging from small pubs to major wholesale bottlers and even other brewers. Guinness still uses a small number of contract bottlers, but other more recently developed products such as Guinness draught bitter and Kaliber are packaged by the company's own packaging division based at Runcorn in Cheshire.

Market changes and threats from competition

While Guinness enjoyed long-term growth and continued success through much of the twentieth century, a rosy future for the company was not always so identifiable. During the 1980s the beer industry in the United Kingdom came under severe attack from international lager brands such as Castlemaine XXXX, Fosters, Miller Lite and others. At one point many industry analysts suggested that the UK beer industry might be so badly damaged that it would struggle to compete. There were additional threats on the horizon. The growing concern about drink-driving was beginning to have an impact on beer sales in pubs across the country. Projecting their research results forward, the beer industry predicted that the volume of draught sales was sure to fall, with the take-home market one of the few beneficiaries, along with soft-drinks manufacturers such as Schweppes and Britvic! More worrying still was the realisation that any growth in the take-home market was likely to be enjoyed by the lager producers as opposed to the beer producers. This was because lager from a can or bottle tasted much the same as lager on draught. The same could not be said for beer from a can. The future looked bleak.

The response: a focused R&D programme

Draught Guinness has a unique appearance which results from the initiation and surging of bubbles of nitrogen and carbon dioxide gas as the beer passes through a special dispensing tap called a font to form a smooth, white creamy head. This creamy top to a pint of Guinness as delivered in the pub is a major factor which creates the flavour differences between draught Guinness and Guinness Original (canned or bottled Guinness).

▶

There was clearly a need to try to improve the taste and appearance of canned or bottled Guinness for the increasing take-home market. The problem was that the thick, creamy head associated with Guinness requires a high shearing force to initiate the break-out of mixed nitrogen and carbon dioxide. This is in contrast to carbonated drinks where the gas comes freely out of the solution (carbon dioxide readily comes out of a glass of lemonade, for example). The task therefore was to find a way of forcing the gas out of the solution. A shearing force similar to that used in the font was required.

Many research projects were started that considered new types of containers that replicated the font used in draught Guinness. The R&D department had been working on this particular problem as far back as the 1960s. In the early 1980s Guinness developed a packaging system that included a small syringe with which the consumer was to inject air into the stout after pouring it. This system was not commercially successful. Other projects looked at methods requiring the consumer to shake the container before pouring. In total over 100 research projects and ideas were tested. Some were very good but prohibitively expensive, making the final product uncompetitive. Others were too complicated, requiring the consumer to carry out several operations before serving.

After four years the research teams had been cut back and morale was low. The problems looked insurmountable. Over £5 million had been spent and research directors and senior managers were beginning to question whether the money should be directed into other projects. The perennial decision of whether to kill the project was discussed. Eventually in late 1987 Alan Forage and his team presented a system to senior management that has become known as the 'In-can system' (ICS). Forage explained:

The 'ICS' itself is a plastic chamber insert with a minute hole which is placed in the bottom of a 500ml can. However, only 440ml of beer is dispensed into the can.

This is to allow for head expansion when the can is opened. Beer containing dissolved gas is filled **under pressure** *into the can and the can is sealed. Once the lid has been put on, the pressures in the can and inside the chamber equilibrate and beer is* **forced** *into the chamber which becomes partially filled. When a consumer opens the can of beer by pulling the ring-pull, the higher pressure in the can is released to atmosphere. The drop in pressure causes an* **imbalance** *between the beer in the can and the beer in the chamber forcing beer out of the chamber through the small hole. It is this process which creates the* **shearing force** *and characteristic 'surge' in draught Guinness. As the beer is forced through this very small hole, nitrogen and carbon dioxide are broken out from their dissolved state.*

(Guinness, 1995)

ICS was developed with a specialist plastics company, McKechnie Plastic Components, that makes parts for the automobile industry. A peripheral structure holds the unit firmly in place when pushed to the bottom of the can. The new product was test-marketed in the Midlands and north of England from April 1988. Results were very encouraging. A few minor changes were made but the concept remained the same. Draught Guinness with ICS was launched nationally in March 1989. The product has been a huge commercial success.

The 'In-can' system

The complete canning system using the ICS is complex. The original canning line had to be considerably altered and involves several operations, including:

- location of plastic chamber in can;
- nitrogen being used to remove all oxygen from the can and insert prior to filling can with beer;

- liquid nitrogen being added which evaporates after the can is seamed to produce a high internal pressure; and
- filled cans being pasteurised at 60°C to give a microbiologically stable product.

The canning line at Runcorn, Cheshire, can now deliver 1,400 cans a minute or more than 23 cans a second (Brown, 1997).

The response of the competition and avoiding patent infringement

If imitation is the highest form of flattery, then Guinness should be pleased. Virtually all the major brewers have responded to Guinness's development by developing their own systems. Some of the best known are Whitbread Draught-flow, Courage Caskpour, Bass Mark II, plus many bottled systems.

There is clearly fierce commercial rivalry between the brewers, hence they try to keep secret the names of the companies which supply their plastic inserts. It is true that the plastic inserts are described in published patents, but as with virtually all production lines there is a huge difference between patent technology and a fully operational canning production line. It is important to note that the ICS as developed by Guinness is not simply the plastic can insert, there is also a great deal of associated technology including filling the can under pressure; use of an inerting tunnel; application of high pressure nitrogen; seaming of the can; and the pasteuriser, all of which contribute to the technology.

Guinness's original patent was comprehensive and covered the plastic insert and most of the associated technology (*see* the Appendix for details of Guinness' original patent application). Those companies which followed were forced to become more ingenious and make their designs more complex to achieve the same result. Many of the technical difficulties have involved minimising the costs associated with canning.

Equipment suppliers have devised clever ways to overcome the patent. Each brewing company in association with insert suppliers has developed individual systems, some using more manual systems with lower equipment costs, others very sophisticated equipment without a large increase in the workforce. The developed cost of the Bass widget is claimed to be £10 million (Wainwright, 1995).

Many of the brewers claim that their widget technology is now superior to that originally developed by Guinness. Whitbread, for example, claims that its two-part injection-moulded widget enables the amount of gas in the can to be carefully preset, offering a more reliable force when the can is opened. Furthermore, because the Whitbread widget is sealed it minimises any air in the can.

Discussion

In many ways Guinness has revolutionised the concept of beer packaging. The can is no longer simply a container but performs a function and is itself an example of new technology. This was underlined when, in 1991, the ICS received the Queen's Award for Technological Achievement.

The product is now sold in more than 50 countries and in March 1993 it launched the sale of its 250 millionth can of draught Guinness. In 1994 it launched a £30-million investment programme in canning facilities at its Runcorn canning factory (*The Canner*, 1994). The wider brewing industry has also benefited from this technological development with higher margins now achievable; the new cans are 20 per cent above the price of the original packaged product.

The inclusion of plastic inserts in a metal can has generated much criticism from the recycling lobby. However, Bass has recently developed an aluminium widget. Also some consumer groups, particularly the Campaign for Real Ale (CAMRA), do not consider the use of widgets as a product improvement. They consider that the beer tastes blander.

▶

In 2004 Drinks group Diageo announced it would close its Park Royal brewery in London which began production in 1938 and was the first site at which Guinness was made outside the Republic of Ireland. The brewing of 4 million kegs will be transferred to the famous St James's Gate site in Dublin as Diageo scales down its draught Guinness production capacity amid declines in consumption in the republic and the United Kingdom. Sales volumes fell 3 per cent in the United Kingdom in second half of 2003, and 7 per cent in the Republic of Ireland. Nevertheless, Guinness is still Britain's fifth best-selling beer – behind Carling, Foster's, Stella Artois and Carlsberg – and the United Kingdom is still the largest market for the stout.

Diageo insists Guinness remains among a handful of its core growth brands otherwise dominated by spirits such as Smirnoff and Johnnie Walker. Global Guinness sales rose 3 per cent in the second half of last year, driven largely by a growing taste for it in Cameroon and Nigeria.

It promotes Guinness Extra Cold as a drink for the summer – much to the annoyance of traditionalists. But in its Irish heartland, Guinness is struggling against a 4 per cent decline in the wider market. As in the United Kingdom, bar sales have fallen as drinkers were lured away by supermarket discounts, and Diageo actually responded by raising the price of Guinness (Bowers, 2004).

Questions

1 Guinness were able to forecast changes in the marketplace, competition and societal changes. Explain these changes and how this helped Guinness develop an effective defence and competitive strategy.

2 To what extent was the Guinness patent effective?

3 What is your view on the patent system, what are its strengths and limitations (*see* Appendix).

4 Many people argue that companies in Europe cannot compete with the Asian economies because labour costs in Europe are too high in comparison. To what extent have Guinness demonstrated that despite high to low costs it is possible to gain competitive advantage?

5 Using the Guinness case, discuss the dilemma of having to decide whether or not to kill a project and the implications of so doing.

6 Show how the Guinness case study illustrates how the traditional view of R&D is still relevant today.

7 To what extent did organisational knowledge and organisational heritage affect the development of the ICS?

Chapter summary

This chapter has introduced the substantial subject of R&D management and some of the challenges that it presents. Emphasis has been placed on highlighting the wide range of different activities undertaken by most R&D functions. Formal management techniques were shown to be an essential part of good R&D management. Companies are unable to justify spending millions of dollars purely on the basis of chance and good fortune. The issue of investment in R&D and industry comparisons was another area of discussion.

The link between R&D and the strategic management activities of the business was also discussed in some detail. This presents its own set of challenges in terms of deciding in which areas to invest and what type of R&D investment to follow. Most companies try to manage a balance of activities, but it is important to be aware of the nature of the pressures placed on management.

Discussion questions

1 Show why R&D management is dependent on industrial context.
2 Discuss the range of operational R&D activities.
3 What was the traditional view of R&D?
4 Not all firms invest in R&D. What should be the level of expenditure on R&D for a firm?
5 What are the main strategic activities of R&D?
6 Discuss some of the strategic pressures on R&D.
7 What is meant by technology leverage?
8 What are the main parts to a patent (*see* Appendix)?

Key words and phrases

Applied research 256	Peripheral technologies 260
Basic research 254	R&D as a percentage of sales 246
Complementary technologies 260	Technical service 256
Core technologies 260	Technology leverage 263
Emerging technologies 260	Technology portfolio 259

Websites worth visiting

Corporate R&D labs www.eas.asu.edu/~kdooley/nsfnpd/corplab.html

European Union, Enterprise and Innovation www.europa.eu.int/comm/enterprise/innovation

European Union, Innovation Directorate www.cordis.lu/fp6/innovation.htm

Pilkington PLC Technology Management www.pilkington.com

Stanford University, explaining innovation www.Manufacturing.Stanford.edu

Technology encyclopedia www.techweb.com

UK Government, Department of Trade and Industry www.Dti.gov.uk/innovation

References

ABCM (1919) 'Report of the British Chemical Mission on Chemical Factories in the Occupied Area of Germany'.

Adler, P.S., McDonald, D.W. and MacDonald, F. (1992) 'Strategic management of technical functions', *Sloan Management Review*, Winter, 19–37.

Ansoff, H.I. (1968) *Corporate Strategy*, Penguin, Harmondsworth.

BCG (1972) *Perspectives on Experience*, Boston Consulting Group, Boston, MA.

Blair, A. (2000) 'Equity markets: Diageo puts a king-sized meal on the menu', *Financial Times*, 24 June, 23.

Bowers, S. (2004) 'Guinness goes home: brewing link with UK severed', *The Guardian*, 16 April.

Brown, D. (1997) 'Nitrogen and its foaming relationship with widgets', *The Brewer*, January, 25–32.

The Canner (1994) 'Widgets rule in UK beer market', March, 28–33.

Chiesa, V. and Masella, C. (1996) 'Searching for an effective measure of R&D performance', *Management Decision*, Vol. 34, No. 7, 49–58.

Cohen, W.M. and Levinthal, D.A. (1990) 'A new perspective on learning and innovation', *Administrative Science Quarterly*, Vol. 35, No. 1, 128–52.

Cordero, R. (1990) 'The measurement of innovation performance in the firm: an overview', *Research Policy*, Vol. 19, No. 2, 10–21.

EIRMA (1985) 'Evaluation of R&D output: working group report, 29', European Industrial Research Management Association, Paris.

Geroski, P., Machin, S. and van Reenen, J. (1993) 'The profitability of innovating forms', *Rand Journal of Economics*, Vol. 24, 198–211.

Guinness (1995) Promotional material issued to the industry to support the product launch.

Hickman, L.A. (1990) *Technology*, McGraw-Hill, Maidenhead.

The Independent (1992) 'R&D Scoreboard'; 10 June, 20.

Lancaster, A. (1997) 'An investigation into the evaluation of an organisation's research and development performance', BA Business Studies undergraduate dissertation.

Mansfield, E. (1991) 'Social returns from R&D: findings, methods and limitations', *Research, Technology Management*, November/December, 24.

Mansfield, E., Raporport, J., Schnee, J., Wagner, S. and Hamburger, M. (1972) *Research and Innovation in the Modern Corporation*, Macmillan, London.

Marsh, P. (1997) 'Engineering a product switch', *Financial Times*, 19 November, 16.

McGrath, M.E. and Romeri, M.N. (1994) 'The R&D effectiveness index', *Journal of Product Innovation Management*, Vol. 23, No. 2, 213–20.

Meyer-Krahmer, F. (1984) 'Recent results in measuring innovation output', *Research Policy*, Vol. 13, No. 3, 12–24.

Mitchell, G.R. (1988) 'Options for the strategic management of technology', *UNESCO Technology Management*, Interscience Enterprises Ltd, Geneva.

Porter, M.E. (1985) *Competitive Advantage: Creating and Sustaining Competitive Advantage*, Free Press, New York.

Quintas, P., Weild, D. and Massey, M. (1992) 'Academic–industry links and innovation: questioning the science park model', *Technovation*, Vol. 12, No. 3, 161–75.

Rosenbloom, R.S. and Cusumano, M.A. (1988) 'Technological pioneering and competitive advantage: the birth of the VCR industry', in Tushman, M.L. and Moore, W.L. (eds) *Readings in the Management of Innovation*, HarperCollins, New York.

Roussel, P.A., Saad, K.N. and Erickson, T.S. (1991) *Third Generation R&D*, Harvard Business School Press, Boston, MA.

Scholefield, J.H. (1993) 'The development of a R&D planning model at ICI', *R&D Management*, Vol. 23, No. 4, 20–30.

Twiss, B. (1992) *Managing Technological Innovation*, 4th edn, Financial Times Pitman Publishing, London.

Video Magazine (1988) 'The format war', April, 50–4.

Wainwright, T. (1995) 'Canned beers get a head', *Beverage World International*, July/August, 39–46.

Weild, D. (1986) 'Organisational strategies and practices for innovation', in Roy, R. and Weild, D. (eds) *Product Design and Technological Innovation*, Open University Press, Milton Keynes.

Williams, D.J. (1969) 'A study of the decision model for R&D project selection', *Operational Research Quarterly*, Vol. 20.

www.innovation.gov.uk/projects/rd_scoreboard(2003).

Further reading

For a more detailed review of the R&D management literature, the following develop many of the issues raised in this chapter:

Day, G.S. and Schoemaker, P.J.H. (eds) (2000) *Wharton on Managing Emerging Technologies*, John Wiley, New York.

Roussel, P.A., Saad, K.N. and Erickson, T.J. (1991) *Third Generation R&D*, Harvard Business School Press, Boston, MA.

Shavinina, L. (2003) *The International Handbook on Innovation*, Elsevier, Oxford.

Tushman, M.L. and Moore, W.L. (eds) (1988) *Readings in the Management of Innovation*, HarperCollins, New York.

9

Managing R&D projects

The past 10 years have witnessed enormous changes in the way companies manage their technological resources and in particular research and development. Within industrial R&D the effect is a shift in emphasis from an internal to an external focus. Contract R&D, R&D consortia and strategic alliances and joint ventures now form a large part of R&D management activities.

The need to provide scientifc freedom and still achieve an effective return from any R&D investment, however, remains one of the most fundamental areas of R&D management. The use of formal planning techniques for R&D is viewed by many as a paradox: the introduction of any planning mechanism would surely stifle creativity and innovation. And yet R&D departments do not have unlimited funds, so there has to be some planning and control. This chapter explores the problems and diffculties of managing R&D projects within organisations.

Chapter contents

Learning objectives

When you have completed this chapter you will be able to:

- recognise the changing nature of R&D management;
- recognise the factors that influence the decision whether to undertake internal or external R&D;
- recognise the value of providing scientific freedom;
- examine the link with the product innovation process;
- recognise the significance of evaluating R&D projects; and
- explore the various ways of funding R&D.

Successful technology management

Organisations that manage products and technologies and have been built on a strong research and development base are constantly looking for opportunities to diversify horizontally into new product markets. Their strategic management activities seek to mobilise complementary assets to successfully enter those markets. For example, Eastman Kodak's knowledge of manufacturing photographic film enabled it to move into the manufacture of computer floppy disks. Similarly, in production-based technologies, key opportunities lie in the technological advances that can be applied to products and production systems, enabling diversification vertically into a wider range of production inputs. The injection-moulding process has had many adaptations, enabling its use in an increasing range of manufacturing techniques. However, companies do not have a completely free choice about the way they manage their technologies (Pavitt, 1990):

> *In many areas it is not clear before the event who is in the innovation race, where the starting and finishing lines are, and what the race is all about. Even when all these things are clear, companies often start out wishing to be a leader and end up being a follower!*

There are two key technology risks that technology managers have to evaluate (Malerba and Orsenigo, 1993; Breschi and Malerba, 1997; Dosi, 1988). First, 'appropriability risks' reflect the ease with which competitors can imitate innovations (*see* Chapter 6). They are typically managed through patent and copyright protection or through controlling complementary assets (such as branding, distribution, specialised services, etc), as discussed by Teece (1986). In the pharmaceutical industry, for example, patent protection is relatively effective because minor changes in the structure of therapeutic drugs can have major consequences for their operation in the human body (Gambardella, 1995). As a result, drug discovery firms are able to specialise in highly risky activities without needing to develop complementary assets to protect their innovations.

The second risk is 'competence destruction'. This reflects the volatility and uncertainty of technical development that vary greatly between technologies, both in terms of the technological trajectories (*see* Chapter 6) being followed and market acceptance. Where technological uncertainty is high, it is difficult to predict which investments and skills will be effective and firms have to be able to change direction at short notice. Consequently, the managers of firms attempting to develop radically discontinuous innovations are faced with the need to attract and motivate expert staff to work on complex problems when unpredictable outcomes may involve redundancy and/or organisational failure.

These two kinds of technology risk tend to be inversely related. Investments in developing highly uncertain technologies are usually undertaken when appropriability risks are limited (e.g. intellectual property protection is available, such as pharmaceuticals and software), while firms developing innovations that are more open to such risks tend to focus on more cumulative and predictable technologies (e.g. food industry and other fast-moving consumer goods (fmcg) areas). Companies racing to produce highly radical, discontinuous innovations have to be flexible in their use of key resources, such as highly expert technologists, and in changing direction, while those developing more imitable technologies have to develop complementary competences (branding, distribution) and integrate them through organisational routines. By making innovations more customer-specific and bundling additional services with them, such companies increase their organisational specificity and limit the ease with which they can be imitated (e.g. Coca-Cola, Unilever). However, these kinds of entrepreneurial technology firms are more organisationally complex than radically innovative companies and have to develop stronger coordinating organisational capabilities (Mason *et al.*, 2004; Casper and Whitley, 2004).

The above discussions reveal the weaknesses in some of the commonly accepted views of technology strategy promoted by many business schools and management consultants. It is not helpful to the organisation to try to predetermine whether its technology strategy should be to lead or to follow, to develop a product or a process. Technology cannot be developed to order or acquired to fill a position in a matrix. It can only be successful if it is fully integrated into the company's business. This means that the company needs a range of complementary assets in other areas such as marketing and distribution, in order to exploit its technology successfully. Developing these skills and capabilities and integrating them into the company takes time. Often these characteristics will be determined by the company's size, its previous activities and its accumulated competencies. However, it is these latter factors and not the company's strategy that will determine whether it will successfully exploit its technology.

As virtually all practitioners realise, there is no easy formula for success. In a review of the literature on technology management, Pavitt (1990) identified the following necessary ingredients for successful technology management:

- the capacity to orchestrate and integrate functional and specialist groups for the implementation of innovations;
- continuous questioning of the appropriateness of existing divisional markets, missions and skills for the exploitation of technological opportunities; and
- a willingness to take a long-term view of technological accumulation within the firm.

The changing nature of R&D management

R&D activities have changed dramatically since 1950. The past 10 years have witnessed enormous changes in the way companies manage their technological resources and in particular their research and development. There are numerous factors that have contributed to these changes (*see* Illustration 9.1). Rothwell and Zegveld (1985) identify three important factors.

- *Technology explosion.* They estimate that 90 per cent of our present technical knowledge has been generated during the last 55 years.
- *Shortening of the technology cycle.* The technology cycle includes scientific and technological developments prior to the traditional product life cycle. These cycles have been slowly shortening, forcing companies to focus their efforts on product

Illustration 9.1

Quick-hit chemistry becomes elusive

Finding a new blockbuster drug has become harder now R&D is more complex, more expensive and more time-consuming,

The men and women in white coats are the centre of attention. The world's drugs companies are coming to terms with a difficult conundrum in research and development: despite huge advances in technology and scientific know-how, R&D productivity seems to have stalled.

By some measures, productivity could even be said to have declined. Statistics from the US Food and Drug Administration, the chief industry regulator, show that 'new molecular entities' (NMEs) – drugs that are a good indicator of medical advances and possible blockbuster status – are becoming less frequent. The FDA approved more than 53 NMEs in 1996 but only 27 last year and just nine in the first half of this year. This is in spite of the much-trumpeted unravelling of the human genome, speedier computing, breakthroughs in biochemistry and, most important, billions of dollars more being thrown at the effort by ever-larger, merged drug behemoths.

The large pharmaceuticals companies' amazing growth over the past few years has been fuelled by a series of drugs that they turned into blockbusters – with sales of more than $1bn (£680m) a year. But they now realise that their current R&D effort is not enough to sustain that growth. One explanation for falling R&D productivity is that the quick hits – in gastrointestinal disorders or heart disease, for example – have already been made. Glaxo built its fortune on the ulcer drug Zantac while Eli Lilly's Prozac took the treatment of depression off the psychiatrist's couch and into the family doctor's surgery.

Ben Shapiro, who as head of external development at Merck is responsible for finding outside R&D collaborations to bolster the company's own pipeline, says: 'The first biotech revolution took off a lot of low-hanging fruit.'

Diseases that have yet to be conquered with blockbusters – Alzheimer's, or the various forms of cancer, for example – have been much harder nuts to crack.

There have been considerable technical and scientific advances, most notably in biotechnology, genomics and related fields. But everyone seems to have underestimated how long it will take for the greater knowledge to result in medicines.

John Niblack, head of R&D at Pfizer, says that overall the odds of a drug candidate's success have hardly shifted in the past 20 years. Pfizer is the world's largest pharmaceuticals company after its $84bn acquisition of Warner-Lambert last year. But, says Mr Niblack, of 12 molecules that Pfizer classifies as its best bets – those drugs that have made it to the verge of clinical testing – only one will make it to market. Carl Seiden, analyst at JPMorgan Chase, says: 'The technologies for sifting data have turned out to be expensive. The companies are developing their experience but they don't have it yet.'

Finding molecules that have a beneficial effect on humans has always been somewhat haphazard. All drugs are trying to affect the body in one of two ways: they either enhance a chemical process or stop it. First companies must know as much as possible about biochemical pathways so that they have more places to attack with drugs. Then they must find molecules that can disrupt the processes.

In the past, the search for compounds has often involved random trawling of organic material such as mud or sewage for promising chemical entities. Now scientists are using techniques such as structure-based design to build custom-made molecules in the laboratory.

▶

In addition, methods such as high-throughput screening – which rapidly speeds up trial-and-error assessment of compounds and how they might affect the body's chemistry – have given companies more to work on.

Greater understanding of our genetic make-up is also leading to ideas for drugs that can correct DNA deficiencies before they have caused damage or more precisely identify people at risk from certain conditions.

However, these advances are recent and all target the start of the R&D process. Even without any unexpected obstacles, companies would take a few years yet to turn them into a flow of drugs at the other end of the pipeline.

But there are unexpected obstacles. The first is poisonous – or toxicological – side-effects. As we learn more about the body's biochemistry, we can strive to test better what pathways a drug will disrupt aside from those that it was intended to. Too much chemical action on the side and you may have the medicinal equivalent of chopping off a head to cure a headache.

Advances in biochemistry and genetics mean there are now far more body interactions to study. There are also many more drugs on the market than before and research is required into how each new drug will interact with existing ones. Companies are developing the high-throughput screening for toxicology but it has been a slow process.

Ultimately, the screening will be more productive because drug candidates will fail earlier in the R&D process, thus saving money that would otherwise have been spent on clinical trials. But at the moment the faster techniques are in their infancy.

After a drug candidate is successful in its toxicology trials, it still has to be tested in humans – the trials are increasingly subject to criticism, with 13 leading medical journals warning this week that the promise of big financial rewards is compromising independence. And with companies and regulators more mindful of side-effects, clinical trials are becoming larger and taking longer, another reason why R&D costs are rising. In areas yet to see significant breakthroughs, such as stroke or cancer, large numbers of patients have to be studied for a long time and the effectiveness of a drug is sometimes hard to prove.

Technical advances can help. In osteoporosis, for example, new equipment for measuring bone mineral density has made it easier to test drugs. But by and large, little progress has been made. Mr Niblack says: 'The great last frontier is to improve the scientific precision of doing clinical trials in chronic disease.'

Some in the industry believe that the next leap in R&D productivity could be as much as 10 years away. Meanwhile the strategy for some, such as Pfizer, has been to acquire rivals, hope that the increased market share will ensure their survival, and tough it out.

Source: A. Michaels, 'Quick-hit chemistry becomes elusive', *Financial Times*, 12 September 2001. Reprinted with permission.

development. For example, the market life of production cars has decreased from approximately 10 years in the 1960s to approximately six years in the 1990s. In some cases a particular model may be restyled after only three years.

● *Globalisation of technology*. Countries on the Pacific Rim have demonstrated an ability to acquire and assimilate technology into new products. This has resulted in a substantial increase in technology transfer in the form of licensing and strategic alliances.

Figure 8.3 showed the traditional areas of research activity for universities and industry. University emphasis has been on discovering new knowledge, with industry exploiting these discoveries in the form of products. The last decade has seen a significant increase in collaborative research, with industry sponsoring science departments in universities and engaging in staff exchanges with university departments.

The effect of these macro-factors is a shift in emphasis within industrial R&D from an internal to an external focus. In a study of firms in Sweden, Japan and the United States Granstrand *et al.* (1992) revealed that the external acquisition of technology was the most prominent technology management issue in multi-technology corporations. Traditionally, R&D management, particularly in Western technology-based companies, has been management of internal R&D. It could be argued that one of the most noticeable features of Japanese companies since the Second World War has been their ability successfully to acquire and utilise technology from other companies around the world. Granstrand *et al.* (1992) suggest that the external acquisition of technology exposes technology managers to new responsibilities. Although this implies that acquiring technology from outside the organisation is something new, this is clearly not the case, as the long history of licensing agreements will show. However, the importance now placed on technology acquisition by technology-based companies reveals a departure from a focus on internal R&D and an acknowledgement that internal R&D is now only one of many technology development options available. The technology base of a company is viewed as an asset; it represents the technological capability of that company. The different acquisition strategies available involve varying degrees of organisational and managerial integration. For example, internal R&D is viewed as the most integrated technology-acquisition strategy with technology scanning the least integrated strategy. Technology scanning is rather narrowly defined by Granstrand *et al.* (1992) as both illegal and legal forms of acquiring technological know-how from outside.

The classification of technology-acquisition strategies offered by Granstrand *et al.* (1995) provides an illustration of the numerous ways of acquiring external technology (*see* Figure 9.1). Other classifications can be found in the technology transfer literature:

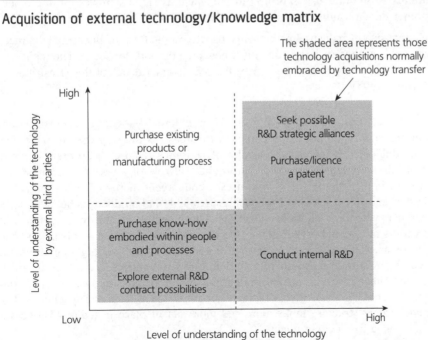

Figure 9.1

Acquisition of external technology/knowledge matrix

Auster (1987); Chesnais (1988); Hagedoorn (1990); Lefever (1992). All these studies, however, offer classifications of only the formal methods of technology transfer. They ignore the many forms of informal linkages, alliances and industry associations that are known to exist and that often result in extensive transfer of knowledge and technology (Kreiner and Schultz, 1990; Rothwell and Dodgson, 1991).

The wide range of activities now being expected from R&D departments and the demands being placed on them are becoming ever more complex. Particular emphasis is being placed on a company's linkages with other organisations. Networking is now regarded as an effective method of knowledge acquisition and learning (Rothwell, 1992; Tidd *et al.*, 2001; Albertini and Butler, 1995). It is argued that the ability to network in order to acquire and exploit external knowledge enables the firm to enter new areas of technological development. The following areas now explicitly require involvement from the R&D department:

- Industry has expanded its support of university research and established numerous collaborations with university departments (Abelson, 1995).

- Industry has increased the number of technological collaborations. R&D personnel are increasingly being involved in technology audits of potential collaborators.

- Research and development personnel are increasingly accompanying sales staff on visits to customers and component suppliers to discuss technical problems and possible product developments.

- The acquisition and divestment of technology-based businesses have led to a further expansion of the role of R&D. Input is increasingly required in the form of an assessment of the value of the technology to the business.

- A dramatic rise in the use of project management as organisations shift to provide customer-driven results (Englund and Graham, 1999).

- The expansion of industrial agreements, usually in the form of licensing, contract work and consultancy, has resulted in a new area of work for R&D. The rapid growth in knowledge-intensive service firms is clear evidence of this (Kastrinos and Miles, 1995).

The focus of these new areas of work is on external knowledge acquisition and assimilation. This is forcing many companies to reassess the way they manage their R&D. In addition, this increased portfolio of activities requires a different range of skills from the individuals involved. The traditional role of a research scientist as a world expert in a particular field, who uses a convergent, narrow-focus approach to uncover new and cheaper ways of producing chemicals and products, is being replaced by researchers who have additional attributes. These include an ability to interact with a wide variety of external organisations, thereby increasing awareness of specific customer needs, market changes, the activities of competitors and the larger environment. Historically, R&D staff faced alternative definitions of career success and reward in career paths either involving increasing administrative responsibility and a path into managerial hierarchy or one involving increasing prestige as technical specialists. This dual-ladder career structure looks more and more out of place in today's varied and rapidly changing R&D environment.

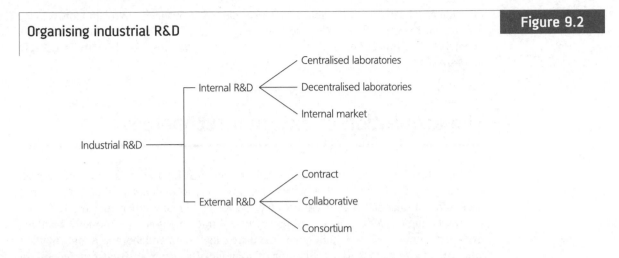

Figure 9.2

Organising industrial R&D

Organising industrial R&D

The increasing emphasis on knowledge acquisition and assimilation is forcing companies to look for ways to improve their effectiveness in this area. Given the growing use of external sources of technology, the R&D manager now has to determine which form of R&D is most appropriate for the organisation. Figure 9.2 shows the many guises of R&D.

Centralised laboratories

The main advantage with centralised laboratories is critical mass. The idea is that far more can be achieved when scientists work together than when they work alone. Those firms trying to achieve technological leadership often centralise their R&D. There is also the possibility that synergy can result, with technologies from different businesses being employed in different unrelated businesses. 3M argue that they gain synergies between businesses resulting in internal technology transfer by having a centralised R&D laboratory (*see* case study in Chapter 12).

Decentralised laboratories

The main advantage of decentralising the R&D function is to reinforce the link with the business, its products and its markets. It is argued that with a large, centralised R&D effort it is often too removed from where the technology is eventually applied. By providing each business or division with its own R&D effort, it is argued that this fosters improved communication and product development. However, the weakness of this closer link is that it can lead to an emphasis on short-term development only.

Internal R&D market

An internal market structure for R&D essentially involves establishing a functional cost centre, where each business pays for any R&D services required. This raises the issue of whether a business is also able to use external R&D services, say from a university. The extent to which this erodes the knowledge base of the organisation, however, is debatable. The limitations of this approach are similar to those for decentralised R&D laboratories.

The acquisition of external technology

So far in this book, we have concentrated on viewing R&D as an activity performed internally by the business. It is necessary, however, to understand that R&D is not necessarily an internal organisational activity. R&D, like any other business function, say marketing or production, can in theory be contracted out and performed by a third party. The previous section highlighted the increasing use of collaborations and strategic alliances to acquire technology (the role of strategic alliances was discussed in detail in Chapter 7). The extent to which it is possible for an organisation to acquire externally developed technology is uncertain and is discussed in Chapters 6 and 10. None the less, many businesses establish research contracts with organisations such as universities to undertake specific research projects.

There is a significant difference between acquiring externally developed technology and external R&D. This difference lies in the level of understanding of the technology involved, often referred to as prior knowledge. To illustrate, the purchase of new computer software will lead to the acquisition of new technology. This is an option available to virtually all businesses, irrespective of their prior knowledge of the technology. However, developing an R&D strategic alliance or an external R&D contract with a third party requires a high level of prior knowledge of the technology concerned. Similarly, the level of prior knowledge of the external third party also influences the choice of method to acquire the technology concerned (Mason *et al.*, 2004).

The matrix in Figure 9.1 offers an insight into the issue of technology acquisition. While the matrix is an over-simplification of a complex subject, it does none the less help to classify the wide range of acquisition options available to companies, from purchasing technology 'off the shelf' to conducting internal R&D. The horizontal axis refers to the level of prior knowledge of the business acquiring the technology. The vertical axis refers to the level of prior knowledge of external third parties.

As was explained in Chapter 3, there are many companies that conduct little, if any, R&D, yet are associated with a wide variety of technology-intensive products. This is particularly the case for supplier-dominated and scale-intensive firms (Pavitt, 1984). Many such companies assemble component parts purchased from other manufacturers and sell the final product stamped with their own brand. Some companies do not even assemble, they simply place their own brand on the purchased product (often called re-badging). In these cases the company concerned usually has commercial and marketing strengths such as service quality and distribution skills. This is similar to own-branding in the grocery market.

The subject of technology transfer is discussed in detail in Chapter 10. It is none the less worth pointing out here that technology transfer usually embraces the activities in the shaded area on the matrix. It is not normally used to describe, say, the purchase of new computer software. Technology transfer is defined as:

The process of promoting technical innovation through the transfer of ideas, knowledge, devices and artefacts from leading edge companies, R&D organisations and academic research to more general and effective application in industry and commerce.

(Seaton and Cordey-Hayes, 1993)

Level of control of technology required

In acquiring externally developed technology, a business must also consider the extent of control over the technology that it requires. For example, if a research project shows promising results that could lead to the development of a new radical technology with many new product opportunities, it is likely that the business would want to keep such research under close control and thus internal. On the other hand, a project with specific technical problems requiring expertise in an area of technology beyond the scope of the business may be ideally suited to a research contract with a university department. Figure 9.3 shows a classification of technology acquisition methods. You will see that they are classified according to the degree of integration with the organisation.

The particular stage of development of the research, or its position in the technology life cycle, will heavily influence the level of control required. For example, is the research at an early stage without any particular product idea in mind (pre-competitive) or is it near completion and shortly to be incorporated in a new product launch (competitive)? Clearly, competitive research will require careful monitoring to ensure that maximum competitive advantage can be secured.

There may also be occasions when the company does not have the in-house expertise to undertake the research. In this case some form of external R&D will be necessary.

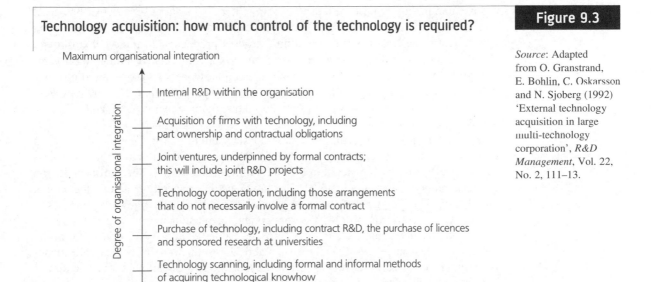

Technology acquisition: how much control of the technology is required?

Figure 9.3

Maximum organisational integration

— Internal R&D within the organisation

— Acquisition of firms with technology, including part ownership and contractual obligations

— Joint ventures, underpinned by formal contracts; this will include joint R&D projects

— Technology cooperation, including those arrangements that do not necessarily involve a formal contract

— Purchase of technology, including contract R&D, the purchase of licences and sponsored research at universities

— Technology scanning, including formal and informal methods of acquiring technological knowhow

Degree of organisational integration

Minimal organisational integration

Source: Adapted from O. Granstrand, E. Bohlin, C. Oskarsson and N. Sjoberg (1992) 'External technology acquisition in large multi-technology corporation', *R&D Management*, Vol. 22, No. 2, 111–13.

Forms of external R&D

Contract R&D

In those situations where the business has a low level of understanding of the technology (bottom left-hand corner of technology acquisition matrix), contracting the R&D out to a third party is often suitable. University research departments have a long history of operating in this area. However, the use of commercial research organisations is rapidly expanding, especially in the field of biotechnology. This method of R&D is also used in urgent situations, when setting up internal research teams would be too slow.

R&D strategic alliances and joint ventures

This area of management was explored in Chapter 7. At this point it is necessary only to be aware of the key advantages and disadvantages of using strategic alliances. This is a generic term for all forms of cooperation, both formal and informal, including joint ventures. With a joint venture, the costs and possible benefits from an R&D research project would be shared. They are usually established for a specific project and will cease on its completion. For example, Sony and Ericsson formed a joint venture in 2001 to develop cell phone handsets. The advantages are usually obvious. In this example, both companies (who were former competitors) were able to share their expertise and reduce the inevitable costs and risks associated with any R&D project. The disadvantages are that either company could inadvertently pass knowledge to the other and receive little in return. It is for this reason alone that many companies still refuse to enter into any form of strategic alliance. It can be usefully explained using game theory principles and in particular the prisoner's dilemma (*see* Chapter 7).

R&D consortia

In this context, R&D consortia are separate from the large-scale technology consortia often found in the Far East. In Japan *keiretsus* (literally meaning societies of business) consist of 20–50 companies, usually centred around a trading company and involving component suppliers, distributors and final product producers, all interwoven through shareholdings and trading arrangements. In South Korea, *chaebols* are similar to *keiretsus* except that they are financed by the government rather than by banks or a trading company and usually the company links are based on family ties (Sakakibara, 2002; Powell, 1996). Such types of business groups are based on common membership and collaborate over a long period of time.

The use of R&D consortia has increased substantially over the past 10 years in both the United States and Europe. Rhea (1991) claims that there have been in excess of 200 R&D consortia registered in the United States since 1984. The European Union offers a number of programmes to encourage R&D cooperation across the Union (*see* Illustration 9.2). One of the most successful, and certainly high-profile, cases is SEMTECH, a consortium of 14 US semiconductor manufacturers. In 1980 nine out of the top 10 silicon chip makers were from the United States. By 1990 five out of the top six were Japanese. SEMTECH was established to try to help the US chip manufacturers. It had substantial funding from the US Defense Department with the aim of creating a viable semiconductor manufacturing equipment and materials industry, thus ensuring that domestic chip producers would not be dependent on Japanese equipment

Illustration 9.2

The development of IMAGE

This shows how pre-competitive R&D collaboration led to the development of an exciting new multi-media product for Olivetti. This cooperation led to further agreements with other firms concerning the manufacturing and marketing of a range of products.

The Olivetti product, called IMAGE, is a software authoring environment for the development of interactive multi-media applications, which enables the user to manipulate graphics, animation, photographs and sound in an integrated manner. The product was eventually launched in 1991 and was one of the first in the field.

The idea for a new multi-media product emerged during the final phases of a research project called MULTOS, financed by the European Union's ESPRIT programme. This programme aims to encourage cooperation between member states in industrial R&D projects, specifically in the area of information technologies. It is managed by DG III, the Directorate General for Industry of the European Commission.

The objective of the project was to develop a basic software system that would store and retrieve multi-media documents. The original group comprised the Crete Research Centre, IEI and Olivetti Pisa Research Laboratories. Each partner would carry out specific research tasks and researchers would meet on a monthly basis to discuss progress. Close contact facilitated the exchange of information and experience, and enabled friendships to develop.

Moreover, there was a common desire to overcome technical problems and develop scientific understanding. The university partners were primarily interested in the theoretical aspects of the MULTOS system, whereas the industrial partners were interested in how the technology could be further developed into products.

This particular project ran from 1985 to 1991 and was very successful. There were two key benefits:

1 Basic R&D was not constrained by costs. This enabled the group to explore the subject rather than focusing on a specific business objective. This type of research (often referred to as 'blue-sky research') is limited in industry today.

2 Individuals received excellent training and experience. The postgraduate researchers involved in the project benefited from wonderful experience of scientific and technical research and the management of an international research project.

The research offered several exciting avenues to pursue, in the fields of software engineering, artificial intelligence, multi-media and office automation. Olivetti Research Labs eventually decided to explore the possibility of a multi-media product.

Source: ESPRIT (1997) *First Open Interconnects for Clustered Systems*, No. 12, DG III, European Commission, Luxembourg, pp. 1–20.

---

sources. SEMTECH has played a major role in developing successive generations of chip-making technology. By 1995, the US semiconductor industry had experienced a dramatic increase in its share of the world market (Corey, 1997).

One of the potential weaknesses of this concept is the potential for reducing competition. The European Union and the US government spend a great deal of time and money trying to detect those organisations operating a cartel. Harsh penalties are usually enforced on any offending organisation. R&D consortia are closely monitored and have to be registered.

The main advantages of this approach are the ability to reduce costs and risks, the ability to access technologies and to influence industry standards on new technology (the experience of the VCR industry and the computer-operating system industry have shown the potential dangers in having competing industry standards). The main disadvantages are similar to those for joint ventures, in that one party may not be able to gain any technological benefit from the consortia. The development of IMAGE is a good example of an effective R&D consortium (*see* Illustration 9.2).

Effective R&D management

Managers of R&D have to try to develop systems and procedures which will enhance the probability of success. To outside observers the research and development process may seem like a random procedure in which inspired scientists, working around the clock, come on major breakthroughs late at night. It is true that R&D is a high-risk activity, but the process is much less random than it first appears. Over the past 40 years there has been extensive research in R&D management and there is an academic journal dedicated to the subject (*R&D Management*). This research has revealed the presence of certain factors in many successful R&D projects and their absence in many failed projects. Table 9.1 summarises these factors.

Table 9.1 Organisational characteristics that facilitate the innovation process and the management of R&D

	R&D requirement	Characterised by
1	Growth orientation	A commitment to long-term growth rather than short-term proft
2	Vigilance	The ability of the organisation to be aware of its threats and opportunities
3	Commitment to technology	The willingness to invest in the long-term development of technology
4	Acceptance of risks	The willingness to include risky opportunities in a balanced portfolio
5	Cross-functional cooperation	Mutual respect among individuals and a willingness to work together across functions
6	Receptivity	The ability to be aware of, to identify and to take effective advantage of externally developed technology
7	'Slack'	An ability to manage the innovation dilemma and provide room for creativity
8	Awareness	High degree of awareness of corporate objectives business strategy
9	Project management	Good project management skills and systems
10	Market orientation	An awareness of the needs and changing nature of the market
11	Diverse range of skills	A combination of specialisation and diversity of knowledge and skills

Source: Adapted from Table 3.4 above (p. 91).

Illustration 9.3

The continued development of aspirin

Through continued research and development, new uses are continually being found for one of the oldest pharmaceutical products – aspirin. Aspirin was first introduced to the market more than 100 years ago in 1897. It was research into salicin, a compound that is found naturally on willow bark, by Bayer, a large German chemical manufacturer, that led to the development of aspirin as we know it today.

The drug was first used as a treatment for arthritis sufferers. Pharmacologist John Vane received the Nobel Prize for chemistry for uncovering how aspirin relieved arthritis. He showed that prostaglandins are released by the body when cells are injured, triggering the symptoms of inflammation, swelling and pain. Aspirin halts the production of these prostaglandins, hence its effectiveness in treating arthritis.

Aspirin has been shown to have a number of additional effects:

- It acts as an analgesic to ease pain
- It acts as an anti-inflammatory to control inflammation
- It acts as an antipyretic to reduce fever
- By thinning the blood it helps to reduce the danger of blood vessels clotting, thereby helping to prevent strokes and heart attacks
- It has also been shown to help reduce colonic cancer
- It is currently being used in the treatment of Alzheimer's disease.

Source: M. Dobson (1997) 'A little miracle', *Sunday Times Magazine*, 16 October, 36.

Effective R&D management can make a considerable impact on the performance of a company. Illustration 9.3 shows how over a period of 100 years R&D has led to many different applications of a drug.

Managing scientific freedom

The idea of applying formal planning techniques to R&D is viewed by many as a paradox. The popular view is that research, by definition, is concerned with uncovering new things and discovering something that previously was unknown. To try to introduce any form of planning would surely stifle creativity and innovation. This leads to one of the most fundamental management dilemmas facing senior managers: how to encourage creativity and at the same time improve efficiency. This dilemma was tackled at a generic level in Chapter 3, so to avoid repetition we will address the problem from an R&D perspective.

R&D managers will argue that the technologist's and scientist's spirit of enquiry must be given room and freedom to exercise. Without the freedom to work on projects that may not appear of immediate benefit to the company, the laboratory may become conservative and uncreative. Furthermore, it may be difficult to attract and retain the best scientists if they are not allowed to pursue those areas that are of interest to them. There are many disputes between research and technology managers and other senior

| Figure 9.4 | Managing scientific freedom within and R&D function |

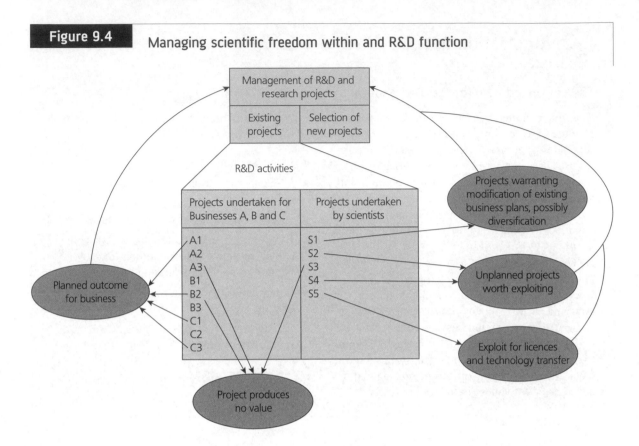

functional managers concerning the extent of time that scientists and research teams should be able to allocate for personal research programmes.

However, R&D managers are realistic: they recognise that few companies, if any, are going to invest large sums of money solely as an act of faith. There are many formal management techniques that are employed to help to improve the effectiveness and productivity of R&D without necessarily destroying the possibility of serendipity.

Virtually all companies accept that a certain amount of time should be made available for scientific enquiry (after all, there are many examples of such research producing profitable outcomes, *see* the 3M case study in Chapter 12). The issue is, *how much time*? One approach, adopted by many technology-intensive companies, such as Siemens, 3M, Ericsson and Nokia, is to consider that a company that invests heavily in R&D is, in reality, managing two types of R&D projects. This can best be shown schematically as in Figure 9.4, which is an extension of Figure 8.6, and shows a variety of project outcomes, which are explained below in Table 9.2.

The R&D projects are divided into two separate groups. The first group is by far the largest, usually accounting for 90 per cent of the R&D budget. It is established in response to requests from the various businesses and supports and maintains the corporate objectives. In Figure 9.4 these projects are labelled A, B and C. The second group of projects are those generated by the scientists themselves, usually as a result of personal interest in the technology. These are labelled S1 to S5. These projects will be generating technology of a commercial value but free from the constraints of corporate

Table 9.2 Research project outcomes

Research Project	Outcome	Action
A1, B2, C1 and C3	Planned outcome for the business	Research project produces desired results for business to incorporate into products
A3, B3 and S3	Project produces no immediate commercial value	Results of project will be examined by other research groups to see if the findings can be used; knowledge remains with R&D
S1	Project warrants changing existing business strategy	In exceptional circumstances the findings from a research project can be so unusual and promising that they warrant a change in business strategy to accommodate possible new product ideas
S5	License technology to third party	When the research results produce interesting technology that is beyond exploitation by the business, it may be possible to generate income from licensing the technology to a third party
S2 and S4	Unplanned projects worth exploiting further	The findings from these personal research projects are so interesting that they require further funding and possible inclusion in business research
A2, B1 and C2	Projects lead to further research projects undertaken by scientists	The findings in themselves are of limited commercial value but stimulate further research projects

objectives. This latter group of research projects is financed by funds that are allocated at the discretion of the R&D manager or more usually an R&D committee or team. Very often these funds represent about 10 per cent of the total R&D budget. This group of research projects has a variety of labels in industry, including blue-sky research, special projects and personal research. Virtually all major technology-intensive companies accommodate a certain amount of time for individuals to pursue their own research projects. Typically, about 10 per cent of a scientist's time will be spent on autonomous research projects.

Twiss (1992) develops this idea of two types of research projects further by suggesting that R&D managers are in effect managing two business activities. The primary activity supports the various businesses and the corporate objectives and the other supports a technology business, involved in generating technology of a commercial value that is unrelated to the corporate objectives.

Skunk works

Technology-intensive companies recognise that if they are to attract and retain the best scientists they have to offer scientific freedom. Moreover, experience has shown that

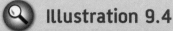

Illustration 9.4

The original skunk works

The name 'skunk works' can be traced back to US aircraft manufacturer Lockheed. It was originally used by Al Capp's 'Li'l Abner' comic strip which featured the 'Skonk works' (sic) where Appalachian hillbillies ground up skunks, old shoes and other foul-smelling ingredients to brew fearsome drinks and other products. Lockheed engineers identified the secret jet aircraft assembly facility as the place where Clarence Johnson was stirring up some kind of 'potent brew'. The skunk works was created by Johnson to design and develop the XP-80 Shooting Star, the US's first production jet aircraft. The nickname stuck, although 'skonk' became 'skunk' in deference to the non-hillbillies working at the Lockheed facility and because Al Capp objected to anyone else using his unique spelling. Cartoonist Capp and the 'Li'l Abner' comic strip departed many years ago, but skunk works is now a registered service mark of Lockheed along with the familiar skunk logo.

Source: Lockheed Martin Corporation (1998), www.lmsw. external.lmco.com/lmsw/html/index.html.

scientists will covertly undertake these projects if autonomy is not provided. There are many examples of exciting technology and successful products that were initiated by scientists operating in a covert manner. In the United States such research projects are referred to as 'skunk works' (*see* Illustration 9.4 for an explanation of its origin).

The link with the product innovation process

Chapters 6, 7 and 8 have all emphasised the accumulation of knowledge as a key part of the R&D process and the process of developing new products. The link between R&D and new product development is often overlooked or frequently they are treated as separate subjects. In practice the two activities are interlinked. This can be simply shown by looking at the extended product life cycle. This well-known conceptual framework purports to capture some of the stages in a product's life from launch to final withdrawal. What is seldom shown is the series of activities prior to the first stage *introduction*. For some products, most notably aircraft or pharmaceuticals, the lead-time prior to launch can be 10 or even 15 years. Figure 9.5 shows the extended product life cycle with some of the key R&D activities incorporated. Mapped on top are the investment and expenditure curves showing the scale of upfront money required in some industries most notably those with long lead times as previously discussed.

Many of the models of NPD emphasise the link to the R&D department. In particular, the network model of new product development shown in Figure 12.14 emphasises this continual interaction throughout the development of the product. Knowledge is accumulated over time as an idea for a product is transformed into a research project.

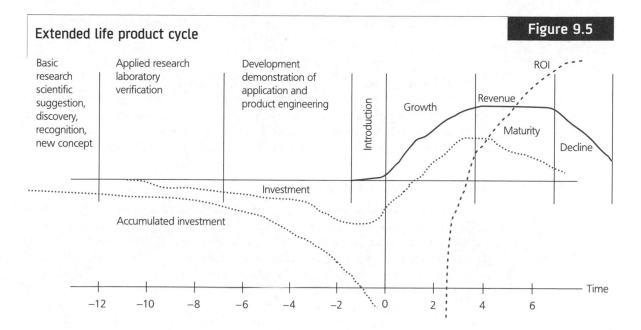

Figure 9.5 Extended life product cycle

The R&D function will be continually consulted on virtually all aspects of the product, including:

- design;
- manufacturing;
- choice of materials to be used;
- required shelf life;
- effects of transportation;
- packaging;
- intellectual property rights; and
- product safety, etc.

It is important to bear in mind that an investment in R&D to develop an existing product further is not generally viewed by product managers as a high-risk activity. The following quote from the brand manager of the makers of one of the leading washing detergents in Europe reflects a commonly held view:

> *We know we can improve the product, our scientists can always improve the product. In fact the launch date for our new improved shampoo has been set but the research is still on-going! The only doubt is the extent of the improvement that our scientists will make.*

A similar example could be drawn from the software industry, which is synonymous with new, improved versions of its software. The key point here is the way R&D investment is viewed. For many firms with years of experience in the management of R&D, an output is expected from their investment in R&D, the only doubt is the detail. Given this perspective on R&D, the following section analyses the range of effects that R&D investment can have on a product's profitability.

The effect of R&D investment on products

Analysis of the products that a company manages will reveal that these contribute in different ways to the overall profit and growth of the company. It is important to recognise that R&D activities can influence this profit contribution in several ways.

Development of existing products

The life cycle of most products lasts for several years. There are some products, especially in the food industry, that seem to have an eternal life cycle. Cadbury's Milk Tray and Coca-Cola are two examples of products that have been on the market for over 100 years. In virtually all other industry sectors, however, a product's market share will slowly fall as competitors compete on price and product improvements (*see* Chapter 12). R&D's role is to extend the life of the product by continually searching for product improvements. The two most common approaches to extend the life of a product are capturing a larger market share and improving profit margins through lowering production costs. For example, the performance of zinc-carbon batteries has improved greatly due to the threat of alkaline batteries like Duracell. This has helped to improve the market share for alkaline batteries. Similarly, personal computer manufacturers such as Dell, Apple, Hewlett Packard and IBM are continually lowering their production costs in order to ensure that their products compete successfully in the PC market.

Early introduction of a new product

Many companies strive to be technological leaders in their industry. Their aim is to introduce innovative products into the market before the competition to gain a competitive advantage. In some industries, such as pharmaceuticals, this approach is very successful. In other sectors being first to market does not always ensure success (*see* Chapter 11 on market entry).

Late introduction of a new product

Deliberately postponing entry into a new market until it has been shown by competitors to be valid reduces the risk and costs. This was the approach used by Amstrad in the UK consumer electronics market. Furthermore, by deliberately slowing down product launches into the market it is possible to maximise profits. For example, software companies have been very successful in launching improved versions and upgrades every six to nine months.

Long-term projects

Looking further into the future, R&D departments will also be developing products that the public do not yet realise they require. This area also includes starting new initiatives and new areas of research. Technology-intensive companies such as Siemens, Microsoft, Airbus and 3M will be working on products for 2010 and beyond.

Evaluating R&D projects

As was discussed in the above section ('The link with the product innovation process') virtually all large technology-intensive firm will have many more ideas that it would wish to fund as research projects; the problem as usual is limited resources. Inevitably choices have to be made about which ideas to support and convert to a funded project and which to drop. There have been many studies on this common problem faced by R&D managers (*see* Carbonell-Foulquie *et al.*, 2003; Farrukh *et al.*, 2000; Cooper 2001). The subject of evaluating research projects is analysed from a marketing perspective in the final chapter of this book on evaluating new product ideas. An R&D perspective is now taken in the following section.

Deciding which projects to select for further resources will inevitably result in dropping others. Typically for every 60 technical ideas considered approximately 12 will receive funding for further evaluation. Of these about six will receive further funding for design and development; half of these will be developed into prototypes and may even go for market testing. But only two will remain for product launch and in most cases only one of these is successful (Babcock, 1996). Figure 9.6 illustrates the drop out rate of project ideas. Dropping an R&D project is theatrically referred to as 'killing a project'. Unsurprisingly it causes considerable anxiety amongst those involved especially when one's fellow scientists have been involved with the project for many months or in some cases years. Evaluating research projects then is a critical issue.

Drop out rates for R&D projects

Figure 9.6

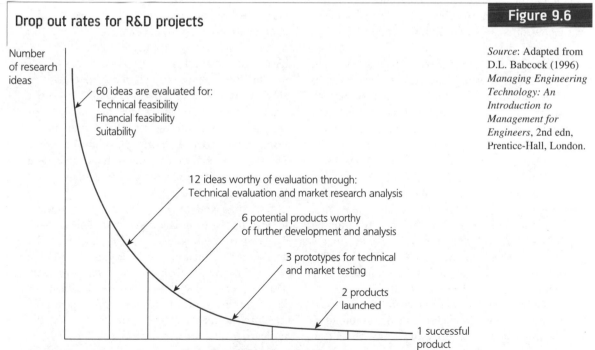

Source: Adapted from D.L. Babcock (1996) *Managing Engineering Technology: An Introduction to Management for Engineers*, 2nd edn, Prentice-Hall, London.

Number of research ideas

60 ideas are evaluated for:
Technical feasibility
Financial feasibility
Suitability

12 ideas worthy of evaluation through:
Technical evaluation and market research analysis

6 potential products worthy
of further development and analysis

3 prototypes for technical
and market testing

2 products
launched

1 successful
product

Evaluation of research project ideas

Evaluation criteria

The evaluation criteria used by businesses varies considerably from industry to industry. There is a considerable body of research devoted to this single area of evaluating research projects. This is not surprising given the long list of famous cases illustrating how many firms rejected projects that later turned into extremely successful products. To this list we must now add that the world's best selling human drug – Pfizer's Viagra – was almost dropped because of the market research findings (*see* Illustration 9.5).

We will look at the range of techniques and methods used by firms later, but it is important to recognise that while many firms may state publicy that they adopt

 Illustration 9.5

Pfizer's Viagra almost slipped away!

Pfizer's Viagra is now part of business folklore in terms of an example of a successful new product. Viagra is now one of the most recognised brands in the world; it has become a social icon with sales in excess of $1.9bn. And it has transformed Pfizer from a medium-sized pharmaceutical firm into the world's leader. However, Viagra was almost dismissed during clinical trials as interesting, but not clinically or financially significant.

The discovery of Viagra was unintended in that in fell out of clinical trials for a new drug being developed for the treatment of angina (angina is defined as brief attacks of chest pain due to insufficient oxygenation of heart muscles). In 1992 following seven years of research a clinical trial was undertaken in Wales for a compound known as UK-92.480. The findings from the trial on healthy volunteers revealed disappointing results. The data on blood pressure, heart rate and blood flow were discouraging. The R&D project was in trouble. Some patients reported side effects of episodes of indigestion, some of aches in legs and some reported penile erections. This final point was listed merely as an observation, at that moment no one said 'wow' or 'great'. Indeed, the decision to undertake trials into erectile dysfunction was not an

obvious one. This was partly because the prevailing view at the time was that most erectile dysfunction was psychological and not treatable with drugs. Few people believed it was possible to produce an erection with an injection of drugs. Pfizer was preparing to drop the angina R&D project due to its disappointing results. It was also considering dropping all studies on the compound even as a possible drug for erectile dysfunction. This was partly because it was not clear that it would have a clinical use. Not all the healthy volunteers had reported erections. How would Pfizer be able to conduct trials for such a condition? Moreover, the market for such a drug was not clear. At that time survey results revealed only 1 in 20 million men suffered from erectile dysfunction; hence even if a medicine could be developed the market would be very small. The R&D team involved in the project managed to gain two years of funding to develop the drug and undertake clinical trials. The rest is, as they say, history. Moreover, the actual market for this type of drug is now known to be far greater than the data had revealed. This is a cautionary tale of the need sometimes to encourage innovation and support scientific freedom in the face of evidence to stop the project.

quantative weighted scoring models or specially adapted software to evaluate all project ideas. Inevitably, as with so many business decisions, there is an element of judgement. After all that is what managers are in position to do – make decisions based on their experience and expertise. This is confirmed by a recent study of R&D decision making in the electronic sensors industry by Liddle (2004). He argues that managers continue to rely on rules of thumb and heuristics for the evaluation of research projects:

> *I just think it's a smell test. Does it sound too good to be true? Does it sound truly incremental to what we're doing? Is it something that sounds worthy of the investment of more time?*
>
> **Extract from an interview with an R&D Manager (Liddle, 2004: 60).**

Whether businesses used formal evaluation models or more informal methods most will involve some or all of the checklist items shown in Table 9.3. This can be developed further using a weighted checklist or scoring model in which each factor is scored on a scale. A relative weight reflecting the importance of that factor is used as a multiple and the weighted scores for all factors are added.

The new product development literature offers a plethora of screening and decision-making methods and techniques aimed at assisting managers in making this difficult evaluation. Cooper (2001) identifies three broad categories of screening methods:

1 benefit measurement models;
2 economic models; and
3 portfolio selection models.

Benefit measurement models

Benefit measurement models are usually derived from a group of well informed and experienced managers identifying variables such as those listed in Table 9.3, and then making subjective assessments of projects. Frequently these variables are brought together in the form of a quantitative or qualitative model that will provide the organisation with a value with which to make comparisons of projects. These models are usually: mathematical, scoring, decision-trees (Holger, 2002).

Financial/economic models

Financial and economic models are the most popular project selection tool. This may not be surprising given that firms are established to make money; however, this type of model is generally accepted as having considerable limitations. This is partly because of the emphasis on financial formulas and their inherent short-term bias. Another limitation of financial models is limited accurate future financial data, which inevitably leads to inaccurate estimates of future revenues, etc.

Portfolio selection models

Portfolio models attempt to find those ideas that 'fit' with the business strategy and attempt to balance the product portfolio. They consider a business's entire set of

Table 9.3 R&D project evaluation criteria

Criteria	Typical questions
1 Technical	Do we have experience of the technology? Do we have the skills and facilities? What is the probability of technical success?
2 Research direction and balance	Compatibility with research goals? Balance of risk in project portfolio?
3 Competitive rationale	How does this project compare relative to the competition? Is it necessary to defend an existing business? Is the product likely to be superior?
4 Patentability	Can we get patent protection? What will be the implication for defensive research?
5 Stability of the market	How stable is the technology? Is the market developed? Is there an industry standard?
6 Integration and synergy	What is the level of integration of this project relative to other products and raw materials? Will it stand alone?
7 Market	What is the size of the market? Is it a growing market? Is there an existing customer base? Is the potential big enough to warrant the resource?
8 Channel ft	Do we have existing customers who might be interested, or do we have to fnd new customers?
9 Manufacturing	Can we use existing resources? Will we require new equipment, skills, etc.?
10 Financial	Expected investment required and rate of return?
11 Strategic ft	Does it support our short-term and long-term plans for the business?

Source: Adapted from R.E. Seiler (1965) *Improving the Effectiveness of Research and Development: Special Report to Management*, McGraw-Hill Book Company, New York.

projects rather than viewing new research projects in isolation. The dimension of balance can be:

- *Newness* – how new is the product likely to be? A radically different product, product improvement, repositioning, etc. (*see* Chapter 12).
- *Time of introduction* – is the new product portfolio going to deliver a constant stream or will it be a case of feast and then famine?
- *Markets* – are the different markets and business areas of the company receiving resources proportionate to their size and importance.

Case study

The role of clinical research in the pharmaceutical industry[1]

Introduction

In August 1997, an advertisement appeared in the world-wide professional journal of the International Association of Physicians in Aids Care (IAPAC) asking more, perhaps, than medical research has ever asked before. It asked for healthy human volunteers who would be willing to test a new AIDS vaccine (Sarler, 1997).

HIV (Human Immunodeficiency Virus, that can lead to AIDS) was discovered in 1984; since then, enormous sums of money have been spent by governments, pharmaceutical companies and other interested parties in the search for a cure and a vaccine. The latest figures from the World Health Organisation show that, world-wide, there are 8,500 new HIV infections a day, the majority of which are in the developing world. What makes HIV so appalling is that it is an infection of the young rather than the old. The syndrome is wiping out people in the prime of life, so the benefits of developing a successful vaccine are clear.

Professor Desrosiers, a microbiologist from Harvard Medical School, has developed a live attenuated vaccine for the monkey equivalent of HIV. This has now been developed further and needs to be tested on humans. Within the pharmaceutical industry this particular stage of research is referred to as clinical trials. The monkey form of AIDS is caused by a slightly different virus from the human one. Past experiments on AIDS in monkeys have had disappointing results; none the less, like all other pharmaceutical drugs, this new attenuated vaccine must undergo clinical trials. These will establish whether or not the vaccine could be beneficial and if this approach could lead to further AIDS vaccines. As will be shown later, the first stage of any clinical trials requires healthy human volunteers.

This highlights an ethical dilemma frequently encountered within research in the pharmaceutical industry. Unlike drug research, which clearly has benefits for the individual recipient, vaccine research has a more altruistic benefit to society at large. This is because a successful vaccine can potentially rid the world of a disease. Like most successful vaccines, such as those for polio, smallpox, yellow fever, mumps and measles, this new vaccine is a live attenuated one. That is, it is a weakened version of the disease.

Pharmaceutical companies are less interested in vaccine research than in drug research. Vaccine production is more expensive than drug manufacture because you have to prove not only that it is safe but that it works. This takes more time and more money.

This very topical and emotive illustration introduces the area of pharmaceutical research, and in particular the area of clinical trials. In the pharmaceutical industry clinical trials form an important part of the research process for developing new products. New product development in the pharmaceutical industry is very different from that in many other industries. This particular case study explores the unique role of clinical research associates in the development of new drugs for the pharmaceutical industry.

Research and NPD in the pharmaceutical industry

The pharmaceutical industry is relatively young. While its origins can be traced to the turn of the century, the industry as it is known today is largely a post-war phenomenon. It grew out of the chemical industry. For example, betablocker

---

[1] This case study has been written as a basis for class discussion rather than to illustrate effective or ineffective managerial or administrative behaviour. It has been prepared from a variety of published sources, as indicated, and from observations.

▶

drugs were developed by ICI and this laid the foundations for its pharmaceutical operations and eventually the formation of Zeneca. The anti-ulcer treatment drug Zantac was the basis for the foundation and growth of Glaxo; this one drug achieved sales in excess of $2 billion per annum. Moreoever, the development of the industry has been fuelled by technological innovation. Figure 9.7 is an overview of new product development in the pharmaceutical industry. The pharmaceutical industry is one of the few industries that follows the classical technology-push model of innovation (*see* Chapter 1). Put simply, scientific research is followed by product development and then marketing. This complete product development process will now be examined in more detail.

The first stage is referred to as pre-clinical scientific research. This involves chemistry, biology, pharmacology (the science of the properties of drugs and their effectiveness on the body) and toxicology (the degree to which a substance is poisonous). In addition, issues of intellectual property and, in particular, the application for patents are key activities. With R&D lasting up to 10 years, it is imperative that a company is able to protect its intellectual property so that it is able to generate some income from its investment. The rising cost of R&D is making this activity even more important. The pie chart in Figure 9.8 shows a breakdown of the main areas of R&D expenditure in the pharmaceutical industry. Experimental research, which includes clinical trials, consumes a large portion of the total funds. Those drug formulations that show promising results are put forward for development and clinical trials. The decision to undertake clinical trials on a potential drug is a critical one because of the high costs associated with these trials.

Figure 9.7	Pharmaceutical product development

Stage of product development	Scientifc Research: Chemistry and Pharmacology		Development: Medical Testing and Clinical Trials				Marketing
Timing	Up to 10 years	1 year	3–10 years				3 years
	Research, including toxicity, formulation and intellectual property	Decision for development	Phase 1: The testing of drugs on healthy volunteers	Phase 2: First testing on patients, usually conducted in hospitals, numbers are low	Phase 3: This involves thousands of patients and is often conducted in general practice	Registration with the Dept of Health	Phase 4: Post-marketing studies. These trials are conducted after the drug has received a product licence. These are used to identify rare adverse events
Rate of dropout: 99%			70%	20%	5–8%		

Figure 9.8	Pharmaceutical R&D expenditure by type

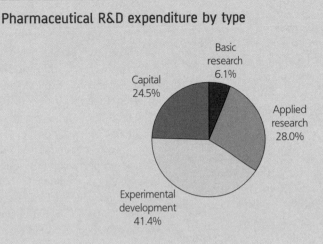

Source: ABPI (1993)
*Pharma Facts and
Figures*, Association
of the British
Pharmaceutical
Industry, London.

Clinical research

The testing of drug formulations on humans is referred to as clinical trials. Within the pharmaceutical industry this is the largest area of R&D expenditure, representing 41 per cent of the total (*see* Figure 9.8). This new product development activity is unique to the pharmaceutical industry. Clinical trials follow four distinct phases.

- *Phase 1 clinical trials*. Phase 1 is the testing of developed drugs on healthy human volunteers. This attempts to establish how the human body handles the new drug and what toxic effects, if any, are experienced. These trials are invariably placebo controlled and involve small numbers of healthy volunteers. These trials are conducted within hospitals and volunteers are often young men, traditionally medical students.

- *Phase 2 clinical trials*. In Phase 2 the drug is tested on patients for the first time. Once again, these trials will usually be conducted in hospitals but will possibly involve a few hundred patients. The objective here is to discover optimum dosage and effects on actual patients.

- *Phase 3 clinical trials*. Phase 3 trials involve thousands of patients and are very expensive. Due to the number of patients required, many of these trials are conducted in general practice. These trials, and the administration of the drug in particular, will be conducted under the same conditions as would exist once the drug has been marketed.

- *Phase 4 clinical trials*. Phase 4 trials are conducted after the drug has received a product licence and has been marketed. Such trials usually involve large post-marketing studies (PMS) to identify rare adverse events.

At the heart of clinical trials is either a general practitioner or a consultant in a hospital. These people are referred to as clinical research investigators and are responsible for the investigation of new treatments in patients. Early investigations are normally conducted in teaching hospitals. Later studies (Phases 2 and 3) involving larger numbers are frequently conducted in district or general hospitals. Pharmaceutical companies developing new drugs have to find investigators to conduct clinical trials on their behalf. Clinical research associates can identify possible investigators and set up clinical trials.

Clinical research associates

Clinical research associates (CRA), sometimes called clinical trial coordinators or scientists, are science graduates (usually in chemistry or pharmacology) often with a PhD and with several years of training within the pharmaceutical industry. Their role involves meeting senior doctors and research scientists. They need to have good interpersonal skills plus skills in analysing scientific results and statistics. A high proportion are female. In the pharmaceutical industry it is common to have senior CRAs managing a small team of CRAs, according to either geographic region or therapeutic group.

The *raison d'être* of the CRA is to coordinate the trial of new drugs. This involves designing the study and preparing the protocol (the design document for the research trial including methodology) and case record forms. CRAs usually select suitable investigators and organise trial supplies of the drug from the pharmaceutical company via the hospital pharmacist. They also negotiate payment for all aspects of the clinical trial. Once the trial is under way the CRA will regularly visit the investigator to discuss its development. Particular attention has to be given to the patients, because frequently it emerges later that patients had taken another drug during the trial (this is often an over-the-counter drug taken innocently at home). This, however, would clearly exclude them from the trial results.

Another major activity of the CRA is to ensure that the trial runs to schedule. Finding patients suitable for a trial is often problematic. Also many clinical research investigators fail to deliver on time, sometimes for justifiable reasons. And frequently the number of patients excluded from a trial, for example due to concomitant medication, will mean that the trial has to be repeated.

Once the clinical trial is complete and the case record forms (CRF) have been filled in, these then have to be analysed with all other trial documentation. This analysis should enable conclusions to be drawn about the drug under investigation. Examples would be: Drug A works better than Drug B, or Drug D and Drug F are equally effective but Drug H causes the following side effects, or Drug T is no better than a placebo or showed no benefit to the patients treated.

Almost all clinical investigators will be very keen to publish the results of any study with which they have been involved. Usually the pharmaceutical company would also be keen to publicise results. This may depend on intellectual property rights issues. Many large pharmaceutical companies favour the idea of a small conference to discuss the development of a new drug. The CRA will have a significant role to play in such an event.

Discussion

In order to perform the necessary clinical trials, the AIDS vaccine under development is clearly going to need healthy human volunteers. At first sight, this may seem like an impossible task. However, so many people have lost loved ones and so many families have been affected by this terrible disease that there are people willing to volunteer. Also further research may enable far safer trials to be established.

The rising cost of healthcare means that pharmaceutical companies are being forced to demonstrate that their new drugs are good value for money. It is therefore important for the results of the clinical trials to show not only that the drugs are not harmful, but also that they are significantly better than existing drugs.

The case illustrates another unique aspect of the pharmaceutical industry and demonstrates why the pharmaceutical industry has lobbied to successfully achieve extensions to their patents where regulatory control takes a long time. They were introduced in Europe in the mid-1990s to compensate patent owners for regulatory delays in approving their pharmaceuticals and agrochemicals. The approvals sometimes took so long that the patent had reached the end of its 20-year life, thus opening the invention to all comers, before the inventor had had much chance to commercialise it.

Patent extensions were designed to provide a level playing field for all pharmaceuticals/agrochemicals patent owners who had suffered regulatory delay exceeding five years, to restore to them an effective 15-year term of protection. The Supplementary Protection Certificate (SPC) takes effect at the instant of patent expiry, and then lasts for the length of time by which regulatory approval exceeded five years. Each SPC therefore has its own fixed duration, but, to protect the public, the maximum duration is five years' effect.

Questions

1 Discuss the unique nature of new product development in the pharmaceutical industry and the role played by the CRA.

2 Compare the product development process with that of a fmcg producer such as Nestlé?

3 Highlight the salient points in the ethical dilemma for pharmaceutical companies that are highlighted in the clinical trials case.

4 What are the limitations of patent extensions?

Chapter summary

This chapter has focused on the key activities of R&D management. It has shown that these have changed significantly over the past few decades. Emphasis has traditionally been placed on internal R&D, but now there is an increase in the use of external R&D. This presents another set of challenges. In particular, when acquiring externally developed technology, a business must also consider the extent of control that it requires over the technology. The need to provide scientific freedom for R&D personnel and the benefits that this brings were also considered.

R&D plays a considerable role in the product innovation process. Indeed, there is often continual interaction with R&D throughout the development of the product. Finally, the chapter considered the various ways of funding the R&D activity. The approach adopted will significantly affect the way R&D is perceived within and outside the company.

Discussion questions

1 Explain why managing an R&D function in 1998 would be different from managing an R&D function in 1978.

2 Discuss the strengths and limitations of undertaking external R&D.

3 What is meant by scientific freedom and why is it important?

4 Explain why the degree of control needed over a firm's technology may vary depending on the technology concerned.

5 Discuss the variety of ways of funding R&D.

6 Explain why many product managers do not view an investment in R&D as a high-risk activity.

Key words and phrases

Centralised laboratories 285	Globalisation of technology 282
Decentralised laboratories 285	R&D consortia 288
Evaluating R&D projects 297	Scientific freedom 291
Extended product life cycle 295	Skunk works 293

 # Websites worth visiting

Association of British Pharmaceutical Industry (ABPI) www.ABPI.org.uk

BTG www.btgplc

European Union, Enterprise and Innovation www.europa.eu.int/comm/enterprise/innovation

European Union, Innovation Directorate www.cordis.lu/fp6/innovation.htm

Patent Office www.patent.gov.uk

Pfizer www.pfizer.com

Pilkington PLC Technology Management www.pilkington.com

Stanford University, explaining innovation www.Manufacturing.Stanford.edu

UK Government, Department of Trade and Industry www.Dti.gov.uk/innovation

 # References

Abelson, P.H. (1995) 'Science and technology policy', *Science*, Vol. 267, No. 27, 1247.

ABPI (2001) *Pharma Facts and Figures*, Association of the British Pharmaceutical Industry, London.

Albertini, S. and Butler, J. (1995) 'R&D networking in a pharmaceuticals company', *R&D Management*, Vol. 25, No. 4, 377–93.

Auster, E.R. (1987) 'International corporate linkages: dynamic forms in changing environments', *Columbia Journal of World Business*, Vol. 22, No. 2, 3–6.

Babcock, D.L. (1996) *Managing Engineering Technology: An Introduction to Management for Engineers*, 2nd edn, Prentice Hall, London.

Breschi, S. and Malerba, F. (1997) 'Sectoral innovation systems: technological regimes, Schumpeterian dynamics, and spatial boundaries' in Edquist, C. (ed.), *Systems of Innovation: Technologies, Institutions and Organizations*, Pinter, London, pp. 130–55.

Carbonell-Foulquie, P., Munuera-Aleman, J.L. and Rodriquez-Escudero, A.I. (2003) 'Criteria employed for go/no-go decisions when developing successful highly innovative products', *Industrial Marketing Management*, June,

Casper, S. and Whitley, R. (2004) 'Managing competences in entrepreneurial technology firms: a comparative institutional analysis of Germany, Sweden and the UK', *Research Policy*, Vol. 33, No. 1, 89–106.

Chesnais, F. (1988) 'Multinational enterprises and the international diffusion of technology', in Dosi, G., Freeman, C., Nelson, R., Silverberg, G., and Soete, L. (eds) *Technical Change and Economic Theory*, Pinter, London, pp. 496–572.

Cooper, R.G. (2001) *Winning at New Products*, 3rd edn, Perseus Publishing, Cambridge, MA.

Cordero, R. (1990) 'The measurement of innovation performance in the firm: an overview', *Research Policy*, Vol. 19, No. 2, 185–92.

Corey, E.R. (1997) *Technology Fountainheads: The Management Challenge of R&D consortia*, Ziff-Davis/Harvard Business School Press, Boston, MA.

Dobson, M. (1997) 'A little miracle', *Sunday Times Magazine*, 16 October, 36.

Dosi, G. (1988) 'Sources, procedures, and microeconomic effects of innovation', *Journal of Economic Literature*, Vol. 26, No. 3, 1120–71.

Englund, R.L. and Graham, R.J. (1999) 'From Experience: linking projects to strategy', *Journal of Product Innovation Management*, Vol. 16, 52–64.

ESPRIT (1997) *First Open Interconnects for Clustered Systems*, No. 12, DG III, European Commission, Luxembourg.

Farrukh, C., Phaal, R., Probert, D., Gregory, M. and Wright, J. (2000) 'Developing a process for the relative valuation of R&D programmes', *R&D Management*, Vol. 30, No. 1, 43–53.

Gambardella, A. (1995) *Science and Innovation: The US Pharmaceutical Industry During the 1980s*, Cambridge University Press, Cambridge.

Granstrand, O., Bohlin, E., Oskarsson, C. and Sjoberg, N. (1992) 'External technology acquisition in large multi-technology corporations', *R&D Management*, Vol. 22, No. 2, 111–33.

Hagedoorn, J. (1990) 'Organisational modes of inter-firm co-operation and technology transfer', *Technovation*, Vol. 10, No. 1, 17–30.

Holger, E. (2002) 'Success factors of new product development: a review of the empirical literature', *International Journal of Management Reviews*, Vol. 4, No. 1, 1–40.

Kastrinos, N. and Miles, I. (1995) 'Knowledge base, technology, strategy and innovation in environmental services firms', paper presented at R&D Management Conference, 20–2 September, *Knowledge, Technology and Innovative Organisations*, Pisa, Italy.

Kreiner, K. and Schultz, M. (1990) 'Crossing the institutional divide: networking in biotechnology', paper for the tenth International Conference, *Strategic Bridging to Meet the Challenge of the 90s*, Strategic Management Society, Stockholm, 24–7 September.

Lefever, D.B. (1992) 'Technology transfer and the role of intermediaries', PhD thesis, INTA, Cranfield Institute of Technology.

Liddle, D. (2004) 'R&D Project Selection at Danahar', MBA Dissertation, University of Portsmouth.

Lockheed Martin Corporation (1998) www.lmsw.external.lmco.com/lmsw/html/index.html.

Malerba, F. and Orsenigo, L. (1993) 'Technological regimes and firm behaviour', *Industrial and Corporate Change*, Vol. 2, 45–71.

Mason, G., Beltramo, J.P. and Paul, J-J. (2004) 'External knowledge sourcing in different national settings: a comparison of electronics establishments in Britain and France', *Research Policy*, Vol. 33, No. 1, 53–72.

Pavitt, K. (1984) 'Sectoral patterns of technological change: towards a taxonomy and theory', *Research Policy*, Vol. 13, 343–73.

Pavitt, K. (1990) 'What we know about the strategic management of technology', *California Management Review*, Spring, 17–26.

Pfizer (2004) Extracts from www.pfizer.com

Powell, W.W. (1996) 'Trust based forms of governance', in Kramer, R.M. and Tyler, T.R. (eds) *Trust in Organisations*, Sage, London, pp. 246–60.

Rhea, J. (1991) 'New directions for industrial R&D consortia', *Research Technology Management*, September–October, 16–19.

Rothwell, R. (1992) 'Successful industrial innovation: critical factors for the 1990s', *R&D Management*, Vol. 22, No. 3, 221–39.

Rothwell, R. and Dodgson, M. (1991) 'External linkages and innovation in small and medium-sized enterprises', *R&D Management*, Vol. 21, No. 2, 125–36.

Rothwell, R. and Zegveld, W. (1985) *Reindustrialisation and Technology*, Longman, London.

Sakakibara, M. (2002) 'Formation of R&D consortia: industry and company effects', *Strategic Management Journal*, Vol. 23, 1033–50.

Sarler, F. (1997) 'Dance with death', *Sunday Times Magazine*, 11 December, 38–44.

Seaton, R.A.F. and Cordey-Hayes, M. (1993) 'The development and application of interactive models of technology transfer', *Technovation*, Vol. 13, No. 1, 45–53.

Seiler, R.E. (1965) *Improving the Effectiveness of Research and Development: Special Report to Management*, McGraw-Hill Book Company, New York.

Teece, D. (1986) 'Profiting from technological innovation: implications for integration, collaboration, licensing, and public policy', *Research Policy*, Vol. 15, 285–305.

Tidd, J., Bessant, J. and Pavitt, K. (2001) *Managing Innovation*, 2nd edn, John Wiley & Sons, Chichester.

Twiss, B. (1992) *Managing Technological Innovation*, 4th edn, Financial Times Pitman Publishing, London.

Further reading

For a more detailed review of the R&D management literature, the following develop many of the issues raised in this chapter:

Day, G.S. and Schoemaker, P.J.H. (eds) (2000) *Wharton on Managing Emerging Technologies*, John Wiley, New York.

Leifer, R. (2000) *Radical Innovation*, Harvard Business School Press, Boston, MA.

Roussel, P.A., Saad, K.N. and Erickson, T.J. (1991) *Third Generation R&D*, Harvard Business School Press, Boston, MA.

Shavinina, L. (2003) *The International Handbook on Innovation*, Elsevier, Oxford.

Tidd, J., Bessant, J. and Pavitt, K. (1997) *Managing Innovation*, John Wiley, Chichester.

10

The role of technology transfer in innovation

Information is central to the operation of firms. It is the stimulus for knowledge, know-how, skills and expertise and is one of the key drivers of the innovation process. Most firms are involved with a two-way flow of knowledge wrapped up as technology in the form of a product or process. Those companies that spend the most on R&D are also some of the biggest licensors of technology; and dynamic, innovative firms are likely to buy in more technology than their static counterparts. This chapter examines the complex subject of technology transfer, increasingly being referred to as knowledge transfer. It explores its role in the innovation process and its influence on organisational learning.

Chapter contents

Learning objectives

When you have completed this chapter you will be able to:

- recognise the importance of the concept of technology/knowledge transfer with respect to innovation management;
- provide a summary of the process of technology/knowledge transfer;
- examine the various models of technology transfer;
- assess the importance of internal organisational factors and how they affect inward technology transfer;
- explain why a 'receptive' environment is necessary for technology transfer;
- identify the different barriers to technology transfer; and
- recognise how tacit knowledge links technology transfer and innovation.

Background

The industrialised world has seen a shift from labour- and capital-intensive industries to knowledge- and technology-based economics. As competition has increased in markets throughout the world, technology has emerged as a significant business factor and a primary commodity. Knowledge transformed into know-how or technology has become a major asset within companies. Technology is vital for a business to remain competitive. In rapidly evolving markets such as electronics and biotechnology, new products based on new technology are essential. Even in mature markets, new technology is necessary to remain competitive on cost and quality.

In the 1960s, 1970s and 1980s many businesses favoured the internal development of technology. But today, with the increasing technological content of many products, many organisations consider internal development too uncertain, too expensive and too slow for the rapid technological changes that are occurring in the market. These drawbacks can be traced to a more fundamental cause – the increasing complexity of technologies and the increasing range of technologies found within products. This has led to a shortening of product life cycles with replacement technologies rapidly succeeding others. The rising costs of conducting R&D have forced many organisations to look for research partners. In addition, companies are finding it increasingly difficult to sustain R&D capability over all areas of their business as the complexity of these areas increases. Internal R&D is increasingly focused on core competencies (*see* Prahalad and Hamel, 1990). R&D in all other business activities is progressively covered by collaborations, partnerships and strategic alliances. While the activity is not new – Alfred Marshal noted the extensive linkages between firms in his work in 1919 (CEST, 1991) – the extent of collaboration appears to be on the increase. Hagedoorn (1990), for example, has shown a marked rise in the amount of collaboration between firms during the 1980s and 1990s.

Many large firms operate in several technology fields and are often referred to as multi-technology corporations (MTC). It is extremely difficult and expensive for such corporations to be technological leaders in every technology within their scope. More and more companies are looking for outside sources of either basic technology to shorten product development time, or applied technology to avoid the costs and delay of research and development. In addition, avoiding 're-inventing the wheel' appears to be high on the list of corporate objectives. Previously, there was one well-known exception to this and that was where a competitor was undertaking similar research. Under these circumstances duplication of research was regarded as inevitable and thus acceptable. However, numerous recent technological collaborations between known competitors, for example IBM and Apple, General Motors and BMW, would suggest that even this exception is becoming less acceptable to industry.

The search for, acquisition and exploitation of developed technology is clearly of interest to virtually all sectors of industry, but it is of particular interest to R&D-intensive or science-based industries. A recent US government study on technology transfer stated: 'Corporations trade in technology in world markets just as they do in other goods and services' (DFI International, 1998: 93).

The dominant economic perspective

It was in the 1980s that governments around the world began to recognise the potential opportunities that technology transfer could bring. This was based on a simple economic theory. Technology which has already been produced, and hence paid for by someone else, could be used and exploited by other companies to generate revenue and thereby economic growth for the economy (*see* Figure 10.1).

It was with this theory in mind that governments began encouraging companies to be involved in technology transfer. They set up a whole variety of programmes trying to utilise technology that had been developed for the defence or space industries (*see* below 'Models of technology transfer'). They also encouraged companies to work together to see if they could share technology for the common good. An example of this was the establishment of Regional Technology Centres (RTC) in the late 1980s around the United Kingdom to serve the various regions. It was even suggested by some commentators that technology transfer could solve the serious problem of the US national debt. In response to this impetus, companies set up their own internal technology transfer departments to try to seek out technology that might be worth exploiting. There were many reports of companies visiting university laboratories and government research

---

| **Figure 10.1** | The economic perspective of technology transfer |

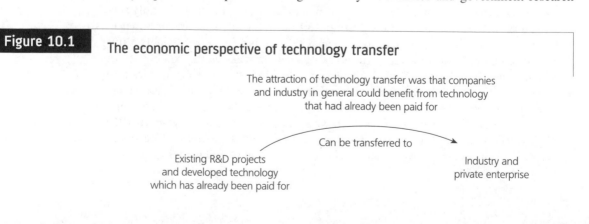

The attraction of technology transfer was that companies and industry in general could benefit from technology that had already been paid for

Can be transferred to

Existing R&D projects
and developed technology
which has already been paid for

Industry and
private enterprise

establishments in an effort to find useful technology. Moreover, the subject of technology transfer began to receive attention from many different quarters. If you were to get the chance to key the words technology transfer into a database of management and science journal abstracts, you would be amazed at the high number of articles that contain these words in their title. Many of these articles were written in the late 1980s.

The alleged panacea for industry's problems did not materialise. Looking back, some still argue that it was a commendable theory, it just did not seem to work in practice. Others argue that the theory was flawed and would never work in practice (Seaton and Cordey-Hayes, 1993); this will be discussed below in the section on 'Limitations and barriers to technology transfer'. There were, however, many benefits that emerged from the energetic interest in technology transfer. One of them was the realisation that successful collaboration and joint ventures could be achieved even with competitors.

Introduction to technology transfer

The concept of technology transfer is not new. In the thirteenth century Marco Polo helped introduce to the Western world Chinese inventions such as the compass, paper-making, printing and the use of coal for fuel. In more recent years, the concept has generated an enormous amount of debate. Many argue that it was a change in US law which led to the surge of interest in the subject. The passage of the landmark National Cooperative Research Act (NCRA) of 1984 officially made cooperation on pre-competitive research legal. This certainly helped raise the profile of the concept of technology transfer (Werner, 1991).

Technology Transfer is the application of technology to a new use or user. It is the process by which technology developed for one purpose is employed either in a different application or by a new user. The activity principally involves the increased utilisation of the existing science/technology base in new areas of application as opposed to its expansion by means of further research and development.

(Langrish *et al.*, 1982)

One of the main problems of research into technology transfer is that over the years the term has been used to describe almost any movement of technology from one place to another, to the ridiculous point where the purchase of a car could be classified as an example of technology transfer. It is true that the technology in question may take a variety of forms – it may be a product, a process, a piece of equipment, technical knowledge or expertise or merely a way of doing things. Further, technology transfer involves the movement of ideas, knowledge and information from one context to another. However, it is in the context of innovation that technology transfer is most appropriate and needs to be considered. Hence, technology transfer is defined as:

The process of promoting technical innovation through the transfer of ideas, knowledge, devices and artefacts from leading edge companies, R&D organisations and academic research to more general and effective application in industry and commerce.

(Seaton and Cordey-Hayes, 1993)

Figure 10.2

The tangibility of knowledge

Source: Adapted from M. Cooley (1987) *Architect or Bee? The Human Price of Technology*, Hogarth Press, London. Used by permission of the Random House Group Limited.

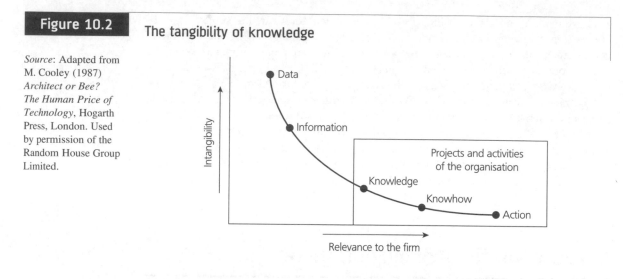

Information transfer and knowledge transfer

It was suggested at the beginning of this chapter that information is central to the operation of firms and that it is the stimulus for knowledge, know-how, skills and expertise. Figure 10.2 helps distinguish information from knowledge and know-how according to its context. It is argued that it is the industrial context which transforms knowledge into action, in the form of projects and activities. It is only when information is used by individuals or organisations that it becomes knowledge, albeit tacit knowledge. The application of this knowledge then leads to actions and skills (projects, processes, products, etc.). Consider Illustration 10.1.

 Illustration 10.1

Pilkington, information and knowledge

Materials have different melting points; for example, glass is molten at 1500°C whereas tin is molten at 180°C. On its own, this is information that can be found in most metallurgy books. Provide an industrial context and the information is transformed into knowledge, know-how and expertise.

Pilkington pioneered the manufacturing process of 'float glass'. This essentially involves heating sand to 1500°C and forcing it out through rollers and over a pool of molten tin to cool prior to being cut to size. This patented process is now universally used by every glass manufacturer in the world. Pilkington developed the process in the 1950s and 1960s and then licensed it to every glass manufacturer in the world. For an entire year, however, the pilot plant had produced nothing but scrap glass. After many operating difficulties, production engineers eventually succeeded in getting the process to work. The company made so much money out of licensing the process that it was able to purchase what was at that time the largest glass manufacturer in the world.

Models of technology transfer

A wide variety of models of technology transfer have been used over the years, particularly in the past 20 years (Dorf, 1988). The following section examines some of these models and offers examples of their application.

Licensing

Essentially, licensing involves the technology owner receiving a licence fee in return for access to the technology. Very often the technology in question will be protected by patents. The details of each licensing agreement will vary considerably. Sometimes the licensor will help the licensee in all aspects of development and final use of the technology. In other cases, the amount of involvement is minimal.

Mutual self-interest is the common dominator behind most licensing contracts, as it is in other business contracts. Licensing is the act of granting another business permission to use your intellectual property. This could be a manufacturing process which is protected by patents or a product or service which is protected by a trademark or copyright. Licensing is the main income generator for the British Technology Group (BTG), a FTSE 100 listed company. It helps businesses and universities generate income from their intellectual property through the licensing of technology to third parties.

Licences to competitors constitute a high percentage of all licences extended; Microsoft's disk-operating system (MS-DOS) is a case in point. These normally arise out of a desire on the part of the competitor to be free of any patent infringement in its development product features or technology. They are also due to the owner of the patent seeking financial gain from the technology.

The licensee must be careful to evaluate the need for and the benefits likely to accrue from the technology before making the commitment to pay. Technology which is only marginally useful, or which may be quickly superseded by new developments in the field, may not be worth a multi-million-dollar licensing agreement. Many companies with sufficient R&D resources believe that patents can be legally breached through creative use of technology. This point is well made in the Guinness case study at the end of Chapter 8. All the other brewers were eventually able to develop their own in-can technology.

Other reasons for licensing are (Rothberg, 1976):

- to avoid or settle patent infringement issues;
- to diversify and grow through the addition of new products;
- to improve the design and quality of existing products;
- to obtain improved production or processing technology;
- to ensure freedom of action in the company's own R&D programme (patents held by other companies may inhibit R&D activities);
- to save R&D expense and delay;
- to eliminate the uncertainty and risk involved in developing alternative processes and technology;
- to accommodate customer needs or wishes; and
- to qualify for government and other desirable contracts.

Science park model

Science parks are a phenomenon that originated in the United States. The idea is to develop an industrial area or district close to an established centre of excellence, often a university. The underlying rationale is that academic scientists will have the opportunity to take laboratory ideas and develop them into real products. In addition, technology- or science-based companies can set up close to the university so that they can utilise its knowledge base. In the United States, where science parks have existed for 40 years, the achievements have been difficult to quantify. Examples are Silicon Valley, a collection of companies with research activities in electronics, and the 'research triangle' in North Carolina, which has several universities at its core. In the United Kingdom, one of the first science parks to be established was the Cambridge Science Park. Over the past 20 years, this has grown into a large industrial area and has attracted many successful science-based companies. Many other universities have also set up their own science parks, such as Southampton, Warwick and Cranfield. It is worth noting that the science park notion separates the innovation process: the R&D is conducted at the science park but manufacturing is done elsewhere (Link and Link, 2003; Dabinett, 1995).

Intermediary agency model

These come in a variety of forms and ranged from Regional Technology Centres (RTC) to university technology transfer managers. Their role, however, is the same: they act as the intermediary between companies seeking and companies offering technology.

Directory model

During the explosion of interest in technology transfer during the 1980s, many new companies sprang up in an attempt to exploit interest in the subject. Companies such as Derwent World Patents, Technology Exchange, NIMTECH and Technology Catalysts offered directories listing technology that was available for licence. Some universities in the United States also produced directories of technology available from the university's own research laboratories. (For an example of the type and range of patents available, *see* Derwent World Patents at www.patentexplorer.com/). The case study at the end of this chapter explores the role of an intermediary (NIMTECH) in helping to provide technology for a small manufacturing company.

Teaching company scheme model

This UK Research Council-funded programme aims to transfer technology between universities and small companies. This is achieved through postgraduate training. Students registering for a two-year MSc at a university are linked to a local company-based research project. The student studies part time for two years with the university, say two days a week, and the other three days are spent at the company working on the project. The university provides support to the student and offers other expertise to the company. These programmes continue to be very successful.

Ferret model

The Ferret model was first used by Defence Technology Enterprises (DTE). DTE resulted from a joint initiative between the UK Ministry of Defence (MOD) and a consortium of companies experienced in encouraging, exploiting and financing new technology. The *raison d'être* of DTE was to provide access to MOD technology and generate commercial revenue. This was achieved through the use of so-called 'ferrets', qualified scientists and engineers who would ferret around for interesting defence technology that could have wider commercial opportunities. The company ceased trading in 1989.

Hiring skilled employees

One of the oldest methods of technology transfer, and one of the most effective according to many research managers, is hiring people with the necessary skills and knowledge. For R&D managers who wish to establish a range of research projects in an area of technology where the company has limited knowledge or experience, this is one of the fastest methods of gaining the necessary technology. People are either recruited from other organisations, including competitors, or from university research departments that have relevant expertise. These people will bring to the organisation their own knowledge, and the ways of working and methods used by their previous organisation – some of which may be replicable, others may not. The role of individual and organisational learning is explored towards the end of this chapter.

Technology transfer units

In the 1980s the US Federal Labs and other research-based organisations, including universities, established industrial liaison units and technology transfer units to bring in technology from outside and/or to find partners to help exploit in-house developments. In the United States, academia has always been subject to financial pressures to generate funds. In Europe, however, universities have traditionally relied on government to fund their needs. With an ever-decreasing pool of resources, universities have recognised the potential benefits from exploiting in-house technology. This has also led to the growth in science parks. Technology transfer units use elements of the intermediary and licensing models.

One of the most successful examples of this approach is the British Technology Group (BTG), a state-owned corporation that was set up to commercialise as much state-funded research as possible, including that undertaken by universities. It was previously known as the National Research Development Corporation. It became so successful and profitable that in 1993 BTG was sold to private investors and it is now operating as a successful public limited company with a FTSE 100 listing. Its main activities are the licensing of new scientific and engineering products to industry and providing finance for the development of new technology (*see* www.btg.co.uk).

Research clubs

This is a UK Department of Trade and Industry (DTI)-funded programme which tries to bring companies together with common interests in particular research areas. Some conduct collaborative research, others exchange information, knowledge and/or experience. This approach adopts the science park model of technology transfer. One of the most successful clubs is the M62 Sensors and Instrumentation Research Club, so called because it originated from a group of companies along the M62 motorway in the north-west of England.

European Space Agency (ESA)

The ESA offers access to space research in virtually all fields of science and technology. This is achieved using a combination of three models: the intermediary agency model, the directory model and the Ferret model (*see* Illustration 10.2).

 Illustration 10.2

FT

Science brought down to earth

Miranda Eadie on a programme to promote terrestrial uses of innovations developed for space missions

For two decades, space technology has provided innovative technical solutions to everyday problems as well as making glamorous space exploration missions possible. The European Space Agency (ESA) has realised, however, that many more earth-based uses for space technology could be found in fields such as medicine, electronics, communications, energy and materials science.

Everyday examples of space technology transfer – the process of applying innovations developed for particular space missions for earth-based use – include the anti-scratch protective layer on plastic contact lenses, air-filled soles of high-tech running shoes, aluminium foil, digital clocks and microwave ovens.

Although technology transfer has occurred informally in space research for several years, many potential terrestrial applications remain unexploited. Lack of time and tunnel vision on the part of research engineers are two of the main reasons for this.

ESA therefore initiated a technology transfer programme in October 1991, with the aim of identifying space technologies that might have civil or commercial applications, and encouraging their transfer.

The initiative is run by Spacelink Europe, a consortium of technology brokers from the UK (JRA Aerospace), France (Novespace), Germany (MST Aerospace) and Italy (D'Appolonia).

Spacelink scouts ESA contractors for possible transfers, catalogues the ideas, contacts non-space companies which may be interested, and eventually negotiates a deal and takes care of inquiries.

The Spacelink catalogue, featuring the space technologies available for exploitation, is called Test (Transferable European Space Technologies) and is published annually. The latest edition, Test 3, contains 60 technologies in many fields, such as optics, sensors, communications, life sciences and robotics. Including the earlier catalogues, there are 170 technologies on offer.

Spacelink's objective is for non-space companies to sign a licensing agreement or form a joint venture with the 'owner' of the technology. This is either the ESA contractor, ESA itself or shared between the two. The technology may be protected by a patent, but this is not always necessary to license the technology.

Although one of the original goals of the programme was for it to become self-financing, through licensing and technology transfer services, its main aim is not economic benefit but to show that space is not just for sending rockets but can have applications on earth.

Anna Marie Hieronimus-Leuba, head of ESA's space commercialisation office, say that it is 'more concerned with showing that investment in space is paying dividends in terms of terrestrial applications, and that it is not just about sending beautiful objects into space'.

The ESA also hopes the programme will increase each of the member states' financial return and share in the technology spin off. It is an ESA policy that each accounting unit paid by a member state into the agency budget awarding industrial contracts should eventually flow back to that member state.

The direct terrestrial applications of space research (weather forecasting, communications via satellites, satellite television, etc.) are more evident than the indirect ones, or spin-offs, which do appear in nearly all fields of science and technology; lucid image processing software, developed for use in remote sensing, has applications in the security forces in number-plate detection, face recognition and fingerprint analysis, Aerocoat fire protection materials, developed to protect equipment on the Ariane space rocket from very high local temperatures generated during the launch phase are now used to protect sensitive equipment in trains for the Channel tunnel link; human waste management systems,

developed for use in space, are now being considered for hospital clean rooms, where hygiene is also a priority; Cream (Cosmic Radiation Effects and Activation Monitor), developed for the Nasa Space Shuttle has been adapted for high flying aircraft and fitted to Concorde; and Radfets, miniature real-time radiation dosimeters used to monitor background radiation on ESA spacecraft, are being developed to measure radiation doses during cancer treatment.

'Technology transfer is a very slow process and financial return cannot be expected in less than four years', says John Rootes, managing director of JRA Aerospace. 'There is a time delay of about a year and a half between the initial contact with a technology, the definition of the licensing agreement and the signing of a contract. A further two years is then needed for the adaptation, testing and fabrication of the technology.'

Although the process is traditionally slow, the programme has advanced more rapidly than expected. When it began, the goal was to secure six transfers in the first three years.

The fact that nine have already been agreed (and that there are many more in the pipeline) indicates great prospects for the programme. The rapidity of these transfers can, in part, be explained by the fact that 40 per cent of them have occurred in the field of software engineering where transfer modifications are minimal.

ESA invested £2m in the programme at its conception. The majority of this is used to pay the members of Spacelink to run the programme but, occasionally, if a transfer looks interesting and there is a shortage of finance to carry it out, ESA may offer some financial support.

This was the case at the Brunel Institute of Bioengineering, where shape memory alloys, originally used to make linear actuators for a space bioprocessing facility, showed prospects in medicine as 'staples' to mend broken bones.

The institute received £12,000 from ESA to develop these staples, and general advice was given with regard to the technology transfer. Financial support was also gained by AEA ▶

Technology after the huge interest shown in its solid lubricants which appeared in Test 1: £5,600 was donated to help pay for a short study into possible terrestrial applications.

Tony Anson, the research engineer at Brunel, is an 'enthusiast' of the programme. He says that besides the programme being an encouraging initiative, the financial support is 'extremely welcome in a country like the UK where the government does not have a particularly philanthropic approach towards research and where there is a dire shortage of funding'. He believes he has a dozen or so technologies which could realistically have a considerable impact in the medical field, if only he could find the money to exploit them.

One of these is the use of shape memory alloys as a prosthesis for hole in the heart. Other transfers which have taken place as a result of the programme include: high stiffness composites developed by Dornier to build space structures for the Rosat X-ray satellite, which are now used for ground-based telescope reflectors and for large screens needed for training systems; ESA's software standards, which have been adopted by many space and non-space companies and which are about to be published by Prentice Hall for world-wide distribution; and image processing software, developed to analyse astronomical images, such as those from Hubble, licensed by Photek for possible application in an image intensification camera.

This camera, which contains a Swedish optical chip, again identified through the programme, could be used for research into arthritis and cancer. The latter examples demonstrate the range of applications for space technology and highlight how separate European initiatives can combine for common good.

ESA ultimately hopes that space industries themselves will strive to identify potential technology transfers as early as possible in the R&D stage. Such lateral thinking should lead to joint development schemes and more marketable products.

Source: M. Eadie, 'Science brought down to earth', *Financial Times*, 15 March 1994. Reprinted by permission.

Consultancy

This area has experienced rapid growth from a non-existent base in the early 1980s to a multi-billion-dollar industry in the 1990s. Although it is management consultancy groups who receive a great deal of attention from the business sections of the quality press, it is the lesser-known technology consultants that have been used and continue to be used by many science-based organisations. Very often they were formerly employed in a research capacity within a large organisation. After developing their knowledge and skills in a particular area of science, they offer their unique skills to the wider industry. R&D research groups within large organisations will often contact several consultants prior to establishing a research project in a particular field related to the consultant's area of expertise. Consultants are able to offer help, advice and useful contacts to get the research project off to a flying start. Frequently they will remain part of the research group during the early years of the project. This is a very popular method of technology transfer and essentially adopts the hiring skilled employees model.

Limitations and barriers to technology transfer

The management of technology transfer has not been entirely straightforward, as is demonstrated in the range of technology transfer mechanisms that have been developed over the last 20 years or so. Research into technology transfer suggests that this is because emphasis has been on providing information about access to technology (Seaton and Cordey-Hayes, 1993). While the provision of technical ideas is a necessary part of technology transfer, it is only one component of a more complex process. Research at the Innovation and Technology Assessment Unit, Cranfield University, over the past 10 years has led to the development of a comprehensive conceptual framework that has helped develop understanding of the complex nature of inward technology transfer and knowledge accumulation.

The conceptual framework, shown in Figure 10.3, views technology transfer and inward technology transfer as a series of complex interactive processes as opposed to a simple decision process. It breaks down the transfer process into a series of subprocesses. The initial framework was developed following a study of the role of intermediaries in the technology transfer process. A mismatch was identified between the needs of potential innovators and the activities of information-centred technology transfer intermediaries (Lefever, 1992). This deficiency was illuminated through the use of the conceptual framework: Accessibility–Mobility–Receptivity (AMR). The research revealed that while much effort appeared to have been directed at providing access to technology, little effort had been aimed at understanding the needs of organisations acquiring technology developed outside the organisation. An organisation's overall ability to be aware of, to identify and to take effective advantage of technology is referred to as 'receptivity'.

The original framework has since been developed further to show the elements which constitute the inward transfer of technology from the viewpoint of the receiving organisation. Figure 10.3 breaks down the receptivity element into four further components. This has provided a useful theoretical framework from which to analyse the notion of technology and knowledge transfer. It is important, however, to understand that this overarching conceptual framework has limitations as a concept. These limitations are a consequence of the fact that, while it expresses the nature of the internal organisational processes and identifies a number of key areas that constitute such processes, it does not itself operationalise these processes. Hence, it functions as a vantage point from which to explore the issues involved.

Subsequent research has uncovered the nature of some of the internal processes of inward technology transfer and has provided an insight into how they affect an organisation's ability to capture, assimilate and apply technology to commercial ends (Trott and Cordey-Hayes, 1996). Research by Macdonald (1992) identified the difficulty of applying other people's technology and the need for this technology to be in such a form that the organisation can reap some benefit. This highlights the importance of viewing technology development as a combination of knowledge, skills and organisations (all embodied in 'organisational know-how') rather than the economist's view of technology as an artefact to be bought and sold. Chapter 6 portrayed the notion of assimilation as an internal knowledge accumulation process, which offers an explanation of how organisations are able to use, manipulate and retain knowledge (Afuah, 2003).

Figure 10.3	Conceptual framework of technology transfer and inward technology transfer

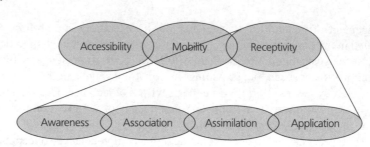

NIH syndrome

One of the best-known barriers to technology transfer is the not-invented-here (NIH) syndrome. This is defined as the tendency of a project group of stable composition to believe that it possesses the monopoly of knowledge in its field, leading it to reject new ideas from outsiders to the likely detriment of its performance (Katz and Allen, 1988). It is general folklore among R&D professionals that groups of scientists and engineers who have worked together for many years will begin to believe that no one else can know or understand the area in which they are working better than they do. In some cases this attitude can spread across the whole R&D function, so that the effect is a refusal to accept any new ideas from outside. This syndrome has been so widely discussed since it was first uncovered that, like many diseases, it has been virtually wiped out. R&D managers still need to be vigilant to ensure that it does not recur.

The next section addresses the issue of receptivity and, in particular, how an organisation's own internal activities affect its ability to transfer technology successfully.

Internal organisational factors and inward technology transfer

Danhof (1949) may be described as one of the first attempts to explore the inward technology transfer process. In his study of the adoption of innovations by industrial companies he identified four different types of company:

- Innovators: the first firm to adopt a new idea;
- Initiators: the firms who adopted the idea soon after the innovators;
- Fabians: the firms who adopted the idea only after its utility was widely acknowledged in the industry; and
- Drones: the last firms to adopt new ideas.

This study revealed that there was considerable difference in the responsiveness of organisations to take up externally developed technology. A similar conclusion was drawn by Kroonenberg (1989) following a study of 3,000 firms in The Netherlands. He suggests that small and medium-sized enterprises (SMEs) can be classified into one of three groups:

1 technology-driven SME;

2 technology-following SME; and

3 technology-indifferent SME.

Both of these studies reveal clear distinctions between firms in either their ability or their willingness to adopt new technology. Establishing the precise nature of the activities that are required to ensure that organisations can either remain as innovators or become innovators has been the subject of numerous studies. Carter and Williams' (1959) study of technically progressive firms uncovered a number of shared characteristics within organisations that facilitate innovation. In a comprehensive review of the technology transfer literature, Godkin (1988) suggests that these same factors would foster technology transfer. The factors are shown below:

- high quality of incoming communication;
- a readiness to look outside the firm;
- a willingness to share knowledge;
- a willingness to take on new knowledge, to license and to enter joint ventures;
- effective internal communication and coordination mechanisms;
- a deliberate survey of potential ideas;
- use of management techniques;
- an awareness of costs and profits in R&D departments;
- identification of the outcomes of investment decisions;
- good-quality intermediate management;
- high status of science and technology on the board of directors;
- high-quality chief executives; and
- a high rate of expansion.

Godkin's classification is one of the earliest studies, specifically on technology transfer, to recognise that the existence of certain activities within the recipient organisation is necessary for successful technology transfer. This point will be explored in detail in the following two sections.

Developing a receptive environment for technology transfer

As was shown above, many of the traditional technology transfer mechanisms concentrate on providing access to technology, with little effort directed towards understanding the needs of organisations acquiring externally developed technology (Seaton and

Cordey-Hayes, 1993). The early literature on inward technology transfer centred on the ability of organisations to access technological knowledge (Gruber and Marquis, 1969) and their subsequent ability to disseminate this information effectively. Allen's work in the 1960s on the role of gatekeepers within organisations exemplifies this (*see* Allen, 1966, 1977; Allen and Cohen, 1969). Seaton and Cordey-Hayes (1993) argue that there has been little thought and research aimed at the difficulties of exploiting externally developed technology. They suggest that this is because technology transfer has largely been seen in terms of providing access to technology. They emphasise the need to view technology transfer as a process.

An organisation's ability to develop new products that meet current market needs, to manufacture these products using the appropriate methods and to respond promptly to technology developments clearly involves more than technical capabilities. However, discussions concerning how organisations utilise their technological base tend to focus on R&D activities and other technical activities alone. Nelson (1991) argues that in industries where technological innovation is important, firms need more than a set of core capabilities in R&D. This point is discussed in detail in Chapter 6.

The notion of receptivity advocated by Seaton and Cordey-Hayes (1993) suggests that there are certain characteristics whose presence is necessary for inward technology transfer to occur. In a similar vein, but within an R&D context, Cohen and Levinthal (1990) put forward the notion of 'absorptive capacity'. In their study of the US manufacturing sector they reconceptualise the traditional role of R&D investment as merely a factor aimed at creating specific innovations. They see R&D expenditure as an investment in an organisation's absorptive capacity and argue that an organisation's ability to evaluate and utilise external knowledge is related to its prior knowledge and expertise and that this prior knowledge is, in turn, driven by prior R&D investment.

Seaton and Cordey-Hayes (1993) argue that inward technology transfer will only be successful if an organisation has not only the ability to acquire but also the ability effectively to assimilate and apply ideas, knowledge, devices and artefacts. Organisations will only respond to technological opportunity in terms of their own perceptions of its benefits and costs and in relation to their own needs and technical, organisational and human resources. The process view of inward technology transfer, therefore, is concerned with creating or raising the capability for innovation. This requires an organisation and the individuals within it to have the capability to:

- search and scan for information which is new to the organisation (awareness);
- recognise the potential benefit of this information by associating it with internal organisational needs and capabilities;
- communicate these business opportunities to and assimilate them within the organisation; and
- apply them for competitive advantage.

These processes are captured in the following stages: Awareness, Association, Assimilation and Application. This four-stage conceptual framework (4A) is used to explore the processes involved in inward technology transfer (*see* Table 10.1).

Table 10.1	4A conceptual framework of technology transfer

Activity	Process
Awareness	Describes the processes by which an organisation scans for and discovers what information on technology is available
Association	Describes the processes by which an organisation recognises the value of this technology (ideas) for the organisation
Assimilation	Describes the processes by which the organisation communicates these ideas within the organisation and creates genuine business opportunities
Application	Describes the processes by which the organisation applies this technology for competitive advantage

Identifying external technology: the importance of scanning and networking

Scanning by individuals on behalf of the organisation is often regarded as an informal and unassigned activity. But in order for individuals to practise the process effectively, organisations must recognise its value (Tidd *et al.*, 2001, Afuah, 2003). However, it is because organisations are unaware of its value that they do not provide support for the process. Research by Oakley *et al.* (1988) on the subject of the search for technical knowledge argues that small firms in particular do not recognise the importance of external technical contacts, suggesting that they do little if any technology scanning.

It has long been recognised that a key characteristic of technically progressive firms is the high quality of their incoming information. In 1959 Carter and Williams reported this in almost 200 firms over a wide range of industries. Many other studies have since demonstrated the importance of external information for successful innovation. For example, SPRU's Project SAPPHO confirmed the need for high-quality external linkages (Rothwell *et al.*, 1974); Peters and Waterman (1982); CEST (1991).

The process of searching for and acquiring technical information is a necessary activity for organisations in order to maintain their knowledge base (*see* Johnson and Jones, 1957). This can be effectively achieved by scanning the technological environment, either through the scientific literature or through interactions with other people (often called networking). Thus, innovation within firms is a process of know-how accumulation based on a complementary mix of in-house R&D and R&D performed elsewhere, obtained via the process of technology scanning.

Each organisational research effort or technological activity represents a fraction of the world's total scientific and technological activity. Organisations are constantly surprised by the amount of technology around that they do not know about. Hence they must somehow ensure that their personnel are aware of technological developments performed elsewhere. During the 1960s and 1970s the question of how to keep personnel aware of technological developments was the subject of intense study (*see* Allen, 1966, 1977; Allen and Cohen, 1969; Tushman, 1977). Some interesting and useful concepts were developed that helped improve our understanding of the complex nature of how individuals within organisations acquire technological information. One of the most effective ways to capture this know-how is through personal interaction (networking).

Figure 10.4 shows the wide variety of sources of information used by firms to help maintain their awareness of technological developments. Different industry sectors have different information requirements. It is self-evident that they produce different products using different technologies and face different market structures. Consequently, research by Bosworth and Stoneman (1996) has revealed that some sectors are extremely reliant on certain external sources of information. The chemical industry, for example, is a high user of scientific and academic journals.

Research at Aston University has also shown that organisations that do not possess boundary-spanning individuals (scanning) will be restricted in the degree to which the organisation becomes aware of and assesses the relevance of innovations in the first place (Newell and Clark, 1990).

Given the importance of an awareness of external information and the role of technological scanning and networking, awareness is seen as the necessary first stage in the inward technology transfer process.

Figure 10.4   Sources of information from scanning and networking

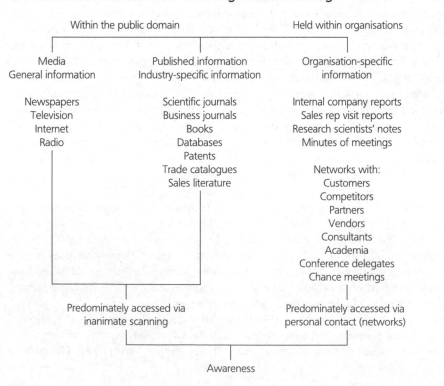

Figure 10.5

A conceptual framework for the development of genuine business opportunities

In order for an organisation to search and scan effectively for technology that will match its business opportunities, it needs to have a thorough understanding of its internal organisational capabilities. This can be effectively achieved via internal scanning and networking, which will enable it to become familiar with its internal activities. The coupling of internal technology scanning with external technology scanning activities can be seen in Figure 10.5 (*see* Trott 1998, for a more detailed explanation of the development of this model.)

Linking external technology to internal capabilities

External scanning without a full understanding of the organisation's capabilities and future requirements is likely to produce much 'noise' along with the 'signal'. 'Tuned scanning', achieved through the internal assimilation of an organisation's activities, as opposed to 'untuned scanning', will produce a higher 'signal-to-noise' ratio (Trott and Cordey-Hayes, 1996).

Inward technology transfer, however, involves more than identifying interesting technology; it is necessary to match technology with a market need in order to produce a potential opportunity for the business. The scanning process needs to incorporate commercial scanning as well as technology scanning so that technological opportunities may be matched with market needs (*see* Figure 10.5).

Such levels of awareness increase the probability of individuals being able to develop and create associations on behalf of the organisation between an internal opportunity and an external opportunity. This process of association is the second stage in inward technology transfer.

Chapter 6 emphasised the importance of recognising that the knowledge base of an organisation is not simply the sum of the individual knowledge bases. Nelson and Winter (1982) argue that such learning by doing is captured in organisational routines. It is these internal activities undertaken by an organisation that form the third stage in the process, assimilation.

Managing the inward transfer of technology

The final stage in the inward technology transfer process is the application of the business opportunity for competitive advantage. This is the stage where the organisation brings about commercial benefit from the launch of a new product or an improved product or manufacturing process. In science-based organisations a combination of credibility and respect, coupled with extensive informal and formal communications among individuals within the organisation, facilitates this process (referred to as an internal knowledge accumulation process). This is not to disregard totally the presence of external influences.

Even in science-based industries few companies are able to offer their researchers total scientific freedom, untouched by the demands of the market. R&D programmes are therefore focused on the business aspirations of the company and its future markets. These are usually set out using the most applicable technology. There is not a constant need for new ideas in technologies beyond these programmes – there are clearly resource limits on R&D departments (*see* Figure 10.6). Inevitably there will be crisis points, where the competition brings out something involving new technology. At these times, there is usually full management commitment and money is invariably made available to bring in new technology quickly to respond to the competition. Here the inward technology transfer processes (as illustrated in Figure 10.6) generally works well due to total commitment from all levels within the organisation.

Where technology is introduced on a more routine basis, a decision has to be made about spending money on a prototype or a demonstrator. The assimilation phase is usually dominated by who will put up the money to try out the new technology. This raises the question: what is the business need and who has the budget to address it and, moreover, do they have any money that can be diverted from something they are already doing to implement this new technology?

Figure 10.6   **The inward technology transfer process**

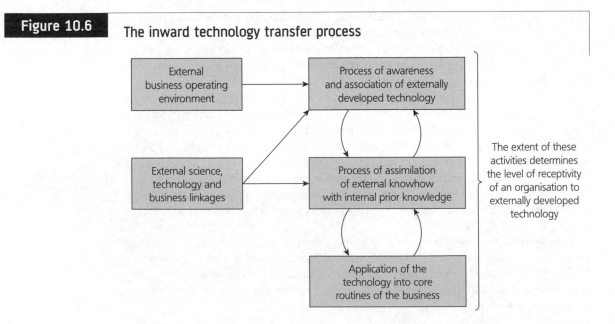

There is also an important distinction to be made here between science-based industries and other less capital-intensive industries. The vast majority of the businesses in the chemical industry, for example, operate and manage manufacturing processes which are highly capital intensive and the plant, when built, is designed to have a life of many years. The building of a new plant is future market-dependent, it sets the need for inward technology transfer and is the catalyst to bringing in new technology. At these times, the businesses tend to be very receptive to new technology, particularly in the concept and design phase of new plant. There exists a window of opportunity for bringing in new, proven-process technology. Internal R&D programmes are generally slightly in advance of this and are engaged in proving the technologies which will be applied in the plant. Without this proof and qualification they would not reach the final application stage. In other less capital-intensive industries these circumscribed windows of opportunity are not so apparent and opportunities may be more consistent.

Thus in addition to the internal processes illustrated in Figure 10.6, there are the inescapable external issues which have been grouped together under the heading of 'external operating climate'. This model explains how internal processes affect an organisation's ability to engage in inward technology transfer and contribute to the development of a receptive environment (Afuah, 2003).

Technology transfer and organisational learning

Several different pieces of research have identified a number of stages that form an inherent part of the knowledge transfer process (Trott and Cordey-Hayes 1996; Gilbert, 1996; Cordey-Hayes *et al.*, 1996). These must occur if the process of knowledge transfer and thus organisational learning is to be complete. While each organisation conducts its activities in different ways, members of that organisation soon adopt the company's way of operating. Organisational know-how is captured in routines, such as particular ways of working. The relationship between knowledge transfer between individuals and groups and the whole organisation may be expressed as two interlinked systems, as in Figure 10.7.

In order for inward technology transfer to take place, members of the organisation must show an awareness of and a receptivity towards knowledge acquisition. Individual learning involves the continual search for new information of potential benefit to the organisation. This frequently challenges existing procedures. Individuals must be continually scanning the internal and external environments for relevant information that can be used to develop associations with internal knowledge. Over time these associations, coupled with additional internal knowledge, can lead to the creation of genuine business opportunities. Having created these opportunities the knowledge can be said to be assimilated at the individual and work group level (this is shown in Figure 10.7 as the first stages in the process of organisational learning). At this point the organisation has not accepted the change nor has it learnt: knowledge has not been transferred, it remains within the work group. However, the idea is implicitly accepted in its adoption by the individual/group.

In order for the organisation to learn, the knowledge must be assimilated into the core routines of the organisation. That is, the knowledge becomes embedded in skills and know-how. It is during application by the work group that knowledge transfers from the individual to the organisation. However, before this knowledge can be assimilated

Figure 10.7	Interlinking systems of knowledge-transfer relationships

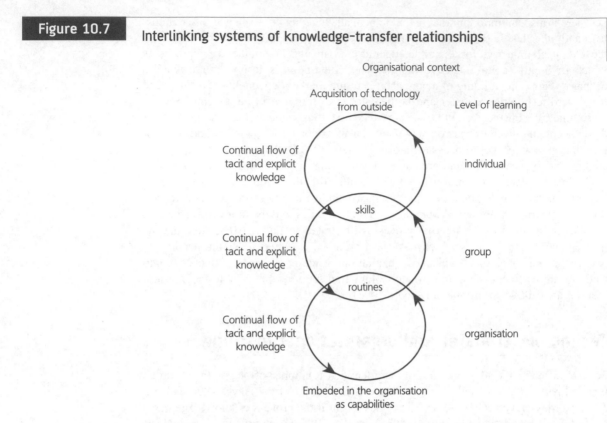

into the core routines of the organisation, there needs to be explicit acceptance by the organisation. There are many examples of individuals bringing technology into an organisation that they believe to be beneficial and yet it does not become accepted by all or part of the organisation. A simple but useful example is that of different versions of software. Several people may have a preference for a certain spreadsheet package, but usually only one version is adopted.

Technological and organisational change can be achieved at the acceptance stage, yet the organisation has not gone through the full learning cycle so this knowledge is not completely transferred into the core routines. Examples of this frequently occur during the implementation of new enterprise resource planning (ERP) systems. There will be some individuals who, because they are closely involved with the new system, will be able to generate enormous amounts of information from it. Others, however, will still be using the previous system and will not be familiar with the new one. It will take several weeks before everyone in the organisation is familiar with the new system and it becomes a 'taken for granted' way of working. The point at which the knowledge becomes embedded in the organisation has recently been referred to as 'tacit know-how' (Howells, 1996; Afuah, 2003).

The way in which the learning cycles link together is illustrated in Figure 10.7. In the manner of double-loop, learning the individual and organisational cycles are inter-related and inter-dependent (Argyris and Schon, 1978). The learning process forms a loop, transferring knowledge from individual into the group. The process of assimilation and adoption of this new knowledge within the inner cycle moves the knowledge into the wider environment and thus into the loop of organisational learning. The role of assimilation has a slightly different emphasis within the individual loops. Assimilation in the individual and group learning cycle refers to assimilation of knowledge from an external source, which may then be applied within the company. Assimilation in the wider cycle relates to assimilation of technology into the core routines of the organisation, which is evidenced by a behavioural change within the organisation. It is only when assimilation in the wider cycle has occurred that learning has truly taken place.

Case study

Sony-Ericsson mobile phone joint venture dependent on technology transfer[1]

This case study provides an excellent example of why firms engage in technology transfer. It also provides practical evidence to illustrate the benefits of technology transfer.

Introduction

In April 2001 Ericsson, the Swedish telecommunications equipment group, and Sony of Japan established a joint venture in mobile phones. The venture, based in London, brought together the two companies' loss-making handset businesses. The news was generally accepted as good for both companies. It would combine Sony's consumer products expertise with Ericsson's extensive knowledge of cell phone networks. Ericsson is the world's leading maker of wireless networks. It would give Ericsson access to Sony's multi-media technology, branding expertise and knowledge acquired from Japan's early start in third-generation cell phone technology. Sony would gain access to Ericsson's telecommunications technology and its distribution. The two companies hoped to create a market leader to threaten the dominance of Nokia of Finland within five years. In 2000 the two companies together shipped 50 million units or $7.2bn-worth of mobile phones, giving them a 12 per cent market share and third position after Nokia of Finland and Motorola of the United States.

The wider business environment, however, was extremely challenging. At the start of the twenty-first century despite the huge growth in cell phones few handset manufacturers were making profits. Nokia was the clear market leader and was producing a profit but Motorola, Phillips, Sony, Ericsson, Siemens, Matsushita, Mitsubishi and others were struggling to deliver profits. Indeed, Ericsson made a loss of £1.6bn on handsets in 2000 and the group announced thousands of job losses. Ericsson suffered from poor handset design, delays in getting them to market and failure to anticipate a market shift to low-end phones. Sony was in a different position. It had well-designed phones but a much smaller global market share – less than 2 per cent – but the impending launch of 3G phones would provide an enormous opportunity for Sony to exploit its multi-media technology portfolio. In particular liquid crystal display technology, digital camera, and music and video technology, all of which are expected to be driving forces behind the launch of 3G.

Rationale of alliance for Sony

The strategic alliance with Ericsson is part of an ambitious expansion led by Nobuyuki Idei, chairman and chief executive, to transform Sony

[1] This case study has been written as a basis for class discussion rather than to illustrate effective or ineffective managerial or administrative behaviour. It has been prepared from a variety of published sources, as indicated, and from observations.

into a global media, communications and network conglomerate. Sony has invested in semiconductors and broadband technology, an online bank and issue a tracking stock to give So-net, its internet service provider (ISP), the means to acquire other ISPs. But, Sony has delivered disappointing financial results for investors over the past few years and Sony will need to accelerate the pace of other changes within the company and develop further new products or else it will fall behind in the next generation of products.

The move into a new business area such as cell phones is welcomed by investors who argue that Sony has been too slow to move away from its traditional businesses such as music stereos, televisions, VCR, DVD and camera recorders. At the same time, market conditions have deteriorated: in consumer electronics, the weakening of consumer confidence after the September 11 attacks on the United States has come on top of already sluggish demand and falling prices.

Certain products, such as low-end stereos made by Aiwa, Sony's 61 per cent-owned subsidiary, are increasingly dominated by low-cost Chinese and South Korean manufacturers. In addition the games division, which in 1998 accounted for 44 per cent of operating profits, has been mired in losses. Increasing competition from Nintendo's GameCube and Microsft's Xbox will put further pressure on Sony's PlayStation2.

Rationale of alliance for Ericsson

For Swedish-based Ericsson, the venture will give it access to Japanese knowledge of third-generation technology which should help it compete in the fiercely competitive handset market. While Ericsson has been dominant in providing technology for the network market, it has increasingly struggled to stay in the top league among handset producers. Ericsson has a long history in microelectronics and its customers come not just from the telecoms industry, but from a variety of other sectors, including avionics, computing, military, and space. None the less, Ericsson has been badly hit by the downturn in the global telecoms equipment market, and it accumulated huge losses in the mobile phone businesses. The group recorded an underlying loss of more than $980m in 2000. Ericsson Microelectronics supplies Ericsson and other customers. It employs 2,500 people and has annual sales of more than SKr5bn. The division makes a range of products such as radio frequency power transistors, as well as chips designed to support 'Bluetooth', a wireless communications standard. Manufacturing is carried out in Sweden, California, Texas and China while design centres are located in Sweden, Norway, Britain and the United States. The business has its headquarters in Kista, a high-technology suburb and major centre of Ericsson operations just north of Stockholm.

The business of making handsets has changed beyond all recognition in recent years from a niche, high-tech activity to the world's biggest consumer electronics industry. As rivals have jumped on the gravy train and developed markets have neared saturation, mobile phones have become commodity items where efficient manufacturing becomes a vital part of staying ahead. In particular, Nokia has demonstrated that the two most important factors in a successful handset business are fashion and speed to market. This is because suppliers have become increasingly reliant on the replacement market since the majority in many countries owns a phone. Ericsson has been grappling with this for some time but has continually failed to find the magic formula for churning out fashionable models fast enough to keep up with changing technology. Notwithstanding the joint venture with Sony, Ericsson intends to retain a large research and development division focusing on handsets, which is vital to ensure its network business stays in touch with consumer demands.

Background knowledge on cell phone technology

Few people realise that a cell phone is much more like a radio than a conventional wired telephone. Indeed, cell phone technology is a development of radio technology rather than wired telecommunications technology. That is, it picks up signals from transmitters. The cell phones we use today were developed from 'Business' radio communication devices such as those as used by taxi firms and emergency services. These allow one party to talk at a time. You push a handset button to talk then release the button to listen. The use of the word 'over' was used to indicate the end of a message. This eliminated echo problems, which took many years to solve before natural, full duplex communications was possible. This proved to be an extremely difficult technical problem to overcome. Simplex, used in business radio, shares a single frequency for both people talking. With cell phones technology the transmitting and receiving frequencies are different, and offset from each other to prevent interference.

Each cell phone requires a cellular system. When we say a cellular system, it means a division of a city or town into small cells. Each cell has a base station that consists of a tower and a small building containing radio equipment, this allows widespread frequency reuse across an area, so that millions of people can use cell phones concurrently. Each cell is typically sized at and covers about a 10-square-miles radius.

Cellular technology uses a principle called frequency reuse to greatly increase customers served. Low-powered mobiles and radio equipment at each cell site permit the same radio frequencies to be reused in different cells, multiplying calling capacity without creating interference. This spectrum-efficient method contrasts sharply with earlier mobile systems that used a high-powered, centrally located transmitter, to communicate with high-powered car mounted mobiles on a small number of frequencies, channels which were then monopolised and not reused over a wide area.

There is a requirement to have a large number of base stations in a city of any size to make cell phone use function conveniently. A typical large city can have hundreds of towers placed in certain regions to cover most of the areas

completely. Central offices called the Mobile Telephone Switching Office (MTSO) handles all of the phone connections to the normal land-based phone system, and controls all of the base stations in the region. Each network operator, such as Vodaphone, 02, Virgin and Orange in the UK runs one (see Figure 10.8).

Moving from cell to cell within a network

All cell phones have special codes related to them. These codes are used to identify the phone's owner, phone and the service provider that they use. Here is what happens when you use your mobile phone:

When a person first turns on their phone, it listens for a System Identification Code (SID) on the control channel. This is a unique frequency that the phone and base station use to send signals to another about things like call set-up and channel changing. If the phone cannot find any control channels to listen to, then it is out of range and will display on the phone a 'no service' message. When it receives the SID, the phone matches up to the SID programmed into the phone. If the SIDs match, the phone realises that the cell it is corresponding with is part of its home system. The phone also transmits a registration request, along with the SID and the MTSO keeps track of your phone's location in a database – this way it is known what cell you are in when it wants to ring your phone. The MTSO gets the call that is calling you and it tries to find you by looking in its system to see which cell you are in. The call is sent to you at that time. You are now talking by two-way radio to a friend!

As you travel and move near the end of your cell, your cell's base station sees that your signal strength is diminishing. In the meantime, the base station in the cell you are moving closer to sees your phone's signal strength increasing. The two base stations coordinate with each other through the MTSO, and at some point, your phone gets a signal on a control channel telling it to change frequencies. This hand-off switches your phone to the new cell without interruption to

▶

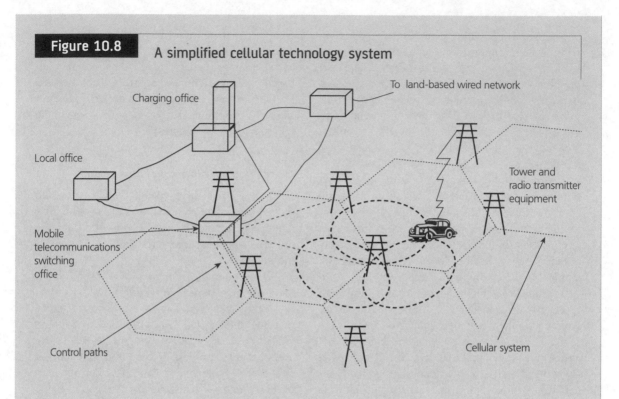

Figure 10.8   A simplified cellular technology system

Charging office

To land-based wired network

Local office

Tower and radio transmitter equipment

Mobile telecommunications switching office

Control paths

Cellular system

you and your call. As you travel, the signal is passed from cell to cell.

Inside a cell phone handset

Cell phones are some of the most intricate devices people play with on a daily basis. Modern digital cell phones can process millions of calculations per second in order to compress and decompress the voice stream. The cell phone comprises the following key individual parts:

- a circuit board containing the brains of the phone;
- an aerial;
- a liquid crystal display (LCD);
- a keyboard (similar to a television remote control);
- a microphone;
- a speaker; and
- a battery.

The circuit board

The circuit board is the heart of the system. The analog-to-digital and digital-to-analog conversion chips translate the outgoing audio signal from analog to digital and the incoming signal from digital back to analog. The digital signal processor (DSP) is a highly customised processor designed to perform signal-manipulation calculations at high speed. The microprocessor handles all of the housekeeping chores for the keyboard and display, deals with command and control signalling with the base station and also coordinates the rest of the functions on the board.

The ROM and Flash memory chips provide storage for the phone's operating system and customisable features, such as the phone directory. The radio frequency (RF) and power section handles power management and recharging, and also deals with the hundreds of FM channels. Finally, the RF amplifiers handle signals travelling to and from the aerial.

The display has grown considerably in size as the number of features in cell phones have increased. Most current phones offer built-in phone directories, calculators and even games. And many of the phones incorporate some type of Personal Digital Assistant (PDA) or Web-browser. Some phones store certain information, such as the SID and Mobile Identification Number (MIN) codes, in internal Flash memory, while others use external cards that are similar to Smart Media cards.

Cell phones have such tiny speakers and microphones that it is incredible how well most of them reproduce sound. The battery is used by the cell phone's internal clock chip.

Technology transfer

The increasing technological content of cell phones, as illustrated above, has forced many firms in the industry to search for technology partners who can provide the additional technology required such as multi-media, digital camera, games, etc. For these firms to try to develop expertise in these areas would be too expensive and too slow for the rapid technological changes that are occurring in the cell phone market. Indeed, the cell phone market is an excellent example of the increasing complexity of technologies and the increasing range of technologies found within products. This has led to a shortening of product life cycles within the cell phone market. Many users now change their handset after 18 months – 2 years. In addition, companies are finding it increasingly difficult to sustain R&D capability over all areas of their business as the complexity of these areas increases. Internal R&D is increasingly focused on core competencies, while R&D in all other business activities is progressively covered by collaborations, partnerships and strategic alliances.

Ericsson is the world leader in cell phone networks and has a long-established reputation in the microelectronics industry stretching back over 50 years. Hence, it has extensive knowledge and expertise of cell phone technology. Sony on the other hand does not, but it does have an extensive portfolio of other technologies that may be useful in third- and fourth-generation cell phones. Some of Sony's technology portfolio includes the following:

- HDTVs, Flat-panel Plasma and LCD WEGA® TVs, FD Trinitron® WEGA® CRT televisions, CRT rear projection TVs, and Grand WEGA® LCD rear projection televisions;
- DVD-video players/recorders, VCRs, Super Audio CD players, and home theatre-in-a-box systems;
- hi-fi components (AV receivers), shelf systems and speakers;
- Walkman® personal stereos, MiniDisc Walkman® players/recorders and personal digital music players;
- Handycam® camcorders;
- Cybershot® and Mavica® digital still cameras;
- Memory Stick® flash media;
- VAIO® desktop and notebook computers;
- CLIÉ™ handheld devices;
- video-conferencing products;
- visual-imaging products;
- professional digital photography systems;
- e-communication and digital signage;
- OEM Li-ion and li-polymer batteries; and
- semiconductor devices, including Sigma RAM memory, ICs, CCD sensors, optical comm. ICs, GPS and cellular/PCs ICs.

New products emerge from Sony-Ericsson

One year after its launch Sony-Ericsson unveiled its first six new handset models, including three with colour screens and one with a built-in camera. At the time Nokia, the market leader, did not have a colour-screen phone on the market, although it was planning to launch a camera-phone by the middle of the 2002.

Sony-Ericsson said it would launch its first 3G handset by the end of 2002. It also unveiled an alliance with Sony's film business to provide games on its new colour-screen phones, which would be based on the films *Men in Black* and *Charlie's Angels*. Further new handset models are planned that will utilise Sony's product design strengths.

In 2002 the launch of next generation mobile services (so called third-generation) was being held up by the financial difficulties of many operators and technical delays in the development of new handsets. The 3G phones were expected to drive demand for a wider range of applications on mobile phones.

Disappointing results

In 2003 Sony-Ericsson announced disappointing end-of-year results. Its market share did not achieve 6 per cent in 2002, compared with a 7–10 per cent target, forcing its owners to plough extra cash into the start-up after it failed to reach profitability as planned. The results placed Sony-Ericsson fifth in terms of market share. The company president, Katsumi Ihara admitted:

'Last year wasn't a good year for Sony-Ericsson, we expected a better business market at the beginning of the joint venture.' But failure is not an option for 2003, he says. 'We cannot accept the fact that Sony-Ericsson can continue to lose money. We need to turn around the business.'

He points to three main causes of the poor performance:

- problems integrating teams from Sony and Ericsson;
- market share losses in China; and
- strong competition in the United States.

The picture emerging in 2003 is very different from the one painted in 2001 when the two firms got together. The product and brand skills of Sony and the telecommunication and distribution skills of Ericsson were thought to be an ideal marriage. Competing with market leaders Nokia, Motorola and Samsung has proved extremely tough. And now other handset makers such as Alcatel and Sagem are beginning to deliver new products into an already crowded marketplace. The signs are worrying for Sony-Ericsson. There may be job losses ahead. Alcatel and Sagem have much lower market share figures than Sony-Ericsson and yet they are both able to deliver profits. Without the success of its T68 handset, which it inherited from the old Ericsson design team, last year's market share would have been several percentage points lower. Kurt Hellström, former Ericsson chief executive and Sony-Ericsson chairman, caused further controversy by suggesting that the Swedish group could halt further investment in the joint venture if there was no evidence of a turnaround.

The joint venture is a long way short of becoming the market leader as was suggested at its launch in 2001 and Sony-Ericsson desperately needs to show that it can manufacture a broad range of compelling phones as it tries to revitalise its flagging market share.

There are some signs of a change of fortunes: market share in China is climbing on the back of sales of its low-end T100 phone and its upmarket colour-screen T68. Also, newly launched handsets such as its top-of-the-range P800 phone, which has been selling well in early trials. Combined with the launch of 'more cute and sexy' models including camera phones 'in all price segments'.

In addition to new products Sony-Ericsson is looking to trim costs by moving more handset production to China and cutting other operational expenses.

Good news at last

In 2003 the Sony and Ericsson joint venture reported its first quarterly profit since its inception two years ago. Sony-Ericsson's sales rose to

€1.3bn. This improvement was particularly due to high demand for its new camera phones in Japan and to the success of its T610 series. This year it has launched five new mobile phones with in-built cameras to take advantage of the growing demand for sending and receiving pictures over mobile handsets. Its Z200 and Z600 Clamshell handsets have also prove extremely popular. It is also planning to launch a series of very low-cost, entry-level phones for markets such India, China and Brazil.

Sony-Ericsson is planning to take more of its mobile phone manufacturing plants under its own control to smooth out supply chain problems and help it take market share. It is in talks to raise its stake in Beijing Ericsson Putian Mobile Communication, a manufacturing facility outside Beijing, and could consider other similar deals in the future. The company is keen to avoid a repeat of 2002, when it failed to take full advantage of booming pre-Christmas demand for phones because of component shortages, and lost market share. However, the decision to bring more factories under direct control is a reversal of parent company Ericsson's policy – in 2001 just before setting up the joint venture – of outsourcing all its handset manufacturing to companies such as 'Flextronics'. About 30 per cent of Sony-Ericsson phones are produced in factories controlled by the company while 70 per cent of production is outsourced. Sony-Ericsson is aiming for 50 per cent production in factories controlled by the company.

Conclusions

In 2004 Sony-Ericsson at last delivered the financial results investors had been waiting for. Units shipped in the first quarter reached 8.8 million, a 63 per cent increase compared to the same period last year. Sales for the quarter were to €1,338 million, representing a year-on-year increase of 66 per cent. In addition, the restructuring measures that were taken in 2003

are now fully contributing to the bottom line. In an overall strong mobile phone market, shipments from Sony-Ericsson reached an all-time high as its product offering in the mid- and entry-level segments continued to gain momentum. Market share is estimated to have increased during the quarter thanks to strong demand and increased operational efficiencies.

The case illustrates how two large multi-technology firms such as Sony and Ericsson, operating in several technology fields found it extremely difficult and expensive to be technological leaders in every technology within their scope. It shows how Sony and Ericsson used technology transfer to enhance their own technology portfolio to shorten product development time and to avoid the costs and delay of research and development.

The longer-term problem for Sony-Ericsson is that it operates in a highly volatile market, that of the technology fashion market. The problem is that fashionable status is ephemeral. Buyers of trendy goods – such as the latest mobile phones – quickly switch to the next 'well cool' item. In the case of handsets, it is usually within 12 to 18 months. One of the questions for Sony-Ericsson is whether it can retain shoppers when they tire of their T610 and other higher-end Sony-Ericsson phones. Will they stick with the brand or move to one of its competitors?

Achieving profitability is obviously good, but whether Sony-Ericsson's business model is sustainable is not answered by one or two quarterly results. It plans to continue to supply a full range of phones, from cheap to expensive. Putting all its efforts into just one segment may make more sense. If Sony-Ericsson can master how to keep fashion victims interested, it may yet become a successful niche player and capture more market share.

An interesting side story to this case is the technology development of cellular technology. It seems that the technology existed for many years and was extremely slow to develop. If one considers that 'one-way business radio' has been

▶

around for 50 years. It seems funding to develop the technology was not forthcoming because people did not perceive how popular cellular radio would become nor how cheap the service would eventually be. If anyone had suspected such a great demand then funding would certainly have flowed much earlier. In the 1970s and 1980s cellular technology was thought of as an evolution of early radio telephones, a better way to provide a few people with a telephone for their cars. It was not thought that cellular technology would revolutionise communications for everyone.

Sources: C. Brown-Humes and M. Nakamoto (2001) 'Ericsson and Sony explore tie-up', *Financial Times*, 20 April; C. Brown-Humes and C. Daniel (2001) 'Ericsson plans micro-electronics division sell-off: unit hit by fall in mobile phone market', *Financial Times*, 20 August; R. Budden (2003) 'Sony-Ericsson seeks success with new phones', www.FT.com, 3 March; A. Harney (2001) 'Ambitious expansion looses its shine', *Financial Times*, 2 October; M. Pesola (2004) 'Sony-Ericsson to raise control', *Financial Times*, 10 March; D. Roberts and C. Brown-Humes (2001) 'Ericsson nears surrender in handset battle', *Financial Times*, 26 January.

Questions

1 Ericsson is the world leader in cell phone networks and has many years of experience of handsets. Explain how Sony's technology portfolio has helped the joint venture.

2 Explain why a cell phone is more like a radio than a wired telephone.

3 Explain why Sony and Ericsson were finding it increasingly difficult to sustain R&D over all of their businesses.

4 Explain why Ericsson is maintaining a large R&D division focusing on handsets when its joint venture with Sony is also conducting R&D and product development of handsets.

5 Many firms are outsourcing more and more of their activities and focusing on core activities. What are the advantages for Sony-Ericsson in bringing manufacturing back under its control?

Chapter summary

Technology transfer has a significant impact on the management of innovation. The process is concerned with facilitating and promoting innovation. The increasing use of strategic alliances means that its importance is set to increase. This chapter has introduced the subject of technology transfer and examined various models of the process. Most models of technology transfer emphasise access to technology rather than trying to understand the receptivity issues of the receiving organisation. The case study showed how effective technology transfer can be in contributing to a firm's success in very competitive conditions.

Discussion questions

1 Why was technology transfer considered to be a solution for budget deficits?
2 Explain the limitations of many of the models of technology transfer.
3 Explain how a firm's internal activities affect its ability to acquire external technology.
4 Explain the importance of tacit knowledge to the technology transfer process.
5 Explain why any technology transferred to an organisation needs to be embedded into its core routines.

Key words and phrases

Knowledge transfer 314	Receptivity 323
Licensing 315	Scanning and networking 325
NIH syndrome 322	Strategic alliance 331
Organisational learning 329	Technology transfer 313

Websites worth visiting

Ericsson www.ericsson.com

European space agency www.esa.com

Information on technology and the market place www.techweb.com

Sony www.Sony.com

Sony-Ericsson www.Sonyericsson.com

References

Afuah, A. (2003) *Innovation Management*, 2nd cdn, Oxford University Press, Oxford.

Agryis, C. and Schon, D.A. (1978) *Organisational Learning*, Addison-Wesley, Reading, MA.

Allen, T.J. (1966) 'Performance of communication channels in the transfer of technology', *Industrial Management Review*, Vol. 8, 87–98.

Allen, T.J. (1977) *Managing the Flow of Technology*, MIT Press, Cambridge, MA.

Allen, T.J. and Cohen, W.M. (1969) 'Information flow in research and development laboratories', *Administrative Science Quarterly*, Vol. 14, No. 1, 12–19.

Bosworth, D. and Stoneman, P. (1996) *Technology Transfer, Information Flows and Collaboration: an Analysis of the CIS*, European Commission, DG XIII: The innovation programme, EIMS Project No. 93/53, Brussels.

Brown-Humes, C. and Daniel, C. (2001) 'Ericsson plans microelectronics division sell-off: Unit hit by fall in mobile phone market', *Financial Times*, 20 August.

Brown-Humes, C. and Nakamoto, M. (2001) 'Ericsson and Sony explore tie-up', *Financial Times*, 20 April.

Budden, R. (2003) 'Sony Ericsson seeks success with new phones', www.FT.com, 3 March.

Carter, C.F. and Williams, B.R. (1959) 'The characteristics of technically progressive firms', *Journal of Industrial Economics*, March, 87–104.

Centre for Exploitation of Science and Technology (CEST) (1991) *The Management of Technological Collaboration*, March, Manchester.

Cohen, W.M. and Levinthal, D.A. (1990) 'A new perspective on learning and innovation', *Administrative Science Quarterly*, Vol. 35, No. 1, 128–52.

Cooley, M. (1987) *Architect or Bee? The Human Price of Technology*, Hogarth Press, London.

Cordey-Hayes, M., Trott, P. and Gilbert, M. (1996) 'Knowledge assimilation and learning organisations', in Butler, J. and Piccaluga, A. (eds) *Knowledge, Technology and Innovative Organisations*, Guerini e Associati, Italy.

Danhof, C. (1949) *Observations on Entrepreneurship in Agriculture: Change and the Entrepreneur*, Harvard Research Center on Entrepreneurship History, Harvard University Press, Cambridge, MA.

DFI International (1998) 'Short- and long-term implications of technology transfer' in *China Technology Transfer Report*, DTI International, London, pp. 93–8.

Dorf, R.C. (1988) 'Models for technology transfer from universities and research laboratories', in *Technology Management*, Vol. 1, Interscience Enterprises Ltd, Geneva.

Gilbert, M. (1996) 'Technological change as a knowledge transfer process', PhD thesis, INTA, Cranfield University.

Godkin, L. (1988) 'Problems and practicalities of technology transfer: a survey of the literature', *International Journal of Technology Management*, Vol. 3, No. 5, 597–603.

Gruber, W.H. and Marquis, D.G. (1969) *Factors in the Transfer of Technology*, MIT Press, Cambridge, MA.

Hagedoorn, J. (1990) 'Organisational modes of inter-firm co-operation and technology transfer', *Technovation*, Vol. 10, No. 1, 17–30.

Harney, A. (2001) 'Ambitious expansion loses its shine: analysts change their tune about Sony's dreams and begin to count the costs of the new mobile phone alliance with Ericsson', *Financial Times*, 2 October.

Howells, J. (1996) 'Tacit knowledge and innovation and technology transfer', *Technology Analysis and Strategic Management Journal*, Vol. 8, 91–106.

Johnson, S.C. and Jones, C. (1957) 'How to organise for new products', *Harvard Business Review*, May–June, Vol. 35, 49–62.

Katz, R. and Allen, T. (1988) 'Investigating the NIH syndrome: a look at the performance, tenure and communication patterns of 50 R&D project groups', in Tushman, W.L. and Moore, M.L. (eds) *Readings in the Management of Innovation*, HarperCollins, New York.

Kroonenberg, H.H. van den (1989) 'Getting a quicker pay-off from R&D', *Long Range Planning*, Vol. 4, 22, 51–8.

Langrish, J., Evans, W.G. and Jerans, F.R. (1982) *Wealth from Knowledge*, Macmillan, London.

Lefever, D.B. (1992) 'Technology transfer and the role of intermediaries', PhD thesis, INTA, Cranfield Institute of Technology.

Lewis, J.D. (1990) *Partnerships for Profit*, Collier Macmillan, London.

Link, A.N. and Link, K.R. (2003) 'On the growth of science parks', *Journal of Technology Transfer*, Vol. 28, 81–5.

Macdonald, S. (1992) 'Formal collaboration and informal information flow', *International Journal of Technology Management*, Special Issue on Strengthening Corporate and National Competitiveness through Technology, Vol. 7, Nos. 1/2/3, 49–60.

Nelson, R.R. (1991) 'Why do firms differ, and how does it matter?' *Strategic Management Journal*, Vol. 12, No. 1, 61–74.

Nelson, R.R. and Winter, S. (1982) *An Evolutionary Theory of Economic Change*, Harvard University Press, Boston, MA.

Newell, S. and Clark, P. (1990) 'The importance of extra-organisational networks in the diffusion and appropriation of new technologies', *Knowledge: Creation, Diffusion and Utilisation*, Vol. 12, No. 2, 199–212.

Oakley, R.P., Rothwell, R. and Cooper, S.Y. (1988) *The Management of Innovation in High Technology Small Firms*, Frances Pinter, London.

Peters, T. and Waterman, R.H. (1982) *In Search of Excellence: Lessons from America's Best Run Companies*, Harper & Row, New York.

Prahalad, G. and Hamel, C.K. (1990) 'The core competence of the corporation', *Harvard Business Review*, Vol. 68, No. 3, 79–91.

Roberts, D. and Brown-Humes, C. (2001) 'Ericsson nears surrender in handset battle: the Swedish group is to outsource some production', *Financial Times*, 26 January.

Rothberg, R. (1976) *Corporate Strategy and Product Innovation*, Free Press, New York.

Rothwell, R., Freeman, C., Horsley, A., Jervis, V.T.P., Robertson, A.B. and Townsend, J. (1974) 'SAPPHO updated: Project SAPPHO phase II', *Research Policy*, Vol. 3, 258–91.

Seaton, R.A.F. and Cordey-Hayes, M. (1993) 'The development and application of interactive models of technology transfer', *Technovation*, Vol. 13, No. 1, 45–53.

Tidd, J., Bessant, J. and Pavitt, K. (2001) *Managing Innovation*, 2nd edn, John Wiley & Sons, Chichester.

Trott, P. (1993) 'Inward technology transfer as an interactive process: a case study of ICI', PhD thesis, Innovation and Technology Assessment Centre, Cranfield University.

Trott, P. (1998) 'Growing businesses by generating genuine business opportunities: a review of recent thinking', *Journal of Applied Management*, Vol. 7, No. 2, 111–22.

Trott, P. and Cordey-Hayes, M. (1996) 'Developing a "receptive" environment for inward technology transfer: a case study of the chemical industry', *R&D Management*, Vol. 26, No. 1, 83–92.

Tushman, M.L. (1977) 'Communication across organisational boundaries: special boundary roles in the innovation process', *Administrative Science Quarterly*, Vol. 22, 587–605.

Werner, J. (1991) 'Can collaborative research work? Success could spawn "collateral benefits" for all industries', *Industry Week*, Vol. 240, No. 13, 47.

Further reading

For a more detailed review of the technology transfer literature, the following develop many of the issues raised in this chapter:

Caspar, S. and Whitley, R. (2004) 'Managing competencies in entrepreneurial technology firms: a comparative institutional analysis in Germany, Sweden and the UK', *Research Policy*, Vol. 33, No. 1, 89–106.

Day, G.S. and Schoemaker, P.J.H. (eds) (2000) *Wharton on Managing Emerging Technologies*, John Wiley, New York.

Kaufman, A., Wood, C.H. and Theyel, G. (2000) 'Collaboration and technology linkages: a strategic supplier typology', *Strategic Management Journal*, Vol. 21, No. 1, 649–63.

Lewis, J. (1990) *Partnerships for Profit: Structuring and Managing Strategic Alliances*, Free Press, New York.

Mason, G., Beltram, J. and Paul, J. (2004) 'External knowledge sourcing in different national settings: a comparison of electronics establishments in Britain and France', *Research Policy*, Vol. 33, No. 1, 53–72.

Nonaka, I. and Takeuchi, H. (1995) *The Knowledge Creating Company. How Japanese Companies Create the Dynamics for Innovation*, Oxford University Press, Oxford.

Shavinina, L. (2003) *The International Handbook on Innovation*, Elsevier, Oxford.

Stock, G.N., Greis, N.P. and Fischer, W.A. (2001) 'Absorptive capacity and new product development', *Journal of High Technology Management Research*, Vol. 12, 77–91.

Part Three

New Product Development

This part reviews and summarises the nature and techniques of new product development. It looks at the process of developing new products and examines many of the new product management issues faced by companies.

Product and brand strategy is the subject of Chapter 11, it addresses the positioning of the product and the importance of brand strategy on the success of any new product. In particular, it examines the influences on product planning decisions and the role of marketing management. All of these heavily influence any decision to develop new products.

Our understanding of the new product innovation process has improved significantly in the past 30 years. During this period numerous models have been developed to help explain the process. These are examined in Chapter 12. Many of these models identify the role of market research to be significant in developing successful new products. Chapter 13 examines the significant role of packaging in new product development. The role of market research is addressed again in Chapter 14, but this time it explores whether there are times when market research may hinder the development of new products.

Chapter 15 moves from the conceptual to the operational level and analyses the particular challenges faced by the new product manager. Taking a practitioner viewpoint, it investigates the activities that need to be undertaken and how companies organise the process. Emphasis is placed on the role of the new product team.

11

Product and brand strategy

The products developed by an organisation provide the means for it to generate income. But there are many factors to consider in order to maximise the product's chance of success in competitive environments. For many technology-intensive frms their approach is based on exploiting technological innovation in a rapidly changing market. Other frms, especially those involved in fast-moving consumer goods (fcmg), will be more focused on meeting and supplying products to meet the rapidly changing needs of their customers. All frms have to consider the market in which they are competing, the nature of the competition and how their capabilities will enable their products to be successful. The positioning of the product and the brand strategy selected are of particular importance and also refect the subject of this chapter.

Chapter contents

Learning objectives

When you have completed this chapter you will be able to:

- explain how product strategies contribute to a firm's performance;
- recognise that new products serve a variety of purposes depending upon what is seen to be the strategic imperative;
- examine the concept of platforms in new product development;
- assess the importance of brand strategy in product development;
- explain how differentiation and positioning contribute to a product's success in the market place; and
- recognise the importance of marketing research for the effective development of new products.

Capabilities, networks and platforms

The company's core capabilities, and those that it can develop or acquire, bound what it can accomplish. However, a broader view brings in the notion of distinctive capabilities. This is wider than technical or operations competence. Kay (1993) suggests that these broader capabilities include an organisation's 'architecture' and this embraces the network of relationships within, or around, the firm. These relationships might cover customers, suppliers, distributors or other firms engaged in related activities. This leads to the perspective that product development, and the competitive rivalry of which it is usually a part, can sometimes be better understood as undertaken by networks of partnerships and alliances rather than by individual, isolated producers (Doyle, 1995).

Chapter 7 introduced the concept of networks and explained that their composition can vary widely. In some high-technology industries a horizontal alliance of competitors or firms might dominate, and perhaps they form a consortium for the research and development of a technology. For example, Kodak, Fujifilm, Minolta, Nikon and Canon were allied in the development of the Advanced Photo System. In other industries it might be a vertical arrangement between suppliers, manufacturers, distributors and possibly even customers. It can be a formal agreement, a loose collection of understandings or a system 'managed' by a powerful member.

Saying this of capabilities leads to complications. If networks are competing, rather than individual firms, then the activities across the network need to be coordinated. Sometimes it is the manufacturer who is dominant and leads and controls the network, as in the motor industry. Sometimes it is a distributor who takes the lead and initiates new product categories, as in food retailing. On occasion a large customer can dominate, show the need for a new product and encourage suppliers to innovate, as in the health service or defence industries. How effectively this leadership and coordination are undertaken influences substantially what products are developed and how they are developed.

Another consideration is that the network members may have a collection of varied motives for being party to the relationship. Through time they may come to stress other motives that may result in their becoming less interested in the network's aims and less willing to cooperate. The network leader therefore needs to spend some time monitoring motives and encouraging, or inducing, full cooperation between all network members. If the network is established for the development of a technology then the partners have other sets of problems once the technology is available. How do they share the results and how do they each go on to establish distinctive, competitive products?

Choosing appropriate partners for the network and keeping them focused are important attributes for network leadership. Developing and refining the network's innovative ability is crucial, and this is not restricted to technical innovation because innovation in business processes and in distribution can also have a large impact.

Capabilities change. Without continuous attention they can become ineffectual or redundant, as the technology or the market requirement moves on. Alternatively, capabilities may be enhanced through internal development, through external acquisition and through the bringing together of new partnerships and alliances so that the network's capability is deeper or wider. Most capabilities thrive through continuity: through continuous incremental enhancement around a technology or a set of related technologies. This is in keeping with the idea of organisational heritage introduced in Chapters 1 and 3.

Product platforms

Emphasis upon continuity in the development of capabilities is also consistent with the idea of an evolving product platform that a 'product family' shares. Muffatto and Rovedo (2000) uses the car industry as the classic example of this idea where several individual models may share the same basic frame, suspension and transmission. As they say, 'a robust platform is the heart of a successful product family, serving as the foundation for a series of closely related products' (p. 31). The Sony Walkman gives another illustration, with its 160 variations and four major technical innovations between 1980 and 1990, all of which were based upon the initial platform (Jones, 1997). Black & Decker rationalised its hundreds of products into a set of product families, with consequent economies throughout the chain from procurement to distribution and after-sales service. In all these cases the evolution of the product platform, along with the evolution of the requisite capabilities, is central to the product development strategy.

This notion may have originated in engineering but it can be applied widely. Mobile phone handsets, food, cosmetics, clothing and furniture manufacturers can be seen to have product platforms and families. Johnson & Johnson and its development of the Acuvue disposable contact lenses provides another example. Thomas (1995) points out that many people needing vision correction did not wear traditional hard or soft contact lenses because of the discomfort and the cleaning requirements. Acuvue uses high quality soft contact lenses sold at a sufficiently low price to allow disposal after a week, without cleaning. This distinctive advantage, which was clearly relevant to many consumers, led to the successful launch in 1987 that defined a new market segment. The original product became the basic platform for continuing innovation that is leading to other new offerings in Johnson & Johnson's vision care product family.

Sometimes entirely new platforms and entirely new capabilities are required. Step changes in the product or manufacturing technology, in the customer need or in what the competition offers, and how it offers it, can demand radical rather than incremental change. The risk is all the more if that means the adoption of new technologies, outside the firm's traditional arena.

If we return to the car industry we see that today products are developed from multiple brand product platforms. Furthermore, products of different brands are developed from inter-firm platform projects. For example, Figure 11.1 shows the Volkswagen Audi Group (VAG) inter-firm product platform development. This shows the one platform supporting several different brands with very different strategic objectives. When the car industry began using product platforms the objective was to obtain commonality and benefits of scale within the company boundary. The basic idea was to differentiate all the components visible to the customer, while at the same time sharing components and production processes across product models (Wheelwright and Clark, 1992; Muffatto, 1999). Some 20 years later, however, the application of the product platform concept is causing concern for many industry analysts, who believe the search for commonality has gone too far at the expensive of brand distinctiveness. The illustration in Figure 11.1 illustrates how the product platform operates across a wide variety of models/brands with different strategies and significant price gaps between the models/brands. According to Muffatto and Rovedo (2000) the benefits gained through using product platforms are:

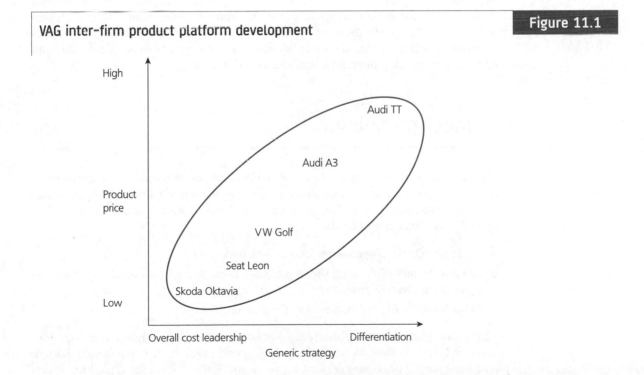

VAG inter-firm product platform development

Figure 11.1

Illustration 11.1

Nestlé Polo's: a new flip top for a new product

Nestlé recently launched a new confectionary product: Polo Holes. The bits left over when the famous mints are pressed. Robinson Plastic Packaging has delivered a transparent, food-grade poplypropylene tube for the launch of this new product. The pack features a flip-top closure with Polo embossing. Robinson Plastic Packaging is part of the Robinson Group and is a dedicated moulder of closures, components and containers for the food, drinks and confectionery industries.

- reduced cost of production;
- shared components between models;
- reduced R&D lead times;
- reduced systemic complexity;
- better learning across projects; and
- improved ability to update products.

When used across firms and models there are many challenges presented. According to Kim and Chhajed (2000) in practice it is difficult to achieve optimum or best solution. Inevitably compromises are sought between engineers and designers from the different brands resulting in decisions that are not in the interest of either brand. Moreover, with inter-firm product platforms some of the sought-after gains such as shared components between models and reduced complexity were not achievable because of the constraint of factory sequencing or architectural structure of the brand.

Product planning

The product planning process takes place before substantial resources are applied to a project. Product planning considers the range of projects that a firm might pursue and over what time frame. It is closely linked to the broader business strategy of the firm and addresses such questions as:

- What product development projects will be undertaken?
- What is the mix of the portfolio of projects (discontinuous new products; platform products; derivative products)?
- What is the timing and sequence of the projects?

The product planning activity clearly requires substantial input from research and development (R&D). It is this link to the technology portfolio of the firm that is so important and needs careful management (*see* Chapters 8 and 9). Deriving a set of products which customers perceive as useful and worth buying may be fortuitous, but more often it is the result of deliberate, systematic endeavour. Organisations choose to compete in one or more product markets using a specified range of technologies (the technology portfolio). They seek to have a set of balanced capabilities that will enable them to match market opportunities by developing attractive market offerings, which customers perceive as conveying valuable benefits. How well they accomplish this, compared with competitors, is a major determinant of success.

The product plan identifies the portfolio of products to be developed by the organisation. The planning process considers product development opportunities from many sources, including marketing, R&D, customers, current product teams and competitor analysis. Usually large firms will have more opportunities than resources to fund and the key question facing product planners is which projects to fund?

The product plan is regularly updated to reflect the changing competitive environment. Indeed, a surprise new product launch by a competitor frequently results in a major change to a firm's product plan. This was the case for Hoover when it responded quickly to Dyson's bagless vacuum cleaner. Product planning decisions generally involve senior management of the firm and form part of the on-going strategy process. When considering product development opportunities they are usually classified as four types:

- *New product platforms*. This type of project involves a major development effort to create a new family of products based on a new, common platform. From an R&D perspective this would be seen as developing a new core technology. The new platform would be used to help existing products compete. An example of this would be Kodak's move into digital photography.

- *Derivatives of existing platforms*. Projects of this type develop an existing platform usually to ensure existing products are updated. This will either provide them with an advantage over the competition or make sure they can compete with the competition. Honda have been extremely successful in utilising their product platform of small petrol engines and applying this technology to a wide variety of market applications from lawn mowers to motorcycles and from outboard motors for boats to chainsaws.

- *Incremental improvements to existing products*. These projects may only involve adding or modifying features of existing products to keep the product line current and competitive. Frequently this may be improving the packaging or reducing the manufacturing cost of producing the product or changing the design slightly. While such changes may seem small they can often have significant impact on sales. The change from see-through cellophane to foil packaging by Walker's made a huge impact on sales. *See also* Nestlé Polos in Illustration 11.1.

- *Fundamentally new products (discontinuous products)*. These projects involve radically different product or production technologies and may help to take the firm into new and unfamiliar markets. Such projects are inherently more risky but may help to secure the long-term future of the firm. This was the case for W.L. Gore & Associates following the development of its breathable fabric 'Gore-Tex'. This new technology has enabled the firm to enter new fabric-based markets. Previously its portfolio of products covered the areas of medical, electronic and industrial.

Illustration 11.2

FT

Apple iPod: from product to platform

To most of us the iPod is a product, a marvel of industrial design that is cute to behold and intuitive to operate. To shareholders of Apple Computer, however, the miniature music player is much more. It is, potentially, a platform. There is more than just semantics at stake. While products stand alone, platforms are the *de facto* standards around which whole markets are built. Steve Jobs, Apple's denim-clad founder and chief executive, should understand the distinction better than anyone.

Apple's website does not exaggerate when it says: 'Apple ignited the personal computer revolution in the 1970s with the Apple II and reinvented the personal computer in the 1980s with the Macintosh.' Yet, today, it accounts for only 3.5 per cent of the PC market. The reason? Apple kept its software to itself, enabling Microsoft to establish its operating systems – first MS-Dos and then Windows – as the platforms on which the $175bn- (£96bn-) a year PC industry is built.

Now that another opportunity is emerging – to establish the iPod as the leading platform for digital music – the question is whether Mr Jobs has learnt from his multi-billion-dollar mistake. At first sight it looks as though he has. Apple has made a series of moves to widen the market for the iPod, most recently its deal this month with Hewlett-Packard, under which HP will sell iPods under its own brand.

Apple has cooperated closely with companies that make add-on products for the iPod. These turn the music player into a voice recorder, a car stereo or an 'album' for digital pictures. The evolution of such an 'ecosystem' of complementary products is one sign of a platform emerging, says Michael Cusumano, professor of management at the Sloan School of Management at the Massachusetts Institute of Technology.

For example, Microsoft worked hard through the 1980s to win over software developers. This ensured there was a steady supply of Microsoft-compatible applications and helped to establish MS-Dos and Windows as industry standards.

But while the development of complementary products is a necessary condition for platform leadership, it is not enough. The test, argues David Yoffie, professor of business administration at Harvard Business School, is whether a company is prepared to put its technology into the hands of rivals. He points to Palm's 1999 decision to license its eponymous operating system for personal organisers to Sony and Handspring. Like the iPod today, Palm's Pilot hand-held organisers led their market in the late 1990s. Like Apple, Palm had worked with outside companies to create an ecosystem of complementary products. By licensing its technology, Palm risked cannibalising sales of its Pilots. Yet it gambled that, in the long run, it could make more money by establishing Palm OS as the dominant platform for hand-held computing.

The jury is still out on Palm's gamble. Slow development of Palm's operating system since 1999 has allowed companies including Microsoft and Symbian to establish rival platforms. Palm was particularly slow to recognise the convergence of hand-held computers and mobile phones. However, these were arguably errors of execution. Palm's platform strategy was clear. Apple has started to move in this direction. Last year, it unveiled a version of iTunes – the online music store with which iPods work – compatible with Windows PCs. At a stroke, this hugely expanded the market.

This month Apple said it would supply iPods for resale by Hewlett-Packard, the world's biggest seller of Windows PCs and, therefore, an arch-rival.

Mr Jobs has even referred to iTunes – which claims a 70 per cent share of legal music downloads – as 'the Microsoft' of its market. The subtext? He sees iTunes as the dominant platform round which a new digital music market will emerge.

The snag is that Apple has still not crossed the Rubicon: it has not risked cannibalising iPod sales in pursuit of the bigger prize. HP will sell Apple-manufactured iPods; it will not be creating its own products using technology licensed from Apple. 'Unless [Apple] does this, it looks like more of the same', says Prof Yoffie. Prof Cusumano agrees: 'If Steve Jobs was serious about establishing the platform for digital music he would be licensing the technology. You have to wonder whether they really understand platform dynamics.'

Both question whether Apple's strong corporate culture would allow it to take such a step. The company's history is one of almost wilful isolation – two decades of integrating proprietary hardware and software to produce what Mr Jobs calls 'insanely great' products. Few would deny that iPod/iTunes is just such a combination. The sales – about 2m iPods so far, 733,000 in the last quarter of 2003 – speak for themselves. It is less clear whether there is an insanely great strategy to match. Apple Computer declined to comment for this article.

In every industry, platform leaders are a cut above the rest. 'Becoming a platform leader is like winning the holy grail: many seek it, but few achieve it', write Michael Cusumano and Annabelle Gawer in *Platform Leadership*.* They might have added that fewer still agree on what a platform is, exactly. One pre-requisite is that a platform has limited value on its own but gains in value when used with complementary products. Thus a computer operating system is a jumble of ones and zeros until coupled with an array of compatible hardware and packages of software. A platform also makes it possible for others to add value. This, says David Yoffie at Harvard Business School, is what differentiates a platform from a mere component.

Also implicit is the idea of market dominance. What economists call 'network effects' give users an incentive to buy into the dominant platform. With dominance comes responsibility. The massive increases in processing power achieved by Intel microprocessors require complementary improvements in memory, display technology and software. The platform leader assumes *de facto* responsibility for driving innovation forward.

E-bay, the online auction site, seems to pass all of the above tests. So does Amazon.com, the online bookseller that acts as e-commerce platform for an increasing number of retailers. Mark Anderson, publisher of Strategic News Service newsletter, points to Salesforce.com as another candidate. The company, which sells sales software to businesses as a subscription service via the Internet, could be viewed as having created a 'sales support platform'. As Mr Anderson writes in his latest newsletter: 'A platform is not a software product, nor is it even a [web]site. Rather, it turns out to be a linkage of services and proprietary advantages which can occur in any market, new or old.'

Source: S. London, 'Apple iPod: from product to platform', *Financial Times*, www.FT.com, 18 January 2004. Reprinted with permission.

* M. Cusumano and A. Gawer (2002) *Platform Leadership: How Intel, Microsoft and Cisco Drive Industry Innovation*, Harvard Business School Press, Boston, MA.

Pause for thought

How do product platforms differ from Umbrella brands such as Nestlé or Kelloggs?

Product strategy

New product strategy is part of a web of strategies. It is linked to, and its objectives are derived from, marketing strategy, technology strategy and the overall corporate strategy. These other strategies provide the role, the context, the impetus and the definition of the scope of new product strategy.

Competitive strategy

New products are not needed just because they are new products. They are required because they serve a customer need and an organisation need. The organisation need will be articulated in the organisation's strategy and there might be comments about striving to lead in the technology, or to be the key innovator, in its mission statement. However, much new product development is not concerned with new-to-the-world innovations, and this is partly because many companies are followers and not leaders in their technology. NPD for a follower can be very different from NPD for a leader. New products perform different roles at different times for different companies. They serve a variety of purposes depending upon what is seen to be the strategic imperative.

Competitive strategy may drive new product planning on a short-term or long-term basis. In the shorter term a defensive posture may suggest that product variants are needed to shore up a declining market share, which is perhaps attributed to a competitor's aggressive new product activities. A reactive strategy could entail filling out product lines with different product sizes or added features that may be intended to deter a new entrant to the market, by not leaving unattended small market segments to be used as an entry point by the new competitor. Such minor product changes could also be employed to secure distributors' loyalty, because they are then able to carry a full range of the product and so be less inclined to stock rival offerings. Imitative products may be brought out, copying competitors, for similar reasons. In these kinds of situations where the new product is a minor modification, however new the advertising proclaims it to be, it is unlikely that the full, classic NPD process would be engaged. There may be little or no research, and market testing may be restricted to determining acceptable price levels or to choosing between alternative advertising messages.

In the longer run competitive strategy may seek a more profound contribution from new products. A strategy may look for new product categories to be developed, within the same or a related technology, or in a new technology area. These new products may appeal to the organisation's traditional customer base or seek new customer segments. This more radical product development would more likely be subject to thorough marketing and technical research, development and testing.

New products can also perform a learning function for the organisation. The development of a pioneering new product platform may at first be tentative, and several alternative concepts for new platforms may be investigated simultaneously. Uncertainties surround such ventures because the new platform may require the development of costly new competences, while simultaneously the nature and the scale of the market opportunity are illusory. The firm may need to develop both new knowledge and new skills in technical, operations and marketing areas. The adequacy of the search for, and the acquisition of, these new skills and knowledge will mark out the leaders.

Product portfolios

Another set of strategic considerations concerns the overall portfolio of products. Analysing the organisation's total collection of products by viewing it as a portfolio, as in an investment portfolio, may give fresh insights. This approach was initiated by the share-growth matrix, or Boston box, which used market share and market growth as dimensions against which to plot the positions of products. A typology was derived with high and low values for each of the two dimensions so that the four quadrants could be contrasted. For example products classified as high share/high growth could be contrasted with those deemed to be low share/low growth. Prospects could also be investigated by comparing where products are positioned presently, where they might be in the future with no change in strategy, and compared with some desired positions. Analyses of this kind might suggest some strategic issues. A clustering of the portfolio in one quadrant might be viewed as unbalanced, and an absence of any products in the two high-growth quadrants might be thought unhealthy.

Such a simple depiction has attracted controversy and alternative models have been suggested using multi-factor dimensions that are composites of variables, such as business strength and market attractiveness. Most of the derivations still employ two dimensions because they can be displayed with ease, but more complex, and some say more realistic, models are multi-dimensional. All these models share a similar aim: to give the strategist an overview that could reveal current or potential problems or opportunities in the product strategy.

This portfolio approach might also be applied to the product families and the platforms upon which they are built, although the selection of appropriate variables to describe the space can be a problem. Thought might be given to the extent to which a wide range of words might be usefully employed to indicate the dimensions, such as: robust, innovative, sophisticated, flexible, generic, evolving, traditional. For example, using relative sophistication (ranging from very sophisticated to unsophisticated) and flexibility (from very flexible to very inflexible) as descriptors of two dimensions might show the majority of product platforms to be unsophisticated and inflexible, with possibly one isolated platform that is sophisticated and flexible. Without qualification that probably means little and it leads to no great revelation. Being unsophisticated is not necessarily a bad thing, it may be just what the customer needs. Regarding the other dimension a very flexible product platform is not necessarily a good thing, it may result in too many compromises that lead to products that are not specialised enough for customer applications. Several such 'mapping' exercises might be tried using different descriptors. A supplementary analysis might trace connections between platforms, any spin-off from them and in addition bring in a time dimension.

Nothing conclusive can be expected from these analyses: they are probing and investigative. The process of taking this broader view of the portfolio draws attention to issues that, with deeper analysis, could be significant. It is this identification of issues that can be critical and can be creative. It can flout any fixation with norms and conventions, which can flourish readily within organisations, and it can underline the point that approaches to product strategy development must be original if they are to lead to distinctive new market offerings.

The competitive environment

The external environment constrains what can be done, for example within the bounds of current understanding of a technology. Sometimes the external environment dictates what must be done, for example following the introduction of a new piece of legislation protecting an aspect of the natural environment, as was seen in the case study in Chapter 1. It can present possibilities and opportunities, such as a breakthrough in an enabling technology or the new affluence of consumers that allows them to be prepared to pay more for products in a particular category. The external circumstances can also pose threats and problems, as when a competitor introduces a significant product advance, or when another rival closes access to materials or to distributors, through its acquisition of companies in those activities.

Close analysis of the present situation in the market is fundamental, along with speculations about how it might progress and because of the potential importance of external events and conditions some type of environmental monitoring, in a strategic sense, has become a key exercise in strategy search. Assessments of the present situation can be extended to conjectures about future environments, and in some industries, such as aerospace or pharmaceuticals, this may require a very long-term view. A range of alternative future scenarios may be built around these conjectures, indicating guesses about what the organisation sees to be the aspects of its environment carrying the most stress. These speculations might deal with some of the following issues.

1 Estimates would be needed about the way the technology will change, and this could be more or less rigorous. It could involve some brainstorming within the organisation and it could seek various forms of external advice from government agencies, research centres, consultants and universities.

2 Estimates might also be made about how the industry competitive structure may alter. Are the same competitors likely to be contending in the market in the future? Are there any indications that any are preparing some kind of strategic shift? Will any withdraw or reduce their activities within the industry? Will there be changes in how companies compete and the positioning they seek in the market? Will there be any new entrants from other industries, or from other countries? Unexpected arrivals in the industry, especially if they are well funded, well managed and they come with a significant innovation, can be particularly troublesome. That was the case when Mars entered the ice cream business and quickly secured a significant market share.

3 Another area of concern could be how any regulatory framework may evolve and this could include the extent to which it would limit activities in the future or open new possibilities.

4 Customer needs may be a further area in which to speculate. Will they become more demanding and require better materials and better performance in the products they use? Will they perceive some emerging technology as a substitute? Will they have new kinds of needs and will there be new kinds of customers?

Taking various combinations of these factors could yield a series of scenarios, and the investigation of the implications for the organisation of each of them could indicate important issues requiring attention. Such future scenarios may throw up attractive or unattractive situations and the organisation may then attempt to do what it can to prepare itself, and to do what it can to increase the likelihood of the former while inhibiting the later. This will help to shape ideas about the potential role for new products and the scope of the problems and opportunities that they are intended to address.

Differentiation and positioning

Product strategy will express how the organisation seeks to differentiate itself, and distance itself, from its competitors and it will be the bedrock of its market positioning. It is axiomatic that for new products to be successful in the market they need to be perceived to be beneficial by prospective buyers. The benefit needs to stand out, to be distinctive and attractive. This distinction needs to be relevant to buyers, and it needs to be seen to be relevant by them. It is pointless being distinctive in a way that consumers believe to be irrelevant or incomprehensible. This point is illustrated in the case study at the end of this chapter.

Differentiation

Broadly, the differentiation sought by competitors could be based upon cost, with a value-for-money proposition, or it could be based upon superior quality, which might encompass better materials, better performance, new features, uncommon availability or better service. A useful perspective on product differentiation is provided by Levitt's idea of product augmentation (Levitt, 1986). He suggests that there are four levels on which products can be considered:

1 *the core product* comprises the essential basics needed to compete in a product market; a car needs wheels, transmission, engine and a rudimentary chassis.

2 *the expected product* adds in what customers have become accustomed to as normal in the product market; for a car this would be a reasonably comfortable interior and a range of accessories.

3 *the augmented product* offers features, services or benefits that go beyond normal expectations.

4 *the potential product* would include all the features and services that could be envisaged as beneficial to customers.

An interesting implication of this categorisation is that it can demonstrate that the position is dynamic because customer expectations change. In the example of the car, where would air conditioning be placed in these categories? Until recently it would have been an augmentation for mass-market vehicles, but it has now become a standard expectation in new cars. Competition drives up consumer expectations. One rival introduces something new and, if it meets customer acceptance, other rivals follow. In

Figure 11.2	Platform development creates the architecture for a family of products

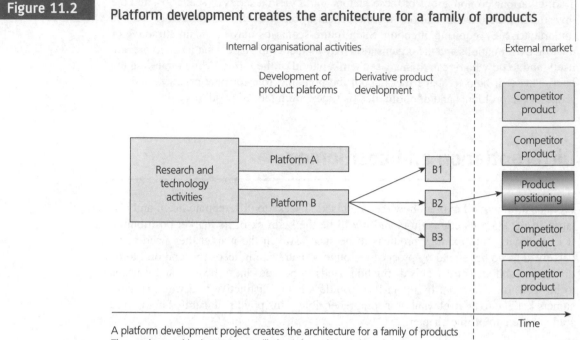

A platform development project creates the architecture for a family of products
The product positioning strategy will also inform the product planning process

consequence augmentations become expectations, and this ratchet effect means there is no equilibrium until the full potential has been realised. Even then changes to the technology, or to another technology, might release an entirely new kind of potential, so that the process continues.

Another implication is that as firms migrate upwards in this process they leave market opportunities for others to exploit. There may be niche markets left for 'unbundled' products or services making low-cost, basic offers with no frills. Airlines are an example.

The choice of differentiation strategy is pivotal. It reaches back to core capabilities and it reaches forward to positioning strategy. The differentiation will not be effective unless it is rooted firmly in the organisation's capabilities, or in the capabilities of the network delivering the new product. Similarly the positioning of the product in the market needs to be built upon, and needs to be consistent with, the differentiation strategy.

Product positioning

Product positioning refers to the perceptions customers have about the product. It is a relative term that describes customer perceptions of the product's position in the market relative to rival products. It is founded upon understanding how customers discriminate between alternative products and it considers the factors customers use in making judgements or choices between products in the market being investigated. These are referred to as the customer's evaluative criteria and they may be the product's physical attributes, but they can include customer assessments about whom the product is meant for, when, where and how it is used and aspects of the brand's 'personality' (e.g. innovative, functional, old-fashioned, exclusive, frivolous, fun).

Positioning studies begin with determining a relevant set of products. The criterion for inclusion is that they must be perceived by customers to be choice alternatives. Then a list of determinant attributes is generated; that is a list of attributes that are salient or the most important to customers in discriminating between the alternatives. With this framework customers' perceptions and preferences are then collected. This could be by survey using a structured questionnaire. Respondents would be asked to scale their feelings about each product on each attribute. They could also be asked their preferred level for each attribute. The output can be portrayed in a diagram (sometimes called a brand map or a perceptual map) showing the locations of each product against the attributes (the dimensions) and relative to the preferred level (the ideal point). This is most readily understood if the analysis is restricted to two dimensions. For example, for a food product the dimensions might be nourishment and calory count and respondents could rate all the brands they know in the category from high to low on these. Some brands may be seen to be highly nourishing with a high calory count and some not so nourishing with a low calory count. Illustrations can be found in Moore and Pessemier (1993) and in Urban and Hauser (1993).

Such a study would show the proximity of, or the distance between, the perceived positions of the products considered. This might show the positions to be crowded in one area, or well spaced. If an ideal point, that is the customers' preferred position, is introduced then the relative distance of each product from this ideal can be measured. If these relative distances accord reasonably with the relative market shares of the products then it could be assumed that the dimensions chosen are a fair representation of the way customers choose in this market. Generally it would be expected that the higher market shares would be won by products nearer to the ideal point.

Customers may be far from unanimous about these perceptions and preferences. If the observations were widely scattered then further research would be needed to understand how customers make their evaluations, and perhaps other dimensions might be tried. If there were several clusters of preferences, each in a different part of the map, this might indicate different market segments. In the food example just above there could be one group preferring a very nourishing product with a low calory count, and another group wanting something nourishing with a high calory count. Mapping product positions against these two ideal points might then reveal one segment to be well served with many products, but an opening for a new product near the other ideal point where there may be no major existing brands.

Positioning strategy depends upon the choice of an appropriate base. This base must be relevant and important to customers and related to how they make choices in that product field. It should also attempt to distance the brand from the positions of rivals. Wind (1982) offers six bases: product feature, benefits, use occasion, user category, against another product or by dissociation from all the other products. Crawford (1997) adds parentage (. . . because of where it comes from), manufacture (. . . because of how it is made), and endorsement (. . . because people you respect say it is good).

Selecting an appropriate positioning can make the difference between success and failure. It determines what the organisation tells the market about the product, whom it tells and how it tells it. Motorcycle producers take various positions. Piaggio's Vespa scooter is aimed at young riders and latterly at women. Susuki is also now targeting women as a distinctive segment. Some of the most expensive machines are now aimed at older men with a revived interest in motorcycling and higher discretionary income. For most products there may be a host of features, benefits and applications; few, if any, products have a single feature, a singular benefit and one narrow application. Choosing from among the possibilities can lead to creative and unique solutions and consequentially to a highly differentiated strategy. It can also result in costly mistakes with products being positioned in strange ways that consumers neither understand nor find credible. As the market grows and matures it may become necessary to consider repositioning. The original differentiation could become less effective as competitors crowd in, or as new types of buyers with different expectations adopt the product. A repositioning exercise could focus upon some reformulation of the product, some change to the image projected, a realignment of the segments targeted or a change to the distribution channels employed.

Competing with other products

Deschamps and Nayak (1995) in their best-selling book on products and brands *Product Juggernauts: How Companies Mobilize To Generate A Stream of Winners* argued that one factor differentiates great companies from the others and that is the products they sell. In a study of leading products they argued that even in basic industries such as chemicals and minerals, suppliers always found ways of differentiating their products from those of their competitors. Deschamps and Nayak identified five distinct product strategies that firms have used in competition, these are shown in Table 11.1.

As products compete with one another they are thus compared with one another. This leads to selection criteria and buyer behaviour. The later is a subject and a textbook in its own right and beyond the scope of this book. It is necessary to note, however, that most models of buyer behaviour recognise two kinds of factors – objective and subjective. Objective factors may or may not be tangible but they must be quantifiable and measurable. By contrast, subjective factors are intangible and are influenced by attitudes, beliefs, experience and associations, which the decision maker holds towards the product. If we leave the subjective criteria to the behavioural sciences and turn our attention to the objective criteria it soon becomes clear that to discriminate between products a performance criteria is required. Many of us would recognise such a list of factors, for we have probably drawn up such a list when going to purchase a personal computer or a car. For the most part, however, such performance criteria do not play a large part in our buying decisions. In industrial markets the reverse is the case and such criteria are the norm. Indeed, in many instances buyers will forward their performance criteria to a list of suppliers and await a quote detailing price, warranties, delivery, etc. Table 11.2 shows typical product performance criteria commonly used by buyers in assessing a product.

Objective product characteristics enable firms to be grouped together so that the whole economy may be classified. The Standard Industrial Classification Manual was first published in the United States in 1945. SIC codes now form part of an international system, making it possible to make precise comparisons between products and services between countries.

Table 11.1 Product strategies

Product strategy	Firm	How?
Product proliferation	Honda Procter & Gamble	On entering the European motorcycle market Honda offered an enormous wide range of engine sizes. When launching their disposable nappy Proctor & Gamble offered a wide range of sizes and gender specifc products.
Value	BMW Toyota	BMW offer a high quality product with emphasis on reliability. It is not the most expensive and emphasis is on value for money. Similarly Toyota use the same product strategy in different market segments.
Design (outward appearance)	Sony Apple	Both Sony and Apple emphasise good design in all of their products, frequently pioneering unique styles and offering elegance and easy-to-use products.
Innovation	3M Merck Phillips	3M and more recently Merck and Phillips have developed reputations for product innovation. This is based on a strong technology culture. This is distinct from design, in that while the product may incorporate a new outward appearance it is the use of new technology that is the focus of the strategy.
Service	American Express Tesco	Both American Express and Tesco continue to be at the forefront of service development. Historically American Express pioneered many service offerings. More recently Tesco (UK retail grocer) compete by continually offering new and improved services to their customers. Their competitors always seem to be trying to catch up.

Table 11.2 Product performance criteria

Product performance factors

1	Performance in operation	9	Safety in use
2	Reliability	10	Ease of maintenance
3	Sale price	11	Parts availability and cost
4	Efficient delivery	12	Attractive appearance/shape
5	Technical sophistication	13	Flexibility and adaptability in use
6	Quality of after-sales service	14	Advertising and promotion
7	Durability	15	Operator comfort
8	Ease of use	16	Design

Source: M. Baker and S. Hart (1989) *Product Strategy and Management*, Prentice Hall, Harlow.

Pause for thought

To what extent is it possible to have several different product strategies within the same firm?

Many products may appear objectively similar such as washing machines. This group of products are often made to a standard size (typically 600mm wide; 500mm depth and 1000mm high). Other performance criteria such as load capacity and spin speed can all be compared; but subjective information is supplied to the customer via branding. The process of branding can take many forms and is not restricted to physical products. Moreover, successful brands are not easily copied. For example, Dyson did not file for patents in the United States, yet through branding has been able to offer a unique product to consumers that competitors have struggled to imitate.

Managing brands

To many, especially the cynical, the word brand is associated with a collection of gimmicks and a lot of advertising to convince the public to buy one manufacturer's product rather than another. To others brands are simply products with brand names or logos. This is partly correct, but there is more to a brand than simply advertising. Even after a huge advertising expenditure a firm would have very few customers if the product in question was faulty or of poor quality. Brands are commonly described in the literature as a multiple-level pyramid, with basic physical attributes forming the base, upon which rests the tangible benefits, the emotional benefits, the brand personality characteristics, with the soul or core of the brand at its apex. Moreover, its not just the marketing function that contributes to the brand as Illustration 11.3 Shows.

A successful brand combines an effective product, distinctive identity and added values as perceived by customers. For some brands that have been managed effectively this can translate into a life of over 100 years and over 200 years in some cases. Table 11.3 illustrates just how long some of the most well known brands have been with us.

Brands and blind product tests

There has been substantial research on the subject of whether consumers are able to recognise brands that they buy frequently from intrinsic attributes alone (taste or smell). The results reveal that from cigarettes to peanut butter and from cola to beer subjects are not capable of recognising their usual brand (Riezebos, 2003). Given these findings one might ask why do consumers continue to pay a premium for particular brands when they cannot taste the difference. Illustration 11.3 discusses the role of brand value.

Table 11.3 Market introduction of brands

Twining	1706	Adidas	1920
Schweppes	1798	Volvo	1926
Levis	1850	Durex	1929
Heineken	1864	Mars	1932
Agfa	1873	McDonald's	1937
Coca-Cola	1886	Playboy	1953
Philips	1891	Benetton	1965
Pepsi-Cola	1898	Nike	1972
Persil	1907	Body Shop	1976
Nivea	1911	Swatch	1982
Boeing	1916	Eternity	1988

Illustration 11.3

The importance of 'brand value'

Price seems so self-evidently to be the reason why goods and services sell that marketers must occasionally feel there is not a great deal more they can add. In sectors as diverse as airlines, call centres, vehicles, electronics, supermarkets and public sector cleaning contracts, low prices attract customers – it is as simple as that.

However, there remain clear limitations on what can be achieved with a relentless focus on low prices. 'If you are going to rely on price as a headline differential, the problem is it leaves you few places to go because there is always someone more clever or more stupid than you', says Mike Snapes, executive chairman of Hillary's Group, the window-blinds specialist.

He argues that in the market for blinds, where so many products 'work and last', quality is no longer a differentiator.

All companies must deliver a satisfactory quality at an attractive price. But beyond that, the aim is to generate a kind of emotional attachment to a name, a level of confidence in a proposition. 'Repeat business is far cheaper to generate than new business, so it is a question of what you surround the product with – the product is now about the overall experience of buying. Do the fitters keep their promises, do they sort out problems quickly, is the process "low hassle"?'

Even in less mature markets, influential voices question how far a good reputation can be built on price alone. Norman Rose, director general of the Business Services Association, an organisation representing companies which provide public services, says there is a popular saying among contractors: the best tender is always the second lowest.

The price has to be right – it has to be affordable and attractive. But times have changed since the old days of compulsory competitive tendering in the 1980s, when the lowest price always won the contract.

'Nowadays, while nobody has money to spare, they [public-sector customers] know that if they just go for the lowest price, they are unlikely to be satisfied.'

A lack of repeat business can be a sign of trying to do things on the cheap, he says.

'If a company only gets first-time deals, it says a lot about them. There is also a growing consideration of "best over the long term".'

Price attracts, but it does not necessarily retain. Raman Roy, chairman and managing director of Wipro Spectramind, India's largest call-centre outsourcing company, has repeatedly emphasised it is not solely lower costs that are spurring the Indian call-centre market. 'They will come for the lower price, but they will stay for the quality of service', he claims.

According to Accenture, the consultancy, the principal reason why the United States has witnessed rising personal incomes and falling spending has little to do with pricing and everything to do with poor customer contact and a lack of innovation.

A survey carried out at the end of 2002 found that customers would cheerfully spend more if companies offered products and services that were 'meaningful' to them. High on the list were issues such as 'improved well-being', 'providing intellectual stimulation' and 'helping people connect with friends and family'.

The study called on companies to reconnect with their customer base by channelling their energies into three specific areas: 'Entry-level luxury', 'life solutions' and innovations in customer interaction.

'Price innovation is not the ideal strategy in an economic environment where consumers are willing to spend more money on products and services that deliver meaningful innovation', says the report, *Consumer Attitudes Towards Innovation*.

Innovation is invariably a longer-term aim. In the shorter term, many companies would far rather pull off what Interbrew achieved with Stella Artois: selling an everyday French beer to the British as a 'reassuringly expensive' premium product.

Dr Sue Eccles, lecturer in marketing at Lancaster University, says the way most consumers remain touchingly wedded to the idea that there is a clear relationship between price and quality guarantees a constant diet of perception management.

Collective assumptions are shaky enough for companies to exploit: 'Price and quality are all to do with the perspective of the consumer', she says. 'There is a widespread belief that price reflects something objective, but that assumption may let us down as any number of blind tests tend to show.'

Price, says Dr Eccles, may be the most firmly established notion in the mind of many customers when they make a decision. Quality is more ethereal – 'acceptable' quality is often good enough. But invariably consumers are willing to pay more to reduce the 'risk factors' involved in a purchase.

When buying something significant, such as a car or clothes, customers are turned away from a low price/acceptable quality product because of social risks. A premium is attached to products with a low social risk/desirability value. The decision becomes one of identity. This explains why issues of 'brand value' and even 'brand experience' play such a dominant role in corporate life.

Calls to increase pricing transparency have produced reams of new information that is easily comparable on the internet; as a result, consumers are better informed.

Yet the arena of perception, the emotional and psychological space inhabited by products, remains a critical factor in the marketing mix.

'Selling is increasingly about reinforcing messages around the price–quality trade-off', says Dr Eccles.

Source: S. Overell, 'The importance of "brand value"', www.FT.com, 19 May 2003. Reprinted with permission.

Branding system

Figure 11.3

Mudumbi, Doyle and Wong (1997) suggest that branding is based on random utility theory, where customers form preferences based on their perception of attributes. Decisions are then made upon these preferences with customers selecting the product with highest expected value or utility. This overview of the branding system is captured in Figure 11.3, with the degree of branding affecting buyer perception and attitudes, buyer behaviour and brand financial performance, and thereby affecting branding strategy.

The brand manager and the firm have to decide the extent to which they wish to invest in their brand and thereby develop it. Such considerations will involve all aspects of the marketing mix and in turn will obviously affect buyer perception. Buyers will then consider the benefits and values that are being promoted and make choices. These choices will affect the returns to the firm and will determine investment decisions for the future of the brand. This is the subject of brand strategy, which we turn to now.

Brand strategy

Brand strategy is the spearhead of the organisation's competitive intentions. It carries the company or product name into the market and shows how it is positioning itself to compete. It involves choices between having no brand name at all, so that the product is sold as a commodity, and the attempt to develop a distinctive brand name with a distinctive set of associations and expectations. In the latter case there are further options. The product could be sold to another party for them to place their trademark or branding on it, or alternatively the complete product, or major components, could be bought-in and then company-branded. There are more choices with the brand name itself. Should the company have a single brand for all its products, such as Kellogg's, or a range of apparently unconnected brands, such as Procter & Gamble? Should it establish a corporate brand as an umbrella with a series of sub-brands under the umbrella, such as Ford? Or should it have a mixed brand strategy with elements of all these approaches?

On one level such consideration might appear to be quite trivial. What's in a name? Think about chocolate confectionary. If Cadbury's decides to launch a new chocolate bar with no Cadbury's identification then would market acceptance be achieved? Will consumers trust it? Will they take the risk and make a first purchase? In any event they probably would not be given the chance to buy because it would not gain sufficient acceptance by distributors. It might achieve limited distribution but it may take a great deal of time to reach full national, let alone international, distribution.

The brand name itself is really a summary; it can stand for a great deal more. It can represent the sum of what people know about the product and its usefulness, quality and availability. It can be surrounded with associations, negative or positive, about how it can be used, where it can be used and the occasions on which it is used. It can be symbolic and loaded with imagery about the kinds of people who use the brand. For some well known brands the few letters in their names can be triggers to wide-ranging perceptions. Focus groups can talk for hours with just the prompt of a few brand names.

It is not just in consumer markets that this power of the brand name is apparent. Inspection of any trade magazine reveals its prevalence in all kinds of markets, and component makers now also attempt to ensure that their brand is evident in advertising and packaging.

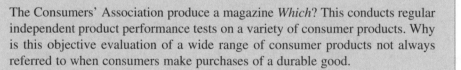

Pause for thought

The Consumers' Association produce a magazine *Which*? This conducts regular independent product performance tests on a variety of consumer products. Why is this objective evaluation of a wide range of consumer products not always referred to when consumers make purchases of a durable good.

Given the significance of brands it is surprising that so many firms make careless mistakes with regard to their brands. According to Helen Rubinstein many firms do not recognise how their departments affect the delivery of the brand. Figure 11.4 helps to show how brands interact with different parts of the organisation. At the centre of this wheel is the finance department as it is guided by the chief executive, who sets financial targets and determines the business objectives. Clearly the finance department has a significant impact on the brand development in particular the degree of investment in brand development.

Brand extensions

A brand extension is the use of an established brand name on a new product in the same product field or in a related field. The brand name might also be stretched to an unrelated product field. A simple brand extension would be when a new or unconventional size is brought out, so that the original brand name is given a prefix (e.g. Giant, Jumbo, Fun), or for some technical products this could be a new alphanumeric code.

Internal and external brand contacts

Source: H. Rubinstein (1996) 'Brand first management', *Journal of Marketing Management*, Vol. 12, 269–80.

Figure 11.4

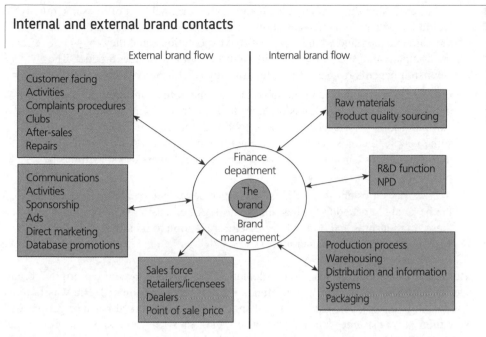

Operating within the same product field, but attempting to attract a new market segment, the extension might have a modified design and there could be added words to the brand name indicating whom it is intended for, such as for men or for women. Daily newspapers extended publication to Sunday and have branded sections, all carrying the original brand name in some way. In the case of an extension to a business computer package it could specify a new application type in the branding.

More radical extensions occur when the brand is stretched or carried into unrelated product fields. Some newspapers, such as the *Daily Telegraph*, started direct marketing operations selling their own brand of clothing. Several fashion houses, such as Boss and Calvin Klein place their brand name wide and far across a range of luxury goods. Wilkinson Sword sell razors and gardening tools under the same brand. Canon market cameras and copiers. Philips use their brand name in diverse electrical and electronic industries. And the Virgin brand name is carried on an airline, a railway, a cola, a retail chain and in insurance.

The rationale behind a brand extension strategy is to take advantage of potential carry-over effects from the original brand. If the original is both well known and well regarded then it probably has a pool of goodwill among consumers and distributors. The extension would be planned to dip into that pool. Three kinds of carry-over effects may be relevant:

1 *Expertise*. If the original had established and maintained itself, probably over a fairly long period, as the best available for that application or usage, then it is likely to have accrued a reputation for high-level competence in its field. Users may feel very comfortable and assured in making repeat buys. This may have been promoted actively and the company may have sought to have itself perceived to be the acknowledged consultant in its area.

An extension that was complementary to the original, and of the same quality, would have its introduction eased owing to a halo-effect. Consumers would know the name already and would have positive expectations, and they may believe that the company that they trusted would not bring out a poor new product. The extension benefits from a trusting relationship established by the original.

2 *Prestige*. Some brands have enviable images and some consumers may believe that these images confer status on those that use them. Some brands benefit from particular kinds of associations and symbolism and they may have become, for some people, the only acceptable product to have in some situations. This does not just apply to consumer markets, organisational buyers can sometimes be just as subjective.

3 *Access*. A well-established original may have developed and held good access to the best suppliers and to the best distributors. An extension would capitalise upon these relationships and it may have a better reception to its initial launch than a new brand that had no reputation.

But brand extensions can also be problematic. The connection with the original brand can be strained and the carry-over effects diminished or eliminated. Bic was famous for its ballpoint pens. Its extension to disposable lighters worked because people still saw them as consistent with the original in being inexpensive, disposable, functional products. But its extension into perfumes failed. Guinness withdrew its Guinness Bitter, and once it did try an apparently contradictory idea with a new version of its original stout called Guinness Light.

In some markets brand extensions are added which contribute little and at times they can be harmful to the original. They can clutter the market and confuse the consumers. A series of lacklustre extensions, and no really new product development, can undermine the credibility of the company among distributors, customers and city analysts.

Market entry

Decisions about how and when to enter the market can make a substantial difference to the new product's prospects. Timing the entry to the market can make or break an innovation. Thoughtless positioning, with little or no distinction, can be harmful to the long-term prospects, whereas astute positioning can have very positive effect. Entry scale, and in particular obtaining and maintaining a strong market presence with high levels of market exposure, can ease the product introduction and stimulate the market's evolution. These three factors are explored in this section.

Entry timing has received particular attention. Commonly it is assumed that early entry is desirable and there is evidence that 'pioneers' accrue 'first mover advantages'. They are able to influence customer expectations and shape how customers make evaluations of products in the new field. They can suggest to consumers the criteria they should employ in making their judgements, and products that are later entrants are then evaluated on that basis. Pioneers can set the standards, establish a distinctive quality position, take the lead in the continuing evolution of the technology, and gain valuable experience in manufacturing and distribution (Buzzell and Gale, 1987). In many mature markets the leaders are those that were the pioneering entrants. However, being too early can be as much of a disadvantage as being too late. A weak, tentative first mover, without the motivation or resources to grow the market, can spend years making losses only to be superseded by a stronger 'fast follower'. Green *et al.* (1995) caution that 'simple nostrums, such as early entry is best, can be dangerous oversimplifications'.

Those that come to the market early, but after the pioneer, can be successful. Procter & Gamble was not the pioneer in disposable napkins or in biological washing powders, but its Pampers and Ariel brands dominate these markets. Japanese competitors displaced Ampex, the pioneer in VCR technology. Commenting on this *The Economist* (1996) said,

> *In many cases, including Ampex's, the first mover was content to have pioneered the technology, believing its breakthrough was enough to bring market leadership. Micro Instrumentation and Telemetry Systems invented the PC in the mid-1970s, but ceded market leadership to latecomers (such as Apple Computer and IBM) that invested heavily to turn the PC into a mass-market product.*

Positioning decisions can be influential and the digital camera industry illustrates this point. Eastman Kodak was the first firm to produce a digital camera for consumers in 1994. It offered 24-bit colour and the ability to connect to a desktop computer via a simple serial cable to download images directly. Today, the market is crowded by firms such as: Fuji, Cannon, Olympus, Hewlett Packard, Nikon, Minolta. According to the *New Zealand Herald* (2004) Sony is the market leader in terms of market share, but Kodak continue to be at the forefront of technology developments. Demand for digital cameras, which record images on memory chips instead of film, continues to grow as consumers become more comfortable with capturing, storing and printing their images. Sony has filed a patent infringement suit against Kodak, intensifying the fight between the two companies. Sony's claims come about a month after Kodak sued Sony alleging it infringed 10 of Kodak's patents related to capturing, printing and storing digital images. Eastman Kodak pioneered this market but has not dominated it. Indeed, the competitors reacted so swiftly that there was little to distinguish the products in the market place.

Scale of entry affects how the product performs and how the market evolves. High levels of effort and resource commitment can stimulate market evolution and a critical factor in this is market exposure. The study by Green *et al.* (1995: 4) of the word processing software market found that,

> *in markets similar to the word processing market explored here, in which basic features and evaluative criteria are quickly established, high levels of market exposure (particularly magazine coverage, but also advertising) during the entry period is associated with a product's long-term performance.*

Getting prospective customers talking and thinking about the product is vital. This may mean the establishment of a strong 'market presence' through press articles, advertising, participation at exhibitions and a highly visible presence in distribution channels.

Launch and continuing improvement

From a business perspective the innovation is not a success until it has established and fixed its place in the market. That depends upon how it is launched, its reception by customers and the continuing attention given to its improvement. The earlier discussion of market entry showed some key factors relevant to the launch strategy, but the act of putting the product onto the market is not an end: it is the beginning of a new phase. Close and constant monitoring of the reactions of customers, distributors and competitors is required to inform the proceeding strategy.

Having the product on the market allows the validation or the rejection of important estimates or assumptions about customer attitudes and behaviour that would have been made during development. It could also reveal unanticipated problems or opportunities. What do customers now understand about the product and has comprehension of its benefits spread in the predicted way? Are there still difficulties? Are they using the product in the ways envisaged? Have customers found problems in using the product that had not come to light before? Do they use it as much as expected and as frequently as expected? Are any potential customers holding back because they see risk in adopting the product, perhaps delaying their acceptance in anticipation of further developments in the technology? Are there enough of those for it to be a problem? Do customers perceive the benefits that were promised, and are these as important to them as hoped originally? Are the benefits now seen as interesting but irrelevant? And are there any problems with the product itself that customers have revealed? Unravelling these questions and dealing effectively with their implications will condition how the prospects for the product evolve.

Many assumptions will also have been built into the operations and marketing plans. Do they stand up? Was the desired positioning achieved, and was that the right positioning decision? Is it now too narrowly defined on a relatively unimportant dimension? Was it conveyed appropriately to distributors and customers? Were the pricing and distribution plans appropriate? Are customer problems being handled efficiently and is the right level of customer service in place? On all these issues the organisation should be learning and responding, tracking and improving.

Thought about how the product and the market will evolve from the launch might give attention to three areas.

1 *Product platform evolution and brand extensions.* What is the next generation of the product? Can the basic product platform be enhanced and should this lead to brand extensions?

2 *Market evolution.* How rapidly will the innovation be diffused? Will there be a lengthy introductory period before any rapid growth? Will new market segments become apparent or can they be created? How should the geographic scope be widened?

3 *Competitive evolution.* How soon will competitors arrive? How predictable is their entry? What distinction, if any, will they bring? What kind of positioning and entry scale are they considering? What entry barriers are in place to deter rivals?

Inauguration is not enough. To be effective the innovation must be well founded in the market and receive customer acceptance, if not their acclaim, and plans need to be made to secure, deepen and widen its market position from the initial launch.

Withdrawing products

Pruning the product range can be an important part of managing the portfolio. Chronic poor sales performance would be a first indicator that consideration should be given to withdrawing products. Prior to that decision careful assessments would be needed of the reasons for the poor performance, of the possible future trends and of the costs and benefits of continuing or withdrawing. In Coca-Cola's case with its bottled water brand Dasani it seems the firm had few options other than to organise a complete product recall as Illustration 11.4 shows.

 Illustration 11.4

FT

Dasani recall leaves Coke dangling over murky water

David Blaine is not the only American export to have misread the UK market in recent months. With the Dasani purified water debacle, Coca-Cola has emulated the US illusionist.

Just weeks after Mr Blaine was ridiculed by Londoners for dangling in a box above the River Thames, a stunt that was viewed more generously in his homeland, Coca-Cola has found itself pilloried for attempting to sell Dasani, an enhanced tap water that was deemed perfectly acceptable in the US.

'Sidcup Spring', the mockers called it, reflecting both the location of the bottling plant and the episode of *Only Fools and Horses*, the classic television comedy show, in which tap water is cheekily marketed under the brand name 'Peckham Spring'.

Whereas Mr Blaine completed his trick as planned, however, Coca-Cola has given its critics fresh ammunition by rushing into a voluntary product recall after discovering that Dasani contained illegal levels of bromate, a chemical that could increase the risk of cancer.

The unanswered question last night was how far up the corporate ladder the consequences would reach. The fault certainly lies with Coca-Cola itself, rather than Coca-Cola

Figure 11.5 Dasani

05/05/2004

►

Enterprises, the member of its bottling network that actually makes Dasani in the UK.

The bromate problem was a consequence of added ingredients supplied by Coca-Cola in the same way that it supplies syrupy concentrate to bottlers for them to make cola.

The legal limit for bromate content is 10 parts per billion, Coca-Cola said. The Dasani it tested prior to the recall contained as many as 25 parts.

The Food Standards Agency, which regulates food safety in the UK, said there was no immediate risk to public health.

It also said that the increased cancer risk to anyone who had drunk Dasani was likely to be 'very small'. Coca-Cola has a free telephone help line for consumers at 0800 227711.

Coca-Cola sells more than 200 million cases of Dasani annually around the world. The company said it was conducting similar tests on Dasani in other markets as a precautionary measure.

Coca-Cola Enterprises said the recall would not affect its balance sheet. The company said it had already tested its Dasani water in North America and found 'no issue at all' concerning bromate.

Coca-Cola said this incident should not hurt the Dasani water brand as 'consumers will understand the facts that this is an isolated incident . . . and it won't have implications outside the UK.'

However, it said it was too early to say whether Dasani would be relaunched in the UK. 'Clearly the focus right now is on withdrawing it', an official said.

Nor was there any immediate official estimate of how much the recall would cost.

The withdrawal began yesterday and was likely to be 80 to 85 per cent complete within 24 hours.

But while the cost of the withdrawal might not be great, the implications for Coca-Cola's attempt to reduce its reliance on sugary carbonated drinks – a particular target for criticism in the obesity debate – could be substantial.

Coca-Cola still has hopes of expanding Dasani in Europe but its ambitions for the UK may now be unrealisable.

Allyson Stewart-Allen, a London-based marketing adviser, said: 'It is now going to be next to impossible for Coke to relaunch Dasani in the UK.'

Neil Hedges, chairman of Fishburn Hedges, the public relations and corporate reputation consultancy, also felt a UK relaunch 'may be just too much for such a new product'.

This is in spite of the fact that Coca-Cola has followed best practice in product recalls by acting swiftly.

'They have done all the right things in terms of withdrawing everything very promptly', he said.

Source: A. Jones and B. Liu (2004) 'Dasani leaves Coke dangling over murky water', www.FT.com, 19 March.

Investigations could first focus on how well the organisation had managed its efforts. It may have lost market share, in which case a series of questions could be posed. Is manufacturing cost out of line with others in the industry? Has there been any decline in quality relative to rivals? Has the product kept up with any evolution in the technology? Have marketing efforts tailed off? Fixing any problems that emerge from these analyses might give the product a new lease of life, and this may be associated with a repositioning exercise. However, if nothing significant is signalled then other possibilities would need to be examined.

If market share was constant but sales were none the less in chronic decline, then this could indicate that the industry, or the particular product form, was passed maturity and entering decline. Predictions about the future industry trend might confirm a pessimistic outlook and the firm would have to decide if it should withdraw quickly, more gradually or try to maintain a position in what may be a much smaller industry in the future.

Exit costs would feature strongly. There may be a complex manufacturing economy within the company with shared processes involving many products. The arbitrary removal of one may throw into jeopardy the economics of the remainder, and so it could be that the product was continued so long as it made some contribution to overheads. The firm may also become an involuntary survivor in the industry because contractual obligations tied it in. These contracts may be with suppliers, customers, distributors or other partners in the network. An inflexible manufacturing plant could also tie it. Reputation could be another issue. The company may not wish to undermine the confidence placed in it by customers or distributors. For example, customers may have high switching costs if they had to buy alternative products and may become resentful if they dropped the product. If the product is part of a wide portfolio then the whole range might suffer if the organisation's reputation were to be damaged.

Alternatively the firm may decide to make an active commitment to stay in the declining industry in anticipation of increasing market share.

Managing mature products

As growth slows and the level of competition intensifies profit margins will come under pressure. Product and brand managers will need to make decisions on the medium- and long-term futures of the brand. Mature products usually make up the majority of a firm's source of cash generative lines (hence the term cash cow in portfolio planning). Profit margins may decline due to increasing number of competitive products, cost economies used up, decline in product distinctiveness, etc. Frequently with the loss-of-profit margins industries tend to stabilise, with a set of entrenched competitors. Indeed, the low margins act as a barrier to entry and those firms remaining in an industry can generate sustained profits over a long period in the maturity and decline stages of a product's life cycle. For example, the 35-mm film processing industry is declining rapidly with the introduction of digital photography. Soon there will probably be a few suppliers only remaining in this once enormous market. Agfa, Fuji and Kodak will probably establish positions in this declining market. Indeed, within the maturity and decline stages of a product's life cycle Schofield and Arnold (1988) distinguish four phases to the mature phase of the traditional product life cycle:

- late growth;
- early maturity;
- mid-maturity; and
- late maturity.

They argue that firms need to be able to recognise the early signs of late growth usually characterised by aggressive price cutting. This continues into the early stages of maturity when the market becomes saturated with little or no opportunity for growth. At this stage firms are forced into taking tactical decisions regarding additional services and promotions. It is also important for firms to be vigilant for changes that take place in the market concerning segments: some segments may decline rapidly while others may still be growing. As the market moves towards mid- and late maturity customers are seen as more discerning and less loyal. Schofield and Arnold argue that several strategies are available to firms managing mature businesses and there are several positive factors:

- price is not important to everyone and probably not to the majority;
- industries that evolve gradually offer time and space for careful strategy selection;
- the market is stable;
- niches once secured require fewer resources to defend them; and
- sustainable real or perceived advantage in cost or performance will attract new business.

Case study

The role of design in the development of a wheelchair for cerebral palsy sufferers[1]

Introduction

Having a new idea and creating a potentially new product is a rewarding experience in itself. This is even more so when the product you have designed and developed can relieve suffering for disabled children. However, even in these instances many product and business decisions still have to be taken. The impact of manufacturing costs on eventual profits can affect considerably the decision about whether the product, despite its apparent benefits, is produced. The commercial viability of any project has to be carefully considered and this is the subject of the following case study, which is based on the film 'Designing for Market' produced by TV Choice (1995).

Cerebral Palsy

Cerebral palsy is a broad term used to describe injuries to the brain, which usually occur at birth or prior to birth. The effect of the condition is a lack of physical control of limbs and difficulty in speaking. Sufferers of the condition were previously referred to as spastics. The term spastic

referred to the muscle spasms that characterise the condition. It is estimated that about 20,000 children suffer from cerebral palsy.

For cerebral palsy sufferers the muscles within the body do not support the bones. In childhood this results in uncontrollable limbs, but later in life the bones themselves often become deformed. These deformities become fixed around puberty. Indeed, buckled and twisted spines are not uncommon in adults with cerebral palsy. Keeping the spine straight as the child grows can help to prevent deformity in the future. It is this theory, together with many years of work as a physiotherapist with children suffering from cerebral palsy, that Pauline Pope developed a wheel-chair that helped to keep the spine straight. Conventional chairs do not provide sufficient support for the body and can contribute to deformed spines as the children grow older. Pope's design was based around the 'motor-cycle' seating position, whereby the seat forces the person to lean forward onto the petrol tank. A similar position is achieved when one sits on a chair with legs astride the back support and chin on the back of the chair (see Figure 11.6).

[1] This case has been written as a basis for class discussion rather than to illustrate effective or ineffective managerial administrative behaviour. It has been prepared from a variety of published sources, as indicated, and from observations.

Figure 11.6 The concept upon which SAM is based centres on the 'motorcycle' seating position which helps to keep the spine straight

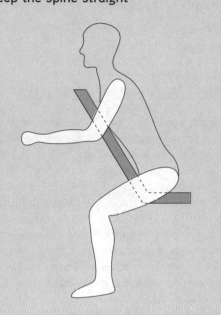

Following many years of experiment and help from an engineer, a successful wheel-chair was produced that contained a moulded seat and chest support. This enabled the child to learn to move their arms, legs and head. Pauline decided to call her chair: Seating and Mobility (SAM). Pauline was pleased with the final design, which provided the necessary support to the child's spine. Unfortunately only six could be manufactured each year on a 'one-off' basis, with each chair being tailored to fit each child.

From tailor-made product to mass-produced product

Armed with a firm belief in the idea as well as the physical product, Pauline decided to approach wheel-chair manufacturers to see whether they would be interested in the large-scale manufacture of the product. 'Sunrise Medical', one of the largest power wheel-chair manufacturers in the United Kingdom, soon expressed interest in the design and signed an agreement with Pauline to explore the possibility of manufacturing the product.

The company was a natural partner for this product as it was already operating in the wheel-chair market and could use its present product platform to develop SAM (see pp. 000–000). One of the first difficulties faced by the company was how to convert a tailor-made product to a mass-produced product which, by definition, is not tailored to individual needs. With the help of computer aided design technology, designers at the company eventually developed a prototype product that incorporated an adjustable seat that could be altered to fit different sizes. The design had several basic components that could be assembled to the required size; in this case foam wedges were used to provide the necessary support.

Commercial viability

Concurrent with the development of the prototype wheel-chair, the marketing manager began to devise a market research study to explore the viability of the product for the company. It was clear to all those who had seen the wheel-chair in use that it brought help to some of the most needy in society. However, it was also clear to everyone involved in the development of the product that the decision about manufacture of the product would depend largely on whether sufficient revenue could be generated to produce a profit for the company. The costs involved in manufacturing suggested a break-even price of approximately £1,500. Revenue generation would depend on two variables: volume and profit margin. Two questions needed to be answered:

- What volume was possible?
- What profit margin was possible on such a product?

There was one additional factor that needed to be considered, and that was the views of several key individuals within the company. As with all new ideas, not necessarily new product ideas, there will usually be resistance from some quarters to any form of change. In this case some of the engineers and designers had come across similar product ideas in the past and, following lengthy explorations, these had been abandoned due to poor revenue projections. Also, the eventual decision regarding manufacture or not would rest with the managing director; initial reactions suggested he was sceptical that the project would be successful.

Product testing

After approximately nine months of further trials and testing the company produced a full-scale prototype product. Pauline, who had been involved closely with the development of the prototype, was pleased with the new SAM. A test run was set up with a 9-year-old girl who was suffering from cerebral palsy. SAM had an electrical power base that propelled the chair and was controlled by a hand operated joy stick. The new design contained an improved contoured seat and extra chest support. After a few minutes of practising with the chair and the controls, SAM was given a ringing endorsement by this young cerebral palsy sufferer. The product was clearly a technical success, but whether the company would be able to generate any revenue from it was still to be established.

Market testing

As the months passed the team were coming under increasing pressure to submit their findings on whether 'Sunrise Medical' should continue with the project. The managing director would soon have to make a decision about the release of further funds. The team decided to undertake some market research to gather feedback from potential customers. Ten specialist Cerebral Palsy centres were identified across the United Kingdom. SAM was taken to each of these centres to collect information on three key areas:

1 interest in the product;
2 likelihood of purchase; and
3 amount willing to pay.

This information should enable the team to decide whether the product could generate sufficient revenue. Unfortunately the results were not encouraging. There was enormous interest in the product; many people including physiotherapists and parents of cerebral palsy sufferers had not seen a product like this before. Many, especially the specialist centres, said they would probably purchase one, and would be willing to pay between £1,500–£2,000. The final figure, however, was disappointing. Sales estimates for the whole market was 150 units. This figure was much smaller than had been expected. The company needed sufficient profit margin to ensure it was able to recover design costs, tooling costs and packaging and distribution costs.

Conclusions

Many readers may find this story disturbing. The fact that due to profit considerations a product, that can help disabled children, was not manufactured on a large scale is sad indeed. This, however, is not a unique case. In the pharmaceutical industry profit considerations lie at the 'heart' of any decision to proceed from research to expensive clinical trials. Moreover, the decision to conduct expensive research into cures for certain diseases such as malaria, will be heavily influenced by whether the intended recipient is able to pay and what the recipient is likely to pay? Many pharmaceutical companies are currently investing large sums of money into research into AIDS. This is not least because many of the intended recipients are in the affluent developed world.

In many ways this case study tells a simple story. That is, it matters little whether the new product is technically advanced or offers significant improvement over existing products, what is important is market demand. The business has a responsibility to its investors – not to take unnecessary risks. Without any evidence of demand the business decided SAM was an unnecessary risk.

Everett Roger's adoption theory (Rogers, 1995) can be used to explain why the market research revealed low expected sales. Rogers argued that first-time purchasers of new products could be classified according to the innovativeness of their adoption behaviour. He presented the adoption behaviour of purchasers of a new product as a time-dependent phenomenon that could be plotted within a normal distribution curve. He labelled the first two segments innovators and early adopters respectively. In this case study these groups did not adopt the product. There was some resistance from experts and physiotherapists working in the field. This was due to lack of knowledge of the product and the benefits that it could bring. Also the product lacked any explicit support from the professional bodies in the field such as the British Medical Council (BAM), the Royal College of Nursing (RCN) or the Chartered Society of Physiotherapists.

Furthermore, there was limited, if any, promotion of the product. This contributed to the low expected sales. The market, in this case the cerebral palsy centres, did not appreciate fully the benefits of SAM and probably needed educating. Clinical support from research papers or health bodies would have helped to assuage some of the scepticism in the market. The pharmaceutical industry has realised this and they are fully aware that in order to persuade general practitioners to recommend their products they have to point to clinical trials and research results.

Source: Reproduced from *Designing for the Market* (video) with permission from TV Choice Ltd. Copies of this film are available from TV Choice Ltd, 22 Charing Cross Road, London, WC2H OHR, www.tvchoice.uk.com.

Questions

1a Can you think of other examples, similar to the wheel-chair in the case study, where a scientific advance and subsequent new product idea is not developed further and introduced to the market place because of commercial arguments?

1b How should companies and society deal with these situations?

2 What market testing was carried out and what conclusions were drawn?

3 Why is the distribution problem so critical?

Chapter summary

Deciding how and on what basis a company wishes to compete with its competitors is of central concern to all companies. Firms need to consider a wide range of factors in order to maximise the product's chance of success in competitive environments. This chapter has shown that a company has to identify the specific ways it can differentiate its products in order to gain competitive advantage.

First and foremost, it has to consider the market in which it is competing, the nature of the competition and how its capabilities will enable its products to be successful. The concept of platforms in new product development was introduced as a way of developing product groups for the future. The positioning of the product and the brand strategy selected were also shown to be of particular importance. Finally, marketing research offers extensive opportunities in terms of information provision. The effective use of this information often leads to the successful development of new products.

 ## Discussion questions

1 If there was a strategic alliance between competitors for the development of a new technology then what are the strategic issues for these firms once that technology becomes available?

2 Apply the notion of product platform to service industries. How relevant is it to financial services or to hotels? What are the issues that would need to be investigated if an idea emerged in a firm in those industries for a novel platform that had no connection with what was done before in that industry?

3 Would you agree that product portfolio analysis is too simplistic to be of much value?

4 Trace the connections between differentiation strategy, core capabilities and positioning strategy. How are they relevant to new product planning?

5 Are brand extensions as relevant in industrial markets as in consumer markets? Do they have a strategic role or are they short-term tactical exercises?

6 What measures would you apply in assessing the success of a new product?

7 What is the point in concept testing if it can only be a crude process with inconclusive results?

8 Are there any ethical issues in the employment of consumer panels in scanner store market tests?

Key words and phrases

Brand extensions 366	Product platform 348
Internal and external brand contacts 367	Product portfolios 355
Market entry 368	Product strategies 354
Mature products 373	Withdrawing products 371
Product differentiation 357	

Web sites worth visiting

Booz, Allen & Hamilton www.bah.com

new ideas to market www.ideo.com

new product development body of knowledge www.npd-solutions.com

product development and management association www.pdma.com

product development forum www.members.aol.com

product development institute www.prod-dev.com

References

Baker, M. and Hart, S. (1989) *Product Strategy and Management*, Prentice Hall, Harlow.

Buzzell, R.D. and Gale, B.T. (1987) *The PIMS Principles*, The Free Press, New York.

Crawford, C.M. (1997) *New Products Management*, 4th edn, Irwin, Burr Ridge, IL.

Deschamps, J.P. and Nayak, P.R. (1995) *Product Juggernauts: How Companies Mobilize To Generate A Stream of Winners*, Harvard Business School Press, Boston, MA.

Doyle, P. (1995) 'Marketing in the new millenium', *European Journal of Marketing*, Vol. 29, No. 13, 23–41.

The Economist (1996) 'Why first may not last', Management focus column, 16 March, 65.

Green, D.H., Barclay, D.W. and Ryans, A.B. (1995) 'Entry strategy and long-term performance: conceptualization and empirical examination', *Journal of Marketing*, October, 1–16.

Jones, T. (1997) *New Product Development*, Butterworth Heinemann, Oxford.

Kay, J. (1993) *Foundations of Corporate Success*, Oxford University Press, Oxford.

Kim, K. and Chhajed, D. (2000) 'Commonality in product design: cost saving, valuation change and cannabilisation', *European Journal of Operational Research*, Vol. 125, No. 3, 602–21.

Levitt, T. (1986) *The Marketing Imagination*, The Free Press, New York.

Moore, L.M. and Pessemier, E.A. (1993) *Product Planning and Management*, McGraw-Hill, New York.

Mudambi, S., Doyle, P. and Wong, V. (1997) 'An exploration of branding in industrial markets', *Industrial Marketing Management*, Vol. 26, 433–46.

Muffatto, M. (1999) 'Introducing a platform strategy in product development', *International Journal of Production Economics*, Vol. 60, 145–53.

Muffatto, M. and Roveda, M. (2000) 'Developing product platforms: analysis of the development process', *Technovation*, Vol. 20, No. 11, 617–30.

New Zealand Herald (2004) 'Sony still on top in digital camera market, finds study', Technology Section, 4 April.

Riezebos, R. (2003) *Brand Management: A Theoretical and Practical Approach*, Prentice Hall, Harlow.

Rogers, E. (1995) *Diffusion of Innovations*, 4th edn, Free Press, New York.

Rubinstein, H. (1996) 'Brand first management', *Journal of Marketing Management*, Vol. 12, 269–80.

Schofield, M. and Arnold, D. (1988) 'Strategies for mature business', *Long Range Planning*, Vol. 21, No. 5, 69–76.

Thomas, R.J. (1995) *New Product Success Stories*, John Wiley, New York.

Urban, G.L. and Hauser, J.R. (1993) *Design and Marketing of New Products*, 2nd edn, Prentice-Hall, Englewood Cliffs, NJ.

Wansink, B. (2001) 'Revitalising mature packaged goods', *Journal of Product and Brand Management*, Vol. 10, No. 4, 228–42.

Wheelwright, S.C. and Clark, K.B. (1992) *Revolutionising Product Development*, The Free Press, New York.

Wind, Y. (1982) *Product Policy*, Addison-Wesley, Reading, MA.

Further reading

For a more detailed review of the product and brand management literature, the following develop many of the issues raised in this chapter:

Baker, M. and Hart, S. (1999) *Product Strategy Management*, Prentice Hall, London.

Shavinina, L. (2003) *The International Handbook on Innovation*, Elsevier, Oxford.

Riezebos, R. (2003) *Brand Management: A Theoretical and Practical Approach*, Prentice Hall, London.

12

New product development

Few business activities are heralded for their promise and approached with more justifed optimism than the development of new products. Successful new products also have the added beneft of revitalising the organisation. Small wonder then that the concept of new product development (NPD) has received enormous attention in the management literature over the past 20 years. The result is a diverse range of literature from practitioners, management consultants and academics. This chapter explores this literature and examines the various models of NPD that have been put forward. It also explains the importance of NPD as a means of achieving growth.

Chapter contents

Innovation management and NPD

When one considers a variety of different industries, a decline in product innovations is matched only by a decline in market share (Ughanwa and Baker, 1989). For example, in 1995 the last remaining British mass manufacturer of motor cars, Rover, saw its market share slowly fall 20 per cent to only 10 per cent over the previous 20 years. Companies need to reach out to the future and develop new products that will enable them to compete over the coming decades. The chief executive of BP Chemicals acknowledged that 'cost reduction is a miserable job but conceptually it is easy' (Houlder, 1994). The message here is that cutting costs, while a necessary part of business management compared to generating new products, is relatively straightforward.

This chapter looks at the exciting process of developing new products. Part One of this book has highlighted the importance of innovation and how the effective management of that process can lead to corporate success. To many people new products are the outputs of the innovation process, where the new product development (NPD) process is a subprocess of innovation. Managing innovation concerns the conditions that have to be in place to ensure that the organisation as a whole is given the opportunity to develop new products. The actual development of new products is the process of transforming business opportunities into tangible products. Figure 12.1 helps to illustrate the link between innovation and new product development.

New product development concerns the management of the disciplines involved in the development of new products. These disciplines have developed their own perspectives on the subject of NPD. These are largely based on their experiences of involvement in the process. Hence, production management examines the development of new products from a manufacturing perspective, that is, how can we most effectively manufacture the product in question. Marketing, on the other hand, would take a slightly different perspective and would be concerned with trying to understand the needs of the customer and how the business could best meet these needs. However, producing what the customer wants may or may not be either possible or profitable. The lack of a common approach to the development of new products is due to this multiple perspective. This is illustrated in Figure 12.2. The variety of views presented on the subject is not a

Figure 12.1 Sales from products introduced within the past four years

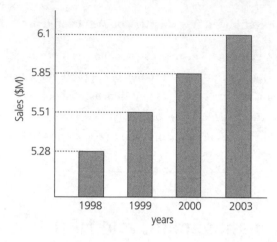

Figure 12.2 A variety of perspectives from which to analyse the development of new products

weakness. Indeed, it should be viewed as a strength, for these different perspectives illuminate the areas that are left in the dark by other perspectives.

Usually, competition between companies is assessed using financial measures such as return on capital employed (ROCE), profits and market share. Non-financial measures such as design, innovativeness and technological supremacy may also be used.

Theoretically it is possible for a firm to survive without any significant developments to its products, but such firms are exceptions to the norm. Where long-term success is dependent on the ability to compete with others, this is almost always achieved by ensuring that your company's products are superior to the competition.

New products and prosperity

The potential rewards of NPD are enormous. One only has to consider the rapid success of companies such as Microsoft and Compaq in the rapidly growing home computer industry. Similar success was achieved by Apple and prior to this IBM, in the

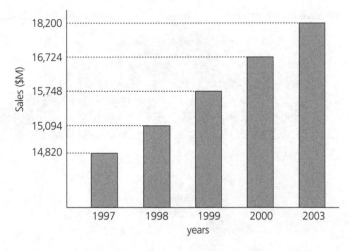

New product contributions to sales, 1997–2003

Figure 12.3

early development of the same industry. This example illustrates an important point, that success in one year does not ensure success in the next. Both Apple and IBM experienced severe difficulties in the 1990s.

Research by Cooper and Kleinschmidt (1993) has suggested that, on average, new products (defined here as those less than 5 years old) are increasingly taking a larger slice of company sales. For 3M, for example, new products contributed to 33 per cent of sales in the 1970s. This increased to 40 per cent in the 1980s and account for over 50 per cent in the 1990s (*see* Figure 12.3). The life cycles of products are becoming increasingly shorter (*see* Chapter 1).

Considerations when developing a NPD strategy

Chapter 6 outlined many of the activities and factors that organisations need to consider in managing a business in the short and long term. In addition, Chapter 11 highlighted many of the factors that a business needs to consider if it is successfully to manage its products. It should be clear that establishing a direction for a business and the selection of strategies to achieve its goals form an on-going, evolving process that is frequently subject to change. This is particularly evident at the product strategy level (Figure 12.4 illustrates the main inputs into the decision-making process). The process of product strategy was highlighted in Chapter 11 and is the creative process of recognising genuine business opportunities that the business might be able to exploit. It is commonly referred to as 'opportunity identification' (Crawford, 1997).

On-going corporate planning

In large organisations this can be a very formal activity involving strategic planners and senior managers with responsibility for setting the future direction of the business. In

| Figure 12.4 | Main inputs into the decision-making process |

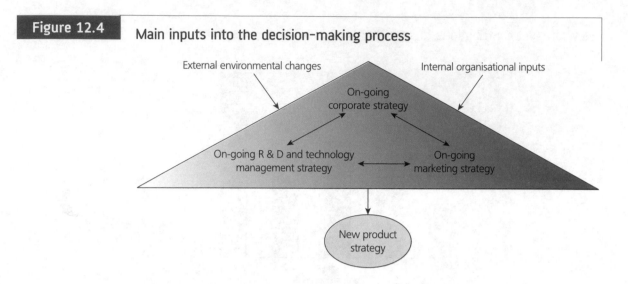

smaller organisations this activity may be undertaken by the owner of the business in an informal, even *ad hoc* way. For many businesses it is somewhere in the middle of these two extremes. The effects of any corporate planning may be important and long-term. For example, the decision by a sports footwear manufacturer to exit the tennis market and concentrate on the basketball market due to changing social trends will have a significant impact on the business.

On-going market planning

Decisions by market planners may have equally significant effects. For example, the realisation that a competitor is about to launch an improved tennis shoe that offers additional benefits may force the business to establish five new product development projects. Two of these projects may be established to investigate the use of new materials for the sole, one could be used to develop a series of new designs, one could look at alternative fastenings and one could be used to reduce production costs.

On-going technology management

In most science- and technology-intensive industries such as the pharmaceutical and computer software industries, this activity is probably more significant than on-going market planning. Technology awareness is very high. The continual analysis of internal R&D projects and external technology trawling will lead to numerous technical opportunities that need to be considered by the business. Say that a recent review of the patent literature has identified a patent application by one of the company's main competitors. This forces the business to establish a new project to investigate this area to ensure that it is aware of any future developments that may affect its position. This area is explored in more detail in Chapter 9.

Opportunity analysis/serendipity

In addition to the inputs that have been classified above, there are other inputs and opportunities that are often labelled miscellaneous or put down to serendipity (*see* Chapter 1). The vice-president of 3M remarked that 'chaos is a necessary part of an innovative culture. It's been said that 3M's competitors never know what we are going to come up with next. The fact is neither do we' (*see* the case study at the end of this chapter).

NPD as a strategy for growth

The interest expressed by many companies in the subject of developing new products is hardly surprising given that the majority of businesses are intent on growth. Although, as was discussed in Chapter 11, this does not apply to all companies, none the less the development of new products provides an opportunity for growing the business. (It is worth reminding ourselves that new product development is only one of many options available to a business keen on growth.)

One of the clearest ways of identifying the variety of growth options available to a business is using Ansoff's (1965, 1968) directional policy matrix. This well-known matrix, shown in Figure 12.5, combines two of the key variables that enable a business to grow: an increase in market opportunities and an increase in product opportunities. Within this matrix new product development is seen as one of four available options. Each of the four cells considers various combinations of product-market options. Growth can be achieved organically (internal development) or through external acquisition. A criticism of this matrix is that it adopts an environmental perspective that assumes that opportunities for growth exist – they may not. Indeed, often consolidation and retrenchment need to be considered, especially in times of economic downturn. Each of the cells in the matrix is briefly discussed below.

Ansoff matrix

Figure 12.5

	Current products	New products
Current markets	1 Market penetration strategy	3 Product development strategy
New markets	2 Market development strategy	4 Diversification strategy

Source: Adapted from I. Ansoff (1965) *Corporate Strategy*, Penguin, Harmondsworth; (1968) *Toward a Strategy of the Theory of the Firm*, McGraw Hill, New York.

Market penetration

Opportunities are said to exist within a business's existing markets through increasing the volume of sales. Increasing the market share of a business's existing products by exploiting the full range of marketing-mix activities is the common approach adopted by many companies. This may include branding decisions. For example, the cereal manufacturer Kelloggs has increased the usage of its cornflakes product by promoting it as a snack to be consumed at times other than at breakfast.

Market development

Growth opportunities are said to exist for a business's products through making them available to new markets. In this instance the company maintains the security of its existing products but opts to develop and enter new markets. Market development can be achieved by opening up new segments. For example, Mercedes decided to enter the small car market (previously the company had always concentrated on the executive or luxury segment). Similarly, companies may decide to enter new geographic areas through exporting.

Product development

Ansoff proposes that growth opportunities exist through offering new or improved products to existing markets. This is the subject of this chapter and, as will become clear, trying to establish when a product is new is sometimes difficult. None the less, virtually all companies try to ensure that their products are able to compete with the competition by regularly improving and updating their existing products. This is an on-going activity for most companies.

Diversification

It hardly needs to be said that opportunities for growth exist beyond a business's existing products and markets. The selection of this option, however, would be significant in that the business would move into product areas and markets in which it currently does not operate. The development of the self-adhesive note pads (Post-It) by 3M provided an opportunity for the company to enter the stationery market, a market of which it had little knowledge, with a product that was new to the company and the market.

Many companies try to utilise either their existing technical or commercial knowledge base. For example, Flymo's knowledge of the electric lawnmower market enabled it to diversify into a totally new market. Indeed, the introduction of its Garden-vac product led to the creation of the 'garden-tidy' product market. While this is an example of organic growth, many companies identify diversification opportunities through acquisition. For example, in the United Kingdom some of the privatised electricity companies have purchased significant holdings in privatised water companies. The knowledge base being utilised here is the commercial know-how of the provision of a utility service (former public service).

Additional opportunities for diversified growth exist through forward backward and horizontal diversification. A manufacturer opening retail outlets is an example of forward integration. Backward integration is involvement in activities which are inputs to the business, for example a manufacturer starting to produce components. Horizontal diversification is buying up competitors (*see* Johnson and Scholes, 1997, for a more detailed discussion of diversification).

A range of product development opportunities

A development of Ansoff's directional policy matrix was Johnson and Jones's (1957) matrix for product development strategies (*see* Figure 12.6). This matrix replaces Ansoff's product variable with technology. It builds on Ansoff's matrix by offering

New product development strategies

Figure 12.6

Increasing technology newness ⟶

Products objectives	No technological change	Improved technology	New technology To acquire scientific knowledge and production skills new to the company
No market change	Sustain	Reformulation To maintain an optimum balance of cost, quality and availability in the formulae of present products	Replacement To seek new and better ingredients of formulation for present company products in technology not now employed
Strengthened market To exploit more fully the existing markets for the present company's products	Remerchandising To increase sales to consumers of types now served by the company	Improved product To improve present products for greater utility and merchandisability to consumers	Product line extension To broaden the line of products offered to present consumers through new technology
New market To increase the number of types of consumer served by the company	New use To find new classes of consumer that can utilise present company products	Market extension To reach new classes of consumer by modifying present products	Diversification To add to the classes of consumer served by developing new technology knowledge

Increasing market newness

Source: S.C. Johnson and C. Jones (1957) 'How to organise for new products', *Harvard Business Review*, May–June, Vol. 35, 49–62.

further clarification of the range of options open to a company contemplating product decisions. In particular, the use of technology as a variable better illustrates the decisions a company needs to consider. For example, Johnson and Jones distinguish between improving existing technology and acquiring new technology, the latter being far more resource intensive with higher degrees of risk. Ansoff's directional policy matrix made no such distinction. Similarly, the market-newness scale offers a more realistic range of alternatives. Many other matrices have since been developed to try to help firms identify the range of options available (*see* Dolan, 1993).

The range of product development strategies that are open to a company introduces the notion that a new product can take many forms. This is the subject of the next section.

Illustration 12.1

FT

New products crucial to success

As a keen cyclist, Yoshizo Shimano knows all about the importance of keeping in touch with his company's products. Mr Shimano is president of Shimano, the world's biggest maker of bicycle components.

Frequently, he borrows a bike from the company's R&D division to keep in touch with what researchers are up to.

'We won't compete with our customers by building complete bikes. But we must keep in mind how our components are going to be used and have a vision of the product that is safe as well as being fun', he says.

Mr Shimano's interest in trying out bicycles containing his company's components underlines how manufacturers must pay increasing importance to bringing out new products.

These must either solve a pressing customer problem or come up with an idea that breaks completely new ground within a few years.

In either case, manufacturers' strategies on new product development are crucial to their chances of long-term success in a world where competition is becoming steadily tougher.

At Shimano, the company says its components feature in roughly one in three of the 110 million or so bikes made globally. Sales from fishing tackle as well as bike components last year came to ¥141bn.

Shimano is quoted on the Tokyo stock exchange, with the family retaining a minority stake.

Mr Shimano says Shimano keeps in touch on product development by talking continually to the 400–500 bicycle manufacturers world-wide it supplies. It makes 13 main types of parts – gears, brake systems and drive chains – each of which can come in up to 100 different variants.

In the early 1990s, the company prospered through the development of products, such as specialist gears, that suited the then fashion for rugged, off-road mountain bikes. Now the mountain bike craze has died away, Mr Shimano says the company is increasing its development of products such as automatic gears that will give cyclists, particularly on congested city roads, safer, smoother rides.

'If the cyclist does not have to bother with changing gears, he can concentrate on other aspects of controlling the bike which is likely to lead to safer journeys', says Mr Shimano.

Medtronic of the US, the world's biggest maker of medical implants, also continues to develop new products. In the late 1980s, most of its annual sales came from heart pacemakers, but a crop of other products will this year contribute to sales up fivefold at more than $5bn.

The company specialises in implanted devices that manage – rather than cure – chronic diseases including heart ailments as well as disorders of the neurological system such as Parkinson's and Alzheimer's diseases.

At the company's Minneapolis research laboratory, proof of the company's commitment to product development is evident in a small human dummy – unkindly christened Sid Seizure.

It acts as a test rig for a novel kind of implantable device for treating epilepsy and could start trials in humans next year. The implant is inserted under the skin by the chest and wired up to receive signals from the brain.

Through this mechanism, the device could tune into the pre-shock signals which indicate an epileptic attack is about to take place. These would trigger a burst of electric pulses from the implant which would counteract the brain signals, so nullifying the attack. If all goes well in the clinical trials, products could be in routine use later this decade.

Scott Ward, vice-president for neurology at Medtronic, says the company is working on a number of similar products that could counter a range of neurology-related problems.

While links with physicians and medical researchers around the world play a big part in such work, another key to Medtronic's product development strategies is its focus on devising tiny implantable pumps and motors which are needed in its implants.

The company says it has to make these items itself – they are too important to be left to outside businesses.

Heraeus, a private German company, also believes in retaining internal competence in new technologies. A world leader in platinum-related materials and engineering, it had sales last year of €8.2bn, of which just over two-thirds came from trading platinum and other related metals, with the rest from a mind-boggling range of products.

They include electrical goods and wiring, dental and medical implants, high-purity quartz glass used for optical fibres and scientific instruments, sensors and specialist lamps. Horst Heidsieck, Heraeus's chief executive, says many of these products are based on physical and chemical processes that led to the formation of the company in 1851.

Mr Heidsieck says the company's long-term strengths in platinum technologies has given it a means to bring out products that exploit the chemical properties of platinum and similar exotic metals in areas such as electrical goods and catalysts.

Source: P. Marsh (2002) 'New products crucial to success', www.FT.com, 21 May.

What is a new product?

Attempting to define what is and what is not a new product is not a trivial task, although many students of business management have had much fun arguing over whether the Sony Walkman was indeed a new product or merely existing technology repackaged. Another example that illustrates this point is the product long-life milk, known in the United States as aspectic milk (sold without refrigeration). This product has been consumed for many years in Europe but it is a relatively new concept for most consumers in the United States. Consumers who drink refrigerated milk may be extremely wary of milk sold from a non-refrigerated shelf (Thomas, 1993). Once again, while clearly this product is not absolutely new, it can be seen that it is more useful from a product manager's perspective to adopt a relativistic view.

It is important to note, as was explained in Chapter 11, that a product is a multi-dimensional concept. It can be defined differently and can take many forms. Some dimensions will be tangible product features and others intangible. Does the provision of different packaging for a product constitute a new product? Surely the answer is no – or is it? New packaging coupled with additional marketing effort, especially in terms of marketing communications, can help to reposition a product. This was successfully achieved by GlaxoSmithKline with its beverage product Lucozade (*see* Illustration 12.2). Today this product is known as a sports drink, yet older readers will recall that the product was originally packaged in a distinctive bottle wrapped in yellow cellophane and commonly purchased at pharmacists for sick children. This illustrates the difficulty of attempting to offer a single definition for a new product.

If we accept that a product has many dimensions, then it must follow that it is theoretically possible to label a product 'new' by merely altering one of these dimensions, for example packaging. Figure 12.7 illustrates this point. Each dimension is capable of being altered. These alterations create a new dimension and in theory a new product, even if the change is very small. Indeed, Johne and Snelson (1988) suggest that the options for both new and existing product lines centre around altering the variables in the figure. Table 12.1 shows what this means in practice.

Illustration 12.2

The repositioning of Lucozade

The repositioning of Lucozade is one of the most famous of recent times. Lucozade was first launched on to the UK market nearly 60 years ago. The product is a carbonated beverage with a high level of glucose. The brand was originally associated with illness and convalescence. In the 1960s and 1970s bottles of Lucozade were a common sight by the side of a hospital bed. Some 20 per cent of sales came from pharmacists. Promotion of the brand focused on slice-of-life situations showing Lucozade as a source of energy when family members, especially children, were recovering from illness. The result was that few brands could claim to have such a strong association with sickness.

SmithKline Beecham (now GlaxoSmithKline) was aware that many consumers purchased the product as a pick-me-up drink as well as for sickness. Following further studies in this area, the company decided to move the product from a sickness product to an in-health product. The end result of this was one of the most recognisable television campaigns of the 1970s. It features a wavy line that went up and down, reflecting different times of the day. Lucozade was promoted as a drink that should be consumed during troughs to help one get through the day. The strap line was: 'Lucozade refreshes you through the ups and downs of the day.' Volume sales increased by 13 per cent in the first year.

This was not the end of Lucozade's repositioning. The move from a sickness drink to an in-health drink was further reinforced when the product was completely redeveloped as a sports drink in the 1980s. Top sports stars were used to promote the product as an energy product to be consumed after and during strenuous exercise.

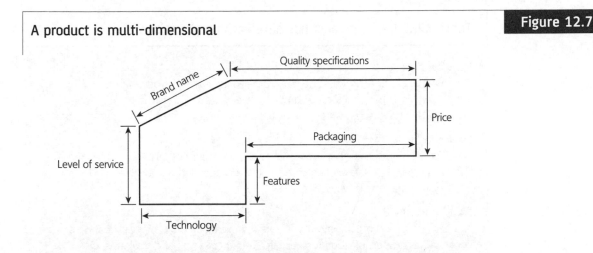

A product is multi-dimensional

Figure 12.7

Table 12.1 Different examples of 'newness'

1   Changing the performance capabilities of the product
    (for example, a new, improved washing detergent)

2   Changing the application advice for the product
    (for example, the use of the Persil ball in washing machines)

3   Changing the after-sales service for the product
    (for example, frequency of service for a motor car)

4   Changing the promoted image of the product
    (for example, the use of 'green'-image refll packs)

5   Changing the availability of the product
    (for example, the use of chocolate-vending machines)

6   Changing the price of the product
    (for example, the newspaper industry has experienced severe price wars)

Source: F.A. Johne and P.A. Snelson (1988) 'The role of marketing specialists in product development', Proceedings of the 21st Annual Conference of the Marketing Education Group, Huddersfield, Vol. 3, 176–91.

Defining a new product

Chapter 1 established a number of definitions to help with the study of this subject and provided a definition of innovation. In addition, it highlighted a quotation by Rogers and Shoemaker (1972) concerning whether or not something is new. It is useful at this juncture to revisit their argument. They stated that while it may be difficult to establish whether a product is actually new as regards the passage of time, so long as it is perceived to be new it *is* new. This is significant because it illustrates that newness is a relative term. In the case of a new product it is relative to what preceded the product.

Table 12.2 A new product has different interpretations of new

New product A
A snack manufacturer introduces a new, larger pack size for its best-selling savoury snack. Consumer research for the company revealed that a family-size pack would generate additional sales without cannibalising existing sales of the standard-size pack.

New product B
An electronics company introduces a new miniature compact disc player. The company has further developed its existing compact disc product and is now able to offer a much lighter and smaller version.

New product C
A pharmaceutical company introduces a new prescription drug for ulcer treatment. Following eight years of laboratory research and three years of clinical trials, the company has recently received approval from the government's medical authorities to launch its new ulcer drug.

Moreover, the overwhelming majority of so-called new products are developments or variations on existing formats. Research in this area suggests that only 10 per cent of new products introduced are new to both the market and the company (Booz, Allen and Hamilton, 1982). New to the company (in this case) means that the firm has not sold this type of product before, but other firms could have. New to the market means that the product has not appeared before in the market. However, the examples in Table 12.2 illustrate the confusion that exists in this area.

The three products in the table are all new in that they did not exist before. However, many would argue, especially technologists, that Product A does not contain any new technology. Similarly, Product B does not contain any new technology although its configuration may be new. Product C contains a new patented chemical formulation, hence this is the only truly new product. Marketers would, however, contend that all three products are new simply because they did not previously exist. Moreover, meeting the needs of the customer and offering products that are wanted is more important than whether a product represents a scientific breakthrough. Such arguments are common to many companies, especially those that have both a strong commercial and technological presence and expertise.

For the student of innovation and new product development, awareness of the debate and the strong feelings that are associated with it is more important than trying to resolve the polemics. Indeed, the long-term commercial success of the company should be the guiding principle on which product decisions are made. However, in some industries, the advancement of knowledge and subsequent scientific breakthroughs can lead to possible product offerings that would help certain sections of the population. Commercial pressures alone would, however, prevent these new products from being offered, as we saw in the Guinness case study in Chapter 8. The science and technology perspective should therefore not be dismissed.

Classification of new products

There have been many attempts to classify new products into certain categories. Very often the distinction between one category and another is one of degree and attempting to classify products is subject to judgement. It is worthy of note, however, that only 10 per cent of all new products are truly innovative. These products involve the greatest risk because they are new to both the company and the marketplace. Most new product activity is devoted to improving existing products. At Sony 80 per cent of new product activity is undertaken to modify and improve the company's existing products. The following classification (Booz, Allen and Hamilton, 1982) identifies the commonly accepted categories of new product developments.

New-to-the-world products

These represent a small proportion of all new products introduced. They are the first of their kind and create a new market. They are inventions that usually contain a significant development in technology, such as a new discovery, or manipulate existing technology in a very different way, leading to revolutionary new designs such as the Sony Walkman. Other examples include Kodak's digital camera, 3M's Post-It notes and Guinness's 'in-can' system.

New product lines (new to the firm)

Although not new to the marketplace, these products are new to the particular company. They provide an opportunity for the company to enter an established market for the first time. For example, Alcatel, Samsung and Sony-Ericsson have all entered the cell phone market to compete with market leaders Nokia and Motorola originators of the product.

Additions to existing lines

This category is a subset of new product lines above. The distinction is that while the company already has a line of products in this market, the product is significantly different from the present product offering but not so different that it is a new line. The distinction between this category and the former is one of degree. For example, Hewlett-Packard's colour ink-jet printer was an addition to its established line of ink-jet printers.

Improvements and revisions to existing products

These new products are replacements of existing products in a firm's product line. For example, Hewlett-Packard's ink-jet printer has received numerous modifications over time and, with each revision, performance and reliability have been improved. Also manufacturing cost reductions can be introduced, providing increased added value. This classification represents a significant proportion of all new product introductions.

Cost reductions

This category of products may not be viewed as new from a marketing perspective, largely because they offer no new benefits to the consumer other than possibly reduced costs. From the firm's perspective, however, they may be very significant. The ability

Figure 12.8	**The average new product portfolio**

Source: Adapted from A. Griffin (1997) 'PDMA research on new product development practices: updating trends and benchmarking best practices', *Journal of Product Innovation Management*, Vol. 14, 429.

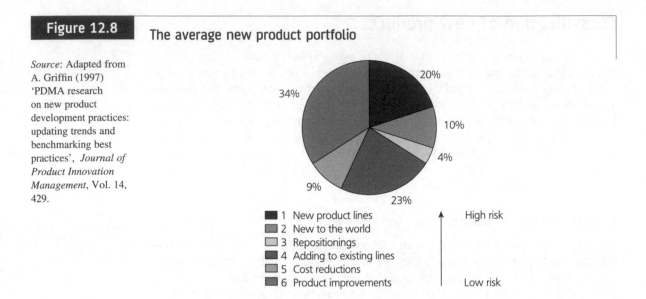

to offer similar performance while reducing production costs provides enormous added-value potential. Indeed, frequently it is this category of new product that can produce the greatest financial rewards for the firm. Improved manufacturing processes and the use of different materials are key contributing factors. The effect may be to reduce the number of moving parts or use more cost-effective materials (*see* Chapter 4). The difference between this category and the improvement category is simply that a cost reduction may not result in a product improvement.

Repositionings

These new products are essentially the discovery of new applications for existing products. This has more to do with consumer perception and branding than technical development. This is none the less an important category. Following the medical science discovery that aspirin thins blood, for example, the product has been repositioned from an analgesic to an over-the-counter remedy for blood clots and one that may help to prevent strokes and heart attacks.

In practice most of the projects in firm's portfolios are improvements to products already on the market, additions to existing lines (line extensions), and products new to the firm but already manufactured by competitors (new product lines). Figure 12.8 illustrates the average project portfolio within firms. Here 70 per cent of new products are improvements, cost reductions and additions to existing lines.

New product development as an industry innovation cycle

Abernathy and Utterback (1978) suggested that product innovations are soon followed by process innovations in what they described as an industry innovation cycle (*see*

Chapter 1). A similar notion can be applied to the categories of new products. The cycle can be identified in a wide variety of industries. New to the world products (Category 1) are launched by large companies with substantial resources, especially technical or marketing resources. Other large firms react swiftly to the launch of such a product by developing their own versions (Categories 2 and 3). Many small and medium-sized companies participate by developing their own new products to compete with the originating firm's product (Category 4). Substantial success and growth can come to small companies that adopt this strategy. Hewlett-Packard has grown into one of the most successful personal computer manufacturers even though it was not, unlike Apple and IBM, at the forefront of the development of the personal computer. As competition intensifies, companies will compete in the market for profits. The result is determined efforts to reduce costs in order to improve these profits, hence there are many cost reductions (Category 5).

Overview of NPD theories

The early stages of the new product development process are most usually defined as idea generation, idea screening, concept development and concept testing. They represent the formation and development of an idea prior to its taking any physical form. In most industries it is from this point onwards that costs will rise significantly. It is clearly far easier to change a concept than a physical product. The subsequent stages involve adding to the concept as those involved with the development (manufacturing engineers, product designers and marketers) begin to make decisions regarding how best to manufacture the product, what materials to use, possible designs and the potential market's evaluations.

The organisational activities undertaken by the company as it embarks on the actual process of new product development have been represented by numerous different models. These have attempted to capture the key activities involved in the process, from idea to commercialisation of the product. The representation of these tasks has changed significantly over the past 30 years. For example, the pharmaceutical industry is dominated by scientific and technological developments that lead to new drugs; whereas the food industry is dominated by consumer research that leads to many minor product changes. And yet the vast majority of textbooks that tackle this subject present the NPD process as an eight-stage linear model regardless of these major differences (Figure 12.8 shows how the process is frequently presented). Consequently this simple linear model is ingrained in the minds of many people. This is largely because new product development is viewed from a financial perspective where cash outflows precede cash inflows (*see* Figure 12.9). This graph shows the cumulative effect on cash flow through the development phases, from the build-up of stock and work in progress in the early stages of production, when there is no balancing in-flow of cash from sales, to the phase of profitable sales which brings the cash in-flow.

Virtually all those actually involved with the development of new products dismiss such simple linear models as not being a true representation of reality. More recent research suggests that the process needs to be viewed as a simultaneous and concurrent process with cross-functional interaction (Hart, 1993).

| Figure 12.9 | Commonly presented linear NPD model |

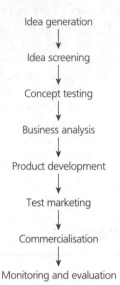

Idea generation

↓

Idea screening

↓

Concept testing

↓

Business analysis

↓

Product development

↓

Test marketing

↓

Commercialisation

↓

Monitoring and evaluation

For the reasons outlined above, the different perspectives on NPD have produced a wealth of literature on the subject (Brown and Eisenhardt, 1995; Craig and Hart, 1992). In addition, the subject has attracted the attention of many business schools and business consultants, all interested in uncovering the secrets of successful product development. Numerous research projects have been undertaken including in-depth case studies across many industries and single companies and broad surveys of industries (e.g. Ancona and Caldwell, 1992; Clark and Fujimoto, 1991; Dougherty, 1990; Zirger and Maidique, 1990).

As a result, research on new product development is varied and fragmented, making it extremely difficult to organise for analysis. Brown and Eisenhardt (1995) have tackled this particular problem head on and have produced an excellent review of the

| Figure 12.10 | Cash flows and new product development |

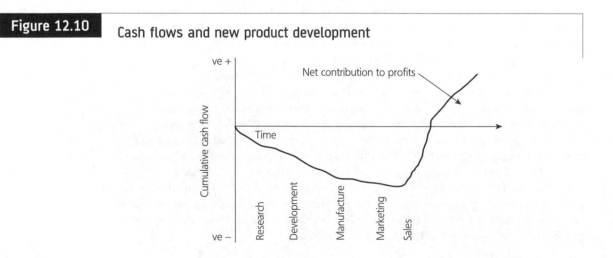

Table 12.3 The three main streams of research within the NPD literature

	Rational planning	*Communication web*	*Disciplined problem solving*
Aim/objective/title	Rational planning and management of the development of new products within organisations	The communication web studies the use of information and sources of information by product development teams	Disciplined problem solving focuses on how problems encountered during the NPD process were overcome
Focus of the research	The rational plan research focuses on business performance and fnancial performance of the product	The communication web looks at the effects of communication on project performance	The third stream tries to examine the process and the wide range of actors and activities involved
Seminal research	The work by Myers and Marquis (1969) and SAPPHO studies (Rothwell *et al.*, 1974) was extremely influential in this feld	Thomas Allen's (1969, 1977) research into communication patterns in large industrial laboratories dominates this perspective	The work by the Japanese scholars Imai *et al.* (1985) lies at the heart of this third stream of literature

Source: S.L. Brown and K.M. Eisenhardt (1995) 'Product development: past research, present fndings and future directions', *Academy of Management Review*, Vol. 20, No. 2, 343–78.

---

literature. In their analysis they identify three main strcams of literature, each having its own particular strengths and limitations (*see* Table 12.3). These streams have evolved around key research findings and together they continue to throw light on many dark areas of new product development.

While this is an important development and a useful contribution to our understanding of the subject area, it offers little help for the practising manager on how he or she should organise and manage the new product development process. An analysis of the models that have been developed on the subject of new product development may help to identify some of the activities that need to be managed.

Models of new product development

Among the burgeoning management literature on the subject it is possible to classify the numerous models into seven distinct categories (Saren, 1984):

1 departmental-stage models;
2 activity-stage models and concurrent engineering;
3 cross-functional models (teams);
4 decision-stage models;

5 conversion-process models;

6 response models; and

7 network models.

Within this taxonomy decision-stage models and activity-stage models are the most commonly discussed and presented in textbooks. Figure 12.9 is an example of an activity-stage model (*see also* Crawford, 1997, and Kotler, 1997, for examples of a decision-stage model).

It is worthy of note that there are many companies, especially small specialist manufacturing companies, that continue to operate a craftsman-style approach to product development. This has been the traditional method of product manufacture for the past 500 years. For example, in every part of Europe there are joinery companies manufacturing products to the specific requirements of the user. Many of these products will be single, one-off products manufactured to dimensions given on a drawing. All the activities, including the creation of drawings, collection of raw materials, manufacture and delivery, may be undertaken by one person. Today, when we are surrounded by technology that is sometimes difficult to use never mind understand, it is possible to forget that the traditional approach to product development is still prevalent. Many activities, moreover, remain the same as they have always been.

Departmental-stage models

Departmental-stage models represent the early form of NPD models. These can be shown to be based around the linear model of innovation, where each department is responsible for certain tasks. They are usually represented in the following way. R&D provides the interesting technical ideas; the engineering department will then take the ideas and develop possible prototypes; the manufacturing department will explore possible ways to produce a viable product capable of mass manufacture; the marketing department will then be brought in to plan and conduct the launch. Such models are also referred to as 'over-the-wall' models, so called because departments would carry out their tasks before throwing the project over the wall to the next department (*see* Figure 12.11).

| Figure 12.11 | Over-the-wall model |

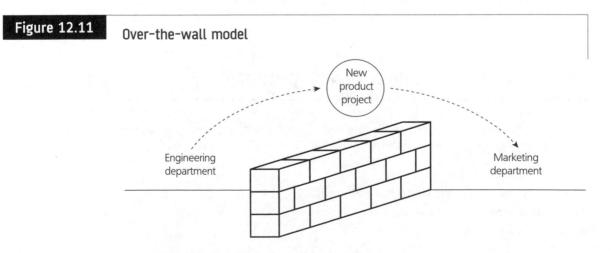

Source: C. Lorenz (1990) *The Design Dimension*, Basil Blackwell, Oxford.

Figure 12.12

Mike Smith's secret weapon: the salutary tale of 'How not to design a swing, or the perils of poor coordination'

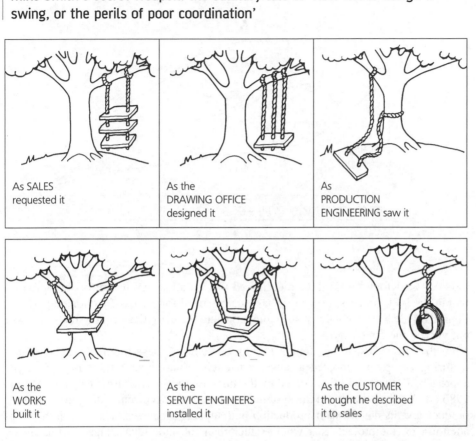

As SALES requested it

As the DRAWING OFFICE designed it

As PRODUCTION ENGINEERING saw it

As the WORKS built it

As the SERVICE ENGINEERS installed it

As the CUSTOMER thought he described it to sales

It is now widely accepted that this insular departmental view of the process hinders the development of new products. The process is usually characterised by a great deal of reworking and consultation between functions. In addition, market research provides continual inputs to the process. Furthermore, control of the project changes on a departmental basis depending on which department is currently engaged in it. The consequence of this approach has been captured by Mike Smith's (1981) humorous tale of 'How not to design a swing, or the perils of poor coordination' (*see* Figure 12.12).

Activity-stage models and concurrent engineering

These are similar to departmental-stage models but because they emphasise activities conducted they provide a better representation of reality. They also facilitate iteration of the activities through the use of feedback loops, something that the departmental-stage models do not. Activity-stage models, however, have also received fierce criticism for perpetuating the 'over-the-wall' phenomenon. More recent activity-stage

| Figure 12.13 | An activity-stage model |

Source: C.M. Crawford
(1997) *New Products
Management*, 5th edn,
McGraw-Hill,
Chicago, IL.

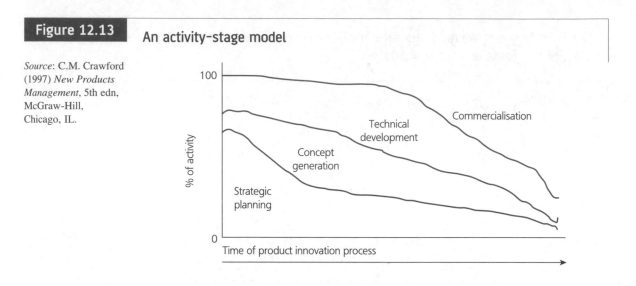

models (Crawford, 1997) have highlighted the simultaneous nature of the activities within the NPD process, hence emphasising the need for a cross-functional approach. Figure 12.13 shows an activity-stage model where the activities occur at the same time but vary in their intensity.

In the late 1980s, in an attempt to address some of these problems, many manufacturing companies adopted a concurrent engineering or simultaneous engineering approach. The term was first coined by the Institute for the Defense Analyses (IDA) in 1986 (IDA, 1986) to explain the systematic method of concurrently designing both the product and its downstream production and support processes. The idea is to focus attention on the project as a whole rather than the individual stages, primarily by involving all functions from the outset of the project. This requires a major change in philosophy from functional orientation to project orientation. Furthermore, technology-intensive businesses with very specialist knowledge inputs are more difficult to manage (the case study at the end of Chapter 15 explores some of these problems). Such an approach introduces the need for project teams.

Cross-functional models (teams)

Common problems that occur within the product development process centre around communications between different departments. This problem, specifically with regard to the marketing and the R&D departments, is explored more fully in Chapter 15. In addition, projects would frequently be passed back and forth between functions. Moreover, at each interface the project would undergo increased changes, hence lengthening the product development process. The cross-functional teams (CFT) approach removes many of these limitations by having a dedicated project team representing people from a variety of functions. The use of cross-functional teams requires a fundamental modification to an organisation's structure. In particular, it places emphasis on the use of project management and inter-disciplinary teams.

Decision-stage models

Decision-stage models represent the new product development process as a series of decisions that need to be taken in order to progress the project (Cooper and Kleinschmidt, 1993; Kotler, 1997). Like the activity-stage models, many of these models also facilitate iteration through the use of feedback loops. However, a criticism of these models is that such feedback is implicit rather than explicit. The importance of the interaction between functions cannot be stressed enough – the use of feedback loops helps to emphasise this.

Conversion-process models

As the name suggests, conversion-process models view new product development as numerous inputs into a 'black box' where they are converted into an output (Schon, 1967). For example, the inputs could be customer requirements, technical ideas and manufacturing capability and the output would be the product. The concept of a variety of information inputs leading to a new product is difficult to criticise, but the lack of detail elsewhere is the biggest limitation of such models.

Response models

Response models are based on the work of Becker and Whistler (1967) who used a behaviourist approach to analyse change. In particular, these models focus on the individual's or organisation's response to a new project proposal or new idea. This approach has revealed additional factors that influence the decision to accept or reject new product proposals, especially at the screening stage.

Network models

This final classification of new product development models represents the most recent thinking on the subject. The case studies in Chapters 7 and 10 highlight the process of accumulation of knowledge from a variety of different inputs, such as marketing, R&D and manufacturing. This knowledge is built up gradually over time as the project progresses from initial idea (technical breakthrough or market opportunity) through development. It is this process that forms the basis of the network models (these models are explored more fully in Takeuchi and Nonaka, 1986; Nonaka, 1991; Hagedoorn, 1990; Trott, 1993; Nonaka and Takeuchi, 1995).

Essentially, network models emphasise the external linkages coupled with the internal activities that have been shown to contribute to successful product development. There is substantial evidence to suggest that external linkages can facilitate additional knowledge flows into the organisation, thereby enhancing the product development process (Cusumano and Takeishi, 1991; Kamath and Liker, 1994; Liker et al., 1995). These models suggest that NPD should be viewed as a knowledge-accumulation process that requires inputs from a wide variety of sources. The model in Figure 12.14 helps to highlight the accumulation of knowledge over time. This may be thought of as a snowball gaining in size as it rolls down a snow-covered mountain.

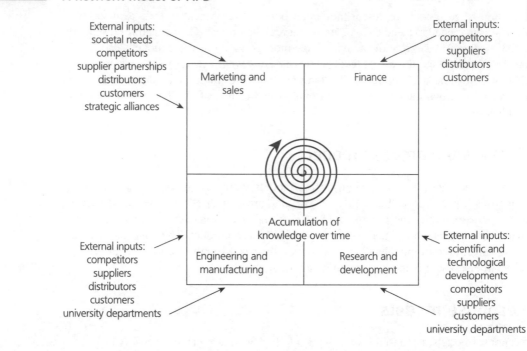

Figure 12.14   A network model of NPD

External inputs:
societal needs
competitors
supplier partnerships
distributors
customers
strategic alliances

External inputs:
competitors
suppliers
distributors
customers

Marketing and sales

Finance

Accumulation of knowledge over time

Engineering and manufacturing

Research and development

External inputs:
competitors
suppliers
distributors
customers
university departments

External inputs:
scientific and technological developments
competitors
suppliers
customers
university departments

Case study

An analysis of 3M, the innovation company[1]

Introduction

Any review of the literature on new product development and innovation management will uncover numerous references to 3M. The organisation is synonymous with innovation and has been described as 'a smooth running innovation machine' (Mitchell, 1989). Year after year 3M is celebrated in the *Fortune* 500 rankings as the 'most respected company' and the 'most innovative company'. Management gurus from Peter Drucker to Tom Peters continually refer to the company as a shining example of an innovative company. This case study takes a look at the company behind some of the most famous brands in the marketplace, such as Scotch videocassettes and Post-It notes. It examines the company's heritage and shows how it has arrived at this enviable position. Furthermore, the case study attempts to clarify what it is that makes 3M stand out from other organisations.

Background

Originally known as the Minnesota Mining and Manufacturing Company, with its headquarters in St Paul, Minnesota, 3M was established in 1902 to mine abrasive minerals for the production of a single product, sandpaper. From these

[1] This case has been written as a basis for class discussion rather than to illustrate effective or ineffective managerial or administrative behaviour. It has been prepared from a variety of published sources, as indicated, and from observations.

Sales over the past five years

Source: Compiled from data from 3M Corp (2004). Financial results from 3M international web page, 3M, www.mmm.com

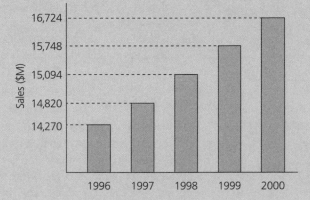

Figure 12.15

inauspicious beginnings, the company has grown organically, concentrating on the internal development of new products in a variety of different industries. The latest review of the company's position reveals that it manufactures over 60,000 products, has operations in 61 countries, employs 70,000 people and has achieved an average year-on-year growth in sales of 10 per cent (*see* Figure 12.15). Its products include Scotch adhesive tapes, fibre-optic connectors, abrasives, adhesives, floppy disks, aerosol inhalers, medical diagnostic products and Post-It notes.

3M gave the world 'wet or dry' abrasives, which did so much to reduce the incidence of respiratory disease in the 1920s. It invented self-adhesive tape in 1925, light-reflective materials in the 1940s and pioneered magnetic recording and photocopying. This heritage established the technology from which many of its products are still derived. To reinforce this impressive performance, 3M is consistently ranked among the top 10 of America's most admired companies in the US journal *Fortune*, in its annual review of the top 500 companies in the United States. 3M is a large and unusually diverse company. The company is currently restructuring, the spin-off of its data storage and imaging businesses forming a new company.

The 3M approach to innovation

Many writers, academics and business leaders have argued that the key to successful innovation is good management (Henderson, 1994). Arguably, this is precisely what 3M has mastered. A closer inspection, however, will reveal that the company has combined a variety of management techniques, such as good communications and the setting of clear objectives with a company culture built on more than 90 years of nurturing ideas and fostering creativity. It uses a combination of structured research and individual freedom to explore ideas by allowing research scientists to spend 15 per cent of their time conducting projects of their own choosing. It is a unique combination of activities that is, by definition, difficult to replicate. They are described in this case study under the following headings:

1 Company heritage and culture
2 The demand for innovation (the 30 per cent rule)
3 Freedom for creativity
4 Tolerating failure
5 Autonomy and small businesses
6 High profile for science and technology
7 Internal technology transfer

Company heritage and culture

Through a combination of formal and informal processes, the company has developed a culture devoted to creating new products and building new businesses. This is partly based on the simple idea of hiring good people and trusting them. Indeed, this is the first goal that is stated in 3M's formal principles of management: 'the promotion of entrepreneurship and the insistence upon freedom in the workplace to pursue innovative ideas' (Osborn, 1988: 18).

The demand for innovation (the 30 per cent rule)

While the sales performance in Figure 12.15 is impressive, it conceals an important statistic; that is, 30 per cent of the company's sales come from products that are less than 4 years old. Indeed, this is a business objective that every 3M business manager has to try to achieve. What this means is that these business managers are under pressure to ensure that not only do they develop new products but that these new products will eventually represent 30 per cent of the business's sales. This objective has been effectively communicated throughout the organisation and is now ingrained within the management style and part of the culture of the company. Hence, the search for new ideas is part of daily activities.

Senior managers from other large manufacturing companies would rightly argue that a similar percentage of sales within their own companies comes from products less than 4 years old. However, the difference between 3M and other organisations is that 3M has developed this approach over many years and has worked hard to ensure that developing new products is much higher on the agenda in management meetings than at other companies. Moreover, the success of the approach is due to the continual reinforcement of the objective. Indeed, the performance of individual business managers is partly judged on whether they are able to achieve the objective.

The 30 per cent objective was first introduced in the 1980s when 25 per cent of sales had to come from products less than 4 years old. This was altered in 1992 to 30 per cent. 3M has recently added another goal, which is to ensure that 10 per cent of sales come from products that have been in the market for only one year.

Freedom for creativity

Scientists and engineers are given time to work on projects and ideas that they consider to be of potential interest to the company and 15 per cent of an individual's work week time may be dedicated to such activities. This is not exclusive to 3M and is common practice in most large R&D laboratories. None the less, it is an effective method of providing room for creativity and another way of showing that the organisation encourages innovative effort. Indeed, it is a method of providing resources to entrepreneurs, allowing them to work on ideas without having to seek out approval from the organisation. Another way of allocating resources is the use of grants. Known as 'genesis grants', these give researchers up to $75,000 to develop their ideas into potential product opportunities.

One of 3M's most famous new products was the result of this practice, the Post-It note. Spencer Silver and Arthur Fry both invoked the 15 per cent rule to allow them to work on the project that eventually led to its development.

Spencer Silver was a 3M research chemist working on adhesive technology. His brief was to produce the strongest adhesive on the market. By some extraordinary mischance he developed an adhesive that had none of the properties he was looking for, but which did have two interesting properties which he had never previously encountered: it could be reused and it left no residue on the material to which it was applied. Yet no one could find a use for it and the idea was shelved.

Art Fry, one of Spencer Silver's colleagues, sang in a choir. Every Sunday he would carefully mark his hymnbook with slips of paper and every Sunday the slips fell out. Then he remembered Spencer Silver's useless adhesive. Applied to paper strips, Art Fry found that they made fine book markers that did not fall out when he opened the book. Post-It brand technology had been developed ten years before Art Fry discovered what to do with it!

In a recent lecture on the subject of innovation, the 3M vice-president for research and development (Coyne, 1996) reported that:

The 15 per cent rule is meaningless. Some of our technical people use more than 15 per cent of their time on projects of their own choosing. Some use less than that; some none at all. The figure is not so important as the message, which is this: the system has some slack in it. If you have a good idea, and the commitment to squirrel away time to work on it, and the raw nerve to skirt your manager's expressed desires, then fine.

Tolerating failure

'It's easier to be critical than creative' is an adaptation of a famous quote from Benjamin Disraeli. It captures the essence of 3M's approach to tolerating failure. Most large companies with large R&D departments will have many on-going new product research projects. Many will consume large amounts of resources and will not result in a new product. This fact is all part of the new product game. Those close to the game are aware of this; at 3M it is argued that everyone is aware of the need to try new ideas. Its founder and early chief executive, W.L. Knight, stated over 60 years ago that:

A management that is destructively critical when mistakes are made, kills initiative, and it is essential that we have people with initiative if we are to continue to grow.

Vasilash (1995) suggests that many of the senior managers within 3M are known to have made at least one mistake in their career while they tried to be innovative, thereby suggesting that W.L. Knight's philosophy continues.

3M has had its share of colossal failures. In the 1920s one of the company's top inventors had an incredible flash of brilliance: maybe people could use sandpaper as a replacement for razor blades. Instead of shaving your face or legs, you could just sand off the whiskers. Every man and woman would need it. The company would sell the product by the ton! Not surprisingly the idea was not realised in practice – but the inventor was not punished for following his idea. For every 1,000 ideas only 100 are written up as formal proposals. Only a fraction of these become new product ventures and over half of the company's new product ventures fail (Coyne, 1996).

Autonomy and small businesses

Like many companies 3M realises that large organisations, with their inevitable corresponding structures and systems, can sometimes inhibit the creative dynamism often required to foster innovative effort. Hence, it has adopted an approach that enables individuals and groups within the organisation to establish small internal venture groups, with managers free to make their own decisions, develop their own product lines and take responsibility for the results, without continuous coordination across the company (Stewart, 1996). This approach attempts to offer an entrepreneurial environment under a corporate umbrella.

Provided that certain financial measures are met, such start-up venture groups follow a well-trodden path: a new business operation starts out as a project, if sales reach $1 million it becomes a fully fledged product. At $20 million, it becomes an independent product department separate from its parent department. If it continues to grow it will be spun off as a separate autonomous division. Currently, divisions characteristically have $200 million in sales.

Experience has taught the company that in the early days of a business's life, many decisions are taken through informal discussions among the individuals involved. There are usually insufficient resources to allow for lengthy and detailed analysis, which is more common in more established businesses.

High profile for science and technology

Although the company was formed around a single technology sandpaper, today 3M makes use of more than 100 technologies such as membranes, biotechnology, artificial intelligence, high-vacuum thin films and superconductivity. These technologies underpin the products that the company develops and manufactures. To support these activities the company invests 6.5 per cent of its annual sales turnover in research and development. This is about twice that of the top 50 industrial companies in the United States. The money is used to employ over 7,500 scientists and technologists in developing new and interesting technology. It is this technological intensity that provides the company with the competitive advantage to compete with its rivals.

It is important to note that while the company is technology-intensive, this does not imply a single-minded, technology-push approach to innovation. The role of the marketplace and users plays an important part in product development. For example, 3M's famous Scotch tape was once manufactured strictly as an industrial product, until a salesman got the idea of packaging it in clear plastic dispensers for home and office use.

Communication and technology transfer

The communication of ideas helps to ensure that a company can maximise the return on its substantial investments in the technology. Very often it is the combination of apparently diverse technologies through technology transfer that has led to major product innovations. For example, microreplication technology is the creation of precise microscopic, three-dimensional patterns on a variety of surfaces, including plastic film. When the surface is changed numerous product possibilities emerge. It was first developed for overhead projectors, its innovative feature being a lens made of a thin piece of plastic with thousands of tiny grooves on its surface. Microreplication helped the plastic lens to perform better than the conventional lens made of heavy glass. 3M became the world's leading producer of overhead projectors. It is this technology, which can be traced back to the 1960s, that has spread throughout 3M and led to a wide range of products, including better and brighter reflective material for traffic signs; 'floptical' disks for data storage; laptop computer screens; and films.

Discussion

While few would argue with 3M's successful record on innovation, there may be some who would argue that, compared to companies such as Microsoft, IBM and GlaxoSmithKline, its achievements in terms of growth have not been as spectacular. However, the point here is not that 3M is the most successful company or even that it is the most innovative, although one could surely construct a strong case, merely that the company has a long and impressive performance when it comes to developing new products.

This case study has highlighted some of the key activities and principles that contribute to 3M's performance. Many of these are not new and are indeed used by other companies. In 3M's case they may be summarised as an effective company culture that nurtures innovation and a range of management techniques and strategies that together have delivered long-term success. Many companies pay lip service to the management principles and practice set out in this case study. There is evidence that 3M supports these fine words with actions.

For further information about 3M and its business activities, visit the 3M international web page at: www.3m.com

Questions

1 There are many examples of successful companies. To what extent is 3M justifiably highlighted as the 'innovating machine'?

2 In the 3M case study, what is meant by the statement: 'the message is more important than the figures'?

3 Discuss the merits and problems with the so called '15 per cent'. Consider cost implications and a busy environment with deadlines to meet. To what extent is this realistic or mere rhetoric?

4 Encouraging product and brand managers to achieve 25 per cent of sales from recently introduced products would be welcomed by shareholders, but what happens if a successful business delivers profits without 25 per cent of sales from recently introduced products?

5 Some people may argue that 3M's success is largely due to the significance given to science and technology and this is the main lesson for other firms. Discuss the merits of such a view and the extent to which this is the case.

Chapter summary

This chapter has considered the relationship between new products and prosperity and shown that new product development is one of the most common forms of organic growth strategies. The range of NPD strategies is wide indeed and can range from packaging alterations to new technological research. The chapter stressed the importance of viewing a product as a multi-dimensional concept.

The later part of the chapter focused on the various models of NPD that have emerged over the past 50 years. All of these have strengths and weaknesses. By their very nature, models attempt to capture and portray a complex notion and in so doing often over-simplify elements. This is the central argument of critics of the linear model of NPD, that it is too simplistic and does not provide for any feedback or concurrent activities. More recent models such as network models try to emphasise the importance of the external linkages in the NPD process.

Discussion questions

1 Explain why the process of new product development is frequently represented as a linear process.

2 Explain why screening should be viewed as a continual rather than a one-off activity.

3 Discuss how the various groups of NPD models have contributed to our understanding of the subject of NPD.

4 Evaluate the wide range of product development opportunities that exist.

5 Examine the concept of a multidimensional product; how is this helpful?

6 Explain Booz *et al.*'s (1982) classification of new products.

7 Why do some marketers and scientists often argue about whether a product is new or not?

8 Discuss some of the strengths of network models of NPD.

Key words and phrases

Activity-stage models and
concurrent engineering   401
Conversion-process models   403
Cost reductions   395
Cross-functional models (teams)   402
Decision-stage models   403
Departmental-stage models   400

Line additions   395
Line extensions   395
Network models   403
New product lines   395
New-to-the-world products   395
Repositionings   396
Response models   403

Websites worth visiting

3M www.3m.com

Booz, Allen & Hamilton www.bah.com

The Design Council www.Designcouncil.com

new ideas to market www.ideo.com

new product development body of knowledge www.npd-solutions.com

product development and management association www.pdma.com

product development forum www.members.aol.com

product development institute www.prod-dev.com

References

3M Company Report (2000) www.mmm.com/profile/report2/chairman.html

3M Corp (2004) Financial results from 3M international Web page: 3M www.mmm.com

Abernathy, W.L. and Utterback, J. (1978) 'Patterns of industrial innovation', in Tushman, M.L. and Moore, W.L. (eds) *Readings in Management of Innovation*, HarperCollins, New York, 97–108.

Allen, T.J. (1969) 'Communication networks in R&D laboratories', *R&D Management*, Vol. 1, 14–21.

Allen, T.J. (1977) *Managing the Flow of Technology*, MIT Press, Cambridge, MA.

Ancona, D.G. and Caldwell, D.F. (1992) 'Bridging the boundary: external processes and performance in organisational teams', *Administrative Science Quarterly*, Vol. 37, 634–65.

Ansoff, I. (1965) *Corporate Strategy*, Penguin, Harmondsworth.

Ansoff, I. (1968) *Toward a Strategy of the Theory of the Firm*, McGraw Hill, New York.

Becker, S. and Whistler, T.I. (1967) 'The innovative organisation: a selective view of current theory and research', *Journal of Business*, Vol. 40, No. 4, 462–69.

Booz, Allen and Hamilton (1982) *New Product Management for the 1980s*, Booz, Allen and Hamilton, New York.

Brown, S.L. and Eisenhardt, K.M. (1995) 'Product development: past research, present findings and future directions', *Academy of Management Review*, Vol. 20, No. 2, 343–78.

Clark, K. and Fujimoto, T. (1991) *Product Development Performance*, Harvard Business School Press, Boston, MA.

Cooper, R.G. and Kleinschmidt, E.J. (1993) 'Major new products: what distinguishes the winners in the chemical industry?' *Journal of Product Innovation Management*, Vol. 10, No. 2, 90–111.

Coyne, W.E. (1996) Innovation lecture given at the Royal Society, 5 March.

Craig, A. and Hart, S. (1992) 'Where to now in new product development?' *European Journal of Marketing*, Vol. 26, 11.

Crawford, C.M. (1997) *New Products Management*, 5th edn, Irwin, Chicago, IL.

Cusumano, M.A. and Takeishi, A. (1991) 'Supplier relations and management: a survey of Japanese transplant, and US auto plants', *Strategic Management Journal*, Vol. 12, 563–88.

Dolan, R.J. (1993) *Managing the New Product Development Process*, Addison-Wesley, Reading, MA.

Dougherty, D. (1990) 'Understanding new markets for new products', *Strategic Management Journal*, Vol. 11, 59–78.

Hagedoorn, J. (1990) 'Organisational modes of inter-firm co-operation and technology transfer', *Technovation*, Vol. 10, No. 1, 17–30.

Hart, S. (1993) 'Dimensions of success in new product development: an exploratory investigation', *Journal of Marketing Management*, Vol. 9, No. 9, 23–41.

Henderson, R. (1994) 'Managing innovation in the information age', *Harvard Business Review*, January–February, 100–5.

Houlder, V. (1994) 'Rewards for bright ideas', *Financial Times*, 18 December.

IDA (1986) *The Role of Concurrent Engineering in Weapons Systems Acquisition*, report R–338, IDA Washington, DC.

Imai, K., Ikujiro, N. and Takeuchi, H. (1985) 'Managing the new product development process: how Japanese companies learn and unlearn', in Hayes, R.H., Clark, K. and Lorenz C. (eds) *The Uneasy Alliance: Managing the Productivity–Technology Dilemma*, Harvard Business School Press, Boston, MA, 337–75.

Johne, F.A. and Snelson, P.A. (1988) 'The role of marketing specialists in product development', Proceedings of the 21st Annual Conference of the Marketing Education Group, Huddersfield, Vol. 3, 176–91.

Johnson, G. and Scholes, K. (1997) *Exploring Corporate Strategy*, 4th edn, Prentice Hall, Hemel Hempstead.

Johnson, S.C. and Jones, C. (1957) 'How to organise for new products', *Harvard Business Review*, May–June, Vol. 35, 49–62.

Kamath, R. and Liker, J.K. (1994) 'A second look at Japanese product development', *Harvard Business Review*, November–December, Vol. 74, 154–70.

Kotler, P. (1997) *Marketing Management*, Prentice-Hall, Englewood Cliffs, NJ.

Liker, J.K., Kamath, R., Wasti, N. and Nagamachi, M. (1995) 'Integrating suppliers into fast-cycle product development', in Liker, J.K., Ettlie, J.E. and Campbell, J.C. (eds), *Engineering in Japan: Japanese Technology Management Practices*, Oxford University Press, New York.

Mitchell, R. (1989) 'Masters of innovation: how 3M keeps its new products coming', *Business Week*, April, 58–63.

Myers, S. and Marquis, D.G. (1969) 'Successful industrial innovation: a study of factors underlying innovation and selected firms', National Science Foundation, NSF 69–17, Washington.

Nonaka, I. (1991) 'The knowledge creating company', *Harvard Business Review*, November–December, Vol. 69, No. 6, 96–104.

Nonaka, I. and Takeuchi, H. (1995) *The Knowledge Creating Company*, Oxford University Press, Oxford.

Osborn, T. (1988) 'How 3M manages innovation', *Marketing Communications*, November/December, 17–22.

Rogers, E. and Shoemaker, R. (1972) *Communications of Innovations*, Free Press, New York.

Rothwell, R., Freeman, C., Horlsey, A., Jervis, V.T.P., Robertson, A.B. and Townsend, J. (1974) 'SAPPHO updated: Project SAPPHO phase II', *Research Policy*, Vol. 3, 258–91.

Saren, M. (1984) 'A classification of review models of the intra-firm innovation process', *R&D Management*, Vol. 14, No. 1, 11–24.

Schon, D. (1967) 'Champions for radical new inventions', *Harvard Business Review*, March–April, 77–86.

Smith, M.R.H. (1981), paper presented to the National Conference on Quality and Competitiveness, London, November, reported in *Financial Times*, 25 November.

Stewart, T. (1996) '3M fights back', *Fortune*, Vol. 133, No. 2, 5 February, 42–7.

Takeuchi, H. and Nonaka, I. (1986) 'The new product development game', *Harvard Business Review*, Vol. 64, No. 1, 137–46.

Thomas, R.J. (1993) *New Product Development*, John Wiley, New York.

Trott, P. (1993) 'Inward technology transfer as an interactive process: a case study of ICI', PhD thesis, Cranfield University.

Ughanwa, D.O. and Baker, M.J. (1989) *The Role of Design in International Competitiveness*, Routledge, London.

Vasilash, G.S. (1995) 'Heart and soul of 3M', *Production*, Vol. 107, No. 6, 38–9.

Zirger, B.J. and Maidique, M.A. (1990) 'A model of new product development: an empirical test', *Management Science*, Vol. 36, 876–88.

Further reading

For a more detailed review of the new product development literature, the following develop many of the issues raised in this chapter:

Grindling, E. (2000) *The 3M Way to Innovation: Balancing people and profit*, Kodansha International, New York.

Hart, S. (1996) *New Product Development, A Reader*, The Dryden Press, London.

Shavinina, L. (2003) *The International Handbook on Innovation*, Elsevier, Oxford.

Swink, M.L., Sandvig, J.C. and Mabert, V.A. (1996) 'Adding "zip" to product development: concurrent engineering methods and tools', *Business Horizons*, Vol. 39, No. 2, 41–50.

Takeuchi, H. and Vanaka, I. (1996) 'The new product development game', *Harvard Business Review*, Vol. 64, No. 1, 137–46.

13

Packaging and product development

Packaging is rarely the first issue one cites when we are asked to consider the reasons why some firms are successful. Yet, when one strolls into McDonald's for a morning cup of coffee one cannot separate the beverage from its packaging: the cup, the lid, the stirrer and the bag in which you carry away your hot drink. The packaging's colourful imagery helps reinforce the brand of McDonald's and does much more such as: keep the drink warm; help to reduce spillage through a lid; enables you to hold the drink without scalding your hand, enables you to add milk and sugar to suit your personal preference. While this is a very simple illustration it reminds us of how easy it is to overlook packaging and its role in product development.

This chapter examines the role of packaging in the product development process and illustrates the importance of packaging in the development of new products in the fast-moving consumer goods (fmcg) sector.

Chapter contents

Learning objectives

When you have read this chapter you will be able to:

- understand the contribution packaging can make to the new product development process;
- recognise the wide range of packaging systems available;
- recognise the significance of the interface between product and channel members;
- recognise how packaging can provide significant scope for added-value benefits; and
- demonstrate what impact packaging has on product development, brand management and channel management.

Wrapping and packaging products

Packaging and its products touch all our lives every day. It is inextricably bound up with all kinds of industries, both large and small. The world packaging industry is estimated to be $900bn (Directories Today, 2003). The UK packaging market in 2001 was reckoned to be worth £9.2bn and the industry employs around 100,000 people (Timms, 2002). Packaging is a vital tool in the marketing mix, too often ignored by companies, but twice as much is annually spent on this as on above-the-line advertising and promotions (Sara, 1990). Moreover, every product produced requires packaging; hence the packaging industry is one of the largest sectors in the world economy.

When it comes to packaging Japan and its long history of craftsmen and designers are unsurpassed in their beautiful and delicate wrappings of even the most fragile of products. Hideyuki Oka's best-selling book *How to Wrap Five Eggs* is a feast of 244 beautiful photographs of traditional delicate Japanese packaging (Oka, 1989). For example, there is an illustration of rope wrapping of dried fish, which provides ventilation thereby preserving the fish for up to six months and it is possible to unwrap just a bit at a time. The skills necessary to produce such exquisite wrapping and packaging of products are remarkable, the passing of which we all will surely lament. The eminent American designer in the foreword of this book asks:

If the craftsmen and designers of old Japan could create beauty with their materials are we today to accept defeat when faced with ours?

In Europe, one of the oldest and simplest forms of packaging, that was the norm in the nineteenth and early part of the twentieth centuries, was to wrap the product in paper. Very few products are still sold this way, even fewer food products. One product that has continued to be packaged in this way, despite fierce competition from substitute products, is butter. It continues to be offered as a block form simply wrapped in paper.

Table 13.1 Maintaining brand leadership through packaging developments, while the product remains unchanged

Brand	Position in 1935	Position in 2002
Bird's Custard	1	1
Heinz Soup	1	1
Kelloggs' Cornflakes	1	1
McVitie's Digestives	1	1
Cadbury's Dairy Milk Chocolate	1	1
Schweppes Mixers	1	1
Kodak Film	1	1

Such simple packaging is rarely selected by many firms today; indeed in most other product categories the world of packaging has changed considerably. In those cases where the product has been competing in the marketplace for many years it has been the development of its packaging that has enabled it to remain competitive, sometimes allowing the product to remain relatively unchanged (*see* Table 13.1). For example, at the beginning of the twentieth century washing detergent was originally sold in paper bags; this was later changed to cardboard boxes, and then plastic bags and more recently resealable plastic containers.

Packaging is a frequently overlooked aspect of managing products. It is not, however, overlooked by those involved in the daily ordering, shipping, storage and display of products. Retailers in particular have the daily, sometimes hourly task of ripping open boxes and lifting consumer products on to supermarket shelves. When one is in daily contact with a wide range of consumer products like this one soon appreciates the importance of packaging. Dented cans, torn boxes and leaky bottles cost P&G, the world's largest producer of fast moving consumer goods, over £50 million a year. It is very much aware of the impact of packaging on its profits. In the late 1990s P&G decided to tackle this issue and changed its policy on so-called 'unsaleables', those products that have damaged packaging. This change in policy had enormous implications for retailers. It introduced a no-returns policy and placed the responsibility of disposing of unsaleables with the retailers. In addition, P&G would pay a quarterly lump sum to retailers based on estimates of unsaleables likely to occur (Narisetti, 1997). The impact on all retailers was significant, but this serves as a reminder of how the issue of packaging affects businesses on a daily basis. In his eleventh edition of *Marketing Management*, Phillip Kotler suggested that packaging was so significant that many marketing managers have called it a fifth P along with price, product, place and promotion (Kotler, 2003: 436).

Packaging has evolved significantly from its uses by primitive societies to carry food and water. Glass containers first appeared in Egypt in 2000 BC and later the French emperor Napoleon awarded 12,000 francs to the winner of a contest to find a better way

Arla's yoghurt for children

Figure 13.1

05/05/2004

to preserve food, which led to a crude method of vacuum-packing (Croft, 1985). Today, where there is competition in virtually all product categories, packaging is often the consumer's first point of contact with the actual product and so it is essential to make it attractive and appropriate for both the product's and the customer's needs. Here then is the first challenge facing any product manager: to ensure the package for the product serves its functional purpose and acts as a means of communicating product information and brand character.

Illustration 13.1 shows how even for an established international brand like Timotei the significance of packaging continues to play a part in the brands growth. Failure to recognise this would have serious implications for the brands future.

If anyone is in any doubt about the importance of packaging in fmcg consider Figure 13.1. This shows Arla's yoghurt for children. The strawberry-flavoured yoghurt is contained in a yoghurt pot shaped in the style of 'Bob the Builder', BBC television's very successful children's television series: a new product created entirely from a change in packaging of the yoghurt. Clearly Arla of Denmark considers that the substantial royalty payments are worth it to secure increased sales of its yoghurt (www.Arlafoods.com). Furthermore, the future of the packaging industry looks exciting with new technologies offering many opportunities for growth. The use of intelligent packaging systems that sense and register changes in the pack contents are now being introduced by food manufacturers. And brand-protection devices such as radio frequency identification (RFID) tags are being added to packaging to prevent counterfeiting (Hancock, 2003).

Illustration 13.1

Why Timotei is packaged differently in India

Over the past five years Unilever has been steadily increasing sales of its international brand of shampoo: Timotei. European readers may be surprised to learn that consumers in India prefer to purchase their shampoo in individual sachets rather than in bottles. Unilever has tried to offer Timotei in a variety of size bottles but consumers prefer the individual sachets. It is true there are a number of explanations for this type of behaviour. First, there is the economics dimension that needs to be considered; that is the up front investment in a bottle of shampoo, which may sit around on a shelf for many weeks. Second, and most importantly for this group of consumers is the small individual sachet provides the correct amount of shampoo without the need to measure out the required quantity!

Source: BBC Radio 4, 'In Business', 6 February 2003.

The basic principles of packaging

The three basic principles of packaging are shown in Figure 13.2; they are:

1 protection (and tamper proofing);
2 containment; and
3 identification

These basic principles need to be met with all packaging at optimal overall cost. Clearly it is always possible to have improved packaging but at what cost and do the benefits enjoyed justify the additional cost? The Kellogg's Rice Krispies illustration (Figure 13.3) shows a cardboard box. The packaging for this product has changed very little since 1933; indeed today Kellogg's continue to use a cardboard box. The brand manager could for example use an aluminium box or a steel box or a polyurethane container (maybe it should), but the firm has decided that the additional cost would not be most advantageous for the firm.

| Figure 13.2 | The basic principles of packaging |

Source: Adapted from B. Stewart (1996) *Packaging as an Effective Marketing Tool*, Kogan Page, London.

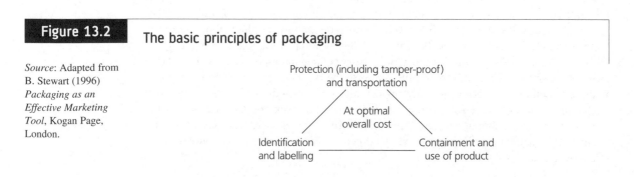

> The changing packaging of Kellogg's Rice Krispies; an illustration of a 1933 packet of Kellogg's Rice Krispies
>
> **Figure 13.3**

Protection

Packaging has a primary role in preserving product integrity by protecting the product against potential damage from climatic, bacteriological and transit hazards, plus any other hazards to which the product is likely to be exposed on its journey from manufacturer to the end consumer. UK multiples recognise that many products perish in the very last stages of their journey following purchase by the consumer. Typically products are accidentally dropped in the supermarket car park during loading into the car or they are attacked by pets or young children in the home prior to reaching the safety of the cupboard!

Tamper-proof packaging

Food producers and retailers have experienced commercial terrorism within their own stores. Sainsbury experienced several attempts in the 1990s to blackmail it out of millions of pounds. Baby food manufacturers such as Cow & Gate and Heinz were pioneers in developing tamper-proof packaging. All of their food products are now sold with tamper-proof packaging, which indicates any tampering to consumers and resellers. These baby food manufacturers use glass jars and metal jar tops with pop-up discs showing when a jar has been opened. In addition extra labelling on the package warns consumers not to purchase the product if the pop-up disc is visible (Morgan, 1997).

Containment

The second principle of any packaging is that of containment, which may seem almost too obvious for consideration. This may help to explain why this basic principle is often overlooked. It is during the use of the product by the consumer that issues of containment becomes all too visible. Fluids such as milk, orange juice and hair spray are obvious examples of products that require a package that contains the product after it has been initially used. Hence, there is a requirement for such packaging to have dispensing and resealing features. Effective containment clearly involves ensuring the pack does not leak, fall apart or otherwise annoy the end user. Caps that do not reseal properly, bags that split on opening, and cartons that fall apart are irritants, and they deter repeat purchases. As consumers we have all struggled to peel the aluminium foil lid off a yoghurt pot. In frustration we use more force only to send the entire contents onto the floor or worst still down the front of our shirt. Similarly we have all cut our fingers on the cardboard cartons of cereal boxes as we struggle to enter the box without ripping the top of the box.

Identification

The third basic principle underlying any form of packaging is that of identification, frequently referred to as labelling. It would be unusual to find an aisle of brown cardboard boxes sitting on shelves in a store but this would be the interesting experience

 Illustration 13.2

When the packaging is an integral part of the product

Books are probably the clearest example of where the packaging forms part of the product. In this case the cover helps to achieve the three basic objectives of packaging: containment, identification and protection. Significant resources are devoted to the task of devising a cover that will help sell a book. See the case study at the end of Chapter 5.

The Guinness 'in-can' system is another good example of a product that cannot be separated from its packaging; it is the particular packaging system that delivers the final product to the consumer. Indeed, it was the development of the product's packaging that itself led to a new product. The Guinness case study can be found at the end of Chapter 8.

Jiff Lemon is one of the few brands to mimic nature quite so unashamedly. Its packaging is in the shape of the fruit and allows the consumer to squeeze it without producing any wastage, and unlike real lemons has excellent storage properties.

Dulux solid emulsion overcomes the problem of dripping paint for the consumer. However, there was a ten-year gap between development of the solid emulsion and the development of the pack that allows access by the roller rather than having to empty the contents of the tin into a roller tray.

The toothpaste pump was developed in Sweden. This type of packaging is the norm for most toothpaste brands. It is an example of a packaging system coming to the aid of an outmoded, inefficient system for dispensing paste.

if products were to go unidentified or unlabelled. Canned food produce is a clear example of the importance of identification. Without the wrap around paper label all tins would appear identical, hence the need to inform the consumer what is inside the packaging. In many fast-moving consumer goods categories great efforts are made to display the actual product or part of the product to the consumer. This role of packaging includes:

- information on how the product is used;
- establishment of brand identity; and
- promotion of sale.

Identity is not simply a function of graphics; it can also be a function of shape. Shape can provide the unique brand identity for a product, or it can place the product in a specific market sector. For example, computer software is an intangible product, but by using a paint tin as packaging for a drawing and paint computer software product Jenkins & Hall Rucker, Rucker Design Group has helped reinforce the tangibility of art (Morgan, 1997).

The underlying principle that ties these three cornerstones of packaging together is that of optimal overall cost. This is an important concept for its implications are far beyond the basic unit cost of the packet. Whatever product is to go inside the package, it has to be filled or placed inside in an efficient operation or significant costs will be incurred at this stage. Similarly if the packet design leads to difficulties or poor performance in storage this will add to the overall costs. It should be clear that selecting the optimal package design to meet all the differing requirements is not a simple task.

Labelling

As well as the functional requirements that the label has to perform such as providing information on the following:

- source of the product;
- contents;
- how to use the product;
- universal product code (Upc) or bar code (used by retailers and producers for price and inventory control purposes);
- warnings;
- certifications;
- how to care for the product;
- nutritional information;
- type and style of the product; and
- size and number of servings.

A famous anecdote that is often told to reinforce the importance of packaging and labelling in particular concerns the ability of labelling to double sales of a product. The story goes that some of the world's leading fast-moving consumer goods manufacturer's were intrigued by an email, which they had received that claimed to be able to double sales. Eventually the firm was contacted and after the payment of appropriate sums of money revealed that by simply using the word 'repeat' on the package consumers would consume double the amount. Whether one believes the story or not the reverse is certainly true. Illustration 13.3 shows how poor labelling can lead to consumer confusion; in this case with pharmaceuticals. Labelling also serves to promote the product, however marketing communication is beyond the scope of this book (*see* Fill, 2001, *Marketing Communications: Context, Strategies and Applications*; Pickton and Broderick, 2002, *Integrated Marketing Communications*).

Illustration 13.3

Pharmaceutical packaging: a case of confusion

The pharmaceutical industry seems to be dominated by packaging initiatives that unnecessarily compromise patient compliance and thus safety. A middle-aged male patient in Ireland reports the challenge he faces daily as a result of inventiveness in product presentation. Currently he is prescribed six not unusual medications for a hypertensive condition and related effects, one replacing a previous drug. The packaging of each is in blister packs, one tablet to be taken per day, but the similarity ends there, as the variety with each manufacturer's packaging is substantial. The utter confusion is clear: no two packages are the same. Whether a blister pack covers one week or two, presentation may be in parallel rows or round the pack. Each pack has to be considered separately, the end of the run of removed tablets identified, and the next to be used identified. The only commonality is that the labelling of days of the week takes the form of three letters (with 'THURS' for Thursday in six cases). The print is always in fine lettering and never larger than 12 point. It is in capitals in six cases, and seldom in a dark colour. The typeface of one pack is such that if 'MON' is viewed upside down, it reads as an imperative 'NOW.' Three products originate or are packed in Ireland, three in England, and one is labelled as 'UK–Ireland' packaging of a French-licensed product. The only correlation is that it is the English products that give Sunday and Monday equal position as the start of the week.

This patient is fit, mentally competent, and has good vision, yet this variety faced at breakfast time and bedtime needs alertness at a time of day when this may be compromised. As pattern of removal is more prominent than indistinct printing, but leads to false decisions given the different patterns of presentation, wrong dosage is very possible and does occur. As these drugs are more likely to be prescribed in the later part of life for elderly or confused patients the risks are obvious, yet unnecessary.

There seems no need for this variety. Pharmaceutical manufacturers are not competing for patients on the basis of consumer choice of packaging, and patients have this non-conformity forced on them. Patients are unnecessarily put at risk by design inventiveness.

Producers of other products based on days of the week, such as diaries, calendars, and television listings, have moved towards a high degree of concordance even though consumers have personal choice. But in pharmaceuticals, where health and life are involved, this is not the case.

Source: M. Rigby (2002) 'Pharmaceutical packaging can induce confusion', letters to the editor, *British Medical Journal*, Vol. 324, 679.

Characteristics of packaging

Packaging provides significant scope for product and brand managers to develop their products. In its most simple form new packaging provides opportunities for making the product available in different quantities. Take a product like milk; it is available in a wide range of forms including: 4-pint containers, 2-litre containers, 1-litre containers, 1-pint containers, 1/2-pint containers and single vacuum-cup sachets for use by the trade in cafes, etc. This wide range of different size of packaging enables the product to be offered to different market segments: the 1/2-pint cardboard package is targeted at the snack/lunch box segment, whereas the larger 4-pint plastic container is targeted at the family home-use segment. Moreover, by considering carefully how your product is offered and used in the market it is possible to gain significant product design advantages. One of the most famous packaging developments occurred in the toilet cleaning products category. The appropriately named Toilet Duck product recognised that by changing the shape of the bottle it was possible to help consumers use the product. The angled spout with a swan-neck shape convinced shoppers that this product would make cleaning toilets easier. This change in pack design from the standard upright shaped bottle revolutionised this product range; now all products in this category have adopted similar shaped packaging. Table 13.2 offers a summary of some of the development opportunities that are available to virtually all fmcg products.

Dispensing

Table 13.5 (p. 434) illustrates a number of products that suffer from poor dispensing. Many manufacturers have attempted to improve this aspect of their products packaging. Most ground roast coffee packaging contains a plastic measuring scoop to facilitate dispensing into a percolator machine; the same cannot be said for rice or other dried pasta products where consumers are unsure about correct quantity. Similarly few people would buy a shower-gel product if it did not incorporate a hook from which to hang the product in the shower thereby facilitating dispensing.

Table 13.2 Fmcg packaging purpose and development considerations

Package purpose	Development considerations
dispense	Access; portion control, e.g. built in measure; pouring
storage	Stackability; location: refrigerator, bathroom, kitchen
stability	Storage life, especially after opening
handling	Ease of use for intended purpose
Opening/resealing	Appropriate to task i.e. frequency of use
After use	Secondary use (e.g. as storage container)
Disposal	Ease of disposal

Storage

Easy product storage is one aspect of packaging purpose that can offer considerable development opportunities. In this case storage refers to storage of the pack by the consumer after purchase. One would rightly question the wisdom of glass containers for products that are frequently used in a bathroom. Similarly the packaging for tinned food facilitates stacking and storage. It is therefore necessary to think through the use of a product rather than simply consider on-shelf appearance, notwithstanding this aspect of merchandising.

Stability

Stability in this case does not refer to physical stability of the package in terms of whether it remains upright; this is covered under storage. Stability in this case refers to shelf-life. There are some obvious examples of packaging development to lengthen the shelf-life for products such as septic packaging for milk and orange juice. Bread manufacturers have also developed foil packaging in attempt to improve the shelf-life of the product after opening. Conversely pharmaceutical manufacturers are in search of almost the opposite objective: packaging that will deteriorate the product as soon as the shelf-life has expired. One of the concerns of pharmaceutical manufacturers is the use of drugs, such as antibiotics, by consumers long after their shelf-life has expired, hence they are developing packaging that turns an unappealing black colour.

Handling

Effective pack handling is also an important issue to consider in adding value and consumer convenience. The built-in carrying handle on a 2-litre or 4-litre milk carton is an obvious example where without it simply taking the product from the shelf would be problematic. Conversely glass bottles of wine are frequently dropped on their journey from shelf to the safety of the consumer's car. Initial pack handling then needs careful consideration when developing packaging, but so to does the ability to direct the product to do its job. Producers of baby products have long recognised this important element in pack design. For example, Johnson & Johnson understand that where baby personal care products are concerned ease of use is essential because at least one hand will be holding the baby.

Opening/resealing

Many products once opened require resealing for use at another time, whether it is a 250-gram tub of yellow spread that has a plastic lid or a shampoo bottle with a screw cap the ability to reseal and re-open a package is a fundamental requirement for many products. Packaging engineers and designers need to think through the product's use from the consumer's viewpoint in order to design-in appropriate re-sealing to the packaging system. An example where this element of packaging has helped manufacturer's add value to their offering is in carbonated drinks – 333-ml cans of carbonated drinks such as Coca-Cola, Pepsi and Irn-Bru retail for 25 per cent less than their screw-cap plastic 333-ml bottle equivalents. Consumers are willing to pay a premium for the ability to drink, seal and re-open the product.

After use and secondary use

The use of some packaging for storage containers has a long heritage and is recognised by many brand managers. The round tins used to package and store loose tobacco have been used by households all over the world for a variety of secondary uses. One of the world's oldest producers and distributors of tea, Twinings, have frequently used their loose tea tins as a promotional incentive. Consumers see value in purchasing the product to obtain a useful steel storage tin complete with hinged lid. At the most basic level, many households reuse polyethylene carrier bags as waste-bin liners.

Disposal

The ability to dispose of packaging easily with the minimum of fuss is a consumer convenience that is often overlooked as an opportunity to add value. The obvious example where disposal takes a high priority is in diapers or nappies. In this case the introduction of a use and dispose product made this necessary but unpleasant activity more convenient for the consumer. In other fmcg areas, there are many opportunities for development. Many plastics-film materials, in particular resist disposal in the waste-bin by expanding rather than being compressed. Similarly the 2-litre or 4-pint milk containers take up considerable space in the waste-bin. Moreover, it is at this stage where environmental concerns are most obvious as consumers begin to consider where the refuse will go next. This subject, however, is vast and beyond the scope of this chapter or book.

Having developed an improved pack design it is necessary to communicate this to consumers, especially if this developed advantage is not obvious. This area of brand management and marketing communications is beyond the scope of this book and readers should consult texts such as: Kotler, 2002, *Marketing Management*; Fill, 2002, *Marketing Communications*; and Pickton and Broderick, 2000, *Integrated Marketing Communications*.

 Illustration 13.4   FT

Laundry, with a minor in linguistics: Once informative, product packaging has gone global and now offers lessons in a dozen different languages

Globalisation has a lot to answer for: Chicken McNuggets, the World Trade Organisation, the rising cost of tear gas. And have you tried washing your clothes with Ariel Futur laundry detergent lately?

Once, the writing on a box of soap powder offered the intrigue and excitement of a minor novel. It told strange tales of miraculous ingredients that lifted hidden dirt and digested stubborn stains, and evoked a thrilling sense of danger

▶

with its heavily emphasised warnings ('DO NOT wash flame-resistant fabrics at temperatures above 50 degrees C' – presumably, for fear of triggering a conflagration).

But pick up a pack of Ariel Futur in Europe today, and you enter a different world: one in which 'future' no longer ends with an 'e', and more regrettably, in which the great soapbox literature of the past has given way to indecipherable pictograms and a babel of tongues.

The product information on a pack of Ariel Futur now appears in 10 languages, with English at the bottom of the list. As a result, it takes 10 times as many words to say anything, so even after the sub-miniaturisation of the text, there is room for only the bare minimum of information.

Gone are the reassuring claims about the product's efficaciousness; there is no hint as to whether the detergent is meant for white or coloured clothes; and English speakers will not know the powder contains enzymes, a skin irritant for many adults and children, unless they turn the pack upside down and scour the small print on the bottom.

Procter & Gamble, the product's maker, has tried to ease the pressure on space by substituting pictograms for some of the instructions. From these, users may deduce that if they want to wash a white T-shirt with a large smudge on the upper left thorax, and if the water that comes out of the taps is mid-grey rather than black (hard) or white (soft), they should use an 88ml dose of power.

But how many households have a device capable of delivering such a precise measure? There is nothing inside the pack to help. And what happens if you throw caution to the wind, take a wild guess, and inadvertently administer a 90ml dose? Do your underpants melt?

Globalisation, of course, is to blame for the Ariel Futur user's predicament. P&G and other companies are trying to maximise profits by selling the same product, in the same packaging, in as many different countries as they can. Thus, the list of ingredients on Unilever's Magnum ice-cream wrapper is translated into 10 languages, and the 20 languages on a pack of P&G's Pampers nappies range from Hungarian to Hebrew.

This does have its benefits. In the UK, P&G now sells its cheese-and-onion flavoured Pringles crisps in bilingual tubs marked 'fromage & oignon', greatly extending Britons' notoriously poor linguistic skills. And no one need wonder how to say 'surfactant' in Finnish any more. (It is 'tensideja').

Even so, in a week that has brought the ousting of P&G's chief executive after three profit warnings in four months, you have to wonder how far this makes sense. Companies such as P&G are trying to make global citizens of their customers at a time when globalisation has seldom been as unpopular.

Last year, Coca-Cola went through a crisis that, like P&G's, sent its share price tumbling and resulted in the ousting of its chief executive. His replacement, Douglas Daft, has said many times that the company's biggest blunder was going global at a time when the world was going local.

'Think local, act local' is now the mantra at Coca-Cola. They should try it at P&G. It might just sell a little more soap.

Source: R. Tomkins, 'Laundry, with a minor in linguistics', *Financial Times*, 10 June 2000.

Product rejuvenation

All markets inevitably experience periods of both growth and decline. Product managers have been very successful in intervening to help their products increase market share and extend their life in the marketplace. None the less, as growth slows and products enter maturity, profit margins to the firms and their owners, in particular, will begin to decline. The firms will be putting the product managers under pressure to regain those margins. The product managers will hopefully already have new product development projects in place, but they may wish also to consider rejuvenating the existing product. Developing the packaging is an activity that is frequently overlooked in favour of increased promotional activity or more radical product development activity. Rogers (1962) cites a number of reasons why profit margins decline:

- Increasing number of competitive products leading to over-capacity and intensive competition:
- market leaders under pressure from smaller companies;
- strong increase in R&D to find better versions of the product;
- cost economies used up;
- decline in product distinctiveness;
- dealer apathy and disenchantment with a product with declining sales; and
- changing market composition where the loyalty of those first to adopt begins to waver.

Packaging development provides a relatively inexpensive way of rejuvenating a product. Johnson and Jones' (1957) product-market matrix offers an excellent classification of nine opportunities for growth (*see* Figure 12.6). Packaging, however, is not mentioned. Since this time technology has developed rapidly and the opportunities now available to packaging engineers is simply breathtaking. It is possible to use virtually any material and improved printing techniques provide further flexibility. Illustration 13.5 shows the breathtaking assortment of packaging systems available to the product manager

Illustration 13.5

We need a bottle for our pills, what can you do?

The answer is quite a lot. The following gives an indication of the extent of this variety on offer to the product or brand manager:

- Clic reversible cap child-resistant vials (very small medicine bottle);
- Clear-Vu Screw-Loc child-resistant vials;
- Clear-Vu PET plastic graduated oval bottles;
- ointment jars, dropper bottles, amber glass oval bottles;
- amber glass pill vials and square jars;

- child-resistant and regular continuous thread closures;
- HDPE wide-mouth pharmaceutical rounds; and
- Sani-Glas graduated flint glass oval bottles

Plus many more . . .

D. Luce & Son Inc., a wholesale distributor of prescription packaging and pharmacy supplies since 1943 offers a wide variety of glass and plastic containers, and closures.

Source: www.essentialsupplies.com

considering packaging for what one might consider as straightforward: some pills. Alas, even here the options are considerable.

Indeed, the packaging industry has been one of the fastest growing industries over the past 20 years. A simple but effective illustration of the industry and revenues involved can be found by referring to some trivia from the UK's *Sunday Times* 'Rich List'. Each year this national newspaper produces a list of the wealthiest people in Britain. In 2003 Hans Rausing was second on this list; he is part of the family behind the Tetra Pack empire (*Sunday Times*, 2003). One of the industry's leaders is Smurfit-Stone Container Corporation (Nasdaq: SSCC). It is the world's largest integrated producer of paperboard and paper-based packaging products. In the year 2000 68 per cent of Smurfit-Stone's operating revenue was generated from containerboard and corrugated container sales. Consumer packaging, which includes folding cartons and boxboard mills, accounted for 12 per cent; speciality packaging accounted for 8 per cent; and recycling, 5 per cent.

New product opportunities through packaging

Continual analysis of the market in which current products operate should provide many opportunities for developing the product/brand. This is one of the fundamental responsibilities of the brand manager; in much the same way as scientists are expected to remain up-to-date with scientific developments in their field, so too must brand managers. With this in mind brand managers should be reviewing opportunities continually. Frequently, the decision not to proceed with a business opportunity may be correct, but as was stated earlier, in virtually all cases improvements to a product's packaging are always possible. For example, it is usually possible to improve the way a product is displayed on the shelf or to improve the opening or resealing, etc. Frequently the changes will be minor, but sometimes a change in packaging can lead to a completely new market for the brand. Take the example of 'Celebrations', the new assorted chocolate product from Mars. This has proved to be an extremely successful new product for Mars and has helped the firm establish itself in the chocolate gift-box market; a segment previously unexploited and dominated by its competitors Nestlé with Quality Street and Cadbury's with Roses. If ever there was an example of the power of packaging in new product development this was it. Illustration 13.6 shows how Toblerone changes its packaging to enable it to compete in the gift market.

Altering the packaging of a product can considerably change the target market and the way a product is used. The example of carbonated soft drinks is useful here. Lemonade offered in glass bottles suggests high quality and is aimed at the adult market. Lemonade in PET bottles and aluminium cans is offered to the children's market, whereas PVC bottles are usually targeted at the family 2-litre take-home market. Table 13.3 illustrates the wide range of packaging systems used in a single product category.

Illustration 13.6

Toblerone Multiple Gift Pack

Toblerone is a milk chocolate bar studded with almonds and nougat. It is a Swiss product and unapologetically uses the triangular segments of chocolate to echo the mountains of Switzerland and to distinguish itself from the traditional flat chocolate bar. This distinctive triangular pack, printed in gold and red, has been deliberately untouched for decades. It is an excellent example of visual or design equity; a visual element in a product that is so synonymous with the product that it can only be changed at great risk.

KJS, the new owners of Toblerone, wanted to extend the brand's appeal to higher volume markets, in particular the chocolate gift market. The market leaders in this very large segment were Cadbury's Roses and a new entrant Mars Celebrations.

Blueberry Design in London was commissioned to develop new packaging for the product that would enable it to compete in the gift market. The packaging had to retain the visual equity of the existing single product but in a luxury format to compete with some of the luxury products.

The result was the Toblerone gift pack. A multipack cardboard 'Christmas cracker' shape which contains six 50g bars in one pack.

Source: C.L. Morgan (1997) *Packaging Design*, Watson-Guptill, New York.

Table 13.3 A wide variety of packaging systems are used for soft drinks

Packaging system	Benefits and limitations
Glass bottle	Indicated high quality, can be clear or coloured; not suitable for children's drinks; rigid structure for graphics; recyclable.
PET (Polyethylene terephthalate) bottle	Can be clear or coloured; resealable, suitable for carbonated soft drinks; unbreakable, recyclable, rigid structure for graphics.
PVC (Poly vinyl chloride) bottle	More opaque than PET; less rigid; can have a handle incorporated; cheap; unbreakable.
Aluminium can	Particularly suitable for carbonated soft drinks; unresealable; effective structure for graphics; recyclable.
Steel-mix can	Particularly suitable for carbonated soft drinks; unresealable; effective structure for graphics; recyclable; cheaper than aluminium.
Tetra Pack carton	Ideal for children's drinks; variety of pack sizes; cheap; unresealable; appropriate for long-life drinks; recyclable.

Product and pack size variation

Product and brand managers are constantly searching for ways to increase sales, especially when this is linked to their personal remuneration. By aligning pack sizes with particular consumer life styles it is possible to increase growth through market development. For some consumers making less frequent trips to the store suits their busy schedule, others who have more time to shop and operate with restricted budgets may opt for smaller pack sizes. For large families large pack sizes are bought frequently because consumption is high, whereas for older people living alone the reverse may be true.

Opportunities for size alterations are relatively straightforward for the manufacturer of 'free flowing' consumables such as food and personal care products in the form of liquids, granules and powders. The situation is different with unit products such as disposable nappies or a confectionary chocolate bar. The implications in this category are much more significant and are similar to those of a new product introduction. Indeed, the introduction by Mars of its Celebrations product was essentially a product/pack size alteration.

There is a strong association in the eyes of the consumer between larger pack size and economy; however there are some obvious restrictions in terms of how large a pack should be, such as:

- weight and ease of carrying home;
- storage space within the home;
- product usage versus shelf-life;
- capital outlay; and
- ease of dispensing product from large container.

Clearly larger packs carry a weight penalty and there is a limit to what a consumer can be expected to carry home. Packaging for baby nappies and washing detergents almost excludes those without a car to carry the product home.

Another area where large packs are used is in promotions where packs are frequently sold with a 25 per cent free content. Once again for 'free flow' consumables (such as cereals or shampoo) this is a relatively easy option to exploit, but for unit consumables, such as confectionary chocolate bars, the implications are akin to a new product introduction.

The example of the Mars Celebration new product illustrates the opportunities that exist in exploiting smaller product/pack varieties. Small containers are often associated with 'precious' products, and indeed many 'exclusive' brands of perfume are packaged in this way. The travel market is another segment where small containers have obvious advantages. One product that utilises both small packaging and product variants is Kellogg's cereal variety pack. This product provides the fascination of miniaturised products of their full-size counterparts, and product variants within one unit pack. Variety packs provide opportunities for manufacturers to move less popular products.

Illustration 13.7

Dulux emulsion paint – new package development

It is attention to the detail and painstaking analysis that frequently leads to effective results. This was the case when ICI owners of the Dulux paint brand began looking at ways to try to differentiate its product from that of the competition. After all, paint is hardly a new product – it has been around for hundreds of years. There have been developments in paint technology such as the introduction of emulsion paint and more recently the move to more aqueous-based paints. None the less, in 2000 when product managers at Dulux began reviewing their emulsion product it was, as usual, the ability to differentiate the brand amongst the competition that would allow it to charge a premium for its product and increase its market share. The emulsion market is crowded and competition from DIY store brands such as B&Q, Homebase, Wicks, etc. is fierce. Furthermore, many consumers perceive emulsion to be a commodity product such as coffee, and so the argument goes: 'coffee is coffee – why would anyone pay more for one type of coffee?' But, as all students of marketing know, this is precisely the role of brand management to develop the brand and position it in the market place so that consumers are willing to pay a premium for it. With this in mind Dulux Emulsion brand and product managers set about examining their product.

They started by examining the end use of a tin of emulsion paint. The paint is probably going to be used by homeowners decorating their own property. The influence of successful television programmes such as the BBC's 'Changing Rooms' cannot be overlooked. Frequently, the house will be furnished and the task is to improve the appearance of the room. None the less, avoiding spillage and mess is a high priority of users. Indeed, they will usually put down sheets of newspaper and dustsheets to avoid drips of emulsion on furniture (so called non-drip paints have been on the market for many

years but drips still occur). The tin will need a handle to facilitate lifting and carrying from floor to stepladder etc. The lid must be secure to enable users to close with confidence it will not leak and yet must be able to be re-opened. Frequently, the user will struggle with a screwdriver to open the tin. When this has been achieved the user searches for a stick or maybe the same screwdriver to stir the contents of the tin. Those studying carefully will not have forgotten the lid, which needs to be placed somewhere, paint-side up! Hopefully, where someone will not walk on it or put their hand on it. And let us not forget the stick that was used to stir the emulsion, where does that now go? When the emulsion is used, excess emulsion has to be removed from the brush by scraping it across the top of the tin. This causes paint to build up in the rim that eventually overflows down the side of the tin or hardens slowly making re-sealing the lid difficult. After the painting is complete the tin will be stored in the garage.

This analysis of emulsion paint in use quickly revealed to Dulux brand and product managers that the existing packaging was failing in many areas and numerous opportunities existed to create consumer benefits through packaging improvements. Not all of these have been developed and some will be developed over time because brand managers have to consider *optimal overall cost* (*see* Figure 1.1):

- a genuine 'non-drip' emulsion paint;
- change tin to enable access to tin with roller;
- a hinged lid;
- provision of stirring stick;
- safety catch on lid to reassure closure;
- indicator on tin showing when past shelf-life; and
- transparent tin showing colour of contents.

Packaging systems

Whether one is considering the packaging for a new product or reviewing the packaging of an existing product it is worth remembering that all packaging can be improved. There is, however, the optimal overall cost to consider (*see* Figure 1.1). The type of materials used and the package system selected are inextricably linked together, particularly when one considers the high-volume automated production lines that will be used for fmcgs. Any large-scale capital expenditure will require careful analysis and justification, hence product and brand managers need an understanding of the variety of packaging systems available. Table 13.4 provides a summary of the most common forms of packaging and their key attributes in fmcgs.

Table 13.4 Packaging systems

Packaging system	Product example	Key attributes
Steel and aluminium tins and cans	Carbonated soft drink	Unresealable (single serve); effective structure for graphics; recyclable.
Folding cartons	Frozen cheesecakes; cereal boxes; Easter eggs.	Versatile; fnal shape often a box but features such as handles can be added; cardboard engineering and new coatings provide additional opportunities.
Rigid boxes	Polystyrene boxes for chicken pieces and minced beef.	Still used for premium products; stackability; separate lid;
Hanging-pack formats:	Popular within the DIY market.	Inexpensive; ideal for small low cost items.
– Blister packs	Children's small toys; batteries.	Versatile blister from PVC usually mounted onto a backing card.
– Skin packs	Often used in promotions to put two products together, e.g. jar of coffee and a packet of biscuits.	Versatile blister from PVC, similar to above without the backing card mount; forms a 'covering skin' around the product.
– Cartons	Small cartons of DIY products such as screws, nails, etc.	All advantages of cartons plus ability to hang.
Flowraps	Chocolate bars.	Inexpensive, good graphics available; variety of flms available.
Glass bottles and jars	Premium products; wine; baby food.	Traditional, facilitates tamper proofng.
PVC bottles and jars	Personal care products; carbonated drinks.	More opaque than PET; less rigid; can have a handle incorporated; cheap; unbreakable.
PET bottles and jars	Premium personal care products; carbonated drinks.	Can be clear or coloured; resealable; unbreakable; recyclable; rigid structure for graphics.
Flexible tubes	Toothpaste; pharmaceutical creams.	Convenience of application; resealability.
Thermoform/fll/seal	Yoghurt pots; pharmaceutical products.	Simple; facilitates in-house packaging; cost-effective.
Composite containers	Pringles	A spirally wound paper-based tube with plastic end caps.
Bags	Potato chips; rice; sugar; fertiliser; retailer carrier-bags.	Wide variety of fnished products available from high-quality paper carrier-bag with rope handle to thin polyethylene carrier-bag.

Retailer acceptance

When considering a product's packaging it is desirable if not essential to get input from members of the distribution channel from an early stage. After all, it is resellers and wholesalers who have to handle, store and deliver the product to the retailer. Consideration must therefore be given to storage space, ease of stacking and handling. A triangular-shaped box may be an interesting design for a new brand of soup but if distributors and resellers have difficulty storing and stocking it they may decide not to purchase it and stock it in their stores.

For a new product to become successful it must, of course, be accepted by the final user, but success is also dependent on acceptance of the new product by the channel members through whom it passes in reaching the final customers. Whereas final users are most concerned about how the product will perform when used, channel members are much more interested in how the product will sell, whether it will be easy to stock and display and most important, whether it will be profitable. This is especially the case when it comes to consumables, which is the business of the supermarkets. Such retailers are overwhelmed by products that consumers hardly ever buy. Research from Kurt Salmon Associates found that almost 25 per cent of the 30,000 products in a typical supermarket sell less than one unit a month. And 85 per cent of the sales are generated by just 7 per cent of the products (Schiller *et al.*, 1996). No wonder retailers are sceptical of more new products.

Levels of anxiety increase still further for manufacturer brands when they consider the rise of the distributor brands or store brands. Distributor brands or store brands sell in supermarkets typically for about 10–20 per cent less than manufacturers' brands, yet the profit margins realised by supermarkets are usually about 10–15 per cent higher than for manufacturer' brands. A significant amount of shelf space is given over to the store's own brands, thus making any request for additional shelf space more likely to be rejected.

While the manufacturer may view the idea of having 10 flavours of ice cream as an excellent marketing idea, the retailer would prefer fewer flavours as they see different flavours simply competing with one another and not contributing to turnover. From the retailer's perspective they want to:

- stock only product lines that sell;
- reduce quantity purchased; and
- stock goods that produce high levels of profit.

Retailers do recognise that they have to offer a service to the consumer and so they have to stock a variety of products, but manufacturers must recognise that the retailer will frequently see things differently. Understanding the problems retailers face will help in developing effective packaging. For example, one needs to consider how a retailer would prefer (probably intends) to stock and display the goods. Consider a pizza. Is this product to be displayed lying flat on a shelf with the facing edge being the side of the box or is to be displayed standing on its end with the full pizza facing outwards? The manufacturer may prefer the exciting toppings on the pizza to be facing out, but the retailer may argue that a lack of shelf space prevents this option from being considered. Such constraints may force manufacturers to alter their packaging.

Table 13.5 Ten of the most irritating packages

	Product package	Problem/difficulty
1	4-pint milk plastic containers	Leakage
2	Single-portion vacuum-formed cup for milk	Difficult to open
3	Biscuit wraps	Difficult to open
4	Frozen vegetables in bags	Cannot reseal
5	Sugar, flour and rice bags	Cannot be resealed
6	Audio cassettes that are tightly shrink-wrapped	Difficult to open
7	Vacuum-packed roasted coffee	Difficult to open and to dispense
8	McDonald's Happy Meals	Excessive packaging
9	Pickled onions in glass jar	Difficult to remove screw-top lid
10	Toothpaste tube	Excessive waste, unable to access all the contents

Source: P. Trott (2003) 'Packaging and new product opportunities', University of Portsmouth Business School, Working Paper Series No. 00123.

Revitalising mature packaged goods

The idea of the product life cycle implies that the brand will eventually die, but there is no reason why a brand should die if it is attached to a product people want to buy. One only has to look around at the brands on our shelves and one is immediately struck by the longevity of many brands (*see* Chapter 11). None the less many brands do lose sales and become labelled mature or, worse, old! In such circumstances brand managers need to use a variety of tools and skills if they are to successfully revitalise these mature goods. There are three key areas that need to be addressed:

- reminding consumers about the brand;
- improving where the product is sold; and
- improving the packaging.

The first of these is largely a promotional tactic and beyond the scope of this book. According to Wansink and Huffman (2001) it is the simple act of promoting an old brand, which consequently results in significant increases in sales. It is almost as if the consumer has forgotten about the brand and, when they are reminded of its existence they buy it because they have not had it for a while.

Illustration 13.8

Packing in freshness with foil at Walkers Crisps

Walker's was founded in 1948 in Leicester, England. It sold potato chips (crisps) at a price premium because it argued that its crisps were fresher than the competition. This small but significant price premium enabled the firm to spend more on advertising than the competition, which in turn drove up sales. In 1989 PepsiCo acquired Walker's and set about expanding the brand. PepsiCo identified that Walker's would be able to reinforce their freshness advantage through improving the packaging of their product. The standard packaging across the industry for crisps was see-through cellophane. Walker's introduced foil packaging,

which kept the product fresher for longer. Moreover, it was seen as an innovative product development and indeed was promoted as such. By 1994 Walker's was the biggest food brand in the United Kingdom in terms of unit sales. Since this development Walker's have developed the brand further using by Gary Lineker (UK soccer hero) and later Michael Owen (England international soccer player) to promote the brand.

Source: K.L. Keller (2003) *Building, Measuring and Managing Brand Equity*, 2nd edn, Prentice-Hall, Englewood Cliffs, NJ.

Case Study

Halfords Motor Oil: Redesign and rebranding of an existing product[1]

Introduction

Halfords is Britain's number one retailer of car parts, cycles and accessories. With over 400 stores in Britain, it attracts more than 1.2 million customers through its doors every week and is one of the largest non-food retailers in the United Kingdom. It boasts around 12,000 product lines, an annual turnover of in excess of £500 million and a company history spanning more than a century; many analysts view it as a British business institution.

For many British car users, especially the DIY enthusiast, when they require something for their car Halfords would be one of the first retailers they would consider. Yet, surprisingly in the 1990s Halfords own brand of motor oil

did not sell well and preliminary market research revealed that it was not valued highly by its customers. Some executives at Halfords considered it surprising that, given that oil was largely a commodity product like bread and milk, sales of their own-brand oil was disappointing. The company set out to investigate what could be done to increase sales.

Background

Founded as a local hardware store in Birmingham in 1892 by F.W. Rushbrooke, Halfords has since grown to establish its position as the leading retailer of car parts, cycles and accessories in the UK. It was not until 1965 that the business

[1] This case has been written as a basis for class discussion rather than to illustrate effective or ineffective managerial administrative behaviour. It has been prepared from a variety of published sources, as indicated, and from observations.

▶

became known as Halfords Limited. The years that followed saw Halfords open its 300th store and become part of the Burmah Group in 1969. The business moved to a custom-built head office and warehouse in Redditch, Worcestershire, where it remains to this day.

The 1980s was a decade of change for Halfords, as it was one of the first retail groups to make the move from the high street to edge of town locations, recognising customers' needs for bigger stores, more choice and convenient parking. It also introduced its well-known blue, red and white corporate identity. Two more changes of ownership followed with the Ward White Group purchasing the business in 1984 and then the acquisition of the Group by The Boots Company in 1989. Since then, Halfords has gone from strength to strength, leading the revolution in out-of-town retailing, generating consistent growth in sales and profits over the last 10 years and clearly establishing itself as the UK market leader. In April 2000, Rod Scribbins became managing director, overseeing the rollout of the company's ambitious 'Arcade' superstore programme. Within 'Arcade' stores customers benefit from added features including sub-shops for Bikehut, Audio, Parts, Ripspeed and Touring. More product ranges, specialist staff who are enthusiasts in their particular areas and a brighter, more contemporary shopping environment, are all changes that have been introduced.

In September 2002, Halfords was acquired by CVC Capital Partners from The Boots Company and Rod Scribbins was appointed chief executive. Halfords head office employs 600 people, supporting over 400 stores with a total staff of 9,000.

The problem

As is often the case in such apparent positive positions, all is not well in the Halfords garden. Scratch beneath the surface and problems and missed opportunities abound. One in particular is the focus of this study: motor oil. Given that Halfords is the largest retailer of motor oil in the United Kingdom one might expect sales of its own brand of motor oil to be significant. This however, was not the case, indeed sales from its own brand were very disappointing. This is somewhat surprising given that sales from store brands in the United Kingdom are generally good. That is, compared with some European countries the UK consumer has a favourable view towards store brands and in many product categories, from clothes to food, consumers readily purchase a store brand. Why then not motor oil? Moreover, Halfords saw this as a business opportunity they wished to exploit, but how? Was there something particularly unusual about motor oil? Who were the competitors? What were the other brands? Was this a market in which Halfords could be competitive? So many questions, and at present so few answers. The one question that had been answered by the managing director of Halfords was that the business should exploit this opportunity.

Design brief

Halfords decided that it did not have sufficient expertise in-house to tackle the task of exploring the task of rebranding and repackaging a major product. The firm commissioned the international design group Pentagram with a brief to redevelop its brand of motor oil. This would probably involve redesigning the container, relabelling it and repositioning it in the market. The decision to use an external agency is not uncommon and is the approach followed by most large retailers. Such product design expertise is rarely found in-house and such projects are commonly contracted to third-party experts.

Research

The brief to Pentagram was clear, but before the firm could start it needed to understand the situation better. Indeed, it needed to be sure that it was going to address the problem and not a symptom of the problem. Pentagram undertook its own market research on retailing motor oil and undertook a series of in-depth interviews with consumers in the form of focus groups to try to uncover some of the issues surrounding motor oil.

The team soon uncovered that the industry is confronting a number of changes. In particular there is an overall decline in sales as modern cars require less servicing and less frequent top-ups and changes. On the other hand, within this declining market premium grade motor oils rather than standard-grade are becoming more prevalent. Furthermore, the industry is dominated by some of the largest firms in the world most notably the world's oil companies. Over many years these firms have developed a range of brands that are synonymous with motoring. This association is reinforced through extensive advertising and sponsorship of motoring events in particular Formula One motor racing. Indeed, most oils carried 'flashy' Grand Prix-style branding. It seemed that this did nothing to help consumers select the correct oil. The brand leaders in Europe are:

- BP and Castrol;
- Shell Oils; and
- Exon (Esso) Mobil.

BP recently announced a major sponsorship deal with David Beckham as *The Guardian* recently announced (Day, 2002):

> *Not content with posing smothered in baby oil for a magazine cover shoot, David Beckham has signed up to endorse an oil more associated with the grime of the garage – BP's Castrol brand. The England and Real Madrid football star has signed a two-year sponsorship deal with oil giant BP to promote the Castrol lubricant.*

The Pentagram team next had to investigate the product in terms of what it does.

What motor oil does in your engine

Motor oil lubricates the hundreds of moving parts in your engine to keep them from wearing out before their normal lifetime. It must also help to cool the engine, and keep hot combustion gases out of the crankcase. And it cleans up water, soot, carbon, lead salts and acids that get into every engine. Thus, the right motor oil helps the engine run better and last longer.

To help oil do these jobs better, certain chemicals, called additives, are put into it. For example, cleaning additives, called detergents or dispersants grab dirt and sludge particles as they are generated in the engine and hold them in suspension until they are removed when you change oil. Other additives fight oxidation, rust, corrosion and foaming to prolong engine life. But additives are used up in doing their work, and can only be replaced by changing the oil. To summarise, engine motor oil is required for:

- lubrication of the moving engine parts to prevent wear;
- reducing friction;
- maintaining engine cleanliness;
- protecting against engine rust and corrosion;
- cooling engine parts;
- sealing combustion gases;
- permitting easy starting; and
- extending engine life.

Different types of engine oils

There are different types of oil and consumers have to pick the oil that is best for their own usage and application. They have to choose an oil depending upon how they use their car, and the outdoor temperature they are driving in.

Outdoor temperature

As the temperature changes, the viscosity or fluidity of the oil changes. Think of the oil in the engine as being like molasses in a bottle.

When the bottle of molasses is removed from the refrigerator, it is very thick or viscous and moves slowly. But if it is warmed up, it becomes thinner and flows easily. The same is true of oil in an engine. When it is cold, the oil will be thick. If it is too thick, it may not even allow the engine to turn over and start. On the other hand, if it is too thin, it may allow the engine to start but it could be too thin when the engine warms up to do its work properly.

Viscosity measurements designate thickness and thinness

To tell consumers how thick or thin an oil is, the Society of Automotive Engineers (SAE) has established a viscosity classification that appears on the top of oil cans. The numbers consumers see go from 5W, which would be for very thin oil used in extremely cold weather conditions, up to a 50, which would be for very thick oils that have special uses such as very hot applications or racing engines. These numbers designate the SAE viscosity grade. Most people use a multi-graded oil that covers the highest and lowest temperatures that will be encountered.

This background information was useful and helped the team paint a picture of the product, the brands and the market. It also revealed that 50 per cent of cars required premium grade oil, yet 75 per cent of sales was standard grade. It seemed that many consumers were not buying the correct oil, moreover Halfords was not selling its most profitable lines.

It was now necessary to uncover the views of consumers; in particular the team were aware that many motorists did not buy motor oil and left this to the annual service of their car. What soon became clear following discussions with retailers was that there were essentially three types of buyers of motor oil:

1　DIY enthusiast – regular purchaser of motor oil. This group undertook their own servicing of their vehicle.

2　DIY part-timer. This group did not service their own vehicle but regularly checked their vehicle and would top-up their engine with oil if necessary.

3　Emergency. This group only purchased oil in an emergency.

The Pentagram team soon recognised that the largest retail purchasers of motor oil was the DIY group. The DIY part-timer with limited knowledge tended to purchase the branded product, whereas the DIY enthusiast armed with more knowledge would make their purchase decision based on performance and price. This was the group that the Pentagram team decided would be most likely to purchase the Halfords store brand. Even here, however, price itself would be insufficient. There needed to be additional qualities that would convince the DIY enthusiast to select the Halfords brand ahead of the branded oils.

Consumer testing

Pentagram set up a series of consumer focus groups to try to explore the issues that influence purchase and to explore how consumers use the oil. The discussions soon revealed that price was a significant factor in the decision-making process. Many questioned the high price of the manufacturer's brand. Yet, when asked about store-branded oil, few had even tried it. Indeed, knowledge about the properties and performance of motor oil was low and many were buying the incorrect oil for their car. Interestingly the Halfords brand seemed to hold up well under analysis and was regarded as a trusted brand. These findings were confirmed in other focus groups. This presented some interesting challenges for the Pentagram team. Consumers feel the leading manufacturer brands of oil are expensive, yet few had tried the store brands. Also, there was an opportunity to offer some clear relevant product information regarding performance and selection of oil. Yet the Halfords brand was highly regarded and many consumers regularly purchase store brands in other product areas. The studies looking at how consumers used the oil revealed little other than problems with pouring a heavy 5-litre container. This was well documented and almost an accepted part of the process of using motor oil. But, maybe this was a way for Halfords to challenge the leading brands. It was also noticed that it seemed the only way to determine how much oil was in a can was to lift it up and feel the weight. If the Halfords brand of oil could solve the pouring problem and make this task simple, provide a viewer for oil level and offer some better information and labelling regarding properties and performance, maybe this would encourage people to try the Halfords brand.

New packaging

Pentagram decided to look closely at the possibility of improving considerably the dispensing of oil from the container into the engine. Further studies revealed that the problem seemed to centre on the inability to accurately direct flow of oil. A longer neck like a tea pot spout would help, but so would a better hand position on the can to control the flow of oil in much the same way as one would using a bottle (*see* Figure 13.4). The packaging designers came up with the idea of an additional long spout that could be attached to the neck of the container. This would certainly improve direction of flow. The problem with this was the additional cost of screw threads on the detachable long spout. Also in tests consumers suggested it was unnecessarily fiddly to have

Drawings for new packaging of oil container

Figure 13.4

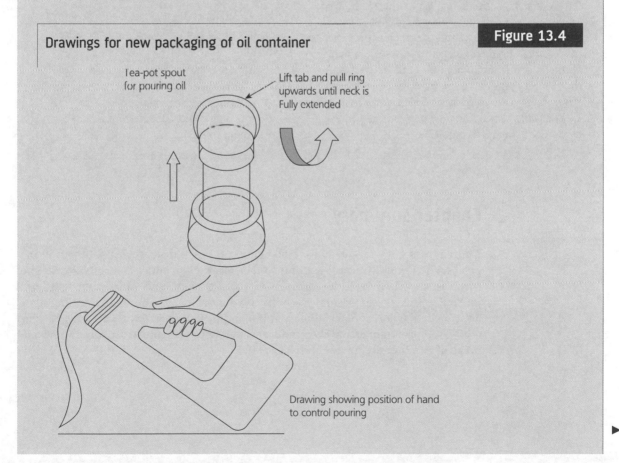

Tea-pot spout for pouring oil

Lift tab and pull ring upwards until neck is Fully extended

Drawing showing position of hand to control pouring

to unscrew and screw on another spout. The obvious solution was a long spout for pouring that was integral to the container in some way but how? Eventually the designers developed the 'pull-up teapot pouring spout'. The traditional screw cap top has been replaced with a push-on top; this reduces cost by dispensing with the need for a screw thread. A ring tab is then pulled revealing a long neck about 50 cm in length giving sufficient direction in pouring (*see* Figure 13.4). In addition the handle for the container is in line with the spout helping to direct flow of oil. The issue of labelling was solved simply by offering three types of motor oil. A premium-grade oil for most 16-valve petrol engines, a diesel grade for diesel engines and one for standard grade. The three different oils were offered in three different colours making them different and distinguishable on the shelf. The final container also incorporated a viewer for oil level. All these packaging attributes propelled the Halfords brand up the sales league, and many of the leading manufacturer brands have been forced to incorporate them into their own brands. After one year volume of sales increased by 18 per cent, its value by 44 per cent and profits by 54 per cent (PSAG, 1997).

Discussion

This case clearly illustrates the value of packaging and labelling in product development. The motor oil itself remained unchanged, but the packaging and labelling of the oil was considerably altered enabling Halfords to reposition its oil as a slightly more up-market store-brand oil. Initial sales were very encouraging and if copying is viewed as a form of flattery then Halfords is surely content.

Questions

1 Discuss how Halfords used packaging as a strategic tool.

2 Should Halfords have explored the possibility of developing a new brand of motor oil?

3 Use the attributes in Table 13.2 to explore whether more radical packaging could be developed for this product category.

4 Arguably this was a product whose sales were declining and could have been dumped. Can you think of any other 'mature' products that could benefit from an investment in packaging design?

Chapter summary

This chapter has explained how packaging can be used strategically to maintain a product's competitive position and to develop new product concepts. Packaging receives surprisingly little coverage in management and marketing texts and journals; this is surprising given its pivotal role. Traditionally packaging is approached from a marketing communications perspective. This chapter has addressed packaging from the producer's perspective to illustrate some additional areas of product design and development.

Discussion questions

1 Explain the various ways that packaging be used as a strategic tool.

2 Discuss the importance of fostering channel-member support in the early stages of the development of a new product.

3 Is it practical to elicit channel-member input into the manufacturer's product planning and development process? What problems might this cause?

4 Fitting new products to the channel members' assortments may sometimes be a problem. When might this be the case?

5 Private label or store brands sell in supermarkets typically for about 10–20 per cent less than manufacturers' brands, yet the profit margins realised by supermarkets are usually about 10–15 per cent higher than for manufacturers' brands. Explain why both parties need each other.

6 Select a package of any consumable product. Assess its contribution to brand equity. Justify your decisions.

7 Name an example of a brand article where product design is actively deployed to communicate the brand values. Discuss which brand values are involved and how product design is used.

8 Discuss how packaging can be used to enhance a brand's image.

9 Discuss the factors that may lead to declining profit margins for mature products.

Key words and phrases

The basic principles of packaging 418	Product and pack size variation 430
After use/secondary use 425	Product rejuvenation 426
Dispensing 423	Retailer acceptance 433
Disposal 425	Revitalising mature packaged goods 434
Handling 424	Stability 424
Opening/resealing 424	Storage 424

Websites worth visiting

Design company www.Pentagram.com

Institute of Packaging www.iop.co.uk

Packaging consultancy firm www.pira.org.uk

Packaging supplier www.essentialsupplies.com

Role of manufacturing in design www.Manufacturing.Stanford.eduirl

References

Croft, N. (1985) 'Wrapping up sales', *Nation's Business*, October, 41–2.

Day, G.S. (1999) *The Market Driven Organisation*, The Free Press, New York.

Day, J. (2002) *Media Guardian*, 30 April.

Directories Today (2003) www.directories-today.com/i_packaging.htm

Fill, C. (2002) *Marketing Communications: Context, Strategies and Applications*, 3rd edn, Prentice Hall, London.

Hancock, M. (2003) *Consumer Technologies will Spur Growth in Profit through Innovation*, PIRA, London.

Johnson, S.C. and Jones, C. (1957) 'How to organise for new products', *Harvard Business Review*, May–June, Vol. 35, 49–62.

Keller, K.L. (2003) *Building, Measuring and Managing Brand Equity*, 2nd edn, Prentice-Hall, Englewood Cliffs, NJ.

Kotler, P. (2003) *Marketing Management*, 11th edn, Prentice Hall, London.

Morgan, C.L. (1997) *Packaging Design*, Watson-Guptill, New York.

Narisetti, R. (1997) 'P&G to stores: keep the dented Crisco cans', *Wall Street Journal*, 21 March, 5.

Oka, Hideyuki (1989) *How to Wrap Five Eggs*, Weatherhill, Tokyo.

Pickton, D. and Broderick, A. (2000) *Integrated Marketing Communications*, Prentice Hall, London.

PSAG (1997) Packaging Solutions Advice Group (PSAG). 'Pack to the Future' is a series of discussions on design, branding and packaging issues hosted by the Packaging Solutions Advice Group. 'Strategic Shifts in Retail Brands' was held at the Design Show at the Business Design Centre on 28 October 1997.

Rigby, M. (2002) 'Pharmaceutical packaging can induce confusion', Letters to the editor, *British Medical Journal*, Vol. 324, 679.

Rogers, E. (1962) *Diffusion of Innovations* (3rd edn, 1983; 4th edn 1995), The Free Press, New York.

Sara, R. (1990) 'Packaging as a retail marketing tool', *International Journal of Physical Distribution and Logistics Management*, Vol. 20, No. 8, 10–21.

Schiller, Z., Burns, G.L. and Miller, K. (1996) 'Make it simple', *Wall Street Journal*, 9 September, 98.

Stewart, B. (1996) *Packaging as an Effective Marketing Tool*, Kogan Page, London.

Sunday Times (2003) 'Sunday Times Rich List 2003', 8 May.

Timms, S. (2002) Address by Minister for Trade to DTI Packaging Industry Conference, DTI Conference Centre, London, 4 July.

Trott, P. (2003) 'Packaging and new product opportunities', University of Portsmouth Business School, Working Paper Series No. 00123.

 Further reading

For a more detailed review of the packaging management literature, the following develop many of the issues raised in this chapter:

Kumar, N., Scheer, L. and Kotler, P. (2000) 'From market driven to market driving', *European Management Journal*, Vol. 18, No. 2, 129–41.

Nancarrow, C., Wright, L.T. and Brace, I. (1998) 'Gaining competitive advantage from packaging and labelling', *British Food Journal*, Vol. 100, No. 2, 110–18.

Shavinina, L. (2003) *The International Handbook on Innovation*, Elsevier, Oxford.

Underwood, R.L. (2003) 'The communicative power of product packaging: creating brand identity via lived and mediated experience', *Journal of Marketing Theory and Practice*, Vol. 11, No. 1, 62–77.

Underwood, R.L. and Klein, N. (2002) 'Packaging as brand communication: effects of product pictures on consumer responses to the package and brand', *Journal of Marketing Theory and Practice*, Vol. 10, No. 4, 58–69.

Underwood, R.L. and Ozanne, J.L. (1998) 'Is your package an effective communicator? A normative framework for increasing the communicative competence of packaging', *Journal of Marketing Communications*, Vol. 4, 207–20.

Vartan, C.G. and Rosenfield, J. (1987) 'Winning the supermarket war: packaging as a weapon', *Marketing Communications*, Vol. 12, No. 5, 31–6.

Wansink, B. and Huffman, C. (2001) 'Revitalising mature packaged goods', *Journal of Product and Brand Management*, Vol. 10, No. 4, 228–42.

14

Market research and its influence on new product development

The role and use of market research in the development of new products is commonly accepted and well understood. There are times, however, when market research results produce negative reactions to discontinuous new products (innovative products) that later become profitable for the innovating company. Famous examples such as the fax machine, the VCR and James Dyson's bagless vacuum cleaner are often cited to support this view. Despite this, companies continue to seek the views of consumers on their new product ideas. The debate about the use of market research and, more importantly, what type of research in the development of new products is long-standing and controversial. This chapter will explore these and other related issues.

Chapter contents

Learning objectives

When you have completed this chapter you will be able to:

- understand the contribution market research can make to the new product development process;
- recognise the benefits and weaknesses of consumer new-product testing;
- understand the significance of discontinuous products; and
- recognise the role of switching costs in new product introductions.

Market research and new product development

Business students in particular are very familiar with the well-trodden paths of arguments about the need for market research. Indeed, they are warned of the dangers and pitfalls that lie ahead if firms fail to conduct sufficient market research. Compelling and potentially alarming stories are used to highlight the importance of market research. One of these is presented in Illustration 14.1.

Chapters 11 and 12 outlined the activities involved in the development of new products. In this chapter it is necessary to examine in more detail some of these activities and to identify areas of potential difficulty. Figure 12.8 outlined the key activities of the new product development process. Within the product concept generation stage, however, there is a significant amount of internal reviews and testing. Figure 14.1 expands this stage into a series of further activities. As can be seen from the diagram, it is extremely difficult to delineate between the activities of concept testing, prototype development and product testing. The activities are intimately related and interlinked. There is a considerable amount of iteration. Product concepts are developed into

 Illustration 14.1   FT

The traditional view of new product testing

McDonalds recently admitted to making a big mistake with a new product. Several years ago it was considering launching the McPloughmans, a cheese and pickle salad sandwich. The McPloughmans was developed to compete with the UK's supermarket chains in the cold sandwich market. Unfortunately, had the company conducted market research it would have found that this product was not highly desirable. Indeed, their customers did not want the product and their staff were embarrassed to sell it. From now on, said the company, rather than relying on 'gut-feeling' that it knew what its customers wanted McDonalds intended to conduct rigorous fact-based market research.

Source: *Financial Times*, 28 October 1994. Reprinted with permission.

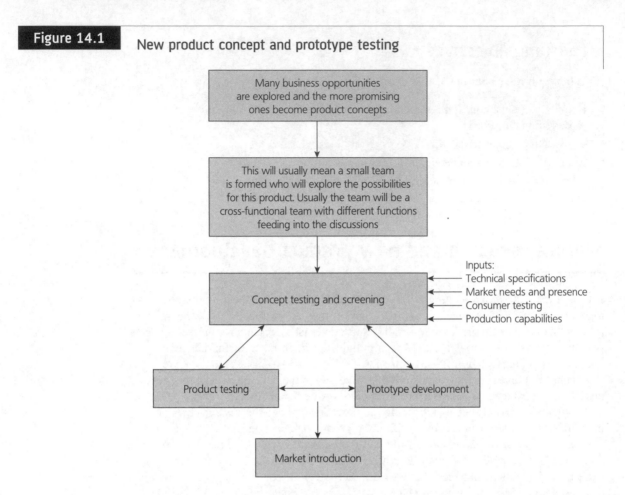

Figure 14.1	New product concept and prototype testing

prototypes only to be quickly redeveloped following technical inputs from production or R&D. Similarly, early product prototypes may be changed almost on a daily basis as a wide variety of market inputs are received. This could include channel members who have particular requirements and early results from consumer tests may reveal a number of minor changes that can be made simply and quickly by prototype designers.

The purpose of new product testing

The main objective here is to estimate the market's reaction to the new product under consideration, prior to potentially expensive production and promotional costs. To achieve this objective it is necessary to consider a number of other factors:

1 The market:
   current buying patterns;
   existing segments; and
   customer's view of the products available.

2 Purchase intention:
   trial and repeat purchase;
   barriers to changing brands; and
   switching costs (more about this later).

3 Improvements to the new product:
   overall product concept; and
   features of the product concept.

All these factors are linked and are usually covered in consumer new product testing and referred to as *customer needs and preferences*. This, however, raises an important question: the type of needs required would surely depend on the type of product under consideration and the consumer. King (1985) argues needs can be classified into three types:

● Basic needs are those that a customer would expect. For example, a customer would expect a new car to start every time.

● Articulated needs are those that a customer can readily express. For example, a customer may express a desire for additional features on a motor vehicle.

● Exciting needs are those that will surprise customers and are not being met by any provider at present. In the example here it may be finance packages enabling easy and quick purchase of a new car.

While this is helpful it is the so-called 'exciting needs' that all new product developers want to uncover. For success will surely come to those who are able to understand these needs and use them in the next generation of new products. This, however, is extremely difficult to capture. Some of the techniques and concepts used in consumer product testing are reviewed in the following sections.

Testing new products

Have you ever been stopped in a supermarket and asked for your opinion on a new food product? This is more than a diversion from the chore of shopping – you could be tasting the next big product. For example, all food manufacturers hope it will be their company that will develop the next 'Flora' or 'Sunny Delight' (two of the most successful new food products of the past ten years). In-store tasting is a serious business and millions of pounds are spent on this activity to create new foods that will tempt consumers. This is the accepted and well-known face of consumer research. Indeed, the food industry is one of the most prolific developers of new products and a heavy user of consumer research. Frequently the process involves enhancing an existing winner or repackaging tried and tested products. 'Flora' was one of many 'yellow spreads' but the brand has become so successful that it has been extended to other product lines including cheese.

Food manufacturers are continually seeking to add value to their products. This clearly enhances their profit margins, but competition in food retailing is fierce and retailers have been able to put pressure on manufacturers to keep prices down. Indeed,

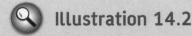

Illustration 14.2

Robinsons Fruit Shoot

Fruit Shoot from Robinsons was launched in 2001 and is now a £60 million super brand, achieving value sales growth of 44 per cent during the past year. Its success has been atributed to the unique design and packaging of the drink. Prior to Fruit Shoot most children's drinks were packaged in paper board cartons with straw. Fruit shoot revolutionised the market by using a colourful resealable plastic bottle (see Figure 14.2). In the UK Fruit Shoot is bought by over half of all households with kids and achieves 98 per cent awareness amongst children, according to Britvic. During 2003 and 2004 Fruit Shoot has incorporated two new flavours and this redesign promises to maintain and continue the strong growth of the brand.

Figure 14.2   Fruit Shoot

Source: www.Britvic.com (2004).

during 1999 and 2000 average food retail prices actually fell. Initially manufacturers pushed down their own costs in an attempt to improve margins, but when these could be reduced no further manufacturers turned to new product development to enable them to add value and command a higher price. Frequently the success of the product lies in the packaging as Illustration 14.2 shows.

Put crudely, to command a higher price a manufacturer of, say, baked beans will have to develop different forms of packaging, add curry, meat balls, etc., all of which will have been tested by the taste buds of consumers first. But if a product is not liked by consumers should it always be dumped and labelled 'bad idea'? In the food industry a disliked new flavour crisp may indeed be a 'bad idea' and a potential flop if the product gets to market, but in other industries initial rejection by consumers may not be a good indication of future success. The Dyson case study at the end of this chapter is a good illustration of a successful product that was initially rejected by manufacturers, retailers and some consumers, yet it turned out to be a success. There are, of course, many other well-known cases such as the fax machine. Peter Drucker once observed that 'one can use market research only on what is already in the market'. He supported his point by saying that American companies failed to put the fax machine on the market 'because market research convinced them there was no demand for such a gadget'.

Techniques used in consumer testing of new products

The following is a brief guide to some of the research techniques used in consumer testing of new products. Some products and services go through all the stages listed, but few do or should go through all these. The techniques would have to be adapted to meet the specific requirements of the product or service under consideration.

Concept tests

Qualitative techniques, especially group discussions, are used to obtain target customer reactions to a new idea or product. Question areas would cover:

- understanding and believability in the product;
- ideas about what it would look like;
- ideas about how it would be used; and
- ideas about when and by whom it might be used.

This would help to reveal the most promising features of the new product, and groups to whom it might appeal. It might be argued that the assessment of *purchase intent* is the primary purpose of concept testing, so that products and services with poor potential can be removed. The most common way to assess purchase intention is to provide a description of the product or take the product to respondents and ask whether they:

- definitely would buy;
- probably would buy;
- might or might not buy;
- probably would not buy; or
- definitely would not buy.

Test centres

These are used for product testing when the product is too large, too expensive or too complicated to be taken to consumers for testing. One or more test centres will be set up and a representative sample of consumers brought to the test centre for exposure to the product and questioning about their reaction to it. See the development of the cerebral palsy wheelchair at the end of Chapter 11.

Hall tests/mobile shops

These are commonly used for product testing or testing other aspects of the marketing mix such as advertising, price, packaging, etc. A representative sample of consumers is recruited, usually in a shopping centre, and brought to a conveniently located hall or a mobile caravan, which acts as a shop. Here they are exposed to the test material and asked questions about it.

Product-use tests

These are frequently used in business-to-business markets. A small group of potential customers are selected to use the product for a limited period of time. The manufacturer's technical people watch how these customers use the product. From this test the manufacturer learns about customer training and servicing requirements. Following the test the customer is asked detailed questions about the product including intent to purchase.

Trade shows

Such shows draw large numbers of buyers who view new products in a few days. The manufacturer can see how buyers react to various products on display. This technique is convenient and can deliver in-depth knowledge of the market because the buyers' views may differ considerably from those of the end-user consumers.

Monadic tests

The respondents are given only one (hence the name) product to try, and are asked their opinion of it. This is the normal situation in real life when a consumer tries a new product and draws on recent experience with the product they usually use, to judge the test product. The method is not very sensitive in comparing the test product with other products because of this.

Paired comparisons

A respondent is asked to try two or more products in pairs and asked, with each pair, to say which they prefer. This is less 'real' in terms of the way consumers normally use products, but does allow products to be deliberately tested against others.

In-home placement tests

These are used when an impression of how the product performs in normal use is required. The product(s) are placed with respondents who are asked to use the product in the normal way and complete a questionnaire about it. Products may be tested comparatively or sequentially.

Test panels

Representative panels are recruited and used for product testing. Test materials and questionnaires can be sent through the post, which cuts down the cost of conducting in-home placement tests. Business-to-business firms may also have test panels of customers or intermediaries with whom new product or service ideas or prototypes can be tested.

When market research has too much influence

It is argued by many from within the market research industry that only extensive consumer testing of new products can help to avoid large-scale losses such as those experienced by RCA with its Videodisc, Procter & Gamble with its Pringles and General Motors with its rotary engine (Barrett, 1996). Sceptics may point to the issue of vested interests in the industry, and that it is merely promoting itself. It is, however, widely accepted that most new products fail in the market because consumer needs and wants are not satisfied. Study results show that 80 per cent of newly introduced products fail to establish a market presence after two years (Barrett, 1996). Indeed, cases involving international high-profile companies are frequently cited to warn of the dangers of failing to utilise market research (e.g. Unilever's Persil Power and R.J. Reynold's smokeless cigarette).

Given the inherent risk and complexity, managers have asked for many years whether this could be reduced by market research. Not surprisingly, the marketing literature takes a market-driven view, which has extensive market research as its key driver. That is, find out what the customer would like and then produce it (the market-pull approach to innovation). The benefits of this approach to the new product development process have been widely articulated and are commonly understood (Cooper, 1990; Kotler, 1998). Partly because of its simplicity this view now dominates management thinking, but unfortunately this sometimes goes beyond the marketing department. The effect can be that major or so-called discontinuous innovations are rejected or accepted based on consumer research.

Advocates of market research argue that such activities ensure that companies are consumer-oriented. In practice, this means that new products are more successful if they are designed to satisfy a perceived need rather than if they are designed simply to take advantage of a new technology (Ortt and Schoormans, 1993). The approach taken by many companies with regard to market research is that if sufficient research is undertaken the chances of failure are reduced (Barrett, 1996). Indeed, the danger that many companies wish to avoid is the development of products without any consideration of the market. Moreover, once a product has been carried through the early stages of development it is sometimes painful to raise questions about it once money has been spent. The problem then spirals out of control, taking the company with it. Illustration 14.3 highlights many of the difficulties facing firms introducing new products.

The issue of market research in the development of new products is controversial. The marketing literature has traditionally portrayed new product development as essentially a market/customer-led process, but paradoxically, many major market innovations appear in practice to be technologically driven, to arise from a technology seeking

Illustration 14.3

Stay tuned to consumer taste

Eight out of 10 new products are commercial failures. Gabriele Marcotti looks at the reasons why so many companies get it wrong

In Thomas Edison's time it must have seemed as if something new was coming along every year: telephone, lightbulb, car and aircraft were all introduced within a relatively short time.

Today we are told we live in a rapidly changing, technology-driven world, hungry for better, more powerful products. More money than ever is spent on research, development and invention. Yet it is generally accepted that eight out of 10 new products fail.

Worryingly, the ratio has remained constant over the past 30 years. Two conclusions can be drawn: either consumers are not as interested in innovation as we think or they are not being offered the right products.

Establishing a set of parameters to determine what products can succeed is the ambition of many innovation-driven corporations. It is a tortuous ballet of constant negotiation between inventors, developers, accountants and market researchers. Experts agree it does not work as well as it should.

'Quite honestly, I don't know of any corporation that is happy with its current strategy', says Vijay Jolly, professor of strategy and technology management at the International Institute for Management Development in Lausanne, Switzerland.

Art Fry knows a thing or two about innovation. Eighteen years ago he invented the Post-It Note on behalf of 3M. The US company has long been admired for its success in introducing new products. It operates a 15 per cent rule: all employees are encouraged to spend 15 per cent of their work time free from supervision, working on their own projects.

'People hate change and many companies still don't really understand that,' explains Mr Fry. 'People follow their own established patterns. They figure that even if a new product is better, perhaps all the work involved in learning how to use it and getting accustomed to it simply isn't worth it.'

Val Tsourikov, chief executive of Invention Machine Corporation, a company that aims to rationalise the innovation process, agrees. 'Every person on this planet has a certain psychological inertia', he says. 'If I spend several days learning something, I want to use it, I don't want to change. If you give me another product, I need to start all over again.'

If Mr Tsourikov and Mr Fry are correct, it would appear there is little point in trying to innovate, especially with radical ideas.

Not necessarily, maintains Professor Jolly, who has identified three elements crucial to success: 'The first is what I call the use paradigm. What is the product going to be used for and how. Take multi-media functions, for example. Some contend that they are part of the personal computer paradigm, that people will access and use them as they do with PCs. Others believe it's a television paradigm, it's a passive process rather than an interactive one. Either way, you need to be very clear about what your product is for.

'Another factor to keep in mind is that more often than not, class association is more important than value added. That is, when designing a product, avoid making it unique. People will accept a substitute for an existing product much more easily if they can relate it to the existing product. Of course, it has to be a better substitute as well. The only exception to this is when the value added of the new product is immensely greater, but that is extremely rare.'

Bearing this in mind, consumers will reject, say, a pyramid-shaped television even if it is

10 per cent 'better' than existing ones, because it will not have the required class association. According to Prof Jolly, a conventional-looking television that is just 2 per cent better has more chances of success than the pyramid TV.

'The third element is that too often research focuses on customer needs rather than consumer demand,' he says. 'Simply because our research indicates the consumer needs a product does not mean he knows he needs, and thus demands, it.'

Of course, this is where advertising and marketing can convince the consumer the product is useful to them. Yet they must also convey exactly what the product does and why it is better – not an easy task, especially when faced with budget constraints or a product that no one has seen before.

Mr Fry recalls: 'We were lucky with Post-Its: the unit cost was so low we could just mail out free samples and people were willing to try them. We ended up with a 90 per cent repurchase rate.'

A free giveaway would be difficult to implement in something like the pyramid TV scenario, which is why innovation is rare and usually limited to large corporations when it comes to expensive products.

Yet even a corporate juggernaut would be wary about investing in the pyramid TV, according to Perry Lowe, Professor of Marketing at Bentley College in Boston, Massachusetts: 'A large company would not develop something like that, unless it had a tremendous upside. They wouldn't want to cannibalise sales of existing televisions and they probably don't need the extra volume.'

So is our pyramid TV doomed forever, even though it is better than existing televisions? Not necessarily, says Prof Lowe: 'It could be developed by a small entrepreneur, maybe one who relies on passion and instinct rather than market research. With a little luck and a lot of persistence he could find backing from a venture capitalist. But that's really a recent development and one pretty much limited to the US.'

The picture Prof Lowe paints is one where corporations, hindered by the inefficiency of their research and marketing departments and their lack of patience with products that do not offer immediate returns, are becoming increasingly ineffective at fuelling technological progress. Instead, the process is aided by venture capitalists who, in turn, sell out to the corporations once the product succeeds. Creation is being replaced by acquisition.

Source: G. Marcotti, 'Stay tuned to consumer taste', *Financial Times*, 31 March 1998. Reprinted with permission.

a market application rather than a market opportunity seeking a technology. This, of course, is the antithesis of the marketing concept, which is to start with trying to understand customer needs. The role of market research in new product development is most clearly questionable with major product innovations, where no market exists. First, if potential customers are unable adequately to understand the product, then market research can only provide negative answers (Brown, 1991). Second, consumers frequently have difficulty articulating their needs. Hamel and Prahalad (1994) argue that customers lack foresight; they refer to Akio Morita, Sony's influential leader:

Our plan is to lead the public with new products rather than ask them what kind of products they want. The public does not know what is possible, but we do.

This leads many scientists and technologists to view marketing departments with scepticism. Frequently they have seen their exciting new technology rejected due to market research findings produced by their marketing department. Market research

---

Illustration 14.4

GlaxoSmithKline

GSK have known for many years that consumers are fickle. Many years after the launch of its very successful Aquafresh striped toothpaste GlaxoSmithKline undertook consumer research to try to explore product development opportunities. Some of the findings were surprising. Consumers questioned the need or benefit of having stripes in the paste. Yet, in store trials when given the opportunity to purchase a single colour paste consumers continued to purchase the striped toothpaste. A similar reaction was recorded when consumers were asked about flavouring of the toothpaste. Consumers suggested that they would prefer a wider variety of flavours such as strawberry or banana rather than mint, yet when other flavours were offered few consumers purchased them. The product manager emphasised the need to check consumer rhetoric with their actions.

Source: P. Trott and A. Lataste (2003) 'The role of consumer market research in new product decision-making: some preliminary findings from European firms', Entrepreneurship, Marketing and Innovation Conference, University of Karlsrühe, 8–9 September, conference proceedings.

---

specialists would argue that such problems could be overcome with the use of 'benefits research'. The problem here is that the benefits may not be clearly understood, or even perceived as a benefit by respondents. King (1985: 2) sums up the research dilemma neatly:

> *Consumer research can tell you what people did and thought at one point in time: it can't tell you directly what they might do in a new set of circumstances.*

The illustration above, from GlaxoSmithKline, consumer healthcare highlights the difficulties of trying to understand consumer research:

Discontinuous new products

Major innovations are referred to as discontinuous new products when they differ from existing products in that field, sometimes creating entirely new markets and when they require buyers to change their behaviour patterns. For example, the personal computer and 3M's Post-It notes created entirely new markets and required consumers to change their behaviour. Such products usually require a period of learning on the part of the user. Indeed, sometimes the manufacturer has to explain and suggest to users how the product should and could be used. Rogers' (1995) study on the diffusion of innovations as a social process argues that it requires time for societies to learn and experiment with new products. This raises the problem of how to deal with consumers with limited prior knowledge and how to conduct market research on a totally new product or a major product innovation. The two major difficulties are:

1 the problem of selection of respondents; and

2 the problem of the understanding of the major innovation.

Confronted with a radically new technology, consumers may not understand what needs the technology can satisfy, as was the case with the fax machine or the Post-It note. This is because consumers are not able to link physical product characteristics with the outputs of the innovation. For example, when consumers first saw a fax machine all they saw was a bulky expensive machine that looked like a copier. They were not able to imagine using it, hence they were not receptive to the new idea. Research has shown that experts are better able to understand potential benefits than those with less product knowledge. The type of research technique selected is crucial in obtaining accurate and reliable data.

Market research and discontinuous new products

In the case of discontinuous product innovations, the use and validity of market research methods is questionable (von Hippel and Thomke, 1999; Elliot and Roach, 1991). As far back as the early 1970s Tauber (1974) argued that such approaches discourage the development of major innovations. It may be argued that less, rather than more, market research is required if major product innovations are required. Such an approach is characterised by the so-called technology-push model of innovation. Products that emerge from a technology-push approach are generated with little consideration of the market. Indeed, a market may not yet exist as with the case of the PC and many other completely new products. Frequently, consumers are unable to understand the technology in question and view new products as a threat to their existing way of operating. Martin (1995: 122) argues that:

> *customers can be extremely unimaginative . . . trying to get people to change the way they do things is the biggest obstacle facing many companies.*

Many writers on this subject argue that potential consumers are not able to relate the physical aspects of a major innovative product with the consequences of owning and using it (Ortt and Schoormans, 1993). Others argue that while market research can help to fine-tune product concepts it seldom is the spur for an entirely new product concept. Consequently most conventional market research techniques deliver invalid results (Hamel and Prahalad, 1994).

More recently, new approaches are being recognised in the area of discontinuous product innovations. One technique adopts a process of probing and learning, where valuable experience is gained with every step taken and modifications are made to the product and the approach to the market based on that learning (Lynn *et al.*, 1997). This is not trial and error but careful experimental design and exploration of the market often using the heritage of the organisation. This type of new product development is very different from traditional techniques and methods described in most marketing texts.

Circumstances when market research may hinder the development of discontinuous new products

Product developers and product testers tend to view the product offering in a classical layered view, where the product is assumed to have a core benefit and additional attributes and features are laid around it, hence layered view. Saren and Tzokas (1994) have argued that much of the problem is due to the way we view a product. They state that we often view it in isolation from:

● its context;
● the way it is used; and
● the role of the customer–supplier relationship.

This contributes to misleading views on new products. Figure 14.3 illustrates the tripartite concept that captures the three views highlighted by Saren and Tzokas. The significance of this alternative view is that it highlights the reality of any product's situation. That is, product developers and product testers need to recognise that a product will be viewed differently by channel members than by end-users. For example, end-users will be concerned about how the product will perform, whereas channel members are more interested in how the product will *sell*, whether it will be easy to *stock and*

| Figure 14.3 | The tripartite product concept |

Source: Adapted from M.A.J. Saren and N. Tzokas (1994) *Proceedings of the Annual Conference of the European Marketing Academy*, Maastricht.

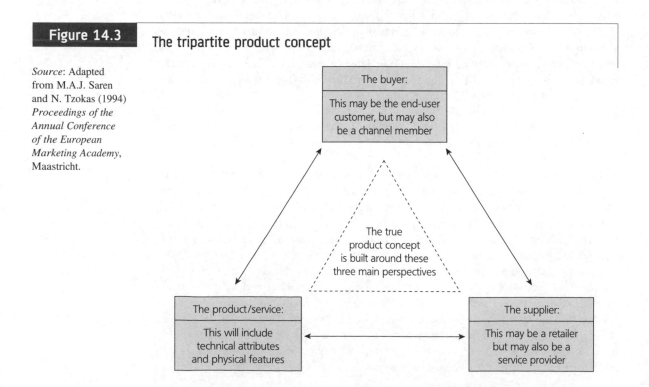

display, and most important, whether it will be *profitable*. The Dyson case study at the end of this chapter illustrates the difficulties in trying to convince retailers to stock a new, slightly unusual product with which they are not familiar.

Technology-intensive products

Adopting a technology-push[1] approach to product innovations can allow a company to target and control premium market segments, establish its technology as the industry standard, build a favourable market reputation, determine the industry's future evolution, and achieve high profits. It can become the centrepiece in a company's strategy for market leadership. It is, however, costly and risky. Such an approach requires a company to develop and commercialise an emerging technology in pursuit of growth and profits. To be successful, a company needs to ensure its technology is at the heart of its competitive strategy. Merck, Microsoft and Dyson have created competitive advantage by offering unique products, lower costs or both by making technology the focal point in their strategies. These companies have understood the role of technology in differentiating their products in the marketplace. They have used their respective technologies to offer a distinct bundle of products, services and price ranges that have appealed to different market segments. Such products revolutionise product categories or define new categories, such as Hewlett Packard's laser-jet printers and Apple's (then IBM) personal computer. These products shift market structures, require consumer learning and induce behaviour changes, hence the difficulties for consumers when they are asked to pass judgement.

This is particularly the case if the circumstances relate to an entirely new product that is unknown to the respondent. New information is always interpreted in the light of one's prior knowledge and experience. In industrial markets the level of information symmetry about the core technology is usually very high indeed (hence the limited use of market research), but in consumer markets this is not always the case. For example, industrial markets are characterised by:

● relatively few (information-rich) buyers;
● products often being customised and involving protracted negotiations regarding specifications;
● and, most importantly, the buyers usually being expert in the technology of the new product (i.e. high information symmetry about the core technology).

In situations of low information symmetry consumers have difficulty in understanding the core product and are unable to articulate their needs and any additional benefits sought. Conversely in situations of high information symmetry consumers are readily able to understand the core product and hence are able to articulate their needs and a wide range of additional benefits sought, for example in tasting new food products.

Furthermore, discontinuous product innovations or radical product innovations frequently have to overcome the currently installed technology base – usually through

---

[1] The technology-push approach to NPD centres on trying to deliver the most effective technology available.

displacement. This is known as the *installed base effect*. The installed base effect is the massive inertial effect of an existing technology or product that tends to preclude or severely slow the adoption of a superseding technology or product. This creates an artificial adoption barrier that can become insurmountable for some socially efficient and advantageous innovations. An example of this is the DVORAK keyboard, which has been shown to provide up to 40 per cent faster typing speeds. Yet the QWERTY keyboard remains the preference for most users because of its installed base, i.e. its widespread availability of keyboards that have the QWERTY configuration (Herbig *et al.*, 1995).

The idea of being shackled with an obsolete technology leads to the notion of switching costs. Switching is the one-time cost to the buyer who converts to the new product. Porter (1985) notes that switching costs may be a significant impediment to the adoption of a new consumer product. Buyer switching costs may arise as a result of prior commitments to a technology (a) and to a particular vendor (b) (Jackson, 1985). Computer software is an obvious example where problems of compatibility frequently arise. Similarly, buyers may have developed routines and procedures for dealing with a specific vendor that will need to be modified if a new relationship is established. The effect of both types of switching costs for a buyer is a disincentive to explore new vendors. There is a clear dilemma facing firms: market research may reveal genuine limitations with the new product but it may also produce negative feedback on a truly innovative product that may create a completely new market. The uncertainty centres on two key variables:

1 information symmetry about the core technology between producer and buyer; and

2 the installed base effect and switching costs.

Breaking with convention and winning new markets

There is evidence to suggest that many successful companies were successful because they were prepared to take the risky decision to ignore their customers' views and proceed with their new product ideas because they passionately believed that it would be successful. Subsequent success for these new products suggested that the firm's existing customers were unable to peer into the future, recognise that a different product or service would be desirable and articulate this to the firm. On reflection this seems a lot to ask of customers, and indeed is extremely difficult.

Between 1975 and 1995, 60 per cent of the companies in the *Fortune* 500 listing were replaced. Irrespective of their industry, new entrants either created new markets or recreated existing ones. Compaq overtook IBM to become the world's largest manufacturer of personal computers; Dyson overhauled Hoover's established position of market leader to become the new market leader in vacuum cleaners; Xerox lost out to Canon who quickly became the bestseller in copiers; and there are many other examples. So why is it that established highly respected firms fail to recognise the future? In the cases already mentioned hindsight suggests that more resources should have been devoted to innovation, but that is not all. Established businesses that have been successful for many years also develop comfortable routines and become complacent. Hierarchies, systems, rulebooks and formulae work pretty well for controlling and improving the efficiency of repeated actions. They are hopeless for inventing, experimenting with and developing something that has never happened before (*see* 'The dilemma of innovation management', Chapter 3). Furthermore, a growing number of academics (Christensen, 1997; Hamel and Prahalad, 1994) argue that a particular problem exists because firms rely too heavily on market research and that some of the techniques reinforce the present and do not peer into the future. It is well known that market research results often produce negative reactions to discontinuous new products (innovative products) that later become profitable for the innovating company. Indeed, there are some famous examples such as the fax machine, the VCR and James Dyson's bagless vacuum cleaner. Despite this, companies continue to seek the views of consumers on their new product ideas. The debate about the use of market research in the development of new products is long-standing and controversial.

In his award-winning 'business book of the year'[2] Clayton Christensen (1997) investigated why well run companies that were admired by many failed to stay on top of their industry. His research showed that in the cases of well managed firms such as Digital, IBM, Apple and Xerox, 'good management' (sic) was the most powerful reason why they failed to remain market leaders. It was precisely because these firms listened to their customers and provided more and better products of the sort they wanted that they lost their position of leadership. He argues that there are times when it is right not to listen to customers. Indeed, many companies share the same ideas about who their customers are and what products and services they want. The more that companies share this conventional wisdom about how they compete, the more they fight for incremental improvements in cost reductions and quality, and the more they avoid the discontinuous disruptive new products. Illustration 14.5 highlights the dangers of falling into this trap.

It is not surprising that many firms try to meet the needs of their customers. After all, successful companies have established themselves and built a successful business on providing the customer with what he or she wanted. IBM and Hoover, for example, became very good at serving their customers. But when a new, very different, technology came along these companies struggled. These large successful companies have been fighting known competitors for many years through careful planning and reducing costs. Suddenly they were faced with a completely different threat: new, smaller firms doing things differently and using unusual technologies. In IBM's case it was personal computers and in Hoover's case it has been bagless vacuum cleaners.

If sufficient care is not exercised by managers market research can be used to support conservative product development decision making. The previous sections have highlighted the difficulty faced by many managers in the field of new product development. In many crucial new product development decisions, the course of action that is most desirable over the long run is not the best course of action in the short term. This is the dilemma addressed in the debate about short-termism, that is, an emphasis on cutting costs and improving efficiencies in the immediate future, rather than on creativity and the development of innovative new product ideas for the long term. What is of concern is not the desire to cut costs but the apparent disregard of the implications and damage

[2] Christensen (1997) was awarded the *Financial Times* business book of the year award in 1999.

Illustration 14.5

How to discover the unknown market

Companies know that to succeed, they must innovate. Yet too often they compete head-to-head for a bigger share of existing markets. In a six-part weekly series, W. Chan Kim and Renee Mauborgne show how companies can identify opportunities for distinctive products or services and break free from the competitive pack.

The internet, the euro, globalisation, deregulation, the crisis in Asia, Russia and Brazil, the green movement – in this fast-changing economy, why does your company deserve to thrive? Because it has a lot of resources? A strong brand name? Has been in operation for 100 years? Or because it is the most efficient in its industry? None of these will be sufficient. Think of Compaq overtaking International Business Machines to become the world's largest personal computer maker, or Virgin Atlantic Airways successfully challenging the far larger British Airways. Xerox had a strong name in copiers, as did Hoover in vacuum cleaners. But that did not stop either Canon or Dyson becoming bestsellers in their respective industries. If the traditional routes to success are no longer enough, what will ensure future success? Look at the companies that are rising. Merrill Lynch may be the biggest bull on Wall Street, but the market capitalisation of Charles Schwab, the online broker, recently exceeded Merrill Lynch's. And Schwab has created more new jobs over the past decade, not to mention garnering more positive press coverage.

The market capitalisation of Intel, the world's largest semiconductor manufacturer, exceeds that of all the companies in India combined. Compaq earned a place on the *Fortune* 500 just three years after its inception, and from 1991 to 1997 grew from a $3bn to a $25bn enterprise based almost entirely on internal growth.

Between 1975 and 1995, 60 per cent of the companies on the *Fortune* 500 were replaced.

Irrespective of their industry, what is common to the new entrants to the list is that they either created new markets or recreated existing ones. By contrast, the declining companies were competing for a bigger share of existing markets.

What is astounding here is the rapidity with which those rising companies create and accumulate their wealth. The wealth-generating power of innovation in this knowledge economy is beyond doubt.

Imagine a market universe that is made up of known and unknown market space. While known market space embraces all markets that exist today, unknown market space embraces those that are not yet in existence. Any market in existence today, however, once belonged to unknown market space. Today gas-fired electricity plants may be the largest market for natural gas in North America, but this market did not exist a decade ago until Enron created it. Or think of one of the fastest-growing segments in the car market today, multi-purpose vehicles. A little over a decade ago this market did not exist; nor did the market for fun fashionable watches that Swatch created, or routers, switches and other networking devices Cisco designed. The list goes on. Yet while wealth and excitement increasingly come from exploring unknown market space, companies have a poor understanding of how to go about it. Almost all of the work in the field of strategy is about exploiting known market space. Companies are advised to enter an industry with high growth and profit potential, and position themselves in it to outdo existing rivals. No wonder companies' strategies tend to regress towards capturing a bigger share of existing markets.

Knowing how to position a company in known market space provides little insight into how to create new market space. There is a huge gap between what companies need to create wealth in the future and what the current body of knowledge on strategy has to offer.

This gulf came through in our interviews with more than 500 senior managers across the globe: while more than 80 per cent saw creating new market space as a key strategic priority, an even higher percentage were at a loss as to how to systematically achieve this end.

For the past decade, we have studied companies that have successfully created new markets and recreated existing ones. Our aim was to develop a robust analytical framework that companies can apply to break out of existing boundaries. We have identified six basic paths, applicable to all industries.

Contrary to most companies' imaginations, none requires any special vision or foresight about the future; all come from looking at familiar data from a new perspective.

In a drive to match their rivals, many companies share the same ideas about who their customers are and what products and services they want. The more that companies share this conventional wisdom about how they compete, the more they fight for incremental improvements in cost or quality.

Has your company fallen into this trap of competitive improvements? Do you know how to break from the competitive pack? Is your company lagging behind in profitable growth? Do you want to go for a step change, but do not know how?

In the next few weeks, we will show how your company can break free from competitive convergence and go for breakthrough profitable growth.

The first path examines how Bloomberg, SAP, Canon and Philips Lighting created new market space by re-defining the buyer group of their industry.

Source: 'How to discover the unknown market', *Financial Times*, 6 May 1999. Reprinted with permission.

that such policies may bring about, and in particular the neglect of the company's ability to create new business opportunities for the future well-being of the company.

To return to a point made earlier by Akio Morita, Sony's influential leader. Morita argued that the public did not know what was possible and it was the firm that should lead the customer. This point is explored more fully by Hamel and Prahalad (1994: 108) who argue that firms need to go beyond customer-led ideas if they wish to be successful in the future. They are brutal in their criticism of customers' ability to peer into the future:

> *Customers are notoriously lacking in foresight. Ten or fifteen years ago, how many of us were asking for cellular telephones, fax machines and copiers at home, 24 hour discount brokerage accounts, multivalve automobile engines, video dial tone, etc.?*

Successful companies of the future will be those that are part of its creation. This means developing products that will be used in the future. Companies need to continually challenge existing products and markets. This can be achieved by pushing at the boundaries of current product concepts. Some firms have recognised this and are putting the most advanced technology they have available into the hands of the world's most sophisticated and demanding customers. IBM and Xerox have learnt through bitter experience what it is like to lose out to newcomers with new ideas and new technology. They know that today's customers may not be tomorrow's.

Using a simple two-by-two matrix (Figure 14.4) showing needs and customers, Hamel and Prahalad have shown that however well a company meets the articulated

| Figure 14.4 | Gaining new customers of the future |

Source: S. Hamel and
C.K. Prahalad (1994)
'Competing for the
future', *Harvard
Business Review*,
Vol. 72, No. 4, 122–8.

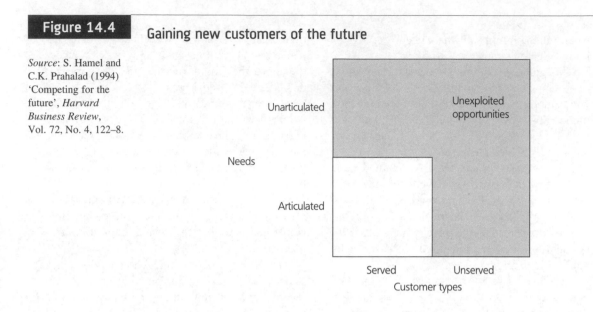

needs of current customers, it runs a great risk if it does not have a view of the needs customers cannot yet articulate: in other words the products of the future.

When it may be correct to ignore your customers

Many industry analysts and business consultants are now arguing that the devotion to focus groups and market research has gone too far (Christensen, 1997; Martin, 1995; Francis, 1994). Indeed, the traditional new product development process of market research, segmentation, competitive analysis and forecasting, prior to passing the resultant information to the research and development (R&D) department, leads to commonality and bland new products. This is largely because the process constrains rather than facilitates innovative thinking and creativity. Furthermore, and more alarming, these techniques are well known and used by virtually all companies operating in consumer markets. In many of these markets the effect is an over-emphasis on minor product modifications and on competition that tends to focus on price. Indeed, critics of the market-orientated approach to new product development argue that the traditional marketing activities of branding, advertising and positioning, market research and consumer research act as an expensive obstacle course to product development rather than facilitating the development of new product ideas.

For many large multi-product companies it seems the use of market research is based upon accepted practice in addition to being an insurance policy. Many large companies are not short of new product ideas – the problem lies in deciding in which ones to invest substantial sums of money (Cooper, 2001; Liddle, 2004), and then justifying this decision to senior managers. Against this background one can see why market research is so frequently used without hesitation, as decisions can be justified and defended. Small companies in general, and small single-product companies in particular, are in a different situation. Very often new product ideas are scarce; hence, such companies frequently support ideas based upon their intuition and personal knowledge of the product.

The significance of discontinuous new products is often overlooked. Morone's (1993) study of successful US product innovations suggests that success was achieved through a combination of discontinuous product innovations and incremental improvements. Furthermore, in competitive, technology-intensive industries success is achieved with discontinuous product innovations through the creation of entirely new products and businesses, whereas product line extensions and incremental improvements are necessary for maintaining leadership (Lynn *et al.*, 1997). This, however, is only after leadership has been established through a discontinuous product innovation. This may appear to be at variance with accepted thinking that Japan secured success in the 1980s through copying and improving US and European technology. This argument is difficult to sustain on close examination of the evidence. The most successful Japanese firms have also been leaders in research and development. Furthermore, as Cohen and Levinthal (1990, 1994) have continually argued, access to technology is dependent on one's understanding of that technology.

Striking the balance between new technology and market research

Market research can provide a valuable contribution to the development of innovative products. The difficulties lie in the selection and implementation of research methods. It may be that market research has become a victim of its own success, that is, business and product managers now expect it to provide solutions to all difficult product management decisions. Practitioners need to view market research as a collection of techniques that can help to inform the decision process.

The development and adoption process for discontinuous or complex products is particularly difficult. The benefits to potential users may be difficult to identify and value, and usually because there are likely to be few substitute products available it is difficult for buyers to compare and contrast. Sometimes product developers have to lead buyers/consumers and show them the benefits, even educate them. This is where some marketing views suggest the process is no longer customer-led or driven by the market, and they would argue that what is now occurring is a technology-push approach to product development. Day (1999) suggests that on closer examination there are a number of false dichotomies here:

- that you must either lead or follow customers;
- that you cannot stay close to both current and potential customers; and
- that technology-push cannot be balanced with market-pull.

It is true, as we have seen in this chapter, that customers respond most positively to what is familiar and comfortable and that customers view the high costs of new technology (including switching costs) in a largely negative way. Firms need to try to understand how customers will view innovations in the marketplace, this may include adoption influences such as consumption pattern, product capability and technological capability (Veryzer, 2003). Valid good management should be capable of selecting the appropriate market research techniques to avoid superficial consumer reactions. A thorough understanding of all aspects of the market and the needs of users should inform managers that it is possible to provide customers with what they want and lead them through education.

The argument about current markets and future markets is powerfully made by both Christensen (1997) and Hamel and Prahalad (1994). The suggestion here is that firms become myopic towards their current customers and fail to see the larger slowly changing market. The case of IBM in the 1980s is often given here. It surely is a responsibility of senior management to try to understand the wider and future environment of the firm. This may be very easy to record, but in practice it is extremely difficult to carry out. There are real dangers for all firms here. For example, discontinuous new technologies may require huge changes for firms, and one can see that for many the easy option is to hope the new technology fails and the firm can carry on as normal. Failure to change and adopt may result in more cases like IBM, Xerox, Hoover and many financial service firms that failed to respond to on-line banking. Once again it should be possible for a well run company to fully exploit its current markets and develop and enter the markets of the future. For example, both Kodak and Fuji have exploited the massive changes in the photographic market with the introduction of digital photography.

Finally, the arguments about market-pull or technology-push never seem to go away. But readers of this book should now be clear that this is a stale argument. What is required is an understanding of innovation. While it is clear that in some industries the role of science and technology is far greater than in other industries, innovation requires inputs from both. It is true there are many firms in the pharmaceutical sector who argue that their approach to product development is to start with brilliant science and to look for ways of using it in new drugs; and that the role of marketing and sales is to develop sales of these products. While this approach may work for a few, even in this industry sector there are many firms who operate differently. Some of the most successful pharmaceutical firms including GlaxoSmithKline, Pfizer and Merck work very closely with buyers and users to develop new drugs and to improve many existing ones. Indeed, the success of one of the world's bestselling drugs, 'Viagra', is surely testament to the benefits of working closely with the market.

The challenge for senior management

Innovation is clearly a complex issue and sometimes it is a concept that sits uneasily in organisations. Indeed, some writers on the subject have argued that organisations are often the graveyard rather than the birthplace for many innovations. Applying pressure on product managers to seek high profits from quick volume sales rather than develop business opportunities for the future is a common mistake made by senior management. Similarly a heavy reliance on market research to minimise risk when developing new product ideas also contributes to an early grave for product ideas. The use of financial systems that minimise risk and avoid investment in more long-term projects is another common preference, which frequently emanates from senior management.

Correcting such ills will never be easy, but given the strategic importance of innovation it is a challenge senior management must take up. The adjustments which need to be made in order to encourage innovation in large companies may break some of the established rules of corporate life. They will require changes to internal systems and structures and the culture of the organisation. However, without such changes, potential innovations will continue to be squeezed out by the system, and thus rob the company of the most effective means of survival (Brown, 1991).

Case study

Dyson, Hoover and the bagless vacuum cleaner[1]

This case study illustrates many of the obstacles and difficulties of launching a new product. The product in question used new technology that was initially rejected by existing manufacturers. It was priced at more than double that of existing products, but eventually captured more than 50 per cent of the UK vacuum cleaner market in less than four years.

Introduction

Conventional wisdom would surely suggest that Dyson Appliances Ltd would fail within a few months. After all, it appeared to be a small company with an eccentric manager at its helm, trying to sell an over-priced product of limited appeal in a very competitive market with less expensive, conventional, mass-market products made by respected manufacturers whose names were, quite literally, household words. The result was very different. The story of the Dyson bagless vacuum cleaner is not a classic tale of 'rags to riches'. The charismatic inventor James Dyson was afforded many privileges and opportunities not available to most. It is, none the less, a fascinating story and illustrates many of the difficulties and problems faced by small businesses and 'lone inventors'; and demonstrates the determination, hard work and sacrifices neces-

sary in order to succeed. The cliché *against the odds*, which Dyson (1998) used as the title of his autobiography, is certainly appropriate and tells the story of the development and launch of the first bagless vacuum cleaner – the Dyson DC01.

This case raises several significant research questions in the field of innovation management. First, how and why did senior executives at leading appliance manufacturers across Europe, such as Electrolux, Bosch and Miele, decide not to utilise the technology offered to them by Dyson? Second, how and why did senior buyers for many retail chains across the United Kingdom fail to recognise the potential for the DC01? Third, technology transfer experts would point out that the Dyson vacuum cleaner is a classic case of technology transfer – a technology developed for one industry, i.e. dust extraction from sawmills, is applied to a different use in a new industry. Hence, it is technology transfer that needs to be championed and supported further by governments. Fourth, as a mechanism for protecting intellectual property, it seems that patents depend on the depth of your pocket. That is, they are prohibitively expensive and are almost exclusively for the benefit of large multi-national organisations. What can be done to help small businesses without such large pockets and unlimited financial resources? And finally, many commentators would argue Dyson was successful partly

[1] This case has been written as a basis for class discussion rather than to illustrate effective or ineffective managerial or administrative behaviour. It has been prepared from a variety of published sources, as indicated, and from observations.

▶

because he had some influential contacts that he had established – he was fortunate. But there may be a hundred failed Mr Dysons littering the business highways who did not have such contacts. How can governments try to facilitate inventors like Dyson and ensure that more innovations succeed (thereby developing the economic base of their country)?

Reaping the rewards from technological innovation

Since Dyson's entry into the domestic appliance market two of the largest world players in the vacuum cleaner market have responded to the challenge laid down by James Dyson's bagless vacuum cleaner, launched in the United Kingdom in 1993. Dyson now accounts for a third of all vacuum cleaner sales in the United Kingdom. In 1998 Dyson Appliances sold nearly 1.4 million units world-wide. Revenues for the year were £190 million but surprisingly net income was £29 million – 15 per cent of sales (*see* Figure 14.5).

Background

Prior to the development of the bagless vacuum cleaner James Dyson had already demonstrated his prowess as a designer and businessman. He was responsible for the 'ballbarrow', a wheelbarrow that revolutionised that market by using a ball rather than a wheel. This was to provide the financial foundation for the development of the bagless vacuum cleaner. That particular experience taught James Dyson many lessons. One in particular is worth mentioning. The patents for the ballbarrow were owned by the company that James Dyson helped to set up. He eventually parted with this company but unfortunately lost all control of the patents as they belonged to the company and not to himself. Dyson was determined that any future patent would personally belong to him and not a company.

For those who may not recall their British social and economic history, Hubert Booth developed the first vacuum cleaner at the end of the nineteenth century. Vacuum technology uses the principle of a vacuum (the absence of everything, even air). Vacuum cleaners actually create a partial vacuum, or more accurately, an area of reduced air pressure as air moves outward within the fan. Airflow is created as air with normal air pressure moves towards the area with the reduced air pressure. A few years later in 1902 the British Vacuum Cleaner Company was offering a vacuum cleaning service to the homes of the affluent and wealthy. A large horse-drawn 5-hp engine would pull up outside your home and a hose would be fed into the house where it would begin to suck out all the dust. By 1904 a more mobile machine was available for use and was operated by domestic servants. As popularity of the technology increased, additional manufacturers began entering the market. Electrolux introduced a cylinder and hose vacuum cleaner in 1913 and in 1936 Hoover an upright cleaner with rotating brushes. This was known as the Hoover Junior and was the bestselling vacuum cleaner in the United Kingdom. Indeed, virtually all vacuum cleaners since this time are variations on that Hoover Junior design. That was until the late 1970s and early 1980s when James Dyson developed a vacuum cleaner using cyclonic forces and avoided the need for a bag to collect dust.

When it comes to cleaning performance, there is a tendency to look primarily at the power of the suction motor and the amount of bristles on the brush roll. While these are important considerations, the quality and size of the paper bag are very important factors as well. The paper bag in a vacuum cleaner consists of a special paper enclosure into which the dirt and air are directed as part of the filtering system. The paper used is specially processed to permit the air to pass through it while retaining as much of the dust and dirt as possible. The quality of the bag's filter media affects both its ability to retain the fine dust and allergens and its ability to allow air to flow easily through it. The size of the bag will also

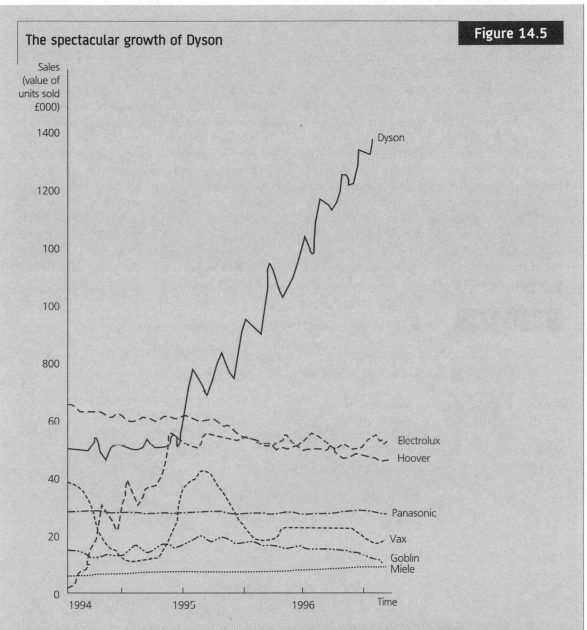

The spectacular growth of Dyson

Figure 14.5

affect how easily the air flows. A good-quality paper bag is a very important vacuum cleaner component, which needs to be regularly replaced. The Dyson vacuum cleaner maintains its performance during the vacuuming process because it has no bag, hence there is no reduction in suction due to clogging of the pores of the bag, a feature that is characteristic of the bagged cleaners.

The development of a bagless vacuum cleaner

It is the bag component of a vacuum cleaner that Dyson focused on to revolutionise the vacuum cleaner appliance industry. Put simply he tackled the key dilemma for vacuum cleaners – how to collect dirt and dust, yet at the same time allow clean air to pass through. This was achieved by abandoning the use of bags to collect dirt. Instead he adapted the use of centrifugal forces. Many of us will have enjoyed cyclonic forces personally. One of the oldest fun rides at fairgrounds involves a large drum in which people stand with their backs against the outer wall. When the drum spins the floor is lowered and people remain pressed against the outer wall. The exhilaration and excitement clearly results from being forced against a wall, unable to move one's head or arms due to the huge forces that are created. Yet the fascinating aspect here is that the drum's speed is no more than 33 kph (20 mph).

It is this principle that is used to separate the heavy dust particles from the air allowing the clean air to continue through the machine. The air, which has no mass, is not forced against the side walls of the container and takes the easiest route in the centre and thus out through the hole at the bottom (*see* Figure 14.6). This approach had been used in a variety of industries to collect dust, for example, in sawmills, but this was on a large scale (30m by 10m) and involved substantial pieces of equipment. The difficulty was applying this technology to a small domestic appliance.

If anyone still thinks that innovation is about waking up in the morning with a bright idea and shouting 'Eureka!' they should consider carefully James Dyson's difficult road to success. Between 1978 and 1982 he built over 1,000 prototype vacuum cleaners, spent over £2 million and experienced many years of sweat and headaches before eventually developing a

| Figure 14.6 | Basic operating principle of Dyson bagless vacuum cleaner |

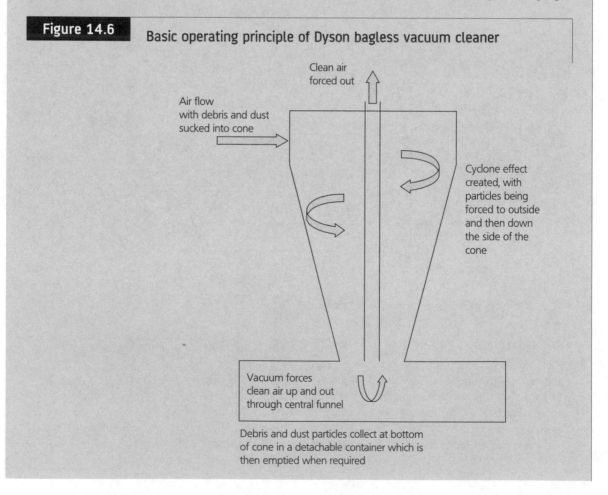

successful prototype. But this was merely the start of an even longer project to get manufacturers to buy the licence to manufacture. Indeed, over 10 years later Dyson decided to mass produce the product for the UK market himself.

The story begins in 1978 with James Dyson at home with his young family helping with some of the chores around the home. Like many families at the time, the Dysons owned a Hoover Junior upright vacuum cleaner. Dyson noticed that when a new bag is fitted to the vacuum cleaner it works well, but quickly loses much of its suction. He soon had the vacuum cleaner in pieces on his workbench and was amazed to realise that the standard vacuum cleaner technology relied on holes in the bag to allow clean air to pass through. As soon as these clogged up (which starts to occur immediately) suction begins to deteriorate. Moreover, he quickly discovered that all bagged vacuum cleaners operate on the same principle. How, then, can this limitation be overcome? The idea came to Dyson while he was investigating a problem at his ballbarrow factory. To improve toughness the product was powder-coated and then heated. This involved spraying the powder coating, which was messy. To overcome this problem an industrial vacuum cleaner was required. The suppliers of the powder coating informed Dyson that most of their larger customers use cyclones to collect the powder. Such cyclones are also used in a variety of industrial settings such as sawmills to extract dust from the air. This information was the beginning of what turned out to be a 15-year project.

Cyclonic cleaning systems separate the dust particles from the airflow by spinning the air within a separation chamber. The Dyson system operates as follows.

Any dirt and air enters the nozzle near the floor and travels through the hose towards the separation chambers. It first enters the primary dirt-separation chamber where the larger dirt particles are deposited. From there the air with the remaining fine dirt and dust travels to the cyclonic chamber. Once in the cyclonic chamber, the spinning action separates most of the fine dirt and dust particles from the airflow. The spinning causes centrifugal force to act upon the dust particles, moving them outward while the air exits from the inner part of the chamber (see Figure 14.6).

The Dyson vacuum cleaner uses two cyclones and several filters to capture dirt and dust. While the first cyclonic chamber captured large dust particles some fine dust particles were escaping with the air. The answer was a second, smaller, cyclone and Dyson spent many months developing this idea. The key problem was in the application of the theory, that is, having dust pass through one cyclone and then another all in a small domestic appliance. After months, and eventually years, of further trials and errors the development of a cyclone within a cyclone was born (the dual cyclone). As dirt and air is sucked into the machine the first cyclone separates the large dust particles and these come to rest at the bottom of the canister. The remaining air and fine dust (including cigarette smoke) is then carried into a second cyclone which separates the even finer dust particles from the air.

The technology also uses several replaceable filters to remove even smaller particles of dust. Since the air is quite clean, it is then allowed to flow through the motor to cool it. After leaving the motor the air is filtered by an HEPA (High Efficiency Particulate Air) exhaust filter to remove even more fine particles and carbon from the motor brushes before it leaves the vacuum cleaner.

In search of a manufacturer – 'don't let them get you down'

Thanks to experience gained with other products, most notably the ballbarrow, Dyson was able to ensure that patent applications were in place prior to negotiations. This is essential if you wish to ensure that large multi-national companies are not going to steal your intellectual property. From Dyson's experience he would argue that they would probably try to steal it regardless of any protection one held.

▶

Dyson was offering a licence to manufacturing companies that included exclusive rights to his patents. In return Dyson would receive a percentage of their profits from the sale of the manufactured product. Dyson was looking for a five- to ten-year licence with a royalty of 5 per cent of the wholesale price and £40,000 up front. In addition he was offering his help in the development of the product from its prototype form. Unfortunately Hoover, Electrolux, Goblin, Black and Decker, AEG, Vax and many others all declined. There were many different reasons given. Sometimes the companies appeared to be arrogant and dismissed Dyson as a 'loony crank'. What was surprising was that throughout, companies appeared to be obsessed with finding fault with the product. On other occasions the company expected Dyson to hand over the patents for very little financial reward. Frequently there were difficulties in agreeing to meet. This was due to problems of protecting the intellectual property that would flow from a meeting between the R&D experts of the company in question and Dyson.

Many of the objections, limitations and problems with the prototype may have been justified. One may even argue that the agreement sought by Dyson was ambitious. There is also one other key issue – the bags. The Dyson product was proposing to eliminate vacuum bags, but this was a very profitable business for vacuum cleaner manufacturers. They were unlikely to relish this prospect.

Breaking through in Japan

If things were not going well in the United Kingdom and Europe fortunately Dyson had a breakthrough in Japan. Apex Inc. agreed, after several arduous weeks of negotiations, to a licence to manufacture and sell in Japan. The product was to be called 'G-Force'. The successful licensing of the technology to a Japanese manufacturer in the late 1980s helped Dyson to secure much-needed revenue at a time when

he was beginning to consider throwing in the towel. This small level of income also provided the encouragement he needed to start planning the establishment of manufacturing facilities in the United Kingdom. What is interesting about the licensing arrangement in question is that Dyson was uncertain that licensing revenues received reflect the true sales figures. As with all licensing and royalty agreements, there is a significant element of trust required. For example, authors trust their publishers that sales of their book will be accurately recorded and appropriate royalties paid. There is, however, the small matter of who establishes the level of sales. This, of course, is taken by the publisher who then pays the royalties to authors. This 'high-trust' relationship also operates with other licensing agreements where royalties are paid per item sold.

Entering the UK market and manufacturing in the United Kingdom

With a small amount of revenue starting to trickle in Dyson decided that it was time to start in Britain. The existing appliance manufacturers had expressed no interest, hence Dyson planned to manufacture the product in Britain by offering the product to existing contract manufacturers. Essentially Dyson decided to offer a series of contracts to two existing manufacturing companies, one to mould the component parts and another to assemble. For the existing moulding and assembly companies it was additional capacity. Unfortunately the companies selected by Dyson caused further problems. First, the quality of the completed product was not acceptable to Dyson. Second, the companies seemed to be squeezing Dyson's work in between existing long-standing contracts. In the end Dyson decided that he would prefer to manufacture and assemble the product himself. He purchased the moulds from the plastic moulding company and attempted to establish a factory in the United Kingdom, the rationale being that this would at least ensure that he was in control of his own destiny and would not have to rely on others. Further difficulties, however, were encountered by Dyson. First, he found that it is extremely difficult to borrow money – even with a proven successful product. Dyson explored the possibility of setting up a factory in an area where government development grants are available. For example, he tried South Wales but David Hunt, the then Welsh Office Minister, refused his application for a grant.

The project had now consumed 12 years of his life and had cost £2 million. Once again Dyson was forced to consider whether it was all worth it.

After months of negotiations Dyson's local bank manager agreed to lend him some more money and he was able to set up his manufacturing factory in Wiltshire. Soon Dyson was producing his own product in his own factory and the first Dyson bagless vacuum cleaner rolled off the production line in 1992.

Trying to sell to the retailers

Armed with a shiny new DC01 under his arm James Dyson began visiting the large UK white-goods retailers such as Currys, Dixons and Comet to arrange sales orders. Unfortunately Dyson was disappointed at their reaction. Quite simply, the retailers were not convinced that the UK consumer would be willing to pay possibly three times as much for a vacuum cleaner. Moreover, Dyson's bagless product was twice the price of the brand leader. The response was almost universal:

> *Consumers are very happy with this one – why should they pay twice as much for yours? And anyway, if your idea was any good Hoover or Electrolux would have thought of it years ago.*

Eventually, several of the home catalogue companies agreed to feature the product. In addition, an electricity board shop in the Midlands also agreed to stock a few products. Initially, sales were slow but gradually they increased.

Eventually John Lewis, the national department store, agreed to take the product. From here sales began to take off.

In terms of marketing and promoting the product what is interesting is that, to date, the company has spent virtually nothing on promotion. Dyson has always adopted a strong product orientation and has believed that if a product is good enough it should require very little promotion. It is this approach which Dyson adopted for the bagless vacuum cleaner. Despite the use of revolutionary technology Dyson decided against large advertising budgets and instead relied upon a few press releases and features in newspapers.

The competition responds

With Dyson beginning to challenge the once-comfortable dominant position of Electrolux and Hoover, both companies mounted a strong defence of their products' technology, claiming that their traditional vacuum cleaning technology was more effective than the Dyson. Much of the debate, usually via press advertisements, centred on cleaning effectiveness. Hoover and Electrolux were able to make some headline-grabbing claims, in particular, that their products had more suction power, and hence, were better. Certainly the traditional vacuum cleaner with a bag had an initial high level of suction power, but this was necessary because the bag soon clogged up, reducing the level of suction. There are two different ways of viewing cleaning effectiveness. The most common use has to do with the ability of a vacuum cleaner to pick up dirt from the surface being cleaned. The other is the ability of the filtering system to clean the air so that a minimum amount of dirt and allergens is recirculated back into the home. The variable that is significant in a vacuum cleaner, however, is the flow of air and is measured in cubic metres per minute (CMM). It is one of the most important aspects of vacuum cleaner performance. Airflow in a vacuum cleaner is inversely

▶

| Figure 14.7 | Cleaning performance of five vacuum cleaners |

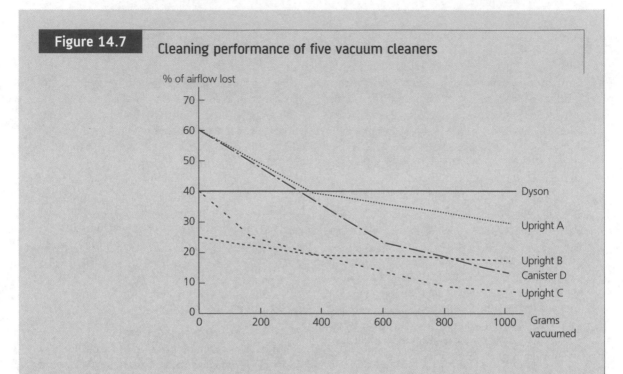

proportional to the total resistance within the system and directly proportional to the suction created by the suction motor.

Figure 14.7 depicts cleaning performance after vacuuming 100 grams of ASTM (American Society for Testing and Materials) Test Dirt. You will see that the Dyson machine maintains a steady airflow while other 'bagged' machines lose airflow.

Hoover's bagless vacuum cleaner

With sales and market share continuing to decline (*see* Table 14.1) Miele and Hoover attempted to fight Dyson in the vacuum cleaner market by developing similar bagless vacuum technologies. Hoover embarked on a technology transfer exercise to utilise technology first developed for the oil industry. The centrifugal force technology (similar to that used by Dyson) was used to separate gas or sand from crude oil. This technology has now been applied to Hoover's

Table 14.1 With sales declining Miele and Hoover have attempted to take on Dyson in the vacuum cleaner market

	Volume (%)	Value (%)
Dyson		
Total market	33.5	53.5
Upright	51.6	66.9
Cylinder	13.6	29.8
Hoover		
Total market	12.3	9.2
Upright	16.5	10.2
Cylinder	8.2	7.1
Miele		
Total market	2.1	2.6
Cylinder	6.1	10.4

Source: 'A dirty business', *The Guardian*, 16 March 1999.

range of Triple Vortex vacuum cleaners in an attempt to compete with Dyson's own patented centrifugal force technology (*see* Hoover.co.uk, 2000). Interestingly, Hoover's technology dispenses with the need for any filters. This may provide the advantage Hoover requires to re-establish itself as a key player in the vacuum cleaner market. Dyson is claiming, however, that Hoover's technology infringes his patents and is currently fighting this lawsuit.

Dyson has had several legal battles with his competitors over patent infringement and advertising standards. In January 2000 the Advertising Standards Association (ASA) ruled in favour of Dyson regarding an advertisement from Electrolux that claimed its vacuum cleaner was the most powerful. The ASA ruled that power of the motor was no indication of vacuum cleaner effectiveness (*Sunday Times*, 2000).

Conclusions

James Dyson certainly believes it was worth it in the end. But during the 15-year period there were probably many occasions when he felt like giving up or more likely would have sold out for a few hundred thousand pounds. The period 1980–92 was very difficult, not just for himself but also for his family, and enormous pressures were placed on them. Fortunately they survived, arguably someone without the background, resources and contacts would have failed. Many people have great ideas but only a few achieve success. Very often it is due to the determination of the individual involved, sometimes events seem to conspire against even the best efforts of the individual.

Dyson invests heavily in R&D and believes that this is the key to success. Not all firms support this view. The level of investment in R&D varies considerably. The high value he places on

creativity sets Dyson apart from other firms and helps to explain his insistence on maintaining what in Britain are considered insanely large annual investments in research and development. Nearly 17 per cent of revenues regularly goes to supporting the company's R&D efforts, a figure some ten times greater than the average in the United Kingdom. As a result of these ongoing research expenditures, a company that started with just one product now offers more than a dozen – all either upright or canister vacuum cleaners, each a more refined and technologically advanced model than its predecessors.

Questions

1 How can businesses try to ensure that their senior managers (both buyers and new business development managers) do not dismiss exciting technology and with it potentially profitable business?

2 How can governments try to assist inventors like Dyson and ensure that more innovations succeed in their country, and thereby developing their economic base?

3 What is the role of patents? To what extent is it an effective system for protecting intellectual property?

4 Explain the rationale behind Electrolux and Hoover's decision not to purchase the license from Dyson. Given Hoover's recent development of the Triple Vortex vacuum cleaner how do you assess this decision? What level of royalty would have been reasonable for both parties, that is, Dyson and Hoover?

5 Why is negotiating a licence for a new product so difficult?

Chapter summary

This chapter has shown that great care must be exercised in market research, for there are times when market research results produce negative reactions to discontinuous new products (innovative products) that later become profitable for the innovating company. Like any activity that contributes to new product development, it has strengths and weaknesses. Many of these weaknesses are highlighted when the new product is discontinuous. Finally, some new products have particularly difficult problems to overcome if they are to be successful, like high switching costs. If these are recognised in advance, however, it is possible to overcome even these significant challenges.

Discussion questions

1 Explain why consumer market testing might not always be beneficial.

2 We are told that many new products fail, but is this because many firms are impatient. Discuss whether firms should allow more time for their product to be adopted and whether they would end up with a successful product.

3 Explain why discontinuous new products present a different challenge.

4 Discuss the advantages of the tripartite product concept in developing new products.

5 Discuss the dilemma faced by all firms of trying to listen to customers' needs and wants and yet also trying to develop new products for those customers that they do not yet serve.

6 Explain why some writers argue that organisations are the graveyard of product innovations rather than the birthplace.

Key words and phrases

Concept testing 451	Switching costs 460
Discontinuous new products 456	Tripartite product concept 458
Installed base effect 460	Unarticulated needs 464
Market research 447	

Websites worth visiting

Britvic plc www.Britvic.com

The Design Council www.Designcouncil.com

Product development association www.pda.com

Product development forum www.members.aol.com

Product development institute www.prod-dev.com

References

Barrett, P. (1996) 'The good and bad die young', *Marketing*, 11 July, 16.

Britvic (2004) www.Britvic.com

Brown, R. (1991) 'Managing the S curves of innovation', *Journal of Marketing Management*, Vol. 7, No. 2, 189–202.

Christensen, C.M. (1997) *The Innovator's Dilemma: When New Technologies Cause Great Firms to Fail*, HBS Press, Cambridge, MA.

Cohen, W.M. and Levinthal, D.A. (1990) 'A new perspective on learning and innovation', *Administrative Science Quarterly*, Vol. 35, No. 1, 128–52.

Cohen, W.M. and Levinthal, D.A. (1994) 'Fortune favours the prepared firm', *Management Science*, Vol. 40, No. 3, 227–51.

Cooper, R.G. (1990) 'New products: What distinguishes the winners', *Research and Technology Management*, November–December, 27–31.

Cooper R.G. (2001) *Winning at New Products*, 3rd edn, Perseus Publishing, Cambridge, MA.

Day, G.S. (1999) *The Market Driven Organisation*, The Free Press, New York.

Dyson, J. (1998) *Against the Odds*, Orion Books, London.

Elliot, K. and Roach, D. (1991) 'Are consumers evaluating your products the way you think and hope they are?' *Journal of Consumer Marketing*, Vol. 8, No. 1, 5–14.

Francis, J. (1994) 'Rethinking NPD; giving full rein to the innovator', *Marketing*, 26 May, 6.

Guardian (1999) 'A dirty business', 16 March, 22.

Hamel, G. and Prahalad, C.K. (1994) 'Competing for the future', *Harvard Business Review*, Vol. 72, No. 4, 122–8.

Herbig, P., Howard, C. and Kramer, H. (1995) 'The installed base effect: implications for the management of innovation', *Journal of Marketing Management*, Vol. 11, No. 4, 387–401.

www.Hoover.co.uk (2000)

Jackson, B.B. (1985) *Winning and Keeping Industrial Customers*, Lexington Books, Lexington, MA.

King, S. (1985) 'Has marketing failed or was it never really tried?', *Journal of Marketing Management*, Vol. 1, 1–19.

Kotler, P. (1998) *Marketing Management*, Prentice Hall, London.

Liddle, D. (2004) 'R&D Project Selection at Danahar', MBA Dissertation, University of Portsmouth.

Lynn, G.S., Morone, J.G. and Paulson, A.S. (1997) 'Marketing and discontinuous innovation: The probe and learn process', in Tushman, M.L. and Anderson, P. (eds) *Managing strategic innovation and change, a collection of readings*, Oxford University Press, New York, 353–75.

Martin, J. (1995) 'Ignore your customer', *Fortune*, Vol. 8, No. 1, 121–25.

Morone, J. (1993) *Winning in High-tech Markets*, Harvard Business School Press, Cambridge, MA.

Ortt, R.J. and Schoormans, P.L. (1993) 'Consumer research in the development process of a major innovation', *Journal of the Market Research Society*, Vol. 35, No. 4, 375–89.

Porter, M.E. (1985) *Competitive Advantage*, Harvard Business School Press, Cambridge, MA.

Rogers, E. (1995) *The Diffusion of Innovation*, The Free Press, New York.

Saren, M.A.J. and Tzokas, N. (1994) *Proceedings of the Annual Conference of the European Marketing Academy*, Maastricht.

Sunday Times (2000) 'Dyson bags ruling on Electrolux', Business Section, 24 January, 1.

Tauber, E.M. (1974) 'Predictive validity in consumer research', *Journal of Advertising Research*, Vol. 15, No. 5, 59–64.

Trott, P. and Lataste, A. (2003) 'The role of consumer market research in new product decision-making: some preliminary findings from European firms', *Entrepreneurship, Marketing and Innovation Conference*, University of Karlsrühe, 8–9 September, conference proceedings, Karlsrühe.

von Hippel, E. and Thomke, S. (1999) 'Creating breakthroughs at 3M,' *Harvard Business Review*, Vol. 77, No. 5, 47–57.

Further reading

For a more detailed review of the role of market research in new product development, the following develop many of the issues raised in this chapter:

Hamel, G. and Prahalad, C.K. (1994) 'Competing for the future', *Harvard Business Review*, Vol. 72, No. 4, 122–8.

Hutlink, E.J., Hart, S., Henery, R.S.J. and Griffin, A. (2000) 'Launch decisions and new product success: an empirical comparison of consumer and industrial products', *Journal of Product Innovation Management*, Vol. 17, No. 1, 5–23.

Kumar, N., Scheer, L. and Kotler, P. (2000) 'From market driven to market driving', *European Management Journal*, Vol. 18, No. 2, 129–41.

Shavinina, L. (2003) *The International Handbook on Innovation*, Elsevier, Oxford.

Swink, M. (2000) 'Technological innovativeness as a moderator of new product design integration and top management support', *Journal of Product Innovation Management*, Vol. 17, No. 1, 208–20.

Veryzer, R. (2003) 'Marketing and the development of innovative products', in Shavinina, L. (ed.), *The International Handbook on Innovation*, Elsevier, Oxford.

15

Managing the new product development team

The popular phrase 'actions speak louder than words' could be a subtitle for this chapter. While the previous four chapters in the third part of this book helped to identify some of the key factors and activities involved in the new product development process, it is the execution of these activities that will inevitably lead to the development of a new product. The focus of this chapter is on the management of the project as it evolves from idea into a physical form. Many companies have become very good at effective NPD, demonstrating that they are able to balance the many factors involved.

Chapter contents

Learning objectives

When you have completed this chapter you will be able to:

- examine the key activities of the NPD process;
- explain that a product concept differs significantly from a product idea or business opportunity;
- recognise that screening is a continuous rather than single activity;
- provide an understanding of the role of the knowledge base of an organisation in the new product development process; and
- recognise that the technology intensity of the industry considerably affects the NPD process.

New products as projects

Over the past 50 years a large number of models and methods have been developed to help improve a company's performance in new product development (Craig and Hart, 1992). However, despite the positive influences these models may have on companies' efforts, Mahajan and Wind (1988) have shown low rates of usage in their study of *Fortune* 500 companies. More recently, Nijssen and Lieshout (1995) have shown in their study of companies in the Netherlands that the use of NPD models has a positive effect on profits.

The previous chapters have outlined some of the conditions that are necessary for innovation to occur and have shown various representations of the new product development process. However, while these conditions are necessary, they are insufficient in themselves to lead to the development of new products. This is because, as with any internal organisational process, it has to be managed by people. The concepts of strategy, marketing and technology all have to be coordinated and managed effectively. Inevitably, this raises issues in such areas as internal communications, procedures and systems. This is where the attention turns from theory and representation to operation and activities.

We have seen that a product idea may arise from a variety of sources. We have also seen that, unlike some internal operations, NPD is not the preserve of one single department. And it is because a variety of different functions and departments are involved that the process is said to be complicated and difficult to manage. Furthermore, while two separate new products may be similar generically, there will frequently be different product characteristics to be accommodated and different market and technology factors to be addressed. To be successful new product development needs to occur with the participation of a variety of personnel drawn from across the organisation. This introduces the notion of a group of people working as a team to develop an idea or project proposal into a final product suitable for sale. The vast majority of large firms create new project teams to work through this process. From initial idea to launch, the

---

Table 15.1 NPD terminology

NPD terminology	Definition
Business opportunity	A possible technical or commercial idea that may be transformed into a revenue-generating product.
Product concept	A physical form or a technology plus a clear statement of benefit.
Screening	A series of evaluations, including technical, commercial and business assessments of the concept.
Specifications	Precise details about the product, including features, characteristics and standards.
Prototype/pilot	A tentative physical product or system procedure, including features and benefits.
Production	The product produced by the scale-up manufacturing process.
Launch	The product actually marketed, in either market test or launch.
Co-joint analysis	A method for deriving the utility values that consumers attach to varying levels of a product's attributes.
Commercialisation	A more descriptive label would be market introduction, the phase when the product is launched and hopefully begins to generate sales revenue.
Commercial success	The end product that meets the goals set for it, usually profit.

---

project will usually flow and iterate between marketing, technical and manufacturing groups and specialists. The role of the new project team is at the heart of managing new products and is the focus of the case study at the end of this chapter.

The key activities that need to be managed

The network model of NPD shown in Figure 12.14 represents a generalised and theoretical view of the process. To the practising manager, however, this is of limited practical use. Business managers and the managers of project teams need to know what particular activities should be undertaken. From this practitioner standpoint it is more useful to view the new product development process as a series of linked activities.

Figure 15.1 attempts to identify and link together most of the activities that have been associated with the NPD process over the years. This diagram represents a generic process model of NPD. It is not intended to be an actual representation of the process as carried out in a particular industry. Rather, it attempts to convey to the practitioner how the key activities are linked together to form a process. Some of these labels differ

The NPD process as a series of linked activities

Figure 15.1

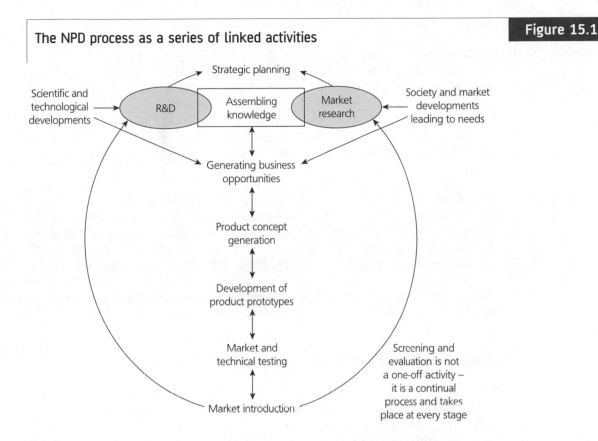

between industries and a good example of this is in the pharmaceutical industry. Final testing of a product is referred to as the clinical trial, where the product is used by volunteers and the effects carefully monitored. In the automotive industry final testing may involve the use of consumers trying the product for the first time and offering their reflections on the design and ergonomics.

One of the most comprehensive studies on new product success and failure was undertaken by Cooper in 1979. In this study 12 activities were identified: initial screening; preliminary market assessment; preliminary technical assessment; detailed market study; financial analysis; product development; product testing (in-house); product testing (with customer); test marketing; trial production; full-scale production; and product launch. Since this a number of different studies have highlighted the importance of some of these activities over others. Other studies have shown that firms frequently omit some of these activities (Cooper, 1988a,b; Sanchez and Elola, 1991). Students of new product development are left with an unclear picture of which activities are necessary and which are performed. The answer is context-dependent and, in particular, industry-dependent. Some industries no longer use test marketing, for example, whereas for others it is still a very important activity. This is explained below.

This section will examine the activities that need to be performed by businesses and NPD teams. The early activities are defined as the 'assembly of knowledge' and the 'generation of business opportunities'. These activities usually occur before a physical representation of the product has been developed. Up to this point costs have been relatively low, especially when compared to subsequent activities. These activities, defined here as product concept development and development of product prototypes, transform what was previously a concept, frequently represented by text and drawings, into a physical form. The product begins to acquire physical attributes such as size, shape, colour and mass. The final activities are market and technical testing and market introduction. It is worthy of note that these activities may occur at an earlier stage and that any of these activities can occur simultaneously.

Chapter 12 reviewed the wide range of models that have been developed to try to further our understanding of this complex area of management. Hopefully you will recognise the new product development process as a series of activities that transform an opportunity into a tangible product that is intended to produce profits for the company. In practice, the process is difficult to identify. Visitors who ask to see a company's NPD process will not see very much, because the process is intertwined with the on-going operation of the business. Furthermore, the process is fluid and iterations are often needed. Developments by competitors may force a new product idea due for impending launch back to the laboratory for further changes. The model in Figure 15.1 highlights many of the important features and also identifies the importance played by the external environment. From an idea or a concept the product evolves over time. This process involves extensive interaction and iteration, highlighted by the arrows in the diagram.

Assembling knowledge

The vast majority of marketing textbooks fail to identify the first activity of the NPD process, the assembling of knowledge (Kotler, 2003; Brassington and Pettitt, 2003). It is from an organisation's knowledge base that creativity and ideas for new products will flow. Chapter 6 emphasised the importance of an organisation's knowledge base in underpinning its innovative ability. Without the continual accumulation of knowledge, an organisation will be hindered in its ability to create new product ideas. Figure 15.2 shows a wide range of activities that together help to maintain a company's knowledge base.

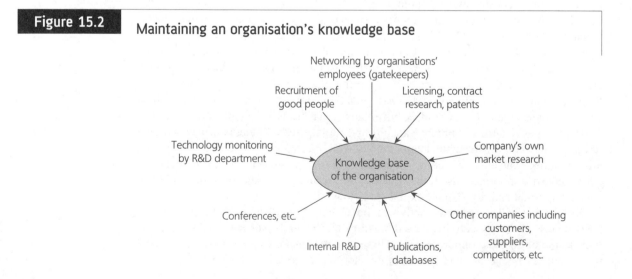

Figure 15.2 Maintaining an organisation's knowledge base

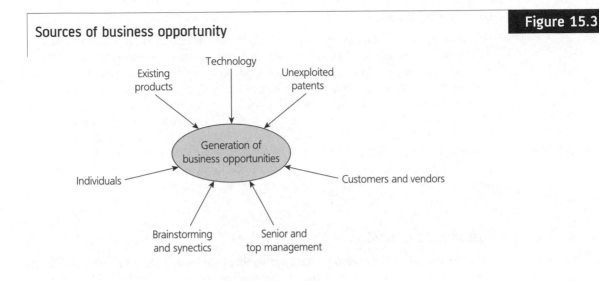

Figure 15.3

Sources of business opportunity

The generation of business opportunities

The generation of business opportunities is the next activity in the process of new product development. This was discussed in Chapters 6 and 12. You should therefore be aware of the concept, even if the process is not fully clear. This stage in the NPD process is also referred to as opportunity identification (OI). It is the process of collecting possible business opportunities that could realistically be developed by the business into successful products. This definition contains several caveats, which helps to explain the difficulty that faces businesses. New product ideas can emerge from many sources, as illustrated in Figure 15.3. Although this classification is not intended to be exhaustive, the figure identifies many of the key sources for product ideas which are explained below.

Existing products

Many new ideas will come from a company's existing range of products. Very often small changes to a product result in the development of new lines and brands. This was the case for Unilever, which since 1930 has added detergents to its original product line of bar soap. It has also developed new brands of detergent from its original detergent Persil, such as Surf.

Technology

The most obvious source of ideas is the company's own R&D department which is funded to research technology and develop new product ideas. It is also the responsibility of the R&D department to keep abreast of external technological developments of interest to the company. This is frequently referred to as technology assessment. Opportunities for the transfer of technology to the company need to be continually reviewed. This is explored in further detail in Chapters 9 and 10.

Unexploited patents

For those companies that invest heavily in R&D, the development of patents is part of the day-to-day operation of a busy research and development laboratory. Many of these patents could be used in the eventual development of a new product; many, however, will not. Research and development laboratories continually scan patent databases, such as Derwent in the United States, for listings of interesting patents. In so doing, they can identify patents that have not yet been exploited and use them to develop new product ideas. This highlights and emphasises an earlier point made in Chapter 6 about the dual benefits of investment in R&D. In order to scan, search and identify interesting and potentially useful patents, a company needs to be knowledgeable in that area. Without this prior knowledge scanning patent databases would be akin to looking at a foreign language that one does not understand.

Customers and vendors

Eric von Hippel's (1988) famous study of medical equipment manufacturers and users identified that the highest percentage of new product ideas originated with customers (the users). It has, however, since been suggested that this was a particular trait of that industry. It is, none the less, an important contribution to the debate about the origin of new product ideas. Indeed, in many other industries, especially fast-moving consumer goods (fmcg) industries, consumers are carefully studied to try to identify possible product ideas. For example, Procter & Gamble and Unilever continually visit consumers in their homes to watch and analyse the way they clean their furniture and do the laundry. Such studies have produced numerous product ideas, as was highlighted in the case study at the end of Chapter 6. In addition, customer complaints about products are an excellent source of ideas. Many product packaging improvements have been the result of customer complaints. For example, many of the multiples have responded to complaints from customers about leaking liquid containers, such as those for milk and orange juice, and have developed improved packaging as a result.

Salesforce

Vendors (sales representatives) are a particularly good source of new product ideas. Gordon (1962) has shown the important role played by this group in generating new business opportunities. They spend a large part of their time with customers discussing their own products and learning about competitors' products. Many companies insist that their sales representatives provide weekly reports on all the companies they have visited, noting any possible product development opportunities. For example, sales representatives from Shell, BP and Hoechst frequently visit manufacturing companies which use chemicals in their manufacturing operations. It is during discussions with these manufacturers about the effectiveness of the chemicals that ideas for product modifications are generated. Several new chemicals have been developed for specific companies and later launched nationally or internationally as a new product.

This raises an important point about the role of sales representatives, especially in technology-intensive industries. They are expected to be qualified scientists or engineers who subsequently undergo extensive commercial training in marketing and sales. Such highly trained people are in stark contrast to the popular image of a sales representative often depicted as a smooth-talking second-hand car salesman!

Senior and top management

Many company leaders have taken personal responsibility for technological innovation in their companies. As far back as the 1950s, Alistair Pilkington continued to push the float glass process in Pilkington Glass against severe opposition. His idea was eventually successful. Akio Morita adopted a similar approach at Sony with the development of the Walkman, even though initial market research suggested that there was limited demand for such a product. However, not all leaders are successful. Edwin Land, former CEO of Polaroid, pushed his idea of instantly developed movies against fierce opposition, but the product was a major failure.

Those companies that have developed a reputation for innovation and new product development, such as Siemens, Nokia and 3M, rely on their senior management to concentrate on providing an environment for innovation to flourish. This is emphasised in the case study at the end of Chapter 12.

Brainstorming and synectics

Brainstorming is a creativity exercise used with groups of about six to eight people. The idea is for people to use their own imagination and creativity and to build on the ideas of others in the group. There is usually a chairperson who asks for and records ideas relating to a specific problem. People within the group are encouraged to be liberal and uninhibited with their suggestions. A slightly more involved and subtle approach called synectics has been developed by Gordon (1962), who suggest that if the problem under investigation remains a secret, more imaginative ideas will flow.

Individuals

In addition to the R&D department, sales representatives and marketers, product ideas can originate from areas not usually associated with product development. Accountancy departments, secretarial support staff and contract hire personnel have all been identified as originators of ideas for new products. Many inventors have remarked, after the event, that the original idea was conceived outside company time and far away from the company. Everyone has the ability to be creative.

Developing product concepts: turning business opportunities into product concepts

This activity involves transforming a list of ideas into potential product concepts. In some cases the identification of an opportunity is sufficient to reveal the product required. For example, a paint manufacturer may uncover a need for a new form of paint that will not drip on to carpets and clothes, is easy to apply, will wash off users' hands and clothes if spilt and is hard-wearing like conventional paints. In other cases the concept is clear but the details need to be added. For example, a domestic appliance manufacturer may discover that some of its customers have expressed interest in a domestic water-cleaning device. In this case, the manufacturer is clear that the appliance will need to be fitted in the home but much more information is required. Sometimes it may not be clear at all what form the product will take. For example, a chemical manufacturer may uncover an opportunity in the treatment of water for industry. The eventual product could

Table 15.2 A new product concept		
Need	*Form*	*Technology*
A new low-fat yellow spread	A soft yellow spread that can be applied like margarine	An emulsion of fat droplets in water

take many different forms and use many different technologies, chemical treatment, mechanical treatment, etc. The idea is a long way from an actual product.

For a product idea to become a new product concept, Crawford (1997) argues that three inputs are required: form, technology and need.

> **Form:** *This is the physical thing to be created (or in the case of a service, the sequence of steps by which the service will be created). It may still be vague and not precisely defined.*
> **Technology:** *In most cases there is one clear technology that is at the base of the innovation (for the 3M Post-It it was the adhesive; for the instamatic camera it was the chemical formulation which permitted partial development in light).*
> **Need:** *The benefits gained by the customer give the product value.*

The following example illustrates this point. A dairy food manufacturer may uncover an idea for a new type of yellow spread (butter or margarine). All the details for the product remain unknown. Once the details are known the product idea is said to be a product concept. In this case, the product concept could be an opportunity in the yellow spreads market for a low-fat spread that can be applied like soft margarine (an emulsion of fat droplets in water), which has a buttery taste (*see* Table 15.2).

It is important to remember that an idea is just that, an idea, whereas a concept is the conjunction of all the essential characteristics of the product idea. This usually incorporates form, technology and need but lacks detail. The underlying message here is that product ideas without details are often more like dreams and wishes. For example, an aircraft manufacturer may wish for a noise-free aircraft engine, or a pharmaceutical company may wish for a cure for AIDS.

The screening of business opportunities

Screening product ideas is essentially an evaluation process. It is important to note that it is not a single, one-off activity as portrayed in many textbooks. It occurs at every stage of the new product development process (and is covered in Chapter 9 under evaluating R&D projects) and involves such questions as:

● Do we have the necessary commercial knowledge and experience?
● Do we have the technical know-how to develop the idea further?
● Would such a product be suitable for our business?
● Are we sure there will be sufficient demand?

The main purpose of screening ideas is to select those that will be successful and drop those that will not – herein lies the difficulty. Trying to identify which ideas are going to be successful and which are not is extremely difficult. Many successful organisations have made serious errors at this point. The Research Corporation of America (RCA) identified the huge business opportunity of radio and television but failed to see the potential for videocassette recorders (VCR). Kodak and IBM failed to see the potential in photocopying but Xerox did not. The list grows each year and while the popular business press are quick to identify those companies which make a mistake they are not so quick to praise those companies which identify successful business opportunities. 3M, for example, recognised a business opportunity in self-adhesive notes. Even here, persistence was required on behalf of the individuals involved. This was because, initially, the company was not sure about the idea (*see* Chapter 12).

Distinguishing between dreams and reality

Recognising what is a possible product and what is fantasy is an important part of the screening process. There are many examples of businesses rejecting a new product idea (business opportunity) because they did not believe it would work. Some of these are so famous they are known outside the world of business: Xerox and the computer graphical interface; Dyson and the bagless vacuum cleaner; Whittle and the jet engine. There must be a distinction between those opportunities that the business could develop into a product and those which it could not, and recognition of those that are likely to generate revenue and those that will not.

Market research will clearly provide valuable market analysis input at this stage to help in the decision process. This is covered in Chapter 9 along with other activities often associated with the screening activity, such as concept testing, product testing, market testing and test marketing. Organisations use a variety of different labels for very similar activities. The following represents an overview of many of the activities associated with the screening process.

Initial screen, entry screen or preliminary screen

This represents the first formal evaluation of the idea. Each of the ideas that came from the pool of concepts has to be given an initial screen. This will involve a technical feasibility check and marketing feasibility test, plus a comparison with the strategic opportunity. This would include evaluating whether the particular product would fit with the business's existing activities. The advantage of early screening is that it can be done quickly and easily and prevents expenditure on product ideas that are clearly not appropriate.

Customer screen, concept testing

This can vary between informal discussions with potential customers and feedback on developed prototypes. Concept testing is extremely difficult and mistakes are very easy to make. People have difficulty reacting to an entirely new product concept without a learning period, as discussed below.

Technical screen, technical testing

This activity can vary from a few telephone calls to technical experts to extensive analysis by an in-house R&D department or an analysis by a third party such as an independent consultant (often a university laboratory). This chapter and Chapter 9 discuss the activity of technical testing during which evaluations are continually undertaken.

Final screen

This normally involves the use of scoring models and computer assessment programs. Various new product ideas are fed into the program and a series of questions and assessments, with different weightings, are made, resulting in a scoring for each. One of the most serious criticisms of scoring models is their use of weights, because these are necessarily judgemental.

Business analysis

This may involve the construction of preliminary marketing plans, technical plans, financial reviews and projected budgets. All of these may raise potential problems that were previously unforeseen. It is not uncommon for new products to reach the mass-production stage only to encounter significant manufacturing difficulties, often when production is switched from one-off prototypes to high-volume manufacture.

Development of product prototypes

This is the phase during which the item acquires finite form and becomes a tangible good. It is at this stage that product designers may develop several similar prototypes with different styling. Manufacturing issues will also be discussed such as what type of process to use. For example, in the case of a tennis racket, engineers will discuss whether to manufacture using an injection-moulding or compression-moulding process. During this activity numerous technical developments will occur. This will include all aspects of scientific research and development, engineering development and design, possible technology transfer, patent analysis and cost forecasts.

Rapid prototyping

Reducing the time to develop products is a top priority for firms especially in consumer markets. Pamela Buxton (2000) argues that time to market is no longer measured in years but months. In the food industry 'own label' development is extremely rapid. Brand management firms like Procter & Gamble, Unilever and Biersdorf have all reduced their product development times. Ten years ago development took eighteen months to two years. Now this has been cut to six to nine months. Industry analysts now argue that it is better to get to the market 90 per cent correct and grab the market opportunity rather than wait longer and enter the market 100 per cent correct (Buxton, 2000). It is not only the fmcg industries that are under pressure to reduce NPD times. Domestic appliance manufacturers such as Siemens, Hoover and AEG are also responding to the need to get new products into the marketplace more quickly.

One area that has seen a significant development is the area of rapid prototyping. This is the process of developing a range of prototypes quickly for consideration by the firm. Stereolithography (SLA) is the most widely used rapid prototyping technology. Stereolithography builds plastic parts or objects a layer at a time by tracing a laser beam on the surface of a vat of liquid photopolymer. This class of materials, originally developed for the printing and packaging industries, quickly solidifies wherever the laser beam strikes the surface of the liquid. Once one layer is completely traced, it is lowered a small distance into the vat and a second layer is traced right on top of the first. The self-adhesive property of the material causes the layers to bond to one another and eventually form a complete, three-dimensional object after many such layers are formed.

Stereolithography allows you to create almost any 3-D shape you can imagine. If you can get it into a computer-aided design (CAD) program, you can probably create it. Hoover used stereolithography during the development of its Vortex vacuum cleaner. This helped it get a product from drawing board to the retailer in 12 months. It was able to develop a range of prototype vacuum cleaners and test them before deciding on the most suitable design. Once produced the object has the strength of polystyrene plastic. Which means that it can be drilled, mounted and cut. It enables the firm to try out the prototype in actual use. For example, a chair manufacturer will produce different arm-rest shapes using stereolithography and try them out on actual chairs to see how they feel.

The basic stereolithography process goes like this:

● create a 3-D model of your object in a CAD program;
● a piece of software chops the CAD model up into thin layers – typically 5–10 layers per millimeter;
● the 3-D printer's laser 'paints' one of the layers, exposing the liquid plastic in the tank and hardening it;
● the platform drops down into the tank a fraction of a millimetre and the laser paints the next layer; and
● this process repeats, layer by layer, until the model is complete

It is not a particularly quick process. Depending on the size and number of objects being created, the laser might take a minute or two for each layer. A typical run might take 6–12 hours.

Stereolithography is generally considered to provide the greatest accuracy and best surface finish of any rapid prototyping technology. Over the years, a wide range of materials with properties mimicking those of several engineering thermoplastics have been developed. Limited selectively colour-changing materials for biomedical and other applications are available, and ceramic materials are currently being developed. The technology is also notable for the large object sizes that are possible.

Technical testing

Closely linked to the development of product prototypes is the technical testing of a new product. It is sometimes difficult to distinguish between where prototype development finishes and testing begins. This is because in many industries it is frequently an on-going activity. Take the motor vehicle industry as an example. Engineers may be developing a new safety system for a vehicle. This might involve a new harness for the seat belt and a new airbag system. As the engineers begin designing the system they will be continually checking and testing that the materials for the belt are suitable, and that the sensors are not so sensitive that the airbag is inflated when the vehicle goes over a bump in the road. There will, of course, be final testing involving dummies and simulated crashes, but much of the technical testing is on-going.

Market testing and consumer research

These activities have been covered in Chapter 14, so they will only be dealt with briefly here. The traditional approach to NPD involved a significant stage devoted to market testing. Developed products were introduced to a representative sample of the population to assess the market's reaction. This was usually carried out prior to a full-scale national launch of the product. This was the commonly accepted approach, especially in fast-moving consumer goods industries such as confectionery, household products, food and drink. More significantly, manufacturers have emphasised the need to be first into the market and have often skipped the test market. Linked to this is the fear that a test market may reveal a new product to competitors who may be able to react quickly and develop a similar product. Furthermore, the use of direct marketing and the Internet has seen many new products being introduced via these developing channels.

In today's fiercely competitive marketplace products tend to go straight from consumer research and product development to national launch:

> *Marketers claim that consumer research techniques are now so sophisticated that full-blown tests are no longer necessary. Besides, once they have invested in R&D plus new plant, and created an advertising campaign, they might as well go national immediately. The fixed costs are so high that you might as well get on with it, says Mark Sherrington of marketing consultancy Added Value.*

(*Management Today*, 1995)

The debate about the benefits and limitations of consumer research has raged for many years (*see* Chapter 14 for much more on this). Put simply, critics associated with the consumerism movement claim that most new products are actually minor variations of existing products. They further argue that consumers are not able to peer into the future and articulate what products they want. They suggest that the major innovations of the twentieth century, such as electricity, frozen food, television, microcomputers and telecommunications, have been the result of sustained technological research uninhibited by the demands of consumers. Marketers, on the other hand, argue that without consumer research technologists will produce products that are not what the market wants. There are many examples to support both arguments. The Sony Walkman is often cited by those critical of consumer research, since the product was initially rejected on the basis of insufficient features such as the ability to record, etc. Similarly, the Disk camera, developed by Eastman Kodak between 1980 and 1988, is used by supporters of consumer research to highlight the potential disaster of not seeking consumers' views. It was a very small instamatic camera designed to appeal to those seeking a simple-to-use machine. Unfortunately, it produced grainy photographs.

Research by Christensen and Bower (1995) and Daily (1996) suggests that listening to your customer may actually stifle technological innovation and be detrimental to long-term business success. Ironically, to be successful in industries characterised by technological change, firms may be required to pursue innovations that are not demanded by their current customers. The results of this study suggest that managers may sometimes be wise to ignore the advice of their existing customers, who are primarily interested in incremental product improvements. This argument of not relying too heavily on the market derives further support from research conducted by Schmidt (1995) (*see* Illustration 15.1). This revealed that for industrial products, technical activities are more important than marketing activities such as market assessment, detailed market study, product testing with customer and test marketing. Indeed, Schmidt argues that inadequate focus on the technical activities and excessive focus on marketing activities and the marketing concept are myopic.

Illustration 15.1

Be wary of consumer research

If consumer research had been conducted at the turn of the century, the responses garnered from people as they walked along dusty dirt tracks meandering across the meadows of England would have halted research into the motor car. If asked whether they would like to have a noisy, dirty machine that would be responsible for thousands of deaths and cause enormous amounts of pollution, their answer would probably have been 'no thank you'. Chapter 14 explores the issue in more detail.

Market introduction

Commercialisation is not necessarily the stage at which large sums of money are spent on advertising campaigns or multi-million-pound production plants, since a company can withdraw from a project following the results of test marketing.

It is important to remember that for some products, say in the pharmaceutical business, the decision to finance a project with 10 years of research is taken fairly early on in the development of the product and this is where most of the expense is incurred. With other fast-moving consumer goods, like foods, advertising is a large part of the cost, so the decision is taken towards the launch phase.

Launch

We must not lose sight of reality. Most new products are improvements or minor line extensions and may attract almost no attention. Other new products, e.g. a major cancer breakthrough or rapid transport systems without pollution, are so important that they will receive extensive television news coverage.

Illustration 15.2

James Dyson and the dual cyclone vacuum cleaner

James Dyson has become a household name. This development of a revolutionary vacuum cleaner had a dramatic impact on the domestic vacuum-cleaner market and brought enormous success to his company. The product is a vacuum cleaner without a bag for collecting dirt. It eliminates the main problems associated with conventional vacuum cleaners of burst bags and blocked air flow and provides virtually 100 per cent suction power. It is the first technological breakthrough in the industry since the invention of the vacuum cleaner in 1901.

The product took five years to develop and included over 5,000 prototypes. It involved designers, engineers and scientists but, as is so often the case, the most difficult part of the project, according to Dyson, was trying to get retailers to stock the product. It was almost a 'Catch 22' situation, with retailers refusing to stock until convinced by sales figures. From the retailers' perspective, they saw this new product as very expensive – it was double the price of the best – selling units.

Eventually several electricity board retail chains and two big mail-order catalogues agreed to take the product. This provided publicity. It is now an enormous success and the market leader, overcoming resistance from three very big international brands. Technological innovation has provided differentiation and competitive advantage.

Source: J. Dyson, (1997) *Against the Odds*, Orion Books, London.

NPD across different industries

It has been stressed throughout this book that innovation and NPD in particular are context dependent. That is, the management of the process is dependent on the type of product being developed. A simple, but none the less useful, way of looking at this is to divide the wide range of activities involved in the development of a new product into technical and marketing activities. Figure 15.4 shows the NPD activities divided into the two categories. Against this are placed a variety of industries to illustrate the different balance of activities. It becomes clear that industrial products (products developed for use by other industries), such as a new gas-fired electricity generator, have many different considerations from those of a new soft drink. In the latter case there will be much more emphasis on promotion and packaging, whereas the electricity generator will have been designed and built following extensive technical meetings with the customer concentrating on the functional aspects of the product. Clearly, in between these two extremes the balance of activities is more equal. In a recent study of NPD involving 12 firms across a variety of industries, Olson *et al.* (1995) found that cross-functional teams helped shorten the development of times of

Figure 15.4

Classification of new product development activities across different industries

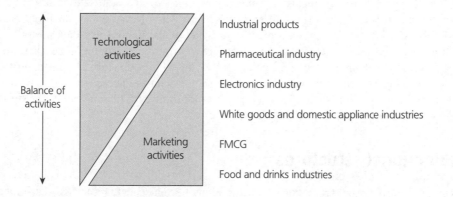

truly innovative products. More bureaucratic structures may provide better outcomes for less innovative products.

Organisational structures and cross-functional teams

Industrialists and academics have for many years been interested in the subject of how organisations are structured and the relationships that occur between individuals and functions. The nature of the industry in general and the product being developed in particular will significantly influence the choice of structure. Moreover, the organisation structure will considerably affect the way its activities are managed. It is not possible to alter one without causing an effect on the other. For example, the introduction of concurrent engineering techniques means that companies will need to be less reliant on functional operations and adopt the use of project management and cross-functional teams. Organisational structures and teams will therefore be examined together in this section.

Teams and project management

The use of teams within organisations is certainly nothing new. In sport having between five and fifteen individuals all working together has been the foundation for games all over the world. Similarly, within organisations teams have been used for many years, especially on large projects. In industry, however, the concept of having teams of individuals from different functions with different knowledge bases is a recent development. Jones (1997) suggests that in the field of medicine the practice of having a group of experts from different functions working together on a project has been around for many years. In manufacturing industries the use of cross-functional teams has occurred in parallel with the introduction of concurrent engineering.

New product project teams in small to medium-sized organisations are usually comprised of staff from several different functions who operate on a 'part-time' basis. Membership of the project team may be just one of the many roles they perform. In larger organisations, where several projects are in progress at any one time, there may be sufficient resources to enable personnel to be wholly concerned with a project. Ideally, a project team will have a group of people with the necessary skills, who are able to work together, share ideas and reach compromises. This may include external consultants or key component suppliers.

Functional structures

Unlike the production, promotion and distribution of products, NPD is a cross-disciplinary process and suffers if it is segregated by function. The traditional functional company structure allows for a strong managerial layer with information flowing up and down the organisation. Each function would usually be responsible for one or more product groups or geographical areas (*see* Figure 15.5).

Another common approach used by many large manufacturing companies is to organise the company by product type. Each product has its own functional activities. Some functions, however, are centralised across the whole organisation. This is to improve efficiency or provide common features (*see* Figure 15.6). This type of structure supports the notion of product platforms (*see* Chapter 11) where a generic group of technologies are used in a variety of products. Sony, Philips and Nokia all have centralised R&D activities where the majority of products are developed allowing for a high degree of technology transfer between product groups. This is one of the key arguments in favour of a centralised R&D function, of which more later.

It is important to note that while many organisations have clearly defined company structures, closer inspection of the actual activities within these companies will invariably reveal an informal structure that sits on top of the formal structure. This is made up of formal and informal communication channels and networks that help to facilitate the flow of information within the organisation (*see* Figure 15.7).

| Figure 15.5 | Functional company organisation |

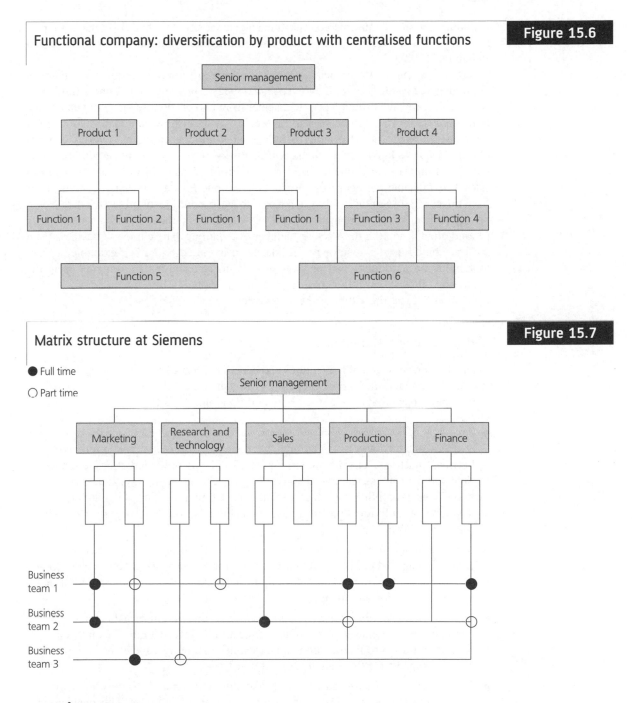

Figure 15.6

Functional company: diversification by product with centralised functions

Figure 15.7

Matrix structure at Siemens

Matrix structures

The use of a matrix structure requires a project-style approach to NPD. Each team will comprise a group of between four and eight people from different functions. A matrix structure is defined as any organisation that employs a multiple-command system including not only a multiple-command management structure but also related support mechanisms and associated organisational culture and behaviour patterns (Ford and Randolph, 1992).

Matrix structures are associated with dual lines of communication and authority (Tushman and Nadler, 1978; Lawrence *et al.*, 1982). They are seen as cross-functional because they involve bringing people together from two or more separate organisational functional areas. This can be seen in Figure 15.7, which shows the matrix structure at Siemens. The traditional hierarchy is functional, while the horizontal overlay consists of business areas known as business teams. Business team 1 comprises one full-time member from marketing, one full-time member from R&D, one full-time member from sales, one full-time member from production and one full- and one part-time member from finance. Between them this group would manage a number of projects. There would be a team leader for each business team. However, this person would not necessarily be, and often is not, the most senior member of the group. The choice of business team leader is based on the type of project the team is undertaking. For example, a team looking at the introduction of new products is likely to be led by someone from the marketing function, even though there will almost certainly be someone more 'senior' from another function within the business team.

Matrix structure at Siemens

The following are some of the features and benefits of a matrix organisational structure that have been identified in the literature. However, for a full review of matrix organisation and project management see Ford and Randolph (1992).

- *Provision of additional channels of communication*. The combination of a matrix structure and business teams ensures that there is extensive lateral communication between functions. The diagram in Figure 15.7 shows how marketing personnel involved in business teams 1, 2 and 3 bring back to the marketing function knowledge of activities of the other functions. Communication skills are also developed as individual business team members learn the 'languages' of the other functions (Allen, 1984).

- *Increase in informal communication channels*. In addition to the increase in formal linkages, there is also an increase in informal networks between personnel from different functions. These develop from friendships and cooperation formed as a product of formal linkages.

- *Increase in information loads*. The increase in formal and informal channels of communication means that individuals collect more information. This information is brought back into the function and disseminated among colleagues in the group. There is support for this view in Joyce (1986).

- *Increase in diversity for individuals*. Some individuals may be involved in two or three business teams. Their role may be part time or full time. This enables them to work with a variety of people from different backgrounds and disciplines across the organisation. This type of working environment enlarges an individual's experience and outlook and provides them with an improved understanding of the organisation's entire activities (Kolodny, 1979).

Corporate venturing

The idea behind corporate venturing is that fledgling businesses should be given the freedom to grow outside the constraints of an existing large, established organisation. Conventional management thinking argues that new ventures should be sheltered from the normal planning and control systems, otherwise they will be strangled. Ideally, they should be given high-level sponsorship from senior management, but must be able to manage their own relationships with other companies. Many large organisations such as Nokia, IBM and General Electric have a long experience of corporate venturing stretching back to the 1960s. However, following some high-profile failures, most notably by Shell in the mid-1980s, corporate venturing fell out of favour. More recent research suggests that the record of corporate venturing compared to external venture capitalists shows that the latter do no better than the corporations (Lorenz, 1993).

An internal corporate venture is a separate organisation or system designed to facilitate the needs of a new business. Companies usually adopt an internal corporate venture when the product involved is outside their existing activities. The case study at the end of Chapter 12 shows how 3M use internal corporate venturing to help transform business ideas into genuine businesses. (For a more detailed discussion on the role of new ventures, *see* Tidd *et al.*, 2001.)

Project management

Whichever organisation structure is adopted, the project itself has to be well planned, managed and controlled. It is the setting of achievable targets and realistic objectives that helps to ensure a successful project. In addition, ensuring that resources are available at the appropriate time contributes to good project management.

Many organisations have tried and tested project management programmes and organisational systems to help ensure that projects are well managed. But even in these well run organisations there will often be individual project managers who build a reputation for delivering on time and for being able to turn a doubtful project into a successful project. This introduces the subject of managing people within organisations. This is not the place to explore these issues which are at the heart of theories of organisational behaviour. They are comprehensively examined by others such as Mullins (2003).

Reducing product development times through computer-aided design

When concurrent engineering is used in conjunction with other management tools the results can be very impressive. For example, the aerospace and automobile industries have been using computer-aided design (CAD) for more than 15 years. In both these industries product development times are relatively long, sometimes lasting 10 years. The ability to use CAD lies at the heart of broader efforts to compress product development times and share information across an organisation. This is even more important when there are several companies involved in the manufacture of a single product. The Airbus consortium of companies which manufactures aircraft has been using CAD to help with its very complicated product data management (PDM). This is particularly useful in helping speed up engineering and manufacturing processes. In addition, the Airbus Concurrent Engineering (ACE) project is helping to develop common product development processes across the consortium (Baxter, 1997).

The marketing/R&D interface

The case study at the end of this chapter highlights some of the difficulties of managing cross-functional teams in technology-intensive industries where the technology being used is complex and difficult to understand for those without scientific training. In such industries, scientists and engineers are often heard berating their commercial colleagues for failing to comprehend the technical aspects of the project. This introduces a common difficulty: the need to manage communication flows across the marketing and R&D boundaries. This problem was first recognised as important in the 1970s (Rubenstein *et al.*, 1976) and remains a critical issue in new product development (Souder and Sherman, 1993).

The main barriers to an effective R&D/marketing interface have been found to be related to perceptual, cultural, organisational and language factors (Wang, 1997). Marketing managers tend to focus on shorter time-spans than R&D managers, who adopt much longer time-frames for projects. In addition, the cultural difference results from the different training and backgrounds of the two groups. For example, scientists seek recognition from their peers in the form of published papers and ultimately Nobel prizes, as well as recognition from the company that employs them. Marketing managers, on the other hand, are able only to seek recognition from their employer, usually in the form of bonuses, promotions, etc. The organisational boundaries arise out of departmental structures and the different activities of the two groups. Finally, the language barrier is soon identified in discussions with the two groups, because while marketers talk about product benefits and market position, R&D managers talk the quantitative language of performance and specifications.

The extent of the integration required between marketing and R&D depends on the environment within which product development occurs. In many technology-intensive industries where the customer's level of sophistication is low, the extent of integration required may be less than that needed where the customer's level of sophistication is high and the technology intensity of the industry low. For example, in the pharmaceutical industry (high level of technological intensity) customers' sophistication is low because they are unable to communicate their needs. They may want a cure for cancer but have no idea how this can be achieved. On the other hand, in the food industry (low level of technological intensity) customers are able to articulate their needs. For example, they can explain that a particular food might taste better or look better if it contained certain ingredients. (For a more detailed discussion on the difficulties of managing the relations between R&D and marketing, *see* Bruce and Cooper, 1997.) Table 15.3 illustrates some commonly held beliefs by marketing colleagues and R&D colleagues about one another.

Table 15.3 How marketing and R&D perceive each other

Marketing people about technical people	Technical people about marketing people
Have a very narrow view of the world	Want everything now
Never fnish developing a product	Are focusing on customers who do not know what they want
Have no sense of time	Quick to make promises they cannot keep
Are interested only in technology	Cannot make up their minds
Do not care about costs	Cannot possibly understand technology
Have no idea of the real world	Are superfcial
Are in a different world	Too quick in introducing new products
Always looking for standardisation	Want to ship products before they are ready
Should be kept away from customers	Are not interested in the scientist's problems

High attrition rate of new products

As new product projects evolve and progress through each stage of development, many will be rightly cancelled or stopped for a wide variety of reasons. The failure of a product idea to be developed into a product is not necessarily a bad thing. Indeed, it may save the company enormous sums of money. This is explored more fully in Chapter 8. More serious problems arise when, as often happens, new products are launched in the expectation of success, but then ultimately fail leaving high costs to be met by the company. Sometimes a product can cause harm and suffering, but these are rare; the example of the Thalidomide drug is a chilling reminder of a product failure.

Clearly, product ideas are rejected throughout the new product development process. Figure 15.8 shows the traditional view of the rising cost of new product development as it moves closer to launch. This is based on fmcg industries which involves high-cost promotional campaigns. Arguably, the cost curve for science-intensive industries is inverse, with high costs being associated with R&D activities and relatively low-cost promotional activities towards the end of the development.

Studies of why new products fail are difficult to undertake. This is partly due to an unwillingness by companies to let outsiders know that they have been unsuccessful. Also, it is difficult to untangle what happened and identify the cause of failure. With hindsight things often do not look the same. People are, in many cases, very defensive about their role in the development of a new product. There is always a reluctance to be associated with failure. Studies by Cooper (1998a), Urban *et al.* (1987) and Crawford (1997) have identified many of the often cited reasons for failure. These are listed in Table 15.4.

There is much debate about the failure rates of new products, which vary widely. The collection of data on this issue is problematic, with a wide range of different

Figure 15.8   Product failures

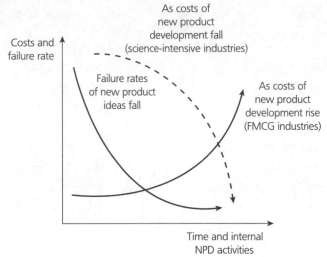

Table 15.4 Reasons for new product failure

1 Product offers nothing new or no improved performance

2 Inadequate budget to develop ideas or market the product

3 Poor market research, positioning, misunderstanding consumer needs

4 Lack of top management support

5 Did not involve customer

6 Exceptional factors such as government decision (e.g. new law on hand-gun control may seriously affect the manufacturer of a new hand-gun)

7 Market too small, either forecasting error with sales or insuffcient demand

8 Poor match with company's capabilities, company has insuffcient experience of the technology or market

9 Inadequate support from channel (a problem experienced by Dyson)

10 Competitive response was strong and competitors were able to move quickly to face the challenge of the new product (P&G highlighted weaknesses with Unilever's Persil Power)

11 Internal organisational problems, often associated with poor communication

12 Poor return on investment forcing company to abandon project

13 Unexpected changes in consumer tastes/fashion

Illustration 15.3

Coke cans plans for Dasani in France

Coca-Cola has shelved plans for a spring launch of its Dasani bottled mineral water in France – regarded by the company as its most important product debut there since Diet Coke – and Germany.

The US drinks company's decision yesterday followed the recall of the brand in the UK after a health scare. Plans for a relaunch there have been dropped.

It said: 'Although this is an isolated and resolved incident in Great Britain, Coca-Cola has also decided to postpone the introduction of the Dasani brand in France and Germany, as the timing is no longer considered optimal.' It added, however, that it would launch in France and Germany later and claimed the brand might yet have some future in the UK.

Coke withdrew Dasani last week after discovering in it illegal levels of bromate, a chemical that could increase the risk of cancer. It followed ridicule in the media after it became known the product was processed tap water from Sidcup, south-east London.

The Dasani for continental Europe, however, would have been sourced from a spring in Belgium. However, few analysts believed the brand could have competed against Perrier, Evian and Vittel in France after its UK difficulties. The company said it had spent about £1.75m on marketing Dasani in the UK before withdrawal. It would not give an estimate of the cost of the UK recall.

Source: J. Johnson and A. Jones, 'Coke cans plans for Dasani in France', *Financial Times*, 25 March 2004. Reprinted with permission.

---

definitions being used across industries and countries. Some companies now claim a maximum failure rate of 10 per cent. This is a long way from the failure rate, often quoted in the popular business press of 90 per cent. Products rarely fail in the market-place: weak products are usually eliminated prior to entry to the market. Consequently any such failures command huge publicity, as Illustration 15.3 shows.

The article from the *Financial Times* shows that even multi-national companies with an impressive heritage of developing brands and managing products can make mistakes. For Coca-Cola the difficulties encountered with its Dasani brand potentially highlight a poor match with its perception in Europe and the new product. Dasani has been very successful in the United States. Indeed sales in 2003 place it second in terms of market share of bottled water. It could simply be a combination of poor marketing communications and public relations and maybe some misfortune. But, it could also signify a more serious concern. That is, the reluctance on the part of the European consumer to separate Dasani from its parent brand Coca-Cola. In the bottled-water market the association with all things pure may be particularly necessary, hence Evian's association with the Alps and Buxton's association with the hills in the peak district in Britain. In Europe it may be that Coca-Cola may have to work particularly hard to distance itself from Dasani. This may lead some to question the financial benefits of entering the very competitive European bottled-water market.

Case study

The use of cross-functional teams in new product development[1]

Part of this case study is presented as a discussion between the research and development manager and the production manager and reads like a short story. The names used are fictitious, but it is based on an original piece of research (Lothian, 1997) and explains some of the problems of managing cross-functional teams. It also highlights a common problem with business research, that practice very often differs from theory and rhetoric. The company in question is an internationally recognised manufacturer of computer hardware.

Background

In order to ensure that the time spent on new product development is kept to a minimum, companies are increasingly adopting concurrent engineering techniques and cross-functional teams (CFT). This case study explores the use of cross-functional teams in the development of new products. It analyses the effectiveness of cross-functional teams and identifies several limitations. Indeed, the case highlights how CFT can hinder NPD if used incorrectly.

The company, hereafter referred to as Xrend, is a leading manufacturer of advanced information technology products. It specialises in data capture, storage and delivery, via products such as hard disk drives. The market in which the company operates is expanding rapidly and many opportunities exist for future developments. A closer inspection of the company's arrangements, however, revealed that it was heavily dependent on one customer which accounted for about 80 per cent of its turnover. This source of business was set to decline over the next five years and this had led to a realisation that the development of

new products was urgently required. The company had embarked on an appraisal of its new product development operations and had decided that it needed to be overhauled. Cross-functional teams were to be at the centre of the company's new product development activities.

The introduction of cross-functional teams and concurrent engineering at Xrend

Prior to the implementation of CFT, the company structure was most akin to a matrix structure with functions such as accountancy, marketing and manufacturing lying across projects. The individual functions had their own hierarchies and line-management structures. Such a structure is not uncommon in many technology-intensive manufacturing companies.

The introduction of CFT led to significant changes, particularly as the teams were not directly accountable to the functions, instead being accountable to project managers. This case focuses on the activities of one particular CFT. This team, called Centris, was given the responsibility of developing small storage units for large computer machines. The team consisted of eight members, who were project team leader, test engineer, development engineer, manufacturing engineer and representatives from marketing, field support, materials and procurement. Each team member was expected to be actively involved in the project. In addition, they were required to represent their functional department and ensure their interests were considered by the team. This was fine in theory but practice, as will be seen, was very different.

---

[1] This case has been written as a basis for class discussion rather than to illustrate effective or ineffective managerial administrative behaviour. It has been prepared from a variety of published sources, as indicated, and from observations.

When practice differs from theory

George Richardson placed both hands on top of his head and looked towards the sky.

'It's amazing', he said. 'How can it be that for the past year we have had a cross-functional team that is not a cross-functional team?'

Adam Wilson responded to the general manager's enquiry explaining that everyone had thought the Centris team was operating in a cross-functional way but it is only now emerging that the team had not actually been operating as it should.

Adam Wilson, production manager, had been called in to see the R&D manager following the publication of an internal report highlighting the weaknesses of the Centris new product team. Centris had been the first team to adopt the cross-functional approach to new product development. The report had not been full of praise. It had raised several issues, the most important of which was that the team had not been operating in a cross-functional manner. Adam Wilson offered a brief summary of the report's findings:

'The problem, George, is that the team has not yet been able to adapt to working in teams of people with diverse backgrounds. Some of the technical people feel the commercial people don't understand what is being said.'

'So what's new?' joked George.

'The point is,' replied Adam, ignoring George's facetiousness, 'that the Centris team has tried to overcome this difficulty by setting up so-called "off-line" meetings.'

'What are off-line meetings?' snapped George.

Adam realised he would have to explain from the beginning. 'At first the Centris team used daily team meetings to discuss current issues as they arose. This gave each team member the opportunity to participate in the development of the project. As the project progressed a variety of difficulties and challenges would present themselves to the team. The issues raised ranged from financial and design requirements to manufacturing limitations. The point here is that many of the discussions involved detailed technical issues.

Many of the team members felt that they were unable to contribute to these discussions because they felt they were outside their area of expertise. The team felt that already precious time was being used in an unproductive manner. In an attempt to reduce this unproductive time, the team decided that, as and when required, off-line meetings (OLMs) would be established to address those particular issues that required specialist input. OLMs would consist of members who could add value to the discussions. In effect, this meant those with prior knowledge and shared common knowledge – functional members.'

'This seems to be understandable and reasonable', interjected George.

'Indeed, at first this seemed to be an effective use of limited resources', Adam continued. 'The Centris team would continue to meet daily and as and when particular difficulties arose an OLM was established to investigate. Unfortunately, the OLM began to cannibalise the cross-functional nature of the Centris team. For example, the marketing engineer has reported that decisions were occasionally made without his input. This reduces product integrity.'

'What does that mean?' demanded George.

'It's a marketing term. Essentially product integrity depends on a link between the customer's expectations and product performance. The marketing engineer should have been providing this link, but it seems that at times the link was not in place. Within six months from the start of the Centris team the OLM approach to difficulties has become the dominant means of problem resolution. Indeed, in many ways, it is the success of the OLM that has led to the downfall of the Centris team. The team's approach to problem solving had gone full circle.'

Adam reached for a marker pen and drew a diagram to emphasise the point (*see* Figure 15.9).

Adam continued, 'You see, the cross-functional nature of the team exists in name only. To all those outside the company, even to many inside the company, the Centris team is a cross-functional team. It consists of a variety of members from different functions and has regular meetings.

▶

Figure 15.9   Functional approach to cross-functional back to functional

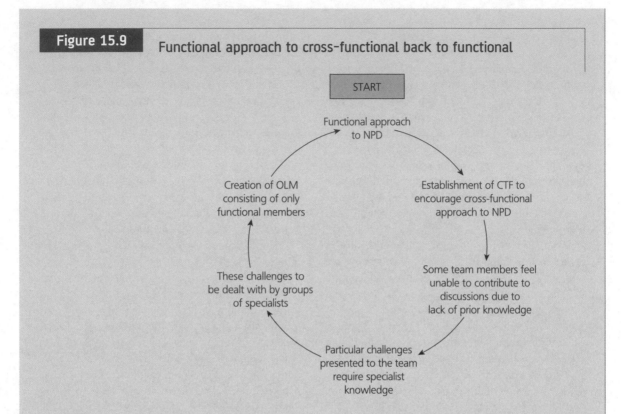

It appears to operate in a cross-functional way. Indeed, even some of the members of the Centris team believe they are engaged in NPD using CFT. Individuals within the team, however, did wonder to themselves how their new method of working differed from their previous style of operating! The answer, of course, is not much.'

George sat upright, transfixed, nodding and agreeing with Adam's explanation. Adam continued in lecturer mode now that the attentive student was keen to learn more. 'What this means is that the excluded members of the OLM are no longer exposed to information flows in the team. Given the arguments for CFT – that they help to create new knowledge and facilitate the dissemination of it throughout the organisation – the effect of the use of OLM is to reduce cross-functionality; reduce knowledge-creating potential; and reduce "product integrity".'

Adam scribbled these last three points on the whiteboard underneath his previous drawing. 'The overall effect has been to reduce the effectiveness of NPD by limiting interaction and the cross-fertilisation of ideas between different functions.'

Discussion

Scratching beneath the surface

This case study highlights a potential hurdle over which many stumble when studying aspects of business management. The popular business press and other publications for executives are full of prescriptions for business problems. Very often they recommend the adoption or implementation of a new management technique (cynics would refer to these as fads). On the face of it many businesses may be using this new technique. Had Xrend been approached regarding the use of CFT the response would surely have been affirmative. Scratch beneath the surface, however, and all is not as it first appears. Many studies of business management, especially those involving large surveys using postal questionnaires, suffer from this potential weakness. That is not to say that all such surveys are flawed, clearly, this is not so. It is, however, worthy of note, that it is healthy to enquire and to question the methodology used. The student of management should adopt a critical and inquisitive approach, especially when analysing the literature.

The reduction of knowledge-creating potential

The case study clearly shows that CFT by name is not necessarily cross-functional by nature. Indeed, at Xrend, decision making was dominated by the 'off-line' meetings, which occurred at a functional level, and the benefits of cross-functional teams were never realised. Regular meetings took place and team members engaged in detailed discussions, but problems that arose were dealt with in a functional manner. Hence, there was little cross-functional knowledge being created. Technical experts were reluctant or unable to engage in discussions with non-technical experts. It was as if they were operating as an exclusive group and restricting entry. Such behaviour can hinder organisational learning. Dougherty (1990) and Nonaka (1991) have identified that new knowledge is created through the frequent interaction of individuals who are able to combine their own knowledge and perspectives with others and that CFTs are an ideal mechanism to foster this activity.

The role of experts and professionalism

The notion of professionalism and the exclusion of non-experts have received a great deal of attention in the literature. Danziger and Kramer (1985) refer to this notion as the 'skill bureaucracy', whereby groups of people create a bureaucracy around skills as well as jargon as a means to exclude, thereby making it very difficult for those without those skills or jargon to participate. They go on to argue that certain professions (medicine, law, education) use this approach as a means of exclusivity.

Managing teams

The membership of the Centris project team remained constant throughout the project's life. This facilitated continuity and fostered good working relationships among team members. It was, however, in contrast to the approach used by other organisations. For example, Deschamps and Nayak (1995) reported that Ford used an American football-style approach to its projects, adding and discarding members as the project progressed.

Cultural issues and heritage of working practices

Many organisations have evolved from much smaller beginnings, yet many of their internal working practices have remained and they contribute to the organisation's heritage (*see* Chapter 1). Hence, any organisational change needs to consider these characteristics and peculiarities. In this case the functional method of working was heavily ingrained in the culture of the organisation. Thus the change to CFT was far more difficult than it might have been for other organisations.

Questions

1 Discuss the dilemma of trying to ensure that members of a team are, on the one hand, able to make meaningful contributions to the group of specialists and, on the other hand, unable to make a contribution through a lack of shared knowledge.

2 What went wrong in the case?

3 List the advantages and the limitations of cross-functional teams.

4 Explain how cross-functional teams help to reduce the product development time.

5 Explain the important role of a hybrid manager in cross-functional teams.

Chapter summary

The main focus of this chapter has been an examination of the activities of the NPD process. Adopting a practitioner standpoint, the new product development process is viewed as a series of linked activities. Emphasis is placed on the iterative nature of the process and many of the activities occur concurrently. A new product needs to be viewed as a project that acquires knowledge gradually over time as an idea is transformed into a physical product. The knowledge base of the organisation will provide for a diverse range of contributions to a project. Furthermore, during this process there is continual evaluation of the project.

This chapter also offered a view of NPD across a variety of industries. The key point here is that the balance of technical and commercial activities will clearly vary depending on the nature of the industry and the product being developed.

 ## Discussion questions

1 Explain why there is not one best organisational structure for new product development.
2 Explain why the image of sales representatives as second-hand car dealers is at best misleading and at worst pejorative and incorrect.
3 Explain why screening in the development of a new product needs to be viewed as a continual process.
4 What are the differences between the way scientists view innovation and the way marketing people tend to view it?
5 'New products are a necessary evil.' From whose viewpoint are they necessary and whose viewpoint are they evil?
6 Why do so many new products fail?

Key words and phrases

Business opportunity 488	Matrix structure 497
Corporate venturing 499	Product concept 487
Cross-functional teams 495	Prototype 490
Marketing/R&D interface 500	Screening 488

 ## Websites worth visiting

The Design Council www.Designcouncil.com

Examples of design: 4c Design www.4Cdesign.co.uk

How stereolithography works www.computer.howstuffworks.com/stereolith.htm

Inventions, designs, patents www.iacllc.com

Product Development Association www.pda.com

Stanford University, explaining innovation: www.Manufacturing.Stanford.edu

References

Allen, T. (1984) *Managing the Flow of Technology*, MIT Press, MA.

Baxter, A. (1997) 'Designs for survival', *Financial Times*, 20 November, 16.

Brassington, F. and Pettitt, S. (2003) *Principles of Marketing*, 3rd edn, Financial Times Pitman Publishing, London.

Bruce, M. and Cooper, R.C. (1997) *Marketing and Design Management*, Thomson Business Press, London.

Buxton, P. (2000) 'Time to market is NPD's top priority', *Marketing*, 30 March, 35–6.

Christensen, C.M. and Bower, J.L. (1995) 'Customer power, strategic investment, and the failure of leading firms', *Strategic Management Journal*, Vol. 17, 197–218.

Cooper, R.G. (1979) 'The dimensions of industrial new product success and failure', *Journal of Marketing*, Vol. 43, 93–103.

Cooper, R.G. (1998a) 'The dimensions of industrial new product success and failure', *Journal of Marketing*, Vol. 43, No. 3, 93–103.

Cooper, R.G. (1998b) 'Predevelopment activities determine new product success', *Industrial Marketing Management*, Vol. 17, No. 3, 237–47.

Craig, A. and Hart, S. (1992) 'Where to now in new product development?' *European Journal of Marketing*, Vol. 26, 11.

Crawford, C.M. (1997) *New Products Management*, 5th edn, Irwin, Chicago, IL.

Daily, C. (1996) 'Is the customer always right? (Effects of customers' influence on product development strategies)', *Academy of Management Executive*, Vol. 10, No. 4, 105.

Danziger, J.N. and Kramer, K.L. (1985) 'Computerised data-based systems and productivity among professional workers – the case of detectives', *Public Administration Review*, Vol. 45, No. 1, 196–209.

Deschamps, J.P. and Nayak, P.R. (1995) *Product Juggernauts: How Companies Mobilize to Generate a Stream of Market Winners*, Harvard Business School Press, Boston, MA.

Dougherty, D. (1990) 'Understanding new markets for new products', *Strategic Management Journal*, Vol. 11, 59–78.

Dyson, J. (1997) *Against the Odds*, Orion Books, London.

Ford, R.C. and Randolph, W.A. (1992) 'Cross functional structures: a review and integration of matrix organisations and project management', *Project Management Journal*, Vol. 18, No. 2, 269–94.

Gordon, W.J. (1962) 'Defining a creativeness in people', in Parnes, S.J. and Harding, H.F. (eds) *Source Book for Creative Thinking*, Scribners, New York.

Jones, T. (1997) *New Product Development: An Introduction to a Multifunctional Process*, Butterworth-Heinemann, Oxford.

Joyce, W.F. (1986) 'Matrix organisation: a social experiment', *Academy of Management Journal*, Vol. 29, No. 3, 536–61.

Kolodny, H.F. (1979) 'Evolution to a matrix organisation', *Academy of Management Review*, Vol. 4, No. 4, 543–53.

Kotler, P. (2003) *Marketing Management*, 11th edn, Prentice-Hall, Englewood Cliffs, NJ.

Lawrence, P.R., Kolodny, F.H. and Davis, S.M. (1982) 'The human side of the matrix', in Tushman, M.L. and Moore, W.L. (eds) *Readings in the Management of Innovation*, HarperCollins, New York.

Lorenz, C. (1993) 'The best way to rear corporate babies', *Financial Times*, 8 October, 23.

Lothian, I. (1997) 'New product development at Xyratex: a study of cross-functional teams', BA Business Studies dissertation, University of Portsmouth.

Mahajan, V. and Wind, Y. (1988) 'New product forecasting models: directions for research and implementation', *International Journal of Forecasting*, Vol. 14, 341–58.

Management Today (1995) 'Why new products are bypassing the market test', October, 12.

Miles, L. (1995) 'Mothers and fathers of invention', *Marketing*, 1 June, 26.

Mullins, L.J. (2003) *Management and Organisational Behaviour*, 6th edn, Financial Times Pitman Publishing, London.

Nijssen, E.J. and Lieshout, K.F. (1995) 'Awareness, use and effectiveness of models for new product development', *European Journal of Marketing*, Vol. 29, No. 10, 27–39.

Nonaka, I. (1991) 'The knowledge creating company', *Harvard Business Review*, Vol. 69, No. 6, 96–104.

Olson, E.M., Orville, C.W. and Ruekert, R.W. (1995) 'Organising for effective new product development: the moderating role of product innovativeness', *Journal of Marketing*, Vol. 59, 48–62.

Rubenstein, A.H., Chakrabarti, A.K., O'Keefe, R.D., Souder, W.E. and Young, H.C. (1976) 'Factors influencing innovation success at the project level', *Research Management*, Vol. 19, No. 3, 15–20.

Sanchez, A.M. and Elola, L.N. (1991) 'Product innovation in Spain', *Journal of Product Innovation Management*, Vol. 11, No. 2, 105–18.

Schmidt, J.B. (1995) 'New product myopia', *Journal of Business and Industrial Marketing*, Vol. 10, No. 1, 23.

Souder, W.E. and Sherman, J.D. (1993) 'Organisational design and organisational development solutions to the problem of R&D marketing integration', *Research in Organisational Change and Development*, Vol. 7, 181–215.

Tidd, J., Bessant, J. and Pavitt, K. (2001) *Managing Innovation*, 2nd edn, Wiley, Chichester.

Tushman, M.L. and Nadler, D. (1978) 'An information processing approach to organisational design', *Academy of Management Review*, Vol. 3, 613–24.

Urban, G.L., Hauser, J.R. and Dholaka, N. (1987) *Essentials of New Product Management*, Prentice-Hall, Englewood Cliffs, NJ.

von Hippel, E. (1988) *The Sources of Innovation*, Oxford University Press, New York.

Wang, Q. (1997) 'R&D/marketing interface in a firm's capability-building process: evidence from pharmaceutical firms', *International Journal of Innovation Management*, Vol. 1, No. 1, 23–52.

Further reading

For a more detailed review of the new product development literature, the following develop many of the issues raised in this chapter:

Christensen, C.M. (2003) *The Innovator's Dilemma: When New Technologies Cause Great Firms to Fail*, 3rd edn, Harvard Business School Press, Boston, MA.

Cooper, R. (1999) 'The invisible success factors in product innovation', *Journal of Product Innovation Management*, Vol. 16, No. 2, 85–96.

Cooper, Robert G. (1999) 'From experience: the invisible success factors in product innovation' *Journal of Product Innovation Management*, Vol. 16, No. 1, 115–33.

McDonough III, Edward, F. (2000) 'Investigation of factors contibuting to the success of cross-functional teams', *Journal of Product Innovation Management*, Vol. 17, No. 3, 221–35.

Shavinina, L. (2003) *The International Handbook on Innovation*, Elsevier, Oxford.

Appendix

Guinness patent

(12) **UK Patent Application** (19) **GB** (11) **2 183 592** (13) A

(43) Application published **10 Jun 1987**

(21) Application No **8529441**

(22) Date of filing **29 Nov 1985**

(71) Applicant

Arthur Guinness Son & Company (Dublin) Limited,

(Incorporated in Irish Republic),

St. James's Gate, Dublin 8, Republic of Ireland

(72) Inventors

Alan James Forage,

William John Byrne

(74) Agent and/or Address for Service

Urquhart-Dykes & Lord, 47 Marylebone Lane,

London W1M 6DL

(51) INTCL

B65D 25/00 5/40

(52) Domestic classification (Edition I)

B8D 12 13 19 7C 7G 7M 7P1 7PY SC1

B8P AX

U1S 1106 1110 1111 B8D B8P

(56) Documents cited

GB 1266351

(58) Field of search

B8D

B8P

Selected US specifications from IPC sub-class B65D

(54) **Carbonated beverage container**

(57) A container for a beverage having gas (preferably at least one of carbon dioxide and inert (nitrogen) gases) in solution consists of a non-resealable container 1 within which is located a hollow secondary chamber 4, eg a polypropylene envelope, having a restricted aperture 7 in a side wall. The container is charged with the beverage 8 and sealed. Beverage from the main chamber of the container enters the chamber 4 (shown at 8a) by way of the aperture 7 to provide headspaces 1a in the container and 4a in the pod 4. Gas within the headspaces 1a and 4a is at greater than atmospheric pressure. Preferably the beverage is drawn into the chamber 4 by subjecting the package to a heating and cooling cycle. Upon opening the container 1, eg by draw ring/region 13, the headspace 1a is vented to atmosphere and the pressure differential resulting from the pressure in the chamber headspace 4a causes gas/beverage to be ejected from the chamber 4 (by way of the aperture 7) into the beverage 8. Said ejection causes gas to be evolved from solution in the beverage in the main container chamber to form a head of froth on the beverage. The chamber 4 is preferably formed by blow moulding and located below beverage level by weighting it or as a press fit within the container 1 by lugs 6 engaging the container walls, the container being preferably a can, carton or bottle. The chamber 4 may initially be filled with gas, eg nitrogen, at or slightly above atmospheric pressure, the orifice being formed by laser boring, drilling or punching immediately prior to locating the chamber 4 in the container 1.

The drawings originally filed were informal and the print here reproduced is taken from a later filed formal copy.

(12) UK Patent Application (19) GB (11) 2 183 592 (13) A

(43) Application published **10 Jun 1987**

(21) Application No **8529441**

(22) Date of filing **29 Nov 1985**

(71) Applicant
Arthur Guinness Son & Company (Dublin) Limited,

(Incorporated in Irish Republic),

St. James's Gate, Dublin 8, Republic of Ireland

(72) Inventors
Alan James Forage,
William John Byrne

(74) Agent and/or Address for Service
Urquhart-Dykes & Lord, 47 Marylebone Lane,
London W1M 6DL

(51) INT CL[4]
B65D 25/00 5/40

(52) Domestic classification (Edition I)
B8D 12 13 19 7C 7G 7M 7P1 7PY SC1
B8P AX
U1S 1106 1110 1111 B8D B8P

(56) Documents cited
GB 1266351

(58) Field of search
B8D
B8P
Selected US specifications from IPC sub-class B65D

(54) Carbonated beverage container

(57) A container for a beverage having gas (preferably at least one of carbon dioxide and inert (nitrogen) gases) in solution consists of a non-resealable container 1 within which is located a hollow secondary chamber 4, eg a polypropylene envelope, having a restricted aperture 7 in a side wall. The container is charged with the beverage 8 and sealed. Beverage from the main chamber of the container enters the chamber 4 (shown at 8a) by way of the aperture 7 to provide headspaces 1a in the container and 4a in the pod 4. Gas within the headspaces 1a and 4a is at greater than atmospheric pressure. Preferably the beverage is drawn into the chamber 4 by subjecting the package to a heating and cooling cycle. Upon opening the container 1, eg by draw ring/region 13, the headspace 1a is vented to atmosphere and the pressure differential resulting from the pressure in the chamber headspace 4a causes gas/beverage to be ejected from the chamber 4 (by way of the aperture 7) into the beverage 8. Said ejection causes gas to be evolved from solution in the beverage in the main container chamber to form a head of froth on the beverage. The chamber 4 is preferably formed by blow moulding and located below beverage level by weighting it or as a press fit within the container 1 by lugs 6 engaging the container walls, the container being preferably a can, carton or bottle. The chamber 4 may initially be filled with gas, eg nitrogen, at or slightly above atmospheric pressure, the orifice being formed by laser boring, drilling or punching immediately prior to locating the chamber 4 in the container 1.

The drawings originally filed were informal and the print here reproduced is taken from a later filed formal copy.

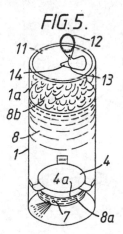

FIG. 5.

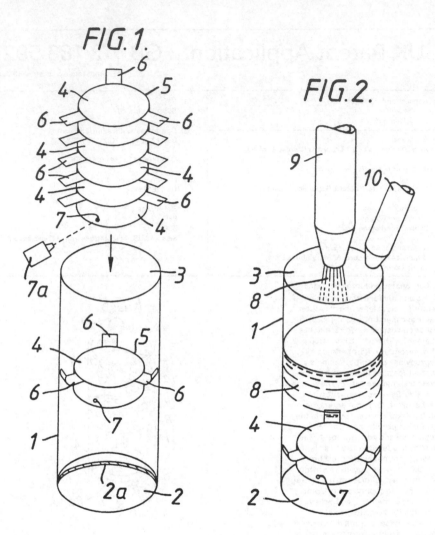

FIG.1.

FIG.2.

Reference to UK Patent Application 2,183,592A is made with kind permission of Guinness Brewing Worldwide Limited and their Patent Attorneys, Urquhart-Dykes & Lord.

SPECIFICATION A beverage package and a method of packaging a beverage containing gas in solution

Technical field and background art

This invention relates to a beverage package and a method of packaging a beverage containing gas in solution. The invention more particularly concerns beverages containing gas in solution and packaged in a sealed, non-resealable, container which, when opened for dispensing or consumption, permits gas to be evolved or liberated from the beverage to form, or assist in the formation of, a head or froth on the beverage. The beverages to which the invention relates may be alcoholic or non-alcoholic; primarily

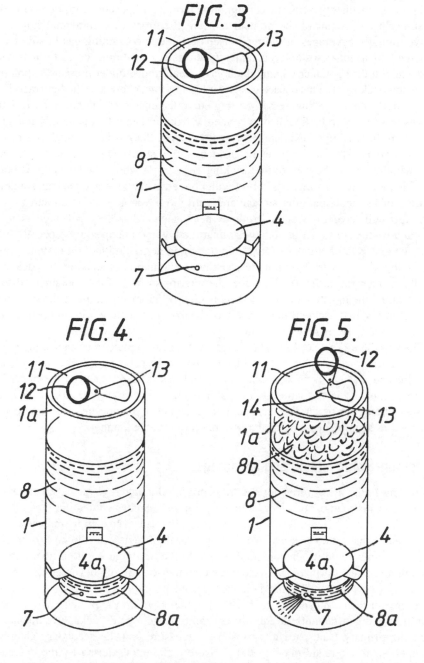

FIG. 3.

FIG. 4.

FIG. 5.

the invention was developed for fermented beverages such as beer, stout, ale, lager and cider but may be applied with advantage to so-called soft drinks and beverages (for example fruit juices, squashes, colas, lemonades, milk and milk based drinks and similar type drinks) and to alcoholic drinks (for example spirits, liquers, wine or wine based drinks and similar).

It is recognised in the beverage dispensing and packaging art that the characteristics of the head of froth which is provided on the beverage by the liberation of gas from the beverage immediately prior to consumption are an important consideration to the consumer's enjoyment of the product and are therefore of commercial importance. Conventionally beverages of the type discussed above containing gas in solution and packaged in a non-resealable container (such as a can, bottle or carton) provide a headspace in the container within which gas is maintained under pressure. Upon opening of the package, the headspace gas is vented to atmosphere and the beverage is usually poured into a drinking vessel. During such dispensing of the beverage it is usual for gas in solution to be liberated to create the froth or head. It is generally recognised that when dispensing a beverage as aforementioned, the gas is liberated as a result of the movement of the beverage over a surface having so-called gas nucleation or active sites which may be the wall of the drinking vessel into which the beverage is poured. There is therefore a distinct possibility with conventional beverage packages that upon opening of the container after storage and until the beverage is poured there-from, the beverage will have little or no froth or head–such a headless beverage is usually regarded by the consumer as somewhat unattractive and unappealing especially where the beverage is to be drunk directly from the container. Admittedly it may be possible to develop a head or froth within the container by agitating or shaking the package (so that the movement of the beverage over the interior surface of the container causes the liberation of the gas in solution) but this is clearly inconvenient once the container is opened and is inadvisable if the package is shaken immediately prior to opening as the contents tend to spray or spurt on opening.

There is therefore a need for a beverage package and a method of packaging a beverage containing gas in solution by which the beverage is packaged in a non-resealable container so that when the container is opened gas is liberated from the beverage to form or assist in the formation of a head or froth without the necessity of an external influence being applied to the package; it is an object of the present invention to satisfy this need in a simple, economic and commercially viable manner.

Statements of invention and advantages

According to the present invention there is provided a beverage package comprising a sealed, non-resealable, container having a primary chamber containing beverage having gas in solution therewith and forming a primary headspace comprising gas at a pressure greater than atmospheric; a secondary chamber having a volume less than said primary chamber and which communicates with the beverage in said primary chamber through a restricted orifice, said secondary chamber containing beverage derived from the primary chamber and having a secondary headspace therein comprising gas at a pressure greater than atmospheric so that the pressures within the primary and secondary chambers are substantially at equilibrium, and wherein said package is openable, to open the primary headspace to atmospheric pressure and the secondary chamber is arranged so that on said opening the pressure differential caused by the decrease in pressure at the primary headspace causes at least one of the beverage and gas in the secondary chamber to be ejected by way of the restricted orifice into the beverage of the primary chamber and said ejection causes gas in the solution to be evolved and form, or assist in the formation of, a head of froth on the beverage.

Further according to the present invention there is provided a method of packaging a beverage having gas in solution therewith which comprises providing a container with a primary chamber and a secondary chamber of which the volume of the secondary chamber is less than that of the primary chamber and with a restricted orifice through which the secondary chamber communicates with the primary chamber, and charging and sealing the primary chamber with the beverage to contain the gas in solution and to form a primary headspace in the primary chamber, and charging the secondary chamber with beverage derived from the primary chamber by way of said restricted orifice to form a secondary headspace in the secondary chamber whereby the pressures in both the primary and secondary chambers are at equilibrium and gaseous pressures in both the primary and secondary headspaces are at a pressure greater than atmospheric so that, when the container is broached to open the primary headspace to atmospheric pressure, the pressure differential caused by the decrease in pressure at the primary headspace causes at least one of the beverage and gas in the secondary chamber to be ejected into the beverage of the primary chamber by way of said restricted orifice and the said ejection causes gas to be evolved from solution in the beverage in the primary chamber to form, or assist in the formation of, a head of froth on the beverage.

The present invention is applicable to a wide range of beverages of the type as previously discussed and where those beverages contain gas in solution which gas is intended to be liberated to form or assist in the formation of the head or froth on the beverage. Understandably the gas in solution must not detract from, and should preferably enhance the characteristics required of the beverage and be acceptable for use with food products; preferably therefore the gas is at least one of carbon dioxide and inert gases (by which latter term is included nitrogen) although it is to be realised that other gases may be appropriate.

The present invention was primarily developed for the packaging of fermented beverages such as beer, ale, stout, lager and cider where among the desirable qualities sought in a head are a consistent and regular, relatively fine, bubble size; a bubble structure which is substantially homogeneous so that the head is not formed with large irregularly shaped and random gaps; the ability for the head or bubble structure to endure during a reasonable period over which it is likely to be consumed, and a so-called 'mouth-feel' and flavour which may improve the enjoyment of the beverage during consumption and not detract from the desirable flavour characteristics required of the beverage. These desirable qualities are of course equally applicable to non-fermented beverages, for example with so-called soft drinks. Conventionally, beverages of the type to which the invention relates are packaged in a non-resealable container which when opened totally vents the headspace to atmosphere, contain carbon dioxide in solution and it is the liberation of the carbon dioxide on opening of the package and dispensing of the beverage into a drinking vessel which creates the froth or head; however, the head so formed has very few of the aforementioned desirable qualities – in particular it is usually irregular, lacks homogeneity and has very little endurance so that there is a tendency for it to collapse after a short period. It has been known for approximately 25 years and as discussed in our G.B. Patent No. 876,628, that beverages having in solution a mixture of carbon dioxide gas and inert gas (such as nitrogen or argon) will, when dispensed in a manner whereby the mixed gases are caused to evolve to develop the head or foam from small bubbles containing the mixture of carbon dioxide and, say, nitrogen gases, provide the desirable qualities for the head as previously discussed. Commercially the formation of the head by the use of mixed gases as aforementioned has been widely employed in the dispensing of beverage in a draught system and on demand from a bulk container (such as a keg or barrel) where the gases are caused to evolve by subjecting the beverage to intense shear forces in passing it under pressure through a set of small holes. Beverages, particularly stout, having a mixture of carbon dioxide and nitrogen gases in solution and dispensed in draught using the aforementioned technique have met with considerable commercial success and it was soon realized that there was a need to make available for consumption a similar beverage derived from a small non-resealable container suitable for shelf storage and retail purposes.

Research has indicated that to achieve the initiation of a head on a beverage containing carbon dioxide and inert gas such as nitrogen in solution it is necessary to provide so-called 'active sites' which are regions where the beverage is subjected to a high local strain (such a strain being higher than the cohesive force of the beverage). In these conditions the beverage prefers to generate a bubble of mixed gases instead of 'bending around' the active site. It was found that an active site could be solid, liquid or gas such as granules, restrictor holes, rapid streams of liquid or bubbles and the like. It was also found that ultrasonics could produce a 'ghost' active site by the formation of extreme pressure gradients. There has however been a problem in providing an 'active site' in a beverage packaged in a non-resealable small container in a manner which is commercially and economically acceptable. During the past 25 years considerable expenditure has been devoted to research and development in an attempt to overcome the aforementioned problem. For example, our G.B. Patent No. 1,588,624 proposes initiating the evolution of mixed carbon dioxide and nitrogen gases from a beverage by subjecting the beverage to ultrasonic excitement, by injecting a gas, liquid and/or foam into the beverage by use of a syringe-type device, or by pouring the beverage over an excitation surface such as polystyrene granules. Although these latter proposals were successful in achieving the desired head formation, the necessity to use ancilliary apparatus had commercial disadvantages (for example, it is unreasonable to expect a retail customer to have available an ultrasonic signal generator; also the steps required to effect initiation of the head following opening of the beverage package involved an inconvenient discipline and time factor). In a further example our G.B. Patent No. 1,266,351 relates to a non-resealable package containing beverage having mixed carbon dioxide and inert gases in solution; in this disclosure a can or bottle has two chambers of which a larger chamber contains the beverage while the smaller chamber is charged under pressure with the mixed gases. On opening of the can or bottle to expose the larger chamber to atmosphere, its internal pressure falls to atmospheric permitting the pressurized gas in the small chamber to jet into the beverage by way of a small orifice between the two chambers. This jet of gas provides sufficient energy to initiate the formation of minute bubbles and thereby the head from the evolution of the mixed gases in the beverage coming out of solution. By this proposal the small gas chamber is initially pressurized with the mixed gases to a pressure greater than atmospheric and from a source remote from the beverage; as a consequence it was found necessary, particularly in the case of cans, to provide a special design of two chambered container and an appropriate means for sealing the smaller chamber following the charging of that chamber with the mixed gases (such charging usually being effected, in the case of cans, by injecting the mixed gases into the small chamber through a wall of the can which then had to be sealed). Because of the inconvenience and high costs involved in the development of an appropriate two chambered container and the special facilities required for charging the mixed gases and sealing the container, the proposal proved commercially unacceptable.

The container employed in the present invention will usually be in the form of a can, bottle or carton capable of withstanding the internal pressures of the primary and secondary chambers and of a size suitable for conventional shelf storage by the retail trade so that, the overall volume of the container may be, typically, 0.5 litres but is unlikely to be greater than 3 litres.

By the present invention a two chambered container is employed as broadly proposed in G.B. Patent No. 1,266,351; however, unlike the prior proposal the secondary chamber is partly filled with beverage containing gases in solution and the beverage in the secondary chamber is derived wholly from the beverage in the primary chamber so that when the contents of the primary and secondary chambers are in equilibrium (and the primary and secondary headspaces are at a pressure greater than atmospheric) immediately prior to broaching the container to open the primary headspace to atmosphere, the pressure differential between that in the secondary headspace and atmospheric pressure causes at least one of the beverage and the headspace gas in the secondary chamber to be ejected by way of the restricted orifice into the beverage in the primary chamber to promote the formation of the head of froth without the necessity of any external influence being applied to the package. The pressurisation of the headspace gas in the secondary chamber is intended to result from the evolution of gas in the sealed container as the contents of the container come into equilibrium at ambient or dispensing temperature (which should be greater than the temperature at which the container is charged and sealed). Consequently the present invention alleviates the necessity for pressurizing the secondary chamber from a source externally of the container so that the secondary chamber can be formed as a simple envelope or hollow pod of any convenient shape (such as cylindrical or spherical) which is located as a discrete insert within a conventional form of can, bottle or carton (thereby alleviating the requirement for a special structure of can or bottle as envisaged in G.B. Patent No. 1,266,351).

Although the head or froth formed by pouring wholly carbonated beverages tends to lack many of the desirable qualities required of a head as previously discussed; our tests have indicated that by use of the present invention with wholly carbonated beverages (where the head is formed by injection of gas or beverage from the secondary chamber into the primary chamber) the resultant head is considerably tighter or denser than that achieved solely by pouring and as such will normally have a greater life expectancy.

The beverage is preferably saturated or supersaturated with the gas (especially if mixed carbon dioxide and insert gases are employed) and the primary chamber charged with the beverage under a counterpressure and at a low temperature (to alleviate gas losses and, say, at a slightly higher temperature than that at which the beverage freezes) so that when the container is sealed (which may be achieved under atmospheric pressure using conventional systems such as a canning or bottling line), the pressurisation of the primary and secondary headspaces is achieved by the evolution of gas from the beverage within the primary and secondary chambers as the package is handled or stored at an ambient or dispensing temperature (greater than the charging temperature) and the contents of the container adopt a state of equilibrium. As an optional but preferred feature of the present invention, following the sealing of the container, the package may be subjected to a heating and cooling cycle, conveniently during pasteurisation of the beverage. During such a cycle the gas within the secondary chamber is caused to expand and eject into the primary chamber; during subsequent cooling of the package, the gas in the secondary chamber contracts and creates a low pressure or vacuum effect relative to the pressure in the primary chamber so that beverage from the primary chamber is drawn into the secondary chamber by way of the restricted orifice. By use of this preferred technique it is possible to ensure that the secondary chamber is efficiently and adequately charged with beverage and has the desired secondary headspace.

The restricted orifice through which the primary and secondary chambers communicate is conveniently formed by a single aperture in a side wall of the secondary chamber and such an aperture should have a size which is sufficiently great to alleviate 'clogging' or its obturation by particles which may normally be expected to occur within the beverage and yet be restricted in its dimensions to ensure that there is an adequate jetting effect in the ejection of the gas and/or beverage therethrough from the secondary chamber into the primary chamber to promote the head formation upon opening of the container. The restricted orifice may be of any profile (such as a slit or a star shape) but will usually be circular; experiments have indicated that a restricted orifice having a diameter in the range of 0.02 to 0.25 centimetres is likely to be appropriate for fermented beverages (the preferred diameter being 0.061 centimetres). It is also preferred that when the package is positioned in an upstanding condition in which it is likely to be transported, shelf stored or opened, the restricted orifice is located in an upwardly extending side wall or in a bottom wall of the secondary chamber and preferably at a position slightly spaced from the bottom of the primary chamber. It is also preferred, particularly for fermented beverages, that when the contents of the sealed package are in equilibrium and the package is in an upstanding condition as aforementioned, the restricted orifice is located below the depth of the beverage in the secondary chamber so that on opening of the container the pressure of gas in the secondary headspace initially ejects beverage from that chamber into the beverage in the primary chamber to promote the head formation. It is believed that such ejection of beverage through the restricted orifice is likely to provide a greater efficiency in the development of the head in a liquid supersaturated with gas than will the ejection of gas alone through the restricted orifice; the reason for this is that the restricted orifice provides a very active site which causes the beverage to 'rip itself apart' generating extremely minute bubbles which themselves act as active sites for the beverage in the primary chamber, these extremely minute bubbles leave 'vapour trails' of larger initiated bubbles which in turn produce the head. Since the extremely minute bubbles are travelling at relatively high speed during their injection into the beverage in the primary chamber, they not only generate shear forces on the beverage in that chamber but the effect of each such bubble is distributed over a volume of beverage much larger than the immediate surroundings of an otherwise stationary bubble.

A particular advantage of the present invention is that prior to the container being charged with beverage both the primary and secondary chambers can be at atmospheric pressure and indeed may contain air. However, it is recognised that for many beverages, particularly a fermented beverage, prolonged storage of the beverage in contact with air, especially oxygen, is undesirable as adversely affecting the characteristics of the beverage. To alleviate this possibility the secondary chamber may initially be filled with a 'non-contaminant' gas such as nitrogen (or other inert gas or carbon dioxide) which does not adversely affect the characteristics of the beverage during prolonged contact therewith. The secondary chamber may be filled with the non-contaminant gas at atmospheric pressure or slightly greater (to alleviate the inadvertent intake of air) so that when the container is charged with the beverage, the non-contaminant gas will form part of the pressurised headspace in the secondary chamber. As previously mentioned, the secondary chamber may be formed by an envelope or hollow pod which is located as a discrete insert within a conventional form of can, bottle or carton and such a discrete insert permits the secondary chamber to be filled with the non-contaminant gas prior to the envelope or pod being located within the can, bottle or carton. A convenient means of achieving this latter effect is by blow moulding the envelope or pod in a food grade plastics material using the non-contaminant gas as the blowing medium and thereafter sealing the envelope or pod to retain the non-contaminant gas therein; immediately prior to the pod or envelope being inserted into the can, bottle or carton, the restricted orifice can be formed in a side wall of the pod or envelope (for example, by laser boring). Immediately prior to the container being sealed it is also preferable to remove air from the primary headspace and this may be achieved using conventional techniques such as filling the headspace with froth or fob developed from a source remote from the container and having characteristics similar to those of the head which is to be formed from the beverage in the container; charging the primary chamber with the beverage in a nitrogen or other inert gas atmosphere so that the headspace is filled with that inert gas or nitrogen; dosing the headspace with liquid nitrogen so that the gas evolved therefrom expels the air from the headspace, or by use of undercover gassing or water jetting techniques to exclude air.

Although the secondary chamber may be constructed as an integral part of the container, for the reasons discussed above and also convenience of manufacture, it is preferred that the secondary chamber is formed as a discrete insert which is simply deposited or pushed into a conventional form of can, bottle or carton. With cans or cartons such an insert will not be visible to the end user and many bottled beverages are traditionally marketed in dark coloured glass or plastics so that the insert is unlikely to adversely affect the aesthetics of the package. The discrete insert may be suspended or float in the beverage in the primary chamber provided that the restricted orifice is maintained below the surface of the beverage in the primary chamber on opening of the container; for example the insert may be loaded or weighted to appropriately orientate the position of the restricted orifice. Desirably however the insert is restrained from displacement within the outer container of the package and may be retained in position, for example at the bottom of the outer container, by an appropriate adhesive or by mechanical means such as projections on the package which may flex to abut and grip a side wall of the outer container or which may engage beneath an internal abutment on the side wall of the outer container.

Drawings

One embodiment of the present invention as applied to the packaging of a fermented beverage such as stout in a can will now be described, by way of example only, with reference to the accompanying illustrative drawings, in which:

Figures 1 to *4* diagrammatically illustrate the progressive stages in the formation of the beverage package in a canning line, and

Figure 5 diagrammatically illustrates the effect on opening the beverage package prior to consumption of the beverage and the development of the head of froth on the beverage.

Detailed description of drawings

The present embodiment will be considered in relation to the preparation of a sealed can containing stout having in solution a mixture of nitrogen and carbon dioxide gases, the former preferably being present to the extent of at least 1.5% vols/vol and typically in the range 1.5% to 3.5% vols/vol and the carbon dioxide being present at a considerably lower level than the amount of carbon dioxide which would normally be present in conventional, wholly carbonated, bottled or canned stout and typically in the range 0.8 to 1.8 vols/vol (1.46 to 3.29 grams/litre). For the avoidance of doubt, a definition of the term 'vols/vol' is to be found in our G.B. Patent No. 1,588,624.

The stout is to be packaged in a conventional form of cylindrical can (typically of aluminium alloy) which, in the present example, will be regarded as having a capacity of 500 millilitres and by use of a conventional form of filling and canning line appropriately modified as will hereinafter be described. A cylindrical shell for the can 1 having a sealed base 2 and an open top 3 is passed in an upstanding condition along the line to a station shown in Figure 1 to present its open top beneath a stack of hollow pods 4. Each pod 4 is moulded in a food grade plastics material such as polypropylene to have a short (say 5 millimetres) hollow cylindrical housing part 5 and a circumferentially spaced array of radially outwardly extending flexible tabs or lugs 6. The pods 4 are placed in the stack with the chamber formed by the housing part 5 sealed and containing nitrogen gas at atmospheric pressure (or at pressure slightly above atmospheric); conveniently this is achieved by blow moulding the housing part 5 using nitrogen gas. The volume within the housing part 5 is approximately 15 millilitres. At the station shown in Figure 1 the bottom pod 4 of the stack is displaced by suitable means (not shown) into the open topped can 1 as shown. However, immediately prior to the pod 4 being moved into the can 1 a small (restricted) hole 7 is bored in the cylindrical side wall of the housing part 5. In the present example, the hole 7 has a diameter in the order of 0.61 millimetres and is conveniently bored by a laser beam generated by device 7a (although the hole could be formed by punching or drilling). The hole 7 is located towards the bottom of the cylindrical chamber within the housing part 5. Since the hollow pod 4 contains nitrogen gas at atmospheric pressure (or slightly higher) it is unlikely that air will enter the hollow pod through the hole 7 during the period between boring the hole 7 and charging of the can 1 with stout (thereby alleviating contamination of the stout by an oxygen content within the hollow pod 4).

The hollow pod 4 is pressed into the can 1 to be seated on the base 2. Conventional cans 1 have a domed base 2 (shown by the section 2a) which presents a convex internal face so that when the pod 4 abuts this face a clearance is provided between the hole 7 and the underlying bottom of the chamber within the can 1. It will be seen from Figure 1 that the diameter of the housing part 5 of the pod 4 is less than the internal diameter of the can 1 while the diameter of the outermost edges of the lugs 6 is greater than the diameter of the can 1 so that as the pod 4 is pressed downwardly into the can, the lugs 6 abut the side wall of the can and flex upwardly as shown to grip the can side wall and thereby restrain the hollow pod from displacement away from the base 2.

The open topped can with its pod 4 is now displaced along the canning line to the station shown in Figure 2 where the can is charged with approximately 440 millilitres of stout 8 from an appropriate source 9. The stout 8 is supersaturated with the mixed carbon dioxide and nitrogen gases, typically the carbon dioxide gas being present at 1.5 vols/vol (2.74 grams/litre) and the nitrogen gas being present at 2% vols/vol. The charging of the can 1 with the stout may be achieved in conventional manner, that is under a counterpressure and at a temperature of approximately 0°C. When the can 1 is charged with the appropriate quantity of stout 8, the headspace above the stout is purged of air, for example by use of liquid nitrogen dosing or with nitrogen gas delivered by means indicated at 10 to alleviate contamination of the stout from oxygen in the headspace.

Following charging of the can 1 with stout and purging of the headspace, the can moves to the station shown in Figure 3 where it is closed and sealed under atmospheric pressure and in conventional manner by a lid 11 seamed to the cylindrical side wall of the can. The lid 11 has a pull-ring 12 attached to a weakened tear-out region 13 by which the can is intended to be broached in conventional manner for dispensing of the contents.

Following sealing, the packaged stout is subjected to a pasteurization process whereby the package is heated to approximately 60°C for 15–20 minutes and is there-after cooled to ambient temperature. During this process the nitrogen gas in the hollow pod 4a initially expands and a proportion of that gas passes by way of the hole 7 into the stout 8 in the main chamber of the can. During cooling of the package in the pas-teurisation cycle, the nitrogen gas in the hollow pod 4 contracts to create a vacuum effect within the hollow pod causing stout 8 to be drawn, by way of the hole 7, from the chamber of the can into the chamber of the pod so that when the package is at ambient temperature the hole 7 is located below the depth of stout 8a within the hollow pod 4.

Following the pasteurisation process the contents of the can 1 will stabilise in a con-dition of equilibrium with a headspace 1a over the stout 8 in the primary chamber of the can and a headspace 4a over the stout 8a in the secondary chamber formed by the hollow pod 4 and in the equilibrium condition. With the sealed can at ambient tem-perature (or a typical storage or dispensing temperature which may be, say, 8°C) the pressure of mixed gases carbon dioxide and nitrogen (which largely results from the evolution of such gases from the stout) is substantially the same in the headspaces 1a and 4a and this pressure will be greater than atmospheric pressure, typically in the order of 25lbs per square inch (1.72 bars).

The package in the condition shown in Figure 4 is typically that which would be made available for storage and retail purposes. During handling it is realised that the package may be tipped from its upright condition; in practice however this is unlikely to adversely affect the contents of the hollow pod 4 because of the condition of equi-librium within the can.

When the stout is to be made available for consumption, the can 1 is opened by rip-ping out the region 13 with the pull-ring 12. On broaching the lid 11 as indicated at 14 the headspace 1a rapidly depressurises to atmospheric pressure. As a consequence the pressure within the headspace 4a of the secondary chamber in the pod 4 exceeds that in the headspace 1a and causes stout 8a in the hollow pod to be ejected by way of the hole 7 into the stout 8 in the primary chamber of the can. The restrictor hole 7 acts as a very 'active site' to the supersaturated stout 8a which passes therethrough to be injected into the stout 8 and that stout is effectively 'ripped apart' to generate extremely minute bubbles which themselves act as active sites for the stout 8 into which they are injected. These minute bubbles leave 'vapour trails' of larger initiated bubbles which develop within the headspace 1a a head 8b having the previously discussed desirable characteristics.

It is appreciated that the headspace 1a occupies a larger proportion of the volume of the can 1 than that which would normally be expected in a 500 millilitre capacity can; the reason for this is to ensure that there is adequate volume in the headspace 1a for the head of froth 8b to develop efficiently in the event, for example, that the stout is to be consumed directly from the can when the tear-out region 13 is removed. Normally however the stout 8 will first be poured from the can into an open topped drinking vessel prior to consumption but this pouring should not adversely affect the desirable characteristics of the head of froth which will eventually be presented in the drinking vessel.

In the aforegoing embodiment the can 1 is charged with stout 8 (from the source 9) having in solution the required respective volumes of the carbon dioxide and the nitrogen gases. In a modification the can 1 is charged with stout (from source 9) having the carbon dioxide gas only in solution to the required volume; the 2% vols/vol nitrogen gas necessary to achieve the required solution of mixed gas in the packaged stout is derived from the liquid nitrogen dosing of the headspace in the can.

CLAIMS

1 A beverage package comprising a sealed, non-resealable, container having a primary chamber containing beverage having gas in solution therewith and forming a primary headspace comprising gas at a pressure greater than atmospheric; a secondary chamber having a volume less than said primary chamber and which communicates with the beverage in said primary chamber through a restricted orifice, said secondary chamber containing beverage derived from the primary chamber and having a secondary headspace therein comprising gas at a pressure greater than atmospheric so that the pressure within the primary and secondary chambers are substantially at equilibrium, and wherein said package is openable, to open the primary headspace to atmospheric pressure and the secondary chamber is arranged so that on said opening the pressure differential caused by the decrease in pressure at the primary headspace causes at least one of the beverage and gas in the secondary chamber to be ejected by way of the restricted orifice into the beverage of the primary chamber and said ejection causes gas in the solution to be evolved and form, or assist in the formation of, a head of froth on the beverage.

2 A package as claimed in claim 1 in which the container has a normal upstanding condition with an openable top and said secondary chamber has an upwardly extending side wall or a bottom wall within which said restricted orifice is located.

3 A package as claimed in either claim 1 or claim 2 in which with the pressures within the primary and secondary chambers substantially at equilibrium the restricted orifice is located below the depth of the beverage within the secondary chamber.

4 A package as claimed in any one of the preceding claims wherein the secondary chamber comprises a hollow and discrete insert within the container.

5 A package as claimed in claim 4 in which the insert floats or is suspended in the beverage in the primary chamber and means is provided for locating the restricted orifice below the surface of the beverage in the primary chamber.

6 A package as claimed in claim 5 in which the insert is weighted or loaded to locate the restricted orifice below the surface of the beverage in the primary chamber.

7   A package as claimed in claim 4 wherein means is provided for retaining the insert at a predetermined position within the container.

8   A package as claimed in claim 7 wherein the container has a normal upstanding condition with an openable top and said insert is located at or towards the bottom of said container.

9   A package as claimed in either claim 7 or claim 8 wherein the insert comprises a hollow pod or envelope having means thereon for retaining it in position within the container.

10 A package as claimed in claim 9 wherein the retaining means comprise flexible tab means which engage a side wall of the container to retain the insert.

11 A package as claimed in any one of claims 4 to 10 wherein the insert comprises a hollow moulding.

12 A package as claimed in claim 11 when appendant to claim 10 in which the container has a side wall and the moulding is substantially cylindrical with radially extending tabs engaging the wall of the container.

13 A package as claimed in any one of claims 4 to 12 in which the container has a base on which the insert is located and said restricted orifice is located in an upwardly extending side wall of the insert spaced from said base.

14 A package as claimed in any one of the preceding claims in which the beverage has in solution therewith at least one of carbon dioxide gas and inert gas (which latter term includes nitrogen).

15 A package as claimed in claim 14 in which the beverage is saturated or supersaturated with said gas or gases.

16 A package as claimed in any one of the preceding claims in which the container is in the form of a can, bottle or carton.

17 A package as claimed in any one of the preceding claims in which the restricted orifice comprises a circular aperture having a diameter in the range of 0.02 to 0.25 centimetres.

18 A package as claimed in any one of the preceding claims and comprising a fermented beverage having in solution therewith carbon dioxide in the range 0.8 to 1.8 vols/vol (1.46 to 3.29 grams/litre) and nitrogen in the range 1.5% to 3.5% vols/vol.

19 A beverage package substantially as herein described with reference to the accompanying illustrative drawings.

20 A method of packaging a beverage having gas in solution therewith which comprises providing a container with a primary chamber and a secondary chamber of which the volume of the secondary chamber is less than that of the primary chamber and with a restricted orifice through which the secondary chamber communicates with the primary chamber, and charging and sealing the primary chamber with the beverage to contain the gas in solution and to form a primary headspace in the primary chamber, and charging the secondary chamber with beverage derived from the primary chamber by way of said restricted orifice to form a secondary headspace in the secondary chamber whereby the pressures in both the primary and secondary chambers are at equilibrium and gaseous pressures in both the primary and secondary headspaces are at a pressure greater

than atmospheric so that, when the container is broached to open the primary headspace to atmospheric pressure, the pressure differential caused by the decrease in pressure at the primary headspace causes at least one of the beverage and gas in the secondary chamber to be ejected into the beverage of the primary chamber by way of said restricted orifice and the said ejection causes gas to be evolved from solution in the beverage in the primary chamber to form, or assist in the formation of, a head of froth on the beverage.

21   A method as claimed in claim 20 which comprises subjecting the sealed container to a heating and cooling cycle whereby gas within the secondary chamber is caused to expand and eject by way of the restricted orifice into the primary chamber and subsequently to contract and create a low pressure effect in the secondary chamber relative to the primary chamber to draw beverage from the primary chamber into the secondary chamber by way of said restricted orifice.

22   A method as claimed in claim 21 in which the heating and cooling cycle comprises pasteurisation of the beverage.

23   A method as claimed in any one of claims 20 to 22 in which the container has an upstanding condition with an openable top and which comprises locating the restricted orifice within an upwardly extending side wall or bottom wall of the secondary chamber.

24   A method as claimed in any one of claims 20 to 23 which comprises charging the secondary chamber with beverage from the primary chamber to the extent that the restricted orifice is located below the depth of beverage in the secondary chamber.

25   A method as claimed in any one of claims 20 to 23 which comprises forming the secondary chamber by a discrete hollow insert located within the primary chamber of the container.

26   A method as claimed in claim 25 in which the hollow insert is to float or be suspended in the beverage in the primary chamber and which comprises loading or weighting the insert to locate the restricted orifice below the surface of the beverage in the primary chamber.

27   A method as claimed in claim 25 which comprises retaining the insert at a predetermined position within the container.

28   A method as claimed in any one of claims 25 to 27 which comprises forming the hollow insert having the restricted orifice in a wall thereof and locating the insert within the primary chamber prior to the charging and sealing of the primary chamber.

29   A method as claimed in any one of claims 25 to 28 which comprises forming the hollow insert by blow moulding.

30   A method as claimed in claim 29 which comprises blow moulding the hollow insert with gas for dissolution in the beverage so that said gas is sealed within the secondary chamber, and forming said restricted orifice in the wall of the insert immediately prior to locating the insert in the primary chamber.

31   A method as claimed in claim 30 which comprises sealing said gas in the secondary chamber at atmospheric pressure or at a pressure slightly greater than atmospheric.

32   A method as claimed in any one of claims 25 to 31 which comprises forming the restricted orifice in the hollow insert by laser boring, drilling or punching.

33   A method as claimed in any one of claims 25 to 32 in which, prior to it being sealed, the container has an upstanding condition with an open top through which the primary chamber is charged with beverage and which comprises locating the insert through said open top to provide the secondary chamber within the container.

34   A method as claimed in claim 33 when appendant to claim 27 which comprises press fitting the insert within the container so that during its location the insert engages with a side wall of the container to be retained in position.

35   A method as claimed in any one of claims 20 to 34 which comprises, prior to sealing the primary chamber, purging the primary head space to exclude air.

36   A method as claimed in any one of claims 20 to 35 in which the gas comprises at least one of carbon dioxide gas and inert gas (which latter term includes nitrogen).

37   A method as claimed in claim 36 in which the beverage is fermented and has in solution carbon dioxide in the range 0.8 to 1.8 vols/vol (1.46 to 3.29 grams/litre) and nitrogen in the range 1.5% to 3.5% vols/vol.

38   A method of packaging a beverage as claimed in claim 20 and substantially as herein described.

39   A beverage when packaged by the method as claimed in any one of claims 20 to 38.

Printed for Her Majesty's Stationery Office by
Croydon Printing Company (UK) Ltd, 4/87, D8991685.
Published by The Patent Office, 25 Southampton Buildings, London, WC2A
1AY, from which copies may be obtained.

Index